The Complete

Meat

Cookbook

The Complete *Meat* Cookbook

A Juicy and Authoritative Guide to
Selecting, Seasoning, and Cooking Today's
Beef, Pork, Lamb, and Veal

Bruce Aidells and Denis Kelly

PHOTOGRAPHS BY BEATRIZ DA COSTA

ILLUSTRATIONS BY MARY DEPALMA

HOUGHTON MIFFLIN COMPANY
NEW YORK   BOSTON

For information about permission to reproduce selections from
this book, write to Permissions, Houghton Mifflin Company,
215 Park Avenue South, New York, New York 10003.

Visit our Web site: www.houghtonmifflinbooks.com.

Library of Congress Cataloging-in-Publication Data
Aidells, Bruce.
The complete meat cookbook : a juicy and authoritative guide to selecting, seasoning,
and cooking today's beef, pork, veal, and lamb / Bruce Aidells and Denis Kelly ;
photographs by Beatriz Da Costa.
p. cm.
Includes index.
ISBN 0-618-13512-X
1. Cookery (Meat) I. Kelly, Denis, 1939– . II. Title.
TX749.A36 1998
641.6'6—dc21   98-28216   CIP

Designed by Susan McClellan

Cover photograph by Beatriz Da Costa
Braised Lamb Shanks with Fennel and Small White Beans
Food Styling by Anne Disrude
Prop Styling by Betty Alfenito

Printed in the United States of America

WCT 10 9 8 7 6 5 4 3 2 1

TO LONI KUHN

(1932 – 1997)

Loni, this book is dedicated to you.

Loni Kuhn, our dear friend, encouraged us to share our cooking and recipes with others. Her cooking school made us put our recipes on paper. Her own wealth of recipes was vast, and she shared many of the best with us here and in our other books. Unfortunately, she died before she had a chance to put her own work into a book.

Good bread, good meat, good God, let's Eat!

—Irish-American Grace

Ess Gesundteheit!
(Eat in good health!)

—Yiddish Expression of Hospitality

Some hae meat and canna eat,
And some wad eat that want it,
But we hae meat, and we can eat,
And sae the Lord be thankit.

—Scottish Grace

Contents

Introduction

FRANKLY, WE LOVE MEAT. And we know we're not alone: most people today and throughout history have relished the sensation of biting into a juicy beefsteak, a succulent pork chop, or a spicy lamb kebab. This book is written for those who share this carnivorous inclination. Whether we cook and enjoy meat every day, once a week, or only on special occasions, meat is an important and enjoyable part of our diet.

Like most Americans of our generation, we grew up eating plenty of tender steaks, thick chops, and rich Sunday roasts, cooked simply and without much seasoning. In fact, in our households, everybody thought garlic was a kind of salt. Those of us who weren't lucky enough to be Italian, Polish, or "ethnic" ate pretty bland food: meat and potatoes and overcooked vegetables. Meat was the centerpiece of almost every meal: the prime rib on Sunday, beautifully browned and glistening with crisp fat; lusciously tender brisket and pot roasts; pork chops with cream gravy and mashed potatoes; juicy meat loaf and hamburgers; the thick porterhouse steak Dad grilled on the barbecue on summer afternoons.

Even though it was often not well seasoned, the meat was wonderful: juicy and tender and full of flavor. Even humbler cuts such as Swiss steak or spareribs were marbled with plenty of fat to provide flavor and tenderness. They could be cooked to the medium or even well-done stage without much seasoning and still be delicious. Fattened on corn in the Midwest and cut to order by the neighborhood butcher, this high-quality meat became the symbol of American prosperity.

Unfortunately, the meat we remember with such nostalgia is not the same as what we eat today. Because of pressures to lower the fat in the American diet, producers have been breeding and raising animals to be leaner. Mom would have scorned most of the beef, pork, and lamb we buy in the supermarket. She chose cuts with rich, intramuscular fat that gave them juiciness and tenderness. When we cook meat now using recipes from older cookbooks, we're often disappointed. Pork comes out of the oven hard, dry, and juiceless; beef and lamb lack the succulent texture and robust flavors we remember.

A NEW APPROACH

The new meat demands a new approach, and that's our mission in this book: to show you how to prepare today's cuts so that they're tender, juicy, and full of flavor. Both of us have been chefs in San Francisco Bay area restaurants and have taught and written about food during an exciting time in American cooking. We've developed our own ways to cook meat successfully, and we'll pass these tricks on to you. We'll also tell you about techniques we've learned from the masters—friends and fellow cooks.

Like everyone else in America, we crave spice and liveliness in our food. We still hanker for Mom's comfort food, but we now want it enlivened and interesting, cooked with flair and originality. Here we've gathered it all: the exotic recipes as well as many new interpretations of classic dishes that Mom used to cook: Not-Like-Mom's Meat Loaf, with wild mushrooms and pancetta, for instance, or Catahoula's Smoky Short Ribs with New Orleans Red Gravy, made with black coffee and jalapeños. Most can be quickly prepared by the everyday cook who has to feed a family after a hard day's work or who wants to entertain friends at a weekend dinner or barbecue with a minimum of fuss. We've provided tips and suggestions for cooking the more time-consuming dishes such as braises and stews in easy stages with minimum preparation times. We've also included some recipes for special occasions and holidays and for large crowds of hungry friends and relatives.

THE FLAVOR STEPS

Our flavor steps for each recipe will show you how to add intense and delicious tastes to meat. Seasoning is essential to successful meat cookery, and we'll show you how to do it well. Seasonings can be as simple as dry rubs—combinations of spices and herbs rubbed on the meat's surface—or marinades of fresh herbs and acidic ingredients such as wine or soy sauce. We'll also show you how to put juiciness and flavor back into all-too-lean pork chops and pork loin with solutions of salt, water, sugar, and spices, called flavor brines. We'll provide you with rubs, marinades, and flavor brines for every type of meat, from savory Santa Maria Barbecued Tri-Tip in Orange-Ginger Marinade to tender Lamb Kebabs with Cranberry-Onion Marinade to spicy and succulent Tuscan Herb-Infused Roast Pork and Dan's Grilled Rosemary-Cured Lamb Shoulder Chops.

We'll teach you how to cover thin cuts with tasty glazes or crusts to keep them moist and how to bring a new dimension to meats of every kind with savory stuffings. Finally, we'll share our favorite recipes for sauces and salsas that add excitement to meats, as in Gordon's Grilled Rib-Eye Steak with Chile-Tomato Vinaigrette, Grilled Pork Steaks in Yucatán Marinade with Orange-Pineapple Salsa, and Roast Rack of Lamb with Tapenade. Whether it's down-home cooking updated from Mom's kitchen or cutting-edge cuisine with exciting new tastes, we'll show you how to transform even the humblest cuts into memorable meals. You'll also learn how to use meat economically, how to determine the best cooking method for each cut, and how cooking times and techniques have changed.

MEAT AND A HEALTHY DIET

Because it's important to learn how to integrate meat into a healthy diet, we'll show you how fat levels can be controlled and how meat can be mixed with a variety of other ingredients as a condiment or flavoring. Many of our recipes are specially annotated to indicate that they have less than 10 grams of fat per serving. Pork tenderloin, a lean cut, for example, is cooked in myriad ways: sautéed with tomato and basil sauce over fresh pasta or roasted with Chinese ginger-lemon sauce or grilled with a rosemary and fennel seed crust. We'll demonstrate how all kinds of cuts, from steaks to roasts to spareribs, can be prepared with a minimum of added fat and a maximum of flavor.

HOW TO TALK TO THE MEAT GUYS

Most important, we'll teach you how to talk to the meat guys. The marketplace is changing rapidly, and the different cuts, grades, and brands can be confusing. In earlier times, butchers bought whole carcasses from local meat packers and slaughterhouses and cut them up themselves; they could be relied on to give good advice and pass on their knowledge. Now most meat comes to shops and supermarkets already cut and boxed, and all too many butchers merely wrap the meat and know little about the product they sell. We'll guide you in the search for quality meat and tell you what to look for and what to ask about. By the time we're through, you'll know all about the major cuts, the USDA grades, and how to select and buy the best meat available, whether from an old-fashioned butcher or from the supermarket.

MYTHBUSTING

Along the way, we'll be demolishing a number of the cherished myths of meat cookery: the sorts of things that Grandma insisted on and Mom went along with, such as not salting meat before cooking and cooking pork chops until they are completely white. We'll knock down these misconceptions one by one as we investigate the new world of meat cookery.

Using This Book

IN THE NEXT CHAPTER, you'll learn the basics—everything you need to know before you start cooking. Within the main chapters for beef, pork, lamb, and veal, the recipes are organized by cut, and within that by cooking method, with dry-heat cooking coming first (broiling, pan-broiling, sautéing, grilling, roasting), followed by moist-heat methods (poaching, braising, stewing).

At the end of the book is a Seasoning Chart that lists dry rubs, marinades, and brines and the best cuts to use with each (see page 577). You can consult the chart first, if you want a certain flavor with a cut of meat, or go directly to a particular recipe and then try other suggested variations. A list of mail-order sources for herbs, spices, smoked meats, and other ingredients is also included.

THE RECIPES

When the cooking procedures, times, and techniques are essentially consistent for a cut of meat, we give you a Master Recipe. Variations simply involve changes in herbs, spices, and other flavoring ingredients and/or adding or substituting other ingredients. The techniques, procedures, and cooking times are usually not affected. Once you know the Master Recipe, you can create your own variations and improvise with confidence.

SPECIAL FEATURES

Most recipes are conveniently categorized to guide you quickly to dishes that fulfill a particular requirement. Recipes are cross-referenced by their main characteristics, and each recipe may have more than one important feature.

- **Cooking on a Budget**—dishes that cost less than $2 per serving
- **In a Hurry**—dishes that take less than 30 minutes to prepare
- **Low-Fat**—dishes that have less than 10 grams of fat per serving
- **Fit for Company**—dishes for entertaining or special occasions
- **Good for a Crowd**—dishes that are easily produced on a large scale

- **Two for One**—recipes for meals designed to be turned into other dishes, with both recipes included
  - **Rewarms Well**—dishes that benefit from being made in advance
  - **Meat as a Condiment**—recipes featuring meat as a flavoring, not the main ingredient, with less than 2 ounces of meat per serving
  - **Mom's Comfort Food**—rich and satisfying, just like Mom used to make
  - **Great Leftovers**

A Few Words about Ingredients

■ **Salt:** Most recipes call for ordinary table salt; some specify kosher salt. Kosher salt is a high-quality salt with few impurities and a good "salty" flavor. It can be used in any recipe. Various types of sea salt are also quite flavorful and can be used in most recipes.

■ **Fat:** We've designed our recipes to use as little added fat as possible. We trim fat from the meat before cooking and skim the fat from stocks and sauces before serving. We have tried to limit any additional fat to small quantities of healthful oils for cooking or salad dressings.

■ **Oil:** Most of our recipes call for olive oil or vegetable oil. Use a good-quality extra-virgin olive oil if possible. Corn, canola, peanut, and other mild-flavored oils can also be used in most recipes. We sometimes call for Asian sesame oil; this is a highly flavored oil available in Asian groceries and some supermarkets and from mail-order sources.

■ **Butter:** We don't often use butter, but when we do, we suggest you use the unsalted kind. It is fresher, with a better flavor than salted—but salted butter will also do. Adjust salt accordingly.

■ **Stock:** We prefer to use homemade stocks, but you can use canned stocks in most recipes. We suggest low-sodium chicken stock. Canned vegetable stocks can also be used. Be sure not to add too much salt if you are using any canned stock, as some become quite salty if reduced to make a sauce.

■ **Herbs and Spices:** Many of our recipes call for fresh or dried herbs. Generally you can substitute half as much of a dried herb for a fresh one, since drying concentrates flavors. Dried herbs and spices lose much of their flavor after one or two months on the shelf. Buy them in small quantities and store them in tightly closed jars. Fresh herbs are now widely available (and are easy to grow in a window box or backyard garden); they are preferable in most cases to the dried.

DON'T CALL THEM LEFTOVERS

WHEN YOU COOK ROASTS, STEWS, AND EVEN STEAKS, there is usually meat left over. But don't think "leftovers." Think of this as an opportunity to make an even tastier dish the second time around. Delicious meat from a previous meal can be combined with other ingredients such as pasta, rice, potatoes, and vegetables to make an entirely new dish, not the dreaded leftovers we had to eat as kids. Give a savory pasta served with cooked short ribs and fresh tomato sauce an appetizing new name like Short Rib Ragout with Pasta (page 223) and serve it to family or guests. Some dishes made from previously cooked meat, in fact, are so good that we often make the original dish just to get to eat the second one. Tostada Salad (page 130) and hearty sandwiches like Cuban Roast Pork Sandwich with Mojo Sauce (page 361) and Lamb and Caponata Sandwich (page 488), to name just a few, fall into this category.

To avoid the unpleasant "refrigerator" taste of rewarmed meat, which sometimes plagues cuts cooked by dry-heat methods, such as steaks and roasts, we often recommend that you use them at a cold room temperature in sandwiches and salads. If you cook roast beef chunks in chile con carne or leg of lamb in a curry for a long time over low heat, you won't have to worry, however. Or you can spice up leftover gravy with some chiles and salsa and reheat pieces of pork, beef, or lamb to fill burritos or tacos, or chop roast beef, pork, or veal and mix it with flavorful ingredients to make a hash or to fill small meat pies such as pasties or empanadas.

Braised dishes such as pot roasts and stews can be rewarmed successfully in the sauce or gravy they were cooked in and are often even better the next day. Care should be taken, however, just to warm the meat, not overcook it. Heat only the portions you need for a single meal to avoid cooking the meat over and over.

Bruschetta Steak Sandwiches (*page 109*)

Sautéed Lamb Chops with Balsamic Vinegar and Fresh Mint Vinaigrette (*page 458*)

Thai-Style Barbecued Baby Back Ribs (*page 382*)

Veal and Asparagus Stew in Lemon Sauce (*page 562*)

Tuscan Roast Rack of Veal (*page 552*)

Calves' Liver in Mustard Sauce (*page 573*)

Roast Rack of Lamb with Herb and Bread Crumb Crust (*page 482*)

Sautéed Pork Chops Normandy Style (*page 271*)

Meat Basics

A Little History
Meat and the Human Diet

ET'S FACE IT: from the cave to the condo, we human beings have always been meat eaters. No matter what tales you've heard about some mythic past life of gentle fruit-eating primates, whenever human beings have had the chance, they've eaten meat on a regular basis. Paleoanthropologists think that humankind's great evolutionary leaps were a direct result of the successful pursuit of protein in the form of meat. They feel that the key to humanity's development over the ages has been access to animal proteins through scavenging and hunting in the beginning, then the domestication and exploitation of selected species after the agricultural revolution.

Our remote ancestors took the first step when they moved out of the forest, where their fruit-based diet had been supplemented by occasional, opportunistic meat eating—pretty much the way chimpanzees eat today. Out on the savanna, huge herds of grazing animals gave early hominids easy access to large amounts of meat on a regular basis. The skulls and jawbones of *Homo erectus,* the first true human, show that teeth adapted for meat eating and larger brain cavities developed simultaneously. Meat seems to have provided the evolutionary push that resulted in larger brains, full bipedalism, and complex social organization.

These early humans were omnivorous hunter-gatherers who lived on meat, fruit, roots and tubers, and seeds and leaves. If you examine our diet today, you can see how little we've changed: on a typical day we might eat steak (meat), potatoes (tubers), and carrots (roots) for dinner, along with a salad (leaves) dressed with oil (from seeds) and vinegar (from fruit), and bread (made from seeds of wheat, a form of grass). Even junk food reflects our all-too-human tendency to binge on fat ("Have some more buffalo hump, my dear?") and sugar ("Look at all those ripe plums, yum!") whenever we have the chance.

Most of humanity's existence has been spent in this hunting-gathering stage, a period that stretches from the emergence of *Homo erectus* about one and a half million years ago to the Neolithic agricultural revolution, about 9000 B.C. The agricultural diet is an upstart. Contrary to what we usually think, hunter-gatherers had it pretty good. They thrived on a variety of foods gathered from the immediate environment. And they hunted the surrounding countryside for rodents and other small animals, birds, deer, wild cattle, bison, even mammoths and mastodons. If we judge from contemporary hunter-gatherers in southern Africa, the Amazon, or Australia, we see that procuring sufficient food doesn't take all that much time—about 12 hours a week, according to some estimates—so the hunter-gatherer family has plenty of time for leisure and play, to tell stories, weave baskets, or lie around in the shade inventing culture.

Anthropologists have been debating about the ideal human diet, just like everyone else. Since most of our time as a species has been spent in the hunter-gatherer stage, some suggest that the diet that sustained us for most of our existence must represent the ideal. Paleoanthropologists have found that the hunter-gatherers were significantly taller than early farmers, who derived most of their sustenance from cultivated grains, with very little animal protein in their diet. The hunter-gatherers had strong bones and excellent teeth, unlike the farmers.

THE IDEAL HUMAN DIET

To know what man ate before he invented agriculture is to know his diet during the millions of years during which he adapted to a particular choice of foods. We may thus assume that this choice represents something like his "ideal" diet, and might well form the basis of the advice that the nutritionist is asked to give in formulating diets for health. . . . On this basis, the nutritionist would suggest that a diet that contained a fairly high proportion of meat would be basically the diet most suitable for human animals.

—From "Archaeology and the Nutritionist: The 'Ideal' Diet," by John
Yudkin, in *The Domestication and Exploitation of Plants and Animals,*
edited by Ucko and Dimbleby

THE AGRICULTURAL REVOLUTION: A DECLINE IN HUMAN DIET?

Hunter-gatherers had become skilled hunters by the late Ice Age. They followed and harvested the large herds that gathered along the edge of the ice, using finely crafted flint spearheads and the *atlatl*, or spearthrower, a startling bit of technology that dramatically increased the power of the hunter. Later, bows, nets, and snares gave early humans regular sources of meat for eons in Europe, the Mideast, and Africa. With the change in climate after the last Ice Age and the gradual extermination of large prey through overhunting, humankind gradually began to adopt another, more sedentary way of life that exploited stands of wild grasses (wheat, barley, corn), legumes (lentils, peas, beans), nuts, and fruits. Human beings continued to hunt, but they also began to manage herds of small animals such as sheep and goats, snared small game, and fished and gathered mollusks from rivers, lakes, and seas.

This new pattern of village life led to the Neolithic agricultural revolution, which resulted in regular sources of storable food for the first time in human history. Grain-based agriculture evolved in the Near East and produced the surplus of wealth that led to the origins of city life—in a word, civilization. But with the great revolution in food production came nutritional problems: a diet based largely on carbohydrates (starches and sugar) was nutritionally inferior to the "ideal" diet of the hunter-gatherers, with its high protein and vitamin levels. As Arno Karlen sums it up in *Man and Microbes,* "As agriculture spread from its sources in the Near East, China, and Mexico, life expectancy in much of the Neolithic world dipped from the usual forty years of hunter-gatherers to about thirty."

NO MORE FREE LUNCH

By the time the great agriculturally based civilizations of Mesopotamia, Egypt, and the Indus had arisen, sheep, goats, pigs, and the wild ox, or aurochs, had been tamed and domesticated. This meat on the hoof was the main source of protein to supplement a diet based on wheat, barley, and other grains. But meat is "expensive" in ecological terms. A large quantity of vegetable food over a long period of time is needed to produce edible protein in the form of meat. So, in time, given the expensive (and perishable) nature of this food, access became restricted to an elite—a condition that would last until the changes wrought by the next great human upheaval, the industrial revolution. Only the aristocracy of priests, warriors, or landowners ate meat on a regular basis; the lower classes of laborers, farmers, and peasants subsisted largely on grains, with meat eaten only at festivals or other special occasions.

The high-protein diet was restricted to the upper classes up to modern times. Animals were slaughtered on a regular basis only for castle and abbey tables in the Middle Ages. Hunting was the preferred mode of recreation for the nobility during the feudal period, a pastime that provided a valuable by-product in the form of meat. Peasants were not allowed access to game, and laws against poaching helped to preserve the elite's monopoly on protein. About the only time most of the peasantry saw meat was on feast days, and their physical and mental development suffered accordingly.

Not until the industrial revolution did meat come regularly to ordinary tables. In the United States during the nineteenth century, immense farms in the Midwest began to produce great quantities of corn and other grains using mechanized harvesters and modern fertilizers. The grain was fed to the surplus cattle in the West and the meat was shipped to market in refrigerated train cars. Thus the whole populace, rich and poor, had access to plenty of meat and protein for the first time, resulting in a great revolution in diet and public health.

Modern meat has its drawbacks, surely: we worry about its ecological impact and its effect on our cholesterol levels. But we have a largely healthy population in twentieth-century America, with children increasing in stature and life expectancy generation by generation. For those of us who are the children of immigrants—who fled famine and the cultural and economic oppression of a system that limited meat eating and other "luxuries" to an elite—unlimited hamburgers are satisfying. Sinking your teeth into a tender steak fulfills a deeply human need that goes back to *Homo erectus* crouched by a fire on the open plain. Is it any wonder that we prefer meat cooked on a grill to any other type? Isn't that rare porterhouse we wolf down at the Sunday barbecue a celebration of our ancestry?

THE QUEST FOR FLAVOR

One of the great sources of flavor and probably the most revolutionary addition to American cooking arrived with the huge influx of Italians (mostly from the poorer south of that country) in the early twentieth century. Meat-and-potatoes Americans fell in love with garlic, oregano, and spices with their first taste of garlic bread and pizza. Italian chefs also brought us "new" vegetables like zucchini, broccoli, bell peppers, and mushrooms—a welcome alternative to canned peas and spinach, products of the American tendency to cook vegetables into tasteless mush. Garlic and herb pastes and oil-based marinades are two of the most important Italian contributions to meat cookery.

The Chinese restaurant was another eye-opening place where Americans found startling new dishes with exotic ingredients. Chinese cooks rely on fresh vegetables and little bits of meat, highly seasoned and quickly cooked, to provide lively food that awakens the taste buds and pleases the eye. Stir-frying and

MOM'S STANDBY
Garlic Salt on Everything

WHEN I WAS GROWING UP IN LOS ANGELES, my mother had just one spice in the kitchen: a popular brand of garlic salt. She'd take a steak or chop or roast, sprinkle it liberally with the seasoned salt and a little pepper, then cook the meat medium-well. It always came out juicy and full of flavor. Now I know why: it was the meat itself. Mom carefully chose the cuts for our family from the neighborhood butcher, who knew her well and provided her with quality. These days it's hard to find an old-fashioned butcher, but if you do, cling to him (or her—the times are a-changing, even with butchers).

This early real-garlic deprivation is probably why I went overboard in the garlic department when I got to Berkeley. I joined up with the garlic crazies and was a member of the Lovers of the Stinking Rose, an organization dedicated to garlic excess at every level (would you believe garlic ice cream?). My first (and so far only) movie role was in Les Blank's ode to garlic, *Garlic Is as Good as Ten Mothers*. If you look closely, you can see me cooking up a storm (I'm the big guy with the beard and leather cap) with Anzonini, a colorful flamenco singer and dancer. Anzonini, a Gypsy from Andalusia who lived in Berkeley, was one of those master meat cooks who taught us the tricks of adding flavor and character to meat by using spice rubs, herb pastes, and marinades. You'll see many of these seasoning strategies in this book; they're the basis of our flavor steps at the beginning of each recipe.   *B.A.*

grilling marinated meat on skewers are two Asian techniques that are particularly appealing.

Both Mexican and Southwest cooking have shown us how fiery chiles, herbs like oregano, and spices like cumin can be used to flavor meat that's added to basic ingredients like beans, rice, and corn. These hot cuisines are also surprisingly healthful, using meat sparingly with fresh vegetables and starches; they continue to inspire many of our most creative chefs.

The cuisines of Louisiana, both Cajun and Creole cooking, rely on dry rubs of various chile peppers, herbs, and spices to season meats before grilling, broiling, or braising. The spicy crust seals in juices and is especially suitable for the leaner meats.

ECLECTIC INFLUENCES

In the last 20 years, the range of flavors available to Americans has been increased dramatically in the way it always has, by new waves of immigration. After the Vietnam War, large numbers of Southeast Asians moved to the United States. They carried with them their foodways, bringing new ingredients and cooking styles. Vietnamese, Thai, Cambodian, Burmese, and other Southeast Asians opened restaurants, just as the earlier Italians, Chinese, and Mexicans had, introducing their spicy cuisines to eager American diners.

The titillating flavors of Thai food in particular are making their way into home cooking. Even supermarkets now offer lemongrass, galangal, fish sauce *(nam pla),* Thai basil, and coconut milk. Highly seasoned pork or beef is often grilled and served on salads or with lightly cooked vegetables. The combination of bits of spicy meat in a hot, sweet sauce with crisp vegetables laced with chiles, mint, and basil is irresistible. Other Asian cuisines, such as Korean and Japanese, offer soy-based marinades that add intense and delicious flavors to meats of all types.

As Americans travel throughout the world, we're constantly discovering new tastes and rediscovering some of the earlier popular cuisines in their authentic settings. We rave about Calabrian *salsicce* (highly spiced fresh sausage), Tuscan *fagioli* (white beans in virgin olive oil), or Sicilian *caponata* (a sweet-and-sour eggplant relish). We love Mexican favorites like tacos and tamales, but we're also eager to try regional delights like Yucatán banana leaf tamales or the fabled seven *moles* (elaborate stews) of Oaxaca.

As a result, a new style of meat cookery is emerging, eclectic and universal, merging American ingredients and traditions with new and exciting herbs, spices, and techniques in a never-ending quest for flavor.

What Matters Most in Buying Meat

W HAT *IS* QUALITY MEAT? Is it the top grade or the cut with the highest price? For many people, quality means bright red meat devoid of all visible fat. This pretty meat, which breeders have worked so hard to produce, toughens easily and lacks flavor—qualities we'd like to avoid.

Of course, many factors affect quality in meat: the age of the animal and its breed, its diet, the conditions of slaughter, the temperature at which the meat is stored, whether the meat has been aged, and how it was packed and shipped. All these are important for quality (and mostly unknown to the consumer), but the single most important factor in determining tenderness and flavor is what part of the carcass the meat comes from and how you cook each cut. You'll learn all about this and the USDA (U.S. Department of Agriculture) grading system in the chapters on individual meats.

Consumers can't be expected to know the answers to all these questions, so we must educate ourselves—one reason you're reading this book—and rely on professional butchers who have been properly trained. There was a time when each neighborhood had its premier butcher shop. Over the years, you got to know your butcher and formed a relationship based on trust and the exchange of information. When you weren't happy with what you got, you let the butcher know about it and got better meat the next time. If you're one of the fortunate few who still has an old-fashioned butcher shop in your neighborhood, let him or her know you care about quality and cultivate this valuable relationship.

If, however, like most of us, you buy your meat from a supermarket, you have to work to make sure you get the quality and service you need. There always *is* a butcher back there. Don't just grab a package of meat and run; try to get to know the meat cutters and, especially, the manager. Give them feedback about the meat you buy and ask questions: Where on the carcass does this cut come from? What is the grade of the meat? Who is the supplier? Like any professional butcher, your supermarket meat manager should be an individual of high integrity, knowledge, and skill. A good butcher is like a good auto mechanic, a jewel beyond price, someone who can be important to your enjoyment of life and to your pocketbook. Be persistent and demand quality in meat and you will find it.

Surprisingly, many warehouse club stores offer consumers very fine meat: USDA Choice beef and excellent pork from the best packers. You usually have to buy sub-primal cuts (see opposite page) or rather large amounts of cut meat, but it's often worthwhile to use what you need immediately and then double-wrap and freeze the rest for up to three months. The prices are very

Miss Sullivan Visits
O'Leary the Butcher
(Poor Devil)

MY AUNT NORA was a formidable presence. A maiden lady, a full six feet in her sensible oxfords, with jet-black hair, a pale Irish complexion, and fierce dark eyes, Aunt Nora strode through our neighborhood in Brooklyn, intimidating everyone from the kids playing stickball to the cop on the beat. You heard, "Good day to you, Miss Sullivan," and "How are you this fine day, Miss Sullivan?" on every side as she swept through the crowds of shoppers on 4th Avenue with me and my sisters in tow, on her way to buy the groceries for the week. But while she merely cowed kids, cops, and the neighbors, she put the fear of God into the shopkeepers, especially Mr. O'Leary, the butcher.

When she entered his shop, O'Leary, himself a stately and imposing man (have you ever seen a lean butcher?), would come out from behind the cooler, bowing and wringing his huge hands. "Ah, Miss Sullivan, I've been saving a beautiful roast for you today," he'd exclaim with notes of hope in his voice. "I'm sure you have, Mr. O'Leary," she'd reply with more than a hint of disdain, "and now let's have a look at it."

O'Leary would scurry back into the walk-in refrigerator and emerge with a huge, perfectly aged, 7-bone rib roast, deep red meat encircled with ivory fat, and present it to Aunt Nora like a work of fine art. She'd look at it scornfully, prod the edge of fat, peer intently until she discovered a trace of gristle or a chunk of extra fat, and dismiss it with a wave of her hand. "Is this the best you can do, Mr. O'Leary?" she'd say. And O'Leary, shoulders sagging, losing hope, would enter the walk-in again and again, emerging with roast after roast, until one barely met with Aunt Nora's approval.

"This just might do," she'd finally say, "if you trim it well and deliver it too, and mind, I'm not paying for all that fat and bone." O'Leary and the other butchers would be all smiles now, bowing us out, bestowing pieces of bologna on us kids and savory bits of beef kidney to take home for the cats as we left.

And the next day, for Sunday dinner, Aunt Nora would season the glorious roast with just a touch of salt and pepper and roast it and roast it and roast it until it was a deep brown on the outside and just as brown all the way through. My father (a budding gourmet of the new school) would try to convince her to leave the meat just a bit pink this time, and I, as I got older, would plead for some herbs or a bit of garlic.

Aunt Nora would listen carefully, nod once or twice, and then dismiss us with a sniff and a toss of her head. My father and I were Kellys, after all, a clan from far to the north of Kerry, the Sullivan homeland, and therefore suspect with our foreign ways and sophisticated (and most likely depraved) tastes for red meat and exotic seasonings. Foreigners might put garlic and herbs in their food and eat their meat blood-red, but the Sullivans were respectable folk from the true heart of Ireland who would cook their meat until it was done, make plenty of gravy for the mashed potatoes, and boil the carrots and peas until you could chew them without breaking a tooth.

After dinner, the Sullivan uncles would doze in their armchairs with copies of the *Daily News* over their faces while we kids played John McCormack records on the ancient wind-up Victrola until Aunt Nora called us for just a little dessert of peach cobbler with fresh peach ice cream to round off the meal.

D.K.

reasonable. As with other butchers, you can (and should) ask about quality and give them feedback about what they sell.

The Moment of Decision: How to Choose Good Meat

There you are in front of the seemingly endless meat case in the supermarket or standing in front of that upscale butcher who has just called out your number in the crowded shop: what do you look for to get that great steak or chop? What do you tell the butcher, and how can you know that he or she is on your side? How can you be sure you'll end up with a delicious and tender piece of meat to serve at the feast you are planning?

Well, the short answer is: you can't be absolutely sure, even with the finest butcher and the highest grade of meat. We live in an imperfect world, and many variables that go into getting tender and flavorful meat into the marketplace. But there *are* some things you can do to increase your chances of finding tasty and tender meat.

The first thing is to read What Matters Most in Buying Beef (or Pork or Lamb or Veal) at the beginning of each chapter. Look for the qualities for each type of meat: the color of external fat should be white rather than yellow and it should be well trimmed; the color of the meat should be suitable to the type—cherry red to brownish red for beef or lamb, pale pink for pork and most veal; the texture should be fine-grained, not coarse; there should be flakes of intramuscular fat called marbling running through; in general, the meat should look appetizing and appealing.

Buy the highest USDA grade available that is compatible with your pocketbook. If you are not sure, ask the butcher and insist on getting answers. Don't be impressed by supermarket "fantasy" names such as Butcher's Choice or Five Star Prime. These terms are intentionally misleading—trying to get you to think that the market is selling you USDA Choice or Prime grades of beef. If you have a question about a cut or grade, ask the butcher or push the buzzer in the supermarket.

Several beef companies and a few lamb and pork suppliers are now offering specially labeled and branded meats. Many use the word "natural" to describe their meat—a term the government has defined to mean meat raised with minimal processing and without the use of artificial ingredients.

Some companies, such as Coleman Natural Meats and Maverick Ranch Natural Beef, have gone a step further to produce beef free of hormones and antibiotics as well as any pesticide residue. Generally speaking, branded beef will give you a better result than the usual supermarket meat. You might want to try a brand when you see it and decide for yourself. Brands found in regional marketplaces include: Bradley Ranch (B3R Brand) in Texas, Nieman-Schell and Harris Ranch in California, and Brae Beef on the East Coast. Some brands are specific to special meat breeds of cattle, such as Certified Black Angus, Farmland Black Angus, and Certified Hereford Beef. Other brands include Laura's Lean Beef, Double Diamond Brand, and supermarket brands such as Ralph's California Beef and Ukrop's Own Beef in Virginia. Formula-fed veal is sold under the Provimi and Blue Dutch labels, and range-fed veal is available from specialty producers such as Summerfield Farms by mail-order (see Sources, page 584). Summerfield Farms, Jameson, and other specialty producers also offer high-quality lamb. Amish farmers in the Northeast supply some superb pork to specialty stores. This is not a complete list: you may well find other specialty sources of fine meat.

But probably the most important factor in getting good meat onto the table is picking the right cut for the cooking method and recipe. Consult Cooking Today's Meat (page 51) and choose the cut carefully. If you are going to grill a steak tonight, don't pick a piece of bottom round, pretty though it might be. Look for a thick, well-marbled T-bone or porterhouse. We suggest preferred cuts in each recipe; also consult the introductions for the various meats to which cuts are suitable for which cooking methods.

THE FLAVOR STEPS

How can we coax the flavor we crave from the new, leaner meat? There are three ways: seasoning the meat before cooking, introducing flavors during the cooking process, and adding flavor ingredients after cooking.

We firmly believe that all meat should be seasoned before cooking to achieve the maximum flavor. At the simplest, this will mean using salt, pep-

HOW TO READ A RETAIL LABEL

THE NAMES OF THE VARIOUS CUTS OF MEAT can be confusing, varying widely from one part of the country to another or even from market to market. Label standards provided by the National Livestock and Meat Board are a first step toward uniformity throughout the United States. The label will help you to identify the primal cut, or area of the carcass that the labeled piece of meat came from, and thus determine the suitable method of cooking by consulting our introductions for each type of meat. The label doesn't, however, provide information about the grade, supplier, and other issues of quality.

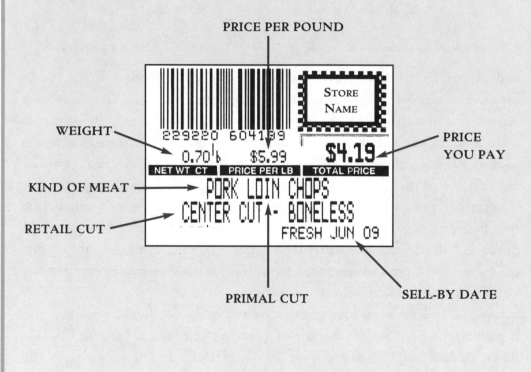

PRICE PER POUND

STORE NAME

WEIGHT

229220 604189

0.70 lb $5.99 $4.19

NET WT CT   PRICE PER LB   TOTAL PRICE

PRICE YOU PAY

KIND OF MEAT — PORK LOIN CHOPS

RETAIL CUT — CENTER CUT — BONELESS

FRESH JUN 09

PRIMAL CUT

SELL-BY DATE

per, and perhaps an herb or spice. More elaborate dry rubs of spices and herbs, herb pastes, wet marinades, coatings, stuffings, and so forth will be listed at the beginning of many ingredients lists as a **Flavor Step.**

Salt is the most important seasoning for meat, and salting meat *before* cooking is the most essential flavor step. Doesn't salting meat before cooking make it lose its juices and become dry and tough? As you'll see if you try our taste experiment (see opposite page), this is simply not true.

When meat cooks at relatively high temperatures, as in grilling, panfrying, or roasting, it begins to brown, sending up wonderful aromas and developing savory flavors. From a chemist's point of view, the browning involves chemical reactions in the amino acids that make up meat proteins, the caramelization of sugars from the meat (yes, there *is* some sugar inherent in meat), and the melting and mixing of fats with the proteins. When meat is salted before browning, the salt seems to accentuate the taste, becoming incorporated into the overall flavor profile. In other words, instead of just tasting salty, salt seems to mellow and round out the flavors produced by the browning process. When the meat is salted after browning, the salt is not so easily incorporated into the overall flavor profile. The palate simply tastes salt layered on top of the other complex flavors, only a shadow of the full potential flavor.

But why take our word for this? Conventional wisdom tells us otherwise. And after all, every palate is unique, and perhaps what tastes good to us may not taste good to you. Conduct your own taste test and see what you think.

Pepper has an entirely different effect on meat, depending on whether it is added before or after cooking, perhaps because of the complex nature of the spice. In contrast to salt, pepper seems to have much less flavor when added before cooking than when it is added after. For that reason, we add a little bit more freshly ground pepper to meat after cooking to pick up some of the aromatic elements lost in the cooking process. Pepper fanciers may want to try a taste test of their own, using different amounts on preseasoned and postseasoned meats and perhaps experimenting with different types of pepper (white, black, red, green) and grinds (coarse, medium, fine).

Besides salting and peppering meat, there are several other valuable techniques for introducing flavor into meat before cooking.

Dry Rubs are mixtures of spices and/or herbs that are rubbed or sprinkled over meat before cooking. Depending on the recipe, the meat can sit in the refrigerator for a day or two or can be cooked immediately. The longer the meat is exposed to the spices and/or herbs, the more they will permeate.

LOW-SODIUM DIETS

IF YOU'RE ON A LOW-SALT DIET, by all means use salt sparingly (you can halve the amounts we call for), but when you use your careful ration, do so where it will have the most impact on flavor. Just sprinkle a little salt on your meat before you cook it. And remember, when you eliminate salty foods from your diet, your sensitivity to salt will increase, so that just a little will go a long way. Some cooks use sea salt or other more intensely salty salt to get more bang per grain.

SALT *BEFORE* YOU COOK

T O BE OBJECTIVE and make this a controlled "blind" experiment, you'll need at least two people and a 1-inch-thick New York (strip) steak. You will also need a heavy skillet or ridged broiling pan, salt, and a pepper mill.

Cut the steak in half to make two 1-inch-thick steaks without fat or gristle of equal size and thickness. Season one steak on both sides with enough salt and pepper to provide a light, uniform sprinkling over the meat. Heat your pan over high heat for 5 minutes. Add the two steaks—the preseasoned one and the unseasoned one—and cook for 3 to 4 minutes on one side. Turn the meat over and cook it for 3 to 4 minutes more. You should have two rare steaks with a nicely browned, but not charred, surface. (Cook 4 to 5 minutes per side for medium-rare.) Now, sprinkle the unseasoned steak with about the same amount of salt and pepper you used on the other one. Label the preseasoned steak A and the postseasoned steak B.

Place both steaks on a platter and turn your back. Have your "assistant" cut equal slices of meat from each steak without telling you which is which. Taste each piece and write down your responses to A and B, but don't tell your partner what you think. Then have your assistant turn his or her back on the steaks after showing you which one was seasoned before cooking and which was seasoned after. Repeat the same blind tasting with your partner and have him or her write down the responses without telling you. Before showing each other the results, try to articulate what differences, if any, there were between the two steaks and why (or if) you preferred one over the other. Then reveal the results and see if you agree or disagree that the preseasoned piece is more flavorful.

After trying this experiment many times, we've found that presalted (and otherwise preseasoned) meat is much more flavorful and juicy than meat seasoned after cooking.

Think of spice and herb rubs as dry flavor marinades for meat, poultry, or even fish. Either a dry rub or a wet marinade could be used on the same cut of meat, depending on the flavor profile and texture desired. Dry rubs are better for extremely tender cuts such as beef fillet, since too much time in an acidic marinade can make already tender meats mushy and unpalatable.

Wet Marinades are used primarily to flavor meat, but they do have some tenderizing effect, especially on thinner cuts and meat of moderate tenderness ("in-between" meats) such as beef sirloin, chuck, top round, and flank steaks or lamb shoulder chops. Their tenderizing properties come from the acidic ingredients, which may include citrus juices, vinegar, wine, beer, or soy sauce.

With modern meats, tenderizing is not needed as much as in the past, but adding robust flavors is even more important. A few words of caution: some recipes call for marinating for hours or even overnight. Be sure to refrigerate any meat that is marinated for more than two hours to prevent spoilage. Remember that marinades containing high amounts of acid can make small, tender pieces soft and gummy if they're left in the marinade too long.

Marinades are not really useful for tenderizing large cuts such as roasts, since the marinade does not penetrate deep into the meat. And they don't work for tough cuts such as brisket or shank, which have so much connective tissue that no amount of marination will make them tender. These cuts should always be cooked by moist-heat methods with either a dry rub or wet marinade applied for flavor.

Pastes are variations of wet marinades. Delicious pastes are made with rehydrated dried chiles, garlic, onions, ginger, and/or fresh herbs such as basil or cilantro. They are pureed with spices and sometimes oil or other liquids in a food processor or blender. The paste is rubbed over the meat, which is left to marinate for a few hours or overnight in the refrigerator before cooking, depending on the recipe. Most of the paste clings to the meat to form a flavor crust as the meat is grilled or roasted.

Brining is a time-honored technique for both preserving and adding flavor to meat. Traditionally, high concentrations of salt and, sometimes, sugar and spices are either dissolved in water or rubbed directly on the meat. When the high levels of salt penetrate to the center, the meat is cured, and it can be smoked, air-dried, or cooked and eaten as is. This pickling or curing process helps to preserve meat because some of the water is replaced by salt, making conditions unsuitable for bacterial growth. Ham, bacon, salami, and corned beef (see Make Your Own Corned Beef, page 201) are all examples of brined and cured meats.

Brines have another function: flavor, juiciness, and the texture of meats (especially pork) are all enhanced if the meat spends just hours or up to a few

THE MYTHS OF TENDERIZING

For a tough cut of meat, the only way to make it tender is to braise it or stew it slowly. The following timesavers may be popular, but they don't work.

■ Don't buy "tenderized steaks." Sometimes called minute steaks or cutlets, these are thin, tough cuts that have been run through a commercial tenderizer or pounded with a serrated meat hammer. Cardboard tastes better.

■ Avoid chemical meat tenderizers. Usually made from papaya enzymes, they give meat a soggy texture and unpleasant flavor.

days in a highly flavored brine with a lower salt content than the traditional cure. In this case, some salt and the spices in the brine penetrate the meat. And most important, water from the brine enters the meat to give it a firm and juicy texture. We call this technique **Flavor Brining** (see page 254). Flavor brines work because the free water in the meat cells has a higher concentration of dissolved substances than the brine, so that water from the brine is drawn into the meat by osmosis. As a result, the meat will actually end up weighing more.

Stuffing is another old but wonderful technique for increasing flavor and juiciness in meat. The stuffing can be as simple as a mixture of chopped herbs, garlic, and bread crumbs or as elaborate as a combination of ground meats, cognac, and truffles. A stuffing not only enhances flavor but can also improve the appearance and make an ordinary flank steak or breast of veal into a beautiful and elegant dish: *Matambre* (page 120) and Stuffed Veal for Passover (page 570) are but two examples. There's no reason to limit yourself to the traditional stuffings: prosciutto, coppa (cured pork shoulder), bacon, ham, cheese, anchovies, roasted vegetables, or even dried or preserved fruits can all be used to add excitement to even the most mundane meat.

Braising and **Stewing** not only produce a flavorful liquid but also enhance the texture and taste of the meat as it soaks up the stock. In braising, the meat is browned before cooking in liquid; this is one of the most successful ways to provide rich, intense flavor, especially for the less tender cuts. By using the coordinated timing techniques described in this book, you can take advantage of this magnificent cooking method without spending too much time in the kitchen.

Beefsteak Florentine (*page 106*)

Boneless Short Ribs with Tomato and Fennel (*page 222*)

Roast Leg of Lamb (*page 486*)

California Beef Stew with Zinfandel and Roasted Winter Vegetables (*page 208*)

Pork Loin and Coleslaw Sandwich (*page 310*)

Nogales Steak Tacos (*page 102*)

Moroccan Lemon Tagine (*page 503*)

Braised Pork Butt with Port and Prunes *(page 366)*

Sauces can enhance the flavors of meat. Barbecue sauces are simple and tasty. We rarely make elaborate, classic French sauces unless we think they're essential for flavor and don't contribute too much fat. We prefer simpler pan sauces based on the cooking juices from properly seasoned and cooked meat with a little wine, beer, or cider added.

Condiments complement and brighten flavors. Examples include vinaigrettes, mustards, salsas, relishes, horseradish sauces, chutneys, ketchups, soy-based dipping sauces, and flavored oils such as truffle oil and rosemary oil.

Highly Flavored Side Dishes enhance grilled and roast meat: salads, herbed fresh tomatoes, or flavored mashed potatoes complete the plate.

Cooking Today's Meat

NO MATTER WHAT PIECE OF MEAT YOU BUY, the most important factor in tenderness and flavor is cooking it to the proper stage of doneness, using the method appropriate to the cut. Heat makes meat tender and gives it that delectable color, flavor, and aroma. But the cook has to determine what form the heat will take, depending on where on the carcass the meat comes from. Choosing between cooking by dry heat (broiling, sautéing, stir-frying, grilling, roasting) or moist heat (braising, poaching) is all-important: grilling a piece of tough bottom round will give you inedible results; braising a piece of lean pork loin has a similar effect.

Meat is basically composed of muscle protein organized into bundles, connective tissue (collagen and elastin), fat, blood, and water. Cooking changes the elements; it also makes meat more tender and safe to eat, and it maximizes flavor.

DRY OR MOIST HEAT?

Heat affects tenderness in two opposing ways, depending on whether it is dry or moist. When a lamb chop is grilled or a prime rib roasted, dry heat is applied directly. The proteins that make up the muscle component begin to change and unfold. Eventually, the meat shrinks and loses moisture, fat, and juiciness. At internal temperatures under 120°F (very rare), not much moisture has been lost. But by the time a chop or roast reaches 160°F (well-done), a great deal of the juice has leached out into the pan. So when you apply dry heat directly to lean meat, as in grilling or roasting, don't let it get much over medium-rare (130° to 140°F), or it will become dry and tough.

Moist heat, in the form of heated liquid or steam, converts the tough collagen in the meat to gelatin over a period of time. This is what makes your tough pot roast tender when it's braised or stewed. The softening process starts to occur at 160°F. Even though it's softened, however, the meat will become dry if cooked above this temperature unless it has sufficient intramuscular fat (marbling) to replace the lost moisture. That's why a fattier cut like chuck makes a more juicy pot roast than the leaner bottom round.

If you have a tender cut of meat with very little connective tissue, such as top loin steak or rib-eye roast, cook it with dry heat to an internal temperature that preserves moisture and accentuates tenderness, 120° to 140°F. Tougher cuts high in collagen, such as brisket or chuck, should be cooked with moist heat to an internal temperature that promotes the breakdown of collagen but leaves enough internal fat to compensate for the increased water loss, 155° to 165°F.

In dry-heat cooking, the exterior is browned by the caramelization of the inherent sugars in the meat and by a series of complex chemical reactions called the Maillard reaction. As the moisture on the meat's surface begins to evaporate, the juices concentrate and mix with any seasonings to form an appetizing brown crust. This provides the luscious flavor and intense "meaty" flavor we find so irresistible in a grilled steak or richly browned roast.

When meat is cooked by moist heat, however, it develops a different flavor profile than when it is cooked by dry heat. You can combine the two methods and brown the meat first to contribute some of the flavors to the broth or sauce, as is usually done with pot roasts and stews. As the meat cooks slowly in the broth, it absorbs the flavors from the liquid so that it becomes tender and delicious, with a robust sauce.

NUTRIENTS

In general, cooking meat does not deplete its nutritive value. Since fat is melted and extracted, cooking can actually reduce the fat level; cooked meat usually has less fat and fewer calories than raw meat. But highly overcooked meat, such as pot roast cooked in a pressure cooker, can lose 70 percent of the vitamin thiamin, which is destroyed by high heat—one reason we don't recommend pressure cookers for meat cookery. Other vitamins, such as B_{12} and B_6, however, are not as unstable at high heats, but all these vitamins are water-soluble and can leach out into cooking liquids. Thus the cooking liquids are valuable for their nutrients as well as their flavor; serve them as a broth or sauce or use them later in a soup.

SAFETY CONSIDERATIONS

Except for pork, which has to be cooked to a high enough temperature to eliminate any risk of trichinosis (see page 245), the prevalent opinion up to a few years ago was that most meat needed only to be cooked long enough to satisfy the taste of the diner. In fact, some classic beef dishes such as steak tartare and carpaccio feature raw beef.

In recent years, however, outbreaks of an infectious strain of *E. coli* bacteria (*E. coli* 0157:H7) in ground meats has brought the idea of eating any raw or undercooked meat into question. The USDA has taken a strong position by publishing doneness temperature recommendations that require all ground meat and hamburger to be cooked to 160°F, or well-done, and any cut of meat to at least 140°F, or what most chefs would call medium.

Never a bastion of culinary taste, the USDA declares that 140°F is rare, but no self-respecting chef of our acquaintance would ever offer anybody the light pink steak you get at 140°F and make that claim. In most steak houses

THE MEAT COOK'S SECRET WEAPON

THERE IS ONE INDISPENSABLE TOOL for the modern meat cook: the digital instant-read thermometer. We don't mean those old bulky, grossly inaccurate thermometers you jam into the roast and leave to get spattered with grease in the oven. A little better are the more recent instant-read thermometers with a circular dial on the top. You poke them deep into the center, avoiding the bone, and they give you a reasonable idea of its temperature. They're pretty accurate and can generally be depended on. But because they need to be plunged deep to register correctly, they can't be used for thinner cuts like steaks and chops.

What you really need to be a great meat cook is a *digital* instant-read meat thermometer. It is battery-powered (with a watch/camera battery) and displays temperatures electronically to two decimal points. Most have a range from -40° to +300°F, with a deviation of less than 0.1°F. It can provide an accurate reading when only about ¼ inch of the tip is inserted, so it works for steaks, chops, and burgers.

These newfangled gadgets are not expensive ($10 to $20) and will prove to be one of the best cooking investments you've ever made. Most of our recipes assume you've used one of these. We don't think you can be a successful meat cook without one.

you'd get it thrown back at you, or at least returned with a frosty glare. So what is one to do?

With large chunks of meat such as roasts or steaks, the interior portion of the meat is essentially germ-free. Only the surface of the meat can come in contact with microorganisms such as bacteria, and only a minimal amount of the meat is exposed. In most cooking methods for these cuts, the heat at the surface is high enough to kill bacteria, thus ensuring healthy eating no matter what the internal temperature. Even low-temperature roasting (250° to 275°F) provides enough heat to kill food-borne pathogens. There is always some risk of bacterial contamination, albeit quite small, so you must make up your own mind. You can follow the USDA's recommendations and be absolutely safe. Or accept some risk and eat a porterhouse the way you want it: rare and juicy and delicious.

Ground meat is another story. Here each individual particle of meat and fat has been exposed to the natural germ-filled environment of the butcher shop or packing house where it was ground. While the surface bacteria of a steak will be destroyed by cooking, bacteria in the interior of a hamburger can still be viable and dangerous. The USDA recommendation of 160°F internal temperature, or well-done, ensures safety. Exposure to 155°F for 15 seconds will kill bacteria, and one minute at 150°F is also sufficient. The USDA recommendation thus allows for a margin of error.

How to Tell When It's Done

WE DON'T THINK THOSE OLD-FASHIONED CHARTS that tell you to cook a piece of meat for so many minutes per pound are very useful. They not only refer to the fattier meats of previous decades but were never very accurate in the first place. We strongly encourage you to measure the internal temperature of virtually any cut by using a digital instant-read meat thermometer (see page 53) to determine its degree of doneness. In each of our recipes, we give you a *minimum* amount of time for cooking. The meat might not even be rare at this point. After this minimum time, begin checking the temperature, referring to the Doneness Chart on the following pages.

On this chart, we have included the temperatures recommended by the USDA, which tend to be 10° to 15°F too high, because of the government's concern for safety. We provide the temperatures for doneness used by today's chefs and meat cooks—rare in a good restaurant won't be anywhere near the 140°F the USDA recommends. It's up to you to decide whether it's more important to enjoy a rare steak or be totally sure the meat is risk free, if over-cooked.

You can use this chart for steaks or chops as well as roasts. Steaks and chops thicker than 1¼ inches do benefit from a rest of 5 to 10 minutes before serving. Roasts should be allowed to rest for 15 to 30 minutes so that the juices can redistribute and carryover (residual) heat can finish the cooking. Their internal temperatures will increase 5° to 10°F. For large roasts (8 pounds or more), such as a standing rib, a 45-minute rest is not uncommon. The final internal temperature will probably be at least 15°F higher than when the meat was removed from the oven. In all cases, cover the meat loosely with foil to keep the surface from cooling too quickly. In general, the higher the temperature of the oven, the greater the residual heat and the higher the final temperature the meat will reach after resting.

THE DONENESS CHART

VERY RARE

	REMOVE FROM HEAT	IDEAL TEMPERATURE (AFTER RESTING)	USDA RECOMMENDS
Beef steaks/lamb chops	115° to 120°F	115° to 120°F	none
Beef/lamb roasts	110° to 115°F	115° to 125°F	none

Very rare (what the French call *bleu*) should be reserved for beef or lamb. The center of the meat will be soft and the color of raw meat (cherry red for beef, purple red for lamb). The rest of the meat will be bright pink and quite juicy. We find that when large roasts such as prime rib are removed from the oven at 110° to 115°F, they often reach a final temperature of 125°F or more after 20 to 30 minutes of rest and may be considered rare rather than very rare. The internal temperatures of very large roasts (8 pounds or more) that rest for 45 minutes may increase by 15°F.

RARE

	REMOVE FROM HEAT	IDEAL TEMPERATURE (AFTER RESTING)	USDA RECOMMENDS
Beef steaks/lamb chops	120°+ to 130°F	125°+ to 130°F	140°F
Beef/lamb roasts	115°+ to 120°F	125° to 130°F	140°F

Beef and lamb are the only meats cooked to the rare stage (*saignant* in French). The meat will be fairly soft and bright pink to red in the center, not blood-red as in very rare. Some blood-red areas may remain near the bones and in the very center of large roasts. The meat is very juicy.

MEDIUM-RARE

	REMOVE FROM HEAT	IDEAL TEMPERATURE (AFTER RESTING)	USDA RECOMMENDS
Beef steaks/lamb chops/veal chops	130°+ to 135°F	130° to 140°F	150°F
Beef/lamb/veal roasts	125°+ to 130°F	130° to 140°F	150°F

Beef, lamb, and veal can be reliably cooked to this popular degree of doneness. The meat is quite pink in the center with no blood-red areas and has begun to turn grayish around the edges. It is firmer than rare but still quite juicy. Often lamb described as "rare" in restaurants is served at this temperature.

MEDIUM

	REMOVE FROM HEAT	IDEAL TEMPERATURE (AFTER RESTING)	USDA RECOMMENDS
Beef steaks/lamb/veal chops	135°+ to 150°F	140°+ to 150°F	160°F
Beef/lamb/veal roasts	130°+ to 140°F	140° to 150°F	160°F

Meat defined as medium has a wider temperature range (15 degrees) than rare or medium-rare. This doneness is fine for fattier cuts of beef, lamb, or veal, such as cross-rib roast, prime rib, leg of lamb, or rack of veal. The meat will be pink in the center and gray at the periphery, the texture quite firm, the grain compact. Pale veal may need to be cooked to 145° to 155°F to develop its best flavor. Pork is safe to eat at 145° to 150°F, but most cuts need higher temperatures for the best flavor. Pork chops may be eaten in this range, since they risk drying out beyond 155°F.

MEDIUM-WELL

	REMOVE FROM HEAT	IDEAL TEMPERATURE (AFTER RESTING)	USDA RECOMMENDS
Beef steaks/lamb/veal/pork chops less than 1¼ inches	150°+ to 165°F	155° to 165°F	170°F
Beef/lamb/veal/pork roasts/ pork chops 1¼-1½ inches or more	145°+ to 155°F	150° to 165°F	170°F

Beef or lamb should be cooked by moist or very slow heat to this range; otherwise, the meat will be dry. Fatty cuts such as lamb shoulder or beef chuck will still be juicy, however. The meat will usually be uniformly gray, with a pinkish tint near the bones. Pork and milk-fed veal are best cooked to this temperature; the juices may be faintly pink. The meat should still have some juiciness. Pork loin, especially boneless pork loin, should reach a final temperature of 150° to 160°F; remove it from the oven at 145° to 150°F. Thick pork chops (1¼ inches) may be cooked to 145°F and allowed to rest for 5 or 10 minutes for a final temperature of 150°F.

WELL DONE

	REMOVE FROM HEAT	IDEAL TEMPERATURE (AFTER RESTING)	USDA RECOMMENDS
Pork/veal roasts	165°+	170° to 185°F	170°

Meat is overcooked at this stage unless it is fatty and naturally juicy, as are cuts like spareribs or Boston butt. Pork loin or chops will be hard and dry.

Choosing the Right Cooking Method

Master Techniques

COOKING WITH DRY HEAT

DRY HEAT IS MOST SUCCESSFULLY APPLIED to tender cuts of meat, although moderately tough cuts such as beef rump or bottom round can be made tender if roasted very slowly (see Slow-Roasting, page 66). Dry heat is the best way to produce a browned exterior and the desirable "browned meat" flavors.

Tips for Success

■ Many cuts of **beef** are ideal for this method: steaks, rib roast, cross-rib roast, sirloin, and top round.

■ Virtually all **pork** cuts are tender enough to cook by dry heat, except for the shanks, hocks, and some parts of the neck and shoulder.

■ Almost all parts of **lamb** are also tender enough to be cooked using dry heat, except the shanks and neck.

■ **Veal** loin, leg, and some parts of the shoulder can be cooked by dry heat.

■ All **ground meats,** including **sausage,** can be cooked with dry-heat methods.

BROILING

■ **Best cuts:** lamb and veal chops, beef steaks, kebabs, burgers.

Many cookbooks recommend broiling steaks, chops, and other small pieces of tender meat. Cooking meat by radiant heat from direct exposure to a flame or heating element, usually below the oven of a gas or electric range, has long been popular. Many people assume broiling is healthier than cooking in a frying pan, since fat drains away through the grill. But home-broiled steaks and chops often end up dry and chewy, not luscious and tender like the steak house product.

It's not the home cook's fault, though. The broilers of most stoves, gas or electric, just don't put out enough heat. Instead of searing the surface of the meat, they sweat out valuable juices into the broiling pan or onto the surface of the meat, where they evaporate. These home broilers reach only 500° to 550°F, whereas commercial restaurant broilers get up to 700°F. With care, however, you can achieve adequate results with a home broiler, although we recommend pan-broiling for most chops or steaks.

For best results, steaks or chops should be at least ¾ inch thick and up to 1½ inches. A 2-inch-thick steak can be broiled successfully if care is taken to turn it frequently to prevent charring. Pork chops are difficult to broil both because they are so lean and because it's hard to get to exact cooking temperatures—overcooking will dry out the meat. We suggest you cook pork chops by sautéing or grilling in a covered barbecue.

Master Technique

- Prepare the meat as directed below.
- Preheat the broiler at the highest level for 15 minutes, with the broiling rack and pan in place, to achieve maximum heat. (Consult the manufacturer's directions to see if the broiler door should be left ajar.) Lightly oil the meat on both sides so that it does not stick to the rack and to aid in the browning.
- Place the broiling pan about 3 inches from the heat source, so that a 1-to-1½-inch-thick steak is 1½ to 2 inches from the heat. For a thicker steak, place the pan about 3¾ inches from the heat.
- After the meat has browned nicely on one side, 3 to 4 minutes, turn it over with tongs and brown the other side. Check often for doneness with an instant-read meat thermometer.
- Turn the meat once or twice more during cooking to keep the surface from burning. For a 2-inch-thick steak, after the steak has browned on both sides, move the broiling pan or rack so that the meat is about 3 inches from the heat source to prevent the outside from burning before the inside is done; turn the steak two or three times.

PREPARING MEAT FOR DRY-HEAT COOKING

- Remove the meat from the refrigerator an hour before cooking. Trim excess fat.
- Season all sides of the meat with salt and pepper or the herb or spice rub of your choice. If it has been in a wet marinade, pat dry.
- Use a large enough cooking vessel so there will be no overcrowding, which steams meat rather than browns it.
- Use an instant-read thermometer to check for doneness. Consult the Doneness Chart (page 56) for suggested internal temperatures.

Let the meat sit, loosely covered, for 5 to 15 minutes (depending on size) to absorb juices and let the internal temperature equilibrate.

■ Remember that broiled meat, like other meats, should sit, covered loosely, for 5 minutes or so to let the juices settle and become distributed throughout the meat. The internal temperature will rise 5°F or more, depending on the thickness and cut.

PAN-BROILING

■ **Best cuts:** steaks 1½ to 2 inches thick, chops ¾ to 1¼ inches thick, and burgers ¾ to 1 inch thick.

This is our preferred method for cooking steaks, chops, or burgers for a small group (one to four people). Pan-broiling is quick and easy, and it doesn't heat up the kitchen. The only disadvantage is a bit of smoke, which can cloud up your kitchen and set off your smoke alarm if you don't have a good exhaust fan.

If you like your meat at all well-done, we don't recommend pan-broiling steaks or chops thicker than 1¼ inches, because the surface will burn and toughen before the interior is done to your liking. That's also why we don't generally recommend pan-broiling pork chops, although thin, boneless pork chops can be cooked by this method. Sautéing (see opposite page) is a better method for most pork chops.

Master Technique

■ Use a heavy cast-iron skillet or heavy ridged pan or grill designed for pan-broiling made of cast iron or heavy coated aluminum. The weight of the pan is important so it will hold and distribute the heat evenly; don't try to pan-broil using a thin frying pan. Nonstick pans are often too thin.

■ Prepare the meat as directed on page 59.

■ Use a large enough pan so that there will be no overcrowding. A 12-inch skillet will hold six to eight lamb chops, a good-size steak such as a T-bone, or four veal chops.

■ Heat the pan over the highest heat until it is quite hot. An edge of meat touched to the pan should spatter briskly, not just make a hissing sound.

■ For most meat you won't need any oil, but for very lean cuts such as a veal chop or lean filet mignon, brush the meat with a little olive or vegetable oil. Some people rub a piece of fat over the surface of the hot pan, but this is usually not necessary and will cause more smoking. Another method is to sprinkle a little salt in the pan to prevent the meat from sticking; we don't think this is necessary either, and it can add too much salt to the meat.

■ Put the meat in the pan, making sure the pieces are not touching each other. Cook the meat uncovered over high heat for about 2 minutes. Turn and sear the other side for 2 minutes more. This should be sufficient time to cook a 1-inch-thick steak or chop to the medium-rare stage. For thicker pieces of meat, turn the heat down to medium-high and turn the meat often to prevent burning or charring.

■ Test the meat often with an instant-read meat thermometer and cook it until it reaches the desired temperature (see the Doneness Chart, page 56). For a 1¼-inch-thick steak or chop, this should take about 3 to 5 minutes more cooking after the initial searing for 2 minutes on each side. If fat accumulates in the pan, pour it off so that the meat broils and does not fry.

■ Set the meat aside, covered loosely with foil on a warm platter, for about 5 minutes (10 minutes for a really thick steak). Remember, the internal temperature will rise about 5°F as the meat rests. You can use this time to make a pan sauce.

SAUTÉING

■ **Best cuts:** thick small steaks such as filets mignon, chops; especially useful with thicker pork chops.

This technique is much like pan-broiling, except that a small amount of oil is added to the pan. It is a little gentler on the meat and can provide juicy results even with lean cuts. Sautéing also provides tasty drippings that you can easily turn into a pan sauce.

Master Technique

■ Trim and season the meat as directed on page 59.

■ Sear it over high heat in a small amount of oil or melted fat from the meat in a heavy frying pan. Avoid searing only in butter, since it will burn at high temperatures. If you want a buttery flavor, use half butter and half oil or stir a little butter into the sauce just before serving.

■ Depending on the thickness and type of meat, continue to cook it uncovered over high heat, turning often, until done. For thicker meat, lower the heat and cover to cook to the desired doneness, using an instant-read thermometer to check.

■ Add a little wine or stock to the covered pan, if you wish, and make a sauce with the pan juices, seasonings, and stock or wine, following the directions in the individual recipe.

PANFRYING

- **Best cuts:** thinner cuts of veal, pork, and beef.

Similar to sautéing, this technique uses considerably more oil in the pan. The meat, often breaded or battered (chicken-fried steak and Wiener schnitzel are examples), is fried in ¼ inch of oil over medium-high heat to create a crisp crust and nicely cooked interior.

Master Technique

- Meat should be turned often and the heat regulated to prevent burning. An instant-read meat thermometer should be used to determine doneness.

STIR-FRYING

- **Best cuts:** flank steak cut into strips across the grain, beef fillet trimmings, pork tenderloin strips.

This ingenious Asian method fries small pieces or strips of meat and vegetables separately in a small amount of oil, most often in a wok. It's really a form of sautéing over very high heat. You can also use a large frying pan for stir-frying, especially over an electric burner. Ultrahigh heat sears the food and gives it a lovely browned flavor. To avoid burning, the bits of food are kept in constant motion by stirring and tossing. Very little oil and only a small amount of meat are used, making stir-frying a quick and healthful way to cook. The meat and vegetables are then combined in a savory sauce incorporating other flavorful liquids. Stir-fried dishes are best eaten over rice or noodles.

Master Technique

- Heat a wok or large frying pan over the highest heat possible. Chinese chefs say, "Hot wok, cold oil," so pour in a little peanut oil (a tablespoon or two) when the pan is very hot.
- Toss in your meat, which may or may not be marinated in a soy-based sauce. Sear and brown the meat, stirring it up against the sides of the pan if you are using a wok. Remove the meat with a slotted spoon.
- Add whatever vegetables you like to the pan—sliced white and green onions, chopped garlic, broccoli, snow peas, water chestnuts, bok choy, or what you will, and stir vigorously until barely tender but still crisp.
- Return the meat to the pan and pour in a few tablespoons of soy and/or stock, along with a little cornstarch dissolved in water if you want a thicker sauce. Stir everything together over high heat for a minute or two, and serve immediately.

GRILLING

Grilling has become the most popular method of cooking meat in America, both indoors and outdoors. Basically, indoor gas and electric grills should be thought of as broiling apparatuses with the source of heat reversed (below rather than above the meat). They often provide more heat than the old-fashioned broilers in kitchen ranges and can give better results if enough heat can be applied to the meat. For indoor grills, follow the directions for Broiling on page 58.

An outdoor grill can be anything from a hibachi to a humongous barbecue costing thousands of dollars, but we especially like versatile kettle barbecue grills, both charcoal and gas versions, which offer some of the best ways to cook meat, either by grilling over direct heat or by roasting with indirect heat. Meat cooked in a kettle grill picks up a delicious smoky flavor, is juicy and tender, and can be cooked without extensive flaming or charring. The key to success is to cook with the cover on in most cases. The cover allows you to control the air flow around the coals and to moderate the heat to reduce flare-ups, which can burn the surface. An instruction manual comes with most kettle barbecues, and it's essential reading, since every grill is different. Follow those directions when cooking and use our suggestions below.

In general, we have found that while you can leave the cover off for the first minute or two of cooking to sear the surface of the meat, this step isn't really necessary because you can sear with the cover on right from the start—and that way you'll avoid meat-charring flare-ups. Two different techniques are used to cook all meats, sometimes alone and sometimes in combination. These are direct cooking (grilling directly over coals) and indirect cooking (roasting).

Direct Cooking over Coals

■ **Best cuts:** 1½-to-2-inch-thick steaks, pork, lamb or veal chops, burgers, kebabs, sausages.

In direct cooking, the meat is grilled right over the hot coals or the gas broiler. This is the preferred method for steaks, chops, and other small pieces of tender meat. The following directions are for charcoal grills; follow the manufacturer's instructions for gas grills.

Master Technique

■ Build a charcoal fire so that half of the grate is spread with only a single layer of coals and the other half with two or three layers. Leave some space around the edge of the grill with no coals. The single layer will be your area of moderate heat, the multilayered section will provide high heat, and the area with no coals can be used to keep fully cooked pieces of meat warm while the others finish. (Food kept warm there will continue to cook, however, so don't leave it too long. You can transfer the meat to a warm platter, covered with foil, if the other pieces take much longer to cook.)

■ When the coals have a light coating of gray ash, test the fire for temperature levels. With the grill off, hold your hand at the level of the rack over the high-temperature area of the coals. If your hand gets too hot by the time you can count to two, the heat is sufficient. If not, wait a while and try again or add more coals to the high-temperature area.

■ Put the rack on and let it heat for a minute or two. Put the meat over the high-temperature area and cover the grill immediately, leaving the top vents open. If the meat flares up, close one or two of the vents in the top part of the kettle lid to cut off air flow; this should stop flaming quickly. Open the vents again and regulate flaming as needed. Both top and bottom vents should be kept fully open while you are direct-grilling, except for brief periods to control flaming.

■ After 2 minutes, turn the meat and sear on the other side. If the meat is more than 1½ inches thick or if it seems to be cooking too fast and flaming excessively, transfer it to the moderate-heat area and continue to cook it, with the grill covered, to your desired degree of doneness.

■ If you like your meat rare, start to check it with an instant-read meat thermometer after the initial searing, or 4 or 5 minutes of cooking. Continue to flip the meat over frequently, checking the temperature as it cooks. Remove pieces of meat from the area with hot coals as soon as they are 5° to 10°F below the desired doneness level and place them on the warming area on the outside edge of the grill. The internal temperature will continue to rise as the remaining pieces of meat cook. Steaks and chops thicker than 1½ inches should be removed from the grill and allowed to rest for 10 minutes or so on a warm platter, loosely covered with foil. Thinner pieces of meat, kebabs, burgers, and sausages should rest for about 5 minutes before serving.

Indirect Cooking

■ **Best cuts:** tri-tip, beef rib roast, pork tenderloin, pork loin, pork shoulder, rack of lamb, leg of lamb.

This is a popular way to cook meat in a covered barbecue and is ideal for large pieces that require longer cooking times, more than 15 minutes or so. The meat is centered on the grill with a drip pan beneath and the coals are heaped up on either side of the pan. The meat actually roasts and takes on the aromas of smoke from the charcoal and from any hardwood chips added to the fire.

If you love the smell and taste of wood smoke in meat, as we do, then you may want to use soaked wood chips or chunks for either direct or indirect grilling. For short cooking periods, wood chips soaked in water for 30 minutes or so work well; larger wood chunks burn longer and more slowly for extended cooking times (see individual recipes for more details). Wood chips or chunks can be replenished through the access holes next to the handles of the grill or by removing the cooking grill briefly. Use only hardwoods such as hickory, alder, apple, oak, cherry, pecan, or mesquite. These chips and chunks can be purchased at hardware stores or specialty markets.

Master Technique

■ Start a fire with 40 to 60 charcoal briquettes, depending on the size of the kettle barbecue (follow the manufacturer's directions). Leave all the vents open. When the coals are covered with gray ash, push equal amounts to either side of the bottom grate and place an aluminum drip pan in the middle. You can buy or make one: form a sheet of heavy foil into a rectangular pan about 10 by 18 by 4 inches.

■ Place the grill rack on top so that the access holes next to the handles are over the coals on either side. If you roast for longer than an hour, use these holes to add more coals. You may want to sear smaller pieces of meat, such as rack of lamb, pork tenderloin, or beef fillet roast, directly over the coals to brown them. Larger pieces such as pork loin, leg of lamb, and standing rib roast can be cooked the whole time over indirect heat—the longer cooking period will brown them sufficiently.

■ After you've seared a smaller piece of meat, move it over the drip pan; or place a larger cut over the drip pan in the center of the grill to start. Place the cover on the grill with all the vents open and keep the meat covered at all times. If the meat seems to be cooking too fast, or is smoking and sizzling excessively, or if the drippings in the pan catch fire, partially close the upper vents. If that doesn't reduce the flames, partially close the lower vents (which directly control the amount of oxygen getting to the fire), too. Once the flaming dies down, the vents can be opened again.

■ Test the meat with an instant-read thermometer. Small roasts such as rack of lamb may take as little as 15 minutes to cook after the initial searing, so start checking them early. Tri-tip roasts may take only 30 to 40 minutes; and a large prime rib roast may have to cook for 2 to 3 hours. If you apply glazes, sauces, or marinades that contain sugar, brush them on only during the last 10 to 15 minutes of cooking to prevent charring.

BARBECUING, OR SLOW-ROASTING, IN A COVERED GRILL
■ **Best cuts:** tough, fattier meats like beef brisket, pork spareribs, pork butt, beef ribs, and lamb shoulder.

Barbecuing, as opposed to outdoor grilling, is the long, slow roasting of meat or poultry using charcoal and/or wood chunks both as a heat source and for flavoring. Slow barbecuing is best done over indirect heat in a kettle barbecue or a specially built brick barbecue. You may choose to add liquid to the drip pan used in this procedure. Ideally the temperature of the barbecue should be maintained at 200° to 275°F throughout the cooking period, which can be lengthy. For a full discussion, see Slow-Cooked Barbecued Spareribs— The Real Way, page 376.

OVEN-ROASTING
■ **Best cuts:** large pieces of meat that are at least 2 or 3 inches thick and are moderately to very tender.

Occasionally, thin, flat pieces of meat such as flank steak are turned into roasts; they're either rolled into a cylindrical shape or stuffed to increase their girth. Ideal cuts should have ample marbling, since they run the risk of drying out unless they're cooked only to very rare. In the case of lean cuts such as pork loin, great care must be taken so that the meat doesn't exceed 155°F and become dry and tough.

In the old days, roasting took place not in ovens but on spits rigged in large fireplaces, some big enough to roast whole oxen. The cook patiently tended to the meat, turning the spit, basting, and prodding it until it reached perfection. Spit-roasting is still a delicious way to cook meat and is practiced today in some of the world's finest restaurants in Madrid, southern France, northern Italy, and Greece, where whole suckling pigs and lambs, huge chunks of beef, chickens, rabbits, and even venison and wild boar are turned slowly over glowing fires, sending off billowing clouds of aromatic smoke. Here at home, many restaurants now feature spit-roasting as a specialty. Some gas grills come with electric spits installed, and if you're lucky enough to have one, follow the manufacturer's directions. Many of our dry rubs and marinades are suitable for spit-roasting, especially those for larger pieces of lamb or pork.

BASTING: A WASTED EFFORT

MANY RECIPES call for basting roasts with wine, stock, or other liquids or fat. This is thought to keep them moist and add flavor. We don't think basting does much for roasted meat—it just washes away seasonings from the surface and doesn't contribute to juiciness at all. For perfect results, the trick is not to overcook the roast.

Basting the surface of the meat during dry-heat cooking should not be confused with the cooking method that we call wet basting (see page 72), in which the meat is cooked in a liquid.

Most of us, though, rely on ovens to do our roasting. Ironically, some of the old practices of spit-roasting are still with us, such as basting meat as it cooks, in most cases an unnecessary step (see Wet Basting, page 72, for some exceptions).

Because it's next to impossible to judge the degree of doneness of roasted meat from appearance, an accurate instant-read meat thermometer is a must.

Successful roasting depends on two key variables: the internal temperature of the finished meat (degree of doneness) and the oven temperature. The lower the temperature, the slower the cooking. Less moisture and fat are lost, and the finished roast will be tender. If you cook two identical roasts to an internal temperature of 135°F (medium-rare), roasting one at 450°F for a short period of time and the other at 250°F for a longer period, the longer-cooked roast will be more succulent. It will also have less weight loss from exuded moisture and fat, will be consistently pink throughout its interior, and will be more tender than the roast cooked at 450°F. The roast cooked at 250°F, however, will have very little external browning and less "cooked meat" flavor than the higher-temperature roast.

Basically, roasting can be divided into three methods: high-temperature roasting (at 450°F and above), moderate-temperature roasting (300° to 350°F), and low-temperature roasting (250° to 275°F). Each method has its own merits and its own applications, which we will discuss here in general terms. Consult the individual recipes for specific recommendations and details.

High-Temperature Roasting (450°F and above)

■ **Best cuts:** very tender meats such as tri-tip, beef fillet, New York strip, beef top loin, eye of prime rib, lamb loin, rack of lamb—cooked no more than medium-rare to medium.

Because high-temperature roasting doesn't enhance tenderness, it works only for those cuts that are already very tender. Even though this method can cause shrinkage and moisture loss, the roasting times are so short for such cuts that this usually isn't a problem. The browning and caramelization of the surface provide delicious flavors, and the pan drippings can often be used to make a wonderfully intense gravy. Some smaller cuts such as rack of lamb may be in the oven for only 20 to 30 minutes, not enough time to develop a rich, brown crust. You can brown these first in a skillet for maximum flavor and appearance. Remember that meat cooked at high temperatures should rest for at least 10 minutes so that the juices can settle. The internal temperature might rise as much as 10°F, so be sure to compensate. For example, if you want to end up with medium-rare meat—135°F—take it out of the oven when the internal temperature reaches 125°F.

Some recent cookbooks advocate roasting all meats in a very hot oven (500°F). Although we agree that this method can create a delicious, heavily browned crust of caramelized juices and seasonings, it's very difficult to achieve the proper degree of doneness. Just a few extra minutes of roasting in such a hot oven can mean the difference between a perfectly cooked prime rib and an overdone disaster. Furthermore, large cuts of meat such as prime rib or leg of lamb roasted in a hot oven should be allowed to rest for 20 to 45 minutes to distribute the internal juices and finish carryover cooking. Depending on how large the piece of meat is, the internal temperature could rise from 15° to as much as 25°F during this time, leading to problems. If you want to cook a whole prime-rib roast to rare using this method, to ensure a final temperature of 130° you'd have to remove the meat from the oven when its internal temperature was 105°F—barely above body temperature.

High-temperature roasting also can cause splattering, smoking, and a dirty oven—a nuisance if you have a sensitive smoke alarm and don't have a self-cleaning oven.

Moderate-Temperature Roasting (300° to 350°F)

■ **Best cuts:** tender pork such as pork loin or tender pieces of veal like the rack; beef sirloin or rump roast; large cuts such as leg of pork, a whole 7-bone standing rib roast, a large beef top round (10 to 15 pounds), or a big leg of lamb.

Since lean meats such as pork loin can dry out easily, they can benefit from the gradual, steady application of moderate heat. Because these roasts are usually fully cooked at about 130° to 140°F, they're in the oven long enough to brown well. In the case of beef or lamb, even though the meat may be cooked only to the medium-rare stage, it will be in long enough (usually more than 2 hours) to develop a savory brown crust. In the case of smaller roasts, such as beef rump or sirloin tip that will cook for less than 2 hours, you may want to sear them first in a heavy skillet to brown the surface and then continue cooking to the desired degree of doneness in a moderate oven.

English Method of Roasting (High-Temperature Searing Followed by Moderate Roasting)

■ **Best cuts:** standing rib roasts, beef top loin roasts.

This is the time-honored technique used by English cooks for roasting beef and is our preferred method. Although there is a little more shrinkage than in the moderate-heat method, the rich brown crust that results more than compensates for the slight loss of juiciness. A large chunk of tender meat (7 to 10 pounds) is seasoned and then seared in a hot (450° to 500°F) oven. The temperature is then lowered to 350°F, and the browned roast allowed to reach its final internal temperature. This method provides the advantage of high heat for the flavor and moderate heat for tenderness, juiciness, and careful control of degree of doneness.

Slow-Roasting (250° to 275°F)

■ **Best cuts:** tougher, less expensive cuts of beef from the chuck and round.

The chuck roasts most suitable for slow-roasting are (in order of preference): bone-in blade roast, cross-rib roast, chuck-eye roast (somewhat fattier than the others), chuck fillet or chuck tenderloin (often labeled mock tender or mislabeled chuck eye), shoulder or arm roast, and boneless center blade roast. From the round (a bit less flavorful): top round, eye of the round, and bottom round (the least tender cut of all). Other good roasts for this method come from the sirloin and rump: sirloin tip, top sirloin, rump roast, and bottom rump roast.

Slow-roasting is particularly useful for lean beef cooked for cold rare roast beef sandwiches or salads, where little or no fat is wanted. There's less shrinkage with slow-roasting, so you get juicier results. Although the meat can be roasted at 200°F, most home ovens are not accurate at these low temperatures and bacterial contamination could occur, so 250° to 275°F is the best range.

Commercial meat plants cook meat this way to minimize shrinkage and maximize tenderness. The trade-off is that the meat doesn't brown and develop the luscious flavors that we find so desirable. To compensate, you can first roast the meat at 250°F to an internal temperature of 110°F. At that point, leave the meat in the oven and turn up the temperature to 500°F to complete the cooking and brown the surface. For a small (2-to-3-pound) roast, this browning should take about 15 minutes if the meat is to be cooked to the medium-rare stage, 135°F. Like all roasts, the meat should be allowed to rest under foil for 15 or 20 minutes before carving, so remove it at 5° to 10°F below the desired final internal temperature.

In general, slow-roasting is not a good idea if you want well-done meat (more than medium, or 145°F), since even fatty cuts like chuck will dry out with such long cooking. It's better to use moist-heat methods such as pot-roasting. Cuts with more flavor and a higher level of intramuscular fat are better cooked by this method than leaner cuts such as round or sirloin.

COOKING WITH MOIST HEAT

COOKING MEAT IN A MOIST ENVIRONMENT of liquid or steam is best for tough cuts, because the moist heat softens and dissolves the collagen or connective tissue. The heat must be applied gently—a simmer, not a boil—since high levels of moist heat can toughen and shrink muscle fibers.

BRASING AND STEWING

■ **Best cuts:** beef chuck, beef round, lamb shoulder, cuts from the pork leg or shoulder, veal shoulder and breast.

Braising means cooking in liquid in a sealed container—pot-roasting and stewing are notable examples. In pot-roasting, larger chunks of meat are cooked in a flavored liquid, then sliced and served with gravy made from the cooking liquid. Stewing involves smaller pieces of meat and more liquid. Most braises and stews call for searing or browning the meat first and then cooking it in water, stock, wine, or other liquids, usually enhanced with aromatic vegetables such as onions, carrots, and garlic. A few stews, such as Moroccan lamb tagine or French veal stew—*blanquette de veau*—do not require browning first.

The less liquid used in a braise, the more intensely flavored the sauce. It's a good idea to braise meat in a pot the meat fits snugly so that you won't have to use a lot of liquid. Our recipes recommend various liquids for braising, but you can vary them to suit your taste and needs. Traditional braising liquids are water, stock, wine, beer, and tomato and other juices. These often incorporate intensely flavored liquids such as soy sauce, liqueurs, and brandy, chile purees, and Worcestershire sauce. When the tender meat is removed, the braising liquid can be made into a sauce by degreasing and then boiling it to concentrate the flavors, a process called reduction. The liquid can also be thickened with cornstarch or flour, but in most cases this is not necessary.

Braising can take place on top of the stove at a slow simmer or in a moderate oven, 325° to 350°F. A heavy lidded pot, casserole, or Dutch oven gives the best results. Almost all braised dishes are best made a day or so ahead to develop flavor.

Master Technique

■ Before it's browned, wipe the meat dry and season it with salt and pepper or a dry rub, or dredge with flour. The meat may be marinated first (consult individual recipes). Marinated meat should be brought to room temperature and thoroughly dried before cooking.

■ We suggest using olive oil or vegetable oil for searing, although some cooks still prefer fat rendered from the meat to be cooked. Avoid butter and margarine, which have a tendency to burn.

■ Heat the oil over medium-high heat in a heavy lidded pot or Dutch oven until a piece of meat sizzles briskly when it touches the pan. Put the meat into the pot, being careful not to crowd the pieces if using smaller pieces rather than one large cut (overcrowding lowers the heat and causes the meat to steam and sweat). Turn the meat frequently as it browns to avoid burning.

■ Remove the meat from the pan when it has browned, pour off most of the fat, and then sauté aromatic vegetables such as onions, carrot, and garlic in the remaining fat. Some chefs like to sprinkle sautéed onions with a little sugar; the resultant caramelizing adds attractive colors and flavors to the braise. You can also leave a tablespoon or two of fat in the pan and set the meat on a bed of chopped savory vegetables for further cooking, with some chopped ham or prosciutto for extra flavor.

■ Return the meat to the pot and add the braising liquid. For a stew, the liquid should just cover the pieces of meat. For pot-roasting and braising larger pieces of meat, the liquid should be ¼ to ½ inch deep. To braise meat on top of the stove, bring the liquid to a boil, reduce the heat to a bare simmer, cover, and cook until the meat is tender; if necessary, replenish the liquid in the pot and turn the meat from time to time to keep it moist. To braise meat in the oven, preheat the oven to 325° to 350°F. Place the pot with the browned meat, vegetables, and cooking liquid in the oven, cover, and cook until the meat is tender. Replenish the liquid if necessary and turn the meat from time to time.

■ If you want to serve vegetables with your stew or pot roast and you are cooking it on the stovetop, add them to the pot during the last 45 minutes of cooking; estimate about ¼ pound of vegetables per ¾ pound of meat. If you are braising in the oven, we recommend that you cook the vegetables separately on top of the stove and add them to the pot toward the end of the cooking period.

POACHING

■ **Best cuts:** tougher pieces of meat such as beef brisket, corned beef, beef shank, beef bottom round, veal shoulder, breast of veal, lamb shoulder, pork neck, and ham hocks.

This gentle method of cooking immerses meat in liquid at low temperatures, 170° to 180°F, thereby softening the connective tissue without toughening muscle fibers. Although it's usually reserved for tough cuts, poaching can also be used successfully with certain tender meats such as beef fillet.

Many types of flavored broths can be used as the poaching liquid. The meat is rarely browned before poaching and the resulting broth is rich in flavor—often it's served as a soup course before the meat or incorporated into a sauce or gravy.

Many cultures, including our own, have one-pot dishes based on poached meat and vegetables: New England boiled dinner, French *pot-au-feu,* Italian *bollito misto,* Austrian boiled brisket, Spanish *cocido madrileño.* While many recipes have "boiling" in their name, the technique is really poaching at low temperatures.

WET BASTING

■ **Best cuts:** moderately tough meats such as lamb shoulder or veal shoulder and some of the more tender cuts of beef chuck.

Frequent basting with liquids such as wine, water, stock, or beer while the meat roasts in an open pan filled with ¼ inch of liquid is another form of moist cooking. Some of the liquid in the pan evaporates and fills the oven with steam, while basting moistens the surface of the meat. Basting with butter, oil, or even fat, however, doesn't work because it doesn't create the moist environment and steam that help to tenderize the meat. Wet basting also provides an intensely flavored liquid that can easily be turned into a delicious sauce. Meats cooked by this method are usually roasted in a moderate oven (300° to 350°F) to the medium-well stage of doneness.

STEAMING

This method is not often used with meat, but it can be used to warm already cooked meats such as corned beef, pastrami, or ham. Steam can also be used to cook raw corned beef or really tough cuts like pork trotters (pig's feet), beef shank, or lamb neck.

PRESSURE-STEAMING/PRESSURE-COOKING

We don't recommend pressure-cooking for meat since it's very hard to control the level of doneness. All too often meat is overcooked to the point where it begins to disintegrate. But a pressure cooker can be used for extremely tough cuts—trotters, hocks, shanks, brisket, or neck. It can also be used to make quick stews.

MICROWAVING

We are not enthusiastic about cooking meat in a microwave, since it usually comes out looking and tasting like a wet rag. However, microwaving can be a useful method for warming braised meat.

▪ Beef ▪

America's Most Popular Meat

WHEN WE REMEMBER GREAT MEALS OF THE PAST, the centerpiece usually is beef in some form or another—that great prime rib for Christmas dinner, a juicy steak hot from the barbecue, or Mom's succulent pot roast.

Beef is still our national favorite; each day 76 million portions are served in the United States. We may eat leaner beef and less of it than we used to, but we continue to enjoy its hearty taste in many forms. In restaurants, beef is still the king of the menu, and more and more of us opt for steak when dining out. Steak houses are the hottest sector of today's restaurant business, and they appropriate much of the country's prime beef, which is increasingly hard to find in supermarkets—one reason why so many of us order it when we dine out.

One of meat's main attractions is its versatility. The tender cuts from the sirloin, loin, or rib that provide steaks or roasts are delicious when cooked only briefly over high heat and are a fast source of potent flavor. The tougher cuts lend themselves to pot-roasting, stewing, braising, and slow-roasting—dishes that can be conveniently made ahead and rewarmed.

And let's not forget the hamburger, America's—and the world's, it seems—favorite food. Not only do Americans of all ages line up at the hamburger stand, but we now see the golden arches everywhere from the Champs-Élysées to Tiananmen Square. The citizens of Minsk recently rioted in the streets, competing to be the first in town to munch a Big Mac.

A Colorful History

CATTLE FROM LASCAUX TO LAREDO

The wild bulls that leap out from the painted walls of prehistoric caves in the South of France and Spain—Lascaux, Chauvet, Altamira—seem strangely familiar, with their widely curving horns, strong shoulders, thin withers, and lean, rangy bodies. After you contemplate them for a while, you realize with a start that they remind you of Texas Longhorns—descendants of these ancient cattle that adapted and readapted to the wild to survive in burning heat and bitter cold and to defend their young against predators. Cattle are the most powerful animals that humans have sought to exploit and dominate over the centuries. They have served as sources of meat, milk, hide, horn, labor, and, often, religious awe from before the beginnings of civilization to the present day.

The wild ox *(Bos primigenius),* called the aurochs or urus, is the ancestor of most of today's domestic cattle *(Bos taurus).* Wild cattle were hunted and, we can infer from the cave paintings, venerated by humankind for many thousands of years. They were one of the last of the major species to be domesticated, most likely in Mesopotamia, Egypt, and northern India some time between 6000 and 4000 B.C. The herding and exploitation of cattle for meat and milk and as work animals spread rapidly into Europe, the Far East, and Africa, where breeding with native species resulted in the ancestors of modern cattle. Wild cattle existed in Europe into historical times. In the first century B.C., Julius Caesar compared them to elephants in power and ferocity in his *De Bello Gallico,* and Pliny the Elder described the aurochs's remarkable strength and swiftness. Wild bulls were hunted by Charlemagne in the ninth century and were still found in the forests of eastern Poland as late as the seventeenth century.

BULL GODS AND CATTLE DANCERS

Cattle, and especially bulls, have been a source of religious awe from Cro-Magnon times. Ancient Egyptians worshiped a specially selected Apis bull as an incarnation of the god Osiris. Lithe, young cattle dancers are depicted vaulting over the horns of bulls on the walls of Minoan palaces, and Greek myth describes the Minotaur, half-man, half-bull, at the center of the labyrinth in Crete. Roman soldiers worshiped and sacrificed the bull as part of the cult of Mithra, which was especially popular in Spain. In India, humped cattle, or zebu *(Bos indicus),* descended most likely from the wild Malaysian *banteng,* are sacred and wander through the streets at will. And today's bullfight, with its elaborate rituals and costumes, such as the running of the bulls in

Pamplona, shows humanity's longstanding fascination with this animal and its powers.

Whole cultures have centered on cattle herding. A man's wealth is counted by the number of his cows among the Masai and Dinka tribes of Africa today just as it was by the Celts of pre-Roman Europe. Young Masai warriors live with their cows and subsist on a diet of blood and milk; Dinka villagers travel with the herds and derive most of their nourishment and material culture from their cattle.

OXEN PULLED THE PLOW, BUT THE MEAT WAS TOUGH

Cattle provided the draft animals for most of Europe from Roman times until relatively recently. Plows were pulled and wagons drawn by slow but powerful oxen, or castrated bulls. Cattle were killed and eaten only when their work as milk cows or draft animals was over, which made for chewy and stringy beef. In the days before refrigeration, slaughtering an ox or cow meant that hundreds of pounds of meat had to be consumed quickly. Thus beef, probably as tough as shoe leather (another bovine product), was eaten only on special feast days by the peasantry or by aristocrats when the hunt didn't go well. Oxen were often roasted whole on huge spits in castle fireplaces, carved, and served to the lords and ladies and hordes of hungry retainers.

During the later Middle Ages, the expansion of cities created markets for beef, mutton, and other agricultural products. Each year in the fall, stock raisers from the lord of the manor to the lowliest peasant had to decide how many animals to keep over the winter. Feed was scarce and expensive, so animals were slaughtered and the meat preserved by smoking or salting for family use. The surplus cattle, pigs, sheep, and geese were sent to market over long drovers' roads that led to the cities. In fact, English cattle drovers were the original cowboys.

ENGLISHMEN: LEGENDARY BEEFEATERS

The English have always loved meat, especially the famous roast beef of Old England (usually cut from either the short loin or from the standing rib) still featured today in many London restaurants. Beef eating in England began to take on almost legendary status in Elizabethan times: it was credited with creating the bluff well-being and ruddy health of the English yeoman and the unflappable courage of the English soldier, or Beefeater. Prosperous merchants used their new wealth to buy meat for the table, and their foreign visitors were amazed at the great quantity (and high quality) of the beef they were served.

AMERICAN BEEF: FROM LONGHORNS TO MODERN BREEDS

American colonists, like their English forebears, ate plenty of beef, though it was the pig, which thrived on American corn, that provided most of their meat. Colonists along the eastern seaboard brought mixed-purposed cattle breeds from England and the Continent: Durhams and other English Short-horns and Holsteins suitable for milk and meat and for service as draft animals. Later eastern farmers imported pure meat breeds, such as the Scottish Black Angus and white-faced English Herefords, which have blocky bodies, thick and bulky loins, and a tendency to layer on intramuscular fat, making them rich and tender. These breeds did much to improve the quality of meat from American herds.

But it was the Texas Longhorn, derived from the Spanish cattle brought over by the conquistadors, whose abundance and availability fueled America's love of beef. These half-wild cattle, whose precursors were the original wild cattle of the Iberian Peninsula seen on prehistoric cave walls, thrived in the sparse pastures and desert scrubland of Texas and the Southwest. By the time of the Civil War, millions of the Longhorns roamed through Texas, tended by Mexican and Texan ranchers who raided each other's loosely controlled herds across an ill-defined border. With the dislocation caused by the war, these half-wild cattle became even wilder and their numbers increased at an amazing rate. Some estimates put the number of cattle ranging through Texas after the war at 45 million or more.

The problem facing Texan and other western ranchers was how to get this huge surplus of meat on the hoof to markets in the East. The answer lay in the system of railroads that developed during the war to supply the Union's war machine. Radiating from Chicago to the South, West, and East, the rail-roads provided the means of getting cheap and plentiful beef to the cities, with their rapidly expanding population. In the stockyards of Chicago and Kansas City, the cattle were first fattened on corn and other agricultural products of the Midwest, then shipped to markets. With the advent of refrigerated freight cars, cattle could be slaughtered by meat packers at the railheads and fresh and wholesome meat shipped to butchers throughout the country.

DUDES OUT WEST
Aristocrats on the Range

NOT ALL THE RANCHERS OF THE WILD WEST were rough-and-tumble types. The English, Europeans, and moneyed Easterners saw the range and its millions of cattle as an investment opportunity and a way to get in contact with the primitive life of the Noble Savage extolled by Rousseau. They had the money; the West provided land, cattle, and plenty of prospects. So they arrived with suitcases, portmanteaux, valets, wine cellars, whole arsenals of weapons, and plenty of attitude—amazing, amusing, and often angering the locals.

One of the more flamboyant of the aristocratic ranchers, the Marquis de Morès (with the suitably ornate name of Antoine Amédée Marie Vincent Amat Manca de Vallombrosa), set up quite a spread out in the Little Missouri Valley of the Dakota badlands; it included a château with Oriental rugs, fine china, and a splendid wine cellar. He stocked his 10,000-acre ranch with prime cattle, sheep, and horses and decided to go into competition with meat packers like Armour by setting up his own slaughterhouse at a nearby railhead. He boasted: "My father-in-law has 10 million dollars and can borrow 10 million more. I've got old Armour and the rest of them matched dollar for dollar." De Morès even formed his own Northern Pacific Refrigerator Car Company, with his immensely rich father-in-law, and sold shares in the venture to eager eastern and European investors.

Trouble ensued, however, with local ranchers and their hired hands. Shootouts with neighbors—the Marquis was described as being "armed like a battleship"—brought on legal problems, and the slaughterhouse scheme proved financially disastrous. The terrible winter of 1886–87, called the Great Die-Up by northern ranchers, was the last straw for the Marquis and many other cattle entrepreneurs. He and his father-in-law called it quits and retired from the field. The Marquis continued his life of adventure, however. He died some years later in a battle with Tuareg warriors in the remote Sahara, Colts blazing, game to the end.

COWPOKES AND CATTLE DRIVES

Getting the cattle to the railroads from Texas, however, was another story—one that has created the myth of the cowboy and the cattle drive so often depicted in movies, from *Red River* to *Lonesome Dove*. Driving cattle to market is an ancient profession, as we have seen, but the English drovers did not have to contend with Comanches, Kansas bushwhackers, rustlers, rattlesnakes, swollen rivers, and dusty deserts.

A series of trails arose to get cattle to the railroads. The first was the Shawnee Trail, which dated back to the 1840s and led through Kansas to railheads at Kansas City, Sedalia, and St. Louis. This route was cut off by the Civil War; Union raiders who remained after the bitter fighting on the Kansas-Missouri border made it difficult for Texans (mostly ex-Confederate soldiers) to get through unscathed after the war. The focus shifted west to the Chisholm Trail, which led through the Indian Territory to Abilene, a dusty town that became a thriving cattle emporium overnight. Over 50 percent of Texas cattle moved up the Chisholm Trail after the war, although the Western Trail to Dodge City and the Goodnight-Loving Trail to Denver soon became popular as the railheads moved west.

These trails and the cattle drives created the modern image of the cowboy: brave and hard, self-reliant, and quick to go for his Colt to defend the herd or his honor. While Hollywood has had much to do with creating the myth, there is reality behind the legends. These itinerant agricultural laborers *were* brave and rugged individuals who did much to create the modern meat industry—and almost as much for Hollywood. Many early stars such as Tom Mix were real cowboys drawn to the emerging movie industry to work as wranglers in the first Westerns. Wyatt Earp died (with his boots off, we presume) in the 1920s in Hollywood.

CATTLE BARONS AND RANGE WARS

Cattle barons such as Charles Goodnight, a tough and taciturn range rider who created the Goodnight-Loving Trail, Richard King, whose immense King Ranch still produces fine beef, and Abel Shanghai Pierce, a ex-seafarer with a swashbuckling past, are just a few of the colorful and powerful men who created the modern beef industry. Along with British and European entrepreneurs like the Scottish land shark Murdo Mackenzie and the aristocratic Marquis de Morès and moneyed Easterners like Teddy Roosevelt, they transformed cattle ranching in the last half of the nineteenth century. Their methods ranged from legal (hard work, tough bargaining, defending their property from rustlers) to the not-so-legal (theft, arson, and murder). But as a result of their efforts and the many wars for dominance of the open range, this disparate group of sagebrush capitalists came to control huge amounts of land and millions of cattle. With the coming of barbed wire in the 1870s, they were able to fence the once-free range and build huge commercial empires, many of which, like the King Ranch in South Texas, remain prosperous today.

NEW BREEDS AND STEAK HOUSES

The cattle barons also gave us what we now think of as American beef. Toward the end of the nineteenth century, they introduced Herefords, Durham, Angus, and other meat breeds to the West. They bred these and drought-resistant Asian humped breeds, or Brahmans, with native stock to create a new type of western cattle that incorporated the Longhorns' ability to survive difficult conditions with the foreign breeds' capacity to fatten easily and provide more tender meat. Even when Longhorns were fattened on corn and grain, their meat was tough and stringy. British breeds and the new hybrids produced the tender beef that Americans came to love: rich, well-marbled meat with a deep, beefy flavor.

With the great surplus of beef reaching the eastern markets, the hordes of immigrants that were flooding into America in the latter part of the nineteenth century had the opportunity to eat meat on a regular basis for the first time. In cities like New York and Chicago, restaurants specializing in beef, or steak houses, became the symbol of the good life for many working-class Americans. A steak dinner was the reward for a week's hard work, and orgies of steak eating often marked holiday festivities. Not much has changed. Even with all the emphasis today on keeping lean and eating green, steak houses continue to thrive and a thick steak is still the dinner of choice for many Americans out for a night on the town.

THE HAMBURGER: AN AMERICAN SUCCESS STORY

Even more popular than steak, however, is that great icon of American food, the hamburger. The simple patty of ground beef served on a bun has become the symbol of America, with critics taking aim at it whenever they want to show what's wrong with our cooking (and our way of life). But hamburgers are famous for a good reason: they can be delicious if prepared with imagination, seasoned skillfully, and carefully cooked.

The American hamburger is thought to have its origins in the seagoing practice of grinding tough, hard, salted beef to tenderize it, then mixing it with onions and soaked bread crumbs, and frying it as patties or ersatz steaks.

Many immigrants first encountered this dish on the Hamburg-American liners that brought so many of them to the United States in the late nineteenth century. When they landed in America, the newcomers kept their taste for this hamburger steak, a luxury for those who rarely ate meat. They continued to make it, using the cheap and ample supplies of fresh beef shipped from western markets. The popularity of the hamburger steak gradually moved west, and in the 1930s, chains like White Tower spread its fame.

The burger's apotheosis came with the creation of the drive-in restaurant in Southern California after World War II. Now embellished with lettuce, tomato, onions, pickles, and gooey dressing, hamburgers became the quintessential food of the drive-in crowd in the go-go '50s and the swinging '60s and soon became the perfect food for rebelling teenagers everywhere. The burger was cheap, it was fun to eat, it was trendy, and with a malt and fries it was exactly what your long-suffering mother didn't want you to eat! With the industrializing and standardizing of the burger that began at a little drive-in in San Bernardino adorned with golden arches, the American hamburger conquered the world.

The New Lean Beef
A Nutritional Profile

W E'RE NO LONGER EATING QUITE THE SAME BEEF that the cattle ranchers provided up to the 1950s and 1960s, the heyday of American beef consumption. With declining beef sales from health concerns, the ranchers responded by raising leaner beef cattle by keeping them for less time in feedlots and breeding their herds with leaner European cattle such as Charolais, Limousin, and Chianina, which have wide loins and provide bigger but leaner steaks and roasts than other breeds.

As a result, depending on the grade, today's beef has considerably less intramuscular fat than in previous times. The widely available grade Select has on average only about two thirds the fat of the highest Prime grade.

Although beef often gets a bad rap for its high fat content, when you take a closer look it isn't the villain it's been made out to be. Lean beef has about twice the saturated fat of skinless chicken breast. But if we compare leaner cuts like beef round and sirloin with fattier chicken parts such as skinless thighs, we find that they have only about two-thirds the saturated fat.

Some of the leanest cuts of beef are among the tastiest and tenderest. These are (beginning with the leanest): top round, sirloin tip, sirloin, top loin (New York strip), beef tenderloin (fillet). All can be cooked as steaks or roasts. Even chuck or pot roast, when braised and trimmed of fat, meets the low-fat criterion of less than 180 calories and less than 8 grams of fat per 3-ounce serving. You can lower the fat content of the dish even more—about ½

THE RIGHT KIND OF FAT

W E ALL WANT FATLESS MEAT, but we also want our steaks to be butter-tender, juicy, and delicious. Both are not possible. Consumers tend to judge meat by how much visible external *inter*muscular fat there is on a steak; this kind of fat can be trimmed off. Instead, they should look for the *intra*muscular fat, or marbling, which determines juiciness and tenderness.

If you want to lower the fat content of cooked meat, follow our suggestion to cut off most of the external fat. But for tender meat, look for and welcome marbling; just a little fat streaked throughout the meat keeps it juicy and tender.

BEEF AT A GLANCE

■ **Look for:** Slightly moist meat, light cherry red to brownish red color, marbled interior fat, white external fat. Smooth, tight grain in the meat. Should smell clean and fresh.

■ **Avoid:** Sticky or wet meat, very deep purple red meat, dark splotches, yellow fat with browning or darkening. Stale or sour odors (take meat back to the store if it smells unpleasant).

■ **Overlooked Cuts:** Tri-tip, skirt steak, hanger steak.

■ **Best Buys:** Chuck steaks, shank, brisket, beef ribs.

■ **Luxury Cuts:** Filet mignon, standing rib roast, top loin roast.

■ **Storage:** Two to four days refrigerated; well-wrapped and frozen, up to six months.

gram per serving—by trimming the meat of external fat before cooking, the method we recommend in most of our recipes.

Beef not only is packed with protein but also contains high levels of dietary nutrients such as vitamin B_{12} and iron. And it contains them in far higher amounts than chicken: available iron, for example, is two and a half times higher in beef, while vitamin B_{12} is eight times higher. And beef has much more flavor than the bland and ubiquitous boneless, skinless chicken breast we find all too often on our plates.

What Matters Most in Buying Beef

FRESHNESS DENOTES QUALITY. Good beef should smell fresh with no stale, sour, or off odors. The surface of the meat should be moist, but never sticky or dripping wet. Depending on the cut, the texture should be fine-grained, although certain cuts such as brisket, flank, or shank may have a coarser texture. The fat should be white with no brown or darkened areas that suggest dried out, older meat. When you buy meat that is already wrapped, there shouldn't be excessive liquid in the package, indicating previously frozen and thawed meat.

Color isn't a very reliable indicator of quality, since many butcher cases use special lighting to give meat a misleading bright red hue. If you can take the package out of the meat case, the beef should be light cherry red to brownish red in natural light. Very dark or deep red beef could indicate tough and tasteless meat from dairy cows. In some supermarkets and wholesale club stores, large pieces of meat, such as whole strip loins, are often sold in vacuum-sealed bags (Cryovac). The lack of oxygen in these packages gives the meat a dark purplish color, but when the bag is opened, it returns to its characteristic reddish color. Also, the meat may give off a strong odor from the liquid accumulated in the bag. This will dissipate after a few minutes of exposure to air.

The best and most critical judgment of quality comes from your taste buds after you've cooked the meat. The meat should deliver the taste, tenderness, and juiciness you are looking for in good beef. If it doesn't, let the butcher know you are unhappy and why.

A Quick Anatomy Lesson for the Busy Cook

BEFORE YOU PURCHASE ANY PIECE OF BEEF, you have to know what you are going to do with it. You certainly wouldn't want to buy a butter-tender beef fillet to make a pot roast. Not only would the meat fall apart during the long, moist cooking but it would be a complete waste of a very expensive cut. And you definitely wouldn't choose a beef brisket to slice up into steaks for the grill. You'd go broke paying dental bills for all those guests who broke their teeth or sprained their jaws gnawing on that tough meat. Where on the steer the meat comes from is the most important factor in determining how tender it will be and how it should be cooked.

GENERAL GUIDELINES

Tenderness depends on the amount of work a particular muscle does. The areas along the back of the steer (the loin, ribs, and rump) don't get as much exercise as the neck, shoulders, brisket, and flanks. Tender steaks and roasts cut from the animal's back can be cooked quickly by dry-heat methods such as grilling, frying, and roasting. Tougher cuts require the moist, slow heat of braising and stewing to be cooked to perfection. The advantage of these tough cuts, however, is flavor: muscles that do more work have more of that rich beef taste. Think of filet mignon versus pot roast: the steak is tender, light, and tasty; the braised meat intense, luscious, hearty. The trick is to know what part of the animal the meat comes from and to cook it in just the right way.

But you don't have to become an expert in anatomy to understand the important cuts of beef. In fact, there are really only eight basic areas of the steer that you need to know about. Meat packers call these areas the **primal**

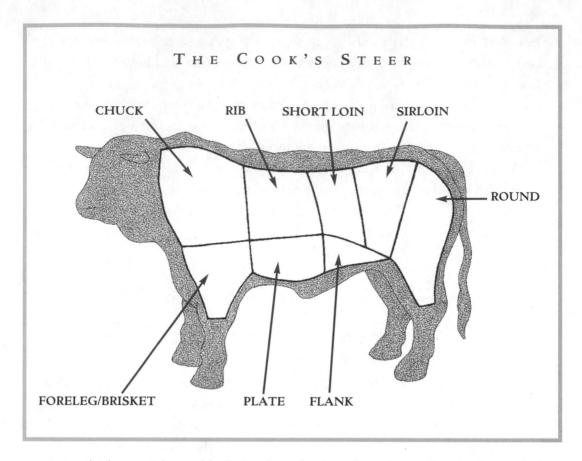

THE COOK'S STEER

CHUCK   RIB   SHORT LOIN   SIRLOIN

ROUND

FORELEG/BRISKET   PLATE   FLANK

cuts, which are either sold wholesale or broken down into sub-primal cuts and sold to markets and, increasingly, consumers. The three primal areas that make up the back are called the **rib, short loin,** and **sirloin.** Steaks and roasts are cut from these areas (see How to Choose a Great Steak, page 92, and How to Choose a Great Roast Beef, page 172, for individual cuts). Meat from the sections along the back will have a fine, close-grained texture and usually a single eye of muscle.

The **chuck (shoulder), brisket/foreshank, flank,** and **plate** areas from the shoulder and sides of the steer yield tougher cuts, ideal for stews, pot roasts, and other braises. They are also the main sources of ground beef. The texture of the meat is more coarsely grained, and the cuts usually have several muscles interwoven with connective tissue, which needs slow heat to become tenderized or dissolved. Although they start out tough, these flavorful cuts can become silky smooth and fork-tender when properly cooked.

Meat that makes up the **round (leg),** along with some areas of the chuck and flank, are in-between in terms of tenderness. While not as tender as the short loin and rib, they have a good, meaty flavor and can be cooked by dry-heat methods. The texture and flavor of these slightly tougher cuts can be vastly improved by marinating: top round, often sold as London broil, is a good example. Rump roast is especially delicious with a dry marinade and slow roasting (325°F) to medium rare. Round steaks and bottom round can be a bit dry and tough and are best braised.

Grades of Beef

ALL MEAT AND POULTRY is slaughtered and processed under the inspection of the United States Department of Agriculture, or USDA. Meat packers can choose whether they wish to have their meat graded for quality.

Grading has nothing to do with the wholesomeness of the meat and the conditions under which it was slaughtered and packed. No matter what its quality grade, all meat sold in the United States has to meet strict sanitary requirements all the way from the slaughterhouse to the butcher's case.

Federal quality grading of beef is based on the age of the animal, the degree of intramuscular fat (marbling), and the conformation, or physique, of the animal. Younger animals will be more tender with more marbling, and the age of the animal has a direct effect on the juiciness and flavor of the meat. High-quality beef carcasses will have a broad and substantial back, or loin, area, which provides meat that is both flavorful and tender.

Although there are eight grades, in reality most of the meat falls into the top three grades. To be officially graded, the meat should bear the USDA initials and grade. To be certain, you can ask your butcher to show you the quality grade that is stamped directly on the exterior fat.

Only about 2 percent of today's beef is of the highest USDA grade, or **Prime**. Most of this very expensive meat is sold to overseas buyers from Japan, leaving very little for the retail trade. Virtually all of the remaining Prime beef ends up on restaurant tables. About 45 percent of the carcasses are graded **Choice**, while 21 percent are stamped with the **Select** grade.

Since only the top two grades demand a premium price to justify the cost of grading, many packers instruct the inspectors not to bother putting a grade on carcasses that are not Choice or Prime. These ungraded carcasses are called **No Roll**, since the rolling stamp of the inspector is not applied to the exterior fat of the carcass. Much of the beef in America, especially in supermarkets, is sold ungraded but would have been Select if graded. Often it bears a label that falsely implies a high USDA grade (see box, page 88).

Prime, the top grade, has the highest level of marbling. If you can find a butcher who will sell you some real USDA Prime beef, try it for a T-bone or porterhouse steak or a prime rib. Since it is so expensive, Prime beef is almost always sold as steaks and roasts, so you won't see tougher cuts identified as

BEWARE FANTASY NAMES

MANY LARGE SUPERMARKETS TODAY purchase almost exclusively No Roll, or ungraded, beef. Supermarket butchers then give this leaner, cheaper, and tougher meat what the trade calls fantasy names, which imply grading and quality: Butcher's Prime, Market Choice, and Lean Select. These terms have no legal meaning. "Lean" doesn't necessarily mean good, and "Butcher's Prime" doesn't guarantee meat that's tender, juicy, or tasty. If the meat is inadequate, tell the butcher and take your business to someone who sells USDA-graded meats. Since ungraded meats cost the supermarket less, you should expect to pay less for them, which is not always the case.

This practice of selling ungraded meat with fantasy names is misleading and should be discouraged. Since there is a reliable system of federal guidelines in place, all retail sellers of meat, including the large grocery chains, should use the USDA grading system so that customers know just what kind of meat they are buying, and prices should reflect quality.

Prime. If you happen to know a butcher who deals in Prime beef and cuts up his own carcasses, see if he'll sell you some of the tougher cuts, such as short ribs or chuck. They should be extra juicy with a great, beefy flavor.

Choice represents 67 percent of all graded beef (but remember that this figure is skewed: most beef would be Select if graded). Since you probably won't be able to find Prime beef, seek out Choice as the best alternative. It comes from young animals with minimal to moderate marbling and good conformation. Choice is also the most varied category: some packers offer subgrades in Choice that indicate more marbling, such as Top Choice. Once again, try to find a butcher who knows meat and will talk to you about it; have him or her select the best of the Choice meats available.

Like Prime, Choice is usually found on the more tender and expensive cuts, but even for tougher cuts such as brisket or chuck, it is worth seeking out. Owing to the good level of marbling, you'll end up with juicy and more flavorful pot roasts and braises. Some of the warehouse clubs are now selling Choice beef exclusively, either as sub-primal cuts such as strip loin or packaged in smaller amounts.

Meat packers who feel that they can provide a consistently high-level product in the Choice category have **branded** their meat. Examples include Harris

Ranch in California or Certified Black Angus from a breed with a high degree of marbling. These brands generally cost a little more, but they are usually of high quality and often provide meat that is well aged and nicely trimmed.

Select (once called **Good**) is leaner meat. Select steaks have little marbling and only a few flakes of white, intramuscular fat. Because Select meat is so lean, it can be easily dried out when overcooked by dry-heat methods. It has less flavor and juiciness overall than the higher grades. Tender cuts such as steaks and roasts are best when not cooked beyond medium. Tougher cuts can be braised or stewed and often taste as good as Choice when properly prepared.

As a comparison, a Choice rib-eye steak will have about 5 percent intramuscular fat or marbling; a Select rib-eye will have 3½ percent. Naturally lean cuts such as the top round, however, would be about equal in marbling, with the Select having only 0.5 percent less intramuscular fat than Choice.

Lower grades such as **Standard**, **Commercial**, **Utility**, **Cutter**, and **Canner** rarely reach the butcher's retail case today. Cattle from the lower grades (usually old dairy cows and worn-out bulls) sell at such low prices that no meat packer wants to pay to have them graded. These cattle most often end up as ground beef or in canned soups, hot dogs, and dog food.

In addition to USDA grading, some meat is slaughtered and processed under religious restrictions. **Kosher** meat is butchered under the supervision of special rabbis and is subject to specific Jewish laws. Only certain parts of the carcass may be consumed (for example, from the tenth rib forward), all blood must be drained from the animal, and the meat must be consumed with-

HOW MUCH BEEF TO BUY

ALTHOUGH MOST NUTRITIONAL DATA are based on a 3-ounce cooked boneless serving, this may be too small for most people, especially the more hearty trenchermen. We call for larger portions, usually 4 or more ounces or a little more per serving. Use our recipes as a guide and then consider the appetites at your table. Ravenous teenagers will require a haunch or two per raging appetite. Young executives just back from the health club might call for only a neatly trimmed morsel for fastidious dining. Appetites vary more than you would think, and hot or cold weather can also make a difference, so adjust accordingly. But always remember, it's better to have a little too much than too little. Leftover beef is never a problem (see page 16).

in 72 hours of slaughter. **Halal** meat is also religiously supervised by butchers who follow strict Islamic practices.

Aging Beef for Flavor

Aging beef by keeping it unwrapped under refrigeration (below 36°F but above freezing) for extended periods of time increases its tenderness because natural enzymes are released that help soften the connective tissue in the muscles. Not only is dry-aged beef tender, but a great deal of moisture evaporates (there may be as much as a 20 percent weight loss), concentrating the flavor. The meat mellows, and the rich, beefy taste is accentuated.

There was a time in the not-so-distant past when all good butchers aged their beef, sometimes for as much as six weeks. Today most butchers no longer have the room or the wherewithal to provide dry-aged beef for their customers, although some fine steak houses and prime rib restaurants dry-age their own meat or purchase it from specialty meat purveyors in New York or Chicago. True dry-aged beef is rare, but it is worth knowing about.

Aging is suitable only for the highest grades of beef (Prime or Choice) that will be cooked by dry heat and, because of its considerable cost, should be limited to the best cuts of the rib and short loin. Since there is a lot of shrinkage and trimming in this process, significant weight is lost. This makes dry-aging beef expensive, which is another reason the practice has largely died out.

For those of us who love fine beef, however, there is no substitute for dry-aging. You may still find a cooperative butcher who will allow you to purchase a piece of high-grade beef; ask him or her to dry-age it for you. But remember, you'll have to pay for the gross weight of the meat at the beginning of the aging process to compensate for the weight lost to evaporation and trimming.

As they say in the race car commercials, don't try this at home! Aging meat is for professionals, not for the home cook. If you can get a butcher to do it for you, fine, give it a try. But don't stick a steak in the back of the fridge for a couple of weeks and expect to get a palatable product. The meat needs to hang in a professional refrigerator under the supervision of a butcher to be flavorful and safe.

REFRIGERATING BEEF

FRESH BEEF CAN BE STORED for three to four days in the refrigerator; ground beef should be used within two days. Store meat in its original tray in the coldest part of the refrigerator, at 36° to 40°F. If you don't intend to use the beef within a few days of purchase, it's best to freeze it immediately to ensure optimum quality. Well wrapped, beef will keep frozen for three to six months.

Cooked beef should be kept whole, if possible, loosely wrapped in plastic wrap or foil and stored in the coldest part of the refrigerator. Meat cooked in liquid can be left in the sauce or gravy and rewarmed when needed. Remove any congealed fat and heat slowly in the liquid on the stove or in a microwave. Cooked meat should be eaten within four or five days or frozen as soon as it's cooked and cooled, for up to two or three months.

WET-AGING

Some butchers store their beef at 36°F in its original vacuum pack for two weeks. This form of aging will help to tenderize the meat by the same enzymatic processes involved in dry-aging. But because wet-aging involves no loss of moisture through evaporation, the flavors do not become concentrated as they do with dry-aging. You might want to ask a butcher to set aside a sub-primal cut such as a whole top loin (strip loin), beef tenderloin, or prime rib and age it for you in his or her refrigerator. We don't think wet-aging produces the same flavor as old-fashioned dry-aging, but you could try it and see.

Most meat we purchase these days is not deliberately aged. It will most likely be 4 to 10 days old, depending on how fast the shop turns its inventory and how long it takes to get from the packing house to the meat case. Above all, don't confuse old meat with aged meat. Old meat, sometimes marked down in supermarket cases, simply means meat that is getting near the end of its shelf life and the butcher wants to get rid of it. If you buy this meat, be careful. Plan to use it the same day and discard or return it if it is sticky and has any off odors. This is not what is meant by aged meat; it's simply meat that is getting ready to go bad.

How to Choose a Great Steak

AFTER GROUND BEEF, steaks make up the largest segment of all beef sold, and you can easily taste why. Beefsteaks are tender and flavorful, versatile, and easy to prepare. But different portions of the carcass are sold as steaks, and they are not all alike. Here's how to find and cook a great steak.

The word "steak" refers to an ancient Saxon practice of cooking strips of beef on a stick, or stake, over an open fire. This popular mode of cookery resulted in the whole animal being cut up into bits, or *steiks,* that could be skewered and broiled. But the early Britons soon found that not all steaks are equal: flavor and tenderness depend on where the meat comes from on the animal.

You'll find a lot of discussion and differences of opinion among steak lovers. Some prefer the very tender and almost fatless filet mignon, while others opt for more flavorful and somewhat chewy flank or chuck steaks. The rich flavors of porterhouse and the closely related T-bone are steak house favorites, although fattier rib steaks provide a luscious texture and wonderfully tender meat. To buy bone-in or boneless, to grill or pan-broil, to marinate or not to

THE TENDERNESS SCALE

NOT ALL STEAKS ARE EQUAL: flavor and tenderness depend on where the meat comes from on the animal. The list below was developed from a study at Texas A & M University in 1990 and ranks steaks according to tenderness:

Very Tender
  Fillet, or Tenderloin, Steak
Tender
  Chuck Top Blade Steak*
  Top Loin (New York Strip)
   Steak
  Porterhouse/T-bone Steak
  Rib Steak/Rib-Eye Steak

Moderately tender
(in-between meat
improved by marinating)
  Chuck-Eye Steak
  Round Tip Steak
  Top Sirloin Steak

Note: Top blade steak varies quite a bit, so you must decide if the meat provides adequate tenderness. It also has a vein of gristle down the center that must be cut away.

PAMPERED CATTLE

A FEW RANCHERS are producing very heavily marbled beef from the Japanese Wagu breed (also called Kobe beef). In Japan, some growers feed their pampered steers bottles of beer and massage them daily, something American ranchers don't do. This fabled beef is *very* expensive but exquisitely tender. It can be found in some Japanese groceries and in super-premium butcher shops in Los Angeles and New York—for example, Balducci's in Manhattan.

marinate, are all points for discussion—you'll find passionate adherents of every steak and cooking style at the table, each convinced that his or her steak is the best.

As you can see from the Tenderness Scale, fillet steak or tenderloin is by far the most tender. We both like these steaks because they have ample marbling and good flavor. They are best cooked rare to medium-rare, either grilled or pan-sautéed. Fillet steaks are also sold as filet mignon and tournedos. A large, six-inch section of the fillet is often grilled and served as châteaubriand, usually for two, with a rather elaborate preparation of vegetables and garnishes.

SHORT LOIN STEAKS

In general, the best and most expensive steaks come from the short loin located in the middle of the back, which gets very little exercise. A characteristic T-shaped bone separates the **tenderloin**, or **fillet**, muscle from the larger top loin (called **strip** or **New York**). Bone-in steaks from the short loin with only a bit of tenderloin attached are called **T-bones**, while those with a greater proportion are referred to as **porterhouse**. A bone-in steak without any tenderloin attached goes by many different names: **bone-in top loin**, **New York strip loin**, **shell steak**, **strip steak**, **Delmonico steak**, and **club steak**. Take the bone away and the top loin steak gets called everything but late for dinner. Depending on what part of the country you're from, it can be called a **Kansas City steak, New York strip steak, boneless club steak, ambassador steak, veiny steak,** or **strip steak.** (See Steaks at a Glance, page 98, for a list of steak names and synonyms.) Whatever you call them, these tender steaks from the short loin are excellent and ideal for grilling or pan-broiling. The meat is also firm enough for marinating.

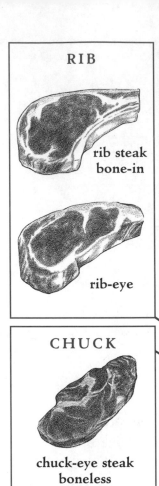

RIB

rib steak
bone-in

rib-eye

SHORT LOIN

T-bone

porterhouse

top loin bone-in
(New York strip steak)

tenderloin
(fillet) steak

SIRLOIN

sirloin steak

culotte (tri-tip)
steak

CHUCK

chuck-eye steak
boneless

chuck blade steak
boneless

chuck shoulder
next to the prime rib

flatiron
(top blade chuck steak)

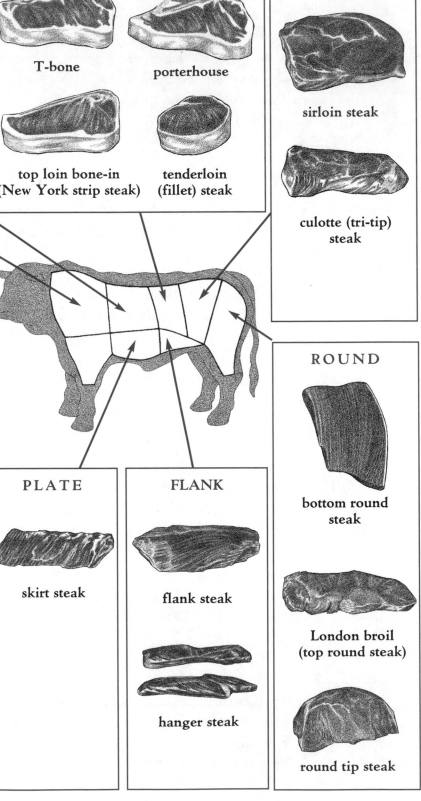

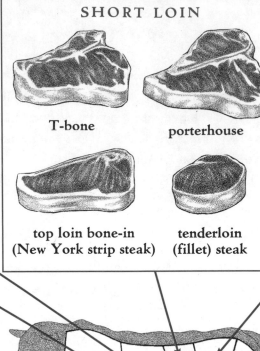

PLATE

skirt steak

FLANK

flank steak

hanger steak

ROUND

bottom round
steak

London broil
(top round steak)

round tip steak

RIB STEAKS

After the short loin, steaks cut from the rib section, where the muscles do a bit more work, are of excellent quality. Bruce prefers the **bone-in rib steak**, while Denis likes the **rib-eye**, the same steak without the bone. These steaks are vastly improved by a dry rub or marinade (see page 579 for suggested marinades). To keep the name confusion at its usual high level: rib steaks are also called **market steaks**, **Spencer steaks**, **Delmonico steaks** (yes, that also refers to the top loin steak—we said it was confusing, didn't we?), **beauty steak**, and *(en français)* **entrecôte**.

HANGER, FLANK, AND SKIRT STEAKS

More tasty than the previous areas but less tender are **hanger steak**, **flank steak**, and especially **skirt steak**—chewy cuts from the chest and side of the animal that have rich, deep, beefy flavors. All these cuts become sublime when marinated overnight in the refrigerator. The popular **London broil** originally was a flank steak in a tangy marinade, which was then grilled and sliced across the grain. Nowadays, however, London broil can mean any lean and less tender steak from the top round, sirloin, or even the shoulder. These cuts are meant to be marinated, grilled, or broiled and then thinly sliced. We prefer to use the tastier flank steak for London broil, since top round steaks often turn out dry and flavorless. The flank steak is easy to recognize by its characteristic longitudinal grain.

SIRLOIN STEAK

Located in the hip area, the sirloin is a transitional cut from the more ten-

NAME GAMES

Time was, when you ordered a New York steak in a restaurant in the Big Apple, they'd look at you as if you were crazy or at least a tourist. If you asked for a Kansas City steak in Kansas City, you got nowhere. But now Kansas City and New York both call the boneless top loin, or strip steak, by their own city name. And in northern California, requesting a New York cut sirloin steak will get you not the top loin but the top half of the sirloin. And a New York tip steak will come from the sirloin tip, not the top loin. Maybe the best thing to do is to order your steak as one wise and extremely carnivorous friend of ours always does: "Give me the best and thickest steak in the joint and cook it till it just stops mooing!"

der, less active muscles of the back and short loin to the more heavily exercised ones of the rump and leg. When it comes to value, **sirloin steak** is the most popular steak sold at retail. It is relatively cheap, with little waste, and can be cooked by dry-heat methods such as grilling, broiling, and pan-broiling. The steaks cut from the tri-tip end of the bottom sirloin, called **culotte**, or **tri-tip,** steaks, are quite tasty when seasoned with a spice rub and grilled.

For our taste, sirloin steak, especially if it is Select grade, can be overly lean and somewhat dry, especially if cooked beyond medium. Wet or dry marinades are essential if you want to make this cut tasty and juicy.

As for its various names, the sirloin can be confusing, since it consists of several muscles that can be cut in different ways. Sirloins were once easily identified by the bit of bone included, but now the bone is removed at the packing house. Boneless versions today are called: **top butt steak, top sirloin butt, sirloin butt steak, hip sirloin,** or **center-cut sirloin** as well as **London broil**. The least desirable but still flavorful **sirloin** is the area next to the leg or round. Like top round steaks, these are flavorful marinated, grilled, and sliced across the grain.

ROUND STEAKS

The leg, or round, area at the hind section of the cow produces not only **top round steaks** (often sold as London broil) but also a steak called a **round tip,** which is often cut thin for a quick sauté or stir-fry. Like so many other steaks, however, these steaks have several other names to add to the confusion (see Steaks at a Glance, page 98). Top round steaks are very lean and can become tough if overcooked. They are much improved if marinated overnight in the refrigerator (see Grilled Bourbon-Marinated Top Round Steak, page 124). **Bottom round** is best braised, as it is too tough for cooking by dry-heat methods. **Round steak,** usually sold bone-in, is a single steak consisting of **top round, bottom round**, and often a piece of the **eye of the round.** It is ideal for braising and is often cooked as **Swiss steak.**

CHUCK STEAKS

You may have noticed from the Tenderness Scale (page 92) that steaks cut from the chuck, or shoulder, can be tender and delicious. And they can be very kind to the pocketbook. **Chuck steaks** offer intense beef flavor and are quite cheap in comparison to short loin steaks. They are chewier, however, and can contain bits of gristle and fat. One bit of warning: a single chuck steak can contain pieces of several muscles of varying degrees of tenderness. You want to be sure to buy steaks that include just those particular cuts that are suitable for dry-heat cooking (see Making the Cut, page 134).

GIT ALONG LITTLE BEEFALO

EVERAL YEARS BACK, some ranchers began raising a cross between beef cattle and buffalo that they called beefalo. This meat is leaner than beef and has some of the wonderful qualities of buffalo. Unfortunately, it's not broadly distributed, but it's worth a try if you can find some. Farm-raised buffalo is also available in many markets. It has a dense texture and a delicious, slightly gamy flavor. Cook it as you would lean beef.

The first slices of **chuck shoulder next to the prime rib** include some of the rib bone. Because the meat here is an extension of the rib-eye, it is almost as tender and just as delicious as a rib-eye steak—but costs much less. See if you can find these **rib-bone chuck steaks;** we think you'll find they are special. Boneless, these steaks are often called **chuck blade boneless steaks.** When the tough under blade is removed, they are sold as **chuck-eye steaks** and also go by a few other names (see Steaks at a Glance, page 98). Since tenderness in chuck steaks can vary so much, we suggest marinating these tasty steaks overnight in the refrigerator before grilling or broiling.

The chuck area also contains the shoulder blade, a flat bone with a ridge down the center. The bone divides two muscles, the flatiron and the chuck mock tender. The flatiron has the shape of an old-fashioned iron and can be sliced into steaks called **flatiron steaks** or **blade steaks.** As you can see from the Tenderness Scale (page 92), these **top blade chuck steaks** can be quite tender, but they have one minor flaw: a small line of gristle running down the center. You can easily remove it with a sharp knife before or after cooking. Flatiron steaks take well to marinades and are excellent grilled. They are quite reasonably priced and can be downright cheap if you cut your own from the center of a blade roast (see Making the Cut, page 134). The name **chuck mock tender** is misleading. It really isn't tender and is best used for braised steak, pot roast, or stew. You sometimes see these as **chuck fillet steaks,** and they are best avoided when cooking with dry heat.

Steaks at a Glance

BEEF CUT	Stir-Fry	Sauté	Pan-Broil	Broil	Grill	Braise	Marination Recommended
SHORT LOIN							
T-Bone/Porterhouse		x	x	x	x		
Tenderloin Steak	x	x	x	x	x		
AKA: Filet Mignon, *Fillet de Boeuf,* Fillet Steak, Châteaubriand							
Top Loin Steak, Boneless	x	x	x	x	x		
AKA: Ambassador Steak, Strip Steak, Boneless Club Steak, Hotel-Style Steak, Kansas City Steak, New York Strip Steak, Veiny Steak							
Top Loin Steak, Bone-in	x	x	x	x	x		
AKA: Chip Club Steak, Club Steak, Country Club Steak, Delmonico Steak, Shell Steak, Sirloin Strip Steak, Strip Steak							
RIB							
Rib Steak	x	x	x	x	x		x
Rib-Eye Steak	x	x	x	x	x		x
AKA: Beauty Steak, Delmonico Steak, Market Steak, Spencer Steak							
PLATE							
Skirt Steak	x	x	x	x	x		x
AKA: Fajita Meat, Inside Skirt Steak, Outside Skirt Steak, Philadelphia Steak							
Hanger Steak		x	x	x	x		x
AKA: Hanging Tenderloin, Butcher's Steak, Hanging Tender							
FLANK							
Flank Steak	x		x	x	x	x	x
AKA: Flank Steak Fillet, Jiffy Steak, London Broil							
SIRLOIN							
Sirloin Steak	x	x	x	x	x		x
AKA: Flat-Bone Steak, Pin-Bone Steak, Round-Bone Steak, Wedge-Bone Steak							
Top Sirloin Steak, Boneless	x	x	x	x	x		x
AKA: Sirloin Butt Steak, London Broil							
Tri-Tip Steak	x	x	x	x	x		x
AKA: Culotte, Triangle Steak							
ROUND							
Round Tip Steak, Thin Cut	x	x	x	x	x		x
AKA: Ball Tip Steak, Beef Sirloin Tip Steak, Breakfast Steak, Knuckle Steak, Sandwich Steak, Minute Steak							
Round Steak						x	
AKA: Full-Cut Round Steak							
Top Round Steak	x	x	x	x	x	x	x
AKA: Top Round London Broil							
Eye Round Steak						x	
CHUCK							
Top Blade Steak, Boneless	x	x	x	x	x	x	x
AKA: Flatiron Steak, Book Steak, Butler Steak, Lifter Steak, Petite Steak, Top Chuck Steak Boneless, Blade Steak							
Shoulder Steak, Boneless		x	x	x	x	x	x
AKA: Clod Steak, English Steak, London Broil, Shoulder Steak Half Cut							
Chuck Arm Steak						x	
AKA: Arm Swiss Steak, Chuck Steak for Swissing, Round Bone Steak							
Chuck-Eye Steak, Boneless	x	x	x	x	x	x	x
AKA: Boneless Chuck Fillet Steak, Boneless Steak Bottom Chuck, Boneless Chuck Slices							
Chuck Mock Tender Steak						x	
AKA: Chuck-Eye Steak, Chuck Fillet Steak, Fish Steak, Chuck Tender Steak							
Chuck 7-Bone Steak		x	x	x	x	x	x
AKA: Center Chuck Steak							

OUR FAVORITE STEAKS

Bruce: I like to gnaw on bones and am a firm believer in the saying, "The closer to the bone, the sweeter the meat." So my favorite steak is the porterhouse, which includes pieces of both the fillet (tenderloin) and the top loin (New York or strip steak). Both of these muscles are very tender and juicy, and they have a particularly mellow and beefy flavor. I love porterhouse when it's cut at least 2 inches thick and cooked on the grill as in Beefsteak Florentine (page 106). Another tasty and often neglected steak that I'm particularly fond of is chuck steak, especially one cut from near the prime rib (you can recognize this by the substantial chunk of rib bone attached). I like the chuck because its intense flavor takes well to so many marinades, especially those with citrus, soy sauce, or even whiskey (see Bourbon Marinade, page 124). Although you may find an occasional bit of gristle, chuck steaks offer a great steak-eating experience.

Denis: I really love hanger steak, the thick strip of meat that hangs from the skirt steak, or diaphragm. Along with skirt steak, this has the most flavor of all the steaks. Hanger steak is also called hanging tenderloin, flap meat, or butcher's steak, the latter because this tender meat is usually taken home by butchers and hardly ever appears in the meat case. Ask your butcher to save some for you. If you can't find this steak, try the similarly flavored skirt steak.

The trick with steaks like the hanger or skirt is to cook them very briefly over high heat, preferably mesquite charcoal. Once cooked, these steaks can be sliced into strips and tucked into tortillas with as many pickled jalapeños as you can stand. Be sure to cook these steaks no more than medium-rare or they get sawdust dry.

THE ULTIMATE STEAK TACO

ONE SUMMER IN MY EARLY COLLEGE YEARS, three friends and I decided to take off on an adventure. I borrowed the family '57 Ford, and we piled in and headed across the great desert that separates Los Angeles from Tucson, Arizona.

We ended up in Mexico, in the border town of Nogales. One day we woke up famished after our siestas and decided to find this great steak place we'd been hearing about all week. The joint was jumping, tables were filled and noisy, and a mariachi band was wandering from table to table playing loudly and singing enthusiastically. (We soon found out you had to pay to get them to go away.)

In one corner was a large barbecue pit, where the pit master, a wizened and dignified old man, was grilling huge steaks over glowing logs of mesquite. In another corner sat a table with large earthenware bowls filled high with charred pasilla and Anaheim chiles. Old women peeled off the burnt skin, cutting the bright green chiles into strips, and piled them on brightly colored platters. At another table, more women patted and baked corn tortillas on a big *comal*, or griddle, while the aromatic smoke from the grilling steaks and chiles swirled around and around in the cooling shade of the patio.

As soon as we sat down, ice-cold bottles of Carta Blanca appeared, along with an immense basket of thick, warm tortilla chips sprinkled with crumbly white cheese and a stone mortar filled with coarsely chopped guacamole. There was no menu and no ordering. All the customers knew what they were there for; you had the sense that you were in good hands and that everything would work out for the best.

After a couple more rounds of beer and chips, a towel-lined basket arrived, filled with warm tortillas folded around melting chunks of mild but tangy white cheese. And soon after, the smiling waitress brought bowls of fire-roasted chiles and a huge platter holding two of the biggest steaks we had ever seen. These were followed by bowls of boiled pinto beans, red and green salsas, and red onions pickled with lime juice. The table setting was simple: big hand-painted plates, bigger napkins, and very sharp steak knives.

It didn't take long for us to figure out the program. You opened up one of the folded tortilla/cheese setups and added sliced chiles and as many strips of grilled steak as you could cram inside, leaving just enough room for some salsa and pickled onions. (The beans were eaten as a side dish.) And then you chomped down, trying to get as much as possible of the delicious mixture into your mouth at once. You washed everything down with cold beer, built another steak, cheese, and chile combo, and continued on. And on. And on.

After we polished off the steaks, platters of freshly sliced papayas and mangoes sprinkled with lime juice and powdered chiles refreshed our palates and cleared our heads. We'd found our adventure, so we squeezed back into my father's Ford and headed north.

More than three decades have gone by, but I often remember those great steak tacos. I'd like to believe that the little hilltop patio restaurant still exists and is still serving that tasty meat and that someday I'll return. But until then, it's possible to create a reasonable facsimile. Heat up the grill, turn on some mariachi music, pop open a few Carta Blancas or Coronas, and get ready for the Ultimate Taco. *B.A.*

Nogales Steak Tacos

Flavor Step ■
NOGALES STEAK MARINADE

6 garlic cloves, mashed
with 1 teaspoon kosher
salt in a mortar or on
a cutting board

¾ cup fresh sour orange
juice (from Seville
oranges) OR ¼ cup
fresh orange juice plus
½ cup fresh lime juice

2 tablespoons tequila
(optional)

2 tablespoons ground
chiles (ancho or
New Mexico)

1 cup chopped fresh
cilantro

1 tablespoon chopped
fresh oregano or
1½ teaspoons dried

2 teaspoons salt

1 tablespoon coarsely
ground black pepper

¼ cup olive or vegetable
oil

2 ¾-to-1-inch-thick chuck
steaks, cut closest to the
prime rib, OR two 1-to-
1¼-inch-thick rib steaks
(each about 1½ pounds)
Salt and freshly ground
black pepper

24 corn tortillas, preferably
handmade (or the
freshest machine-made
you can find)

Serves 6 to 8
■ COOKING ON A BUDGET (CHUCK STEAKS)
■ FIT FOR COMPANY ■ GOOD FOR A CROWD

THE STEAKS WE ATE IN NOGALES were most likely chuck steaks cut from the area closest to the prime rib. Look for chuck steaks with a good portion of rib bone and very little of the blade bone—or you can use bone-in rib steaks. The marinade in this recipe will tenderize the somewhat tougher chuck steaks adequately, but it adds flavor to the more tender rib steaks, too. This is also a superb marinade for fajitas made from skirt or flank steak. Chiles and other Mexican ingredients are available in Latino groceries or by mail-order (see Sources, page 584). Begin the recipe the day before you plan to serve it. *(See photograph, page 46.)*

■ **Flavor Step** ■ Mix all the ingredients in a bowl and whisk together, or put the ingredients into a food processor and pulse briefly. Lay 1 steak in a nonreactive dish. Puncture the meat all over on both sides with a fork or skewer. Pour over half the marinade. Put the other steak on top and repeat the process. Reverse the steaks to make sure that both are well coated with the marinade. Cover with plastic wrap and refrigerate overnight, turning the steaks occasionally to ensure full penetration of the marinade.

About an hour before grilling, remove the steaks from the refrigerator. Soak 6 mesquite wood chunks or 2 cups of mesquite, oak, or hickory chips in water. Fire up a covered charcoal grill with about 60 briquettes or the equivalent of mesquite charcoal. When the coals are completely covered in gray ash and you can hold your hand over them only for a count of two, scatter the mesquite chunks or chips over the coals.

Remove the steaks from the marinade and pat dry with paper towels. Season lightly with salt and pepper. Put the steaks on the grill and cover the kettle immediately. Adjust the vents so that no flare-ups occur. Cook until steaks are done to your liking, 6 to 8 minutes per side for medium-rare to medium (consult the Doneness Chart, page 56). Set the steaks aside on a platter and cover loosely with foil to keep warm while you prepare the tortilla/cheese setups.

Preheat the oven to 300°F. Briefly heat each tortilla over the direct heat of the grill to soften it (or heat each tortilla in a heavy skillet over high heat to soften). Heat the tortillas only enough to make them pliable, so they don't crack when folded over the cheese. Place 2 pieces of cheese on each tortilla and fold in half. Wrap 6 or so folded tortillas in foil, and keep warm in the oven. Repeat the process for all 24 tortillas. It takes about 10 minutes to heat the folded tortillas in the oven and barely melt the cheese—don't keep them in the oven too long or the cheese will ooze out. Pay attention to timing: if you put the tortilla packets in the oven when the steaks are done and let the steaks rest for 10 minutes, that should work out fine. You can leave the tortillas in their foil packets for serving or, if you'd like to be more authentic, wrap them in large cloth napkins or dish towels.

To serve, cut the steaks against the grain into strips 3 to 4

1 pound mild white cheese, such as *queso asadero*, California Monterey Jack, or Wisconsin Muenster or brick, cut into ¼-by-1-by-3-to-4-inch strips

6 fire-roasted pasilla chiles or 10 Anaheim chiles (see below), sliced, OR equivalent canned green chiles, preferably Ortega brand, sliced

GARNISHES

1 cup Lime-Pickled Red Onions (page 104)
Guacamole
Salsas of your choice, such as green chile salsa and salsa cruda

FIRE-ROASTING CHILES OR BELL PEPPERS

CHAR AND BLISTER THE PEPPERS, turning occasionally, over an open flame or under a hot broiler. Put them into a plastic or paper bag for 10 to 15 minutes or so to sweat and loosen the skins. Scrape off the skins and remove the stems and seeds. You can wash the peeled peppers under cold running water if you want, but this can reduce the flavor slightly. Ortega brand canned fire-roasted green chiles are an acceptable substitute for fresh mild chiles.

Be careful when handling hot chiles. Use rubber gloves or wash your hands thoroughly after touching them.

inches long and about ¼ inch thick. Put the bones on a separate platter. Set out the fire-roasted chiles, pickled onions, tortilla/cheese setups, guacamole, and salsas, and encourage your guests to go for it. Pass around the steak bones for true carnivores to gnaw on and toss over their shoulders to the dogs. Beer (preferably Mexican) goes great here, but a spicy Zinfandel would also be delicious.

LIME-PICKLED RED ONIONS
Makes 1 cup

TRY THESE ZESTY ONION SLICES in tacos, burritos, and quesadillas. They're great on sandwiches of all sorts too, from roast beef to grilled Cheddar cheese. You can also use them to liven up grilled fish or chicken breasts.

    1   large red onion, thinly sliced
    ¼   cup fresh lime juice
    1   tablespoon olive oil
    ½   teaspoon salt
    2   tablespoons chopped fresh cilantro
    1   teaspoon chopped fresh oregano or ½ teaspoon dried

Mix all the ingredients together and let the onion marinate for at least 3 hours at room temperature. The onion will keep for up to 4 days, covered, in the refrigerator.

Gordon's Grilled Rib-Eye Steak with Chile-Tomato Vinaigrette

Serves 4
■ FIT FOR COMPANY ■ IN A HURRY

GORDON HEYDEN is one of our chef buddies, and he has a love of hearty food and robust flavors. He has cooked all over the world, but his true love is American Southwestern cooking, with its bright and fiery tastes and vibrant contrasts.

Although we use rib-eye steak in this recipe, you can substitute New York strip (top loin) or fillet steaks with equally good results. For a satisfying Southwestern meal, serve the steaks with corn on the cob, a salad, and some cooked beans or Mexican-style rice; or serve with the accompaniments suggested for Nogales Steak Tacos (page 102).

──────────

■ Flavor Step ■ Season the steaks generously with salt and pepper or rub all over with the spice rub and set aside.

To make the Chile-Tomato Vinaigrette: Combine the chile, shallots or green onions, oregano, and vinegar in a small bowl. Gradually whisk in the olive oil. Right before serving, stir in the tomatoes and season with salt and pepper to taste.

Grill the steaks over a medium-hot charcoal fire until medium-rare to medium (see Grilling, page 63) or pan-broil them (see Pan-Broiling, page 60).

Place the steaks on individual plates and spoon a quarter of the vinaigrette over each; garnish with oregano sprigs, if you like.

4 8-ounce boneless rib-eye steaks, 1-1¼ inches thick

■ Flavor Step ■
Salt and freshly ground black pepper OR Southwestern Spice Rub (page 128) OR Spice Rub for Pork or Beef (page 375)

CHILE-TOMATO VINAIGRETTE
1 fire-roasted Anaheim or other mild green chile (see page 103), chopped, OR ¼ cup canned diced mild green chiles

1½ tablespoons minced shallots or green onions or scallions

1 teaspoon chopped fresh oregano or ½ teaspoon dried

1 tablespoon balsamic vinegar

3 tablespoons olive oil

1 cup halved cherry tomatoes
Salt and freshly ground black pepper

Oregano sprigs for garnish (optional)

Beefsteak Florentine

3 tablespoons of the best
   extra-virgin olive oil
   you can afford,
   preferably Tuscan

2 teaspoons kosher or
   other coarse salt

1 teaspoon freshly ground
   black pepper

1 tablespoon minced garlic
   (optional)

1 2-to-2½-inch-thick
   (or thicker) porterhouse
   steak (2-3 pounds)
   Lemon wedges for
   garnish

Serves 4 to 6
■ FIT FOR COMPANY

IN ITALY, the justly famous *bistecca alla fiorentina* is nothing more than a thick porterhouse steak generously seasoned with salt and pepper, rubbed with extra-virgin olive oil, and grilled over hardwood coals, preferably olive wood. It is simply garnished with lemon wedges and served to appreciative diners. What makes the steak so wonderful is the exquisitely tender and very flavorful Chianina beef, which is usually cooked blood-rare.

Side dishes in a typical Florentine trattoria would be the Tuscan favorites: stewed white beans slathered with plenty of extra-virgin olive oil, spinach or other tender greens sautéed in olive oil, and garlic and oven-roasted potatoes flavored with fresh rosemary. The wine of choice: a fine Chianti Classico, Chianti Rufina, or Chianti Montalbano from the hills near Florence.

To reproduce this Florentine specialty in America, we suggest you buy the best grade of porterhouse you can find (at least USDA Choice) as thick as you can get it (at least 2 inches). To enhance the flavor, rub the meat with olive oil and minced garlic, and marinate it in the refrigerator for up to two days. Grilling the meat over charcoal with some wood chips added will give it a bit of the flavor of the olive wood fire (if, perchance, you come across some olive wood, use it by all means; if not, oak or hickory will do fine). If you don't have time for the two days of marinating, then let the meat rest for an hour or two at room temperature after seasoning with the olive oil and optional garlic. (See photograph, page 41.)

■ **Flavor Step** ■ Mix together the oil, salt, pepper, and the optional garlic in a small bowl. Put the steak in a shallow bowl

GRILLED FILLET OR TOP LOIN STEAK

OTH FILLET AND TOP LOIN (New York strip) steak are excellent when prepared like Beefsteak Florentine marinated overnight in a garlic and oil mixture or brushed generously with olive oil, garlic, salt, and pepper, and then grilled. Try to find steaks that are at least 1½ to 2 inches thick. For best results, cook the steaks no more than medium-rare (see Grilling, page 63, for details). Serve the steaks with lemon wedges, with Salsa Verde (page 122), or with Nancy's Mushroom Vinaigrette (page 108).

or a dish and rub the mixture all over the meat. Marinate at room temperature for 1 to 2 hours or, better still, covered in the refrigerator for up to 2 days. Turn the meat from time to time to coat both sides evenly.

Remove the steak from the refrigerator at least an hour before cooking. When you are ready to grill, prepare a charcoal fire so that you have areas of higher and lower heat (see Grilling, page 63).

Drain off any excess oil from the steak. Sear the steak over the high-heat area of the grill for 3 to 4 minutes per side. Remove the grill rack and sprinkle 2 cups soaked hickory or oak chips on the low-heat part of the fire. Replace the grill and place the steak over the low-heat area. Cover the grill, but turn the steak frequently: this should take 10 to 20 minutes more, depending on the thickness of the steak and the heat of the fire. Check the interior of the meat with an instant-read meat thermometer, and remove the steaks at 5° to 7°F below the desired degree of doneness (see the Doneness Chart, page 56). Let the steak rest, covered loosely with foil, for 10 minutes or so before carving.

To carve, cut the loin meat and the fillet meat away from the bone. Cut into ½-inch-thick slices. Arrange the meat on a platter with the lemon wedges and pass the bone to the hungriest (or loudest) carnivore at the table.

NANCY'S MUSHROOM VINAIGRETTE
Enough for 4 to 6 fillet steaks

IF YOU'RE TIRED of the same old brown mushroom sauce or mushroom cream sauce, try this light and vibrant vinaigrette. The recipe comes from Bruce's wife, Nancy Oakes, who uses a host of vinaigrettes to enliven her entrees at Boulevard, her restaurant in San Francisco. This vinaigrette is good with grilled or pan-broiled steak as well as roasted beef fillet, strip loin, and prime rib. It also makes a nice accompaniment to grilled veal and lamb chops.

The sauce can be served hot, warm, or at room temperature. It does not benefit from being made ahead, though, so it's best to prepare it just before you cook the meat.

½ ounce dried porcini, morel, or shiitake mushrooms
About 1 cup boiling water
¼ cup dry vermouth or dry sherry
2 cups chicken or veal stock OR canned low-sodium chicken broth
2 tablespoons olive oil, plus ¼-½ cup olive oil
¾ pound medium fresh mushrooms, sliced
1 tablespoon minced shallots or garlic
2 tablespoons red wine vinegar, or more to taste
1 tablespoon balsamic vinegar
Salt and freshly ground black pepper

Place the dried mushrooms in a glass measuring cup or bowl. Add enough boiling water to cover and soak for at least 30 minutes.

Remove the soaked mushrooms with a slotted spoon. Chop them and set them aside. Carefully pour the soaking liquid into a saucepan, leaving the last bit of liquid and any grit behind. Add the vermouth or sherry and the chicken or veal stock and bring to a boil. Continue to boil until the flavors are concentrated and the sauce is reduced to about ½ cup. Set aside while you cook the mushrooms.

Heat the 2 tablespoons olive oil in a large skillet over medium-high heat. Add the fresh mushrooms and shallots or garlic and cook and stir for 2 to 3 minutes. Put in the reserved dried mushrooms and continue to cook for 2 to 3 minutes more. If any liquid accumulates in the skillet, pour it into the saucepan with the reduced sauce. Boil the sauce briefly, if you wish, to intensify the flavors further.

Pour the reduced sauce over the mushrooms and add both vinegars. Using a whisk, beat in enough of the remaining oil to form a slightly thick, homogeneous vinaigrette. Taste for salt and pepper and red wine vinegar and serve.

Bruschetta Steak Sandwiches

Serves 4

■ IN A HURRY ■ FIT FOR COMPANY

BRUSCHETTA, the crunchy Italian garlic toast often served with antipasto, also makes a great base for a open-faced steak sandwich. With some stewed white beans and a glass of Chianti, this can be a delightful lunch or summer dinner. *(See photograph, page 17.)*

1 steak, about 2 pounds, pan-broiled, grilled, or broiled
8 1-inch-thick slices of French or Italian bread
 Olive oil
 Salt
2 large garlic cloves, cut in half lengthwise
 Arugula or watercress
 Salsa Verde (page 122) OR Tomato-Olive Salsa (see below; optional)

Cook the steak as you like it, following the directions in the recipe. While the meat is resting, brush the bread generously with olive oil and grill over medium coals or in a preheated broiler until the surface is crisp and golden, 1 to 2 minutes on each side. Remove the toasts, sprinkle them with a little salt, and then rub them all over with the cut edges of the garlic cloves.

Place 2 pieces of toast on each plate with a layer of arugula leaves or watercress on top. Slice the steak into ¼-inch-thick slices and cover the greens with the steak. Serve as is or garnished with one of the salsas.

TOMATO-OLIVE SALSA

Makes 1½ cups

THIS TANGY SALSA is wonderful with steak, grilled pork chops, or veal chops.

1 cup seeded and diced vine-ripened tomatoes
3 tablespoons pitted and chopped kalamata olives
2 tablespoons chopped fresh basil
1 tablespoon finely chopped red onion (optional)
2 tablespoons extra-virgin olive oil
2 teaspoons red wine or balsamic vinegar
 Salt and freshly ground black pepper to taste

Combine all the ingredients in a small bowl. Mix them gently and serve at once.

Sautéed Filet Mignon

2 1¼-to-1½-inch-thick
   filet mignon steaks
   (1-1½ pounds)

■ **Flavor Step** ■
Salt and freshly ground
black pepper
1 teaspoon chopped fresh
   rosemary

2 tablespoons olive oil

**BALSAMIC VINEGAR
PAN SAUCE**
2 teaspoons minced garlic
¼ cup dry vermouth
¼ cup beef or chicken
   stock
2 teaspoons soy sauce
1 tablespoon balsamic
   vinegar
1 tablespoon butter
   (optional)
   Salt and freshly ground
   black pepper

Serves 2
■ IN A HURRY ■ FIT FOR COMPANY

MASTER RECIPE

SAUTÉING MEANS FRYING in a small amount of fat. This differs from pan-broiling, which sears the meat in a hot dry pan. Sautéing works well with lean cuts of beef such as fillet. A flavorful fat such as butter or olive oil will add extra dimension to the meat, and the pan drippings can easily be turned into a simple sauce. This is a quick and convenient method for cooking for two to four diners.

Sautéing is the preferred method of steak cookery in French cuisine, with its emphasis on sauces. Besides filet mignon, this method works well with top loin (New York strip) and culotte steaks.

■ **Flavor Step** ■ Season the meat generously with salt and pepper. Sprinkle with the rosemary.

In a medium, heavy skillet, heat the oil over medium-high heat. Put in the steaks and fry them for 4 to 5 minutes per side for medium-rare (the internal temperature should be 120° to 130°F). Remove and cover loosely to keep them warm while you prepare the sauce.

To make the Balsamic Vinegar Pan Sauce: Pour off all but 1 tablespoon of the fat, leaving any meat juices in the pan. Reduce the heat to medium and sauté the garlic for 15 seconds, stirring. Add the vermouth and scrape up any browned bits from the bottom of the pan. Raise the heat to high and reduce the vermouth to a syrup. Pour in the stock, soy sauce, and vinegar. Boil until the sauce just reduces to a syrup. Remove from the heat and stir in the butter, if you wish. (It adds fat but gives the sauce a velvety texture.) Taste for salt and pepper. Pour over the steaks and serve.

Sautéed Filet Mignon with Artichoke and Mushroom Ragù

Serves 4 to 6

■ FIT FOR COMPANY

THIS SIMPLE RAGÙ of artichokes and mushrooms makes a colorful presentation. Serve with sautéed potatoes.

Sauté the filet mignon as in the Master Recipe (page 110), but omit the Balsamic Vinegar Pan Sauce.

■ **Flavor Step** ■ Pour off the fat from the pan, leaving any meat juices behind. Add the olive oil and reduce the heat to medium. Put in the garlic and shallots and sauté for 30 seconds. Increase the heat to high, add the mushrooms, and cook for 2 minutes, stirring from time to time. Scrape up any browned bits from the bottom of the pan.

Put in the artichokes, along with a pinch each of salt and pepper. Reduce the heat to medium and sauté the artichokes for 3 minutes, stirring occasionally. Add the stock and sage and bring to a boil. Reduce the sauce, stirring often, until it becomes syrupy. Stir in the red pepper strips and remove from the heat. Taste for salt and pepper. Spoon over the steaks and serve.

2 1¼-to-1½-inch-thick filet mignon steaks (1-1½ pounds)

■ **Flavor Step** ■
ARTICHOKE AND MUSHROOM RAGÙ

1 tablespoon olive oil

1 teaspoon minced garlic

1 tablespoon chopped shallots

¼ pound mushrooms (brown, white, or portobello), thinly sliced

2 artichoke bottoms, cooked and thinly sliced, OR 8 fresh or frozen cooked baby artichoke hearts

Salt and freshly ground black pepper

½ cup chicken stock

Pinch of dried sage

12 strips fire-roasted red bell pepper (see page 103)

Sautéed Filet Mignon with Corn and Chile Cheese Sauce

4-6 1¼-to-1½-inch-thick
   filet mignon steaks
   (2-3 pounds)

CORN AND CHEESE SAUCE

2 ears corn, shucked,
   OR 2 cups frozen corn,
   defrosted

2 tablespoons butter

1½ cups finely chopped
   onions

4 fire-roasted Anaheim or
   other mild green chiles
   (see page 103),
   chopped, OR 4 canned
   mild green chiles,
   chopped

1 medium tomato, peeled,
   seeded, and chopped

¾ pound mild cheese such
   as *queso asadero*,
   Monterey Jack, or mild
   Cheddar, shredded

¾ cup crème fraîche, sour
   cream, or heavy cream,
   or more if necessary

A few tablespoons of
   half-and-half (optional)

Salt and freshly ground
   black pepper

Tabasco or other hot
   sauce to taste (optional)

1 mild green chile
   (as above), cut into
   strips, for garnish

Serves 4

■ FIT FOR COMPANY

FRESH SWEET CORN with mild cheese and chiles makes an ideal sauce for fillet steaks with their rich, beefy flavor. The sauce is also delicious over boiled or baked potatoes and makes great nachos when poured over tortilla chips. For a lighter presentation, leave out the cheese and cream and increase the tomatoes to three.

Sauté the filet mignon as in the Master Recipe (page 110), but omit the Balsamic Vinegar Pan Sauce.

To make the Corn and Cheese Sauce: If using fresh corn, bring a pot of salted water to a boil, add the corn, and cook for 5 minutes. Remove the corn from the water and when cool enough to handle, cut the kernels from the cob and put into a small bowl. Using the back of the knife, scrape each cob over the bowl to release the milky liquid. Set aside.

Melt the butter in a medium skillet. Put in the onions and cook for 5 minutes over medium heat, stirring often, until soft. Add the corn, with any liquid, and cook for 2 minutes, stirring from time to time. Stir in the chopped chiles and tomato and simmer until most of the liquid has evaporated. Reduce the heat to medium-low and add the cheese and *crème fraîche,* sour cream, or cream. Stir until the cheese melts and the sauce is smooth and creamy. Add more cream or half-and-half, if the sauce seems too thick. Season to taste with salt and pepper and Tabasco, if you'd like it hotter.

Spoon some of the sauce onto each serving plate and arrange a steak on top. Garnish with the green chile strips and pass the rest of the sauce on the side.

Marinated Flank Steak

Serves 4

■ COOKING ON A BUDGET ■ IN A HURRY ■
■ LOW-FAT (DEPENDS ON MARINADE)

MASTER RECIPE

FLANK STEAK is an ideal cut for marinating. Because the steak is relatively thin and porous, the marinade can penetrate the meat thoroughly. The texture is firm but not too chewy, so the meat doesn't fall apart or become mushy after marinating. Its rich, beefy flavor is complemented well by most marinades, especially those containing soy sauce.

■ **Flavor Step** ■ Pierce the steak all over on both sides with a sharp fork or skewer. Place it in a zipper-lock bag or shallow glass baking dish. Pour over the marinade and refrigerate overnight (cover if using a dish). Shake and turn the bag or turn the meat occasionally. Let it come to room temperature before cooking.

To grill the steak: See Grilling, page 63. Pat the steak dry. Grill the steak over medium-hot coals in a covered or uncovered barbecue or directly over the flames of a gas grill. Flank steak is best cooked medium-rare and should never be cooked more than medium; the internal temperature should be 130° to 135°F. This should take roughly 4 to 5 minutes per side on a standard grill. Allow the steak to rest for 5 minutes, covered loosely with aluminum foil, before carving into ¼-inch-thick diagonal slices across the grain.

To broil the steak: See Broiling, page 58. Pat the steak dry. Place the steak on a preheated rack in a broiler pan about 3 inches from the flame and broil for 4 to 5 minutes per side for medium-rare to medium. Follow the directions above to determine doneness, then let the steak rest and carve as above.

1 1-to-1¼-pound flank steak

■ **Flavor Step** ■

A marinade such as Teriyaki Marinade (page 115), Korean Marinade for Beef (page 217), Nogales Steak Marinade (page 102), Bourbon Marinade for Steak (page 124), OR any of the marinades for chuck steak (see Seasoning Chart, page 577), OR your favorite steak marinade (do not use one containing red wine, which would give the meat a bitter flavor)

Marinated Flank Steak with North African Marinade

■ **Flavor Step** ■
NORTH AFRICAN
MARINADE

1 cup finely chopped
   onions

1½ tablespoons finely
   chopped fresh ginger

1 tablespoon minced garlic

½ cup olive oil

6 tablespoons fresh lemon
   juice

2 tablespoons soy sauce

1 tablespoon dry sherry

¼ cup chopped fresh
   cilantro

1 tablespoon chile powder,
   preferably Gebhardt

1 tablespoon ground
   cumin

1 teaspoon turmeric

1 teaspoon dried marjoram

¼ teaspoon saffron
   (optional)

2 teaspoons *Harissa*
   (page 505), or other
   hot sauce (optional)

2 teaspoons salt

1 teaspoon freshly ground
   black pepper

2 1-to-1¼-pound flank
   steaks

Serves 4 to 6, with leftovers
■ GOOD FOR A CROWD ■ GREAT LEFTOVERS

THIS MARINADE is also excellent for butterflied leg of lamb, lamb kebabs, or veal shanks. The recipe makes enough marinade for a 4-to-5-pound butterflied leg of lamb or 3 to 4 pounds of lamb or veal shank. (Any leftover marinade can be kept refrigerated for 7 to 10 days.)

■ **Flavor Step** ■ Combine all the ingredients in a bowl and mix well. Marinate the flank steak as directed in the Master Recipe (page 113). Grill as directed.

Teriyaki Flank Steak

Serves 4
■ COOKING ON A BUDGET ■ IN A HURRY ■
■ LOW-FAT ■

THE MARINADE IS ALSO EXCELLENT with other types of steak and with pork fillets, chicken, and salmon.

■ Flavor Step ■ Combine all the ingredients in a bowl and mix well. Marinate the flank steak as directed in the Master Recipe (page 113).

Grill as directed.

1 1-to-1¼-pounds flank steak

■ Flavor Step ■
TERIYAKI MARINADE
½ cup soy sauce
¼ cup sake or dry sherry
2 tablespoons light or dark brown sugar
3 garlic cloves, minced
2 tablespoons minced fresh ginger
2 tablespoons Asian peanut oil

MARINADES AND RUBS SUITABLE FOR FLANK STEAK

Nogales Steak Marinade (page 102)
North African Marinade (page 114)
Teriyaki Marinade (see above)
Bourbon Marinade for Steak (page 124)
Southwestern Spice Rub (page 128)
Spicy Beer Marinade (page 138)
Chipotle-Orange Marinade (page 138)
Korean Marinade for Beef (page 217)
Tequila and Lime Marinade (page 292)
Yucatán Marinade (page 294)
Spice Rub for Pork or Beef (page 375)
Thai Marinade for Pork (page 382)

Teriyaki Roll-Ups

4-6 10-to-12-inch flour
    tortillas

JAPANESE-STYLE
STIR-FRIED VEGETABLES

1 tablespoon vegetable oil

2 cups thinly sliced onions

3 tablespoons soy sauce

1 tablespoon light or dark
    brown sugar

1 tablespoon dry sherry

1 teaspoon minced garlic

2 teaspoons minced fresh
    ginger

1 tablespoon rice wine
    vinegar

2 cups broccoli florets

4 medium zucchini,
    thinly sliced

6 green onions or
    scallions, cut into
    2-inch pieces

1 cup small snow peas,
    stems and strings
    removed

3 cups hot cooked rice

1¼ pounds Teriyaki Flank
    Steak (page 113) or any
    other marinated flank
    steak, hot or cold,
    sliced into strips on the
    diagonal

Makes 4 to 6 Roll-ups
■ LOW-FAT ■ GREAT LEFTOVERS ■ IN A HURRY
    ■ MEAT AS A CONDIMENT

YOU CAN USE leftover Teriyaki Flank Steak for these Asian-style burritos or just about any marinated flank steak, leftover or freshly grilled. Simply put, these roll-ups are great sandwiches that can be eaten for a snack or lunch or even a complete meal. Serve them for a simple backyard barbecue or as couch potato fare to devour in front of a TV football game.

Wrap the tortillas in foil and heat for 10 to 15 minutes in a 350°F oven.

To make the vegetables: Heat the oil in a large skillet or wok over medium-high heat. Add the sliced onions and cover the pan. Cook for 10 minutes, stirring often, until they are very soft. Stir together in a small bowl the soy sauce, brown sugar, sherry, garlic, ginger, and vinegar and add to the pan when the onions are soft. Bring to a boil. Add the broccoli, cover, and cook for 3 minutes. Put in the zucchini and cook 1 minute more. Add the green onions or scallions and snow peas and cook 1 minute more, stirring well.

To assemble the roll-ups: Place a hot tortilla on a flat surface. Spoon about ⅔ cup hot rice on one half of the tortilla, leaving a 2-inch border around the side. Cover the rice with 3 or 4 slices of steak and then with the vegetables and some of the pan sauce. Fold in the sides of the tortilla and roll it up into a tight burrito. Serve at once.

Note: *To reheat leftover steak, warm the slices by tossing them in the pan with the vegetable mixture when you add the green onions.*

Thai Beef Salad

■ In a Hurry ■ Cooking on a Budget
■ Fit for Company

THIS REFRESHING SALAD can be made with a freshly cooked steak such as flank steak or with leftover steak or roast beef. Ideally, the beef should be marinated in Thai Marinade for Pork (page 382) before cooking, but any flavorful steak marinade will do, since the meat will pick up Thai flavors from the dressing. The spicy salad makes a lively centerpiece for a lunch or light summer supper; it can also be served as a first course for an Asian banquet. Accompany the salad with a fruity Gewürztraminer from California's Anderson Valley.

Thai ingredients are available from Asian groceries or by mail-order (see Sources, page 584).

Thinly slice the beef across the grain and then cut it into ½-inch-wide strips. Set aside.

Place all the vegetables, including the shredded lettuce, in a large bowl and set aside.

To make the Thai Salad Dressing: Whisk all the ingredients together in a small bowl.

To assemble the salad: Spread a lettuce leaf on each of four serving plates. Add the sliced beef and dressing to the vegetables and toss well. Put one quarter of the mixture on each of the lettuce leaves. Garnish with the mint leaves, the optional cilantro sprigs, and the cherry tomatoes, and serve.

¾-1 pound steak, marinated (see opposite) and grilled, OR ¾-1 pound leftover cooked steak or roast beef
1 cup thinly sliced unpeeled English or Japanese cucumbers
½ cup shredded carrots
1 cup thinly sliced red onions
4-6 cups shredded iceberg lettuce

Thai Salad Dressing
⅓ cup fresh lime juice
¼ teaspoon dried red pepper flakes
2 teaspoons light or dark brown sugar
1 2-inch piece of lemongrass, tough outer part removed, tender center very thinly sliced, OR 2 teaspoons thinly sliced lime zest
½ teaspoon minced garlic
3 tablespoons Thai or Vietnamese fish sauce (*nam pla* or *nuoc mam*)
1 tablespoon peanut oil
3 tablespoons chopped fresh Thai basil or other basil

4 large iceberg or red lettuce leaves

Garnish
20 fresh mint leaves, cilantro sprigs (optional), and 12 cherry tomatoes, halved

A RARE EXPERIENCE

I T WAS, AS THEY SAY IN THE STORIES, long ago and far away. My wife, Kathy, and I were teaching in a university in the far north of the continent, and we had decided to go out for our first night on the town. The main drag of the rugged mining community was grim and dark on a cold September night, but the red neon sign saying STEAKS was bright and inviting.

When we took a look at the menu, I felt pretty good about the restaurant. Each cut was listed separately—porterhouse, sirloin, filet mignon, strip—generally a promising sign. Kathy opted for the filet mignon, medium-rare, while I ordered my favorite—rare porterhouse.

After a hungry half hour and a few questions to the harried waitress, the steaks arrived. They looked odd to me—Kathy's filet mignon was a perfect circle, about five inches in diameter and a quarter of an inch thick. Quite brown. Stiff, like cardboard that had been in the rain and then dried in the sun. My porterhouse was more free-form, a bit like the map of Australia, just as brown and hard, resistant to the fork I tried to poke into it. We looked at each other. What were these things on the plates? What had we gotten ourselves into?

After a pained conversation with the waitress and a little poking and probing, along with a few chewy bites, I realized what medium-rare filet mignon and rare porterhouse meant in this steak house. The chef had taken one large, thin piece of tough round steak and cut the filet mignon out with a cookie cutter or some such other tool. It was round, it was steak, thus filet mignon. The porterhouse aroused his artistic side, and he cut that out free-form, perhaps using some kind of picture or diagram of a porterhouse from *The Chef's Companion* or *The Meat-cutter's Union Gazette*.

He then proceeded to grill the steaks, most likely on one of those stovetop griddles you see in roadside diners, until Done. Done. Done. It is possible that there was some pink in the porterhouse, some hint that the animal it came from was once alive and vital. Perhaps. I didn't see any, and as I reflect, I hardly ever remember seeing pink meat in all our years under the northern lights.

Thus began my steak-ordering act. I would say to the waitress, "I want you to understand that I am a bit crazy (my beard and long hair and disheveled appearance in those days helped to reinforce this impression). I love to eat raw meat. I'm just crazy that way. Tell the chef to take the steak and just drop it onto a hot grill for a second or two, then turn it over for another second, and put it on a plate for me. Raw is what I want, you understand, just a little color on the outside, OK?"

The waitress would write most of this down, glancing nervously toward the bartender, ready to run or shout for help. I imagined her notes for the chef: Crazy. Eats raw meat. Porterhouse. Grill two seconds. Watch out!

When the steak arrived, sometimes I could see traces of pink underneath the brown crust. Sometimes. Mostly the steak was gray, as usual. Tough. Dry. "Do you want the steak sauce?" the waitress would ask warily. I'd nod wearily. "Yeah, I'll take the sauce, and another large ale, please."

I got into trouble, though, when we visited a Chicago steak house while we were on vacation. I ordered a porterhouse, and out of habit, I went into my crazy-for-raw-meat act. The waitress said matter-of-factly, "If you want raw, you'll get raw," not at all concerned or surprised. This should have warned me.

And raw it was. My porterhouse hung over the sides of the plate: two inches thick, rimmed with hard white fat, red and bloody, with just a few scorch marks here and there. "Here's your porterhouse," the waitress said loudly, "raw, just like you ordered." The room grew still; people craned up out of their chairs to look. "Please convey my compliments to the chef," I said bravely, "and ask him to cook this magnificent steak just the way he likes it."

And he did. And it was good and rare and juicy. We decided then that maybe we'd been up north a little too long and started thinking about heading south to California.

D.K.

Matambre
(Rolled Stuffed Flank Steak)

■ Flavor Step ■

3 tablespoons olive oil

1 teaspoon minced garlic

2 teaspoons salt

1 teaspoon freshly ground
   black pepper

1 1½-to-2-pound flank
   steak (the largest
   you can find)
   Salt and freshly ground
   black pepper

MATAMBRE STUFFING

⅓ pound prosciutto, dry
   coppa, or cooked
   country ham, thinly
   sliced
   Large leaves from a
   bunch of spinach, stems
   removed, well washed

½ cup chopped fresh basil

¼ cup chopped fresh
   parsley

1 cup fresh bread crumbs

2 tablespoons minced
   garlic

½ cup freshly grated
   Parmesan cheese

2 tablespoons olive oil

1 additional tablespoon
   olive oil (if roasting
   the *matambre*)

Serves 6 to 8
■ FIT FOR COMPANY

atambre—flank steak that's butterflied and stuffed with fresh herbs, vegetables, and meats—comes from Argentina, where beef cooking (and eating) is a high art. Masterful Argentine cooks have come up with a whole host of stuffing ingredients: blanched root vegetables, fresh greens, thinly sliced coppa, or cured pork shoulder (found in Italian delicatessens), sliced bacon or pancetta, sausages of various types, hams of every variety, *brasciola* (air-dried beef), hard-boiled eggs.

Our recipe comes from Pam Barnett, the banquet chef at Boulevard restaurant in San Francisco and a long-term friend. Pam is one of those dedicated chefs who spends her days off cooking elaborate meals for friends. *Matambre* is one of her favorite party dishes: in the winter, she roasts it in the oven; on hot summer days, she prefers to cook it over indirect heat in a kettle barbecue. You can serve this with Salsa Verde (page 122) rather than the sauce in the recipe if you like. Try it with a Cabernet Sauvignon from Argentina or Chile.

■ **Flavor Step** ■ Combine the marinade ingredients in a small bowl. Set aside while you prepare the steak.

Butterfly the flank steak by slicing through it horizontally, leaving the meat attached at one end. Open it out, cut side up. Season the cut side lightly with salt and pepper.

To make the stuffing: Lay the slices of prosciutto, coppa, or ham over the cut side of the steak. Lay the leaves of spinach over the slices. In a bowl, combine the basil, parsley, bread crumbs, garlic, cheese, and olive oil. Spread over the spinach leaves and roll the steak up tightly like a jelly roll.

Tie the roll in several places and brush the outside all over with the marinade.

To cook on a grill: Prepare a kettle barbecue for indirect cooking (see Grilling, page 63). Sear the *matambre* on all sides directly over the coals, for 5 to 6 minutes total. Move it to the area with no coals, place a drip pan under the meat, and cook with the cover on for another 10 to 15 minutes, or until the meat is rare to medium-rare, 120° to 130°F. Remove the meat from the grill, cover loosely with foil, and let it rest for 10 to 20 minutes. The final internal temperature should be 130° to 135°F. Cut the meat carefully into ½-inch-thick slices and serve with the sauce or with Salsa Verde.

To roast in the oven: Preheat the oven to 350°F. Heat the 1 tablespoon olive oil in a large, heavy skillet over medium-high heat. Sear the beef roll on all sides, 6 to 8 minutes total. If the pan is ovenproof, place it directly into the oven; otherwise, transfer the meat to a roasting pan. Roast for 20 to 30 minutes and then check the internal temperature. Remove the meat when it reaches 120° to 130°F. Cover loosely with foil and let the *matambre* rest for 10 to 20 minutes. Serve with the sauce.

Meanwhile, make the sauce: In a food processor, process the almonds to a thick paste. Add the bread crumbs, olive oil, roasted peppers, and optional red pepper flakes and process until smooth. Taste for salt and pepper.

Note: *To toast almonds, spread them on a baking sheet and roast at 350°F for 10 to 15 minutes, or until they give off a nutty aroma and are lightly browned.*

SAUCE

½ cup toasted almonds (see Note)

¼ cup fresh bread crumbs

2 tablespoons olive oil

1 cup fresh or canned fire-roasted red bell peppers or pimentos (see page 103)

½ teaspoon red pepper flakes (optional)

Salt and freshly ground black pepper

Salsa Verde

Makes about 1 cup

THIS CLASSIC ITALIAN sauce is terrific with grilled beef, pork, or veal. Try it also with poached beef and leftover roast beef.

- 8 anchovy fillets, drained
- ⅔ cup packed coarsely chopped fresh flat-leaf parsley leaves
- ½ cup diced celery, including leafy tops
- ¾ cup olive oil
- 2 tablespoons balsamic vinegar
  Salt and freshly ground black pepper
- 1 garlic clove, minced

In a food processor, finely chop the anchovies. Add the parsley and celery and process until coarsely chopped. Add the oil and vinegar and process for about 30 seconds, until well blended. Taste for salt and pepper. (At this point the salsa can be covered and refrigerated for up to 2 days.) Stir in the minced garlic just before serving.

Beef and Romaine Salad with Blue Cheese and Anchovy Dressing

Serves 4 to 6
■ IN A HURRY ■ COOKING ON A BUDGET

THIS TANGY SALAD is more exciting than the ubiquitous Caesar salad. The pungent flavor of the blue cheese goes well with beef, especially if it's been grilled. Use leftover steak or sliced roast beef. Or grill a steak especially for the occasion. Toss the salad with the dressing first and then lay strips of beef over the top, garnished with chopped chives or green onions or scallions.

You can use Blue Cheese and Anchovy Dressing or your own favorite dressing for Caesar salad.

To make Blue Cheese and Anchovy Dressing: Put the garlic and anchovies in a food processor and process to a paste. Add the mustard, vinegar, oregano, and pepper. With the motor running, pour the oil through the feed tube to make a creamy dressing.

Pour the dressing over the romaine and tomatoes and toss with the cheese to coat the leaves. Lay the beef strips on top and garnish with chives or green onions and serve.

BLUE CHEESE AND ANCHOVY DRESSING

1 garlic clove
4 anchovy fillets
1 tablespoon Dijon mustard
2 tablespoons red wine vinegar or balsamic vinegar
1 tablespoon chopped fresh oregano or 1 teaspoon dried
½ teaspoon freshly ground black pepper
⅓ cup extra-virgin olive oil

1 large head of romaine lettuce, washed, outer bruised leaves removed and discarded, remaining leaves torn into small pieces
2 vine-ripened tomatoes, cut lengthwise into wedges
¼ pound blue cheese, such as Danish Blue, Maytag Blue, or Roquefort, crumbled
½-1 pound cooked steak or roast beef, cut into ¼-inch-thick-by-1-inch-wide strips

GARNISH
Chopped chives or green onions or scallions

Grilled Bourbon-Marinated Top Round Steak

■ Flavor Step ■
BOURBON MARINADE
FOR STEAK

3 tablespoons olive oil

2 tablespoons Dijon
mustard

¼ cup bourbon whiskey

⅓ cup soy sauce

2 tablespoons red wine
vinegar

1 tablespoon Worcester-
shire sauce or A-1
steak sauce

¼ cup light or dark brown
sugar

2 tablespoons minced red
onion

1 tablespoon minced garlic

1 tablespoon minced fresh
ginger (optional)

1 tablespoon salt

2 teaspoons freshly ground
black pepper

1 2-inch-thick top round
or top sirloin steak
(often labeled London
broil) (2-3 pounds)
Salt and freshly ground
black pepper

Serves 4 to 6, with leftovers
■ LOW-FAT ■ IN A HURRY ■ GREAT LEFTOVERS

MUCH OF THE UNIQUELY ROBUST and smoky character of bourbon comes from aging in heavily charred oak barrels. This smokiness makes the whiskey an ideal ingredient in a marinade for grilled meat, since it accentuates the flavors picked up from the smoke of the charcoal and any added hardwood chips. In fact, if you can get some of the charred wood sawdust scraped from old bourbon barrels, you'll have some of the best barbecue smoke around.

These flavors go particularly well with beef. For this dish, choose a top round steak at least 1½ to 2 inches thick, which means you'll be buying quite a large one, 2 to 3 pounds. Keep in mind that top round cut from the hind leg is often marketed as a thick steak misnamed London broil, a term more correctly applied to flank steak. Allow your steak a day or two in the refrigerator to let the marinade penetrate and flavor the meat sufficiently. Don't worry about the leftovers—they make superb beef salads (see pages 123 and 126) or sandwiches. Top round meat is lean, fairly dense, and a little chewy, so it's therefore best cooked medium-rare to medium (125° to 140°F). Other good choices here are top sirloin or chuck steak.

Note: *This steak is a bit too thick to pan-broil successfully.*

■ **Flavor Step** ■ Combine the marinade ingredients in a small bowl. Score both sides of the steak with several ¼-inch-deep gashes; pierce it all over with a skewer or sharp fork.

Place the steak in a zipper-lock bag or shallow baking dish and cover with the marinade. Place the bag or dish (covered) in the refrigerator for 1 or, even better, 2 days; shake the bag or turn the steak from time to time.

To grill the steak: See Grilling, page 63. Remove the steak from the marinade and pat dry. Season lightly with salt and pepper. Grill the steak over medium-hot coals, preferably in a covered kettle barbecue. Turn the steak every 3 to 4 minutes for a total grilling time of 15 to 20 minutes, or until the internal temperature of the center of the steak registers 125° to 140°F on an instant-read thermometer. Remove the steak, loosely cover with foil, and let it sit for 5 to 10 minutes before carving.

To broil the steak: See Broiling, page 58. Remove the steak from the marinade, pat dry, and season lightly with salt and pepper. Broil in a preheated broiler 4 to 5 inches from the heat, turning the steak two or three times, for a total cooking time of 15 to 20 minutes, or until the internal temperature reaches 125° to 140°F.

Slice the steak across the grain into ¼-to-⅜-inch-thick slices. Serve 3 to 4 slices per person. Save any remaining steaks for beef salads or sandwiches.

Steak, Roast Potato, and Grilled Vegetable Salad with Garlic Mustard Vinaigrette

OVEN-ROASTED POTATOES

1½ pounds small red or
    Yukon gold potatoes,
    cut into quarters
¼ cup olive oil
¾ teaspoon salt
1 teaspoon freshly ground
    black pepper
2 tablespoons chopped
    fresh rosemary, thyme,
    or savory or 2
    teaspoons dried

GARLIC MUSTARD VINAIGRETTE

2 garlic cloves, minced
1 tablespoon Dijon
    mustard
1½ tablespoons red wine
    vinegar
½ teaspoon Worcestershire
    sauce
    Pinch of salt
½ teaspoon freshly ground
    black pepper
¼ cup or more olive oil
1 tablespoon chopped
    fresh herbs such as
    basil, thyme, oregano,
    or marjoram

Serves 4 to 6
■ GREAT LEFTOVERS ■ IN A HURRY

THIS IS NOT ONLY a great way to use leftover steak, such as Grilled Bourbon-Marinated Top Round Steak (page 124), Marinated Flank Steak (page 113), or Marinated Chuck Steak (page 136), but also a nice way to serve steak hot off the grill. Although you can serve the salad with leftover boiled potatoes, it's much better with freshly made oven-roasted potatoes. Serve with a hearty California or Rhone Valley Syrah or a hoppy, full-bodied pale ale.

To roast the potatoes: Preheat the oven to 450°F. In a mixing bowl, toss the potatoes with the remaining ingredients until well coated. Spread them on a sheet pan and roast until they are nicely browned on all sides, 20 to 30 minutes. Turn the potatoes often with a spatula as they cook. Set them aside while you assemble the salad.

To make the vinaigrette: Combine the garlic, mustard, vinegar, Worcestershire sauce, salt, and pepper in a small bowl or food processor. Gradually whisk in or process the oil until the dressing is emulsified. Stir in the chopped fresh herbs.

To prepare the steak and grilled vegetables: Prepare all the ingredients and set aside.

To assemble the salad: Mix together the potatoes and grilled vegetables (reserve ¼ cup of the bell peppers or pimento strips) with the green onions or scallions in a large bowl. Toss with all but 2 tablespoons of the dressing. Spoon the salad into a shallow serving bowl or platter. Slice the steak and arrange the slices over the salad. Garnish with the remaining bell pepper or pimento strips. Drizzle the remaining 2 tablespoons of the vinaigrette over the steak and salad. Taste for salt and pepper and serve.

GRILLED VEGETABLES AND STEAK

2 cups grilled vegetables, newly grilled or leftover, such as zucchini, yellow squash, Japanese eggplant, red onions, pattypan squash (see Grilling, page 63), coarsely diced

2 bell peppers (red, yellow, or green), grilled or fire-roasted and peeled (see page 103), cut into thin strips, OR 2 canned pimentos, cut into thin strips

½ cup thinly sliced green onions or scallions or chives

¾-1 pound leftover or freshly grilled steak, preferably marinated, such as Grilled Bourbon-Marinated Top Round Steak OR Marinated Flank Steak

Salt and freshly ground black pepper

Priscilla's Marinated Beef and Black Bean Salad

■ Flavor Step ■
SOUTHWESTERN
SPICE RUB

1 teaspoon ground cumin

1 teaspoon chile powder, preferably Gebhardt

2 teaspoons salt

1 teaspoon freshly ground black pepper

1½ teaspoons light or dark brown sugar

½ teaspoon cayenne pepper

2 teaspoons minced garlic

1 teaspoon minced shallots or green onions or scallions (white part only)

1½ pounds boneless top sirloin, flank, top loin (New York strip), or top round steak

SPICY VINAIGRETTE

1 tablespoon Dijon mustard

¼ cup fresh lime juice

¼ cup olive oil

Serves 6
■ IN A HURRY ■ LOW-FAT

PRISCILLA YEE is a prize-winning cook who has a flair for creating simple but delicious recipes. Here's one with distinct Southwest flavors that combines spicy meat with a warm bean salad. It makes a delightful main course for a light summer dinner or a lively first course for a more elaborate Southwestern banquet. The steak is best grilled over charcoal, but it can also be broiled. The dry spice marinade can be used in many other beef or pork dishes as well.

■ **Flavor Step** ■ Combine the cumin, chile powder, salt, pepper, brown sugar, cayenne, garlic, and shallots or green onions in a small bowl. Rub half of this mixture on both sides of the steak. Let the steak marinate for at least 2 hours at room temperature, or cover with plastic wrap and refrigerate overnight.

To make the Spicy Vinaigrette: Combine the remaining spice rub with the mustard, lime juice, and oil in a food processor or blender and process to blend; or whisk in a bowl until well blended. Set the vinaigrette aside, or cover and refrigerate overnight.

If the steak was refrigerated overnight, remove it from the refrigerator 30 minutes to 1 hour before cooking. Prepare a charcoal grill, preferably a covered kettle style, or preheat the broiler. (See Grilling or Broiling, page 63 or 58.)

Grill the steak over medium-hot coals for 4 to 5 minutes. Turn and grill for 3 to 4 minutes on the other side. The steak is medium-rare when it reaches an internal temperature of 130°F when tested with an instant-read thermometer. Or broil the steak about 3 inches from the heat for 4 to 5 minutes. Turn and broil on the other side for 3 to 4 more minutes for medium-rare.

Meanwhile, make the Black Bean Salad: Put the beans, jicama, bell pepper, and green onions or scallions into a large skillet and set over medium heat. Stir in the vinaigrette and mix well to coat the beans. Cook until the beans are completely warmed through, 3 to 4 minutes, stirring frequently. Remove from the heat and stir in the cilantro, parsley, and diced tomatoes.

To assemble the salad: Spoon the beans into a shallow bowl or platter. Slice the steak diagonally into ¼-inch-thick slices and arrange them over the beans. Garnish with cilantro sprigs, if you want.

BLACK BEAN SALAD

3 cups cooked black beans, homemade or canned (preferably Progresso brand), rinsed if canned

1 cup peeled and diced jicama

1 fresh or canned fire-roasted red or yellow bell pepper (see page 103), diced

½ cup finely chopped green onions or scallions (green part only)

½ cup coarsely chopped fresh cilantro

¼ cup coarsely chopped fresh flat-leaf parsley

2 cups diced seeded ripe tomatoes, drained

Cilantro sprigs for garnish (optional)

Tostada Salad

About 1½ pounds
cooked beef or pork,
cut into ½-by-¼-by-2-
inch strips (3-4 cups)

TORTILLA CHIPS

6 corn tortillas OR
2-3 cups store-bought
tortilla chips
Vegetable oil for deep-
frying (if using fresh
tortillas)

MUSTARD-TARRAGON
VINAIGRETTE

2 tablespoons cider
vinegar
1 tablespoon tarragon
vinegar
1 teaspoon dry mustard,
preferably Colman's
1 teaspoon paprika
1 tablespoon sugar
2 teaspoons kosher salt
¾ cup olive oil

Serves 8
■ MEAT AS A CONDIMENT ■ LOW-FAT
(USING BAKED TORTILLA CHIPS)

THIS SALAD FROM LISA WEISS, our recipe
tester, is so good that if you don't have
any leftover meat, you might be inspired
to cook a steak or a few pork chops just
so you can make it. We prefer to make our own
tortilla chips, but store-bought baked tortilla
chips, widely available these days, will make this
a low-fat dish. Try it with any leftover steak or
meat; it's particularly good with grilled Marinated Flank Steak (page 113) or Cuban Roast
Pork (page 358).

If the meat has been refrigerated, heat it in a microwave or
conventional oven until warmed through, or let it come to
room temperature.

To make the tortilla chips: Cut the tortillas in half, stack
the halves, and cut crosswise into ½-inch strips. Fry the tortillas in vegetable oil heated to 360°F for about 1 minute, or
until crisp. Drain on paper towels. Or purchase chips.

To make the Mustard-Tarragon Vinaigrette: Whisk
the vinegars together with the mustard, paprika, sugar, and
salt. Slowly whisk in the olive oil until the dressing is emulsified.

Place the lettuce and remaining ingredients in a large salad bowl. Add the tortilla chips, meat, and vinaigrette, toss well, and serve.

2-3 heads romaine lettuce,
outer leaves discarded,
washed, and cut
crosswise into ½-inch-
wide strips

½ cup thinly sliced red
onion

4 vine-ripened tomatoes,
peeled, seeded, and
diced

2 avocados, diced

1 cup loosely packed
chopped fresh cilantro

2 fresh or canned fire-
roasted mild green
chiles (see page 103),
cut into strips

1 red bell pepper,
cut into ¼-inch dice

½ cup freshly grated
Pecorino Romano
cheese OR crumbled
queso fresco or feta
cheese

A Real Meal

P AT'S AND GINO'S SIT ON OPPOSITE CORNERS in South Philly that are brightly lit by too much neon. It's best to make a pilgrimage to these venerable shrines of the Philly Cheese Steak late in the evening, when the hunger pangs have set in after a night on the town or an insufficiently satisfying meal of nouvelle cuisine. On a good night, you'll find groups of old Italian men from the neighborhood, waving their arms and arguing about whose steaks are better: Pat's or Gino's. Judging from their age and enthusiasm, these wool-capped *paisans* have been having the same argument for quite a number of years.

One brisk spring night, we pulled up in front of Pat's and got into line behind some of Philadelphia's blue-uniformed finest (the sandwich shops are the safest spots in town, with cops usually lined up with all the other regulars). When our turn came, we ordered a large steak with the works: provolone cheese, grilled green peppers, sautéed onions. You can get the more popular yellow melted fake cheese sauce on the sandwich, but we prefer the actual dairy product to that bright plastic glop. Unless you're a delicate invalid, a kid under four, or just an out-and-out wimp, never order anything less than the large steak—or be prepared for scorn from the sandwich man and ridicule from the regulars. Later you can secretly divide the sandwich with a companion, but be sure to keep out of sight when you do it.

You have to understand what the steak in Philly Cheese Steak really is. Abandon all thoughts of porterhouse, T-bones, or fillets. A Philly steak is composed of the thinnest slices of beef (most likely sirloin). The beef slices are placed on a hot, well-worn griddle and flipped 30 seconds later. At this point the yellow cheesy gunk can be added. Meanwhile, a split roll is handed to the sandwich maker, filled with grilled onions and peppers, and topped with two thin slices of provolone, if that's what you ordered. The meat is scraped off the grill and spread over the onions, peppers, and cheese. The sandwich is quickly wrapped and handed over. At this point, it's up to you to embellish it as you wish. On the counter are trays of pickle relish and hot pickled peppers, with bottles of different hot sauces scattered around. We think the pickled peppers are the best: just tear them apart with your hands and scatter them over the meat. But first you must salt and pepper the sandwich well, since the cooks seem to ignore these seasonings.

All you have to do then is sit down at one of the ubiquitous plastic tables and devour the sandwich. Don't wear your best duds: the sandwiches are really juicy. Rest up for a while at Pat's, sip a birch beer or two, and then saunter across the street to Gino's for a comparative tasting. Then you can join in the argument with the *paisans* and fight for your favorite steak.

Philly Cheese Steaks

■ IN A HURRY ■ COOKING ON A BUDGET

WE'VE TAKEN A FEW liberties with the traditional preparation. Contrary to the usual practice, we salt and pepper the meat and vegetables first, and we have used a much better cheese than the typical bland, rubbery provolone or, even worse, that yellow stuff. Be sure to include pickled peppers—they really make the sandwich sing—and if you have a taste for the hot stuff, sprinkle on plenty of your favorite bottled sauce.

If you're going to use the onion and pepper, sauté them separately in small saucepans with 1 tablespoon olive oil in each until soft, stirring often. The onion will take 10 to 12 minutes, the pepper a little less, 8 to 10 minutes. Sprinkle with salt and pepper and set aside.

Using your thumbs, split the roll or bread open without totally separating the 2 halves. Set aside. Heat the remaining 2 tablespoons olive oil in a skillet over high heat. Put the meat in and sprinkle with salt and pepper. Turn after 30 seconds and season with salt and pepper again. After 30 seconds more, place 2 slices of cheese over the meat, remove from the pan with a spatula, and set aside. Spread the onion and green pepper, if using them, over the roll. Put the meat and cheese on top. Garnish with the optional pickled peppers and hot sauce. Serve at once with plenty of napkins.

FOR EACH SANDWICH

½ cup thinly sliced onions (optional)

½ cup thinly sliced green bell pepper (optional)

4 tablespoons olive oil
Salt and freshly ground black pepper

1 8-to-10-inch Italian roll, preferably very fresh, with a good chewy crust, OR an 8-to-10-inch piece of French baguette

4-5 ounces thinly sliced raw top round, sirloin tip, eye of the round, or boneless eye of chuck

2 slices provolone or Swiss cheese

2-3 red or green Italian pickled cherry peppers, cut into chunks (optional)
Bottled hot sauce (optional)

MAKING THE CUT
The Beef Chuck

CUTTING UP A CHUCK BLADE ROAST into its separate muscles is very easy and will yield delicious and inexpensive steaks, tender meat for kebabs or stir-fries, and lean stew meat. All you need is a sharp knife and a short anatomy lesson.

Here's how to do it: purchase a **chuck 7-bone blade roast**, easily recognized by the number-7-shaped thin piece of shoulder blade that traverses its top third. The thicker the roast, the thicker the pieces you'll end up with. If you want roasts or very thick steaks, try to find a whole chuck 7-bone blade roast or a piece 2 to 3 inches thick. Get one at least 1½ inches thick, in any case. Thinner pieces will naturally yield thinner steaks.

Basically, you need to separate this piece of meat into thirds. The tender top third, the part above the bone, is called the **top blade**. It is divided by a small ridge of bone into the **mock tender** and the **flatiron steak**. The rectangular muscle just beneath the bone is called the **under blade**. This meat is chewier and can be cut up for stew meat or braised whole. The roughly circular bottom piece is quite tender and very tasty. It's called the **chuck-eye** and can be used as a roast or steak, depending on thickness.

To separate the chuck-eye from the under blade, pick up the chuck roast by the blade bone—the roughly circular chuck-eye should begin to pull away. Run your knife along the top of the chuck-eye to separate it **(1)**.

Now that you've removed the chuck-eye section, separate the under blade meat from the top blade by running your knife along the bottom of the blade bone **(2)**.

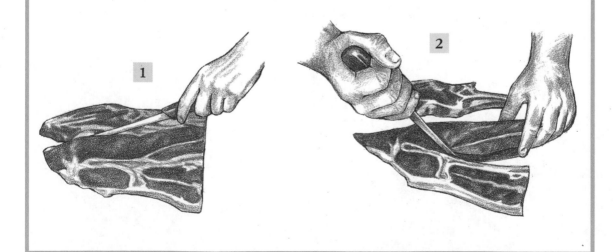

To cut out the flatiron steak and the mock tender, start at the ridge and run your knife along the top of the blade bone to remove each piece (**3**). The mock tender is best braised. The flatiron steak, which has a streak of gristle down the center, can be grilled or made into delicious kebabs or a stir-fry (**4**).

If you like, buy a number of chuck 7-bone blade roasts when they're on sale and then cut up, wrap, and freeze the individual cuts for up to two or three months (see Refrigerating Beef, page 91).

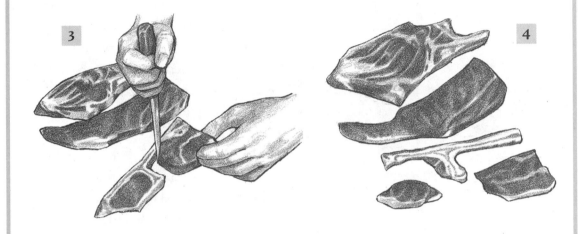

RECOMMENDED MARINADES AND RUBS FOR CHUCK STEAK

Nogales Steak Marinade (page 102)
North African Marinade (page 114)
Teriyaki Marinade (page 115)
Bourbon Marinade for Steak (page 124)
Spicy Beer Marinade (page 138)
Chipotle-Orange Marinade (page 138)
Korean Marinade for Beef (page 217)
Spice Rub for Pork or Beef (page 375)

Marinated Chuck Steak

1 1½-to-2½-pound
(or more) chuck steak,
preferably with some
rib bone attached, ¾-
1¼ inches thick

■ **Flavor Step** ■
Chipotle-Orange or
Spicy Beer Marinade
(page 138) OR your
favorite recipe

Salt and freshly ground
black pepper
(if pan-broiling)

Serves 4 to 6
■ Cooking on a Budget ■ In a Hurry
■ Good for a Crowd

MASTER RECIPE

CHUCK STEAKS are usually cut ¾ to 1¼ inches thick and each may weigh 1¼ to 2½ pounds. Since there is a fair amount of bone and other waste, allow 10 to 12 ounces of chuck steak per serving—that is, about ½ pound of boneless meat for each person. Since the steaks are on the large side, plan on one steak feeding two to three people or more, depending on appetites.

Like flank steak, chuck steak should be marinated for best results (see the suggested marinades and Nogales Steak Marinade, page 102). You may well have leftovers, but the steak is delicious cold in any beef salad recipe (pages 123 and 126) or in steak sandwiches. (You can use the bones for stock.)

Chuck steaks take well to smoke, so we recommend adding a few soaked hickory or other hardwood chips when grilling (see Grilling, page 63). Accompany them with grilled whole green onions or scallions, leeks, or red bell peppers.

■ **Flavor Step** ■ The day before you are going to eat, put the steak in a shallow dish and pierce it all over on both sides with a fork or skewer. Pour the marinade over the steak, cover, and refrigerate overnight, turning the meat occasionally.

About 30 minutes to 1 hour before cooking, remove the steak from the refrigerator.

To grill the steaks: See Grilling, page 63. Chuck steaks are best when grilled over charcoal with the addition of a few soaked hickory or other hardwood chips. These steaks are usually a bit too chewy to be served rare and are best cooked medium-rare to medium.

Remove the steak from the marinade, shake off any excess, and place it directly over the coals of a medium-hot fire. Use a lidded barbecue, if possible, and cover the steak immediately after placing it on the grill; if you're using soaked hardwood chips, sprinkle them over the fire just before adding the steak.

Grill the steak for 5 to 7 minutes on the first side. Turn it over and cook for 5 to 6 minutes more. Test the interior temperature with an instant-read thermometer—it should read 130° to 135°F for medium-rare and 135° to 150°F for medium. Remove the steak to a platter or cutting board. Let rest, loosely covered with foil, for 5 minutes. Cut the meat away from the bones in the largest pieces you can and slice each piece across the grain into ¼-to-½-inch-thick strips. Serve at once.

To broil the steaks: See Broiling, page 58. Preheat the broiler. Remove the steak from the marinade, shake off any excess, and place in the broiler about 3 inches from the flame. Broil for 7 to 8 minutes on the first side, then turn and broil 6 to 7 minutes more for medium-rare to medium. Follow the guidelines above for determining doneness and for carving and serving the steak.

To pan-broil the steaks: See Pan-Broiling, page 60. You will need a ridged or flat cast-iron pan large enough to hold the steak. Remove the steak from the marinade, pat dry with paper towels, and lightly season with salt and pepper to help form a crust. Pan-broil it over high heat for 5 to 6 minutes per side for medium-rare to medium. Follow the directions above for determining doneness and for carving and serving the meat.

Two Marinades for Chuck Steaks

Both of these marinades also work well with top round, sirloin steak, and flank steak.

Spicy Beer Marinade

Makes 2⅓ to 3 cups

1   teaspoon Tabasco sauce
3   tablespoons cider vinegar
1   12-ounce bottle of lager beer
1   tablespoon coarse-grained mustard
1   tablespoon Worcestershire sauce or A-1 steak sauce
½   cup soy sauce
2   teaspoons minced garlic
2   tablespoons minced onion
1   teaspoon salt
1   teaspoon freshly ground black pepper

Combine all the ingredients in a small bowl.

Chipotle-Orange Marinade

Makes 2 to 2½ cups

2   teaspoons grated orange zest
1   cup fresh orange juice
3   tablespoons fresh lemon juice
1   teaspoon minced garlic
⅓   cup vegetable oil
¼   cup soy sauce
1   tablespoon chopped canned chipotle chile in adobo,
    preferably Herdez brand, OR 1 teaspoon red pepper flakes
½   teaspoon salt
1   teaspoon freshly ground black pepper

Combine all the ingredients in a small bowl.

FLATIRON STEAK

Where it comes from: One of two muscles that make up the external top blade area of the chuck or beef shoulder. When boned out, it is a triangular piece of meat that can be roasted or sliced into small steaks.

Why we like it: The whole flatiron muscle is delicious roasted whole or braised as pot roast. The meat is quite tender and can also be sliced into 1-inch-thick steaks for grilling. Its rich beef flavor takes well to marinades, especially those based on soy sauce and incorporating Asian herbs and spices. The line of gristle running down the center of the muscle should be removed before or after cooking.

Price: Inexpensive.

AKA: Top blade steak, blade steak, lifter steak, top chuck steak, book steak, butter steak, petit steak, and other fanciful names.

Flatiron Steak
(Top Blade Steak)

■ Flavor Step ■
Thai Marinade for Pork
(page 382) OR North
African Marinade
(page 114) OR any
of the marinades
recommended for
chuck steak
(see page 135 and
Seasoning Chart, page
577)

4 1¼-inch-thick flatiron
or other chuck steaks
(6-8 ounces each),
trimmed of excess fat

Serves 4

■ COOKING ON A BUDGET

MEAT FROM THE CHUCK, or shoulder, of the steer has a rich, deep, beefy flavor that makes it tastier than other areas often cut as steaks, such as the sirloin or top round.

Our preferred method for cooking steaks from the chuck is grilling, followed by sautéing and broiling. Flatiron and other chuck steaks can also be braised with good results.

■ **Flavor Step** ■ Marinate the steaks as directed in the specific recipe overnight in the refrigerator.

Grill the steaks over direct heat (see Grilling, page 63), sauté (see Sautéing, page 61), or broil them (see Broiling, page 58). Since chuck steaks are somewhat firm and chewy, we recommend that you cook them to the medium-rare or medium stage, or to an internal temperature of 130° to 150°F. Let the steaks rest, covered loosely with foil, for 5 minutes before serving.

If you use the Thai Marinade, serve them with Thai Dipping Sauce (page 383).

Nancy's Chicken-Fried Steak

Serves 4
■ COOKING ON A BUDGET ■ IN A HURRY
■ MOM'S COMFORT FOOD

IF YOU GREW UP ON THE FLAT, sun-parched prairies of Texas and Oklahoma, the mere mention of chicken-fried steak should make your mouth water. This truckers' favorite is served at truckstops and roadside diners from El Paso to the Ozarks; the best versions are crunchy, peppery pieces of beef cut from the bottom round or rump. The steaks are pounded lightly and then floured and deep-fried, hence the chicken-fried moniker.

Like so many of America's comfort foods, chicken-fried steak is poor folks' food—a tough cut of beef tenderized by pounding and then fried up like the South's favorite dish, fried chicken. The thin steaks are usually served with mashed potatoes and cream or country gravy, often with some stewed greens and biscuits.

The trick to success: never use the tenderized cube steaks found in many supermarkets. These come out tasting like cardboard that's been left out in the rain and then covered with wallpaper paste. Instead, cut (or have your butcher cut) ½-inch-thick slices from the bottom round or rump and pound them.

Our recipe comes from Bruce's wife, Nancy Oakes, who turned out many a chicken-fried steak when she ran the kitchen in the back of O'Shea's Mad Hatter's Bar, a lively San Francisco joint that was home to lots of transplanted Texans, quite a few boisterous truckers, and a passel of hungry Irishmen looking for alternatives to corned beef and cabbage. Her secret for a crispy crust: use egg whites and a little cream or half-and-half as the dip with the seasoned flour.

1 pound beef bottom
   round or rump, cut into
   four ⅜-to-½-inch slices
1 cup all-purpose flour
2 teaspoons freshly ground
   black pepper
1½ teaspoons salt
1 teaspoon dried thyme
1 teaspoon cayenne pepper
4 large egg whites, lightly
   beaten
½ cup cream or half-and-
   half
   Vegetable shortening,
   vegetable oil, lard, or
   bacon fat

Trim any external fat from the beef and pound the slices with a meat mallet or the flat side of a cleaver between 2 sheets of plastic wrap to a final thickness of ¼ inch. In a shallow pan or pie plate, combine the flour, spices, and herbs. In another pan or pie tin, whisk together the egg whites and cream or half-and-half. Dip each beef slice first into the flour, shake off the excess, and then dip it into the egg whites and cream and then again into the flour. Place the steaks on a wire rack and let the coating dry for 15 minutes or so.

In a large (12-inch), heavy skillet, heat ½ inch of fat over high heat to 360°F. The fat should be hot enough to sizzle and spurt when a corner of a steak touches it. Fry 1 or 2 steaks at a time, making sure the pan is not too crowded. Cook the steaks for 2 minutes on each side, until the crust is golden brown. Serve with mashed potatoes.

CULOTTE STEAK

Where it comes from: This 1-to-1¼-inch thick steak is cut across the grain from the boneless bottom portion of the sirloin. Before the advent of boxed beef, the tri-tip was attached to bone-in sirloin steaks. This small steak is wonderful when

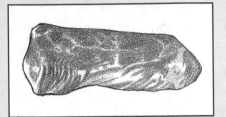

grilled and takes well to marinating. It is loaded with flavor, with virtually no waste. It is also sold separately as a small triangular roast.

Why we like it: Culotte steak's beefy flavor is enhanced by dry rubs and marinades.

Price: Moderately expensive. You can buy the tri-tip whole (often sold in wholesale clubs wrapped in Cryovac) and slice culotte steaks yourself or buy them already cut.

AKA: Not well known in the East. Ask your butcher if you don't see culotte steaks or tri-tip in the meat case. Most large national meat packers call the cut tri-tip or triangle tip.

HANGER STEAK

Where it comes from: Hanger steak is a 1-to-2-pound strip of 1½-to-2-inch-thick muscle attached to and supporting the diaphragm. It hangs off the kidney, just below the tenderloin on the left side of the steer. There is only one hanger steak per animal.

Why we like it: Like the neighboring skirt steak, this slightly chewy meat has a dark color and an intense, beefy flavor. Hanger steak is ideal for marinating and grilling. It is best served medium-rare to medium and sliced across the grain.

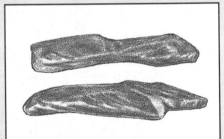

Price: If you are lucky enough to find it, hanger steak will be moderately priced compared to sirloin steak or steaks from the short loin like T-bone and porterhouse.

AKA: Hanging tender, butcher's steak. Offered in French restaurants as *onglet*.

Culotte Steaks with Onion Glaze and Horseradish Bread Crumbs

HORSERADISH BREAD CRUMBS

½ cup soft bread crumbs
   (from day-old bread)
1 tablespoon butter
3 tablespoons bottled
   horseradish, drained
2 teaspoons Dijon mustard
   Salt and freshly ground
   black pepper

4 1½-inch-thick culotte,
   hanging tenderloin,
   filet mignon, or New
   York strip steaks
   (7-8 ounces each)
   Salt and freshly ground
   black pepper
1 tablespoon olive or
   vegetable oil

ONION GLAZE

1 medium onion, thinly
   sliced
2 teaspoons minced garlic
¾ cup dry red wine
   Salt and freshly ground
   black pepper

Serves 4
■ FIT FOR COMPANY ■ IN A HURRY

THE HORSERADISH-AND-MUSTARD-SEA-SONED bread crumbs are also excellent as a con-diment sprinkled over sliced roast beef or leg of lamb. Do not use fine bread crumbs here; the best are homemade bread crumbs about ⅛ to ¼ inch in size. Serve with flavored mashed potatoes, such as roasted garlic mashed potatoes, or mashed potatoes with truffle oil and chopped fresh thyme.

■ **Flavor Step** ■ Preheat the oven to 350°F. Spread the bread crumbs on a cookie sheet and bake for 10 minutes, or until dry and toasted. Melt the butter in a small, heavy skillet over medium heat. Add the bread crumbs, horseradish, and mustard and stir until the crumbs are well coated and golden brown, about 10 minutes. Season to taste with salt and pepper, transfer the crumbs to a bowl, and set aside.

Season the steaks generously on both sides with salt and pepper. In a heavy skillet large enough to hold the steaks without crowding, heat the oil over high heat. Add the steaks and brown them well for 1 minute on each side. Reduce the heat to medium-high and cook for 3 to 4 minutes more per side for rare to medium-rare (120° to 135°F). Transfer the steaks to a platter and keep warm by covering loosely with foil.

To make the Onion Glaze: Pour off all but 1 tablespoon of fat from the skillet and add the onion and garlic. Cook over medium heat until soft, about 5 minutes, stirring from time to time. Pour in the wine and bring to a boil, scraping up any browned bits from the bottom of the pan. Reduce the sauce until it's just a glaze and season with salt and pepper to taste.

Spoon the onion mixture onto a platter; cover with the steaks, sprinkle generously with the bread crumbs, and serve.

How to Choose the Best
Braised Steak

LSO CALLED **Swiss steak** or **smothered steak**, **round steak** is the traditional cut to use for braising. It includes sections of the **top round**, **bottom round**, and sometimes **eye of the round**. Slices that are ¾ to 1¼ inch thick from the bottom round are also good for braising, as are ¾-to-1¼-inch blade steaks cut from the chuck, especially the **mock tender**, **shoulder clod steak**, and **7-bone chuck steak**. You can also ask your butcher to cut ¾-to-1¼-inch slices from the arm area of the chuck, called **arm steak**. Both arm steaks and round steaks can be identified by the characteristically round arm or leg bone. Essentially, braised steak is a pot roast with a thinner cut of meat. You can substitute pot roast recipes for these cuts simply by varying the cooking time according to the thickness of the meat.

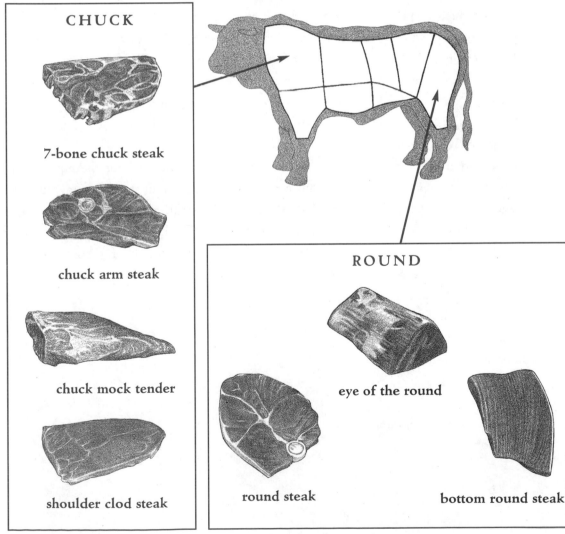

CHUCK

7-bone chuck steak

chuck arm steak

chuck mock tender

shoulder clod steak

ROUND

eye of the round

round steak

bottom round steak

Spanish-Style Oven-Braised Steak

1 2½-pound round steak, chuck steak, or Swiss steak (bottom round)

■ **Flavor Step** ■
Salt and freshly ground black pepper

1 tablespoon olive oil

1 cup dry Spanish sherry or white wine

BRAISING SAUCE

3 fire-roasted red bell peppers (see page 103), cut into ½-inch strips, OR 3 canned Spanish pimentos, cut into ½-inch strips

2 medium onions, thinly sliced

1 cup peeled, seeded, and chopped fresh tomatoes or seeded and chopped canned tomatoes

1 large green bell pepper, cut into ½-inch dice

¼ pound thinly sliced prosciutto or Serrano ham, cut into strips

1 cup beef or chicken stock

2 tablespoons minced garlic

3 bay leaves

½ teaspoon dried marjoram

½ teaspoon salt

½ teaspoon freshly ground black pepper

Serves 4 to 6
■ COOKING ON A BUDGET ■ REWARMS WELL

BOTTOM ROUND (often called Swiss steak), round steak, or chuck steak all work well in this savory dish. It's easy to prepare ahead, rewarms well, and is quite economical—the perfect supper to please a family. Make sure to buy a steak at least 1 inch thick so that the meat doesn't dry out during the long, slow cooking. Accompany this dish with a full-bodied Spanish Rioja or California Zinfandel.

———

■ **Flavor Step** ■ Season the steak generously on both sides with salt and pepper. Preheat the oven to 350°F. Heat the olive oil in a large, heavy skillet over high heat and brown the steak for 2 minutes per side. Transfer the steak to a baking pan or shallow casserole with a tight lid. Pour off the fat from the skillet and add the sherry or white wine. Boil rapidly, scraping up any browned bits from the bottom.

To make the Braising Sauce: Pour the liquid from the pan into a medium bowl. Add all the sauce ingredients and mix well. Pour over the steak and seal the pan tightly with aluminum foil or cover with the lid. (The steak can be prepared to this point and refrigerated for cooking later the same day or the next.)

Put the pan in the oven and bake for 1 to 1½ hours, or until the meat is quite tender. Remove the steak and keep it warm. Pour the sauce into a saucepan and skim off any fat.

To finish the sauce: In a food processor, process the almonds, egg yolks, parsley, and garlic cloves to a paste. Stir this paste into the sauce and simmer over low heat for 10 minutes. Taste for salt and pepper. Pour over the steak and serve with rice or roast potatoes.

SAUCE ADDITIONS

⅓ cup slivered almonds, lightly toasted (see Note, page 121)

3 hard-boiled eggs, yolks only

3 tablespoons chopped fresh parsley

2 garlic cloves
  Salt and freshly ground black pepper

Braised Swiss Steak with Mushrooms and Grappa

■ Flavor Step ■
HERB RUB FOR
SWISS STEAK

½ teaspoon dried sage

½ teaspoon dried thyme

1 teaspoon salt

½ teaspoon freshly ground
black pepper

1 1-to-1¼-inch-thick
braising steak, about 2
pounds, trimmed of
excess fat

Serves 4 to 6, with leftovers
■ COOKING ON A BUDGET ■ REWARMS WELL

I STUMBLED ACROSS THIS RECIPE one day when I was attempting to braise a tough piece of steak in a brandy sauce. When I went to the cupboard to fetch the brandy, all I could find was a dusty bottle of grappa someone had brought as a gift for some long-ago dinner party. I'm not a great fan of this overhyped and often overpriced by-product of the winemaking process and Italian marketing genius, so it just sat there. But when I tried it in the recipe, I learned what grappa should be used for: cooking, not drinking. The results were amazingly good, and I quickly used up that dusty bottle. I now keep a bottle of inexpensive grappa on hand and use it whenever a recipe calls for brandy. You could, of course, just use brandy here if you don't want to go to the trouble of keeping grappa around the house.

For Swiss or any braised steak, use at least a ¾-inch-thick or, better still, a 1¼-inch-thick chuck steak, round steak, slice of bottom round (often called Swiss steak), or rump steak.

B.A.

■ **Flavor Step** ■ In a small bowl, combine the herb rub ingredients and rub all over the steak.

Place the dried mushrooms in a glass measuring cup or bowl. Add enough boiling water to cover and soak for at least 30 minutes.

Heat the oil over medium-high heat in a high-sided skillet or pan with a cover large enough to hold the steak. Put in the steak and sear it for 2 to 3 minutes per side. Remove and set it aside. Put the onions, carrots, and celery in the pan, reduce the heat to medium, and cook for 5 minutes, stirring often. Remove the dried mushrooms from the liquid and add to the pan with the garlic and fresh mushrooms. Fry them for 2 to 3 minutes, stirring often. When you are ready to add the grappa or brandy, pour it into a measuring cup first; don't pour directly from the bottle into the pan, and don't lean over the pan when adding. The spirits may flame up, but don't worry; just continue to cook and shake the pan until the flame goes away. Stir, scraping up any browned bits from the bottom of the pan.

Add the wine, stock, bay leaves, thyme or rosemary, and a pinch each of salt and pepper. Put the steak back in, cover, and cook at a low simmer for 1 hour. Check the steak: when it's fork-tender, it's done. Remove the steak with a slotted spoon and keep warm. Degrease the sauce and reduce it over high heat until it just becomes syrupy. Taste for salt and pepper. Pour over the steak and serve.

You may also refrigerate the steak overnight in its sauce, remove the congealed fat the next day, and reheat the steak in the sauce and serve.

¼ ounce porcini or other dried mushrooms, rehydrated and chopped
2 tablespoons olive oil
3 cups sliced onions
½ cup diced carrots
½ cup diced celery
2 tablespoons chopped garlic
½ pound sliced fresh porcini or domestic white or brown mushrooms
¼ cup grappa or brandy
1 cup white wine
1 cup beef or chicken stock
2 bay leaves
2 sprigs fresh thyme or rosemary or 1 teaspoon dried
Salt and freshly ground black pepper

IRISH UNCLES AND BEEFSTEAKS
AT RYAN'S RIDING EMPORIUM

MY IRISH UNCLES, TOM AND JOHN SULLIVAN, were men of substantial girth and serious demeanor, both dedicated meat eaters and connoisseurs of well-marbled steaks. Tom became a cop at an early age and walked a beat in Brooklyn for 20 years—calm and methodical, a staunch Republican, teetotaler, and upstanding member of the Knights of Columbus and the Sodality of the Sacred Heart. Johnny was a union man from the start; he came up through the ranks and ended as secretary-treasurer of his local, with plenty of scars and stories from the battles with goons and scabs. He was also known to take a drop or two at Roche's Bar on 4th Avenue with Johnny McMannus and the sporting crowd, and he had more than a nodding acquaintance with the Fischetti brothers, who ran the Brooklyn docks.

Tom and John didn't agree on much, especially politics, and the discussions around the Sunday dinner table often got quite lively. But one thing they always agreed on was beef: they would examine a steak minutely and discuss its qualities like art critics with a falsely attributed Rembrandt. They had a decided preference for porterhouse, although they would eat a T-bone in a pinch. They scorned strip steaks (no bone and no fillet), filet mignon (too mushy, too often Frenchified with sauces and foreign junk), sirloin (too tough), and minute steaks (too small and thin). They refused even to consider rump, round, or chuck steaks.

And they weren't shy about quantity, either. I can remember Uncle Tommy sitting down to a Sunday breakfast of fried eggs, potatoes, and toast, with a 2-inch-thick porterhouse hanging over the edges of the plate. And polishing it all off with cup after cup of strong tea while reading the newspaper and reviling that man in the White House, most likely FDR or some other perfidious Democrat. And if this sounds like an unhealthful diet to us these days, consider that Tommy finally left us in the middle of his daily handball game with the retired wise guys at the Brooklyn Y at the age of 89.

Both Tom and Johnny ate steaks on every possible occasion, at home and in restaurants, but their real steak eating took place at the steak feasts, or "beef-steaks," that were thrown by local societies such as the Ancient Order of Hibernians, union locals, and church groups. The most renowned was held every Fourth of July during the '30s, '40s, and '50s out at Ryan's Riding Emporium and Boarding Stables on Sheepshead Bay, where two or three hundred people got together to eat and celebrate the day.

The party began early, with giant fire pits dug in the dunes, where driftwood logs would be burned down to coals. By about noon, heavy metal grates had been dragged over the fire pits, and huge Maine lobsters, clams, crabs, and corn were tossed on them and covered with seaweed and wet burlap sacks. When it was done, the food was raked off onto immense platters and set out on tables, along with melted butter and quartered lemons, for a warm-up course. About this time, kegs of beer would appear, set into washtubs and surrounded by blocks of ice that the kids would chip pieces off all day long to chew on and throw at each other. The band would get going, playing jigs and reels, and some of the friskier young folk would start the dancing.

With the lobsters and so forth, and a few dozen raw oysters finished off, the real eating of the day would commence. Butchers' vans drove over the sand and unloaded trays piled high with steak. The butchers marched to the fire pits, showing off the beautifully marbled porterhouses and T-bones to the hungry crowds. The cooks quickly sprinkled on salt and pepper and tossed the steaks on the grill. And we all crowded round in the fragrant smoke, picking out our steaks and keeping an eye on them as they cooked. The cooks would yell out "medium" or "rare" as they took the steaks from the fire, forking them onto plates held out by eager diners. You took your steak back to the table, where bowls of potato salad and coleslaw were waiting, tried to find some room on your plate for something other than meat, and fell to.

This went on for as long as people could eat, and some, like my uncles, would go back to the fire time and time again, often getting very precise about their choices. "I'll just have that tiny piece there, Pat, and maybe that nice bit of porterhouse with the crisp fat at the edge," they'd tell the cook, usually proffering a pitcher of cold beer as a friendly bribe.

As the sun went down, the music got louder and the older folks began to dance, lining up for the reels and watching grandmas get wild with the jigs and turns. Whiskey was passed around and voices raised in argument and song: "The Tumbled-Down Shack in Athlone," "The Rose of Tralee," "In the Garden Where the Praties Grow." We'd all walk back to the cars in the gathering dusk, remembering famine and exile and ancestors who ate meat once a month if they were lucky, celebrating America with feasting and good times.   *D.K.*

How to Choose the Best Beef for Kebabs

SKIRT STEAK'S SLIGHTLY CHEWY TEXTURE and intense, beefy flavor make it ideal for marinating and threading on skewers. Other in-between cuts—**top round, sirloin steak, tri-tip,** or **chuck steak** from the rib section—make excellent kebabs. These cuts can be marinated to tenderize them just enough to make them suitable for dry-heat cooking such as grilling or barbecuing. More tender cuts such as **top loin steaks** are also delicious as kebabs. Marinating this tender meat for flavor with a wet- or dry-rub marinade makes for wonderful results.

Ideally, kebabs should be cut into cubes about 1½ inches across and cooked in a covered kettle grill until medium-rare to medium. Rare kebabs can be a bit chewy unless you are using top loin; well-done kebabs may become dry and tough.

As with stew meat, avoid buying already-cut kebabs from the butcher. If you cut your own, you can be sure of where the meat comes from, and it will probably be cheaper. It's a little extra work, but worth it.

BUTCHERS' FAVORITE

SKIRT STEAK

Where it comes from: This long, thin flap of tender meat is actually the diaphragm of the steer and is attached to the inside of the rib cage.

Why we like it: The skirt steak has a coarse texture and a rich, beefy taste only matched by hanger steak. Both of these steaks are particularly delicious when marinated, for their loose grain allows them to  absorb the flavors easily. Skirt steak is sold rolled into circular steaks or as is. Because of its appearance, it is called *fajita*, or "belt," in Spanish. This is the authentic meat for the popular Southwestern grill.

Price: Moderate.

AKA: Fajita meat, Philadelphia steak.

Skirt Steak Satay

Serves 8 to 10 as an appetizer,
4 to 5 as a main course
■ FIT FOR COMPANY ■ GOOD FOR A CROWD

S KIRT STEAK is a flavorful strip of beef that comes from the diaphragm of the steer. It can be substituted in any of our recipes calling for marinated flank steak or chuck steak. To make traditional Mexican fajitas, use the marinade from Nogales Steak Tacos (see page 102).

Asian ingredients are available in Asian groceries and specialty shops and by mail-order (see Sources, page 584). You can use the Thai Marinade for Pork (page 382) if you prefer.

──────────

■ **Flavor Step** ■ In a food processor or blender, process the ginger, lemongrass or lime zest, lime or lemon juice, and garlic to a paste. Add the remaining ingredients and process to a smooth sauce. Place the meat in a zipper-lock bag or shallow bowl (cover if using a bowl) and pour in the marinade. Shake the bag or turn the meat to coat thoroughly. Marinate in the refrigerator for at least 4 hours, or overnight. Turn the bag or the meat occasionally.

About 1 hour before cooking, remove the meat from the refrigerator and bring to room temperature. Soak 10 bamboo skewers in cold water for at least 30 minutes so they won't burn.

■ **Flavor Step** ■
SATAY MARINADE
FOR BEEF

2 teaspoons minced fresh ginger

1 stalk lemongrass, tough outer leaves removed and tender inner part thinly sliced, OR 1 tablespoon minced lime zest

1 tablespoon fresh lime or lemon juice

1 tablespoon minced garlic

2 tablespoons Vietnamese or Thai fish sauce (*nuoc mam* or *nam pla*) OR soy sauce

1 tablespoon unsweetened coconut milk

2 teaspoons light or dark brown sugar

1 teaspoon turmeric

1 teaspoon freshly ground black pepper

1½ pounds ¼-to-⅜-inch-thick skirt steak, cut lengthwise into 4-inch-long strips, 1-2 inches wide

SATAY PEANUT SAUCE

1 tablespoon peanut
  or vegetable oil
½ cup finely chopped
  onion
½ teaspoon red pepper
  flakes
1 teaspoon minced garlic
1 teaspoon finely chopped
  lemongrass (tender
  inner part only)
  OR 1 teaspoon minced
  lime zest
¼ cup unsweetened
  coconut milk
1½ tablespoons fresh lime or
  lemon juice, or
  more to taste
1 tablespoon soy sauce
2 teaspoons light or
  dark brown sugar
¼ cup crunchy peanut
  butter
  Salt and freshly ground
  black pepper
  Asian chili paste
  (Sriracha—Thai hot
  chili sauce) or Tabasco
  sauce to taste (optional)

To make the Satay Peanut Sauce: Heat the oil in a small saucepan over medium-high heat. Add the onion, cover, and cook for 3 minutes or until soft, stirring occasionally. Turn the heat to low and stir in the remaining ingredients. Cook, stirring often, until the mixture is smooth and homogeneous. If it seems too thick, add a little water. Taste and correct the seasoning for salt and pepper, spiciness, and/or lime or lemon juice if necessary. Keep the sauce warm over very low heat while you cook the meat.

Remove the beef strips from the marinade and thread them onto the soaked bamboo skewers. Grill the skewers over medium-hot coals (see Grilling, page 63) or broil them in a preheated broiler (see Broiling, page 58) until medium-rare to medium, about 2 minutes per side. Serve the skewers at once with the peanut sauce on the side.

How to Choose the Best
Ground Beef and Hamburger

GROUND OR CHOPPED BEEF is muscle meat that has been ground or chopped in a meat grinder. Federally inspected ground meat by law cannot have more than 30 percent fat, nor can it contain added water, fat, seasonings, binders, or extenders. **Hamburger** is ground beef that may have added fat or seasonings, but no other additives.

Traditionally, the different grades of ground beef are referred to by the primal cuts they supposedly came from, thus implying a level of quality and fat percentage. **Ground beef** is the cheapest and can contain 30 percent fat. **Ground chuck** can contain 20 to 25 percent fat, while **ground sirloin** has 15 to 20 percent fat, and **ground round** 15 percent or less. Unfortunately, labeling styles and percentages of fat differ from area to area and store to store. There are no federal requirements, and there is much leeway in the marketplace. The name of a cut on the label is no guarantee that the meat comes from the primal cut indicated, so implied fat levels cannot always be relied on.

Many stores, however, now label ground beef by percent of lean meat: thus, 70 percent lean contains 30 percent fat, and 85 percent lean has 15 percent fat. Some even sell ground beef that is 95 percent lean—which produces dry and crumbly hamburgers. We think the best percentage is 80 percent lean—that is, 20 percent fat; the minimum fat level should be about 15 percent (85 percent lean) if you don't want a dry and tasteless burger.

Be a smart shopper and look for the percent of fat on the label. Observe the ground meat: if it's full of white specks, there's probably a lot of fat in the blend. When in doubt, ask the butcher to tell you the fat content of his or her ground beef.

COOKING HAMBURGER SAFELY

Hamburger should be handled with greater care than other beef: keep your hands and work surfaces meticulously clean and refrigerate ground beef until just before cooking. Even so, it should be cooked to 160°F internal temperature for complete safety—for once, we agree with the USDA. If you feel you have to eat hamburger that is still pink inside, grind your own from a chunk of previously uncut chuck, using impeccably clean equipment (a food processor or grinder), scalded with boiling water before use. You should also wash your hands, work surfaces, and tools, and rinse off and dry the meat before grinding it.

Hamburger—and life—present risks, and you must be your own judge of what risks you are willing to take. There is always *some* risk, however slight. But dangerous, food-borne illnesses are not common with whole cuts of beef, and tainted hamburger has usually involved sloppy techniques and poor handling of undercooked ground meat by commercial processors. In the Doneness Chart (page 56), we recommend what we consider ideal internal temperatures that will produce properly cooked and flavorful beef. If you want your meat rarer, it's your call.

GRINDING YOUR OWN BEEF

I F YOU WANT TO KNOW exactly what you're getting when it comes to ground beef, grind your own. Our first choice is boneless chuck meat with some of the outer fat, called the fat cap, attached—the resulting grind will have roughly 20 percent fat.

You can use a food processor, which will give you chopped, rather than ground, beef. A really sharp blade is essential; if you plan to do this often, buy a new blade and reserve it just for chopping meat. Or you can use a home meat grinder or a KitchenAid with a grinder attachment. In all cases, make sure all equipment has been scalded with boiling water and is impeccably clean.

To grind beef using a food processor: Chill the bowl and blade in the freezer for 30 minutes. Cut the meat, with the fat, into ¾-inch chunks. Chop small batches of meat and fat together by pulsing the machine until you achieve the desired particle size. Combine the various batches and mix together well. Use immediately, refrigerate for no more than 2 days, or wrap and freeze for later use. Frozen hamburger will keep for up to 3 months.

To grind beef using a meat grinder: Cut the meat with its fat into 1-inch strips. Grind the meat and fat together, using the ¼-inch blade. Mix the batches together and use or store as above.

You can also ask the butcher to grind the meat for you, although you should plan on buying a good amount (at least a few pounds) because some will be left behind in the grinder.

The Classic Hamburger

Serves 4

■ GOOD FOR A CROWD ■ COOKING ON A BUDGET ■
■ IN A HURRY ■

1	pound freshly ground beef chuck

1 teaspoon kosher salt
½ teaspoon freshly ground black pepper
1 tablespoon vegetable oil or melted beef fat (if panfrying)
4 hamburger buns

MASTER RECIPE

WHEN IT COMES TO that American classic, the hamburger sandwich, simplicity breeds perfection. This best of burgers is made from impeccably fresh beef chuck, preferably ground at home (see Grinding Your Own Beef, opposite), mixed with judicious amounts of kosher salt and freshly ground pepper and formed lightly into a ¾-inch-thick patty. It is grilled over charcoal, panfried, or broiled to produce a crumbly brown exterior. Hamburger perfection is achieved when the patty is tucked into a fresh sesame seed bun with sliced, vine-ripened tomatoes, sweet onions, crisp lettuce, and the condiment of your choice.

GARNISH
Sliced tomatoes, sliced sweet onions, lettuce, and condiments of your choice

Combine the meat, salt, and pepper in a large bowl and, using your hands, lightly mix to incorporate the seasonings throughout the meat. Form into 4 equal patties, about ¾ inch thick. Do not pack the patties.

Panfry, using the oil or melted beef fat (see Sautéing, page 61), grill over medium-hot coals (see Grilling, page 63), or broil (see Broiling, page 58) the burgers to the medium stage (see page 56) or to your preference. Serve on the buns, garnished as you like.

MIXING THE SALT, pepper, and other seasonings with the raw meat rather than just sprinkling them on after cooking makes a world of taste difference in burgers. This goes for cheese, too—why not mix in shredded cheese rather than pile it on top to spill and burn? And mixing seasonings with the meat incorporates the flavors of various cuisines into your hamburgers.

CHINESE MUSHROOM BURGER

1 pound ground chuck OR ¾ pound ground chuck plus ¼ pound ground pork

6 Chinese dried black mushrooms or shiitakes, soaked in hot water for at least 30 minutes, drained, stems removed, and finely chopped

¼ cup dark soy sauce

2 tablespoons Scotch whisky (optional)

1 tablespoon Asian sesame oil

3 tablespoons chopped fresh cilantro

2 tablespoons minced green onions or scallions

2 tablespoons minced fresh ginger

1 teaspoon minced garlic

1 tablespoon sugar

1 teaspoon Chinese 5-spice powder

Combine the meat and seasonings and cook as directed in the Master Recipe (page 157). Rather than shaping the mixture into patties, you can use it in a stir-fry.

SUN-DRIED TOMATO BURGER

Combine the meat and seasonings and cook as directed in the Master Recipe (page 157).

1 pound ground chuck

2 ounces prosciutto or pancetta, finely chopped (optional)

3 tablespoons finely chopped oil-packed sun-dried tomatoes

1 teaspoon minced garlic

2 tablespoons freshly grated Parmesan cheese

½ teaspoon salt (¾ teaspoon if you are not using prosciutto or pancetta)

½ teaspoon freshly ground black pepper

GREEK BURGER

Combine the meat and seasonings and cook as directed in the Master Recipe (page 157).

1 pound lean ground lamb, ground chuck, or half of each

2 tablespoons pitted and chopped kalamata olives

1 teaspoon minced garlic

1 tablespoon chopped fresh mint or 2 teaspoons dried

1 tablespoon chopped fresh dill or 2 teaspoons dried

2 teaspoons dried oregano, preferably Greek

1 teaspoon minced lemon zest

1 teaspoon salt

½ teaspoon freshly ground black pepper

SOUTHWEST CHILE BURGER

1 pound ground chuck

1 canned chipotle chile
in adobo, chopped, or
more if you like it spicy

¼ cup chopped fresh or
canned fire-roasted
green chiles
(see page 103)

½ cup shredded Monterey
Jack cheese

1 teaspoon salt

½ teaspoon ground cumin

¼ cup chopped fresh
cilantro (optional)

2 tablespoons minced
red onion

Combine the meat and seasonings and cook as directed in the Master Recipe (page 157).

HUNGARIAN BACON BURGERS

1 pound ground chuck or
¾ pound ground chuck
plus ¼ pound ground
veal

2 ounces uncooked bacon,
finely chopped

1 teaspoon minced garlic

¼ cup freshly grated
Parmesan cheese

1 tablespoon sweet
Hungarian paprika

½ teaspoon salt

½ teaspoon freshly ground
black pepper

2 teaspoons Worcestershire
sauce

2 teaspoons Dijon mustard

Combine the meat and seasonings and cook as directed in the Master Recipe (page 157).

Blue Cheese-Stuffed Burgers

Serves 3 as a main course, 4 as sandwiches

■ FIT FOR COMPANY ■ IN A HURRY
■ COOKING ON A BUDGET

MASTER RECIPE

BY STUFFING A SAVORY MIXTURE between two thin patties of beef and sealing the edges, you can take the humble hamburger to new heights of gastronomical bliss. Stuffed burgers can be an unusual and delicious main course when served with side dishes that complement the stuffing. Or you can turn a stuffed burger into a stupendous sandwich, garnished with condiments to match. Once stuffed and sealed, the burgers can be panfried, grilled, or broiled. For best results, do not prepare the stuffed patties too far in advance—no more than an hour—and keep them refrigerated at all times before cooking. The combination of the pungent blue cheese and beef works very well.

---

1 pound ground beef chuck
¾ teaspoon salt
½ teaspoon freshly ground black pepper
2 teaspoons Worcestershire sauce or A-1 steak sauce

STUFFING

1 cup crumbled blue cheese such as Danish blue, Maytag blue, Roquefort, or Gorgonzola
1 tablespoon butter, softened
¼ cup finely chopped green onions or scallions OR ¼ cup finely chopped sweet onion such as Walla Walla, Vidalia, or red torpedo (optional)

1 tablespoon vegetable oil or melted beef fat (if panfrying)

In a large bowl, combine the meat, salt, pepper, and Worcestershire or A-1 sauce. Form the meat into 6 (for a main course) or 8 (for sandwiches) patties about ⅜ inch thick. Refrigerate the patties while you prepare the stuffing.

To make the Stuffing: Put the cheese in a small bowl and blend in the butter with a fork. Mix in the optional green onions or scallions, using the fork to blend the ingredients to a creamy consistency.

Remove the patties from the refrigerator and place equal amounts of the cheese stuffing on half of them. Cover the stuffing with the other patties and seal the edges by pressing them together with your fingers. Sauté, using the oil or fat, grill or broil to medium, or to your preference (see Sautéing, page 61; Grilling, page 63; or Broiling, page 58).

MUSHROOM-STUFFED BURGER

1 pound ground beef
  chuck
¾ teaspoon salt
½ teaspoon freshly ground
  black pepper
2 teaspoons
  Worcestershire sauce
  or A-1 steak sauce

STUFFING

2 tablespoons butter
¾ pound mushrooms,
  chopped
1 teaspoon minced garlic
1 tablespoon minced
  onion or shallot
2 tablespoons dry
  vermouth or dry
  sherry (optional)
  Salt and freshly
  ground black pepper

Make the patties as directed in the Master Recipe (page 161).

To make the Stuffing: Melt the butter in a skillet over medium-high heat. Put in the mushrooms and cook for 1 minute, stirring frequently. Put in the garlic, onion or shallot, and the optional wine. Stir and cook until the mushrooms have released their juices and they have evaporated, 5 to 7 minutes. Season to taste.

Cool before stuffing and cooking the burgers as directed.

MOZZARELLA AND PESTO-STUFFED BURGER

1 pound ground beef
  chuck
¾ teaspoon salt
½ teaspoon freshly ground
  black pepper
2 teaspoons Worcestershire
  sauce or A-1 steak sauce
1 teaspoon minced garlic

STUFFING

1 cup shredded mozzarella
  cheese
3 tablespoons pesto
1 ounce prosciutto or dry
  coppa, finely chopped
  (optional)

Make the patties as directed in the Master Recipe (page 161), adding the garlic to the meat.

To make the Stuffing: Combine the ingredients in a small bowl and mix well.

Stuff and cook the burgers as directed.

Bacon and Cheddar-Stuffed Burger

Make the patties as directed in the Master Recipe (page 161).

To make the Stuffing: Combine the ingredients in a small bowl and mix well.

Stuff and cook the burgers as directed.

1 pound ground beef chuck
¾ teaspoon salt
½ teaspoon freshly ground black pepper
2 teaspoons Worcestershire sauce or A-1 steak sauce

STUFFING

1 cup grated sharp Cheddar cheese
2 strips bacon, cooked and crumbled
2 tablespoons smoky barbecue sauce (optional)
3 tablespoons finely chopped red onion (optional)

Stuffed Burger Sicilano

Make the patties as directed in the Master Recipe (page 161).

To make the Stuffing: Combine the ingredients in a small bowl and mix well.

Stuff and cook the burgers as directed.

1 pound ground beef chuck
¾ teaspoon salt
½ teaspoon freshly ground black pepper
2 teaspoons Worcestershire sauce or A-1 steak sauce

STUFFING

1 tablespoon chopped capers
2 tablespoons freshly grated Parmesan cheese
½ cup chopped cooked spinach
3 tablespoons toasted pine nuts, walnuts, or pecans (see Note, page 121)
¼ cup shredded Fontina cheese

1 pound ground chuck

½ teaspoon freshly ground
   black pepper

2 teaspoons Worcestershire
   sauce or A-1 steak sauce

3 tablespoons Japanese
   soy sauce

2 tablespoons mirin
   or sweet sherry

1 teaspoon minced garlic

STUFFING

2 tablespoons vegetable oil

2 cups thinly sliced onions

6 dried shiitake
   mushrooms, soaked
   in boiling water for
   at least 30 minutes,
   drained, stems
   removed, and cut
   into strips

1 tablespoon minced
   fresh ginger

2 teaspoons sugar

2 tablespoons soy sauce

1 teaspoon Asian
   sesame oil

TERIYAKI MUSHROOM AND ONION-STUFFED BURGERS

Make the patties as directed in the Master Recipe (page 161), adding the soy sauce, mirin or sherry, and garlic to the beef.

To make the Stuffing: Heat the vegetable oil in a skillet over medium heat and add the onions. Cover and cook for about 5 minutes, until soft, stirring from time to time. Stir in the mushrooms, ginger, sugar, and soy sauce, reduce the heat to medium-low, and cook, uncovered, until the onions are quite soft, about 10 minutes more, stirring often. Stir in the sesame oil.

Cool before stuffing and cooking the burgers as directed.

Beef, Turkey, and Andouille Meat Loaf

Serves 8, with leftovers

■ COOKING ON A BUDGET ■ GOOD FOR A CROWD
■ GREAT LEFTOVERS

ANDOUILLE is a hot and smoky Cajun sausage that's now widely available throughout the United States. Its tangy flavors add a lot to this lively meat loaf, but if you can't find andouille, you can substitute high-quality ham such as country ham or Black Forest ham, or use any other high-quality smoked sausage. Don't try to remove the casing from the sausage. Simply cut it into chunks and coarsely chop it in the food processor.

Creole and Cajun ingredients can be found in many specialty markets or can be ordered by mail (see Sources, page 584).

Preheat the oven to 350°F. Heat the oil in a large skillet over medium-high heat and add the onions with the pinch of salt. Cover and cook for 5 minutes, stirring occasionally. Stir in the optional bell peppers and the garlic and cook for 2 minutes more. Transfer the mixture to a large bowl. Mix in all the remaining ingredients (except those for the glaze). Using your hands, knead the mixture until everything is well blended. On a large baking sheet (with a rim) or a large shallow baking pan, form the meat into a loaf about 10 by 4 by 4 inches high. Place the loaf in the oven and bake for 30 minutes.

Meanwhile, make the Mustard Glaze: Combine all the ingredients in a small bowl.

Brush the glaze all over the top of the meat loaf after the first 30 minutes of baking. Bake the meat loaf for 30 to 45 minutes more, or until the internal temperature is 150° to 155°F. Let the loaf rest for 10 to 20 minutes, loosely covered with foil, before slicing and serving.

2 tablespoons olive oil
1½ cups finely chopped onions
1 teaspoon salt, plus a pinch
½ cup finely chopped red bell peppers (optional)
2 teaspoons minced garlic
1 tablespoon Worcestershire sauce
2 cups soft fresh bread crumbs
½ cup milk
2 large eggs, lightly beaten
1 pound andouille, smoked ham, or other smoked sausage, cut into 1-inch chunks and coarsely chopped in a food processor
1 pound ground beef (85% lean)
1 pound ground turkey
½ teaspoon dried sage
1 teaspoon dried thyme
1 teaspoon freshly ground black pepper

SWEET-AND-SOUR
MUSTARD GLAZE

6 tablespoons Dijon mustard
3 tablespoons light or dark brown sugar
1 tablespoon cider vinegar

Not-Like-Mom's Meat Loaf

1 ounce dried porcini or
  other mushrooms,
  soaked in boiling water
  for at least 30 minutes
1 cup soft fresh bread
  crumbs
½ cup heavy cream
2 tablespoons olive oil
1 cup finely chopped
  onions
2 garlic cloves, minced
½ pound fresh shiitake,
  porcini, or other wild
  mushrooms, stems
  removed if using
  shiitakes; thinly sliced
2 large eggs, lightly
  beaten
1 tablespoon Worces-
  tershire sauce
¼ cup chopped fresh
  parsley
1 teaspoon dried thyme
1 tablespoon kosher salt
1 teaspoon freshly ground
  black pepper
1 pound ground beef
  round (85% lean)
1 pound ground pork
1 pound ground veal
  or turkey
3 slices pancetta, bacon,
  or lean salt pork,
  about ⅛ inch thick

Serves 8, with leftovers
■ GOOD FOR A CROWD ■ GREAT LEFTOVERS

NO DOUBT ABOUT IT, Mom made a great meat loaf, but wild mushrooms give this delicious version flavors she never dreamed of. We like to make plenty, because the leftovers are wonderful in sandwiches. Try cold slices on split baguettes with garlic mayonnaise, sliced red onions, and cornichons. It is excellent served hot with a fresh tomato or marinara sauce. Beaujolais is the perfect wine here, whether you serve the meat loaf hot or cold.

Remove the dried mushrooms from the soaking liquid. If using shiitakes, remove and discard the stems. Chop the mushrooms and set aside. (Save the soaking liquid for use in soups, stews, or pasta sauces.)

In a small bowl, soak the bread crumbs in the cream while you prepare the rest of the ingredients.

Preheat the oven to 350°F. In a large skillet, heat 1 tablespoon of the olive oil over medium heat. Add the onions and sauté until softened, about 5 minutes. Add the garlic and sauté for 2 minutes longer, stirring frequently. Remove the onions and garlic to a large bowl and set aside. Add the remaining 1 tablespoon olive oil to the pan and increase the heat to high. Put in the soaked dried mushrooms along with the fresh mushrooms and sauté, stirring constantly, until the mushrooms release their liquid and it evaporates, about 5 minutes. Add the mushrooms to the onions in the bowl.

Stir in the eggs, Worcestershire sauce, parsley, thyme, salt, and pepper. Mix well, then add the ground meats and soaked bread crumbs with any liquid. Knead gently, using your hands, until everything is well blended. Rinse a large loaf pan (10 by 5 by 4 inches) with cold water and pack the meat into it. Invert the loaf onto a foil-lined baking sheet (with 1-inch sides) or a shallow baking dish or gratin pan and remove the loaf pan. (Or you can form a loaf on the baking sheet or in the pan.)

Place the slices of pancetta, bacon, or salt pork on top of the meat and bake for 1 to 1½ hours, or until the internal temperature is 155°F. Remove the meat loaf from the oven and let it rest, loosely covered with foil, for 10 to 20 minutes before slicing.

Bucci's Italian-American Meatballs

1 pound ground beef
    chuck mixed with
    ½ pound mild or
    hot Italian sausage,
    removed from its
    casing, OR 1½ pounds
    ground beef chuck

2 large eggs, lightly
    beaten

1 cup fresh bread crumbs

2 teaspoons minced garlic

2 tablespoons minced
    onion

⅓ cup finely chopped
    fresh parsley

½ cup freshly grated
    Parmesan or Asiago
    cheese

2 tablespoons finely
    chopped sun-dried
    tomatoes in oil
    (optional)

1 teaspoon salt
    (1½ teaspoons if using
    only ground beef)

2 teaspoons chopped fresh
    herbs such as basil,
    marjoram, or sage or
    any combination of
    these, OR ½ teaspoon
    dried basil, marjoram,
    or sage

1 teaspoon freshly ground
    black pepper

2 tablespoons olive oil

Serves 4 to 6

■ COOKING ON A BUDGET ■ GOOD FOR A CROWD

BUCCI IS THE OWNER-CHEF of a popular Bay Area restaurant specializing in light and spicy Italian food, and if she has a first name, we've never heard it. Her family emigrated from Sicily and landed in America, like so many others, dirt poor. The Buccis settled in the aptly named Syracuse, New York, and created a happy and healthy life that involved plenty of hearty food. Their large garden supplied the table with fresh vegetables every day, and they made their own sauces and canned everything they could, from tomatoes and bell peppers to pickled garlic and pepperoncini. And they ate meat once a week or so, usually in the form of meatballs. As Bucci says, "When things got a little tight, the meatballs contained a lot more bread crumbs. When times were flush, we could afford more meat in them. But no matter what, they always tasted great."

We still enjoy these meatballs at Bucci's restaurant served in a red sauce over spaghetti— with plenty of meat in them and lots of spice and flavor. Bucci likes to mix ground beef with hot or mild Italian sausage made from either pork or turkey. You could try this or use all ground beef.

In a large bowl, combine all the meatball ingredients except the oil, kneading and squeezing the mixture until everything is well blended. Moisten your hands with water and shape the meat into 1½-inch balls.

Heat the oil in a large skillet over medium-high heat and brown the meatballs on all sides for 5 to 7 minutes. Alternatively, you could place the meatballs in a lightly oiled, shallow roasting pan and brown them in a preheated 450° to

500ºF oven for about 10 minutes, shaking the pan from time to time.

You can eat the meatballs as is (if so, cut into one to see that they are cooked all the way through; if not, cook a little longer). Or you can simmer them, as traditional Italian-American cooks do, in a tomato sauce. You could also pour an Italian-style tomato sauce over the meatballs and bake them, covered, for 30 minutes at 350ºF. Use your own favorite sauce or our quick tomato pan sauce.

To make Quick Tomato Pan Sauce: Remove the meatballs from the skillet and set them aside. To the fat in the pan, add the onions, celery, and garlic. Cover and cook over medium heat for 5 minutes, stirring occasionally. Pour in the red wine and bring to a boil, scraping up any browned bits from the bottom of the pan. Cook until the wine is reduced to about ¼ cup. Add the stock and tomatoes, bring to a boil, and reduce the heat to a simmer. Add the basil and a pinch of salt and pepper.

Put the meatballs back into the pan and simmer over low heat for 30 minutes. Remove them with a slotted spoon and keep them warm. Skim any fat from the sauce, bring it to a boil, and reduce it until syrupy, if desired. Taste for salt and pepper. Spoon over the cooked pasta of your choice (1 pound for four people) and add a couple of meatballs to each plate.

QUICK TOMATO PAN SAUCE

1 cup chopped onions

¼ cup chopped celery

1 tablespoon chopped garlic

1 cup dry red wine

1 cup beef or chicken stock

3 cups canned crushed tomatoes in puree

1 tablespoon chopped fresh basil or 1 teaspoon dried

Salt and freshly ground black pepper

Italian Stuffed Cabbage

1 large Savoy or green
    cabbage (3-4 pounds)

2 tablespoons olive oil

2 cups finely chopped
    onions

½ cup finely chopped
    carrots

1 tablespoon minced garlic
    Salt and freshly ground
    black pepper

1 cup chopped cooked
    fresh or frozen spinach,
    drained and squeezed
    dry

1 pound ground beef
    (or 1½ pounds if
    not using sausage)

½ pound mild or hot
    Italian sausage,
    removed from casings
    (optional)

1 cup freshly grated
    Parmesan cheese

3 ounces dry coppa,
    prosciutto, or pancetta,
    finely chopped

1¼ cups soft bread crumbs
    (from day-old bread)

1 teaspoon dried sage

1 teaspoon dried thyme

2 large eggs, lightly
    beaten

2 cups chicken stock

½ cup dry white wine

4 bay leaves

**Serves 6 to 8 as an appetizer,
4 as a main course**
■ REWARMS WELL ■ COOKING ON A BUDGET
■ GREAT LEFTOVERS

TO CELEBRATE MY WIFE Nancy's 40th birthday, we took a trip to the Piedmont area of northern Italy. We had lunch in a rustic cafe, where a tiny and very lively Italian grandmother reigned supreme in the kitchen. One dish stays in my memory more than all the others: a simple appetizer of stuffed cabbage, simmered in a savory broth and then briefly passed under a broiler to crisp a topping of Parmesan cheese. You can make this Italian stuffed cabbage using Pam's Veal Meatballs (page 567), Bucci's Italian-American Meatballs (page 168), or this one, which comes pretty close to the original.

In Italy, the crinkly Savoy cabbage is preferred for stuffing, but you can also use ordinary green cabbage. Choose smaller leaves if you want to make appetizer-size cabbage rolls, large leaves if you want to serve the rolls as a main course. The rolls can be made up and frozen for later use, and leftovers warm up well. A good accompaniment for a main course would be boiled red potatoes, served in the same bowl. Barolo is great with this dish, but for an appetizer you might want to match it with a lighter Piedmontese favorite, Dolcetto.

B.A.

Put the cabbage into a large pot, core side down, and cover with water. Cover the pot and bring to a boil. Lower the heat to a simmer and cook for 10 minutes. Stab the cabbage in the core with a large fork and remove it from the water. Cool under running water. Gently peel off as many leaves as you can, one at a time, without tearing them, cutting them free from the core. Repeat the blanching process until you are down to the small inner leaves. (Save these and the core to chop and use in a soup.) Set the leaves aside while you make the filling.

Heat the oil in a large skillet over medium-high heat and add the onions and carrots. Cover and cook until the vegetables begin to soften, about 5 minutes, stirring often. Stir in the garlic and a pinch each of salt and pepper and cook for 1 minute more. Transfer to a large bowl and add the spinach, ground meat, sausage if using it, ¾ cup of the Parmesan, chopped cured meat, bread crumbs, sage, thyme, 1 teaspoon pepper, and the eggs. If you're using all beef and no sausage, add 2 teaspoons salt; with sausage, 1¼ teaspoons of salt should be sufficient.

Preheat the oven to 325°F. To assemble the cabbage rolls, use about ⅔ cup of filling for large leaves and about ¼ cup for smaller, appetizer rolls: place the filling on the base of each leaf, fold over the sides, and roll the leaf up to make a tight packet. As you complete each roll, place it seam side down in a large baking dish, casserole, or Dutch oven.

Pour the stock and wine over the cabbage rolls and scatter the bay leaves in the baking dish. Cover and bake for 1½ hours, or until the cabbage rolls are quite tender. (At this point, the stuffed cabbage can be cooled in the broth and then refrigerated, to be rewarmed later.)

Meanwhile, preheat the broiler. Remove the cabbage rolls with a slotted spoon, letting any liquid drain back into the dish, and put them into a broiling pan. Keep the broth warm. (Allow 2 large rolls per serving for a main course, 1 or 2 small rolls for an appetizer; any extra rolls can be cooled and refrigerated.) Sprinkle with the remaining ¼ cup Parmesan cheese. Broil for 2 minutes or so to brown the cheese lightly.

Serve the cabbage rolls in shallow bowls with some of the broth.

To rewarm cabbage rolls, spoon some of the broth over the rolls. Warm briefly in a microwave or reheat, covered, on top of the stove for 10 minutes or so. Finish them under the broiler with grated cheese as described above.

How to Choose the Best Roast Beef

OR FLAVOR, PRESENTATION, AND A GREAT BEEFY TASTE, nothing beats a **standing rib roast**. Also called **prime rib**, this is the roast of choice for family gatherings and celebrations such as Christmas, Hanukkah, or rich Uncle Harry's retirement party (it's hoped he'll pick up the tab, because cheap it ain't). A rib roast makes a dramatic centerpiece, a source of admiration and conversation (Uncle Harry can be a bit boring, you know), and fantastic roast beef sandwiches from the leftovers.

The entire primal rib area is cut from the upper rib section of the back of the steer and is made up of ribs 6 through 12. The ribs are numbered from the head to the tail. A full **7-bone prime rib** can tip the scales at over 16 pounds. Rib roasts are also sold in smaller pieces of 2 to 6 ribs. The best portion is made up of ribs 10 through 12, toward the back of the rib section. This 3-rib roast is referred to as the **small end of the ribs** and is the area adjacent to the short loin, which contains the T-bone, porterhouse, New York, and fillet steaks. Meat from this area is tender and flavorful; the roast will be leaner than one cut from the large end and should not have big chunks of fat. If you'd like a small rib roast, this is the one to purchase (ask the butcher to be sure).

The **large end of the rib** (ribs 6 through 9) lies adjacent to the chuck and contains a good amount of fat between smaller lean areas. The meat has plenty of flavor and is quite tender, but there is more waste with this roast than with the small end roast. If you purchase a bone-in rib roast, be sure to ask the butcher to trim off the feather, or chine, bones to make carving easier.

While all of these roasts are usually sold with bones, they can be bought boneless. For most occasions, we prefer bone-in roasts, since we feel that they give fuller flavor and convey the heat better into the roast. And, of course, an added benefit is that the gnawers get to chew on the bones.

One of the most flavorful and common boneless roasts from this area is the **rib-eye**, a large muscle next to the rib bone. It is surrounded by about a ½-inch layer of fat sandwiched between a flap of lean meat and another external layer of fat; these are cut away and removed, leaving only the tender rib-eye muscle. The rib-eye makes a delicious roast with very little waste and can be cut to any size, depending on the number of diners. If you buy a whole rib-eye, you can cut the size roast you want and slice the rest for rib steaks. It is a rather expensive cut, though, and does not make as spectacular a presentation as a bone-in rib roast.

A roast that is becoming very popular is the **bone-in rib-eye**, which combines the best features of a boneless and bone-in roast. This roast is a rib-eye

RIB

whole standing
rib roast
(prime rib)

rib roast,
small end

rib roast large end

rib-eye roast

rib-eye bone-in

SHORT LOIN

whole fillet
(tenderloin)

top loin roast

tenderloin roast

SIRLOIN

tri-tip
(triangle roast)

sirloin roast

sirloin tip roast

ball tip roast

ROUND

rump roast

top round roast

eye of the round roast

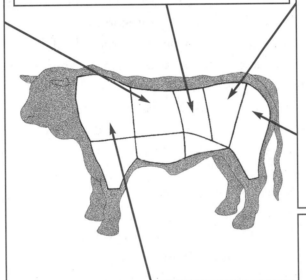

CHUCK

cross rib roast (shoulder clod)

with rib bones attached, but the external fat and flap of meat have been trimmed and the chine bones removed so that it is easy to carve. It is smaller than the prime rib of old, with a lot less fat and bone. It makes a handsome and convenient roast, and it has the added advantage of delicious bones.

Unless you are cooking an intimate Christmas dinner for two, you should buy at least a 3-rib prime rib roast or the boneless equivalent. Even if you are only cooking for four people, it never hurts to have a little leftover beef for a quick sandwich or snack. The ideal standing rib roast should contain 3 to 5 ribs. A 3-rib roast will weigh 6 to 7 pounds, a 5-rib roast 10 to 12 pounds, and a full 7-bone prime rib can weigh 14 to 16 pounds, depending on the size of the animal and how well trimmed the roast is. Figure on feeding 1 to 2 persons per pound, which should leave you a little for leftovers. If your family and friends are real meat eaters, however, a 10-to-12-pound roast will feed 10 to 15 people. See page 178 for roasting directions.

Another expensive but superb boneless roast beef is the **top loin roast** from the short loin area. This is also called a **New York strip,** or **shell roast,** depending on the usual geographic idiosyncrasies.

Since the advent of the club store, discount warehouse store, and super grocery store, a whole top loin can easily be found packed in Cryovac for a very reasonable price. Weighing between 8 and 10 pounds, this tender cut can be roasted whole for a special holiday meal. It's a more elegant and flavorful roast than even prime rib, and, since it has no bones, the top loin is easily carved for a dramatic presentation. The lack of bones also makes a top loin roast cheaper per portion than prime rib, which has a high waste-to-meat ratio. An added plus: if you don't want to serve the whole top loin as a roast, you can cut off 1¼-inch-thick steaks for another meal and leave a 4-to-6-pound piece to serve as a roast. See page 189 for roasting directions.

The **whole fillet,** or **tenderloin,** a cylindrical boneless cut from the short loin sold whole or in roast sections, is probably the easiest and quickest cut of beef to roast. It's flavorful and very tender. The only drawback is that fillet is quite expensive. But its lack of waste and ease of preparation make it the perfect elegant centerpiece for a dinner party; roasted, it cooks quickly in a hot oven. A whole fillet weighs about 6 pounds and feeds 10 to 12 people; a 3-to-4-pound piece should feed 6 to 8. If you buy it whole, trim most of the fat and any silverskin (the membrane under the fat). Since the ends taper, you can roast it and have varying degrees of doneness, or fold the thin ends under and tie at each end. See page 181 for roasting directions.

While not as tender as rib roasts, roasts cut from the sirloin are considerably less expensive, have little waste, and can be quite tasty when prepared correctly. Weighing 3 to 8 pounds, these roasts are boneless, usually rolled and tied, and are called **sirloin tip**, **ball tip roast**, and **sirloin roast**. To add extra flavor, we like to marinate them in a dry rub or wet marinade (see page 188). The increasingly popular **tri-tip** (see page 184) is a small triangular roast from the bottom sirloin area that is excellent roasted at high temperature (see page 187) or grilled (see page 185).

The chuck area of the steer also provides a flavorful roast, usually sold as a **cross rib roast**, or **shoulder clod**. We cook this as we do the sirloin roasts (see page 189 for directions). These cuts also make wonderful pot roasts.

The round, or leg, area produces a number of tasty boneless roasts: the **rump roast**, the **top round**, the **ball tip roast**, and the **tip roast**. Since they are all quite lean, care must be taken to keep them juicy and flavorful. Top round is the cut used by restaurants and *hofbraus* specializing in roast beef sandwiches. This boneless roast is easy to cut thinly on an electric slicer and makes excellent beef sandwiches when piled high with condiments. **Eye of the round** also comes from the leg. This lean, boneless roast is easy to carve, but the lack of fat often makes it too dry and somewhat lacking in flavor. These lean roasts are best cooked in a slow oven to the medium-rare stage (see Slow-Roasting, page 69).

Barbecued Beef Ribs

■ Flavor Step ■

¼-½ cup Dry Rub for Roast
 Beef (page 178) OR ¼-
 ½ cup dry rub of your
 choice (see Seasoning
 Chart, page 577)

4-5 pounds beef ribs cut
 from the standing rib
 roast, left in racks

MUSTARD-SHERRY SAUCE FOR BEEF

¼ cup olive oil

2 cups finely chopped
 onions

2 tablespoons finely
 chopped garlic

¼ cup Worcestershire sauce

¼ cup dry sherry

¼ cup soy sauce

2 tablespoons cider
 vinegar

3 tablespoons light or dark
 brown sugar

½ teaspoon cayenne pepper

1 teaspoon freshly ground
 black pepper

½ cup Dijon mustard

2 tablespoons finely
 chopped fresh thyme
 or 2 teaspoons dried

1 tablespoon crushed
 fennel seeds

 Salt

 Tabasco sauce to taste
 (optional)

■ COOKING ON A BUDGET ■ GOOD FOR A CROWD

WE WERE ASTONISHED one day when we shopped for pork spareribs at a local supermarket. They were about $2.50 per pound, but next to them were small slabs of beef ribs cut from the standing rib roast, packaged and frozen, for a mere 70 cents per pound. Even though it would take a pound of the ribs to serve one person, this was still an unbelievable bargain and one we couldn't resist.

Best of all, the meat on the beef ribs was tender and well flavored. And the ribs could be cooked quickly over direct heat instead of the two hours or more required to cook pork spareribs correctly. They're also delicious roasted in a 350°F oven for about 45 minutes to 1 hour.

We like beef ribs flavored first with a dry rub and then grilled over the coals, with a brushing of barbecue sauce just at the end of cooking. Use any of our barbecue sauces or a good store-bought variety or this tangy Mustard-Sherry Sauce.

━━━━━━

■ **Flavor Step** ■ Rub the dry rub all over the ribs. Cover and marinate for at least 30 minutes at room temperature or, preferably, overnight in the refrigerator. Be sure to let the ribs come to room temperature for an hour before cooking if they've been refrigerated.

To make the Mustard-Sherry Sauce: Heat the oil in a medium saucepan over medium-high heat. Add the onions and cook until soft, about 5 minutes, stirring often. Stir in the garlic and cook for 1 minute. Add the remaining ingredients except the salt and Tabasco, stir well, and bring to a simmer. Cook for 15 to 20 minutes, stirring often. Add a little water if the sauce seems too thick. Taste for salt and add Tabasco if you like a hotter sauce. (The sauce can be made ahead and refrigerated for 2 to 3 days in a covered container.)

To grill the ribs: Prepare a medium-hot fire in a covered barbecue (see Grilling, page 63). Add the ribs and cook, with the grill covered, for 8 to 10 minutes per side, taking care not to burn them. Brush with the mustard sauce and cook for about 8 minutes longer, turning the ribs often so they don't burn. Cut into individual ribs to serve. Brush generously with more sauce and serve additional sauce on the side.

Standing Rib Roast

■ Flavor Step ■
DRY RUB FOR ROAST BEEF

(For a 3- or 4-bone roast; double the recipe for a 5-bone or larger roast)

3 garlic cloves, minced

1 tablespoon kosher salt

2 teaspoons coarsely ground black pepper

2 teaspoons chopped fresh thyme or rosemary or 1 teaspoon dried (optional)

1 3-, 4-, or 5-bone standing rib roast (6-12 pounds), external cap of fat and meat removed and fat trimmed to about ½ inch (bone-in rib-eye roast)

A 4- or 5-bone rib roast (8 to 12 pounds) serves 10 to 15; a 3-bone rib roast (6 to 7 pounds) serves about 8

■ FIT FOR COMPANY ■ GOOD FOR A CROWD ■ GREAT LEFTOVERS

NOW THAT YOU'VE INVESTED big bucks in your beautiful prime rib, the good news is that cooking it to perfection couldn't be easier. All you have to do is season it and roast it. The less done, the better.

If you read many meat cookbooks, you'll find plenty of opinions on how to roast prime rib. Many American books say to roast it in a moderate (325°F) oven. Books with a British pedigree say to sear it in a hot oven (450° to 500°F) for a short time and then turn down the heat to moderate (325° to 350°F) and roast until done. For our liking you can't argue with the Brits. After all, they invented roast beef and Yorkshire pudding! By searing in a hot oven and roasting in a moderate one, you are guaranteed a brown, crusty exterior and the wonderful flavors we all crave in roast beef.

The digital meat thermometer that we talk about on page 53 is a must here. You don't want to make a mistake with a piece of meat that you've laid out so much money for.

■ **Flavor Step** ■ Crush the garlic and salt together with a mortar and pestle or mix them well in a small bowl. Mix in the pepper and the optional herbs. Rub all over the roast, especially in any spaces between the meat and bones. Let the roast sit at room temperature for up to 2 hours, loosely covered, before cooking.

Preheat the oven to 450°F. Lay the roast, bone side down, in a large, shallow roasting pan and roast for 15 minutes. Turn the oven down to 350°F (don't open the door). After about 45 minutes, check the internal temperature of the roast with an instant-read meat thermometer. If it is not 115°F, continue roasting, checking every 15 minutes or so, until it reaches 115°F. This temperature will give you a mostly rare roast, except for the end cuts, which will be medium-rare to medium; you can roast it a little longer to 120° to 125°F if you like it a little more done, but be careful not to overcook it. Remove the roast from the oven and cover it loosely with foil. Let it rest for at least 15 minutes and up to 30 minutes. During this time the retained heat will continue to cook the roast and the juices within the roast will stabilize.

After 15 minutes, if you removed the roast at 115°F, the internal temperature will have risen about 10°, to 125°F. After 30 minutes, the internal temperature may even read 130°F, which is still rare to medium-rare. Carve the roast (see page 180), and serve.

CARVING A STANDING RIB ROAST

ONCE THE BUTCHER HAS REMOVED THE FEATHER, or chine, bones that make up part of the spinal column, carving a standing rib roast is a cinch. After roasting and resting, tilt the roast onto the side that had the feather bone. Stab the meat with a large fork and run your knife down parallel to the ribs, separating the large chunk of meat (the rib-eye) from the rib bones. You will end up with a rack of ribs and a boneless roast that can now be tilted back onto its rib side and cut into slices of whatever thickness you desire. The individual ribs can be separated by cutting down between the bones and offered to the bone gnawers among your guests.

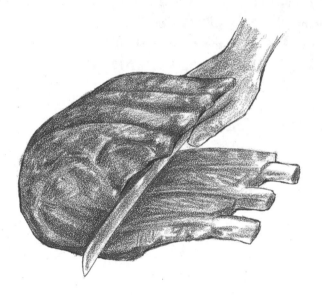

Roast Fillet of Beef

■ FIT FOR COMPANY ■ IN A HURRY

MASTER RECIPE

■ Flavor Step ■
THYME AND GARLIC
PASTE FOR BEEF

1 teaspoon chopped fresh
   thyme or ½ teaspoon
   dried
2 teaspoons minced garlic
1 teaspoon salt
½ teaspoon freshly ground
   black pepper
1 tablespoon olive oil

1 1½-to-2½-pound piece
   of beef fillet
1-2 tablespoons olive oil

BEEF FILLET has such great flavor that it's almost a shame to mask it with a sauce, but the simple Nancy's Mushroom Vinaigrette (page 108) or the Balsamic Vinegar Pan Sauce (page 110) makes a pleasant enhancement. Other good sauces for roast fillet are shiitakes or other wild mushrooms sautéed in butter and garlic, and fire-roasted pimentos or red bell peppers (see page 103), cut into strips and cooked briefly in olive oil with a little dry sherry.

The fillet called for below makes a perfect roast for three to six people; you may even get lucky and have a bit left over for sandwiches or a beef salad.

■ **Flavor Step** ■ Mix the ingredients in a small bowl.

Remove the meat from the refrigerator an hour before cooking.

Preheat the oven to 450°F. Trim the roast of most of the fat, leaving a thin layer. Cut ½-inch gashes in the fat or top side of the meat and rub the Thyme and Garlic Paste into the gashes and all over the surface of the meat. Brush the roast generously with olive oil.

Place the meat on a rack in a shallow pan and put it in the lower third of the oven. Roast for 20 minutes, then check the internal temperature. Remove the meat when the internal temperature reaches 115° to 120°F for rare, 125° to 130°F for medium-rare, or 130° to 140°F for medium. Cover loosely with foil and let the meat rest for 10 to 20 minutes. The temperature will increase another 5° to 10°F or so.

Slice the roast into ½-inch-thick slices and serve as is or with a pan sauce as suggested above.

Fillet Stuffed with Oysters and Tasso

OYSTER AND TASSO
STUFFING

4 tablespoons (½ stick)
butter

2 ounces tasso
(see discussion),
finely chopped

1 teaspoon chopped garlic

¼ cup finely chopped
green onions or
scallions
(white part only)

2 10-ounce jars shucked
small oysters

1 teaspoon chopped fresh
tarragon or ½ teaspoon
dried

1 teaspoon Worcestershire
sauce

1 cup chopped cooked
spinach or one 10-
ounce package frozen
spinach, defrosted and
squeezed dry

About 1 cup soft bread
crumbs (from day-old
bread)

Salt and freshly ground
black pepper

Serves 8 plus
■ FIT FOR COMPANY

IN THE OLD ROUGH-AND-TUMBLE days of the California Gold Rush, a newly wealthy forty-niner was likely to show up at a high-falutin' San Francisco eatery and order a lavish feast of carpetbagger steak washed down with the best Champagne his gold dust could buy. This favorite dish of the high roller was a thick steak with a pocket cut into it that was filled with oysters and grilled. This was luxury indeed; oysters cost a dollar each at the height of the rush and a living wage for most folks was five to ten dollars a week.

Our dish takes the oyster and beef combo one step higher with the addition of tasso, a highly spiced ham used to season many Cajun and Creole dishes. Tasso is available from specialty grocers and by mail-order (see Sources, page 584). You could substitute some heavily smoked ham (Westphalian) dusted with a little cayenne pepper or the popular Cajun sausage, andouille. You could also use this stuffing in a butterflied pork loin or in a roast capon or chicken.

The tasso not only enhances the flavor of the oysters but also complements the flavor of the beef by providing an undertone of smokiness and a jolt of spice. Serve the whole fillet as a *pièce de résistance* for a family get-together or a gathering of special friends. Try a Pinot Noir from California's Russian River or an Oregon Pinot Noir with this special dish.

■ **Flavor Step** ■ Melt the butter in a medium skillet over medium heat. Put in the tasso and garlic and cook, stirring often, for 2 minutes, or until the tasso starts to color slightly. Add the green onions or scallions, oysters with their liquid, tarragon, and Worcestershire sauce and turn the heat to medium-high. Shaking the pan constantly, cook for 1 to 2 minutes, or until the oysters just begin to plump. Transfer the oyster mixture and any liquid to a bowl and add the spinach. Gently stir in just enough bread crumbs to bind the stuffing; it should still be moist. Taste for salt and pepper. Put the mixture in the refrigerator to cool while you prepare the meat.

Preheat the oven to 450°F. Trim the fillet: cut away the side strip of meat if it is attached (it may be saved to make a delicious stir-fry with vegetables). Trim the roast of most of the fat and remove the membrane under the fat, called the silverskin. Butterfly the fillet lengthwise by slicing it horizontally, leaving the meat attached at one side. Open the fillet like a book and spread the stuffing down the center of the cut side of the meat. Tie the roast together in several places with string. Brush generously all over with olive oil. Season the outside of the roast generously with salt and pepper and place it on a rack in a shallow roasting pan.

Put the meat in the oven and roast for 30 minutes, then check the internal temperature in the thickest part of the meat, using an instant-read meat thermometer. When the meat reaches the desired level of doneness (see the Master Recipe, page 181; we recommend medium-rare, i.e., 125° to 130°F), remove it from the oven. Cover the roast loosely with foil and let it rest for at least 15 to 20 minutes. The final temperature should be 130° to 140°F.

Cut the roast into ¾-inch-thick slices and serve.

1 5-to-6-pound whole
   beef fillet
Olive oil for brushing
Salt and freshly ground
   black pepper

About Beef Tri-Tip
(Triangle Roast)

I T'S WORTH THE TROUBLE to seek out tri-tip at your butcher's, since it represents some of the tastiest beef you can find at a reasonable price. In the old days, when butchers cut their meat from the whole beef, they cut sirloins with the bone in, and the tri-tip portion, a triangular chunk of bottom sirloin, ended up as a nondescript part of sirloin steak. Nowadays the sirloin is boned out whole at the packing plant, and the two tri-tips are separated, boned, and sold to butchers whole, thereby creating a new and tender cut. This wonderful 1½-to-2½-pound roast is lean, tender, and full flavored. It has little waste, which makes it perfect to feed four or five persons. If you're fortunate enough to have leftovers from this savory roast, tri-tip makes a great roast beef sandwich and can be used to make tasty beef salads (see pages 117, 123, and 126).

The tri-tip can be easily cooked on a covered grill, so that it is ideal for summer barbecues (see Santa Maria Barbecued Tri-Tip, opposite). Tri-tip takes equally well to dry or wet marinades and is especially compatible with Asian and Southwest flavors. Tri-tip is also sold cut into thick slices as culotte steaks (see Culotte Steaks with Onion Glaze and Horseradish Bread Crumbs, page 144).

Santa Maria Barbecued Tri-Tip

Serves 4 to 6
■ FIT FOR COMPANY ■ GOOD FOR A CROWD ■
■ GREAT LEFTOVERS

I N THE SANTA MARIA VALLEY on California's central coast, the tradition of barbecuing beef goes back to the Spanish *rancho* days. Barbecued tri-tip has long been a specialty of cooks in this region, although sometimes a 2-to-3-inch-thick sirloin steak or top round is used. The traditional accompaniments are salsa cruda made with fresh tomatoes and cooked pinto beans. Bowls of guacamole and warm tortillas are welcome additions. Guests can then fill their own tortillas with hot sliced meat with some salsa and guacamole, just the way Nogales Steak (page 102) is served.

Tri-tip can be grilled directly over the coals, but we feel this thick cut is best cooked over indirect heat in a covered barbecue.

■ **Flavor Step** ■ Combine the ingredients in a small bowl and rub them all over the meat or season with the dry rub; cover and marinate for 2 hours at room temperature or overnight in the refrigerator. If you're using a wet marinade, puncture the roast all over with a meat fork or skewer. Place the meat in a zipper-lock bag or large bowl and pour the marinade over. Cover if using a bowl and marinate for 2 hours at room temperature or overnight in the refrigerator. Turn the meat from time to time to allow the marinade to penetrate evenly. Let the meat come to room temperature before cooking if it's been refrigerated.

To grill over indirect heat: Prepare the grill for indirect cooking (see Grilling, page 63). Remove the meat from the marinade and pat dry. Sear the meat for 2 to 3 minutes on each side directly over the coals and then move it to the area of the grill with no coals. Put a drip pan under the meat,

■ **Flavor Step** ■
1 teaspoon salt
½ teaspoon freshly ground
  black pepper
½ teaspoon garlic powder
    OR
  dry rub of your choice
  (see Seasoning Chart,
  page 577),
  OR Orange-Ginger
  Marinade for Beef
  (recipe follows),
  OR marinade of
  your choice (see
  Seasoning Chart)

1 1½-to-2½-pound beef
  tri-tip, fat trimmed
  to ¼ inch

GARNISHES
Salsa cruda, homemade
  or purchased
Guacamole

SIDE DISHES
Warm tortillas
Cooked pinto beans,
  homemade or canned

cover the grill, and roast for 15 minutes. Then begin checking the internal temperature with an instant-read thermometer: remove the roast when it registers 125° to 130°F for medium-rare (the thinner areas will be medium) or 115° to 120°F for rare. Let the meat rest for 5 to 15 minutes, loosely covered with foil, before cutting across the grain into thin slices. Serve with the garnishes and side dishes.

To grill over direct heat: Set up the grill so there are hotter and cooler areas of the fire (see Grilling, page 63). Sear the meat for 2 to 3 minutes on each side over the hotter area, taking care not to burn the outside (especially if you've used a wet marinade that contains sugar or sweeteners). Transfer the meat to the cooler area and grill it, turning it frequently to prevent burning. After about 20 minutes, begin checking the internal temperature with an instant-read thermometer: remove the meat when it registers 125° to 130°F. Allow it to rest for 5 to 15 minutes, loosely covered with foil, before slicing. Carve and serve as above.

ORANGE-GINGER MARINADE FOR BEEF
Makes about ¾ cup

THIS MARINADE also works well with a cross rib, sirloin tip, or flatiron roast.

1   2-inch piece of fresh ginger, cut into 4 chunks
3   garlic cloves
1   large orange
1   tablespoon Asian sesame oil
¼   cup soy sauce

With the motor running, drop the ginger and garlic through the feed tube of a food processor. Remove a 1-by-3-inch piece of peel from the orange, drop it through the tube, and process to chop the peel. Juice the orange and add the juice to the mixture along with the sesame oil and soy sauce. Pulse once or twice to blend.

Oven-Roasted Tri-Tip

Serves 4 to 6

■ COOKING ON A BUDGET ■ FIT FOR COMPANY

SMALL, TENDER CUTS OF BEEF are best roasted in a very hot oven to develop a crusty, caramelized exterior and a rare and juicy interior: this method is suitable for roasts weighing 1½ to 2½ pounds, such as beef tenderloin, small sirloin roasts, and beef tri-tip. Before roasting, season the meat with salt and pepper or the dry rub of your choice. You can also use a wet marinade (see the chart), but if it contains sugar or other sweeteners, take care not to char the meat. If charring begins to occur, remove the roast from the oven and turn the temperature down to 350°F, then return the meat to the oven once the temperature has dropped.

Tri-tip is an economical and delicious way to serve roast beef dinners for two to six people and should become a regular item on your household menu. Leftovers make great sandwiches and beef salads.

■ **Flavor Step** ■

1 teaspoon salt

½ teaspoon freshly ground black pepper OR dry rub or marinade of your choice (see Seasoning Chart, page 577)

1 1½-to-2½-pound beef tri-tip, fat trimmed to ¼ inch

■ **Flavor Step** ■ If you're using salt and pepper or a dry rub, generously season or rub the meat all over and let it stand at room temperature for up to 2 hours. Or cover the roast and leave it overnight in the refrigerator; let it sit at room temperature for an hour before cooking. If you're using a wet marinade, puncture the roast all over with a meat fork or skewer. Place it in a zipper-lock bag or large bowl and pour the marinade over the meat. Marinate (cover if using a bowl) for up to 2 hours at room temperature or overnight in the refrigerator. If the meat has been refrigerated, let it sit at room temperature for an hour before cooking.

PAN SAUCE
(omit if you use a
wet marinade)
½ cup beef or chicken
   stock
¼ cup red wine
1 teaspoon chopped fresh
   herb of your choice,
   such as thyme or
   rosemary, or ½
   teaspoon dried
1 tablespoon Dijon
   mustard
   Salt and freshly ground
   black pepper

Preheat the oven to 450°F. Remove the meat from the marinade and pat it dry. Discard the marinade. Place the tri-tip, fat side up, on a rack in a shallow roasting pan. Roast for 20 minutes, then begin checking the internal temperature: you should remove the roast at 115° to 120°F for rare, 125° to 130°F for medium-rare (see the Doneness Chart, page 56). Transfer the meat to a carving board or platter, cover loosely with foil, and let it rest for 10 to 15 minutes before carving to allow the residual heat to complete the cooking and the juices to stabilize.

Meanwhile, make the optional Pan Sauce: Pour off any fat from the roasting pan. Place the pan over a burner and add the stock, wine, and herbs. Bring to a boil, scraping up any browned bits from the bottom of the pan. Reduce the sauce almost to a syrup. Whisk in the mustard and taste for salt and pepper.

Carve the meat into thin slices across the grain. If you made the sauce, pour it over the sliced meat and serve.

TRI-TIP DRY RUBS AND MARINADES

Dry Rubs
Southwestern Spice Rub (page 128)
Herb Rub for Pork, Lamb, or Beef
(page 263)
Creole Spice Rub for Pork, Beef
or Lamb (page 328)
Arista Herb Rub for Pork Loin
(page 335)
Garlic and Herb Paste for Pork Loin
(page 336)
Fennel-Sage Rub for Pork or Veal
(page 340)
Herb and Mustard Rub for Pork
(page 366)
Spice Rub for Pork or Beef (page 375)

Wet Marinades
Nogales Steak Marinade (page 102)
North African Marinade (page 114)
Teriyaki Marinade (page 115)
Bourbon Marinade for Steak (page 124)
Spicy Beer Marinade (page 138)
Chipotle-Orange Marinade (page 138)
Korean Marinade for Beef (page 217)
Adobo Marinade (page 286)
Yucatán Marinade (page 294)
Tequila and Lime Marinade (page 292)
Thai Marinade for Pork (page 382)

Whole Roast Top Loin (New York Strip) with Herb Crust

Serves 8 to 12

■ FIT FOR COMPANY ■ GREAT LEFTOVERS ■ GOOD FOR A CROWD

TOP LOIN ROASTS are very tender and, because of their flat, thin shape, they cook quite quickly for the weight of meat they provide. For best results, serve the roast medium-rare. Leftovers make excellent sandwiches or beef salads. This recipe comes from our friend San Francisco chef David Shalleck, who learned this roasting technique while cooking in Italy.

About 2 hours before cooking, remove the meat from the refrigerator.

■ **Flavor Step** ■ Combine the paste ingredients in a small bowl and set aside.

Preheat the oven to 450°F. Brush the vinegar all over the roast. Lay it fat side up on a rack in a shallow roasting pan. Coat the top, ends, and sides of the roast with the herb paste.

Place the meat in the middle of the oven and roast for 15 minutes. Turn down the heat to 350°F and continue to roast for 35 to 45 more minutes. After about 25 minutes, begin to check the internal temperature in the thickest part with an instant-read meat thermometer. Remove the roast from the oven when it reaches 115° to 120°F for rare meat, 125° to 130°F for medium-rare, or 130° to 140°F for medium. Cover the meat loosely with foil and let it rest for 15 to 25 minutes so the meat juices and internal temperatures can equilibrate. The final temperature should be about 10°F higher than when it was removed from the oven.

Carve the meat into ⅜-to-½-inch-thick slices and serve.

1 8-to-10-pound whole beef top loin (New York strip) OR a 4-to-6-pound piece, fat trimmed to ¼ inch

■ Flavor Step ■
HERB AND GARLIC PASTE FOR ROAST BEEF

2 tablespoons minced garlic

2 tablespoons chopped fresh thyme or 2 teaspoons dried

1 tablespoon chopped fresh rosemary or 1 teaspoon dried

2-3 tablespoons salt (depending on size of roast)

1-2 teaspoons freshly ground black pepper (depending on size of roast)

1 tablespoon olive oil

Balsamic vinegar for brushing

How to Choose the Best Pot Roast

FOR OUR MONEY, you can't beat cuts of beef that come from the chuck for pot roasts. Meat from this part of the cow has ample fat, good texture, and a rich, beefy flavor. Pot roast or braised beef made from chuck stays moist and rarely gets dry and stringy as does bottom round or other leaner cuts after long cooking.

The chuck includes the entire shoulder of the animal and can be divided into three areas: the arm, the blade, or upper shoulder blade (which includes the shoulder blade bone), and the neck. **Arm pot roasts** often include part of the round upper leg bone but are also sold boneless as **boneless arm shoulder roasts**. Several muscles make up the blade section, and some are tender enough to be used for steaks and roasts (see How to Choose a Great Steak, page 92, and How to Choose the Best Pot Roast, page 190). The most typical bone-in pot roast from the blade area is called a **blade roast**, named after the characteristic blade bone. One of the best and our favorite cut for pot roast is the **7-bone pot roast**, so called because it includes the blade bone, which is roughly in the shape of the number 7.

Often, pieces of the chuck are sold boneless as flat chunks of meat or rolled and tied. All these cuts make excellent pot roasts and have names like **chuck-eye roast, boneless chuck roast, shoulder pot roast, mock tender, flat-iron roast, cross-rib roast (shoulder clod)**. Just pick out the one with the right size and shape to suit your needs. As long as the meat comes from the chuck, it will serve you well as a pot roast no matter what the name.

Brisket, located slightly below the shoulder, not only provides the best corned beef (see page 201) but is also ideal for pot roast, especially if you leave some fat attached. Brisket is usually sold boneless and is very easy to carve, providing nice uniform slices. It is hard to beat for flavor and texture. The brisket can be purchased **whole** (10 to 15 pounds), or as the **brisket first cut** (the leaner portion is often called the **flat**), or as **brisket front cut**. The latter is our favorite, since this fattier section includes the **deckle point**, a fatty but extremely tasty top piece of brisket.

Some folks swear by the **bottom round**, a boneless solid muscle from the back leg, as ideal for pot roast. We don't agree. There is just too little fat in this area for a flavorful and juicy pot roast. Bottom round is the classic cut used to make the famous German pot roast, sauerbraten. When the meat is marinated for several days in vinegar, wine, and spices, its texture and flavor are much improved. **Eye of the round**, a neighboring lean and boneless cut, suffers from the same tendency to dryness, especially after long cooking. These dry cuts were once improved by the old method of larding, where strips of fat

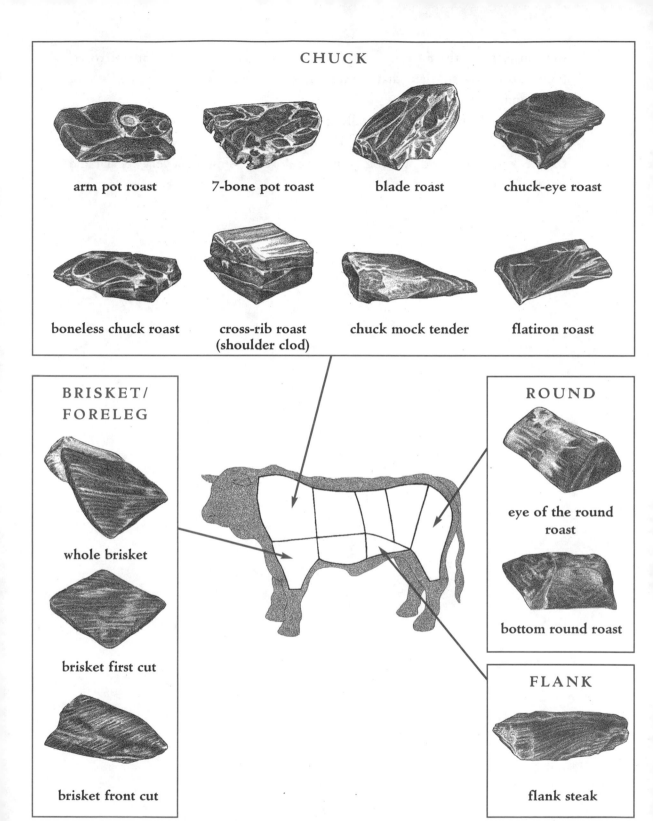

CHUCK

arm pot roast

7-bone pot roast

blade roast

chuck-eye roast

boneless chuck roast

cross-rib roast
(shoulder clod)

chuck mock tender

flatiron roast

BRISKET/
FORELEG

whole brisket

brisket first cut

brisket front cut

ROUND

eye of the round
roast

bottom round roast

FLANK

flank steak

were inserted in the meat before cooking. If you choose round for pot roast, go for **rump roast,** a cut that is more flavorful than bottom round and eye of the round.

Although **flank steak** is usually grilled, often after marinating, it is delicious rolled and tied and braised like a pot roast. A pocket can also be cut in the steak and filled with a savory stuffing before braising for a very special and unusual pot roast.

POT-ROASTING STRATEGIES FOR THE HARASSED HOME COOK

HAVE YOU EVER NOTICED that the recipes for most braised meat dishes, including stews and pot roasts, look pretty much the same? Season the meat, brown it in oil, and remove it from the pot; add the flavoring vegetables (onions, garlic, leeks, celery, carrots), and cook until soft; put the meat back in the pot, add some liquid with herbs and spices, cover, and cook until done. Most of these recipes also say that it's best to make the dish ahead of time, refrigerate it, and serve it a day or so later. The flavor is improved by sitting and mellowing, and you can remove the congealed fat from the surface before reheating.

Did you realize that the beginning steps of browning the meat, cooking the vegetables, and adding the liquid can be accomplished fairly quickly, in 20 to 30 minutes—even less if you prepare the vegetables the night before or in the morning before you leave for work? Once the liquid is added and the pot covered, the dish requires little attention—only time, usually 1½ to 2½ hours.

So here's the strategy: serve your family a relatively simple dinner on Monday night. Use the time you'd ordinarily take to make dinner to prepare the first stages of a pot roast or stew. While the family is eating, put the pot in the oven or over a low flame on the stovetop. Then enjoy a pleasant evening. All this time, the pot roast is cooking itself to tenderness—just check it every so often to see if it is done. When it is, remove the pot from the heat, let it cool for an hour or so, and, before you go to bed, refrigerate it.

The next day, or even a day or two later, remove the pot from the fridge. Remove and discard any congealed fat. Reheat the dish and complete any final steps, such as adding fresh vegetables or thickening the sauce. This final preparation should not take more than 20 minutes or so—less if you use the microwave for rewarming. And there will probably be enough leftovers to feed the family one more meal.

Lisa's Lazy Pot Roast

1 teaspoon dried thyme

1 tablespoon chopped
fresh rosemary or
1 teaspoon dried

1 tablespoon paprika

1 tablespoon kosher salt

1 teaspoon freshly ground
black pepper

1 4-pound boneless beef
chuck roast OR a beef
brisket, trimmed of
most fat

Serves 6, with leftovers
■ MOM'S COMFORT FOOD
■ COOKING ON A BUDGET ■ GREAT LEFTOVERS

OLD-FASHIONED POT ROAST, the kind our moms used to make, is the quintessential comfort food. There's something reassuring about sitting down to a thick slice of braised beef and gravy with mashed potatoes and glazed carrots, even to those of us who look a bit askance at red meat.

Pot roast is economical and makes great leftovers. With this recipe from Lisa Weiss, who valiantly tested recipes for this book, pot roast is a snap. You can make it on a Sunday, if you wish, and serve it to your family later in the week. It makes the best pot roast we've tasted since Mom's (and maybe even that memory's become a little exaggerated over the years).

If you're in a hurry, just eliminate the herb rub. In fact, if you're really in a pinch, don't even bother with the browning. Just put the roast in a heavy casserole, smother it with the onions, and cook it as described below. You'll be amazed at how good it is, and your family will think you've been slavin' away at the stove all day.

■ Flavor Step ■ Combine the herbs, paprika, salt, and pepper in a small bowl. Rub the meat thoroughly with the mixture. You can cook the roast immediately, but it will taste better if it sits for an hour or two at room temperature or overnight in a zipper-lock bag or, well wrapped, in the refrigerator.

Preheat the oven to 350°F. In a large, heavy casserole or a Dutch oven, heat the vegetable oil over medium-high heat. Brown the meat on all sides, about 7 minutes. Remove and set aside. Pour off any fat from the pan and deglaze the pan with the water or stock, scraping up any browned bits with a wooden spoon or spatula. Put the roast back in the pan, cover it with the sliced onions and garlic, cover, and bake for 1 hour.

Remove the cover, turn the roast over so that it is on top of the onions, and continue to cook, uncovered, for another hour, adding more liquid if needed. Stir the onions around after about 30 minutes so they can brown more evenly.

Replace the cover and continue to cook for 1 hour more, or until the meat is fork-tender; brisket will take a little longer than chuck. Remove the meat from the pot and let it rest, covered loosely with foil, while you prepare the sauce. (At this point, you may refrigerate the pot roast for later reheating. Refrigerate the cooking liquid separately. To serve later, remove any congealed fat from the cooking liquid and strain it before using it to reheat the meat gently.)

To serve, strain and defat the sauce. Taste for salt and pepper. Cut the meat into thick slices or separate it into chunks. Spoon some sauce and onions over each serving.

2 tablespoons vegetable oil
½ cup water or beef or chicken stock, or more if needed
5 cups thinly sliced onions (about 3 large onions)
6 garlic cloves, chopped Salt and freshly ground black pepper

PHILADELPHIA MASTERWORK

THE HEART OF SOUTH PHILLY'S ITALIAN MARKET on 9th Street is not very far from the Liberty Bell. At first glance, this street of ramshackle awnings and dilapidated market stalls with piles of refuse everywhere doesn't look much like a thriving commercial area. But its sidewalks are packed with Italian-American shoppers from the neighborhood buying fresh seafood and produce, Italian cheeses, veal, and sausages. It's the bustling cityscape you've seen in the *Rocky* movies—and it's the oldest Italian market in North America.

Italians, like other weary shoppers, need refreshment and nourishment to keep going. So, like many markets, 9th Street and the surrounding area are peppered with take-out windows and lunch counters where you can order a slice of pizza, a meatball hoagie, an Italian lemon ice, or a roast beef sandwich. Our favorite among these bustling joints is Shank and Evelyn's, just around the block from the market, on 10th Street. When you walk into this tiny luncheonette with its four tables and packed counter, it's hard to make your way through the throng of local diners. The menu plastered on the wall is extensive, but most folks in the know order the "roast beef sandwich." The reason for the quotes is that the beef is not really roasted, but rump or round braised slowly to succulent perfection. The waitress is definitely a native speaker: "Watch you guys gonna eat?" she asks. When we reply, "Small roast beef sandwiches," she gives us a look and sizes up our appetites. "Getta coupla large," she says, "with roast peppers 'n onions 'n a side a greens."

When the sandwiches arrive, they're a sight to behold: big pieces of brown-crusted Italian bread with thick slices of juicy pot roast piled in between, interlaced with sweet peppers and onions and dripping with pot juices. On the side there's a mound of bright green chard bathed in olive oil and sprinkled with chopped garlic. If there's a sandwich museum somewhere, this should be one of its masterpieces.

After we polish off this magnificent artwork, we ask what sandwich our waitress and docent prefers. "Get the tripe," she replies, "but it's only on weekends."

Philadelphia "Roast Beef" Sandwich
(Braised Beef and Red Pepper Hoagie)

■ GREAT LEFTOVERS ■ IN A HURRY
■ MOM'S COMFORT FOOD

HERE'S WHAT TO DO with yesterday's pot roast. Just remember: never say "leftovers" when you serve this famous Philly hoagie.

With your thumbs, split the roll or French bread, keeping the two halves attached. Set aside. Reheat the pot roast slices in the braising liquid for 5 minutes in a covered pot or in the microwave for 1 minute in a covered container. Spread the meat over the roll. Spoon all the gravy over the meat and layer on the onion and red pepper. Lightly salt and pepper the sandwich and eat it right away with garnishes.

FOR EACH SANDWICH

1 8-to-10-inch soft Italian or French roll OR piece of French baguette

5-6 ounces thickly sliced cooked pot roast made from chuck, brisket, rump, or round plus ¼ cup of the braising liquid (see Lisa's Lazy Pot Roast, page 194)

½ cup thinly sliced onion from the pot roast OR sautéed until soft in 1 tablespoon olive oil

½ cup sliced red bell pepper, sautéed until soft in 1 tablespoon olive oil, OR ½ cup bottled, roasted red peppers in oil, cut into rough strips

Salt and freshly ground black pepper

GARNISH

Sliced bottled sweet red or yellow peppers

Chopped chard, sautéed with olive oil and garlic

Chinese Master Sauce Braised Beef

■ **Flavor Step** ■

MASTER SAUCE FOR BEEF

2 cups beef or chicken
    stock or water,
    or more if needed

1 cup soy sauce

½ cup oyster sauce

¼ cup Scotch whisky
    or dry sherry

2 tablespoons sugar

8 garlic cloves

4 slices peeled fresh
    ginger, each about
    1 inch in diameter
    and ⅛ inch thick

1 star anise

1 4-inch-long piece
    tangerine peel, dried
    or fresh (optional)

1 2½-to-3-pound piece
    of sirloin tip, eye of
    the round, or beef
    round tip, trimmed
    of most external fat
    and membrane
    Asian sesame oil for
    brushing

Serves 4 to 6
■ REWARMS WELL ■ GREAT LEFTOVERS ■ LOW-FAT

ONE OF THE GLORIES of Viennese cooking is boiled beef: various cuts of beef are gently cooked in flavored stock. French chefs also have a delicious way of poaching beef fillet, called *boeuf la ficelle*. We've combined both techniques with the Chinese method of poaching called Master Sauce cooking (see also Chinese Master Sauce Braised Pork Loin, page 343).

After poaching, the meat can be sliced and served with a drizzle of Asian sesame oil. It's also wonderful rewarmed in the sauce and served over a bed of broccoli florets or poached asparagus.

You can also cook beef in the Chinese Master Sauce for Pork (page 343), which is especially good with tougher cuts such as shin, chuck, or brisket. These cuts should be simmered until almost tender before you turn off the heat and let everything cool to room temperature. This initial simmering might take up to 2 or 3½ hours, depending on the cut, with shin taking the longest and chuck the shortest time.

■ **Flavor Step** ■ Combine all the ingredients in a pot large enough to hold the meat, cover, and bring to a boil. Add the meat. The liquid should come halfway up the side. If not, add more stock or water. Lower the heat and cook at a simmer, covered, for 2 to 2½ hours. Turn the meat over from time to time.

Turn off the heat and let the meat sit in the sauce in the covered pot for 2 to 3 hours to cook slowly and come to room temperature.

Slice the meat and serve brushed lightly with sesame oil or as suggested above.

Note: *To save the Master Sauce, strain it and refrigerate in a covered container for up to 10 days or freeze for later use. When reusing the sauce, taste it and add more liquid and seasonings as needed.*

Mediterranean Brisket

1 8-to-10-pound whole
  beef brisket, with the
  deckle (fatty edge)
  left on

■ **Flavor Step** ■

2 teaspoons salt

1 teaspoon freshly ground
  black pepper

2 tablespoons oil from
  sun-dried tomatoes
  (see below)

3-4 medium onions,
  thinly sliced

2 cups canned tomato
  puree

⅓ cup sun-dried tomatoes
  packed in oil, drained
  and chopped

2 bay leaves

1½ teaspoons dried thyme

2 cups beef stock
  (if using canned broth,
  be careful when adding
  salt or use low-sodium
  stock)

2 cups dry red wine
  Salt and freshly ground
  black pepper

Serves 6 to 8, with leftovers
■ GOOD FOR A CROWD ■ FIT FOR COMPANY
■ REWARMS WELL

THIS RECIPE COMES FROM our tester—and talented home cook—Lisa Weiss. The sun-dried tomatoes give the dish a lively Mediterranean flavor. To quote Lisa, "When I served this dish for the first time, all my guests and family said this was the best brisket I'd ever cooked. The sauce is wonderfully rich and dark. The meat is fork-tender, yet not falling apart, and it's easy to slice."

■ **Flavor Step** ■ Sprinkle the brisket all over with the salt and pepper.

Preheat the oven to 350°F. Heat the oil in a large Dutch oven or roasting pan over medium-high heat. Brown the brisket on all sides, 7 to 10 minutes. Remove the meat and pour off all but 1 tablespoon of fat from the pan. Put in the onions, tomato puree, sun-dried tomatoes, bay leaves, and thyme and stir well to combine. Put the brisket back into the pan and spoon some of the onions and tomatoes over the top. Add the stock and wine and bring to a simmer.

Cover the pot tightly with aluminum foil and put on the lid to form a tight seal. Bake the brisket for 3½ to 4 hours, or until it's fork-tender. Carefully peel back the foil to check. (You can also cut off a small slice and taste it.)

Remove the meat to a platter and cover loosely with foil to keep warm. Degrease the sauce and taste for salt and pepper. To serve, cut the meat into ⅜-inch-thick slices, napped with the sauce. Or refrigerate it, tightly wrapped, to serve the next day. Refrigerate the sauce separately. Before serving, remove any congealed fat, then reheat the meat gently in the sauce or in a microwave.

MAKE YOUR OWN CORNED BEEF

Serves 8 to 10, with leftovers

IT'S NOT DIFFICULT to make your own corned beef, and the results are delicious. We suggest that you use brisket, but you can also use bottom round.

8 cups water, or more if necessary to cover the meat
1¼ cups kosher salt
1 cup sugar
3 tablespoons pickling spices
1 6-to-8-pound whole beef brisket OR piece of
    bottom round, trimmed of excess fat

1 medium onion, spiked with 3 cloves
3 garlic cloves
1 carrot, coarsely chopped
1 celery rib, coarsely chopped
3 bay leaves
1 teaspoon peppercorns

Bring the water to a boil in a saucepan. Add the salt and sugar and stir to dissolve. Stir in the pickling spices. Let cool to room temperature, then refrigerate until cooled to 45°F.

Pour the brine into a large bowl or crock and submerge the meat in it, making sure it stays under the surface by using a heavy plate as a weight. Refrigerate for 8 to 12 days. Stir the brine each day and turn the beef occasionally.

To cook the corned beef, remove the meat from the brine and put it in a large pot. Cover with water and add the vegetables, bay leaves, and peppercorns. Simmer over low heat until tender, 2½ to 3 hours, or more if necessary. Thinly slice across the grain and serve hot or cold.

Pam's Mom's Brisket

■ Flavor Step ■
SAUCE FOR BRAISED
BEEF

1 package dried onion
soup mix

3 medium onions, thinly
sliced

2 celery ribs, chopped

1 cup bottled chili sauce

1 bottle lager beer

½ cup water

1 4-to-5-pound piece of
beef brisket or chuck
OR 6 pounds short ribs,
trimmed of most
external fat
Salt and freshly ground
black pepper to taste
Water or beef stock
if necessary

Serves 6 to 8 with leftovers
■ REWARMS WELL ■ GREAT LEFTOVERS
■ MOM'S COMFORT FOOD

WE USUALLY STAY AWAY from
recipes calling for dried onion soup
and bottled chili sauce, but this
recipe and its many variations have
become family favorites over the years since the
1950s, when they first appeared. *The Joy of
Cooking* and other cookbooks had a lot to do
with their popularity, providing quick and simple recipes for busy homemakers.

It's easy to be snobbish about these dishes,
but some of them just plain taste good. An
added touch: this and other recipes like it benefit from being cooked ahead and rewarmed.
Time-pressured home cooks were not just a '50s
thing; these days, most of us can use all the help
we can get.

You can use this technique with any cut suitable for braised beef or pot roast, and it makes
great short ribs. The advantage of using brisket,
however, is that it can be sliced and rewarmed in
the sauce to make the best French dip sandwich
you ever ate. It's also great in the Philadelphia
"Roast Beef" Sandwich (page 197).

Pam Student is a creative San Francisco chef
who cooked with Nancy Oakes at L'Avenue
restaurant and is now her fellow chef at
Boulevard.

Preheat the oven to 350°F.

■ **Flavor Step** ■ Combine the ingredients in a large
Dutch oven with a cover or a covered casserole. Put the meat
in and spoon some of the sauce over the top.

Cover the pot and bake in the center of the oven for 2½ to 4 hours. Check the meat after 2½ hours to see if it's fork-tender. If not, cook until done.

Ideally, you should refrigerate the meat and sauce overnight, remove the congealed fat, then slice and reheat the meat in the sauce. Or you can degrease the sauce, taste for salt and pepper, slice the meat, and serve it in the sauce immediately. If the sauce seems too thick, dilute it with a little water or stock.

Braciole Braised in Chianti

■ **Flavor Step** ■
ITALIAN STUFFING FOR
BEEF, PORK, OR CHICKEN

½ pound Italian sausage,
 hot or mild, removed
 from casings, OR ½
 pound ground veal,
 beef, pork, or turkey

¼ cup chopped fresh
 parsley

1 cup soft bread crumbs
 (from day-old bread)

½ cup freshly grated
 Parmesan cheese

½ cup finely chopped
 onion

1 teaspoon minced garlic

¼ cup finely chopped
 prosciutto, salami,
 or dry coppa

1 large egg, lightly beaten
 Salt and freshly ground
 black pepper to taste

4 ¼-inch-thick slices of
 beef, cut from the
 rump, bottom round,
 or top round (4-6
 ounces each)
 Salt and freshly ground
 black pepper
 Flour for dusting

Serves 4 to 6
■ FIT FOR COMPANY ■ REWARMS WELL
■ MOM'S COMFORT FOOD

BRACIOLE ARE THIN SLICES of beef filled with a flavorful stuffing and braised. Similar dishes appear in other cultures as roulades, beef olives, roll-ups, beef rolls, or *paupiettes*. The concept is the same whatever the cuisine: use a little meat to feed a lot of people by wrapping thin slices around a stuffing, usually based on bread crumbs, herbs, and, often, sausage. When buying meat to make these dishes, make sure it's composed of a single muscle such a rump or top round so that the slices are even and hold together while cooking. Serve with soft polenta, rice, or pasta.

Any leftovers can be quickly turned into a delicious pasta. Just heat the meat in the leftover sauce (add a little tomato sauce or puree if necessary). Toss some cooked pasta with the sauce, cut the meat into thin slices, and place on top. Garnish with freshly grated Parmesan cheese.

This dish is a family favorite of our friend Bucci, who owns an Italian restaurant in the Bay Area.

■ **Flavor Step** ■ Mix all the ingredients for the stuffing in a large bowl. Set aside.

Trim any excess fat from the meat. Place the slices between 2 sheets of plastic wrap and pound lightly with a meat mallet or the flat side of a cleaver to a thickness of about ⅛ inch; each slice should measure approximately 5 by 8 inches. Season each slice with salt and pepper on both sides. Lay a slice on a flat surface and spread one quarter of the stuffing over the meat, leaving a 1-inch border all around. Fold the sides over the stuffing, then roll the slice up to form a tight packet. With kitchen string, tie the packet securely crosswise in 4 or 5 places and lengthwise in 2 places. Repeat to make three more rolls. Dust the rolls with flour.

To make the Chianti Braising Sauce: In a heavy, high-sided skillet or a Dutch oven, heat the olive oil over medium-high heat. Put in the meat rolls and brown them evenly on all sides, 3 to 5 minutes. Remove the meat and pour off all but about 1 tablespoon of the fat from the pan. Reduce the heat to medium and add the pancetta or bacon. Cook, stirring often, until it just begins to brown and crisp. Add the onions, carrot, celery, and garlic. Cover and cook until the vegetables are soft, stirring occasionally, for about 5 minutes. Pour in the wine and bring it to a boil, scraping up any browned bits from the bottom of the pan. Boil the wine to reduce it by half.

Add the tomatoes, tomato puree or paste, stock, bay leaves, basil, and thyme and return the beef rolls to the pan. Cover, reduce the heat to low, and simmer for 45 minutes to 1 hour, until the beef is tender when pierced with a fork. Transfer the beef to a platter and cover with foil to keep warm. Skim any fat from the sauce and, if needed, boil it to reduce it to a syrupy consistency. Taste the sauce for salt and pepper.

Remove the strings and cut the beef rolls into ½-inch-thick slices. Arrange the slices over soft polenta, noodles, or other pasta or buttered rice and spoon the sauce over.

CHIANTI BRAISING SAUCE

2 tablespoons olive oil

2 slices pancetta or bacon, diced

1 cup finely chopped onions

¼ cup finely chopped carrot

¼ cup finely chopped celery

1 tablespoon minced garlic

3 cups Chianti or other red wine

1 cup fresh tomatoes, chopped and drained, OR canned Italian-style tomatoes

½ cup tomato puree OR 2 tablespoons tomato paste

3 cups beef or chicken stock

2 bay leaves

½ teaspoon dried basil

½ teaspoon dried thyme

Salt and freshly ground black pepper

How to Choose the Best Stewing Beef

NEVER PURCHASE STEW MEAT that is already cut from the butcher's meat case. Not only is it usually more expensive than buying and cutting up your own, but also you have no idea what kind you'll end up with. (The same advice holds true for anything sold as kebabs.) More likely than not, the butcher is trying to unload trimmings from less desirable areas of the steer, such as the bottom round. It will likely be tough and dry meat rather than succulent and tender. Also, most butchers cut their stew meat into chunks that are too small and tend toward dryness.

If you don't want to cut up your own stew meat, purchase a chunk of boneless or bone-in meat from the chuck area and ask the butcher to cut it up for you. You can probably even get most supermarket butchers to do this simple task.

Better still, buy a piece of chuck such as **blade pot roast** and cut it up yourself. This way you get the best meat, and you can also trim off as much fat as you wish and cut the meat into exactly the size pieces you want. Besides meat from the chuck, you can cut up **brisket** for stew. **Bottom round, rump,** and **shank** can also be used, although they are all a bit on the dry side.

If flavor is paramount and you aren't worried about using the leanest possible meat, try our all-time favorite: short ribs, which make the richest and most intensely beefy stew you'll ever taste (see pages 217-25). Purchase nicely trimmed **English-cut short ribs** (the rectangular ones; see page 216), boneless or bone-in, which contain a chunk of the rib, and cut them into stew-size chunks.

If you buy bone-in meat, be sure to season and brown the bones along with the meat. Cook them in the stew to give the sauce extra flavor. If there's any meat left on them, you can gnaw on the bones afterward if you're so inclined.

We like to cut our stew meat into 2-to-3-inch chunks, which hold up better to the long, slow cooking. Smaller pieces (¾-to-1½-inch cubes) cook more quickly and are prone to fall apart in the sauce. No matter what size you use, it will shrink a bit during cooking. Don't worry if the meat seems tough at first; it will become wonderfully tender with longer cooking. Fish a piece out of the pot from time to time and give it a taste. The meat is done when it is soft and tender.

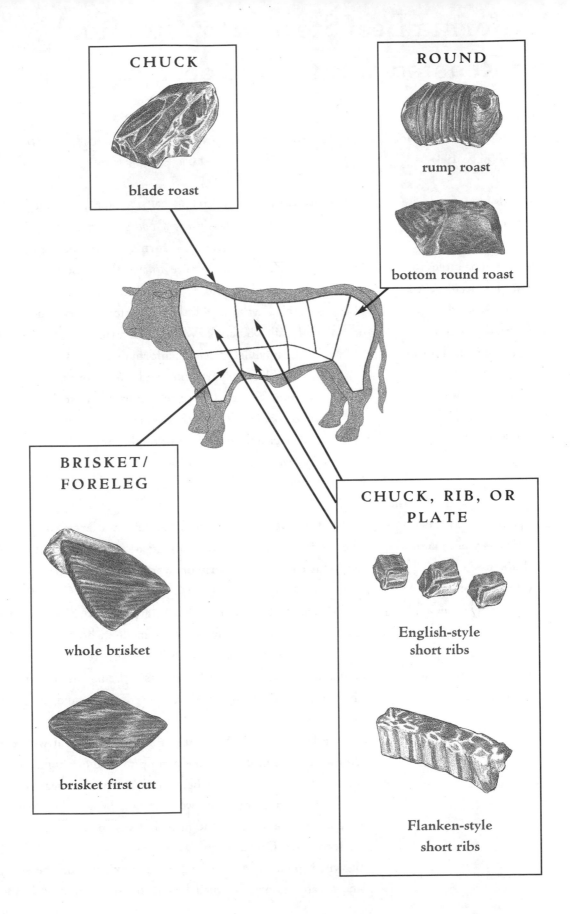

CHUCK

blade roast

ROUND

rump roast

bottom round roast

BRISKET/ FORELEG

whole brisket

brisket first cut

CHUCK, RIB, OR PLATE

English-style short ribs

Flanken-style short ribs

California Beef Stew with Zinfandel and Roasted Winter Vegetables

■ Flavor Step ■
Herb and Paprika Rub for
Beef (page 194)

3-4 pounds beef chuck
    or round, cut into
    2-to-3-inch cubes
3 tablespoons olive oil
¼ pound pancetta, cut
    into ½-inch dice
¼ pound dry coppa,
    cut into ½-inch dice
½ cup flour
3 cups (about 1 bottle
    minus a taste for the
    cook) California
    Zinfandel
2 cups chopped onions
1 tablespoon minced garlic
2 cups chopped canned
    Italian-style tomatoes,
    drained
1 cup beef stock,
    preferably homemade
1 bay leaf
    Salt and freshly ground
    black pepper to taste
    Roasted Winter
    Vegetables (opposite)

Serves 6 to 8
■ GOOD FOR A CROWD ■ COOKING ON A BUDGET
■ FIT FOR COMPANY

THIS IS OUR CALIFORNIA VERSION of the French classic *boeuf bourguignonne*, using the favorite California red varietal, Zinfandel. Be sure to use the same wine you cooked with to accompany the dish—and it doesn't hurt to do a little tasting for quality control while you cook. We suggest a rich, full-bodied Zinfandel from California's Dry Creek Valley, but experiment and use your own favorite. Serve this savory stew over cooked wide noodles along with oven-roasted vegetables and a crusty loaf of sourdough French bread. *(See photograph, page 44.)*

■ **Flavor Step** ■ Put the herb rub in a large bowl. Toss the beef with the mixture, cover, and marinate for up to 2 hours at room temperature or overnight in the refrigerator.

Preheat the oven to 325°F. In a large nonstick skillet, heat 2 tablespoons of the olive oil over medium heat. Put in the pancetta and coppa and cook until the fat is rendered and the pancetta is golden, about 5 minutes, stirring often. Remove the pancetta and coppa with a slotted spoon and drain on paper towels.

In a large, shallow bowl, toss the seasoned meat with the flour. Turn the heat under the pan up to medium-high, shake any excess flour from the beef, and brown the meat on all sides. Take care not to crowd the pan; brown the meat in batches if necessary. As the meat browns, place it in a large casserole or Dutch oven. After all the meat has been browned, pour off all the fat from the skillet, add the wine, and scrape up any browned bits from the bottom. Add the wine from the skillet to the casserole with the beef.

Heat the remaining 1 tablespoon oil in the skillet and sauté the onions over medium heat for 5 to 7 minutes, until they begin to turn golden, stirring often. Add the garlic and cook for 1 minute more. Add the onions and garlic to the casserole along with the tomatoes, beef stock, bay leaf, and drained pancetta and coppa. Bring to a simmer, stirring well. Cover the pan, put the stew in the oven, and bake until the beef is fork-tender, 2½ to 3 hours. Taste for salt and pepper and serve with Roasted Winter Vegetables.

ROASTED WINTER VEGETABLES

4	carrots, cut into 1-inch pieces
2	red onions, cut into 1-inch pieces
3	medium parsnips, peeled and cut into 1-inch pieces
2	large turnips, peeled and cut into 1-inch pieces, OR 8 baby turnips, peeled
5	garlic cloves
¼	cup olive oil
1	tablespoon balsamic vinegar
1	tablespoon finely chopped fresh rosemary
2	teaspoons salt

Preheat the oven to 450°F. Toss the vegetables with the other ingredients. Spread the vegetables out in one layer on a baking sheet or in a shallow baking dish. Roast for about 45 minutes, stirring from time to time, until the vegetables are tender, golden, and somewhat caramelized. Serve hot with stew or at room temperature as a side dish.

Beef Stew with Mushrooms, Onions, and Dark Beer

2 tablespoons olive oil

3 pounds beef chuck, cut into 2-to-3-inch chunks and trimmed of fat

Salt and freshly ground black pepper

2 pounds onions, halved and thinly sliced

7 carrots; 5 cut into ¼-inch dice, 2 cut into 2-inch chunks

¼ pound prosciutto or smoked ham, diced

2 tablespoons chopped garlic

1½ pounds mushrooms, sliced

1 12-ounce bottle of dark beer (see discussion)

2 cups beef or chicken stock, or more if necessary

1 teaspoon dried thyme

3 bay leaves

1 teaspoon Worcestershire sauce

Serves 6 to 8
■ REWARMS WELL ■ MOM'S COMFORT FOOD ■ GREAT LEFTOVERS

THIS RICHLY FLAVORED STEW is our version of the classic Belgian dish *carbonnade flamande,* in which beef is slowly braised on a bed of onions in strong, dark beer. The original version gets a sweet-and-sour effect from the sweetness of the onions and beer, along with a bit of molasses or sugar and vinegar that are often added to the sauce. Ours combines sweet onions and malty beer with the earthiness of mushrooms instead.

We suggest you use a dark lager that's not too hoppy, such as Beck's dark or an amber Oktoberfest-style lager. For a more authentic touch, try abbey ales, such as Orval or Grimberger from Belgium. And by all means, drink the same beer you use in cooking the dish.

In a large Dutch oven or a casserole, heat the oil over high heat. Season the meat generously with salt and pepper and sear it on all sides, 6 to 8 minutes; you may have to brown the meat in 2 batches to prevent crowding. Remove the meat and set it aside.

Put the onions in the pot, cover, and lower the heat to medium. Cook for 10 minutes, stirring frequently and scraping up any browned bits from the bottom of the pot. Stir in the diced carrots (reserve those cut into chunks), along with the prosciutto or ham and the garlic. Cook and stir the vegetables for 5 or 6 minutes, until the onions begin to brown nicely. Add the mushrooms and cook for 1 to 2 minutes more, stirring frequently.

Put the meat back into the pot and pour in the beer and stock to cover (add a little more if necessary). Add the thyme, bay leaves, and Worcestershire sauce. Stir and bring to a boil, then reduce to a simmer. Cover and cook at a low simmer for about 1½ hours, or until the meat is fork-tender.

Remove the beef with a slotted spoon. Degrease the sauce and bring it to a boil. Add the chunks of carrot and boil until the liquid is reduced to a syrupy consistency and the carrots are tender. If the liquid gets too thick before the carrots are cooked, add a little stock or water. Discard the bay leaves. Taste the sauce for salt and pepper. Return the meat to the pot and rewarm it gently before serving.

Chili Colorado, the Lazy Way

4 ancho or mulato chiles
    or other large, dried
    red chiles

4 pounds beef chuck or
    brisket, fat trimmed and
    cut into ¾-inch cubes
    Salt and freshly ground
    black pepper

¼ cup chile powder,
    preferably Gebhardt

2 medium onions,
    coarsely chopped

6 garlic cloves

1 teaspoon cumin seeds

1 teaspoon dried oregano

½ teaspoon ground
    coriander

2 teaspoons salt

1 cup Mexican beer,
    beef stock, or water,
    or more if necessary

2 cups diced red potatoes

2 fresh or canned fire-
    roasted mild green
    chiles, such as Anaheim
    (see page 103), split
    and cut crosswise into
    ¼-inch strips

GARNISH

Fresh cilantro leaves
  (optional)
Finely chopped onions
Sliced avocado
Shredded mild cheese
Hot sauce or salsa cruda

Serves 8, with leftovers
■ REWARMS WELL ■ GREAT LEFTOVERS
■ MOM'S COMFORT FOOD

CHILI COLORADO is a Mexican classic: beef cooked until tender in a red chile sauce. This is the ancestor of all those chile con carnes found all over our country that range from delicious to downright weird (some versions even feature outlandish ingredients such as spaghetti!). The original dish is quite simple and always delicious. First you simmer chunks of beef chuck or brisket in a sauce made of dried red chiles, tomatoes, and liquid (we use Mexican beer, but water or stock will do almost as well).

You can then add cooked pinto beans, if you wish, to make a one-pot meal, or you can finish the dish as we do below with diced potatoes and strips of mild green chiles. The origins of this great dish probably go back to the days when stews cooked slowly in clay pots in adobe ovens: you added what you wanted as they cooked and served them with tortillas to scoop up the savory mixture. As with all braised meats, this stew benefits from being made up a day or two ahead and then reheated before serving. It's also easy to make in stages.

Leftovers can be used as a filling for tacos or burritos. You can also shred the meat to fill enchiladas. Chiles and other Mexican ingredients are available in Latino markets or by mail-order (see Sources, page 584).

Soak the dried chiles in boiling water to cover for at least 15 minutes or up to 1 hour.

Preheat the oven to 350°F. Season the meat all over with salt and pepper. Place it in a casserole or a Dutch oven.

Drain the chiles and remove the stems and seeds. Put the chiles into a food processor, along with the chile powder, onions, garlic, cumin, oregano, coriander, and salt. Pulse the processor to chop the ingredients and then process to a thick paste. If the mixture gets too thick, add a little of the beer, stock, or water. Pour in the remaining liquid and process to blend. Add to the meat in the casserole and mix well. (At this point, you can marinate the meat in the sauce overnight in the refrigerator if you wish.)

Cover the casserole with foil and then put on the lid to make a tight seal. Bake in the middle of the oven for 1½ to 2 hours. Carefully peel back the foil and check to see if the meat is fork-tender; if not, continue to cook until done. Add more beer, stock, or water to the sauce as the meat cooks if it seems too thick.

While the meat is cooking, boil the potatoes in a saucepan of lightly salted water to cover until tender, about 10 minutes.

When the meat is done, degrease the sauce. Stir in the potatoes and green chile strips and bake for 5 more minutes to warm everything through. Taste for salt and pepper. (You can now cool and refrigerate the completed dish, to reheat at a later time if desired.) Serve with Mexican-style rice and cooked pinto beans, with warm tortillas and the suggested garnishes.

Shepherd's Pie

2 cups leftover firm
   mashed potatoes
1 tablespoon olive oil
   or melted butter
1 large egg, lightly beaten
   Salt and freshly ground
   black pepper
   Olive oil

EGG WASH
1 egg beaten lightly with
   1 tablespoon water

   Choice of filling
   (see opposite page)

Serves 4
■ COOKING ON A BUDGET ■ REWARMS WELL

INSTEAD OF THE TYPICAL cafeteria favorite— ground meat topped with mashed potatoes and baked—we like to surround savory leftover braised beef, lamb, or veal with a kind of pie crust made from mashed potatoes. You can use any of the stew or braised meat recipes listed on the opposite page or cut up your favorite pot roast for the filling. The pies can be individual or family size—it doesn't matter, since the method is the same for both. Cut the braised meat into ⅜-inch pieces and trim off any fat.

Preheat the oven to 400°F. Mix the potatoes, olive oil or melted butter, and egg in a bowl until well blended. If the potatoes have been refrigerated, allow them to come to room temperature or warm them slightly in a microwave to make mixing easier. Taste for salt and pepper.

To make individual pies, oil four 2-inch-deep and 4- or 5-inch-diameter gratin dishes; for family style, oil a baking dish 8 by 4 inches (or 8 to 9 inches in diameter). Press some of the potato mixture onto the bottom and up the sides of each dish. The potato should be about ¼ inch thick on the sides and ⅜ to ½ inch thick on the bottom. Spoon in the leftover braised meat and sauce, about ⅓ to ½ cup for individual pies, 5 to 7 cups for a family-size pie. Top the meat with more mashed potato mixture to fully enclose the filling. Brush the top with the egg wash.

Bake for 30 minutes, or until the mashed potato top is browned and the inside of the pie reaches at least 125°F when tested with an instant-read meat thermometer. Let the pie sit at room temperature for 10 minutes. Run a knife around the edge to loosen and turn the pie or pies upside down quickly to unmold. Serve as is or use another plate to invert the pie so that the browned side faces up.

RECOMMENDED FILLINGS FOR
SHEPHERD'S PIE

BEEF

Spanish-Style Oven-Braised Steak (page 146)
Braised Swiss Steak with Mushrooms and Grappa (page 148)
Lisa's Lazy Pot Roast (page 194)
Mediterranean Brisket (page 200)
California Beef Stew with Zinfandel and Roasted Winter Vegetables (page 208)
Beef Stew with Mushrooms, Onions, and Dark Beer (page 210)
Tongue 'n Cheek Stew (page 232)

LAMB

Indian Ground Lamb with Chinese Long Beans and Potatoes (page 473)
Baked Leg of Lamb *Asadar* (page 494)
Braised Boneless Leg of Lamb with 20 Garlic Cloves (page 496)
Lamb Shanks Osso Buco (page 516)
Basque Sheepherders' Lamb Stew (page 524)

VEAL

Braised Shoulder of Veal with Mushroom Gravy (page 556)
Northern Italian Veal Stew with Peas and Roast Portobello Mushrooms (page 564)
Braised Veal Shanks North African Style (page 568)

How to Choose the Best Short Ribs

IT'S HARD TO BEAT SHORT RIBS, with their great beef flavor and succulent tenderness that develops when they are braised in an aromatic liquid. Short ribs are cut from the 12 ribs that extend from the back toward the belly and are found in primal areas such as the plate, rib section, chuck, and brisket. Butchers usually don't distinguish what section of the steer the short ribs are cut from. **English-style short ribs** have a rectangular appearance and include a bit of the rib or are sold boneless. They are cut parallel to the rib bone and between each rib. **Flanken-style** short ribs are cut across the rib bones. Most short ribs are somewhat fatty and should be trimmed of most external fat before cooking.

English-style short ribs

Flanken-style short ribs

Bul-Goki
(Korean Marinated and Barbecued Short Ribs)

Serves 4 to 6
■ COOKING ON A BUDGET ■ IN A HURRY

SHORT RIBS have a wonderful beefy flavor but are usually too tough to cook by dry-heat methods such as barbecuing. Korean cooks, whose national dish is *bul-goki*, have learned how to make short ribs tender by cutting the meat into thin slices across the ribs or by making an accordion cut (see page 219) parallel to the rib bone. They then marinate the meat until it is tender enough to grill. You can also make this dish with thin slices cut from the eye of the chuck, top round, or sirloin. Serve it with steamed fragrant Thai rice, the fiery pickled cabbage known as *kim chee,* and assorted cold vegetables such as cooked spinach with sesame seeds or bean sprouts. Korean and other Asian ingredients can be found in Asian groceries or by mail-order (see Sources, page 584).

A nice accompaniment to short ribs would be whole green onions or scallions brushed with the marinade and grilled alongside the meat. Use large spring onions, if you can find them, or split and cleaned baby leeks.

■ **Flavor Step** ■ In a small bowl, combine the marinade ingredients and whisk well. Set aside while you cut the meat.

■ **Flavor Step** ■
KOREAN MARINADE
FOR BEEF

½ cup Japanese or Korean soy sauce

¼ cup packed light or dark brown sugar

1 tablespoon ketchup

2 tablespoons minced garlic

1 tablespoon minced fresh ginger

2 tablespoons rice vinegar or cider vinegar

2 tablespoons Asian sesame oil

½ teaspoon red pepper flakes (optional)

6 2-to-3-inch-thick English-style (page 216) short ribs (3-3½ pounds total) OR 1½-2 pounds chuck, top round, or sirloin steak, thinly sliced

3 tablespoons finely chopped green onions or scallions (white and green parts)

To make an accordion cut on the short ribs (see illustration, opposite), start nearest the bone of one short rib and make a ¼-inch slice parallel to the bone and about ¼ inch from the bottom of the meat. Leave the bone attached like a hinge (1). Turn the rib over and make a ¼-inch-thick cut in the meat, again stopping about ¼ inch from the bottom edge (2). Turn the rib over and make another similar cut. Continue turning the rib and making ¼-inch-thick cuts that end ¼ inch from the bottom of the meat until you reach the last ¼-inch piece of meat (3). When you unfold the accordion, you should have a strip of meat 8 to 10 inches long (4). Repeat with the other short ribs. Place the meat in a zipper-lock bag or shallow bowl and add the marinade. Marinate (cover if using a bowl) for up to 2 hours at room temperature or overnight in the refrigerator, turning the bag or the meat occasionally.

When you're ready to grill the *bul-goki*, prepare a charcoal grill. (See Grilling, page 63.) Remove the meat from the marinade, discarding the marinade, and pat dry. Grill the slices of meat over medium-hot coals until the surface is brown and bubbly, 3 to 4 minutes per side. *Do not overcook.* The meat is best cooked medium to medium-well.

Remove the meat from the grill and serve at once, garnished with the chopped green onions or scallions. (Alternatively, the meat can be cooked in a preheated broiler, 3 inches from the heat; see Broiling, page 58.)

How to Make an Accordion Cut

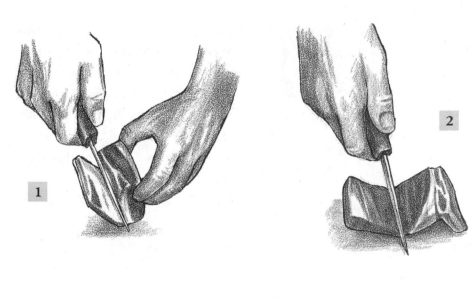

1

2

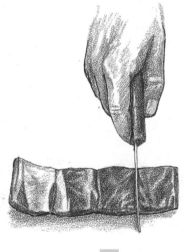

3

4

Korean-Style Oven-Browned Short Ribs

■ Flavor Step ■
KOREAN BRAISING
LIQUID
FOR BEEF OR PORK

10 garlic cloves, peeled

½ cup soy sauce

¼ cup light or dark brown
sugar

3 tablespoons chopped
fresh ginger

6 whole green onions
or scallions

2 tablespoons rice vinegar
or cider vinegar

2 cups water

3 pounds English-style
beef short ribs, boneless
or bone-in, trimmed of
external fat

2-3 tablespoons Asian sesame
oil

Serves 4 to 6

■ REWARMS WELL ■ GREAT LEFTOVERS

THESE LUSCIOUS RIBS are first braised to perfection in a savory stock, then brushed with sesame oil and baked in a hot oven to crisp the outside and intensify their beefy flavor. Simple to prepare, they can be made up a day ahead, then browned in the oven just before you're ready to eat. Serve the ribs in a shallow bowl with the braising sauce and steamed rice and Spinach with Roasted Sesame Seeds (page 221), with chopped green onions served on the side. And don't forget the *kim chee,* fiery Korean pickled cabbage. The same marinade and braising/browning technique works with country-style pork spareribs. Any leftovers can be cut into chunks and stir-fried with vegetables and leftover sauce.

■ Flavor Step ■ Put all the ingredients except the sesame oil into a large pot or Dutch oven, making sure the short ribs are covered by the liquid. If not, add more water and soy sauce. Bring to a boil, reduce the heat to a simmer, and skim off any foam that accumulates on the surface. Continue to cook, uncovered, until the short ribs are quite tender, 1½ to 2 hours.

Preheat the oven to 450°F. Remove the ribs from the braising liquid. Pat them dry and lay them bone side down on a rack above a roasting pan or use the broiling pan provided with your stove. Brush the meat with the sesame oil. Roast the ribs in the middle of the oven until their edges turn crispy, 10 to 15 minutes.

Meanwhile, skim any fat from the surface of the braising liquid. The sauce should have a rich, beefy flavor. If not, boil over high heat to concentrate the flavors. The sauce shouldn't get too thick but remain soupy. Ladle the sauce into shallow bowls and put a rib or two in each. Serve with rice and vegetables.

SPINACH WITH ROASTED SESAME SEEDS

Serves 4 to 6 as a side dish

2 bunches (10 ounces each) washed spinach,
     roots removed, stems attached
3 tablespoons sesame seeds
2 teaspoons Asian sesame oil
     Salt

Place the freshly washed spinach with water still clinging to its leaves in a large lidded pot. Cover and cook over medium-high heat until the spinach is just wilted, stirring from time to time, for about 3 minutes. Drain in a colander and let cool.

Place the sesame seeds in a dry, heavy skillet over medium heat. Toast the seeds, shaking the pan continuously, until they begin to color and give off a nutty aroma, 3 to 5 minutes. Immediately transfer the seeds to a small bowl.

Squeeze as much moisture out of the spinach as you can and chop it coarsely. Combine the spinach, sesame seeds, and sesame oil. Taste for salt and serve.

Boneless Short Ribs with Tomato and Fennel

■ Flavor Step ■
SPICY HERB RUB
FOR BEEF

½ teaspoon dried basil

½ teaspoon dried thyme

¼ teaspoon cayenne pepper

2 teaspoons salt

½ teaspoon freshly ground
   black pepper

2 tablespoons olive oil

3½ pounds boneless
   English-cut short ribs
   (8 rib pieces) OR about
   4½ pounds bone-in
   short ribs

TOMATO AND FENNEL
SAUCE

4 cups sliced onions

¾ cup chopped celery

2 fennel bulbs, diced,
   leafy tops chopped

3 tablespoons chopped
   garlic

½ cup red wine

4 cups diced fresh plum
   tomatoes OR canned
   Italian-style tomatoes

1 14½-ounce can low-
   sodium beef or chicken
   stock OR 1¾ cups
   homemade stock

Salt and freshly ground
   black pepper

Serves 4 to 6, with leftovers
■ TWO FOR ONE ■ COOKING ON A BUDGET
■ REWARMS WELL ■ GOOD FOR A CROWD
■ GREAT LEFTOVERS

BONELESS ENGLISH-CUT SHORT RIBS are best for this recipe (see page 216). If they can't be found, use meaty, lean, bone-in short ribs and remove the bones after cooking (they will give the sauce a little additional flavor).

This recipe is meant to provide two family or company dinners. For the first meal, serve the short ribs whole over a bed of mashed potatoes, couscous, polenta, or bulgur. Use only a portion of the delicious sauce, saving the rest for the second meal, a hearty Italian-style ragout of the diced short ribs served over wide egg noodles. If you have a lot of guests coming to dinner or a particularly large and hungry family, you can serve the whole delectable dish over noodles the first time out. Like most braised dishes, these tasty short ribs are even better made up to a day ahead; just skim off any fat from the surface and reheat before serving. *(See photograph, page 42.)*

In northern California, fennel grows wild from May through September. If you can't find fresh fennel, substitute fennel seeds.

———

■ **Flavor Step** ■ Combine all the herb rub ingredients. Rub over all sides of the short ribs.

Preheat the oven to 350°F. Heat the oil in a large, deep, ovenproof skillet or a Dutch oven over medium-high heat. Add the short ribs and brown on all sides, 7 to 10 minutes. Remove the meat and set aside.

To make the Tomato and Fennel Sauce: Pour off all but 2 tablespoons of the fat from the pan. Add the onions, celery, diced fennel bulbs (reserve the tops), and garlic. Cover and cook for about 5 minutes, until the vegetables begin to soften, stirring occasionally. Pour in the wine and stir well, scraping up any browned bits. Bring to a boil and add the tomatoes, stock, and reserved fennel tops.

Add the short ribs to the pan, cover, and bake for 1½ to 2 hours, or until the meat is quite tender. (You can also cook the short ribs on top of the stove over low heat for about the same length of time.) If the sauce seems too liquid, remove the meat with a slotted spoon and cover loosely to keep it warm. Skim the fat from the sauce and reduce it at a brisk boil over high heat for 10 to 15 minutes, or until it just begins to turn syrupy. Taste the sauce and season with salt and pepper. Serve the ribs and about a third of the sauce, saving the rest for the ragout.

SHORT RIB RAGOUT WITH PASTA

Serves 4

PREPARE THIS RECIPE with leftover short ribs.

> Leftover boneless short ribs (2-4), cut into ½-inch cubes
> 2 cups leftover Tomato and Fennel Sauce
> Low-sodium beef or chicken stock if needed
> Tomato puree if needed
> 1 pound fresh pappardelle or ¾ pound dried wide egg noodles
> ½ cup freshly grated Parmesan cheese

Heat the short ribs in the sauce over medium heat. If the sauce is too thick, dilute it with a little water or stock. If you don't have quite enough sauce (2 cups), add tomato puree as needed.

Meanwhile, in a large pot of boiling salted water, cook the noodles just until done.

Drain the noodles and put on a serving platter. Top with the ragout and sprinkle generously with the cheese.

Catahoula's Smoky Short Ribs with New Orleans Red Gravy

■ Flavor Step ■
FRESH BASIL AND
GARLIC MARINADE
FOR BEEF

15 garlic cloves
1 cup fresh basil leaves
½ cup olive oil

6-8 beef short ribs
     (4-5 pounds), cut
     into 1½-inch pieces
     Salt and freshly ground
     black pepper
2 cups flour
1 tablespoon paprika,
     preferably hot
     Hungarian
1 teaspoon cayenne pepper
2 tablespoons olive oil

Serves 6, with leftovers
■ GOOD FOR A CROWD ■ GREAT LEFTOVERS
■ REWARMS WELL

JAN BIRNBAUM serves up spicy Louisiana-style food at his popular restaurant and saloon, Catahoula, in the tiny town of Calistoga in the northern Napa Valley. Jan was born in Baton Rouge and did his apprenticeship with Paul Prudhomme at K-Paul's in New Orleans. He went on to cook at New York's Quilted Giraffe, Denver's Rattlesnake Club, and San Francisco's Campton Place. Along the way he gained a reputation for creative and exciting food with a Southern flair.

These tangy short ribs come with Jan's famous New Orleans Red Gravy, which you can make yourself or purchase by mail-order from Catahoula (see Sources, page 584). There, Jan serves the ribs with potatoes wrapped in foil with bacon, then roasted in the embers of his brick oven. On the side are roasted red onions and mustard greens sautéed with caramelized leeks. The leftover gravy is also delicious as a barbecue sauce for spareribs or on grilled steak or pork chops; or use it as a braising liquid for pot roast or stew.

■ Flavor Step ■ In a food processor, pulse the garlic until chopped. Add the basil and pulse until chopped. With the machine running, add the olive oil and pulse for a second to mix. Rub this mixture all over the ribs and marinate for up to 2 hours at room temperature or overnight, covered, in the refrigerator. If it's been refrigerated, remove an hour before cooking to allow the meat to come to room temperature.

Remove the ribs from the marinade, shake off any excess, and season them well with salt and pepper. Put the flour in a shallow bowl and mix in the paprika and cayenne. Dredge the ribs in the seasoned flour.

Heat a Dutch oven or a large skillet over medium-high heat. Add the oil and sear the ribs until they are brown and crisp, turning often. Remove the ribs and set aside.

To make the New Orleans Red Gravy: Reduce the heat to medium and add the onions to the pot. Cover and cook for 15 to 20 minutes, stirring often, until they begin to caramelize. Put in the chiles and tomatoes and cook for 15 minutes, uncovered, stirring often. Add the rest of the ingredients except the red wine vinegar and return the ribs to the pot. Reduce the heat, cover, and simmer for 2 hours, or until the ribs are fork-tender. (At this point, you can cool the ribs in the gravy and refrigerate, then finish the dish the next day if you like. Before continuing, remove the ribs from the gravy and remove the excess fat.)

Remove the ribs from the pot and keep them warm; degrease the gravy. Transfer the gravy to a food processor and process to a puree. Add the vinegar and taste for salt and pepper. If the gravy seems too thick, add a little chicken stock or water and reheat if necessary. If it seems too thin, transfer it to a saucepan and boil it to reduce it to a syrupy consistency.

Serve the ribs with the gravy and with the accompaniments described in the discussion if you like.

NEW ORLEANS RED GRAVY

4 large yellow onions, cut into ½-inch dice

2-6 jalapeño chiles (depending on how hot you like it), seeded and sliced

15 plum tomatoes, peeled, seeded, and chopped

8 cups chicken stock, or more if needed

4 cups strong coffee

3 cups red wine

1 tablespoon cumin seeds, toasted and ground (use a mortar and pestle or a spice grinder)

3 bay leaves

¼ cup red wine vinegar

Overlooked but Delicious Cuts

OXTAILS DON'T REALLY COME ONLY FROM OXEN (castrated bulls used as draft animals) but from beef cattle of all types. The tail is skinned and cut into chunks. As unlikely as it may sound, these bits of meat make some of the most delicious braised beef dishes. The reason is simple: oxtails offer rich, beefy flavors and a wonderfully textured sauce because of the amount of collagen they release during cooking. Luckily, in recent years, these once-scorned but delicious morsels have been getting their due from American chefs.

Beef shin meat cut from the foreshanks is quite tough but becomes delicious when braised. It is reasonably priced. When sliced across the bone, the shank also makes a great base for beef stock. Roast the meat and bones in a 450°F oven for 15 minutes to brown and then simmer them with aromatic vegetables to extract their color and rich flavor.

Until very recently, **tongue** from beef and buffalo was considered a delicacy. (After all, there's just one per animal.) Rough-and-ready buffalo hunters argued over who would get the tongue, and discriminating Easterners feasted on pickled tongues shipped to fancy restaurants. When poached slowly for hours, tongue becomes lusciously tender and has a silky feeling in the mouth unsurpassed by any other boiled meat. It is inexpensive, rewarms well, and makes great hot or cold sandwiches, especially when paired with some hot mustard and horseradish.

Although **beef cheeks** may sound awfully odd as a gourmet treat, increasing numbers of restaurateurs and beef lovers are discovering them. These disk-shaped muscles from the cheek weigh ¾ to 1 pound each. Although very tough and full of collagen, when braised for several hours they develop a firm yet soft and silky texture. Stewed or braised, they take on the rich, robust flavor associated with a good pot roast and have a wonderfully dense texture. Cheeks' intense beef flavor makes for great gravy.

Braised Oxtails

Serves 8 or more, with leftovers
■ REWARMS WELL ■ GREAT LEFTOVERS ■
■ COOKING ON A BUDGET ■

I N FANCY RESTAURANTS, the humble oxtail is being given special treatment. Oxtails cook down slowly into a soft and silky tenderness with an intensely flavored, smooth sauce. Like many braised beef dishes, oxtails are best made a day or two ahead, refrigerated, and then rewarmed.

■ **Flavor Step** ■ Combine the herbs, salt, and pepper and sprinkle the mixture all over the oxtails.

In a Dutch oven or large casserole, heat the oil over medium-high heat and brown the oxtail pieces, in batches, for 2 to 3 minutes on all sides, or until nicely colored. Remove the oxtail pieces from the pot with a slotted spoon as they brown.

Pour off all but 2 tablespoons of the fat from the pot and add the onions, leeks, carrots, celery, and garlic. Reduce the heat to medium and cover the pot. Cook the vegetables for 5 to 10 minutes, stirring occasionally, until soft. Stir in the optional porcini or other dried mushrooms, the red wine, stock, and bay leaves. Scrape up any browned bits from the bottom of the pot and bring to a boil. Reduce the heat to a simmer, cover the pot, and cook for 3 hours. Taste the meat to see if it's quite tender and almost falling off the bone; if not, cook until tender. At this point you can cool and then refrigerate the oxtails in their sauce. After a day or two, remove the congealed fat from the surface. Bring the sauce to a simmer and cook the oxtails for 20 minutes, until heated through, then proceed.

Degrease the sauce and remove the oxtails with a slotted spoon. If necessary, reduce the sauce over high heat to a syrupy consistency. Stir the mustard into the sauce, taste for salt and pepper, and return the meat to reheat it. Discard the bay leaves before serving the oxtails and sauce over noodles or mashed potatoes.

■ **Flavor Step** ■
HERB RUB FOR
BRAISED BEEF
2 teaspoons dried thyme
2 teaspoons dried sage
2 tablespoons kosher salt
1 tablespoon freshly
   ground black pepper

5-6 pounds oxtails
2 tablespoons olive oil
2 cups chopped onions
1 cup sliced leeks
   (white part only)
1 cup chopped carrots
¾ cup chopped celery
2 tablespoons minced
   garlic
½ ounce dried porcini
   or other dried mush-
   rooms, soaked in
   boiling water for at
   least 30 minutes,
   drained and chopped
   (optional)
2 cups red wine
2 cups beef or chicken
   stock
3 bay leaves
2 tablespoons coarse-
   grained mustard
   Salt and freshly ground
   black pepper

Braised Beef Shanks with Coconut Milk, Ginger, and Cumin

3 tablespoons butter

2 tablespoons peanut oil, preferably Asian

2½ cups chopped onions

2 carrots, cut into ¼-inch dice

3 garlic cloves, minced

1 tablespoon minced fresh ginger

¼ cup flour

2 teaspoons salt, plus more to taste

1½ teaspoons freshly ground black pepper

4 pounds beef shanks, cut 1½-2 inches thick

2½ teaspoons ground coriander

1 teaspoon ground cumin

½ teaspoon turmeric

½ teaspoon red pepper flakes

1¾ cups beef stock

1½ cups unsweetened coconut milk

1 cinnamon stick, 3 cardamom pods, lightly smashed, and 2 bay leaves, wrapped in a pouch of cheesecloth

Chopped fresh cilantro for garnish

Serves 6
■ REWARMS WELL ■ GREAT LEFTOVERS

THIS DISH COMES FROM our friend and Seattle chef Jeff Bergman. He says, "This braising technique turns these beef shanks into a cool fall or winter supper. I love the marriage of these sweet and savory spices from the Pacific Rim and East India—they awaken the palate and make it sing. Listen for that hum from your guests as they devour everything on the plate!" A side of sautéed snap peas adds great texture and color. Serve rice noodles or fresh Chinese egg noodles instead of rice if you'd rather. Coconut milk is available in some supermarkets and in Asian groceries or by mail-order (see Sources, page 584).

Preheat the oven to 325°F. Melt 1 tablespoon of the butter with 1 tablespoon of the peanut oil in a large roasting pan or Dutch oven over medium-high heat. Add the onions, carrots, garlic, and ginger, reduce the heat to medium, and cook, stirring, until the vegetables soften, about 10 minutes. Remove the vegetables with a slotted spoon and keep warm.

Mix the flour, salt, and pepper together in a shallow bowl. Coat each of the pieces of beef shank in the flour and shake off the excess. Add the remaining 2 tablespoons butter and 1 tablespoon oil to the pot and heat. Over medium-high heat, brown the meat well on all sides, 5 to 7 minutes. Remove the shanks to a platter.

Reduce the heat to medium and add the coriander, cumin, turmeric, and red pepper flakes. Stir for 1 minute to release the oils from the spices. Stir in ½ cup of the beef stock and scrape up any browned bits from the bottom of the pan. Stir in the remaining 1¼ cups beef stock and the coconut milk and bring to a boil.

Return the shanks and vegetables to the pan and add the cheesecloth pouch of spices. Cover the pot, bring it to a boil, and place it in the preheated oven. The shanks should braise until the meat is tender and shrinking away from the bone, 2½ to 3½ hours. Check the shanks from time to time to make sure they aren't sticking to the bottom of the pot.

When the shanks are tender, remove them to a warm platter and cover loosely with foil to keep warm. Degrease the braising liquid if necessary, and reduce it over medium-high heat to thicken slightly. Remove the spice pouch and taste for salt and pepper.

Serve the shanks on warm plates with steamed jasmine rice; ladle the sauce over them, and garnish with the cilantro.

Puebla-Style Tongue in Chipotle Chile Sauce

1 beef tongue, trimmed
   (3-4 pounds)
2 bottles Mexican beer
1 whole head of garlic
2 onions
2 teaspoons salt
1 carrot
1 celery rib
3 bay leaves
1 teaspoon cumin seeds
10 black peppercorns
3 whole allspice or a pinch
   of ground allspice

CHIPOTLE CHILE SAUCE

2 tablespoons olive oil
2 medium onions,
   thinly sliced
2 tablespoons minced
   garlic
2 mild green chiles such
   as Anaheim, canned
   or fresh, fire-roasted
   (see page 103), peeled,
   seeded, and chopped
3 canned chipotle chiles *en
   adobo* (see discussion),
   chopped
1½ cups tongue stock or
   chicken or beef stock
1 28-ounce can solid pack
   tomatoes, drained
2 teaspoons ground cumin
½ teaspoon ground
   coriander
   Pinch of ground allspice

Serves 6, with leftovers
■ REWARMS WELL ■ GREAT LEFTOVERS
■ COOKING ON A BUDGET ■ TWO FOR ONE

IT'S A SHAME that so many people turn up their noses at the idea of eating tongue. Folks from Mexico and Latin America haven't lost their taste for it, however, for they know that it is lusciously tender and its mild flavor takes to a whole host of spices.

Our recipe, from good friend and San Francisco cooking impresario Loni Kuhn, has a decided Mexican flavor. Loni says, "Make sure you end up with plenty of leftovers since this dish makes fantastic tacos and burritos. It rewarms well in the oven, a microwave, or on top of the stove." Serve over rice accompanied by black beans.

Chipotle chiles *en adobo* (smoked red jalapeño chiles in adobo sauce) and other Mexican ingredients can be found in Latino groceries or through mail-order (see Sources, 584).

———

Place the tongue in a large pot. Pour over the beer and add enough water to cover. Add the garlic, onions, carrot, celery, bay leaves, cumin, peppercorns, and allspice. Bring to a boil and skim off any foam. Reduce to a simmer, cover, and cook for 2 to 3 hours, or until the tongue is fork-tender. Take the pot off the heat and let the tongue cool in the cooking liquid. (At this point you may continue with the recipe or cool the tongue in the stock overnight in the refrigerator.) Remove the tongue from the liquid. Reserve the stock. While the tongue is still warm, trim off any bones or fat. With a sharp knife, make a long slit in the skin from the base end. Peel the skin from the tongue with your fingers. Set the tongue aside.

To make the Chipotle Chile Sauce: In a large pan with a cover or a Dutch oven, heat the oil over medium heat. Add 2 tablespoons chopped vegetables from the stock, the onions, and the garlic, cover, and cook for 10 minutes or until the vegetables are quite soft. Add the chiles and cook for 2 minutes more. Place the reserved tongue or chicken stock in a food processor along with the tomatoes, cumin, coriander, and allspice. Process until smooth. Add the tomato mixture to the onions and chiles in the pan and bring to a boil. Season the sauce to taste with salt and pepper. Reduce the heat to a simmer, slice or cube the tongue, and add to the pan. Cover and cook for 30 minutes. Garnish as desired.

Note: *Use the leftover tongue stock to cook lentils or beans to serve as a side dish with rewarmed tongue or combine cooked lentils and tongue for a savory casserole. You could also turn the Chipotle Chile Sauce into a curry sauce by adding a tablespoon or two of curry powder or Garam Masala (page 321) and cooking the sauce for 10 minutes or so.*

Salt and freshly ground black pepper

GARNISH
Chopped cilantro (optional)
Chopped green onions or scallions
Chopped red onions (optional)

Tongue 'n Cheek Stew

1 beef tongue, trimmed

3-4 cups water OR beef
   or chicken stock

2 carrots

2 celery ribs

1 medium onion

2 bay leaves

2 sprigs fresh thyme or
   ½ teaspoon dried

2 teaspoons salt

3 tablespoons olive oil

3 pounds beef cheeks,
   well trimmed and cut
   into 2-inch cubes, OR
   2½ pounds boneless
   chuck, cut into 2-inch
   cubes

2 cups chopped onions

8 garlic cloves, chopped

1 cup dry red wine

4 cups tongue stock
   (see recipe) OR beef,
   veal, or chicken stock

1 4-ounce can tomato
   paste

1 14-ounce can diced
   tomatoes, drained

1½ tablespoons ground
   cumin

   Salt and freshly ground
   black pepper

Serves 4 to 6
■ MAKE AHEAD ■ REWARMS WELL

THIS SAVORY DISH'S ORIGIN is the cowboy favorite called sonofabitch stew that was popular in San Francisco saloons and restaurants in the raucous good old days. The stew was made of the tongue, cheeks, and other favored cuts from the beef carcass, and it was considered quite a delicacy after a diet of tough beefsteaks and chewy stewed meat from range-run cattle.

Our recipe comes from San Francisco's culinary *grande dame* and cooking teacher Loni Kuhn, who got it from the chef at a San Francisco landmark restaurant, Señor Pico, who got it from legendary restaurateur Trader Vic Bergeron, who got it from an old saloon keeper from the wild and woolly Barbary Coast—and God only knows where he got it, maybe from some burned-out chuck wagon cook trading recipes and tall tales for bad whiskey, hands shaking and voice quavering, some bright spring morning in 1910. If you're a fan of boiled or braised meat, don't pass up this recipe. As with most boiled or braised meat, the dish is best made a day ahead and rewarmed.

Place the tongue in a pot and cover it with water or stock. Add the carrots, celery, onion, bay leaves, thyme, and salt. Bring to a boil, reduce the heat to low, and simmer for 2 hours. (If you want to serve the tongue by itself, continue to cook for another 1 to 1½ hours, or until tender.) Remove the tongue from the pot and strain the stock. Reserve 4 cups stock for the stew. When the tongue is cool enough to handle, peel off the skin and trim off any gristle or fat. (See previous recipe.) Cut the tongue into 1-inch cubes and set aside.

GARNISH
Thinly sliced chives
or green onions or
scallions and lime
wedges

Preheat the oven to 325°F. In a large, heavy pot or Dutch oven, heat the oil over medium-high heat. Season the beef cheeks or chuck meat with salt and pepper. Brown the meat on all sides, turning often, 5 to 7 minutes. Remove the meat and set aside.

Pour off all but 2 tablespoons of the fat from the pot and add the chopped onions and garlic. Cover the pot and cook until the onions are soft, about 5 minutes, stirring occasionally. Pour in the red wine and bring to a boil, scraping up any browned bits from the bottom of the pan. Add the 4 cups reserved tongue or other stock, the tomato paste, tomatoes, cumin, and a pinch each of salt and pepper. Put the diced tongue and the beef cheeks or chuck meat back in the pot, cover, and place in the oven.

Cook for 1½ to 3 hours, or until the meat is quite tender— chuck will take considerably less time than cheek meat. When the meat is tender, transfer the pot to the top of the stove and bring to a gentle simmer. Degrease the sauce and taste for salt and pepper. Make the Cornmeal Dumplings (page 234) and add them to the pot just before serving. Pass the chives or green onions and lime wedges at the table.

CORNMEAL DUMPLINGS

Makes 20 to 30 dumplings

THESE CORNMEAL DUMPLINGS are so good, they can turn this most humble of stews into a banquet fit for a trail boss. The dumplings are wonderful in just about any stew or pot roast and make a great side dish for roasts when cooked in stock or gravy. They're substantial, but soft and tender.

- 1 cup flour
- 1 cup cornmeal
- 2 teaspoons baking powder
- 1 teaspoon sugar
- 1 teaspoon salt, or more as needed
- 1 large egg, well beaten
- ¾ cup milk
- 1 tablespoon vegetable oil or butter, melted
  Freshly ground black pepper

In a medium bowl, whisk together the flour, cornmeal, baking powder, sugar, and salt. In a small bowl, beat the egg with the milk and oil or melted butter. Pour the wet mixture into the dry and stir together until well mixed. Drop tablespoon-size dumplings onto the simmering stew (if not making stew, cook the dumplings in a large pot of simmering water or broth). Cover the pot and cook over low heat for 25 minutes, or until the dumplings are firm and floating on the surface. *Absolutely do not lift the cover of the pot to peek.*

· Pork ·

The Most
Versatile Meat

With its ability to absorb a wide variety of flavors, its tenderness, and its innate juiciness, pork lends itself to a wide variety of cooking styles. For this reason it has played a central role in both European and Asian cultures from the earliest times to the present day. This meat takes to strong flavors such as chiles, garlic, and soy sauce. Many savory herbs and spices marry well with pork: sage, rosemary, fennel, paprika, allspice, and cumin, to name just a few. The delicious Tuscan pork dish *Arista* is an example: roast pork loin perfumed with garlic and sage (see page 335). And any French chef will tell you how pork, like veal, can be joined with delicate sauces that incorporate reductions of wine and stock along with mushrooms and truffles. The suggestion of sweetness in the meat also makes it particularly well suited to fruits such as apples, pineapples, and dried apricots.

A central flavoring agent that has always suited pork is salt. Its soft meat and fat can tolerate salt without becoming hard and dry, as beef and lamb often do. Salt-cured pork products have been enjoyed through the ages. The Chinese were probably the first to learn about curing, but making hams, bacon, and other salt-cured products has become almost universal. From Lancashire to Latvia, cured pork was a mainstay: bacon, shoulder, sausages, or ham were often combined with vegetables that could also be stored in cool cellars, such as cabbages, onions, carrots, parsnips, and apples.

What began as a necessity to preserve, however, has been continued because of a preference for flavor. Many of today's cooks, from the professional chef to the backyard barbecuer, have found that lightly curing pork chops, tenderloins, and small roasts by soaking them in a Flavor Brine vastly improves the meat's texture and juiciness (see Flavor Brining, page 254).

Pork's adaptability to a wide variety of ingredients is matched by its unparalleled succulence. All cooks agree that the pig is the most versatile of all the meat animals, since virtually every part of the pig, from the head and jowls through the coveted loin to the flavorful ham and even the tail—everything but the proverbial squeal—is used.

In America, pork's popularity has never waned, from the earliest colonial days to its reincarnation today as "the other white meat." Our current per capita consumption is equivalent to what it was 30 years ago, when meat eating was in its heyday. In the world of gastronomy and fine dining, pork's prestige has grown as well. A few years ago, you rarely saw pork in a fine restaurant. But today many of America's star chefs are making reputations for themselves with signature dishes of pork, often using original and striking brines and glazes for flavor accents. Although pork loin and tenderloin are the most popular cuts, we are starting to see more humble parts, such as shank and spareribs, come back into their own.

A Succulent History

"Pork is the best of meat. It should not be too fat, nor too lean, and the animal not too old. It must be eaten rather cold, without the skin. . . . "   —Hippocrates, the father of Western medicine

OUR DOMESTIC PIGS are descended from the European wild boar, *Sus scrofa*, and the Asiatic wild boar, *Sus vitattus* or *S. indicus*. Depictions of wild boar are found in prehistoric caves such as those at Lascaux, and the boar has been an important, and dangerous, prey of hunters from earliest times to the present. Pigs were probably domesticated as omnivorous scavengers near Neolithic farming communities sometime around the third or fourth millennium B.C.

Early Greek and other ancient cultures valued pork for its nutritious quality, succulent flavor, and versatility. Galen, the Roman physician, recommends pork for those who work hard or perform strenuous exercises in his *De Alimentaria*. And Athenaeus, in his lengthy treatise in praise of good living, the *Deipnosophistae (The Wise Drinkers)*, extols the pig in every form: pickled, salted, smoked, or fresh, roasted, boiled, broiled, and fried.

Greek heroes feasted on pork at their banquets: tender pieces skewered as kebabs, loin cutlets wrapped in fat and broiled, whole pigs roasted on spits, hams and shoulders simmered in cauldrons in savory broths. Odysseus was careful to send the blind harper at a banquet "a piece cut from his loin of pork, crisp with fat." When he returned in disguise to Ithaca, the faithful swineherd Eumaois prepared a welcome-home barbecue: "Taking flesh from every part of the pig, Eumaios wrapped lean strips with fat, floured them with barley meal, and broiled them on the fire. The rest of the meat was sliced and skewered, roasted with care, and heaped onto platters."

ROMAN EPICURES

Apicius, the Roman author of the cookbook *De Re Coquinaria*, written sometime in the late third century A.D., provides many recipes for pork, including roast pork glazed with honey, pork cutlets brined with salt and cumin, stuffed pork roulades in sweet wine, and suckling pig prepared in a mouthwatering variety of ways. Romans of all classes were fond of pork, especially ham and bacon. The common food of many taverns and cookshops consisted of boiled pork with greens, while at aristocratic banquets Roman gourmets dined on the sumptuous presentations described by Athenaeus and Apicius.

The Roman tendency to extremes of gourmandise is satirized by Petronius Arbiter, tutor of the emperor Nero (not the safest of jobs, when you think of it—Petronius did not die well) and author of the *Satyricon*. At a feast thrown by Trimalchio, the epitome of a *nouveau riche* for Petronius, the main course was a huge roast sow surrounded by marzipan piglets. The carver discovered, to his horror, that the pig seemed not to have been gutted, and the feast seemed to be spoiled, with the chef in disgrace. When the pig was cut open, however, whole sausages, blood puddings, small roast birds, and other delicacies tumbled out, to the surprise and delight of the diners. The trick was described earlier by Athenaeus' star chef: the pig is killed and bled by a small cut under the shoulder. The intestines are drawn out through the mouth, washed well with wine and spices, and then replaced. Roast birds, cooked sausages, spices, and gravy are stuffed in via the mouth, and the pig is then roasted whole for the big surprise.

A STAPLE IN ASIA AND EUROPE

In China, pork is one of the building blocks of that great and ancient cuisine. Historians feel that China was one of the sources of the original domestication of the pig, and pig raising is associated with one of the Celestial Immortals and founders of the culture, Fu Hsi. The earliest ideogram denoting "home" in Chinese, in fact, is the sign for a house with a pig under the roof, and pork—fresh or cured, braised, poached, or stir-fried—is used in a vast array of dishes.

Other Asian cuisines, notably Japanese and those of Southeast Asia, use pork more sparingly but in dramatic and delicious ways. Vietnamese Tamarind

Pork Stir-Fry (page 306) and Thai-Style Barbecued Baby Back Ribs (page 382) are tasty examples.

By the time agriculture had fully developed in Europe, the pig was already an important part of everyday life. Each fall pigs were killed before the cold weather set in, and the meat was then salted and often smoked, to keep over the winter. Throughout Europe, the fall slaughtering was an excuse for festivals such as the German *Schlactfest,* the Spanish *matanzas,* and the French *boucherie,* where every part of the pig was consumed with plenty of the local beverages, dancing, music, and good times.

PORK IN AMERICA

Pigs came to America from Europe with the first explorers. Columbus brought eight pigs with him on his second voyage in 1493, and these prolific swine are said to be the ancestors of the pigs that swarmed through the jungles and canebrakes of the Caribbean and South and Central America over the ensuing years. Cortés introduced the pig to Mexico, and on excursions through the region, the brave conquistadores were followed by droves of hogs.

When De Soto arrived in Florida in 1539, he brought 13 sows and 2 boars, which increased to a herd of 300 within a year or so. When the explorer died in 1542 on the banks of the Mississippi, after his 3,000-mile trek through the South and Southwest, 700 pigs were auctioned off to surviving members of the expedition. As an example of the amazing reproductive power of the animal, De Soto's chronicler recorded that more than 400 were killed and eaten, got loose, or were stolen by Indians along the way. These escaped and purloined pigs formed the basis of the population of the semiwild razorbacks that were an important source of food in the American South.

English colonists who immigrated to Jamestown also brought hogs to North America. In 1607, "three sowes in eighteen months increased sixty and od[d] Pigs," we are told, and two years later the colony possessed "five or sixe hundred swine." The animals increased so rapidly that they soon had to be confined to Hog Island, and by 1627, the pigs on the island and in the surrounding forests had flourished so that they were described as "innumerable."

SOUTHERN RAZORBACKS: HAM ON THE HOOF

Conditions in the southern forests were ideal for pigs: plenty of water, a warm and equable climate, and great quantities of food: nuts such as hickory, pecan, and acorns, falls of wild fruit, and abundant vegetation. The inhabitants, from rich planters to Native Americans and settlers of the outback, came to depend on the razorbacks for food. All a settler had to do was go out to the nearest hickory grove and shoot a pig or two to salt down for the winter or coax a pregnant sow into the barn with handfuls of corn for next year's crop of porkers.

Pork—fresh or cured—became one of the main sources of protein in the diet of the American South and is still an integral part of regional traditions. Anyone who drives through the rural South or visits the cities of the region quickly becomes familiar with the iconic pigs—fat and often smiling merrily— that adorn signs advertising the spicy and delicious barbecued pork Southerners are so rightly proud of.

SALT PORK: A YANKEE SPECIALTY

Pigs were also introduced with the first landings in the Massachusetts Bay Colony and in the Dutch colonies in New Amsterdam, and they quickly became an article of trade and an important part of the early commerce of the colonies. Pennsylvania under William Penn was especially prosperous and began exporting live pigs and salted pork to the Caribbean at an early date. American farmers adapted European farming practices to the new continent's conditions and soon had plenty to trade. They found that by penning the half-wild hogs for a few months before slaughtering and fattening them with dried maize or Indian corn, which yielded prodigious and easily stored crops, they could produce huge quantities of meat with little effort or expense. This surplus of corn and pork became the basis for one of the first major exports of the colonies—salted or barreled pork. Salt pork is featured in many Yankee dishes, notably in the famous Boston baked beans.

TO MARKET, TO MARKET

As the industry developed, ports such as Boston, New York, and Philadelphia became processing centers for salt pork for export to the West Indies and England and to supply the trading ships of many nations. Huge herds of pigs were driven to market along the burgeoning turnpike system, to be slaughtered and salted down in barrels in the port cities. We are told in Towne and Wentworth's *Pigs from Cave to Corn Belt* that "the volume of barreled meats rose so rapidly under the presidential administration of George Washington that the hopeful exponents of manifest destiny proclaimed that America would soon eclipse Ireland in the international pork trade." Barreled salt pork also became part of the infamous Triangle Trade: American goods were exchanged in the West Indies for molasses and rum, which were then traded in West Africa for slaves to be sold to planters in the Caribbean and the American South.

PIGWAYS AND HIGHWAYS

The pig played an important role in the settling of the Ohio Valley and the Midwest. As settlers spread across the Appalachians, they brought pigs with them and, as in the South, semiwild "woods hogs" became a mainstay of farmers in the fertile but dangerous forests and meadows of Kentucky, Indiana, and Ohio. Corn was the main crop, and hogs soon became one of the only ways frontier farmers could get their surplus corn to market. In the absence of good roads, farmers had to convert their crops into a movable commodity—either the pig or a more easily transportable one, whiskey. Pigs were seen as "corn on the hoof" and drovers "walked the corn to market," herding hundreds and even thousands of pigs at a time down the primitive trails and later turnpikes that led to the processing centers. These "pigways" became the routes followed by the early railroads and later by the highways and interstates of today's landscape.

PORKOPOLIS: THE RISE OF THE MEAT PACKERS

As the population expanded west, Cincinnati and later Chicago became major centers of pork processing. Early packinghouses in Cincinnati slaughtered and packed millions of pounds of fresh and cured pork each year along with lard, an increasingly lucrative part of the pig. By 1860, the city was slaughtering 400,000 hogs a year and had earned the nickname Porkopolis. Most of the cured meat and lard were shipped down the Ohio River to the Mississippi and then New Orleans for export and for sale in the South. With the Civil War, which blocked the river commerce, and the growing importance of the railroads, Chicago became the most important meat-packing center in the Corn Belt—and eventually Carl Sandburg's "Hog Butcher of the World."

Meat packers such as Philip Armour, Gustavus Swift, and Michael Cudahy began to process pork in extraordinary quantities after the Civil War and, with the coming of refrigeration and canning, created the modern pork industry. These enormous meat processors were able to slaughter and butcher the hogs quickly and efficiently using assembly-line techniques and to ship fresh, cured, or canned meat from the Corn Belt to the rest of the country and the world through the newly developed railroad system. While meat was part of the working man and woman's diet only occasionally in Europe, in America, eating meat in the form of ham or bacon or pork chops or Spam or bologna or hot dogs or hamburger or steak became an everyday occurrence for the first time in history. And the pig, the most efficient meat maker in nature, the American "corn converter," played a huge role in this dramatic change.

The Svelte New Porkers

IN RECENT YEARS there has been another radical change in diet as consumers look for leaner meat of every kind. Pig breeding in America in the twentieth century has shifted in response to consumer demand and as the need for the pig's fat for cooking and as an industrial lubricant decreased.

The modern pig is a much leaner animal than the huge porkers that used to win blue ribbons at the county fair, and when it comes to the table, it's not the rich, fatty, and juicy meat that Grandma served. If you cook it the same way, as many cookbooks recommend, it will be depressingly dry. Pork can still be deliciously juicy, though, if we keep in mind how it has changed and how the cooking techniques have to be modified.

The pig of 30 years ago was a hefty fellow weighing in at nearly 300 pounds when sent to market. Today, at 240 pounds on average, he is svelte compared to his ancestors. Instead of many inches of fat along the ribs, today there's a layer less than an inch thick. The modern pig's lean muscles are larger, and his once-thick back fat is considerably thinner. When dressed out, the carcass weighs about 180 pounds, yielding 105 pounds of lean pork.

What does this new, leaner pig mean from a nutritional standpoint? The good news is that pork compares very well with chicken. The leaner cuts of pork (and the most popular), such as loin chops, loin roasts, and tenderloin, have less overall fat, saturated fat, cholesterol, and calories than equivalent portions of skinless chicken thigh. And what about the ultralean, boneless, skinless chicken breasts that waiflike models and skinny actresses eat in trendy restaurants in Los Angeles and New York? Pork tenderloins—the leanest, most versatile, and tastiest cut of all—have only one more gram of fat per serving with the same number of calories as the skinless chicken breast. The bottom line is that pork can be an excellent source of protein without adding fat to your diet, and it beats the hell out of poached chicken breast for taste!

What Matters Most in Buying Pork

WHETHER YOU'RE STANDING in front of the supermarket meat case or peering at a butcher's display, you have to know what to look for in choosing quality pork. As with all meats, freshness and proper storage are paramount. If the pork has been packed correctly, there shouldn't be excessive moisture in the package, and any liquid should be clear, not cloudy. The meat should be well trimmed, without a lot of fat, and there should be no dark or blemished areas, nor should there be any off odors. The surface should be moist, not slimy or sticky. Reject soft and watery meat, which will undergo considerable shrinkage during cooking and end up dry.

Color and firmness are essential factors in judging quality. Avoid meat that is very pale in color (pinkish gray to grayish pink). Instead, look for pork that is reddish pink. Any fat should be white and smooth. Most important, buy meat that is firm to the touch, lean and fine-grained. As always, buy the freshest you can find—not frozen, if possible.

GRADES OF PORK

Unlike beef and lamb, the top grades of pork are numbered: USDA 1 is the best quality, USDA 4 the lowest. These grades are based on how much lean meat is produced per carcass, with number 1 having the highest proportion of lean to fat. For the consumer, the grading system is more straightforward than with beef, however, for the simple reason that most butchers and supermarkets offer only number 1 pork these days.

PORK AT A GLANCE

■ **Look for:** Firm, slightly moist meat that's pale reddish pink with a fine grain. Shoulder and leg cuts may be slightly darker with a coarser grain. Fat should be white, firm, smooth, and creamy.

■ **Avoid:** Pale, soft pork that looks watery and has excessive fat.

■ **Overlooked Cuts:** Fresh leg or ham, country spareribs, fresh pork shank, Boston butt, picnic ham, fresh picnic shoulder, neck bones.

■ **Best Buys:** Fresh leg or ham, country spareribs, pork tenderloin, Boston butt, ham hocks, picnic ham.

■ **Luxury Cuts:** Crown roast, specialty hams such as prosciutto and Westphalian.

■ **Storage:** For fresh pork, two to four days; raw sausage, five days; bacon and ham, seven days; frozen, four to six months.

A Quick Anatomy Lesson
for the Busy Cook

UNLIKE THE EIGHT primal wholesale cuts that make up the beef carcass, the pig is divided into four primal areas. The hind leg, or **ham**, makes up the largest chunk of the hog carcass. The back, or **loin**, is sold whole or cut into the sirloin end, the center-cut loin, and the blade end. The **belly** contains the spareribs and bacon. The fourth area is the **shoulder** and front leg. The top of the shoulder is called the Boston butt, or Boston shoulder roast, and the arm portion is known as the picnic. Unlike most other meat animals, pork primal cuts are sold in many stores. You can buy a whole ham, fresh or smoked, or a whole loin from old-fashioned pork stores in ethnic neighborhoods and many warehouse clubs. Or you can special-order one from a neighborhood butcher shop.

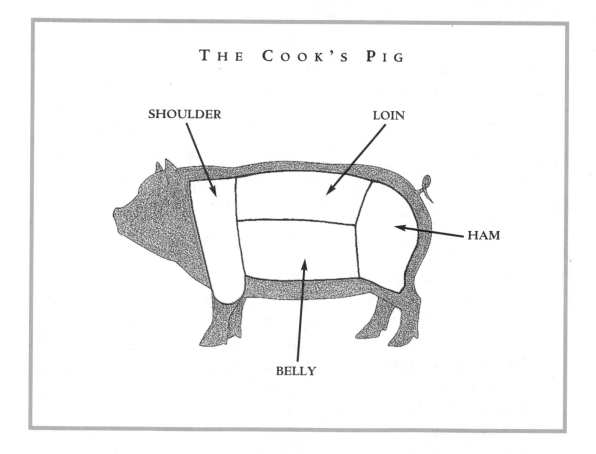

THE COOK'S PIG

SHOULDER

LOIN

HAM

BELLY

Pork Cookery

GENERALLY SPEAKING, the tough, dry pork that is so often encountered on today's tables is not the result of the quality of the meat itself but rather of overcooking. This problem is particularly critical with the leanest and tenderest cuts, so special care must be taken not to overcook pork loin roasts, chops, and tenderloin.

In the old days when pigs were much fattier, the rich and tender meat was very forgiving, staying tasty and juicy even when overcooked to 180°F. Most cookbooks, even some written as late as the 1980s, still tell you to cook pork to these high temperatures.

Unfortunately, leaner cuts like the loin and tenderloin from today's lithe pigs are totally inedible at this high temperature, whether cooked by dry or moist heat. The connective tissue in pork becomes harder and less elastic as its temperature increases to 160°F and above, with the result that it tends to push moisture out of the meat. Hence the all-too-common hard, dry, and chewy pork chop.

TRICHINOSIS

The main reason pork is usually overcooked in America is the fear of the trichinosis parasite. Unfortunately, our government agency responsible for the inspection of pork, the USDA, has neglected to use microscopic or immunological tests for the systematic detection of trichinosis; however, these tests are widely used in European countries. As a consequence, pork processors and consumers have to bear the burden of treating all pork as if it were infected with the trichina worm. Freezing pork at home is not reliable enough to kill trichinae, as some cookbooks say, because home freezers do not consistently get to low enough temperatures to kill the organism.

In reality, though, trichinosis has been almost entirely eradicated in American pork, with only a few cases appearing each year. From 1983 to 1989, there were fewer than 30 cases in the United States, compared to 400 in 1950 alone. Most of the recent incidents have been traced to homegrown pigs that were not inspected or game animals such as bear or wild boar.

DON'T OVERCOOK IT!

Nevertheless, we still need to be cautious, so all pork must be properly cooked for health reasons. But it doesn't have to be incinerated, as many cookbooks would have you do. Trichinae are destroyed at a temperature of 137°F. To be certain, cook the meat to 148°F. This temperature is considered a medium degree of doneness, and the meat is still noticeably pink.

THE OTHER WHITE MEAT
SHOULD END UP SLIGHTLY PINK!

MOST OF US GREW UP hearing our mothers' warnings about undercooked pork: the slightest bit of pink would result in the dreaded trichinosis. And most of our mothers cooked pork to what the cookbooks of the time (and many today) recommended, a gray 180°F.

The overcooking of pork is one of the most pernicious myths of meat cookery and was drummed into a whole generation of cooks. In reality, trichina are killed at 137°F, or medium-rare, and lean cuts such as loin chops and roasts should be taken off the heat at 145° to 150°F, when the meat is slightly pink. Fattier cuts such as the ribs or butt can be roasted or braised to higher temperatures—up to 165°F.

For full flavor and to be sure that the meat is thoroughly done, especially near the bone, pork should be cooked to a final temperature of 150° to 165°F, depending on the cut. For roasts that are allowed to rest for 20 to 30 minutes after leaving the oven, carryover heat will increase the temperature by 5° to 10°F. This means you should actually take a roast out of the oven when it registers 145° to 155°F. Pork cooked to this temperature and allowed to rest to finish cooking may have a faint, pinkish-gray appearance in the center and the juices may be very faintly pink. These colors are perfectly safe; their presence ensures that the pork will be juicy.

Pork chops and smaller lean pieces of pork such as the tenderloin should be cooked to a final temperature at the *lower* end of the range—150° to 155°F (after resting). You can cook larger, fattier roasts such as Boston butt, picnic, and fresh leg of pork to a final temperature at the *higher* end of the range, 155° to 165°F (after a 20-minute rest). To be a consistent and successful cook of pork (and, for that matter, any meat), you *must* purchase a digital instant-read thermometer to take any guesswork out of determining doneness. These thermometers work not only on roasts but also on small pieces of meat.

When you're cooking with moist heat, care must be taken with leaner cuts not to overcook them and dry the meat out. Except for very thick pork loin chops or sirloin chops, moist cooking should be avoided with lean and tender cuts such as tenderloin, since they cook very quickly. Shoulder chops, Boston butt, and shoulder roasts, however, all have sufficient fat so that they can be cooked by moist heat with delicious results.

CHOOSING THE RIGHT CUT

As with beef, the most important factor in getting the right cut is knowing what you wish to make and whether it will be cooked by dry or moist heat. Most cuts can be successfully cooked by dry-heat methods, if care is taken in cooking. Chops and roasts from the loin, leg, and shoulder are all suitable for grilling, broiling, and panfrying as long as they are properly seasoned and not overcooked (see individual recipes for directions). For moist-heat cooking, you need cuts that have ample fat and marbling so that they won't dry out during long cooking. Areas that provide cuts suitable for braising and stewing are the picnic, Boston butt, the blade end of the loin, and the spareribs. Tough cuts such as pig's trotters (feet), hocks, and shanks require long, slow poaching to become tender enough to eat.

GRILLING

Grilling over charcoal or on a gas grill is one of the best ways to cook the most popular cuts such as chops and tenderloins. Pork's mild flavor is deliciously enhanced by smoke from the grill, and the tender meat can be cooked quickly with dry heat. Nonetheless, all the challenges faced when cooking pork by any method are encountered when grilling. In general, we recommend a kettle grill for pork since the heat can be regulated and flare-ups damped down. Most grills are fairly imprecise, and it's difficult to control temperatures and predict cooking times.

GRILL TRICKS

IF YOU'RE USING A COVERED KETTLE barbecue (and we strongly recommend this for pork) and the meat begins to burn, move it off the direct heat, cover the grill, and regulate the vents to control the heat. This indirect method is a bit more like roasting and will take longer, but if you use sugary marinades, it prevents the pork from charring.

If you're not using a kettle barbecue and the meat starts to burn, raise the grill grid so that the meat is farther from the heat source and turn it frequently. Another trick is to have different depths of coals under different parts of the grill (see Grilling, page 63). The areas with thinner layers of charcoal will provide less heat than the thicker layers, so you can move the pieces of meat around to protect them as needed.

Chops cooked to the proper degree of doneness will have a nicely browned surface, with grill marks decoratively crosshatched, if you like to be fancy.

The surface of grilled pork should be crusty and browned, with the juices and seasonings caramelized but not burned or charred. With beefsteaks and lamb chops, it's easy to sear the outside of the meat and leave the inside tender and cooked through, since these meats are usually served rare to medium-rare. For safety reasons, however, we can't leave pork at this stage of doneness, so we have to cook the meat to the medium to medium-well range (145° to 155°F) without burning the surface.

Flavor Steps

For best results, use a dry rub before grilling to enhance the flavors. Juiciness can also be increased by many different marinades. Be judicious, because if the dry rubs or marinades contain sugar or other sweet ingredients such as fruit or ketchup, it's all too easy for the surface of the meat to burn.

Barbecue Sauces and Glazes

If you use a barbecue sauce or glaze that contains sugar or any other sweetening such as molasses or ketchup, do not apply it before or during grilling over direct heat. Brush it on only when the meat is cooked and off the grill or, if you're cooking over indirect heat, for the last few minutes of cooking. If you're wondering why your neighbor Ed's barbecued chicken and spareribs always look (and taste) as if they came out of a blast furnace, this is why—good old Ed likes to slather on the sauce in huge clouds of smoke, sipping his drink and boasting about his barbecuing prowess. If you want your chops to look like Ed's, by all means ladle it on. But if you want juicy and delicious grilled pork (or grilled anything else, for that matter), lay off the sauce, at least until the meat is done.

Fruit Salsas and Glazes, Chutneys, and Condiments

Grilled pork, especially if it's been marinated or highly seasoned with a dry rub, needs no elaborate sauces or accompaniments. But it's delicious with fruit salsas, chutneys of all kinds, glazes, and barbecue sauces. Some of the recipes for pan sauces for pork chops, pork tenderloins, or roast pork loin would be very nice with grilled pork as well.

Grilling Thicker Cuts

The best cuts for grilling are center-cut pork chops, bone-in or boneless, and pork tenderloins that are 1 to 1½ inches thick. These cuts are thick enough to allow for a wider margin of error in timing and will remain juicy. Other pork cuts that can be grilled over direct heat with good results are pork kebabs, baby back ribs, and country-style spareribs and pork steaks cut from the blade end or sirloin end of the loin. Fresh or smoked ham steaks can also be grilled successfully over direct heat, and fully cooked hams, either bone-in or boneless, benefit greatly from grilling with indirect heat.

Grilling Thin Cuts

The most suitable thin cuts for grilling are ¼-to-½-inch-thick boneless pork loin chops or butterflied pork tenderloins, pounded to a ¼-to-½-inch thickness.

Cooking thin cuts requires some skill since there is little margin for error, since they can go from juicy to dried out very quickly on a hot grill. With a little practice, though, you can easily master grilling thin pieces of pork (see How to Cook Thin Pork Chops, page 280). The trick is to concentrate on what you're doing and not get distracted so that you can judge the cooking times carefully.

Roasting on the Grill

A covered kettle grill is ideal for cooking large and/or thick cuts using the indirect method. Technically, this method is really roasting, not grilling, which implies direct heat. But whether you add wood chips or not, pork roasted this way is much more flavorful than when simply baked in the oven. For starters, try cooking a small roast such as pork tenderloin or a 2-to-3-pound piece of pork loin with indirect heat. Flavor the meat first with either a dry rub or brine. With very little effort, you can produce some of the best-tasting pork you've ever eaten. Eventually you may want to roast larger cuts, such as whole racks of center-cut pork loin, fresh or smoked ham, or Boston butts. These are wonderful for company and are no more difficult to cook than small roasts. They simply require a little more time.

BROILING

Broiling is a popular method for cooking tender cuts of pork, but it can present a few problems. Because most home broilers put out insufficient heat, they tend to sweat the meat rather than sear the surface. Their lower than optimal temperatures can cause the juices to ooze out and exacerbate modern lean pork's tendency to dry out during cooking. The best cuts for broiling are the same as those for grilling: pork chops (rib and T-bone, or loin), butterflied pork tenderloin, and pork steaks cut from the Boston shoulder, leg, or sirloin. Ribs can be broiled to crisp the surface, but only after they have been almost fully cooked by baking or parboiling. Broiling can also be used briefly to caramelize a glaze on a pork chop or steak that has been first sautéed.

Broiling Pork Chops

When broiling pork chops, make sure that they are at least ¾ inch thick; 1-to-1½-inch-thick chops are even better. It's hard to control the cooking times of thinner chops and they can easily dry out. Thin chops are far better breaded and panfried or grilled very briefly under a watchful eye (see How to Cook Thin Pork Chops, page 280).

Broiling Pork Tenderloins

To broil pork tenderloins, butterfly them first and watch them carefully so that they don't overcook. In general, you can apply any of the recipes for grilled pork tenderloins, pork chops, and pork steaks to broiling. If you broil the meat 3 to 4 inches from the heat source, the cooking times should be similar to those for grilling. You can use any of the dry rubs, marinades, and brines found in the grilling recipes. As in grilling, be careful not to burn the meat if you're using sweet marinades or glazes.

For best results, use an instant-read meat thermometer when broiling and cook the pork to an internal temperature of 145° to 150°F. Let the meat rest, loosely covered with foil, for 5 minutes or so to distribute the juices and raise the internal temperature before serving.

SAUTÉING

Sautéing is an excellent way to cook pork chops, especially thicker ones (1¼ to 1½ inches thick). The technique is simple: the seasoned chops are cooked in a heavy skillet in a little oil over high heat to sear them on each side, then they are turned while they finish cooking. For thicker chops, we recommend that you cover the pan after the initial searing, lower the heat, and cook until done, usually 6 to 8 minutes, depending on thickness. Use an instant-read meat thermometer to check doneness. Leaner chops such as loin or rib should be removed at about 145°F and should rise to about 150°F after resting.

After the chops have cooked, a little wine or stock can be added to the pan to make a sauce (see Sautéed Pork Chops with Pan Sauce, page 266).

ROASTING

Pork is an ideal meat for roasting—as long as you don't overcook the lean cuts from the loin. To keep them juicy, we recommend searing a loin roast first in a hot oven (400° to 450°F) followed by roasting at a low temperature (300° to 325°F—see Moderate-Temperature Roasting, page 68). This ensures a brown, caramelized exterior and a moist interior. Fattier cuts such as Boston butt and leg can stay juicy when baked at a moderate temperature of 350°F.

To crisp the skin of the leg, you can turn up the heat to 400° to 450°F for the last 10 minutes or so.

BRAISING AND STEWING

Since almost all cuts of pork are tender enough to cook by dry heat, braising in moist heat to tenderize the meat is usually not necessary. Meat cooked in a flavorful liquid even for a brief time, however, will take on the character of the sauce. Pork suitable for braising must contain sufficient intramuscular fat. Unlike tough cuts of beef, which become soft and silky after long cooking, lean pork gets drier and harder as it cooks, eventually falling apart into dry strings. That's because it doesn't contain much collagen, as does beef, but it does have another connective tissue, called elastin, which doesn't dissolve and soften during moist cooking. Instead, it shrinks and gets hard.

The shoulder area has sufficient fat and is ideal for braising. This includes the blade section of the loin adjacent to the Boston butt, the Boston butt, and the picnic. Pork hocks, shanks, and feet are also delicious when braised. Use meat from the shoulder for any pork stew recipe or any recipe that involves the long, moist-heat cooking of pork (see Chinese Red-Cooked Pork, page 357, for example). Spareribs and fresh pork belly can also be delicious braised but can be too fatty for many people's taste.

Pork is often braised in sweet liquids (see Braised Pork Butt with Port and Prunes, page 366) and in broths and stocks with strong flavors (see Pork Adobado, page 286). Like most other braised meat, pork is usually browned first and then simmered in a flavorful broth. Since most pork (except for the shanks) is tender, it takes less time to braise to succulence than other meats.

USING SPICE RUBS OR HERB MARINADES FOR PORK

SPICE RUBS or herb marinades for pork can be used in two ways: (1) to enhance the flavor of the meat but not affect its juiciness or texture; (2) as a light cure to improve the flavor, juiciness, and texture of the chops. If the spice rub or herb marinade is left on the pork for only an hour or two at room temperature or overnight in the refrigerator, it will flavor the pork nicely, but the salt in the rub won't penetrate the meat deeply enough to change its texture. To make it firmer, more tender, and juicy when cooked, the meat must be left in the rub or marinade in the refrigerator for two to four days so that the salt can lightly cure the meat (see page 254 for a discussion of flavor brining).

LESS EXPENSIVE AND DELICIOUS

SOME OF THE LESS EXPENSIVE pork cuts are getting increasingly hard to find in butcher shops and supermarkets because butchers often assume their clientele knows how to cook only the lean cuts like chops, loin, and tenderloin. If you are willing to expand your range, you'll be rewarded with extra-special results. Check out the butchers in the nearest ethnic neighborhood—here on the West Coast we buy a lot of our pork from Chinese stores. Or you should be able to order a fresh ham or pork butt from your neighborhood butcher or market.

PORK LEG OR FRESH HAM

Where it comes from: This is the hind leg of the pig, but fresh, before it is cured and made into what most people think of as "ham." A whole fresh pork leg weighs 15 to 20 pounds and can feed a large gathering. It is also sold in halves as either the shank or butt end. Some clever butchers sell individual muscles such as top round or top sirloin, boned and rolled, as smaller roasts. Thin leg slices can also be used as scallopini or schnitzel.

Why we like it: No pork roast beats the leg for flavor, texture, and just plain pork goodness. We love the robust taste, and if you roast the leg with the skin attached, you'll get irresistible crisp cracklings to munch on. Leftovers make great pork sandwiches. Whole roast leg makes a great center-piece for family feasts such as Christmas or Easter.

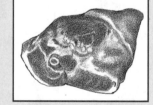

Price: Since very few butchers know how to cut up the leg into smaller roasts, there is not much demand for fresh ham. Most are smoked and marketed as fully cooked ham. Fresh leg of pork is downright cheap when compared with the popular lean cuts like loin—the best pork bargain by far. Getting it, however, can be difficult, and you may need to order this cut ahead.

AKA: Pork leg, leg of pork, fresh ham.

BOSTON SHOULDER ROAST

Where it comes from: The top part of the shoulder includes some of the shoulder blade bone and sometimes a bit of round leg bone. A whole Boston shoulder will weigh 5 to 7 pounds, but it is also sold as half shoulders or boneless Boston shoulder.

Why we like it: Nobody cooks pork better than Chinese chefs, and this is their preferred cut. It has sufficient fat and flavor for both braising and dry roasting, and the rich meat takes well to pungent flavors such as soy sauce, chiles, and ginger.

The shoulder can be braised or roasted well done.

Price: The shoulder is inexpensive to downright cheap, especially on sale. Buy it in quantity when you see it, as it freezes well. It has more waste and external fat than the loin or sirloin but is still a bargain after it is trimmed.

AKA: Boston butt, pork shoulder butt, pork butt.

PICNIC SHOULDER ROAST

Where it comes from: This cut from the arm and foreleg is sometimes sold whole, usually with the bone in. It is also sold in two pieces: the upper arm portion, which is meatier, and the lower foreleg portion, which has a lot of bone, skin, and connective tissue. Usually picnics are sold with some skin attached.

Why we like it: This cut is too tough to be dry-roasted, but its ample fat and skin makes it ideal for braising. The arm area is usually sold bone-in and skinless, while the lower leg portion is sold with the skin on.

Price: Very cheap, although there is a lot of waste, especially if the skin is not something you enjoy. Still, the picnic is worth searching out because the meat takes on a juicy, soft texture when braised and stewed.

AKA: Arm roast.

PORK SHANK

Where it comes from: This is the fore and hind leg from the knee joint to the foot. The feet are cut off and sold separately as pig's feet, or trotters. Shank is usually sold with the skin on. It is often sawed into smaller pieces and smoked to be sold as ham hocks.

Why we like it: Shank meat is tough with lots of connective tissue. It is ideal for long, slow cooking such as braising and poaching. When fully cooked, the shank has an intense flavor and a soft, silky texture—like other shank meat such as lamb or veal (osso buco). It takes well to robust flavors such as sauerkraut and cabbage. The pork shank's large size makes for an impressive presentation.

Price: Shank is cheap, but there is a lot of waste. Figure that you will need about 1 pound per person. Even though the yield is low, the meat is quite rich, so a little actual meat should go a long way.

AKA: Fresh pork hock, pork shin.

Flavor Brining

BRINING PORK BEFORE GRILLING, broiling, sautéing, or roasting is a surefire way to give flavor and juiciness to the meat. This method, which we call flavor brining, to distinguish it from the traditional brining that is done to preserve meat, offers great possibilities to the creative cook. The brine may be sweetened and flavored with honey, molasses, maple sugar or syrup, apple cider, wine, brandy, or beer. Herbs, spices, and fruits may also be added: juniper berries, thyme, bay leaves, pickling spices, chiles, citrus pulp, garlic, aromatic spices, or mustard, to name but a few. All these flavors are carried into the interior of the meat by the process. The most dramatic result of brining is the meat's increased juiciness, however.

It's not necessary to get high levels of salt into brined meat, since the purpose isn't preservation but rather improvement in the texture. Brines used to make Canadian bacon (smoked pork loin) in a commercial smokehouse, for example, will contain one to two cups of salt for each quart of water. The meat is cured in this very salty brine for 6 to 10 days to allow it to absorb the salt and to cure the meat thoroughly so it can be preserved during the cold smoking process. Our recipes for flavor brines, on the other hand, have less than half the minimal level of salt for curing, and the meat soaks in the brine for only a few hours to up to three days, depending on the size and type of meat.

Try brining to see for yourself how marvelous the results are. While long-term, high-salt curing tends to remove water from the meat, the flavor brine actually increases the pork's moisture content and weight.

Be sure that pork chops are at least 1¼ inches thick or, even better, 1½ inches. Take care when brining chops or tenderloins. They can soak up too much of the brine if left too long to cure, becoming overly salty. Timing is critical with these smaller cuts: place the chops or tenderloin in the brine in the refrigerator early in the morning on the day you are going to cook or the night before. After 4 to 6 hours in the brine for chops, 6 to 8 for tenderloin or 2 hours for butterflied tenderloin, and 1 to 3 days for the larger pork loin, take the pork out and panfry a small piece. If the flavor is to your liking, dry off the rest of the pork, wrap it tightly in plastic wrap or foil, and refrigerate it until you are ready to cook. If you would like a more intense flavor, return the pork to the brine to cure longer, up to 24 more hours, then remove the pork from the brine and pat dry. Let the meat come to room temperature before cooking. Grill the pork as described in the master recipes for Grilled Pork Chops (page 264) or Grilled Pork Tenderloin (page 316).

Nancy's Vanilla Brine

Serves 6 to 8
■ FIT FOR COMPANY ■ LOW-FAT

M A S T E R   R E C I P E

N ANCY OAKES, Bruce's wife, uses brines creatively in her San Francisco restaurant, Boulevard. This brine incorporates the wonderful fragrance of vanilla, which melds nicely with pork's sweet flavors.

9 cups hot water

2½ teaspoons pure vanilla extract

½ cup sugar

½ cup kosher salt

2 tablespoons cracked black peppercorns

6 1¼-to-1½-inch-thick center-cut loin pork chops (4-6 pounds total), OR 4 pork tenderloins (1-1¼ pounds each), OR 1 4-to-6-pound piece of boneless pork loin

Stir the hot water, vanilla, sugar, and salt together until the sugar and salt are dissolved. Add the black pepper. Cool to below 45°F in the refrigerator.

Trim any excess external fat from the meat. Submerge the pork in the brine in a large bowl or small crock (make sure the meat stays under the surface during curing by using a heavy plate to weight it down). Refrigerate the pork in the cure. The chops should take 4 to 6 hours in the brine, the tenderloin 6 to 8 hours, and the loin 1 to 2 days. (Bone-in pork can take a day longer in the brine because of the bone, which gives it a larger diameter.) Stir the brine each day and turn the pork occasionally. For cooking instructions, see Grilled Pork Chops (page 264), or Grilled Pork Tenderloin (page 316), or Cured Pork Loin Roasted with Parsnips in Maple-Vanilla Sauce (page 338).

To test brined pork, cut a small piece off the chop, loin, or tenderloin, pat it dry, and panfry it. If the meat is sufficiently salty and flavorful, remove it from the brine and store as above; if not, leave it in the brine and test it again.

Boulevard's Maple Syrup and Apple Cider Brine for Pork

7 cups hot water

½ cup kosher salt

2 cups apple cider

½ cup maple syrup

2 tablespoons coarsely ground black pepper

6 1¼-to-1½-inch-thick center-cut loin pork chops (4-6 pounds total), OR 4 pork tenderloins (1-1¼ pounds each), OR 1 4-to-6-pound piece of boneless pork loin

Serves 6

■ FIT FOR COMPANY ■ LOW-FAT

THIS SWEET-AND-SAVORY brine also hails from Boulevard, Nancy Oakes's popular restaurant. The maple syrup and cider give a real New England autumn flavor to the pork. Serve the meat with baked sweet potatoes and homemade applesauce along with brown bread and a glass of dark ale.

Stir the hot water and salt together until the salt is dissolved. Add the remaining brine ingredients. Cool to at least 45°F in the refrigerator.

Trim any excess external fat from the pork. Refer to the Master Recipe (page 255) for brining directions.

STORAGE TIP

IF YOU'RE NOT READY to cook brined meat after the recommended curing time, remove the meat from the brine, pat it dry, and wrap it in plastic wrap. You can then refrigerate it for a day or two before cooking. It's important that the meat—especially pork tenderloin—doesn't stay in the marinade too long. This soft-textured cut can soak up too much salt and become mushy if left too long in the cure. You can put the tenderloin in brine in the refrigerator the morning of the day you plan to cook it or the night before. Remove it from the brine after about 8 hours and store as described above until cooking.

Honey and Chili Flavor Cure for Pork

Serves 6 to 8

■ FIT FOR COMPANY ■ LOW-FAT

8 cups hot water

½ cup kosher salt

¾ cup honey

1 tablespoon Sriracha (Thai hot chili sauce, see discussion)

1 tablespoon freshly ground black pepper

6 1¼-to-1½-inch-thick center-cut loin pork chops (4-6 pounds total), OR 4 pork tenderloins (1-1¼ pounds each), OR 1 4-to-6-pound piece of pork loin

THE THAI SRIRACHA hot chili sauce called for here is available in Asian groceries or by mail-order (see Sources, page 584). It adds a delicious spicy undertone, but you could substitute 1 tablespoon ketchup and a teaspoon or more of bottled hot sauce.

Stir the hot water and salt together until the salt is dissolved. Add the remaining brine ingredients. Cool to at least 45°F in the refrigerator.

Trim any excess external fat from the pork. Refer to the Master Recipe (page 255) for brining directions.

HOW FLAVOR BRINING WORKS

JANET FLETCHER, a San Francisco food writer and a good friend, summed up what goes on when you flavor-brine pork in an excellent article on the subject in the *San Francisco Chronicle* (March 25, 1998):

> By what mechanism does a little salt water work such magic? "It's our old friend osmosis," says Harold McGee, the Palo Alto specialist in the science of cooking. "If there's more of a diffusible chemical in one place than another, it tries to even itself out."
>
> The muscle absorbs the salt water. There, the salt begins to denature the meat proteins, causing them to unwind and form a matrix that traps the water. And if the brine includes herbs, garlic, juniper berries, or peppercorns, those flavors are trapped in the meat, too. Instead of seasoning on the surface only, as most cooks do, brining carries the seasonings throughout.

Fennel and Mustard Flavor Cure for Pork

8 cups hot water

½ cup kosher salt

½ cup sugar

1 cup Pernod or Anisette

¼ cup Dijon mustard

2 tablespoons crushed fennel seeds

1 tablespoon, more or less, red pepper flakes (optional)

2 tablespoons freshly ground black pepper

6 1¼-to-1½-inch-thick center-cut pork loin chops (4-6 pounds total), OR 4 pork tenderloins (1-1¼ pounds each), OR 1 4-to-6-pound piece of boneless pork loin

Serves 6 to 8

■ FIT FOR COMPANY ■ LOW-FAT

THE FENNEL AND PERNOD add a hint of licorice to this tangy brine. You can increase or decrease the heat level by varying the amount of red pepper flakes, or you can leave them out altogether.

Stir the hot water and salt together until the salt is dissolved. Add the remaining brine ingredients. Cool to at least 45°F in the refrigerator.

Trim any excess external fat from the pork. Refer to the Master Recipe (page 255) for brining directions.

Beer, Chili, and Sage Brine for Pork

Serves 6 to 8
■ FIT FOR COMPANY ■ LOW-FAT

S ERVE THIS SPICY PORK at a Southwestern barbecue with salsa, guacamole, and Black Bean
Salad (page 129).

———————

Stir together the hot water, salt, and sugar until the salt
and sugar are dissolved. Stir in the rest of the brine ingredients. Cool to at least 45°F in the refrigerator.

Trim any excess fat from the pork. Refer to the Master
Recipe (page 255) for brining directions.

5 cups hot water
½ cup kosher salt
½ cup packed light or
   dark brown sugar
3 bottles dark beer
2 tablespoons molasses
1 tablespoon Sriracha
   (Thai hot chili sauce)
   or to taste (optional)
1 tablespoon cracked
   black peppercorns
2 teaspoons dried sage
¼ cup peeled garlic cloves

6 1¼-to-1½-inch-thick
   center-cut loin pork
   chops (4-6 pounds
   total), OR 4 pork
   tenderloins (1-1¼
   pounds each), OR 1
   4-to-6-pound piece
   of boneless pork loin

How to Choose Pork Chops,
Steaks, and Cutlets

JUST AS WITH OTHER MEATS, the best pork chops are cut from the loin and ribs. **Rib chops**, cut from the rib section of the loin, have a large eye of rib meat and the upper part of the rib bone attached. **Loin chops** (from the back) have a T-bone shape and include the loin muscle and some of the ultratender tenderloin. We prefer rib pork chops to loin chops because they have a little more fat and thus less chance of drying out during cooking. Both rib and loin chops should be cut 1¼ to 1½ inches thick; thinner chops tend to cook too quickly. These chops are best cooked by dry heat (grilling, broiling, or panfrying), although if you are careful, you may be able to brown thick pork chops in the pan and then finish off the cooking by braising briefly in a little wine or stock. Both rib and loin chops are also sold as boneless pork chops.

Sirloin pork chops, cut from the sirloin end of the loin, near the hip, are an intermediate cut with more bones than rib or loin chops but with comparable flavor and tenderness. They are delicious when brined or marinated. Like rib and loin chops, they should be cut 1¼ to 1½ inches thick. Sirloin chops should be cooked in moist heat for only a short period because they can easily dry out. Thinly sliced pork cutlets come from the sirloin end of the leg and are often sold as **pork scallops** or **scallopini**. They can be substituted for Wiener schnitzel in any recipe (see How to Cook Thin Pork Chops, page 280). Try to buy scallopini that do not show any connective tissue.

The blade (or chuck) end of the loin, near the shoulder, yields **blade pork chops**, which have a little more fat than rib or loin chops. Since these chops have several muscles and contain more connective tissue, they can be chewy, but they are still tasty when cooked by dry heat. Their flavor and tenderness can be much improved by marinating. They also have enough fat to withstand brining without drying out. **Butterflied or split blade chops**, commonly sold as **country-style ribs**, are an inexpensive, versatile cut that can be grilled, broiled, or braised.

For best results with chops from the rib, loin, or sirloin, we recommend flavor brining (see page 254), which provides flavorful and very juicy chops. As with all lean pork, these chops are best cooked only until lightly pink in the center, 145° to 155°F.

Often when you order "pork chops" in a Chinese restaurant, you will get slices cut from the **Boston butt**. The butt, which is the equivalent of the shoulder chuck in other meat animals, provides some of the best meat on the

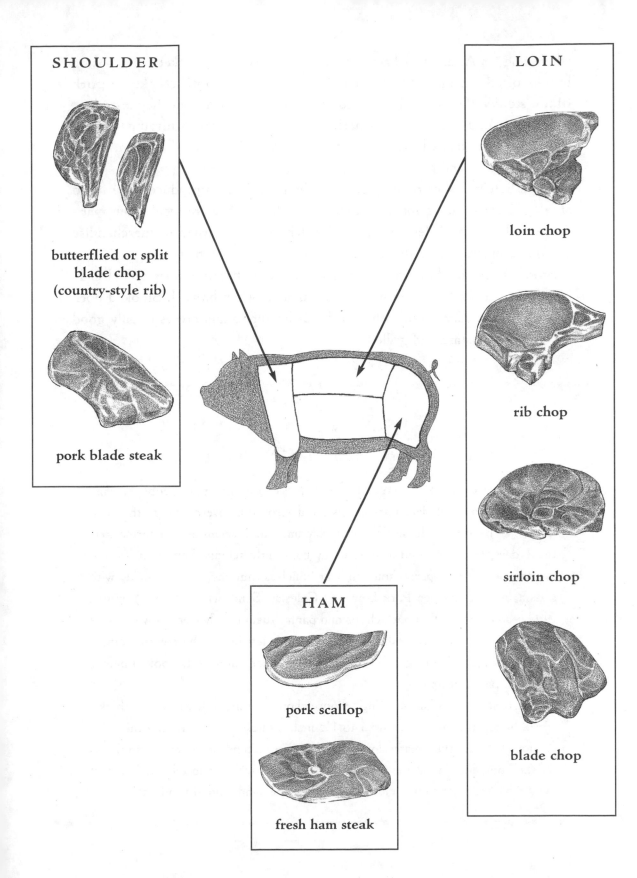

SHOULDER

butterflied or split
blade chop
(country-style rib)

pork blade steak

LOIN

loin chop

rib chop

sirloin chop

blade chop

HAM

pork scallop

fresh ham steak

whole hog, as Asian chefs have long known. In Western markets, the Boston butt is often cut into ½-to-¾-inch slices and sold as **pork steaks** or **pork blade steaks**. These can be cooked by dry or moist heat, but they taste best when marinated in a dry or wet marinade before grilling or panfrying. Or you can remove the blade bone, pound the meat to a thickness of ⅜ inch, bread the pork cutlet, and panfry it.

Some butchers slice round pieces off the fresh ham to produce **fresh ham steaks**. Treat these as you would any pork chop. They are ideal when marinated and grilled. A few enlightened butchers have learned to merchandise individual muscles from the leg such as top round and top sirloin.

Smoked pork chops are also delicious and, because they are already brined and cooked, they do not dry out quickly when braised. Smoked pork chops go particularly well with sauerkraut or apples and are especially good coated with mustard and grilled.

PORK CHOPS THAT DON'T TASTE LIKE STYROFOAM

NO CUT OF TODAY'S LEANER PORK presents more problems than chops. Modern pork chops are destroyed by overcooking—the meat becomes a dense slab of Styrofoam. And it seems as if supermarkets these days have conspired against us by constantly selling chops that are cut too thin to cook properly. You can sear boneless thin chops very quickly with satisfactory results (see Pork Loin and Coleslaw Sandwich, page 310) or you can bread or batter thin pork chops and panfry them briefly (see How to Cook Thin Pork Chops, page 280). But if the bone is left in and the meat is thin, it is next to impossible to get the meat near the bone sufficiently cooked before the main part dries out.

For best results when sautéing, choose chops that are at least ¾ inch thick. Even better, use chops that are 1 to 1½ inches thick. Make sure that they are uniformly thick, since many sloppy butchers have a tendency to cut them thick at the bone and thin at the periphery. Reject such chops and tell the butcher why. You are paying good money and should demand a good product.

HERB RUB FOR PORK, LAMB, OR BEEF

Makes ½ cup

THIS FLAVORFUL RUB can be used on grilled pork chops and grilled pork tenderloin. It's also delicious on grilled lamb chops and rack, shoulder, or leg of lamb, and grilled steak.

2   tablespoons chopped fresh basil or 2 teaspoons dried

2   teaspoons chopped fresh thyme or 1 teaspoon dried

1   tablespoon chopped fresh rosemary or 2 teaspoons dried

1   tablespoon chopped fresh oregano or 2 teaspoons dried

1   tablespoon crushed fennel seeds

1   teaspoon ground coriander

2   teaspoons garlic powder or granulated garlic

2   tablespoons salt

2   teaspoons coarsely ground black pepper

Mix all the ingredients in a small bowl. If you use dried herbs, the rub will keep at room temperature in a sealed jar for up to 2 months. If it's made with any or all fresh herbs, it will keep, sealed, in the refrigerator for about 2 weeks.

Grilled Pork Chops

Dry rub, marinade, or
brine of your choice
(see Seasoning Chart,
page 577)

4 1¼-to-1½-inch-thick
pork chops, preferably
center-cut rib chops, fat
trimmed to ¼ inch

Serves 4
■ IN A HURRY ■ LOW-FAT

MASTER RECIPE

PORK CHOPS, either bone-in or boneless, are the ideal cut of meat for grilling. They take well to marinades (dry and wet) and brines. Chops can be cooked quickly and easily on the grill without charring or under-cooking, and they can be served with a host of sauces and condiments.

By varying your choice of spice and herb rubs and marinades, you can prepare a wide range of differently flavored pork chops using the techniques described in the following pages. Use your own taste and imagination to pair an appropriate condiment or sauce with your favorite spice rub or marinade.

For some of the most succulent and juicy grilled pork chops ever, try brining the chops for three to six hours in one of the recommended brines (see pages 255-59 and the Seasoning Chart, page 577). For a smoky undertone, add 2 cups soaked hickory or oak chips or chunks to the fire just before grilling.

We recommend grilling pork chops in a covered kettle barbecue so you can control the flaming better than on an open grill. You can also use a gas grill with a lid. If flaming occurs under the chops, move them out of the flames and finish by indirect cooking (see Grilling, page 63).

■ **Flavor Step** ■ Coat the chops generously with a dry rub or soak in a marinade for at least 2 hours at room temperature or overnight in the refrigerator. Let refrigerated meat come to room temperature while you build the fire. If you used a wet marinade, pat the chops with paper towels to dry. Or, if you're brining the chops, allow 3 to 4 hours in the refrigerator for ¾-to-1-inch chops and 4 to 6 hours for 1¼-to-1½-inch chops. Remove the chops from the brine before cooking, pat them dry, and let them come to room temperature.

To cook using a kettle barbecue: Build a charcoal fire and spread the coals so that some areas are thicker to provide more intense heat and others have a thinner layer to provide less heat. It's also a good idea to leave part of the grill rack with no charcoal underneath so that you can use the indirect method if necessary. If you are using hardwood chips, follow the directions in the Grilling section on page 63.

When the fire is ready, put the chops directly over the hottest area of the coals. If any flaming occurs, immediately cover the grill with the lid. Sear the chops for 1½ minutes on each side. If flaming continues, move the chops to an area of the grill with less intense heat.

After the chops have been seared, move them, if you haven't already, to a cooler section of the grill. Cover with the lid and cook for 4 to 6 minutes per side, or until they reach an internal temperature of 145° to 150°F. Thicker chops will take longer, thinner ones less time.

To cook using a gas grill: Preheat both sides of the grill for 20 minutes. Shut off one side of the grill when you add the chops. Sear the chops over direct heat for 1½ minutes per side, then transfer to the area of the grill with no flame under it. Cover the grill and cook over indirect heat for 4 to 7 minutes per side, or until the chops reach an internal temperature of 145° to 150°F.

When the chops have reached the desired temperature, remove them from the grill, cover loosely with foil, and let them rest for 5 minutes or so before serving. You may serve them as is or with a condiment or sauce.

Sautéed Pork Chops with Pan Sauce

■ Flavor Step ■

Spice Rub for Pork or
Beef (page 375), OR
Herb Rub for Pork,
Lamb, or Beef
(page 263), OR salt
and freshly ground
black pepper

4 1¼-to-1½-inch-thick
center-cut loin pork
chops, either rib or
T-bone, trimmed
of external fat

1 tablespoon olive oil

MASTER PAN SAUCE
(OPTIONAL)

2 teaspoons finely
chopped garlic

½ cup dry white wine
or dry vermouth

½ cup chicken or beef
stock

1 teaspoon chopped fresh
herbs, such as sage,
rosemary, thyme,
savory, or dill or
½ teaspoon dried
Salt and freshly ground
black pepper to taste

Serves 4
■ IN A HURRY ■ LOW-FAT

MASTER RECIPE

THIS RECIPE and the variations that follow are designed for tender chops cut from the center of the pork loin, rib chops (the best in our opinion), and T-bone chops. The key to successfully cooking center-cut pork chops is not to overcook them. To tell if they are properly cooked, follow our guidelines and timing instructions, and measure the internal temperature of the pork with an instant-read thermometer. For best results and flavor, the internal temperature of these chops should reach 150°F but go no higher than 155°F. Pork cooked to these temperatures is medium to medium-well; it will still have a faint pink tinge and be perfectly safe to eat (the parasite that causes trichinosis is killed at 137°F). If the chops get away from you and reach 160° or even 165°F, they will still most likely be juicy enough to eat, although not ideal. Ignore all cookbooks that tell you to cook pork to 180°F. Pork cooked to this temperature, unless it is quite fatty, like spareribs or belly, is totally inedible.

The Master Recipe can be easily varied in three ways: by changing the herbs and spices used in the flavor step; by changing the liquids, herbs, and spices used in the pan sauce; or by adding fruits, vegetables, or garnishes. Follow the directions for the Master Recipe, using the variations on pages 268-79.

■ **Flavor Step** ■ If using the spice or herb rub, coat the chops generously and let marinate for up to 2 hours at room temperature or overnight in the refrigerator. Let refrigerated meat come to room temperature before cooking. If you used a rub, scrape off any excess and pat the chops dry. If not, season the chops generously on both sides with salt and pepper.

In a large, heavy skillet, heat the oil over high heat. When the pan is hot enough to sear the chops but not burn them, add the chops. They should make a gentle hissing sound when they hit the pan, not an explosive sputter. Adjust the heat if the pan seems too hot or remove the pan from the heat for 30 seconds or so (count this time as part of the overall cooking time). Sear the chops on one side for 1 to 2 minutes, or until beginning to brown lightly. Turn the chops over and sear for 1 minute more.

Reduce the heat so that the chops continue to sizzle—do not turn the heat so low that there are no more sizzling sounds; if the heat is too low, the chops will sweat and juices will exude from the meat and leave it dry. Cover the pan and cook for 3 to 4 more minutes, depending on how thick the chops are. Turn and cook them for 3 to 4 minutes more on the other side. The chops are done when the meat is firm but not hard when pressed with a finger. Better still, test them with an instant-read thermometer—the meat should measure 145° to 155°F and will still be acceptable at 160°F. For the juiciest results, remove the chops from the pan when they register 145°F, cover loosely with foil, and let them rest for 5 minutes or so before serving, to stabilize the juices. After resting they should read 150°F. At this point, you can serve the chops as is or you can make a quick pan sauce.

To make the Pan Sauce: Pour off all but about 1 tablespoon of fat from the pan, leaving any meat juices. Adjust the heat to medium and put in the garlic. Stir and cook for 30 seconds, then add the remaining ingredients, scraping up any browned bits from the bottom of the pan. Bring the sauce to a boil and reduce it over high heat until it just turns syrupy. Put the pork chops back into the pan and turn them several times in the sauce to transfer the flavors. This should take no more than 30 seconds—do not cook the chops in the sauce. Serve the chops with the sauce.

Sautéed Pork Chops with Wilted Greens, Pine Nuts, and Raisins

■ Flavor Step ■
(See Master Recipe,
page 266)

4 1¼-to-1½-inch-thick
center-cut loin pork
chops, either rib or
T-bone, trimmed
of external fat
1 tablespoon olive oil

PAN SAUCE AND GREENS
1 tablespoon olive oil
2 ounces pancetta, diced
(optional)
¼ cup finely chopped onion
2 tablespoons chopped
garlic
¼ cup chicken or beef stock
4 cups spinach leaves
(about 2 bunches)
4 cups coarsely chopped
curly endive, or
Chinese mustard
greens, without stems
(about 2 bunches)
¼ cup golden raisins or
sultanas, steeped in
boiling water for 5
minutes and drained
1 tablespoon white wine
vinegar
¼ cup lightly toasted
pine nuts (see Note,
page 121)
Salt and freshly ground
black pepper

Serves 4
■ IN A HURRY

■ Flavor Step ■ Coat the chops and sauté as directed in the Master Recipe. Remove the chops from the pan and keep them warm.

To make the Pan Sauce and Greens: Pour off all the fat from the pan. Add the olive oil to the pan and heat over medium heat. If you are using the pancetta, sauté it for 5 minutes, stirring often. Remove the pancetta and set it aside; pour off all but 1 tablespoon of the fat. Sauté the onion and garlic in the olive oil or in the remaining tablespoon of fat for about 5 minutes, until the onion is soft. Stir in the stock, scraping up any browned bits from the bottom of the pan, and add both kinds of greens. Cover the pan and cook until the greens are wilted, 3 to 4 minutes. Stir in the raisins and cook for 1 more minute. Stir in the white wine vinegar and toss the greens to coat them well. Add the pine nuts and the pancetta, if you used it, and toss well in the sauce. Taste for salt and pepper. Serve the chops on the greens.

Sautéed Pork Chops with Vermouth and Mustard Sauce

Serves 4
■ In a Hurry

■ **Flavor Step** ■ Coat the chops and sauté as directed in the Master Recipe on page 266. Remove the chops from the pan and keep them warm.

To make the Pan Sauce: Pour off all but about 1 tablespoon of the fat from the pan. Add the garlic and onions, cover the pan, and cook over medium heat for 5 minutes, stirring occasionally. Sprinkle with salt and pepper and the thyme. Stir in the sherry, vermouth, tomato paste, and both mustards, scraping up any browned bits from the bottom of the pan. Cook the sauce over high heat, stirring often, to reduce it almost to a syrup. Remove the pan from the heat and stir in the optional sour cream. Pour the sauce over the chops and serve.

■ **Flavor Step** ■
1 teaspoon finely chopped fresh thyme or
½ teaspoon dried
Salt and freshly ground black pepper

4 1¼-to-1½-inch-thick center-cut loin pork chops, either rib or T-bone, trimmed of external fat
1 tablespoon olive oil

PAN SAUCE
2 teaspoons finely chopped garlic
1 cup finely chopped onions
Salt and freshly ground black pepper
1 teaspoon chopped fresh thyme or
½ teaspoon dried
1 cup dry sherry
½ cup dry vermouth
1 tablespoon tomato paste
1 teaspoon Dijon mustard
1 teaspoon coarse-grained mustard
½ cup low-fat or regular sour cream (optional)

Sautéed Pork Chops with Green Olives, Artichokes, and Lemon Sauce

■ Flavor Step ■

½ teaspoon ground fennel
   seeds (use a mortar and
   pestle or spice grinder)
   Salt and freshly ground
   black pepper

4 1¼-to-1½-inch-thick
   center-cut loin pork
   chops, either rib or
   T-bone, trimmed of
   external fat
1 tablespoon olive oil

PAN SAUCE

½ cup dry white wine
   or dry vermouth
½ cup chicken or beef
   stock
1 teaspoon chopped
   fresh rosemary
1 teaspoon ground fennel
   seeds (see above)
1 cup frozen artichoke
   hearts, thawed and
   quartered
½ cup seeded and diced
   fresh or canned Italian-
   style tomatoes
¼ cup pitted small green
   French or Italian olives
2 tablespoons fresh
   lemon juice
   Salt and freshly ground
   black pepper

Serves 4

■ IN A HURRY ■ FIT FOR COMPANY

■ Flavor Step ■ Coat the chops and sauté as directed in the Master Recipe on page 266. Remove the chops from the pan and keep them warm.

To make the Pan Sauce: Pour off all the fat from the pan. Add the wine or vermouth and stock, rosemary, and fennel seeds, scraping up any browned bits from the bottom of the pan. Reduce the sauce over high heat until it just turns syrupy, then stir in the artichokes, tomatoes, olives, and lemon juice. Cook for 1 more minute to warm everything through. Taste for salt and pepper and serve the sauce over the chops.

Sautéed Pork Chops Normandy Style

Serves 4

■ IN A HURRY ■ FIT FOR COMPANY

SEE THE PHOTOGRAPH ON PAGE 24.

■ **Flavor Step** ■ Coat the chops and sauté as directed in the Master Recipe on page 266. Remove the chops from the pan and keep them warm.

To make the Pan Sauce: Pour off all but 1 tablespoon of the fat from the pan. Sauté the onion, covered, over medium heat for 4 minutes, stirring often. Add the apple slices and cook for 2 minutes more, stirring occasionally. Put in the chicken stock, cider, Calvados or apple brandy, mustard, and ginger, scraping up any browned bits from the bottom of the pan. Add the heavy cream. Reduce the sauce over high heat until it is almost a syrup. Pour the sauce over the chops and serve.

■ Flavor Step ■

½ teaspoon dried sage
  Salt and freshly ground
  black pepper

4 1¼-to-1½-inch-thick
  center-cut loin pork
  chops, either rib or
  T-bone, trimmed
  of external fat
1 tablespoon olive oil

PAN SAUCE

½ cup thinly sliced onion
1 tart apple, peeled, cored,
  and thinly sliced
½ cup chicken stock
¼ cup hard or non-
  alcoholic apple cider
2 tablespoons Calvados
  or apple brandy
2 teaspoons Dijon mustard
  Pinch of ground ginger
¼ cup heavy cream

Sautéed Pork Chops in Tangy Orange Sauce

■ Flavor Step ■
Spice Rub for Pork or
Beef (page 375), OR
Herb Rub for Pork,
Lamb, or Beef
(page 263), OR salt
and freshly ground
black pepper

4 1¼-to-1½-inch-thick
center-cut loin pork
chops, either rib or
T-bone, trimmed
of external fat

1 tablespoon olive oil

PAN SAUCE
½ cup finely chopped
onion

1 cup chicken stock

¾ cup fresh orange juice

1 tablespoon fresh
lemon juice

1 tablespoon orange
marmalade

2 teaspoons arrowroot or
cornstarch, dissolved
in 2 tablespoons cold
water (optional)

Serves 4
■ IN A HURRY ■ LOW-FAT

■ Flavor Step ■ Coat the chops and sauté as directed in
the Master Recipe on page 266. Remove the chops from the
pan and keep them warm.

To make the Pan Sauce: Pour off all but 1 tablespoon of
the fat from the cooking pan. Sauté the onion, covered, over
medium heat for 3 minutes, stirring often. Stir in the remaining ingredients, scraping up any browned bits from the bottom of the pan, and boil the sauce for 2 to 3 minutes, or until
reduced to about 1½ cups. If you prefer a thicker sauce,
whisk in the arrowroot or cornstarch mixture just before serving. Pour the sauce over the chops and serve.

Sautéed Pork Chops in Spicy Gingersnap Gravy

Serves 4
■ In a Hurry

■ **Flavor Step** ■ Coat the chops and sauté as directed in the Master Recipe on page 266. Remove the chops from the pan and keep them warm.

To make the Spicy Gingersnap Gravy: Pour off all but 1 tablespoon of the fat from the pan. Put in the onion and celery and cook over medium heat, stirring to scrape up any browned bits from the bottom of the pan, until soft, about 5 minutes. Stir in the stock, cider vinegar, cayenne, and thyme and bring to a boil. Stir in the crumbled gingersnaps and cook, stirring often, until the sauce thickens to the consistency of heavy cream. If it seems too thick, dilute it with a little more stock. Pour the sauce over the chops and serve.

■ **Flavor Step** ■
Spice Rub for Pork or
Beef (page 375)

4 1¼-to-1½-inch-thick
  center-cut loin pork
  chops, either rib or
  T-bone, trimmed
  of external fat
1 tablespoon olive oil

SPICY GINGERSNAP GRAVY
½ cup finely chopped
  onion
¼ cup finely chopped
  celery
1 cup chicken or beef
  stock, or more if
  necessary
1 tablespoon cider vinegar
¼ teaspoon cayenne pepper
¼ teaspoon dried thyme
4 gingersnaps, crumbled

Sautéed Pork Chops with Maple Bourbon Sauce

■ **Flavor Step** ■
Spice Rub for Pork or
Beef (page 375), OR
Herb Rub for Pork,
Lamb, or Beef
(page 263), OR salt
and freshly ground
black pepper

4 1¼-to-1½-inch-thick
center-cut loin pork
chops, either rib or
T-bone, trimmed
of external fat

1 tablespoon olive oil

PAN SAUCE

½ cup finely chopped
onion

½ cup chicken stock

¼ cup bourbon whiskey

1 tablespoon cider vinegar

1 tablespoon maple syrup
Pinch each ground
ginger and nutmeg

2 teaspoons cornstarch
dissolved in 2
tablespoons cold water
(optional)
Salt and freshly ground
black pepper

Serves 4
■ IN A HURRY ■ LOW-FAT

THIS SAUCE is also excellent with grilled pork chops, smoked pork chops, ham steaks, and brined pork chops (pages 255-59).

———————

■ **Flavor Step** ■ Coat the chops (omit for smoked pork chops and ham steaks) and sauté as directed in the Master Recipe on page 266. Remove the chops from the pan and keep warm.

To make the Pan Sauce: Pour off all but 1 tablespoon of the fat and add the onion. Cook for 3 minutes, covered, over medium heat, stirring occasionally. Stir in the stock, bourbon, vinegar, syrup, and spices, scraping up any browned bits from the bottom of the pan. Boil the sauce for 2 to 3 minutes. It should not become syrupy, but will have an intense flavor nonetheless. If you prefer a thicker sauce, whisk in the cornstarch just before serving. Taste for salt and pepper, pour the sauce over the chops, and serve.

Sautéed Pork Chops with Sweet Apple and Mustard Sauce

Serves 4
■ In a Hurry ■ Fit for Company

THIS SWEET AND TANGY SAUCE can be put together in no time at all and is a real crowd pleaser.

■ **Flavor Step** ■ Coat the chops and sauté as directed in the Master Recipe on page 266. Remove the chops from the pan and keep them warm.

To make the Pan Sauce: Pour off all but 1 tablespoon of the fat from the pan, leaving any meat juices. Adjust the heat to medium and put in the garlic. Stir and cook for 30 seconds. Add the apple juice and the dried apples, scraping up any browned bits from the bottom of the pan. Boil the sauce for 3 minutes and then whisk in the apple jelly, mustard, and cream. Continue to boil until the sauce begins to turn syrupy. Pour over the pork chops and serve.

■ **Flavor Step** ■
Spice Rub for Pork or Beef (page 375), OR Herb Rub for Pork, Lamb, or Beef (page 263), OR salt and freshly ground black pepper

4 1¼-to-1½-inch-thick center-cut loin pork chops, either rib or T-bone, trimmed of external fat
1 tablespoon olive oil

PAN SAUCE
2 teaspoons finely chopped garlic
½ cup apple juice or cider
¼ cup sliced dried apples
1 tablespoon apple jelly
2 tablespoons Dijon mustard
¼ cup heavy cream

Sautéed Pork Chops with Onion and Mustard Sauce

■ Flavor Step ■

½ teaspoon chopped fresh
   or dried dill or
   rosemary

½ teaspoon dry mustard,
   preferably Colman's

½ teaspoon salt

½ teaspoon freshly ground
   black pepper

4 1¼-to-1½-inch-thick
   center-cut loin pork
   chops, either rib or
   T-bone, trimmed
   of external fat

1 tablespoon olive oil

PAN SAUCE

1 cup thinly sliced onions

½ cup white wine or dry
   vermouth

1 tablespoon coarse or
   smooth Dijon mustard

½ teaspoon chopped fresh
   or dried dill or
   rosemary

¼ cup low-fat or regular
   sour cream

Serves 4

■ IN A HURRY ■ MOM'S COMFORT FOOD

THIS PREPARATION IS SO TASTY that you'll have a hard time making pork chops any other way.

■ Flavor Step ■ Coat the chops and sauté as directed in the Master Recipe on page 266. Remove the chops from the pan and keep them warm.

To make the Pan Sauce: Pour off all but 1 tablespoon of the fat from the pan and add the onions. Sauté for 5 minutes and stir in the wine or vermouth, Dijon mustard, and herbs, scraping up any browned bits from the bottom of the pan. Boil the sauce for a minute or two until it begins to turn syrupy. Remove the pan from the heat and stir in the sour cream. Pour the sauce over the chops and serve.

Sautéed Pork Chops with White Wine and Vanilla Sauce

Serves 4

■ IN A HURRY ■ FIT FOR COMPANY

VANILLA COMPLEMENTS PORK nicely and adds a delicious aroma and mysterious flavor to the sauce. This sauce is particularly good with Grilled Pork Chops (page 264) cured with Nancy's Vanilla Brine (page 255) as well. Butter swirled into the sauce just before serving is optional but does bring out the flavor of the vanilla.

Season the chops with salt and pepper and sauté as directed in the Master Recipe on page 266, using the mixture of butter and oil in the pan. Remove the chops from the pan and keep them warm.

To make the Pan Sauce: Pour off all but 1 tablespoon of the fat from the pan and add the shallots. Cook them for 3 minutes, covered. Stir in the wine, stock, apple cider, and vanilla, scraping up any browned bits from the bottom of the pan. Boil the sauce for 2 to 3 minutes, until it is almost reduced to a syrup. If you want a rich, velvety sauce, swirl in a tablespoon of butter at the end. Pour the sauce over the chops and serve.

4 1¼-to-1½-inch-thick center-cut loin pork chops, either rib or T-bone, trimmed of external fat

Salt and freshly ground black pepper
1 tablespoon butter plus 1 tablespoon oil

PAN SAUCE
1 tablespoon finely chopped shallots
¼ cup white wine
½ cup chicken stock
1 tablespoon apple cider
½ teaspoon pure vanilla extract
1 tablespoon butter (optional)

Sautéed Pork Chops with Middle Eastern Apricot Sauce

4 1¼-to-1½-inch-thick
   center-cut loin pork
   chops, either rib or
   T-bone, trimmed
   of external fat
1 tablespoon olive oil

■ Flavor Step ■

½ teaspoon curry powder
   Salt and freshly ground
   black pepper

4 1¼-to-1½-inch-thick
   center-cut loin pork
   chops, either rib or
   T-bone, trimmed
   of external fat

PAN SAUCE

½ cup chopped onion
¼ teaspoon turmeric
¼ teaspoon ground ginger
¼ teaspoon ground
   coriander
   Pinch of ground
   cinnamon
¾ cup chicken stock
½ cup dried apricots,
   cut into strips
½ teaspoon sugar
   Salt and freshly ground
   black pepper

Serves 4
■ IN A HURRY ■ LOW-FAT

THIS DISH HAS HINTS of the flavors of North Africa and goes particularly well with couscous, bulgur wheat, or basmati rice.

■ **Flavor Step** ■ Coat the chops with the curry powder, salt, and pepper. Sauté as directed in the Master Recipe on page 266. Remove the chops from the pan and keep them warm.

To make the Pan Sauce: Pour off all but 1 tablespoon of the fat from the pan and sauté the onion for about 5 minutes, or until soft. Add the spices and cook for 1 minute, stirring to make sure the onion is well coated. Add the stock, apricots, and sugar, scraping up any browned bits from the bottom of the pan. Simmer the sauce until it just begins to turn syrupy. Taste for salt and pepper. Pour the sauce over the chops and serve.

Sautéed Pork Chops with Pineapple

Serves 4

■ IN A HURRY ■ LOW-FAT

YOU CAN USE FRESH or canned pineapple here along with the juice from the canned pineapple or orange juice. The sauce is also excellent with flavor-brined Grilled Pork Chops (page 264), smoked pork chops, or ham.

Season the chops with salt and pepper and sauté as directed in the Master Recipe on page 266. Remove the chops from the pan and keep them warm.

To make the Pan Sauce: Pour off all but 1 tablespoon of the fat from the pan and cook the onion, covered, over medium heat for 5 minutes, stirring occasionally. Add the stock, juice, and pineapple, scraping up any browned bits from the bottom of the pan. Boil the sauce down for 3 minutes. Thicken it slightly by whisking in the cornstarch just before serving. Pour over the chops and serve.

4 1¼-to-1½-inch-thick center-cut loin pork chops, either rib or T-bone, trimmed of external fat
Salt and freshly ground black pepper
1 tablespoon olive oil

PAN SAUCE
½ cup finely chopped onion
½ cup chicken stock
½ cup pineapple or orange juice
½ cup chopped pineapple
1 teaspoon cornstarch dissolved in 1 tablespoon cold water

How to Cook Thin Pork Chops

Salt and freshly ground
black pepper OR dry
rub of your choice
(see Seasoning Chart,
page 577)

4-6 ¼-to-½-inch-thick center-
    cut pork chops, bone-in
    or boneless, trimmed of
    external fat
1 cup flour
1 cup soft bread crumbs
    (from day-old bread)
    OR ¾ cup *panko*
    (Japanese bread
    crumbs)
1 large egg, lightly beaten
    with 1 tablespoon water
    Vegetable oil for
    panfrying
    Lemon wedges for
    garnish

Serves 4
■ IN A HURRY

FOR THE BEST RESULTS, we recommend breading thin pork chops before frying them quickly in hot oil. Breading serves two purposes: it provides a layer of insulation to protect the meat during rapid cooking, and it creates a crust to help keep in the juices. Once breaded and panfried, these thin pork chops taste a lot like Wiener schnitzel and can be used as a cheaper stand-in for veal. We prefer to use soft bread crumbs from day-old bread or the Japanese bread crumbs, *panko,* instead of packaged dried bread crumbs, although they will produce good results too. (*Panko* can be used anywhere bread crumbs are called for; these fine crumbs are wonderful as a breading for fish, chicken, or meat.) Instead of breading, you can use a flavorful paste such as Adobo Marinade (page 286).

■ **Flavor Step** ■ Salt and pepper the chops well or season them with a spice or herb rub.

Place the flour in a shallow pan or plate and put the bread crumbs in another shallow plate or pan. Dredge each chop well in the flour, shaking off any excess. Then dip each chop into the egg, making sure both sides are well coated. Shake off any excess egg and coat each chop on both sides in the bread crumbs, patting them onto the meat. Lay the chops on waxed paper.

Heat about ⅛ to ¼ inch of oil in a 10-to-12-inch nonstick skillet over medium-high heat. Fry the chops until golden on one side, 2 to 3 minutes, then turn and fry on the other for 2 to 3 minutes more. The chops should be faintly pink in the center with a little more pink showing near the bone. Serve them garnished with lemon wedges.

Braised Pork Chops, Steaks, and Other Slabs o' Pork

Serves 4

■ IN A HURRY ■ COOKING ON A BUDGET

MASTER RECIPE

SINCE MANY CUTS OF PORK these days are extremely lean, especially center-cut chops and tenderloin, care must be taken not to dry out and toughen them, even with a short braising period. If you want to braise these leaner cuts, make sure that they're at least 1¼ inches thick or, better, 1½ inches, to give a wide margin of error for the internal temperature. Remove them from the braising liquid when the internal temperature reaches the range of 150° to 155°F and keep them warm while you finish the sauce.

The best cuts for braising for a short time are those that contain enough fat to keep them from drying out if slightly overcooked. These cuts include those from the blade end of the pork loin, usually called blade chops. Steaks cut from the Boston butt, called pork blade steaks, country spareribs (really butterflied blade end chops), fresh ham steaks, and most other slabs of pork also braise well. Depending on the cut you use and the thickness of the meat, cooking times will vary, but in general try not to exceed an internal temperature of 165° to 170°F when braising these fattier cuts.

■ **Flavor Step** ■ Trim the excess external fat from the pork and season well with the spice rub or salt and pepper. If you're using a rub, for more flavor, marinate the pork for 2 hours at room temperature or overnight, wrapped, in the refrigerator. If the meat is refrigerated, bring it to room temperature before cooking.

■ Flavor Step ■

Dry rub of your choice (see Seasoning Chart, page 577) OR salt and freshly ground black pepper

4 1¼-to-1½-inch-thick center-cut pork chops, OR four ¾-to-1-inch-thick pork blade chops, steaks, or shoulder steaks, OR 8 country-style spareribs, OR 2 fresh ham steaks

1 tablespoon olive oil, or more if necessary

PAN SAUCE

Choose a sauce from any of the ones for Sautéed Pork Chops with Pan Sauce (pages 268-79) or Roasted Pork Tenderloin (page 322)

Heat the oil over high heat in a heavy skillet large enough to hold all the pork (or cook the meat in batches, adding more oil if necessary). Put the pork in and sear it for 1½ to 2 minutes per side. Remove the meat and set it aside while you prepare the pan sauce, following the instructions in the specific recipe.

Once you've made the sauce, put the meat back in the pan, cover, and cook at a simmer. For thick, center-cut pork chops, cook for 4 to 5 minutes, turn, and cook for 4 to 5 more minutes for a total cooking time of 11 to 14 minutes. The internal temperature should be 150° to 155°F. For blade chops, country spareribs, and blade and shoulder or ham steaks, cook, turning once after 10 minutes, for a total of about 20 minutes, or until the internal temperature is 155° to 160°F. Transfer the meat to a platter and cover loosely to keep warm.

Degrease the pan sauce and reduce it until it is just syrupy, or finish the sauce as otherwise directed in the individual recipe. Pour the sauce over the meat and serve.

Pork Braised in Port and Balsamic Vinegar Sauce

Serves 4
■ IN A HURRY ■ FIT FOR COMPANY

T HIS TANGY SWEET-AND-SOUR sauce is also delicious with smoked ham steaks, smoked pork chops, or reheated leftover ham, fresh or smoked.

■ **Flavor Step** ■ Season and sear the pork as directed in the Master Recipe on page 281.

After removing it from the pan, pour off all but about 1 tablespoon of the fat. Reduce the heat to medium, add the onions or shallots, and sprinkle with salt and pepper. Sauté for about 5 minutes. Deglaze the pan with the stock, port, and vinegar, stirring well. Bring to a boil, then add the pork, reduce the heat to a simmer, and continue cooking as directed.

■ **Flavor Step** ■
Dry rub of your choice (see Seasoning Chart, page 577) OR salt and freshly ground black pepper

4 1¼-to-1½-inch-thick center-cut pork chops, OR four ¾-to-1-inch-thick pork blade chops, steaks, or shoulder steaks, OR 8 country-style spareribs, OR 2 fresh ham steaks

1 tablespoon olive oil, or more if necessary

1½ cups thawed frozen pearl onions OR 1 cup chopped onions or shallots
    Salt and freshly ground black pepper

½ cup chicken or pork stock

½ cup port wine

2 tablespoons balsamic vinegar

Pork in Fresh Fennel Sauce

■ **Flavor Step** ■
Dry rub of your choice
(see Seasoning Chart,
page 577) OR salt and
freshly ground black
pepper

4 1¼-to-1½-inch-thick
   center-cut pork chops,
   OR four ¾-to-1-inch-
   thick pork blade chops,
   steaks, or shoulder
   steaks, OR 8 country-
   style spareribs, OR
   2 fresh ham steaks

1 tablespoon olive oil,
   or more if necessary

1 cup finely chopped
   onions
1 tablespoon finely
   chopped garlic
½ cup finely chopped
   fennel bulb
   Salt and freshly ground
   black pepper
3 tablespoons Pernod
   or anisette
½ cup chicken stock
¼ cup heavy cream
   (optional)

Serves 4
■ IN A HURRY ■ FIT FOR COMPANY

THE FENNEL AND PERNOD provide an intriguing licorice flavor. The sauce also works well on veal or chicken.

■ **Flavor Step** ■ Season and sear the pork as directed in the Master Recipe on page 281.

After removing it from the pan, pour off all but about 2 tablespoons of the fat. Put in the onions, garlic, fennel, and a pinch each of salt and pepper. Reduce the heat to medium and cook, stirring often, for 5 minutes. Add the Pernod or anisette and boil for 1 minute, shaking the pan. It may flame up; this is OK, just be careful around the flames. Add the stock, boil briefly, and reduce to a simmer. Put the meat back in and finish cooking as directed.

To add the optional cream, remove the pork when it is done and keep warm. Degrease the sauce if necessary, add the cream, and boil until the sauce begins to thicken. Pour the sauce over the pork and serve.

Pork or Veal in Mushroom and Sherry Sauce

Serves 4
■ IN A HURRY ■ FIT FOR COMPANY

THIS WINE SAUCE goes equally well with pork or veal. Try it with pork tenderloin medallions or Sautéed Veal Scallopini (page 547). It's also delicious with sautéed chicken breasts and on grilled halibut or pan-fried prawns.

■ **Flavor Step** ■ Season and sear the pork as directed in the Master Recipe on page 281.

After removing it from the pan, pour off all but about 1 tablespoon of the fat. Reduce the heat to medium and add the garlic and shallots or green onions. Cook for 1 minute, stirring well. Add the mushrooms, sprinkle with salt and pepper, and stir and fry them for 2 minutes more. Pour in the stock and sherry, bring to a boil, and cook until the sauce becomes syrupy. Put the meat back in the pan. Reduce the heat to a simmer, cover, and cook the pork as directed.

■ **Flavor Step** ■
Dry rub of your choice (see Seasoning Chart, page 577) OR salt and freshly ground black pepper

4 1¼-to-1½-inch-thick center-cut pork chops, OR four ¾-to-1-inch-thick pork blade chops, steaks, or shoulder steaks, OR 8 country-style spareribs, OR 2 fresh ham steaks

1 tablespoon olive oil, or more if necessary

1 tablespoon minced garlic
1 tablespoon chopped shallots or green onions or scallions, white part only
½ pound sliced mushrooms Salt and freshly ground black pepper
½ cup chicken stock
½ cup dry or medium dry (amontillado) sherry

Pork *Adobado*

■ Flavor Step ■

ADOBO MARINADE

3 ancho chiles or 5 dried
  New Mexico chiles
  Boiling water as needed
2 canned chipotle chiles
  in adobo (optional)
½ teaspoon ground
  coriander
½ teaspoon cumin seeds
½ teaspoon ground cumin
½ teaspoon dried oregano
1 tablespoon minced garlic
  Pinch of ground
  cinnamon
1 teaspoon salt
1 teaspoon freshly ground
  black pepper
¼ cup vinegar

FOR GRILLING

4-6 ½-inch-thick pork
  chops
  Salt and freshly ground
  black pepper

Serves 4 to 6
■ REWARMS WELL (BRAISED)
■ COOKING ON A BUDGET (BRAISED)
■ GREAT LEFTOVERS

ADOBOS ARE MARINADES or sauces based on vinegar and garlic that are popular throughout the Spanish-speaking world. Chiles, paprika, and annatto seeds are often used for extra flavor and color. In New Mexico, this recipe is made by marinating pieces of pork or beef in a mixture of vinegar and chiles. The meat is slowly simmered and eaten over rice, with *sopaipillas,* or deep-fried bread, on the side.

Another delicious way to use an *adobo* marinade, which we describe here, is on thin pork chops, which are quickly grilled over charcoal and served with a fruity salsa, beans, and rice and a stack of hot corn tortillas.

Leftover braised *adobado* can be chopped and used to fill tortillas for tacos (see Tacos *al Pastor,* page 288) or enchiladas or as a filling for tamales. To give a hot and smoky character to the *adobo* marinade, add the optional chipotles, smoked dried jalapeño chiles that are sold canned in *adobo* sauce (Herdez brand is very good). Dried and canned chiles and other *adobo* ingredients are available in Latino groceries or by mail-order (see Sources, page 584).

■ Flavor Step ■ Cover the chiles with boiling water and let them steep for at least 15 minutes and up to 1 hour. Remove them with a slotted spoon (save the water), slit them open, and scrape away the seeds and stems. Place in a food processor or blender along with the optional chipotles, ¼ cup of the reserved soaking water, and the remaining marinade ingredients. Process until the mixture forms a smooth paste.

Put the meat for braising or grilling in a zipper-lock bag or shallow nonreactive bowl and add the marinade. Cover if necessary, and marinate for about 2 hours at room temperature or, preferably, overnight in the refrigerator.

If it has been refrigerated, bring the meat to room temperature before cooking.

Grilling the pork: Remove the thin pork chops from the marinade and scrape off most of it, leaving some on the chops. Sprinkle with salt and pepper. Prepare a charcoal fire and grill the meat over medium-hot coals for 2 to 3 minutes per side (see Grilling, page 63, and How to Cook Thin Pork Chops, page 280). The meat should measure 145° to 155°F on an instant-read meat thermometer; it may still be a bit pink near the bone. Serve the chops with Peach and Red Onion Salsa (page 293) or Orange-Pineapple Salsa (page 295) and beans, rice, and tortillas.

Braising the pork: Heat the oil in a large, heavy pot or Dutch oven over medium-high heat. Put in the chopped onions, cover, and cook for 5 minutes over medium heat, stirring frequently, until they soften. Add the meat and all the marinade to the pot along with the tomatoes. Adjust the heat to a simmer. Cover and cook for 45 minutes.

Uncover the pot and cook for 30 to 45 minutes more, until the pork is tender and the sauce begins to thicken. If the sauce gets too thick, add a little water. (At this point, the dish can be cooled and refrigerated for later use. Just remove any congealed fat and heat through.)

Skim off any surface fat from the sauce. Taste for salt and pepper and add some hot sauce if you wish—or let guests add their own. Transfer the *adobado* to a serving dish and garnish with sprigs of cilantro. Serve with rice and *sopaipillas* or tortillas.

FOR BRAISING

3 pounds pork shoulder
   butt, trimmed of fat
   and cut into 2-inch
   cubes, OR 4 pounds
   country-style spareribs,
   trimmed of fat

1 tablespoon vegetable oil
1 cup chopped onions
1½ cups peeled, seeded,
   and chopped fresh
   tomatoes or seeded
   and chopped canned
   tomatoes
   Salt and freshly ground
   black pepper
   Tabasco or other hot
   sauce, to taste
   Cilantro sprigs,
   for garnish

Tacos al Pastor

FOR EACH TACO
(2 OR 3 MAKE A SERVING)

2 corn tortillas

2-3 ounces pork marinated in
   adobo (see page 286),
   grilled and cut into
   strips, or leftover
   braised Pork *Adobado*
   (page 286), thinly
   sliced or diced

1-2 tablespoons salsa
   of choice

1 teaspoon finely chopped
   onion

1 tablespoon guacamole
   (optional)

WE ARE FORTUNATE to live in an area peppered with great *taquerías*. These authentic Mexican-American fast-food stands specialize in serving various chopped meats on warm, soft tortillas with a great assortment of fiery salsas. Popular meats are pork *carnitas*, shredded beef, grilled steak, tongue, and pork *al pastor* (shepherd's style).

To make pork *al pastor*, thin slabs of pork are coated in peppery *Adobo* Marinade (page 286) and then stacked on top of each other on a large, vertical skewer in front of a grill (just like Greek *gyros* or Turkish *donnor kebab*). As the meat cooks, slices are cut off the edges, then diced and fried on a griddle along with a couple of corn tortillas. The meat is then scooped off the griddle and tucked into the tortillas with salsa and finely chopped onion.

Pork chops and steaks marinated in *adobo* or leftover braised Pork *Adobado* make a very tasty taco *al pastor*. Once the meat is cooked, simply cut it into thin strips or dice it. Place the spicy pork in a couple of warm corn tortillas, then garnish with a salsa or two and chopped onion and some guacamole, if you like. You can also reheat diced, leftover braised Pork *Adobado* in a little oil in a skillet or in the microwave to make moist and delicious Tacos *al Pastor*.

Warm the tortillas briefly on a dry griddle or heavy skillet and stack one on top of the other. Wrap loosely in a towel.

Heat the meat briefly on a greased griddle or skillet or in a microwave. Spoon the hot meat into the center of the tortillas, fold them over, and garnish with salsa, chopped onion, and the optional guacamole.

Pork Kebabs

CHUNKS OF PORK cut from just about anywhere on the pig are usually tender enough to use as pork kebabs. Kebabs cut from the shoulder, blade end of the loin, and sirloin are economical, but they contain more fat than most people want these days. If you use these cuts, trim as much fat away as you can. Meat from these areas is just chewy enough that it can stand marinating overnight in an acidic marinade.

Center-cut pork loin, tenderloin, or meat from the leg may also be used for kebabs, but be careful not to marinate the tenderloin for too long in a citrus, wine, or vinegar marinade. It's best to use shorter marinating times for chunks from this cut so that the meat doesn't get "overtenderized," or mushy. An hour or two at room temperature, rather than overnight in the refrigerator, is usually sufficient to provide flavor, juiciness, and tenderness. Chunks from all these cuts can also be successfully cured in a brine (page 583) or rubbed with a dry marinade (page 577) and left for a day or so in the refrigerator. As with all lean loin and tenderloin cuts, avoid overcooking them.

Grilled Pork Kebabs

■ Flavor Step ■

Dry rub, marinade, or
brine of your choice
(see Seasoning Chart,
page 577)

1½ pound porks, trimmed
of fat and cut into
1½-inch chunks
(but see discussion
if brining)

Serves 4
■ COOKING ON A BUDGET (SHOULDER)
■ LOW-FAT (DEPENDS ON MARINADE)
■ FIT FOR COMPANY

MASTER RECIPE

KEBABS CAN BE great fun for parties and other get-togethers since they go with so many combinations of marinades, sauces, condiments, and side dishes. We like to provide bowls of various chunky foods to let guests make up their own combinations. You can serve chopped sweet onions and green and red bell peppers alongside chunks of firm, fresh fruit such as pineapples, apples, or peaches. Choices could include pieces of blanched summer squash, highly seasoned homemade croutons, raw or cooked mushrooms, sliced fresh fennel and Belgian endive, raw or lightly cooked Brussels sprouts, radicchio and arugula, and sautéed eggplant.

One of our favorite ways to make kebabs is to alternate pieces of highly seasoned brined or marinated pork with chunks of smoked sausage. Other savory combinations mix pork with seafood, such as lobster, monkfish, shrimp, or scallops. When making up kebabs and accompaniments, it's a good idea to stay with a theme: go Caribbean, for example, with a citrus marinade, fruit salsas, and chunks of pineapple. Or make a Southwestern menu with pork pieces marinated in adobo (see page 286), fresh salsas, and a spicy Black Bean Salad (page 129).

For this recipe, you may want to add 2 cups soaked wood chips such as hickory or oak to a charcoal fire.

■ **Flavor Step** ■ Generously coat the chunks of meat with a dry rub or soak in a wet marinade. In most cases you can marinate the meat for 2 hours at room temperature or overnight in the refrigerator. If you're using pork tenderloin and a high-acid marinade, limit the time to no more than 2 hours at room temperature. If you brine the pork (see page 254), do it before you cut it up, since smaller pieces will get too salty. Brine a 1-pound piece for 8 to 10 hours in the refrigerator, then cut it into cubes. Let any refrigerated meat come to room temperature while you build the fire.

Kebabs are best cooked over direct heat on a covered charcoal or gas grill, although an open grill will also do. If you use a marinade or brine, pat the meat dry with paper towels before cooking. If using wooden skewers, soak them in cold water for 30 minutes. Thread the meat onto the skewers.

To cook using a covered charcoal barbecue: See Grilling, page 63. Prepare a charcoal fire by layering the charcoal to vary the heat sources from high to medium. Put 2 cups soaked wood chips on the coals, if you wish. Put the kebabs on the grill directly over the hottest section. If any flaming occurs, cover the grill immediately or move the kebabs to a cooler portion of the grill. Grill the kebabs for 1 to 1½ minutes on one side, then turn them over. After another minute or so, move them to a cooler part of the grill and put the cover on. Continue cooking, turning the kebabs frequently, until they are nicely browned and reach an internal temperature of 145° to 150°F, 7 to 10 minutes more. Move them to the cooler parts of the grill if they start to burn.

To cook using a covered gas grill: Preheat both sides of the grill for 20 minutes, then shut off half of the grill. Sear the kebabs directly over the heat for 1 to 2 minutes per side. Move them to the cooler side of the grill. Close the grill and roast the meat for 10 to 15 minutes, or until it reaches an internal temperature of 145° to 150°F.

When they are done, remove the kebabs from the grill and let them rest for 5 minutes, loosely covered with foil. Serve with sauces and condiments of your choice.

Grilled Pork Kebabs in Tequila and Lime Marinade

■ Flavor Step ■
TEQUILA AND LIME MARINADE

3 tablespoons fresh
   lime juice
2 teaspoons grated
   lime zest
2 tablespoon tequila
   or mezcal
2 tablespoons olive oil
1 tablespoon minced garlic
1 teaspoon ground cumin
1 teaspoon dried oregano
2 teaspoons salt
1 teaspoon freshly ground
   black pepper

1½ pounds pork, trimmed
   of fat and cut into
   1½-inch chunks
2 green bell peppers,
   cut into 1-inch squares
1 fresh pineapple, cut
   into 1½-inch cubes
   (optional)

Serves 4
■ GOOD FOR A CROWD

THIS TANGY MARINADE is also excellent with country-style spareribs, steaks, and lamb chops. Do not use this marinade, however, with center-cut pork loin; it's too lean and tender and will dry out from the acid in the lime juice.

■ **Flavor Step** ■ Whisk the marinade ingredients together and proceed as in the Master Recipe, page 290.

When you skewer the pork, alternate the pieces of meat with the bell peppers and pineapple.

PEACH AND RED ONION SALSA

Makes 2½ cups

MAKE THIS EASY salsa in July or August, when peaches are at their best—ripe, juicy, and full of flavor. Serve it as a condiment with Grilled Pork Kebabs in Tequila and Lime Marinade (page 292) or marinated Grilled Pork Chops (page 264). Marinating the onion first in lime juice and salt helps to take away the sting of the onion and gives it a lightly pickled flavor.

    ½ cup finely chopped red onion
    ½ teaspoon kosher salt
    1½ tablespoons fresh lime juice
    2 ripe peaches, peeled, pitted, and cut into ½-inch dice
       (about 2 cups)
    1 jalapeño chile, seeded and finely chopped
    1 tablespoon chopped fresh mint
    1 teaspoon sugar, or to taste

In a small bowl, toss the onion well with the salt and lime juice. Let them sit for 30 minutes to pickle slightly.

Just before serving, stir in the remaining ingredients. Use about ½ cup of salsa per serving. The salsa is best made fresh, but it will keep overnight, covered, in the refrigerator.

Grilled Pork Steaks in Yucatán Marinade

■ Flavor Step ■
YUCATÁN MARINADE

1 tablespoon chopped
   fresh oregano or 1
   teaspoon dried

2 teaspoons ground cumin

½ teaspoon ground allspice

2 teaspoons chile powder,
   preferably Gebhardt

½ teaspoon hot pepper
   sauce

2 teaspoons minced garlic

¼ cup fresh orange juice

¼ cup fresh or canned
   unsweetened
   pineapple juice

3 tablespoons fresh
   lime juice

2 tablespoons olive oil

2 teaspoons salt

1 teaspoon freshly ground
   black pepper

3 pounds pork steaks from
   the Boston butt, OR
   picnic shoulder, OR
   country-style spareribs,
   trimmed of most
   external fat

Orange-Pineapple Salsa
   (see opposite page)
8 flour tortillas (optional)

Serves 4 to 6
■ COOKING ON A BUDGET ■ FIT FOR COMPANY

USE PORK STEAKS cut from the shoulder, either from the picnic or Boston butt. For best results, the steaks should be about ¾ inch thick. Country-style spareribs make a tasty variation. A fruit salsa such as Peach and Red Onion Salsa (page 293) or Orange-Pineapple Salsa goes nicely with the spicy steaks. We also like to serve the pork with a salad of jicama, sliced oranges, and sweet red onions, along with Spanish rice. Remember to start marinating the meat a day ahead.

Drink an amber Mexican lager with this spicy dish—Dos Equis, for example.

■ Flavor Step ■ Whisk all the marinade ingredients together in a small bowl. Place the pork in a zipper-lock bag or bowl and pour on the marinade. Marinate overnight (cover if you used a bowl) in the refrigerator, turning the meat several times.

The next day, remove the pork from the refrigerator 30 minutes before grilling. Prepare a fire in a covered charcoal barbecue or gas grill or preheat the broiler.

Meanwhile, make the Pineapple-Orange Salsa and set aside.

Remove the pork from the marinade and pat dry. When the coals are medium-hot, put the steaks on the grill, cover, and cook for 5 to 6 minutes per side, turning the meat 2 or 3 times. Or broil them 3 inches from the flame. The meat is done when it's faintly pink inside but still juicy, about 150°F internal temperature.

Slice the pork into ½-inch strips, leaving some meat on the bones for those who like to gnaw. Serve with the salsa and with flour tortillas if you wish to make some delicious burritos.

ORANGE-PINEAPPLE SALSA

Makes 2½ cups

1   navel orange, peeled and cut into ½-inch dice
1   cup fresh or canned pineapple chunks, cut into ¼-inch dice
1   medium jalapeño chile, seeded and finely chopped
1   cup chopped fresh cilantro
2   tablespoons chopped fresh mint
½   teaspoon ground cumin
2   green onions or scallions (white and green parts), finely chopped

Combine all the ingredients in a festive serving bowl. The salsa can be stored for up to 2 days in the refrigerator.

Baked Pork Steaks with Madeira, Ham, and Tomatoes

4 6-to-8-ounce pork
shoulder steaks, OR
1½-2 pounds country-
style spareribs, OR
1½-2 pounds blade
end or sirloin end
pork chops

Salt and freshly ground
black pepper
2 tablespoons olive oil
1 medium onion, thinly
sliced
½ cup dry white wine or
dry vermouth
1 tablespoon finely
chopped garlic
1 tablespoon coarse-
grained mustard
½ cup sweet Madeira
or sweet sherry
½ teaspoon dried oregano
½ teaspoon dried basil
6 ripe tomatoes, peeled,
seeded, and chopped
(about 1 cup), OR
6 Italian-style canned
tomatoes, drained and
chopped (about 1 cup)
¼ pound thinly sliced
Westphalian ham
or prosciutto, cut
into ¼-inch strips

Serves 4

■ COOKING ON A BUDGET ■ REWARMS WELL

BAKING MEAT IN A SAVORY SAUCE is really a simple form of braising. This technique yields great results and is a real help
to a cook in a hurry. The entire dish can be
assembled in less than 15 minutes the night or
morning before you cook it. Then you can cover
the baking pan with foil and refrigerate it until
you're ready to pop it in the oven.

We recommend pork shoulder steaks or country-style spareribs here—they both have enough
fat so the meat won't dry out if you overcook it
slightly. And the meat is just chewy enough to
benefit from braising. You could also make this
dish with blade pork chops or chops cut from the
sirloin end of the loin. Because center-cut rib or
loin pork chops can dry out when cooked this
way, we don't recommend them for this dish. If
you use them, choose thick chops—at least ¾
inch—and carefully monitor the internal temperature of the meat. It should not exceed 150° to
160°F (depending on the cut) when tested with
an instant-read thermometer. Remove them from
the oven and keep them warm while you finish
the sauce. This sauce would also be good with
ham steaks. Serve the pork and sauce with saffron rice, soft polenta, or a pasta such as ziti,
fusilli, or bow-ties.

Preheat the oven to 350°F. Season the meat generously
with salt and pepper. In a large, heavy skillet, heat the olive
oil over high heat. Put in the meat and brown the chops for
1 to 2 minutes per side, or until lightly colored. Remove and
set aside.

Pour out all but 1 tablespoon of fat from the pan. Add the onion, cover, and cook until soft, about 5 minutes, stirring occasionally. Pour in the wine or vermouth, bring to a boil, and scrape up any browned bits from the bottom of the pan. Pour this mixture into a bowl and add the remaining seasonings. Season with ½ teaspoon salt and ¼ teaspoon pepper. Put the meat into a shallow roasting pan and cover with the tomatoes and ham. Cover the pan with foil. (At this point you can refrigerate the meat to cook later.)

Put the pan in the oven and bake for 15 minutes (if you took the pan from the refrigerator, allow an extra 5 minutes here). Remove the foil and bake for 20 to 30 more minutes. After 20 minutes or so, test the pork with an instant-read meat thermometer. Pork steaks should register no more than 150° to 155°F. The fattier country ribs or blade or sirloin chops can be cooked to 155° to 160°F and still retain their juices. Set the pork aside, loosely covered to keep warm.

Remove the vegetables and ham from the pan with a slotted spoon and reserve. Skim any fat from the surface of the sauce and reduce over high heat until it becomes syrupy. Taste for salt and pepper, stir in the reserved solids, and serve.

Pork Tenderloin Medallions with Fresh Tomato and Basil Sauce over Fresh Pasta

■ **Flavor Step** ■
FENNEL RUB FOR
PORK TENDERLOIN

1 teaspoon salt

½ teaspoon freshly ground
black pepper

½ teaspoon fennel seed,
crushed with a mortar
and pestle

½ teaspoon ground
coriander

¾ pound pork tenderloin,
trimmed of fat and
silverskin, cut into
½-inch medallions

1 tablespoon olive oil

3 large garlic cloves, sliced

2 cups peeled, seeded,
and diced fresh, vine-
ripened tomatoes,
canned Italian-style
tomatoes, OR Oven-
Roasted Tomatoes (see
opposite page)

8 large fresh basil leaves,
cut into thin strips
Salt and freshly ground
black pepper

1 pound fresh pasta,
such as fettuccine
Freshly grated Parmesan
cheese

Serves 4 to 6
■ IN A HURRY ■ LOW-FAT

IDEALLY, THIS DISH SHOULD be prepared in the late summer or early fall, when fresh, vine-ripened tomatoes are easily available. If you can't find vine-ripened tomatoes, use canned Italian-style plum tomatoes or Oven-Roasted Tomatoes. The strength of this dish is based on the freshness and simplicity of the ingredients. Accompany it with a Dolcetto from Piedmont in northern Italy, a Chianti Classico, or a medium-bodied California Zinfandel.

■ **Flavor Step** ■ Combine the spices in a small bowl. Rub the mix onto both sides of the pork medallions and let them marinate for 10 to 20 minutes at room temperature.

In a heavy nonstick skillet, heat the oil over medium-high heat. Brown the medallions for 1½ minutes on each side and set them aside. Turn the heat down to medium and add the sliced garlic. Cook until the garlic becomes fragrant and soft, but do not let it color, 1 to 2 minutes. Add the tomatoes and basil and cook for about 5 minutes, scraping up any browned bits from the bottom of the pan. Return the pork to the pan and cook for 3 minutes more. Taste for salt and pepper.

Cook the pasta, following the instructions on the package. Add the drained pasta to the pork and sauce. Over medium-high heat, toss the pasta until it's well coated with the sauce. Put the pasta and pork in a shallow bowl and garnish with the grated Parmesan. Serve at once.

Oven-Roasted Tomatoes

Makes about 3 cups

ONCE ROASTED, the tomatoes can be packed into containers and refrigerated or frozen to be used as a simple and delicious tomato sauce. Covered, they will last in the refrigerator for about a week, frozen, for up to three months.

> 2 pounds Italian-style Roma (plum) tomatoes, each
> tomato sliced into 2 or 3 thick slices lengthwise
> 2 tablespoons olive oil
> 2 tablespoons finely chopped garlic
> 2 tablespoons chopped fresh herbs such as basil,
> oregano, or thyme or 2 teaspoons dried herbs
> (use individual herbs or combine)
> Salt and freshly ground black pepper

Preheat the oven to 250°F. Spread the sliced tomatoes on baking sheets or roasting pans. Drizzle with the olive oil and sprinkle with the garlic, herbs, salt, and pepper. Roast until the juices given off by the tomatoes have begun to thicken, about 1 hour. Using a spatula, scrape the tomatoes and all the juices into a nonreactive container. Use at once or cover and store in the refrigerator or freezer until needed.

Sautéed Pork Medallions in Tea Sauce with Roasted Sweet Potatoes

■ Flavor Step ■

DRY HERB RUB FOR
PORK TENDERLOIN

1 teaspoon dried thyme,
   oregano, or marjoram

1 teaspoon dried sage

2 teaspoons salt

1 teaspoon freshly ground
   black pepper

2 12-to-16-ounce pork
   tenderloins, trimmed
   of silverskin and fat
   and cut into ¾-inch-
   thick medallions

TEA SAUCE

2 cups strong black currant
   tea, blackberry tea,
   apricot tea, or other
   fruit tea of your choice
   (brewed from 2
   tablespoons tea or
   about 3 tea bags and
   allowed to steep for
   at least 5 minutes)

3 cups chicken stock

½ cup dry white wine

2 tablespoons red currant
   or apricot jam

½ teaspoon dried thyme

1 tablespoon cornstarch,
   dissolved in 2 table-
   spoons cold water

Serves 4 to 6
■ IN A HURRY ■ FIT FOR COMPANY

ARE YOU ONE OF THOSE COOKS who likes to challenge your guests' taste buds and culinary knowledge? Do you love it when your guests say, "What is that flavor, I just can't put my finger on it?" If so, this recipe is for you. Actually, we think you should divulge the secret—that the sauce is made with tea—and that it's really delicious and easy to make. This dish is a fine choice for an elegant small dinner party. Serve the pork over the roasted sweet potatoes and with quickly sautéed bitter greens or spinach. Accompany it with a fragrant Gewürztraminer or dry Riesling from Oregon or Alsace.

■ Flavor Step ■ Combine the spices in a small bowl. Sprinkle the mixture over both sides of the pork medallions. Set them aside while you prepare the sauce and potatoes.

To make the Tea Sauce: Pour or strain the tea, if necessary, into a nonreactive saucepan, add the stock and wine, and bring it to a boil. Cook until the liquid is reduced to 1½ cups. Stir in the jam until it is completely melted. Whisk in the thyme and the cornstarch mixture and boil for 15 seconds or so, until the sauce is thickened and has the consistency of syrup. Remove from the heat.

To make the Roasted Sweet Potatoes: Preheat the oven to 350°F. Brush a large roasting pan with 2 teaspoons of the melted butter. Lay the sliced sweet potatoes in a single layer and brush them with the remaining butter. Sprinkle with the salt and pepper. Bake for 30 minutes, uncovered, or until the sweet potatoes are soft. Pour ½ cup of the tea sauce over the sweet potatoes and bake for 5 minutes more. Turn off the oven. Keep the sweet potatoes warm in the oven while you cook the pork.

Heat the olive oil over high heat in a heavy skillet large enough to hold the pork medallions in a single layer (or, if necessary, cook them in batches). Brown for 1 minute on each side. Reduce the heat to medium and cook for 2 minutes more. Turn the medallions and cook a final 2 minutes, or until the meat registers 150°F on an instant-read thermometer.

To serve, reheat the sauce over low heat. Arrange the medallions in the center of a platter, with the sliced sweet potatoes forming a border around them. Pour the sauce over the pork and serve with sautéed young bitter greens or spinach.

ROASTED SWEET POTATOES

3 tablespoons butter, melted

2 pounds sweet potatoes, peeled and sliced into ½-inch-thick rounds

Salt and freshly ground black pepper

1 tablespoon olive oil

Sesame-Coated Pork Medallions with John's Thai Citrus Glaze

■ Flavor Step ■
ASIAN SESAME COATING

- 1 large egg white
- 1 tablespoon cornstarch
- 2 tablespoons soy sauce
- 1 tablespoon fresh lemon juice
- 1 tablespoon minced fresh ginger
- ½ teaspoon ground Szechuan peppercorns or freshly ground black pepper
- ½ cup sesame seeds

- 1 pound pork tenderloin, trimmed of silverskin and fat and cut into ½-inch-thick medallions

JOHN'S THAI CITRUS GLAZE

- 1 cup fresh grapefruit juice
- ½ cup fresh orange juice
- ¼ cup fresh lime juice
- ¼ cup fresh lemon juice, or more to taste
- 2 teaspoons minced fresh ginger
- 3 tablespoons dark or light corn syrup
- 1 teaspoon Sriracha (Thai hot chili sauce) or other Asian hot chili sauce
- 2 tablespoons Asian fish sauce (*nam pla* or *nuoc mam*)

Serves 4
■ IN A HURRY ■ FIT FOR COMPANY

JOHN ALAMILLA, a chef at Nancy Oakes's restaurant Boulevard in San Francisco who was born and raised in Honduras, has a particular talent for coming up with light and exciting dishes that combine Asian and Caribbean flavors. The citrus glaze in this dish reflects the brightness and spice of Thai cooking, with a tangy Caribbean undertone. It's wonderful on pork, but also goes well with many grilled meats and is especially good with fish or seafood such as calamari. Sriracha Thai chili sauce is available in Asian groceries or by mail-order (see Sources, page 584). It has a unique flavor, but you can substitute an equivalent amount of another Asian chili sauce. You can also find fish sauce in most Asian groceries or order it by mail.

■ **Flavor Step** ■ In a bowl, combine all the ingredients for the coating except the sesame seeds. Add the pork and toss well so that all the pieces are well coated. Let the pork marinate for 30 minutes at room temperature.

Place the sesame seeds on a plate and press the medallions into the seeds so that they are well coated on both sides. Set the medallions aside to dry slightly while you make the glaze.

To make John's Thai Citrus Glaze: Mix the citrus juices with the ginger in a nonreactive saucepan. Bring to a boil and cook over high heat for 10 minutes to concentrate the flavors. Stir in the corn syrup, chili sauce, and fish sauce and continue to boil until the sauce reduces to a very light syrup (the sauce should not be thick enough to coat the back of a spoon). Taste the sauce—it should have a tangy, citrus flavor. Season to taste with sugar and salt and pepper, and if it's not tangy enough, add more lemon juice.

Heat the oil over medium-high heat in a nonstick skillet large enough to hold all the medallions. Put in the pork and fry until toasty brown on one side, about 2 minutes. Turn and cook for 2 minutes more. Add 1 cup of the citrus sauce and cook for 1 minute more, turning the medallions to coat them well.

Divide the lettuce among four plates and top each with 3 or 4 pieces of the pork. Spoon some more sauce over the tops and garnish with the cilantro sprigs. Serve with steamed rice and a stir-fried vegetable of your choice.

Sugar to taste
Salt and freshly ground black pepper to taste

2 tablespoons peanut or canola oil

GARNISH
4 cups shredded iceberg lettuce
Cilantro sprigs

Pork Saltimbocca

6 ½-inch-thick slices of
boneless pork loin
(1¼-1½ pounds total),
trimmed of all
external fat

■ Flavor Step ■
SAGE AND PROSCIUTTO
FILLING

6 thin slices of prosciutto
6 large fresh sage or basil
leaves or 1 teaspoon
dried sage or basil
Salt and freshly ground
black pepper

2 tablespoons olive oil,
or more if necessary
½ cup dry white wine
2 teaspoons minced garlic
¼ pound mushrooms,
thinly sliced (optional)
½ cup veal or chicken stock
Salt and freshly ground
black pepper
1 tablespoon chopped
fresh parsley

Serves 4, with seconds
■ IN A HURRY ■ FIT FOR COMPANY ■ LOW-FAT

NOWADAYS PORK LOIN is so lean and tastes so mild that it can easily be substituted for veal. Veal is traditionally used for this classic dish, but it's more expensive and harder to find than pork. For this, or any veal scallop or cutlet recipe, use ½-inch slices of boneless pork loin or leg pounded to a thickness of about ¼ inch. You can also substitute pounded chicken breasts or turkey cutlets in this and other veal recipes.

Saltimbocca—literally, "it jumps in the mouth"—is a popular Roman dish found in Italian restaurants all over the world. This variation is quite easy to prepare and is perfect for a small dinner party when served with mushroom risotto or over pasta tossed with garlic, olive oil, and parsley. For best results, use fresh sage leaves, but you can substitute a sprinkling of dried sage. For a slightly different flavor, use fresh basil leaves instead of sage. You should use the best prosciutto you can find, preferably Italian, and it should be sliced as thin as possible. If you can't find good prosciutto, use very thinly sliced Westphalian ham.

■ Flavor Step ■ Using the flat side of a cleaver or a meat mallet, gently pound the pork slices between two pieces of plastic wrap so that the slices measure 2½ to 3 inches by 6 to 7 inches. They should be about ¼ inch thick. Cover each slice with a slice of prosciutto and place a sage or basil leaf or a sprinkling of dried herbs on half of each slice. Fold each slice in half over the prosciutto and herbs; it doesn't matter if some of the prosciutto sticks out around the edges. Secure each packet with a wooden toothpick. Season both sides with salt and pepper.

Heat the oil in a large, heavy skillet over high heat. Put in the pork, taking care not to crowd the pan; fry in batches if necessary, adding more oil as needed. Cook the saltimbocca until lightly browned, 1½ to 2 minutes on each side. Remove the pork and set aside. Put in the wine, garlic, and the optional mushrooms and bring to a boil, scraping up any browned bits from the bottom of the pan. Cook for 2 to 3 minutes, until the wine begins to reduce, then add the stock and continue to boil until the sauce just turns syrupy. Taste for salt and pepper. Return the saltimbocca to the pan and heat briefly in the sauce to warm it through. (This time you can crowd the pan if you need to.) Serve the pork covered with the sauce and sprinkled with the chopped parsley.

Vietnamese Tamarind Pork Stir-Fry

TAMARIND MARINADE
FOR PORK

1 teaspoon tamarind paste

1 teaspoon sugar

1 tablespoon Vietnamese
fish sauce (*nuoc mam*)

1 teaspoon minced garlic

1 tablespoon minced
shallots or green onions
or scallions

1 anchovy fillet, mashed
to a paste

1 teaspoon minced fresh
ginger

6 ¼-inch-thick slices of
boneless pork loin
(1-1½ pounds),
cut into ¼-inch-thick
matchsticks

1 tablespoon Asian
peanut oil

1 medium red bell pepper,
cut into 1-inch squares

2 tablespoons Vietnamese
fish sauce (*nuoc mam*)

8 green onions or
scallions, cut into
2-inch pieces

½ cup diced fresh or
canned pineapple

2 tablespoons chopped
fresh mint, for garnish

Serves 4 as a first course,
6 as part of a banquet
■ COOKING ON A BUDGET ■ LOW-FAT

TAMARIND HAS A TANGY, fruity flavor that combines with sweet ingredients for a delicious sweet-and-sour effect. Serve these lively pork strips with rice or noodles as a first course or as part of a Vietnamese banquet with two or three other dishes. Tamarind paste and Vietnamese fish sauce (*nuoc mam*) are available in Asian grocery stores or by mail-order (see Sources, page 584).

■ **Flavor Step** ■ Mix all the marinade ingredients together in a bowl and toss the pork strips in the marinade until they are well coated. Marinate for 30 minutes at room temperature.

Heat 1½ teaspoons of the oil in a wok or heavy skillet over the highest heat. Stir-fry the red bell peppers for 2 minutes. Remove and set aside.

Remove the meat from the marinade, saving the marinade. Add the remaining 1½ teaspoons oil and the meat to the pan and stir-fry until the strips are just cooked through and no longer pink inside, 2 to 3 minutes. Add the reserved marinade, the fish sauce, green onions or scallions, pineapple, and the peppers and cook, stirring often, until most of the liquid has evaporated and the sauce coats the pork, 1 to 2 minutes. Spoon the meat and sauce into a bowl, sprinkle with the chopped mint, and serve.

Thai Red or Green Pork Curry

Serves 4 to 6
■ GREAT LEFTOVERS ■ IN A HURRY
■ MEAT AS A CONDIMENT

THE BRIGHT, SPICY FLAVORS of Thai curry paste can enliven all kinds of meat, poultry, and fish and go especially well with pork. Once you have the curry paste, it's very easy to throw a Thai curry together. You can purchase Thai green curry paste or red curry paste (Mae Ploy brand is a good one) and other Thai ingredients at Asian groceries or by mail-order (see Sources, page 584). Leftover pastes keep in the refrigerator for several weeks.

Although this lively dish is best with freshly cooked pork, you can use leftover roast or grilled pork. We've embellished the recipe with red bell peppers and broccoli, but you can use whatever vegetables you have on hand or in your garden: thinly sliced carrots, shredded cabbage, thinly sliced onions, fresh peas, snow or sugar snap peas, diced zucchini, and cauliflower florets. Serve with steamed Thai jasmine rice.

1-1½ pounds raw pork loin or tenderloin, cut into ¼-inch-thick slices, then cut into ½-by-⅛-inch-thick matchsticks, OR 2-3 cups cubed (¾-inch) cooked pork (roast loin, grilled chops, or tenderloin)
Salt and freshly ground black pepper (if using raw pork)
Vegetable oil for stir-frying (if using raw pork)
1 13½-ounce can unsweetened coconut milk
2-3 tablespoons Thai red or green curry paste
1 teaspoon minced garlic
2 kaffir lime leaves, chopped, or 2 teaspoons chopped lime zest
1 pound broccoli florets
1 red bell pepper, cut into 1-inch squares
Sugar to taste
20 fresh basil leaves, for garnish

If using raw pork, toss the strips with the salt and pepper to season well. Stir-fry the strips in a little oil in a wok or skillet over high heat until they are no longer pink. Set aside.

In a 3-to-4-quart pot, stir together the coconut milk and curry paste. Bring to a boil and add the garlic and lime leaves or zest. Reduce to a simmer and add the freshly cooked or leftover pork. Stir well, put in the broccoli, and cook for 5 minutes. Add the red pepper, stir well, and cook for 2 more minutes or so, until the pepper is still firm but not crunchy. Taste the curry for salt and pepper and sweeten it to your taste with sugar. Ladle it into a bowl, garnish with the basil leaves, and serve.

THE HENDRIX BROTHERS' ULTIMATE PORK CHOP SANDWICH

THE HENDRIX BROTHERS were a matched pair of ancient tavern owners who ran The Hendrix Brothers Regulator, an equally ancient establishment in Bloomington, Indiana. The tavern was named after the brothers themselves and a huge clock labeled The Regulator that hung behind a scarred and beat-up bar running the length of the premises. The brothers were tall, lean, and dour, virtually unspeaking, uttering only an occasional "Uh-huh" or "That'll be a dime [or two bits or six bits]" or "Nope" to most questions. Nothing in the bar cost more than six bits, as I remember, at least nothing that I ever ate or drank. Stroh's or Drewery's beer was a quarter a mug, hot dogs with sauerkraut and raw onions cost fifty cents, and you could get a brain sandwich, pickled pig's feet, ham hocks with lima beans, or a pork chop sandwich from the six-bit menu. Thirst-making snacks such as pickled eggs, pretzels, Polish sausage, or a chunk of rat cheese with crackers and onions could be had for a dime apiece.

Needless to say, The Regulator was a good spot to spend some time when you were short of cash with an empty stomach—a common experience for me in my student days. If you were really down and out, you could make do with a mug of beer and one or two of the salty ten-cent specials. If the scholarship check had just come through or you were flush from tutoring some undergraduate philosophy student in the complexities of the Platonic forms, it was the pork chop sandwich all the way.

Like many Midwestern cooks, the Hendrix brothers had a good hand with pork. They bought the best available, a fat shoat every week or two from Honey James out on Popcorn Road. Honey (he called everybody Honey: "Hi, Honey," he'd say, "what can I do you for today?") had this trading post/grocery store/hardware store/butcher shop about ten miles from town, right across from the Hexagonal Pentecostal Church. He was known to sell the finest and juiciest pork in Marion County, along with range-run chickens, fresh eggs, home-grown tomatoes, and, it was rumored, some pretty good 'shine that his more rural cousins made back in the hills.

The brothers would take some of Honey's best pork loin sliced about a quarter inch thick, season it with salt, pepper, a little bit of sage, and quite a bit of cayenne, dip it into a beer batter, and then deep-fry it for just a minute or two on the broken-down range behind the bar. They'd serve it up on a crusty roll with sliced raw onions and the spicy piccalilli they kept in big crocks. Bread-and-butter pickles and coleslaw completed the presentation.

This was the first pork chop I can ever remember really enjoying. When we ate pork at home, it was usually cooked way past well done and was mighty dry. This chop was still just a little pink inside, burning hot and crunchy, with sweet juices that mingled with the piccalilli and onions. Washed down with the local beer and with maybe some limas and ham hocks on the side, it made a pretty satisfying meal.

I dined at The Regulator regularly for some years until a memorable evening when some good old boys were playing on the stage in the rear, with a Confederate flag nailed to the wall behind them. There was something about leading a charge and trying to tear the flag down, and I seem to remember chairs and bottles flying and somehow ending up on the sidewalk with the Hendrix brothers barring the door, scowling mightily, silent as always. It was farewell to pork chop sandwiches, at least until I started making them myself—almost as good, but never quite the same.

D.K.

Pork Loin and Coleslaw Sandwich

1 pound pork loin, sliced
⅜ inch thick

■ Flavor Step ■
Spice Rub for Pork
or Beef (page 375)

4 egg buns, kaiser rolls,
or other sandwich rolls
Coleslaw and sliced
bread-and-butter
pickles or sour dill
pickle chips

Serves 4 to 6
■ IN A HURRY ■ COOKING ON A BUDGET
■ LOW-FAT

THROUGHOUT THE MIDWEST and South, "pork chop" sandwiches are popular fast-food meals. They're usually made with a thin slice of pork, heavily battered and deep-fried. The sandwiches are tasty, but you can pay a high price in calories and indigestion. Our version, made with highly seasoned slices of pork loin, is much lighter but still packed with flavor. Coleslaw and a side of pickles make it a real treat when served on a soft egg bun or crusty kaiser roll. The pork can be grilled or panfried, depending on your time and preference. *(See photograph, page 45.)*

■ **Flavor Step** ■ Using the flat side of a cleaver or a meat mallet, lightly pound the pork to a thickness of ¼ inch. Generously rub the spice mixture all over the pork and let it marinate for at least 1 hour at room temperature or overnight in the refrigerator, covered with plastic wrap.

Grill the pork slices over a medium-hot charcoal fire (see Grilling, page 63) or panfry in a lightly oiled ridged pan or cast-iron skillet for 30 seconds per side.

To assemble the sandwiches, split the buns or rolls in half. Place a layer of coleslaw on the bottom half of each and cover with 2 or 3 slices of pork. Top with the other halves of the rolls and serve with coleslaw and pickles.

COLESLAW

Serves 4 to 6

FOR THE BEST RESULTS, prepare the coleslaw several hours ahead and refrigerate it or, better still, make it a day ahead.

4 cups shredded green cabbage
2 cups shredded red cabbage
2 green onions, thinly sliced
½ cup thinly sliced red onion

DRESSING
2 teaspoons minced garlic
1 cup mayonnaise
¼ cup sour cream or yogurt
¼ cup light or dark brown sugar
2 tablespoons fresh lemon juice
1 tablespoon cider vinegar
1 teaspoon Worcestershire sauce
½ teaspoon Tabasco
Salt and freshly ground black pepper

Place all the vegetables in a large bowl.

To make the Dressing: Whisk together all the ingredients in another bowl or blend in a food processor.

Toss the vegetables with the dressing and taste for salt and pepper.

How to Choose a Pork Roast

THE CENTER-CUT PORK LOIN is the most common and popular pork roast and is often sold boneless in pieces weighing 3 to 4 pounds. Unfortunately, it dries out easily unless care is taken to prevent it from overcooking. Its texture and flavor are vastly improved by brining (see page 254), and we recommend you routinely add this preparation step when cooking any piece of pork loin. Center-cut pork loin is also sold with the bones attached, which we prefer, since they add juiciness and flavor. Sometimes two boneless loins are tied together to make a **double boneless pork loin, tied**, which is ideal for large groups (see *Arista*, Tuscan Herb-Infused Roast Pork, page 335).

In choosing a pork loin roast, we prefer the section closest to the shoulder, which is likely to be juicier, but since this roast, sold as a **blade end pork loin roast**, has both rib and blade bones, it is more difficult to carve. See if you can find a butcher who will sell you a **boneless blade end pork loin roast** weighing 3 to 4 pounds. More likely you will find a **boneless sirloin pork roast** weighing 2½ to 3½ pounds, which is ideal for a family. We like to roast brined sirloin roast in a covered kettle barbecue over indirect heat for a great outdoor meal.

For a holiday meal or special gathering, a **crown roast of pork** makes a stunning presentation. Cut from the rib section of the loin, this impressive roast is made up of two racks of pork rib chops tied in a circle with space in the middle for stuffing. A crown roast contains at least 16 chops and can be as large as 20 chops, so it is ideal for a large crowd, especially when served with a savory dressing. The roast will weigh in at 8 to 11 pounds and, figuring 1½ to 2 chops per person, a 16-rib roast will feed about 8 to 12, a 20-rib roast 10 to 14. A crown roast is no more difficult or complicated to prepare than any other large roast, which is to say it's a snap. Most specialty butchers are glad to put one together for you by special-order.

The boneless **pork tenderloin** also makes a delicious roast, and it has the extra advantage of being speedy to cook. Don't confuse this thin, cylindrical roast with the pork loin, despite the similarity of their names. The tenderloin is much smaller (¾ to 1½ pounds), whereas a whole loin typically weighs about 7 pounds. Cut from the interior side of the rib bone along the lower and middle back, the tenderloin corresponds to the fillet from the beef.

As with the loin, care must be taken not to overcook this lean and tender meat. Because the tenderloin has such a small diameter, we prefer to tie two together to increase the thickness and prevent overcooking. This preparation gives an added flavor bonus: the roast can be easily stuffed. Like other pork

LOIN

center-cut pork loin,
bone-in

center-cut pork
loin, boneless

crown roast of pork

pork tenderloin

double boneless
pork loin, tied

blade end
pork loin roast

SHOULDER

Boston butt roast

picnic shoulder
arm roast

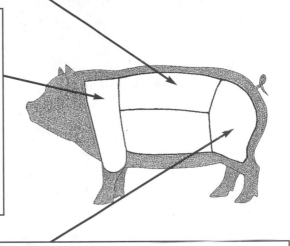

HAM

whole fresh leg of pork
(fresh ham)

top leg (inside)
roast

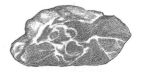

butt half leg of pork

shank end leg of pork

sirloin pork roast, boneless

from the middle back, pork tenderloin is vastly improved by brining (see page 254).

If flavor is your motivator, the **Boston butt** from the shoulder produces the most delicious pork roast, but it has more internal fat than the leg or loin. A whole Boston butt weighs about 6 pounds and is just right for up to eight persons. The added fat ensures that the meat will be juicy even if it is slightly overcooked, making this the ideal cut for those who insist on very well-done pork. You can buy the Boston butt bone-in or boneless. The small blade bone is very easy to remove on your own. Often the Boston butt is cut in half and sold as a 3-to-4-pound roast. You can also occasionally find Boston butt smoked and sold as a **smoked shoulder roll** or **cottage ham**. For braising, a **picnic shoulder arm roast** is a great choice.

When size is no concern, a **fresh leg of pork** (also called **fresh ham**) makes the finest roast of all: you can't beat it for flavor and just plain pork goodness. Like the term tenderloin, ham is confusing since it refers not only to the cured (and often smoked) back leg of the pig but also to the same part when it's not cured—the cut we mean here. This uncured version, essentially a raw leg of pork, is usually referred to as a "fresh ham." In an attempt to straighten things out a bit, we'll call the raw version "leg of pork."

The meat from the leg is juicier and the flavor much more robust than the more expensive and popular pork loin roast. And if you buy your pork leg with the skin attached, you can produce some really delicious cracklings. The problem is that a whole pork leg weighs in at a whopping 20 pounds plus. That's a lot of meat for a small group but just right for a large family holiday. And a whole roast pork leg makes a spectacular presentation for a festive gathering. Leg of pork is also quite cheap—less than half the cost of a standing rib roast, for example, and often less than smoked ham.

If you have the butcher remove the aitch bone (the hip bone), the leg of pork is easy to carve. And if you want to be economic and have at least minimal knife skills, you can turn a whole leg into three or four small pork roasts that are ideal for a family of four to six (see Making the Cut: Pork Leg or Fresh Ham, page 314). If you are lucky enough to live near a market with an enlightened butcher who sells individual pork roasts from the fresh leg, give them a try. The best boneless leg here will be called **top leg (inside) roast**. Smaller bone-in roasts are called **butt half leg of pork** or **shank end leg of pork**. The butt end is more tender and tasty. Some butchers sell the boneless sirloin pork roast from the fresh leg of pork, which also makes an excellent roast.

Pork Tenderloin
The Perfect Cut for the Small Family

THERE ARE MANY ADVANTAGES to pork tenderloin. Because the tenderloin is small and not very thick, it can be cooked quite quickly, a boon to the cook just home from work with a family to feed. Tenderloin's delicate flavor and buttery tenderness also make it an ideal cut for a small dinner party. And the mild character of the meat enables you to pair it with many flavors: fruit, chiles, Indian and Thai spices, mushrooms of all sorts. It can be cooked by any of the dry-heat methods, such as roasting, grilling, or sautéing. This is the leanest cut of pork, with about the same amount of fat as a serving of skinless chicken breast.

At first glance, this ¾-to-1¼-pound cut of lean, tender pork looks expensive. But there is little or no waste and very little fat. A 4-to-5-ounce serving is more than adequate. This works out to about the same cost as a serving of pork chops. You usually don't end up with leftovers, but if you do, tenderloin makes great sandwiches and is perfect for tacos and burritos.

Dry rubs (see page 577) and flavor brines (see pages 255-259) are the best ways to add flavor and juiciness to pork tenderloins. Rubs of herbs and spices can be put on the meat immediately before grilling, but for more flavor, apply the dry rub and then refrigerate the tightly wrapped tenderloin overnight. This is especially important if it is to be left whole and cooked by indirect heat. Brine whole pork tenderloin for 6 to 8 hours in the refrigerator, butterflied tenderloin for a shorter time, 2 to 4 hours. Try lighter brining first, then increase the brining period the next time.

Tenderloins can also be marinated, but a word of caution: since the meat is so tender, it can easily become mushy, especially if you use an acidic marinade ingredient such as citrus, wine, or vinegar. If you choose an acidic marinade, be sure to marinate the meat for no more than an hour or two at room temperature. The only way to tell if a marinade fits the bill is by trial and error, but the general rule for marinating pork tenderloins is that less is better.

Take care when cooking pork tenderloin. Its almost total lack of fat means that it can easily dry out if overcooked. It's best cooked to an internal temperature of no more than 150°F (some restaurant cooks prefer 145°F). Allow the meat to rest for 5 minutes or so after cooking so that the temperature will have risen to about 155°F when you serve it. At this point, the slices will be faintly pink and juicy.

Grilled Pork Tenderloin

■ Flavor Step ■

Dry rub, such as Herb
Rub for Pork, Lamb,
or Beef (page 263),
OR marinade
or brine of your choice
(see Seasoning Chart,
page 577)

2 ¾-to-1¼-pound pork
tenderloins, trimmed
of silverskin and
excess fat

Serves 4 to 6
■ IN A HURRY ■ LOW-FAT (DEPENDING
ON OIL IN MARINADE AND SAUCES SERVED)

MASTER RECIPE

ITS SMALL SIZE, TENDERNESS, and lack of fat make the pork tenderloin ideal for grilling. It can be left whole, seared on the outside, and then roasted briefly by the indirect method to complete the cooking. Tenderloin can also be cooked directly over the coals quickly, and its low fat content means that you don't have to worry so much about flaming.

Pork tenderloins can also be cut into ½-to-¾-inch chunks or medallions that can be cooked on skewers as kebabs. For a full discussion, see Grilled Pork Kebabs (page 290).

If you want to use soaked wood chips for grilling, plan ahead.

■ **Flavor Step** ■ Generously coat the meat with a dry rub or marinate it in a nonacidic marinade for at least 2 hours at room temperature or overnight in the refrigerator. If you use a marinade containing citrus juice, wine, or vinegar, however, marinate it only for up to 2 hours at room temperature. If you choose to brine the pork tenderloins, leave the whole tenderloins in the brine for 6 to 8 hours in the refrigerator, butterflied tenderloin for 2 to 4 hours. Let refrigerated meat come to room temperature while you build the fire. If you're using a wet marinade or brine, remove the meat from the marinade and pat it dry.

To cook over direct heat: Prepare a charcoal fire or covered gas grill as described in Grilled Pork Chops, page 264, and add 2 cups soaked wood chips (oak, hickory) if desired. Put the meat directly above the hottest part of the fire. If any flaming occurs, cover the grill; if you're not using a covered grill, move the pork to a cooler part of the grill. Cook the meat for about 1½ minutes on each side. Move the meat to a cooler part of the grill, cover the grill, and cook for 2 to 3 minutes more per side, until the meat is firm to the touch and registers an internal temperature of 145° to 150°F.

If you are using a gas grill, cook the meat for 1½ minutes per side to sear. Then continue to cook over direct heat for 2 to 3 minutes more per side, covering the grill and moving the meat to the turned-off side of the grill if flaming occurs. Cook the pork for about 3½ to 4½ total minutes per side.

Remove the meat from the grill, cover loosely with foil, and let it rest for 3 to 5 minutes. You can serve the pork tenderloin as is or with a condiment or sauce.

To cook over indirect heat: Build the fire (see Grilling, page 63). Once the coals are burning, mound them into banks on either side of the barbecue grate with a drip pan in between. You can sprinkle 2 cups soaked wood chips (oak, hickory) over the coals at this time, if desired, dividing them equally between the 2 mounds. Sear the tenderloins directly over the hot coals for 1 to 2 minutes per side. Move the tenderloins to the center of the grill, over the drip pan. Cover the grill and roast the meat for 10 to 15 minutes, or until the internal temperature reaches 145° to 150°F. Turn the meat from time to time and renew the wood chips as needed.

If you are using a gas grill, preheat both sides of the grill for 20 minutes, then shut off half the grill. Sear the meat over the flame on all sides, for about 3 minutes total; cover the grill and move the meat to a cooler spot if any flaming occurs. After the meat is seared, move it to the turned-off half of the grill, cover, and cook for 10 to 15 minutes, or until the internal temperature of the meat reaches 145° to 150°F. Turn the meat from time to time.

Remove the meat from the grill, cover loosely with foil, and let it rest for about 5 minutes. Carve the pork into thick slices and serve as is or with a sauce or condiment of your choice.

Grilled Pork Tenderloin with Rosemary and Fennel Seed Crust

2 ¾-to-1¼-pound pork
   tenderloins, trimmed
   of silverskin and fat,
   butterflied by cutting
   lengthwise down the
   center, and pounded
   to a ⅜-to-½-inch
   thickness

■ Flavor Step ■
ROSEMARY AND FENNEL RUB FOR PORK

1 tablespoon olive oil

1 tablespoon fennel seed,
   bruised with the flat
   side of a knife or with
   a mortar and pestle

1 tablespoon chopped
   fresh rosemary or 2
   teaspoons dried

1 tablespoon minced garlic

2 teaspoons kosher salt

2 teaspoons coarsely
   ground black pepper

Serves 4 to 6
■ Low-Fat ■ In a Hurry

YOU CAN ALSO USE this savory herb rub with grilled pork chops, lamb chops, or veal chops. Serve the pork with oven-roasted whole fennel bulbs or fennel bulbs cut into thick slices and grilled. Braised red or green cabbage is a good substitute for fennel bulbs.

■ **Flavor Step** ■ Spread the meat on a plate and rub the olive oil on both sides. Combine the remaining ingredients and rub the mixture all over the pork, pressing it into the meat and any crevices. Let the tenderloins rest for 30 minutes at room temperature.

Grill the tenderloins over medium-high coals for 3 to 4 minutes per side, or until the internal temperature registers 145° to 150°F. Let them rest, covered lightly with foil, for 5 minutes. Serve ½ tenderloin per person.

Pork Tenderloin Tandoori with Cilantro Chutney

Serves 4
■ Low-Fat ■ Fit for Company

ALTHOUGH THE IDEA of using a North Indian tandoori marinade for pork might not be traditional, it is in fact a great way to flavor the meat, especially the lean and succulent tenderloin. For a real feast, serve it with grilled tandoori onions, basmati rice, baked curried cauliflower with yogurt, and flatbread. If you're not a master at making your own Indian flatbread, warmed pita bread does almost as well.

The tandoori marinade is equally good on lamb and can also be used to coat onions and other vegetables such as zucchini and parboiled potatoes before grilling. If you prefer to buy garam masala, it is also available in Asian groceries and by mail-order (see Sources, page 584).

■ **Flavor Step** ■ Whisk all the ingredients for the tandoori marinade together in a small bowl. Place the butterflied tenderloins in a shallow baking dish. Cover them completely with all but ½ cup of the marinade, turning to coat them thoroughly. Cover with plastic wrap and marinate for 2 hours at room temperature or overnight in the refrigerator. Cover and refrigerate the remaining marinade to use later with the onions.

■ Flavor Step ■
TANDOORI MARINADE
1½ cups plain yogurt
¼ cup fresh lime or lemon juice
1 tablespoon minced garlic
1 tablespoon paprika, preferably mild Hungarian
1 tablespoon ground coriander
1 teaspoon ground cumin
1 teaspoon turmeric
1 teaspoon salt
1 teaspoon cayenne pepper or more, to taste
2 teaspoons Garam Masala (page 321)

2 ¾-to-1¼-pound pork tenderloins, trimmed of silverskin and fat, cut in half crosswise, butterflied, and pounded to a ⅜-to-½-inch thickness

2 large onions, cut into ½-inch-thick rounds

Cilantro Chutney (page 320)

About ½ hour before you're going to cook, remove the meat from the refrigerator. The butterflied tenderloins are best cooked over a hot grill, but they can also be broiled (see Broiling, page 58). Heat a charcoal or gas grill to medium-high.

Brush the onion slices generously with the reserved marinade and place them over the fire. Shake most of the excess marinade from the pork tenderloins and place them over the fire. Grill the onions and meat for 2 to 3 minutes per side, or until the meat registers 150°F on an instant-read thermometer; the onions should be lightly colored. Let the meat rest for 5 minutes, covered loosely with foil, before serving. Serve with the chutney on the side.

CILANTRO CHUTNEY

Makes about 2½ cups

1	½-inch piece of peeled fresh ginger
1	garlic clove
1	medium jalapeño chile, seeded and chopped
4	green onions or scallions, cut into 2-inch pieces
1½	cups packed fresh cilantro leaves
¼	cup chopped fresh mint (optional)
1	tablespoon fresh lime or lemon juice
½	teaspoon ground cumin
1	teaspoon salt
1	teaspoon sugar
½	cup plain yogurt

Process the ginger, garlic, and chile together in a food processor or blender. Add the rest of the ingredients except the yogurt and pulse to chop the vegetables and herbs. Add the yogurt and process to form a smooth sauce. Refrigerate until ready to serve. The chutney will keep for 2 days.

GARAM MASALA

Makes ⅓ cup

ROASTING BRINGS OUT THE FLAVOR of the spices in this classic Indian spice mix. It will keep for up to two months in a tightly covered jar.

1   3-inch cinnamon stick
2   tablespoons coriander seeds
1   tablespoon cumin seeds
     Seeds from 15 green cardamom pods
2   teaspoons fennel seeds
1   teaspoon whole cloves
1   teaspoon yellow or brown mustard seeds
2   teaspoons peppercorns

Preheat the oven to 250°F. Spread the spices on a roasting pan and roast in the bottom third of the oven for 30 minutes or so, taking care to shake and stir the spices frequently so that they don't burn.

Place the cinnamon stick between dish towels and hit it with a hammer to break it into pieces. Grind all the spices together to a powder in an electric coffee grinder reserved for that purpose, a spice grinder, or a mortar and pestle. Use immediately or store in a jar with a tight lid.

Roasted Pork Tenderloin

■ **Flavor Step** ■
Spice Rub for Pork or
Beef (page 375), OR
Herb Rub for Pork,
Lamb, or Beef (page
263), OR any of the
marinades for pork
(see Seasoning Chart,
page 580; avoid high-
acid marinades), OR
salt and freshly ground
black pepper

2 ¾-to-1¼-pound pork
  tenderloins, trimmed
  of silverskin and fat
1 tablespoon olive oil

PAN SAUCE
2 tablespoons chopped
  shallots or green onions
  or scallions
½ cup dry white wine
¾ cup chicken stock
  Salt and freshly ground
  black pepper

Serves 4 to 6
■ LOW-FAT ■ IN A HURRY ■ FIT FOR COMPANY

MASTER RECIPE

WHETHER YOU MARINATE IT, rub it with spices and herbs, or just season it with salt and pepper, the way to cook a whole pork tenderloin is basically the same. Once it's cooked, you can slice and serve it as is, with a fruit or vegetable condiment such as Peach and Red Onion Salsa (page 293), or with a sauce made from the pan drippings. All the recipes for sautéed pork chops with pan sauces (see pages 266-79) can be used to make a pan sauce for roast pork tenderloin. If you want to make a pan sauce, we recommend browning the tenderloin in a cast-iron or other ovenproof skillet.

Pork tenderloins can be roasted individually or two can be tied together in a roll to increase the diameter of the slices. In addition, it is very easy to butterfly two whole tenderloins and stuff and tie them together for a meaty and elegant presentation.

You can make any of the variations that follow by changing the Flavor Step and/or Pan Sauce and following the directions in this Master Recipe.

■ **Flavor Step** ■ Rub the herbs and spices over the meat. You may cook it right away or put it into a zipper-lock bag or shallow bowl with the marinade; cover the bowl. Marinate for 1 to 2 hours at room temperature or overnight in the refrigerator, turning the meat occasionally. If the meat has been refrigerated, remove it from the refrigerator 30 minutes before cooking. If the tenderloins have been in a marinade, pat them dry with paper towels. Or you can simply season them with salt and pepper.

Preheat the oven to 400°F. Heat the olive oil in a heavy, ovenproof skillet over medium-high heat. Brown the tenderloins lightly, turning them frequently to brown on all sides, 3 to 4 minutes total. Place the skillet in the oven and roast the pork for 12 to 15 minutes, or until the internal temperature is 145° to 150°F. Let the meat rest on a platter, covered loosely with foil, for 5 minutes before serving.

Meanwhile, make the Pan Sauce: Pour off all but about 1 tablespoon of fat from the pan and place it over medium heat. Add the shallots or green onions and cook for 30 seconds, stirring well. Stir in the wine. Bring to a boil, add the stock, and reduce until the sauce just turns syrupy.

Taste for salt and pepper. Carve the meat into ½-inch-thick slices and nap with the sauce.

Roasted Pork Tenderloin with Blackberry and Black Currant Sauce

■ **Flavor Step** ■
½ teaspoon dried sage
Salt and freshly ground
black pepper

2 ¾-to-1¼-pound pork
tenderloins, trimmed
of silverskin and fat
1 tablespoon olive oil

BLACKBERRY AND BLACK CURRANT PAN SAUCE

2 tablespoon red wine
vinegar
1 cup chicken stock
½ cup *crème de cassis*
(black currant liqueur)
1 tablespoon blackberry
or black currant jam
½ cup fresh or thawed
frozen blackberries
1 teaspoon cornstarch,
dissolved in 2 teaspoons
cold water
Salt and freshly ground
black pepper

■ **Flavor Step** ■ Season and cook the meat as directed in the Master Recipe, page 323.

To make the Pan Sauce: Pour off all the fat from the roasting pan. Deglaze the pan over high heat with a mixture of the vinegar, stock, and liqueur. Stir in the jam and boil the sauce until it begins to turn syrupy. Add the blackberries and cook for 30 seconds to heat them through. Stir in the cornstarch mixture and cook and stir until the sauce thickens. Taste for salt and pepper. Carve the pork into ½-inch-thick slices and pour the sauce and berries over.

Roasted Pork Tenderloin with Chinese Ginger-Lemon Sauce

Serves 4 to 6
■ LOW-FAT ■ FIT FOR COMPANY

■ **Flavor Step** ■ Combine the marinade ingredients in a small bowl. Place the tenderloins in a zipper-lock bag or shallow bowl and pour in the marinade. Cover if necessary and marinate for 2 hours or overnight in the refrigerator, turning occasionally.

The next day, remove the tenderloins from the marinade and pat dry. Reserve ½ cup of the marinade. Roast the pork as directed in the Master Recipe, page 322, but do not brown in oil.

To make the Pan Sauce: While the pork is cooking, combine the ½ cup reserved marinade in a small saucepan with the chicken stock, lemon juice, ginger, sugar, sesame oil, and lemon zest. Bring to a boil and reduce to a simmer.

When the pork is cooked, remove it to a warm platter and cover loosely with foil. Stir the cornstarch mixture into the sauce and cook over medium-high heat, stirring often, until the sauce gets syrupy. Taste for salt and pepper. Carve the pork into ½-inch-thick slices and serve with the sauce.

■ Flavor Step ■
CHINESE GINGER-LEMON MARINADE

- ½ cup soy sauce
- ¼ cup dry sherry
- 2 teaspoons minced garlic
- 4 green onions or scallions (white and green parts), minced
- 2 tablespoons minced fresh ginger
- 2 tablespoons fresh lemon juice

- 2 ¾-to-1¼-pound pork tenderloins, trimmed of silverskin and fat

PAN SAUCE

- ½ cup chicken stock
- 2 tablespoons fresh lemon juice
- 2 teaspoons minced fresh ginger
- 2 tablespoons sugar
- 1 teaspoon Asian sesame oil
- 1 teaspoon minced lemon zest
- 1 teaspoon cornstarch, dissolved in 2 tablespoons cold water
- Salt and freshly ground black pepper

Roasted Pork Tenderloin with Apples

■ **Flavor Step** ■

APPLE BRANDY
MARINADE FOR PORK

2 tablespoon Calvados
or apple brandy

¼ cup apple cider

1 tablespoon cider vinegar

¼ teaspoon ground
cinnamon

½ teaspoon rubbed sage

1 teaspoon freshly ground
black pepper

1 teaspoon salt

2 tablespoons soy sauce

1 tablespoon vegetable oil

2 ¾-to-1¼-pound pork
tenderloins, trimmed
of silverskin and fat

1 tablespoon olive oil

2 Golden Delicious,
Granny Smith, or
McIntosh apples, cored,
peeled, and thinly
sliced

PAN SAUCE

½ cup chicken stock

¼ cup apple juice
Salt and freshly ground
black pepper

THE TENDERLOINS are marinated and then roasted briefly on a bed of sliced apples. The reserved marinade is then used as the basis for a sauce.

■ **Flavor Step** ■ Combine the marinade ingredients in a small bowl. Put the tenderloins in a zipper-lock bag or bowl and pour the marinade over. Marinate overnight (cover the bowl if used) in the refrigerator, turning the meat occasionally.

About 30 minutes before cooking, remove the meat from the marinade, reserving the marinade. Pat the meat dry with paper towels. Brown the tenderloins in the olive oil as directed in the Master Recipe, page 322. Remove the pork from the pan and set aside. Spread the apple slices on the bottom of the pan and put the pork on top. Brush the pork with the reserved marinade and roast at 425°F for 12 to 15 minutes. Transfer the pork and apples to a warm platter and cover loosely with foil while you prepare the sauce.

To make the Pan Sauce: Add the chicken stock to the roasting pan and boil, scraping up any browned bits from the bottom; transfer to a saucepan. Add the reserved marinade and the apple juice to the saucepan and boil over high heat to reduce the sauce almost to a syrup. You should end up with about ¼ cup of sauce. Taste for salt and pepper. Carve the pork into ½-inch-thick slices, arrange the apples on top, and pour the sauce over.

Roasted Pork Tenderloin with Rum, Maple, and Pecan Glaze

Serves 4 to 6
■ FIT FOR COMPANY ■ IN A HURRY

S ERVE THESE PORK TENDERLOINS with Roasted Sweet Potatoes (see page 301). Spoon this sweet and savory sauce over the sliced pork and potatoes. The glaze is also excellent on roast ham or ham steak.

■ **Flavor Step** ■ Rub the sage, salt, and pepper on the tenderloins.

To make the Rum, Maple, and Pecan Glaze: Combine all the ingredients in a saucepan and cook over medium heat, stirring often, until the sugar is melted.

Preheat the oven to 350°F. Brown the pork in the olive oil as directed in the Master Recipe, page 322.

Pour the glaze over the pork in the roasting pan, turning to coat the meat thoroughly. Roast for 15 minutes, or until the pork reaches an internal temperature of 145° to 150°F, basting two or three times with the glaze in the pan.

To serve, carve the pork into ½-inch-thick slices and pour the glaze from the pan over the meat and the sweet potatoes, if you serve them. Adjust salt and pepper if necessary.

■ Flavor Step ■

½ teaspoon rubbed sage
Salt and freshly ground black pepper

2 ¾-to-1¼-pound pork tenderloins, trimmed of silverskin and fat
2 tablespoons olive oil

RUM, MAPLE, AND PECAN GLAZE

1 cup maple syrup
1 cup light or dark brown sugar
½ cup dark rum
2 tablespoons cider vinegar
1 cup chopped pecans
Salt and freshly ground black pepper

Roasted Pork Tenderloin with Oyster Stuffing and Spicy Gingersnap Gravy

CREOLE SPICE RUB FOR
PORK, BEEF, OR LAMB

- 1 teaspoon dried sage
- 1 teaspoon dried thyme
- ½ teaspoon dried rosemary
- 1 teaspoon dry mustard, preferably Colman's
- ½ teaspoon cayenne pepper
- 1 teaspoon granulated garlic or garlic powder
- 2 teaspoons salt
- 2 teaspoons freshly ground black pepper

- 2 ¾-to-1¼-pound pork tenderloins, trimmed of silverskin and fat

OYSTER STUFFING

- 1 tablespoon butter
- ¼ cup finely chopped smoked ham or smoked sausage, such as andouille
- ½ cup finely chopped onions
- 2 tablespoons finely chopped celery
- 1 teaspoon minced garlic
- ½ cup finely diced red bell pepper
- 2 tablespoons finely chopped green onions or scallions (white and green parts)
- ¼ cup chopped mushrooms

Serves 4 to 6
■ FIT FOR COMPANY

O N OUR MANY TRIPS to New Orleans, we've always loved a Creole specialty: stuffed pork chops with a spicy oyster dressing, so we've adapted it to pork tenderloin. The stuffing, of course, can be used with thick pork chops or birds of all kind. It makes a great holiday side dish when cooked alone in an uncovered buttered casserole for 30 to 40 minutes at 350°F. A double recipe ought to be enough for six to eight people.

Butterfly the tenderloin by making a lengthwise cut down the center of each tenderloin to about ¼ inch from the other side. Flatten the split tenderloins with a meat mallet or the flat side of a knife or cleaver to about ⅜ inch thick.

■ **Flavor Step** ■ Combine all the spice rub ingredients and set aside 2 teaspoons of the mixture. Rub the remaining herbs and spices generously all over the meat. (Any extra spice rub that has not come into contact with the meat can be stored, covered, for up to 3 months.) Set the meat aside while you prepare the stuffing.

To make the Oyster Stuffing: In a medium skillet, melt the butter over moderate heat. Add the ham or sausage and cook for 2 minutes, stirring occasionally. Add the onion, celery, and garlic, cover the pan, and cook for 5 minutes, or until the vegetables are softened, stirring often. Stir in the bell pepper, green onions or scallions, and mushrooms and continue to cook, uncovered, for 1 minute. Season with the reserved 2 teaspoons Creole Spice Rub and add the oysters along with their liquid. Cook just until the oysters have become firm and plump, about 2 minutes.

Stir in the corn bread or bread crumbs. The stuffing should be moist enough to hold together when molded on a spoon, but not sopping wet. Add a little water or stock if necessary. Remove the pan from the heat and let cool slightly, then stir in the egg. Taste for salt and pepper. Let the stuffing cool in the refrigerator for 15 minutes or so to firm up.

Preheat the oven to 350°F. Spread the stuffing on the cut side of one of the tenderloins, leaving a ½-inch border around the edges. Lay the other tenderloin cut side down over the stuffing to form a long, flat roast. Tie the roast every 2 inches with cotton string. Don't worry if a little stuffing comes out the ends.

Heat the oil in an ovenproof skillet large enough to hold the roast. Brown the pork over medium-high heat for 1½ minutes per side, or until it's lightly browned all over. Put the skillet in the oven and roast for 20 to 25 minutes, or until the pork (not the stuffing) reaches an internal temperature of 145° to 150°F; the stuffing should measure at least 140°F. Remove the pork and keep it warm while you make the gravy.

Remove the strings and carve the pork into ¾-inch-thick slices. Serve 1 or 2 slices per person and pass the gravy separately.

2 teaspoons Creole Spice Rub (see opposite page)
1 12-ounce jar of shucked small oysters (about 24)
1 cup corn bread crumbs, dried overnight, OR 1 cup coarse bread crumbs, made from day-old French bread
Water or stock to moisten dressing if necessary
1 large egg, lightly beaten
Salt and freshly ground black pepper

1 tablespoon olive oil
Spicy Gingersnap Gravy (page 273)

Roasted Pork Tenderloin Stuffed with Dried Cranberries and Apples

DRIED CRANBERRY AND APPLE STUFFING

2 cups chicken stock

½ cup dried cranberries

½ cup dried apples, cut into ¼-inch dice

1 tablespoon butter

¼ cup finely chopped onion

1 teaspoon minced garlic

½ teaspoon dried thyme

½ teaspoon dried sage

½ teaspoon salt

¼ teaspoon freshly ground black pepper

½ cup fresh bread crumbs

1 large egg, lightly beaten

2 ¾-to-1¼-pound pork tenderloins, trimmed of silverskin and fat

■ Flavor Step ■
Herb Rub for Pork, Lamb, or Beef (page 263)

1 tablespoon butter

Serves 4 to 6
■ FIT FOR COMPANY ■ MOM'S COMFORT FOOD

TO SERVE THIS STUFFING as a side dish with ham, poultry, or roast pork loin, triple the recipe. Cook the stuffing in a covered buttered casserole for 30 to 40 minutes. A triple recipe should be enough for six to eight people.

To make the Dried Cranberry and Apple Stuffing: Bring the stock to a boil in a small saucepan and add the dried fruit. Remove from the heat and let the fruit plump for 15 minutes. Drain the fruit, squeezing out as much liquid as you can, and set it aside. Save the stock to use in the pan sauce.

In a small skillet, melt the butter over medium heat. Put in the onion, garlic, herbs, salt, and pepper. Cover the pan and cook for 5 minutes, stirring from time to time. Stir in the bread crumbs and the reserved fruit. Remove the pan from the heat. Moisten the stuffing, if necessary, with a tablespoon or two or the reserved stock. The stuffing should be moist enough to mound in a spoon, but not sopping wet. Let the stuffing cool for 15 minutes or more in the refrigerator to firm up.

Preheat the oven to 350°F. Butterfly and flatten the tenderloins as described on page 328. Place half the stuffing over the cut side of one of the flattened tenderloins, leaving about a ¾-inch border down each side. Roll up the roast and tie with cotton string every 2 or 3 inches. Repeat for the other tenderloin. Or you can put all the stuffing on the cut side of one tenderloin, cover it with the other, cut side down, and then tie every 2 or 3 inches to make one roast.

■ **Flavor Step** ■ Season the outside of the pork well with all the herb rub.

In an ovenproof skillet large enough to hold both tenderloins or the large roast, heat the butter over medium-high heat. Put in the pork and brown on all sides, about 5 minutes total. Place the skillet in the oven and roast for 6 minutes. Turn the pork over (the bottom tends to burn) and roast for 8 to 10 minutes more, or until the meat has reached an internal temperature of 145° to 150°F. Remove the pork and keep warm while you prepare the sauce.

To make the Pan Sauce: Pour out any fat from the pan and add the white wine. Boil the wine over high heat until reduced by half, 2 to 3 minutes. Add the reserved stock and the cranberry sauce. Stir to melt the jelly and boil until the sauce is just syrupy. Taste for salt and pepper.

Carve the pork into ¾-inch-thick slices and arrange on a platter. Pour the pan sauce over them and serve.

PAN SAUCE

1 cup dry white wine
½ cup jellied cranberry
   sauce
   Salt and freshly ground
   black pepper

Chinese Marinated and Roasted Pork
(Char Su)

■ Flavor Step ■

CHINESE BARBECUED
PORK MARINADE

1 tablespoon minced garlic

2 tablespoons minced
fresh ginger

½ cup soy sauce

¼ cup sweet sherry

¼ cup hoisin sauce

2 tablespoons light or
dark brown sugar

1 tablespoon dry mustard,
preferably Colman's

1 teaspoon Chinese
5-spice powder

2-3 pounds pork tenderloins,
OR 2-3 pounds Boston
butt, butterflied
(have the butcher
butterfly the meat),
cut into 2-by-2-by-12-
inch strips, OR two
1-to-1½-pound slabs
of baby back ribs,
OR 3 pounds country-
style ribs, OR 2 pounds
1½-inch-thick pork
chops

Serves 4 to 8, depending on cut used
■ **Low-Fat (pork tenderloin)**
■ **Cooking on a Budget (country-style ribs)** ■
Good for a Crowd

THE CHINESE HAVE LONG BEEN the world's masters of pork cookery. They know how to bring out its succulent flavor while keeping it juicy and tender. A basic ingredient in many Chinese pork dishes, including soups, sautéed noodles, stir-fries, and stuffings for dumplings, is the marinated roasted pork usually called *char su,* or barbecued pork. Most Chinese chefs prepare *char su* from large strips cut from a butterflied pork shoulder butt. This cut has more fat than the loin or tenderloin, and it is juicier and more flavorful.

This marinade works with the traditional Chinese cut, as well as with spareribs, country-style ribs, baby back ribs, thick pork chops, pieces of boneless loin, or pork tenderloins. Once the meat is marinated, all you have to do is place it on a rack and roast it in the oven to the appropriate degree of doneness, brushing it occasionally with a baste of honey and brown sugar.

Once it's cooked, the pork can be eaten hot or at room temperature. You can serve it sliced over steamed baby bok choy, boiled Chinese broccoli, stir-fried snow peas, or other such vegetables. Serving portions depend on whether the meat has bones or not: a slab of spareribs will feed two or three people; a rack of baby back ribs will feed one or two; ⅓ to ½ pound of boneless meat is a generous serving for one.

■ **Flavor Step** ■ In a medium bowl, whisk together all the marinade ingredients. Place the pork in a large zipper-lock bag or bowl and pour the marinade over. Cover if using a bowl and refrigerate overnight or up to 3 days, turning a few times to coat the pork with the marinade.

About 30 minutes before cooking, remove the pork from the marinade. Preheat the oven to 450°F for pork tenderloin or Boston butt strips, 400°F for ribs or pork chops (the higher temperature may cause the sugar in the marinade to burn, so watch carefully). Place the meat on a rack in a shallow pan lined with aluminum foil.

To make the Honey Baste: Combine the honey and sugar in a bowl. Brush about a quarter of the baste generously over the meat.

Roast the pork tenderloins for 10 to 12 minutes, or until the internal temperature reaches 145° to 150°F, brushing the meat 3 times with the honey baste. Roast any of the other meats to an internal temperature of 150° to 155°F, basting 3 times. Pork chops, baby back ribs, and country-style ribs will take 20 to 30 minutes. Brush the meat with the baste one last time when you remove it from the oven. Allow it to rest, loosely covered with foil, for 5 to 10 minutes before carving.

HONEY BASTE
(Double the recipe
for spareribs)
½ cup honey
¼ cup packed light or
dark brown sugar

TUSCAN TRUCK STOP

SOME OF THE BEST PORK I've ever eaten was in the Tuscany region of Italy, where they call their roast pork *Arista* (from a Greek word meaning "the best"). I had just arrived after a long flight, and it was late morning as I drove my rental car from Pisa to Florence. Since I wasn't ready to face the 100-plus m.p.h. madness of the *autostrada,* I decided to take the side road. The traffic was mostly large trucks that didn't care to pay the tolls and a few small cars filled with folks who wanted to live at a slower pace than most other Italians. So I had plenty of time to peruse the scenery and look for a place to have lunch. When I saw a nondescript restaurant with a whole lot of trucks parked outside, I knew I'd found my spot. In Europe, just as in America, find the truck stops if you want the real (and often the best) food of a region. I pulled over and went inside with the hearty appetite of a truck-drivin' man, ready for whatever they had to offer.

I was seated at a big communal table packed with a group of tough-looking, hungry truckers who were having a very animated discussion about something of great importance to them all. When I asked for a menu, the conversation stopped immediately. "No menu," I was told by everybody at once, "just eat what comes, and you'll eat good here *(mangia bene 'qua)*"—music to my ears.

First came a huge platter of crostini—toasted bread covered with various vegetable purees and toppings: eggplant with garlic and herbs, chickpeas with cumin and black pepper, caramelized onions, white beans and fresh rosemary. Then a big bowl of thick bean and vegetable soup with lots of chopped chard and mustard greens floating on top. And then the main dish appeared: thick slices of faintly pink pork, scented with herbs, floating in meat juices. One bite of the pork and I knew the truck stop rule still worked. The meat was tender and succulent, perfumed with fresh sage and rosemary. The broth was intensely meaty, with the flavors of roasted garlic and black pepper. Served with the pork were a big bowl of Tuscan white beans in fragrant olive oil, a simple green salad, and some perfectly cooked, crisp tiny green beans. With a glass of Tuscan red from the carafe that circulated constantly and some crusty bread to sop up the juices, this truck stop special was one of my most memorable meals in Italy.

I've been back to Tuscany many times and always order *Arista* when I see it on the menu. It's always delicious, although not often up to truck stop standards. I've since learned to make it myself—here's the recipe.   *B.A.*

Arista
(Tuscan Herb-Infused Roast Pork)

Serves 8 (4-pound roast) or
16 (8-pound roast)

■ FIT FOR COMPANY ■ LOW-FAT
■ GREAT LEFTOVERS ■ MOM'S COMFORT FOOD

T HE SECRET HERE is not to overcook the meat and to be quite generous with the seasonings. Any pork left over makes great sandwiches: cold with lemon mayonnaise or tonnato sauce; hot, reheated in the pan sauce.

* * *

■ **Flavor Step** ■ Combine all the ingredients in a small bowl. Rub all over the meat to provide it with a generous coating.

Preheat the oven to 450°F. Brush the meat with 2 tablespoons of the oil. Brush a shallow roasting pan with the remaining ½ tablespoon oil and scatter the sliced garlic on the bottom to provide a bed for the roast. Lay the roast on the garlic, fat side up. Put the pan in the center of the oven and roast for 15 minutes. Turn the oven down to 300°F and roast for 1¼ hours longer if cooking a 4-pound roast, 2 hours longer for a double roast, then test the meat: when the center reads 145° to 150°F on an instant-read thermometer, remove the meat from the oven and cover it loosely with foil while you prepare the sauce.

To make the Pan Sauce: Pour off the fat and add the wine to the roasting pan and bring it to a boil over high heat, scraping up any browned bits from the bottom. Add the stock and cook until the sauce is reduced by half. Strain the sauce, taste for salt and pepper, and serve over ¼-inch-thick slices of the meat.

■ **Flavor Step** ■
ARISTA HERB RUB FOR
PORK LOIN

¼ cup finely chopped fresh rosemary or 2 tablespoons dried

2 tablespoons finely chopped fresh sage or 1 tablespoon dried

2 teaspoons crushed fennel seeds

1 tablespoon kosher salt

1 teaspoon freshly ground black pepper

1 4-pound center-cut boneless pork loin, with a thin layer of fat left intact, OR an 8-pound double pork loin roast, tied and trimmed (double the herb rub recipe)

PAN SAUCE

2½ tablespoons olive oil

10 garlic cloves, thinly sliced

¼ cup dry white wine

1 cup chicken or beef stock

Salt and freshly ground black pepper

Garlic-Roasted Pork Loin

6 garlic cloves

1 tablespoon salt

1 tablespoon finely
   chopped fresh sage
   or 2 teaspoons dried

1 tablespoon finely
   chopped fresh rosemary
   or 2 teaspoons dried

1 teaspoon freshly ground
   black pepper

1 tablespoon olive oil

1 4-to-5-pound center-cut
   pork loin with rack
   of bones removed but
   intact OR a 3½-to-4-
   pound boneless center-
   cut pork loin

Serves 6, with leftovers
■ GREAT LEFTOVERS ■ MOM'S COMFORT FOOD

IT'S HARD TO BEAT a center-cut pork loin infused with garlic and with a rack of roasted bones attached. The bones add extra flavor and juiciness to the finished roast and also enhance a pan gravy, but you can omit them and just follow the sauce directions below. We prefer to have the butcher separate the meat from the bones, leaving the bones intact. We season the meat generously with the paste of chopped garlic and fresh herbs and then reassemble the roast, tying the rack of bones to the meat with cotton twine or kitchen string. This procedure is easier than it sounds and can be done the day before cooking the roast. Preparing it a day ahead also gives the flavors of the garlic and herb paste a chance to penetrate and flavor the meat.

When the roast is properly cooked, the bones may still be a bit reddish; if you want to serve them to your more carnivorously inclined guests to gnaw on, put them back in the oven for 5 minutes or so while the roast rests before carving.

A pan sauce is optional—any of those suggested with sautéed pork chops (see pages 266-79) or roasted pork tenderloin (see pages 322-30) will go well here. Or you can serve the meat and bones as is, with Oven-Roasted Potatoes (page 126) and sautéed greens.

■ Flavor Step ■ Using a mortar and pestle or food processor, mash the garlic and salt together. Add the herbs, pepper, and olive oil and blend to form a paste. Rub the paste all over the meat and on the outside of the bones, if using them. Reassemble the roast and tie the bones to the meat at 2-inch intervals or so. If using a boneless roast, rub the paste all over the meat. Marinate the roast, loosely covered, for about 2 hours at room temperature or, preferably, overnight in the refrigerator.

If the pork was refrigerated, take it out about an hour before cooking. Preheat the oven to 450°F. Lay the roast, bone side down, on a rack in a shallow roasting pan and place it in the center of the oven. Roast for 15 minutes. Turn the heat down to 300°F and roast for 1½ hours longer. The internal temperature of the roast should reach 145° to 150°F. Remove the meat from the oven and cut off the string to separate the bones from the meat. Cover the meat loosely with foil and keep warm for 20 minutes before carving. Or, for a boneless roast, let the meat rest for 15 to 20 minutes, loosely covered with foil, before carving.

If the bones are reddish, put them back in the oven for 5 to 10 minutes while the meat rests. The bones should no longer be red when done. Carve the meat into ¼-inch-thick slices and cut the bones into serving pieces.

Cured Pork Loin Roasted with Parsnips in Maple-Vanilla Sauce

■ Flavor Step ■
Nancy's Vanilla Brine
(page 255) or other
brine of your choice
(see Flavor Brining,
page 254)

1 4-to-6-pound boneless
  pork loin

12 medium parsnips
   (about 2 pounds),
   peeled and cut into
   ½-inch-thick
   diagonal slices

3 tablespoons butter,
  melted
  Salt and freshly ground
  black pepper

Serves 6 to 8, with leftovers
■ FIT FOR COMPANY ■ GREAT LEFTOVERS

THIS RECIPE ILLUSTRATES just how succulent and juicy roast pork can be when cured in a flavor brine. We've used Nancy's Vanilla Brine, but any of the other brines (pages 256-59) would work well too. The sweetness of the parsnips in this dish blends perfectly with the vanilla and maple syrup flavors of the meat and sauce.

■ **Flavor Step** ■ Pour the brine into a large bowl or plastic storage container and brine the pork loin for 1 to 2 days, as described on page 254.

Remove the loin and pat it dry with paper towels. Let the meat rest at room temperature for 20 to 30 minutes while you roast the parsnips.

Preheat the oven to 425°F. Brush the parsnips generously with the melted butter and salt and pepper them well. Spread them in a single layer on a baking sheet or shallow roasting pan and roast for about 15 minutes, or until they begin to brown. Turn them and continue roasting until the other side is browned and they are soft, 10 to 15 minutes. Set the parsnips aside.

Turn the oven down to 350°F. Put the pork, fat side up, in a shallow roasting pan and roast for about 1¼ hours. When the internal temperature reaches 145°F, remove the pork from the oven and cover it loosely with foil. Let the meat rest for 15 to 30 minutes while you prepare the sauce. During this time, the internal temperature of the roast will rise to 150° to 155°F because of carryover cooking.

To make the Maple-Vanilla Sauce: Pour off most of the fat from the roasting pan. Add the garlic and place the pan over medium heat. Cook for 1 minute, stirring. Pour in the stock and scrape up any browned bits from the bottom of the pan. Pour the contents of the pan into a small saucepan. Add the wine, maple syrup, and vanilla and cook over medium-high heat, stirring often, until the flavors are concentrated and the sauce starts to become syrupy. Taste for salt and pepper and stir in the optional butter if you want a silkier sauce.

Meanwhile, rewarm the parsnips in the oven. Arrange them on a platter with slices of the pork loin over them. Pour the sauce over and serve.

MAPLE-VANILLA SAUCE

2 teaspoons minced garlic
1 cup chicken stock
¼ cup dry white wine
1 tablespoon maple syrup
1 teaspoon pure vanilla
    extract
  Salt and freshly ground
    black pepper
2 tablespoons butter,
    softened (optional)

Pork Braised in Milk and Capers

½ teaspoon ground fennel
seeds

½ teaspoon rubbed sage or
dried summer savory

2 teaspoons salt

½ teaspoon freshly ground
black pepper

1 4-pound boneless pork
loin

2 tablespoons olive oil

1 tablespoon butter

½ cup finely chopped
onion or shallots

3 cups whole milk

4 teaspoons capers, rinsed,
drained, and chopped

½ teaspoon fennel seed,
ground in a spice
grinder or with mortar
and pestle

2 bay leaves

1 tablespoon fresh lemon
juice

Salt and freshly ground
black pepper

Serves 6 to 10

■ REWARMS WELL ■ FIT FOR COMPANY

IN THIS CLASSIC BOLOGNESE RECIPE, a well-seasoned pork loin is browned and then braised slowly in milk. The juices of the pork combine with the milk, which becomes rich and caramelized, to form a luscious sauce to go with the succulent, juicy meat. Our friend Loni Kuhn, a San Francisco cooking teacher for more than 20 years, has added a few other ingredients that make a good thing even better. For best results, use only whole milk and serve with your favorite rice dishes: mushroom risotto, for example, or brown rice with roasted vegetables. This would be delicious with a Pinot Grigio from the Alto Adige or Collio in northern Italy or a Pinot Gris from Alsace or Oregon.

■ Flavor Step ■ Combine the seasonings in a small bowl. Trim most of the excess fat from the meat. Sprinkle the herb rub all over the meat.

In a heavy, lidded pot just large enough to hold the pork, heat 1 tablespoon of the oil and the butter over medium-high heat. Put in the roast and brown it nicely on all sides, 7 to 10 minutes in all. If the fat begins to blacken, turn down the heat. Remove the meat and pour off all the fat. Add the remaining tablespoon of oil and lower the heat to medium. Put in the onion or shallots, cover, and cook until they begin to color, stirring often, about 3 minutes. Slowly add the milk, 2 teaspoons of the capers, the fennel seed, and bay leaves. Stir well and scrape up any browned bits from the bottom of the pot.

Turn the heat down to low, put the pork back in, and slowly bring the liquid to a simmer. You don't want to boil the milk, which might scorch and burn. Cover the pot partially to let a little steam escape and cook at a low simmer for 1½ to 2 hours or, more important, until the internal temperature of the meat reaches 145° to 150°F. Remove the pork and keep it warm while you finish the sauce. The final temperature will be 150° to 160°F.

Bring the sauce to a mild boil to reduce it until it forms dark curds. Stir frequently so that the sauce doesn't burn. When finished, the sauce will have a nut brown color with dark curds. Remove any grease from the surface. Stir in the remaining 2 teaspoons capers and the lemon juice and taste for salt and pepper.

To serve, carve the meat and arrange the slices on a platter of flavored white or brown rice (or a combination of both) or garlic mashed potatoes. Spoon the sauce over the meat and serve.

A MASTERFUL SAUCE

CHINESE CHEFS often cook chicken and other poultry in what is referred to as a Master Sauce. This soy-based broth flavors the food as it poaches and, because it cooks so slowly, the meat retains its juiciness. We've adapted this technique for boneless pork loin, which can dry out all too easily if overcooked. One of our favorite ways to use Chinese Master Sauce Braised Pork Loin is to cut the cooked loin into ½-to-¾-inch-thick chops and grill them briefly over gas or charcoal. Brush them frequently as they cook with the reserved sauce. The chops can be eaten as is, with more Master Sauce on the side, or cut into slices, tossed with a bit of the sauce and sesame oil, and served on a bed of wilted spinach.

The Master Sauce gets its name because it can be used over and over again, each time getting richer and more intense. Just strain the sauce after each use and refrigerate or freeze it until the next time you need it. If kept in the refrigerator, it should be used or boiled every five to seven days. Freezing is probably the best way for most of us. Each time you use the sauce, add a little more water, a bit of soy sauce, and a piece of ginger and/or star anise. Taste the sauce whenever you use it and judge what seasonings it needs. Remove any fat from the surface before using the refrigerated sauce or freezing it.

You can also cook beef fillet or eye of the round in this sauce (see Chinese Master Sauce Braised Beef, page 198). Chinese chefs love the taste of beef shin or boneless chuck, which take a bit more time to cook but have intense, beefy flavors.

Chinese Master Sauce Braised Pork Loin

Serves 4 to 6
■ GREAT LEFTOVERS ■ REWARMS WELL ■
■ LOW-FAT ■

Once you've poached the loin in this savory stock, the meat can be sliced and served on a bed of steamed Chinese greens for a delicious, low-fat meal. Or the pork can be cooled to be thinly sliced as part of an appetizer plate. You can also use the tender and juicy meat in a wide variety of Asian dishes, such as soups or noodles with various sauces, or incorporated into tasty salads of all types.

■ **Flavor Step** ■ In a heavy pot just large enough to hold the pork, bring the sauce ingredients to a boil. Add the pork; the liquid should come halfway up the side. Add more liquid if needed. Reduce the heat to a simmer and cover the pot. Simmer for 15 minutes, turn the loin over, and simmer, covered, for 15 minutes more.

Turn off the heat and let the pork sit for 2 to 3 hours in the covered pot to cook slowly as the meat and stock come to room temperature. Turn the meat over from time to time.

Slice the pork. You can brush the slices with sesame oil and sprinkle on some sesame seeds if you wish. Serve the meat at room temperature or slightly warm, reheated in the sauce, or prepare it in any of the ways suggested above.

Note: *To save the Master Sauce, strain it and discard the solids. Store in a covered container in the refrigerator for 5 to 7 days or freeze it. To use, add more stock or water and seasonings as needed and follow the cooking directions.*

■ Flavor Step ■
CHINESE MASTER SAUCE FOR PORK

2 cups water or chicken stock, plus more if needed

1 cup soy sauce

¼ cup rice wine, dry sherry, or Scotch whisky

1 tablespoon hoisin sauce

2 tablespoons sugar

1 cinnamon stick

1 star anise

4 garlic cloves

8 green onions or scallions, roots trimmed

6 slices of peeled fresh ginger, about 1 inch in diameter and ⅛ inch thick

1 2½-to-3-pound piece of center-cut boneless pork loin

Asian sesame oil (optional)

Toasted sesame seeds (optional)

Crown Roast of Pork

Double recipe of Garlic
and Herb Paste for
Pork Loin (page 336)
OR a double recipe of
Arista Herb Rub for
Pork Loin (page 335)

1 8-to-11-pound crown
roast of pork
(16-22 ribs)

STUFFING—ANY OF
THE FOLLOWING
Roasted Winter
Vegetables (page 209),
OR Dried Cranberry
and Apple Stuffing
(page 330; quadruple
the recipe), OR
Sausage, Leek, and
Onion Stuffing
(page 518; quadruple
the recipe)

Pan Gravy (optional
but appreciated,
especially if serving
stuffing; see opposite
page)

Serves 8 to 12

■ FIT FOR COMPANY ■ GREAT LEFTOVERS

YOU'LL PROBABLY NEED to order this roast from the butcher. Many traditional recipes for crown roast of pork call for stuffing the center of the crown and cooking the stuffing with the roast. We do not recommend this practice, since by the time the stuffing is cooked, the meat may be way overdone. Instead, bake a stuffing separately in a casserole and then fill the crown just before serving. Another dramatic and delicious presentation involves filling the center with an assortment of roasted root vegetables or roasted or sautéed whole mushrooms. Another advantage of not stuffing the crown before cooking is that the roast can be baked bone side down, thus eliminating the need to cover the bone ends with foil to prevent burning.

Because more of the meat is exposed to the heat than with a normal bone-in pork loin, the crown roast takes a little less time to reach the desired level of doneness.

Crown roast is delicious with a fragrant Alsatian Gewürztraminer or one from the Anderson Valley in California's Mendocino County.

■ Flavor Step ■ Rub the herb paste generously over all the roast, especially in the crevices between each chop. Either cook the crown immediately or let it marinate for a couple of hours at room temperature or overnight, loosely wrapped, in the refrigerator. The meat should be at room temperature before roasting, so let it sit for an hour or so after removing it from the refrigerator.

Preheat the oven to 450°F. Place the roast, rib bones

down (upside down), in a large, shallow roasting pan. Put in the lower third of the oven and roast for 15 minutes. Then turn the oven down to 300°F and roast the meat for 1½ to 2½ hours more, depending on the size. (If you decide to follow the traditional practice of stuffing the roast beforehand, the full 2½ hours will most likely be needed.) Begin to check the temperature of the unstuffed roast after 1¼ hours. When the meat reaches an internal temperature of 145° to 150°F, remove it from the oven. Let it rest, loosely covered with foil, for 15 to 30 minutes to redistribute the juices and allow carryover heat to finish the cooking to a final internal temperature 5° to 10°F higher. During this rest period you can make a pan sauce if you like.

Meanwhile, cook the stuffing: To serve a stuffing with the roast, pick one of the suggested recipes. Prepare the root vegetables as directed or bake one of the stuffings in a buttered, covered casserole along with the roast for 45 minutes to 1 hour; put the casserole in the oven 15 to 30 minutes before the roast is due to come out of the oven. You can raise the temperature of the oven to 350°F after the roast is removed to speed up cooking. The stuffing is ready when it reaches 150° to 155°F. There is plenty of leeway here, so don't worry about precise timing. You're not making a soufflé—the roast or stuffing can be kept warm as needed to coordinate serving times.

You can also make the stuffing the day before, bake it in a casserole, and refrigerate it overnight. Then all you have to do is warm it through in the oven before serving. Rewarmed stuffing should have an internal temperature of 140°F. You can also prepare the roasted root vegetables a day ahead and rewarm them before serving.

To serve the crown roast, turn it so the rib bones face up and fill the crown with the vegetables or the stuffing of your choice (if you're using one). If you made a pan sauce, serve it on the side. To carve the roast, steady it with a carving fork while cutting between each rib bone to detach the chops. Serve 1 or 2 chops per person, along with any stuffing and/or vegetables.

COOKING PORK ROASTS ON THE GRILL

FOR BEST RESULTS, pork roasts such as loin or Boston butt should be cooked on the grill using indirect heat in a covered kettle barbecue. If you don't have one, you can either butterfly the roast and cook it over direct heat, turning it frequently, or use the grill to brown the exterior and give the meat a smoky tang, then finish the cooking indoors in the oven.

Pork loin is at its juiciest if it's brined first with one of the brines on pages 255-59 or marinated using a dry rub (see Seasoning Chart, page 577). Cook the loin with moderate heat using the indirect method (see Grilling, page 63) and soaked wood chips (such as hickory or oak) to achieve a smoky flavor. The loin should be cooked, as you would indoors, to a temperature of about 145°F—this may take 1½ to 2½ hours, depending on the weight of the meat and the temperature of the grill. Allow the cooked pork to rest for at least 15 minutes, loosely covered with foil, before carving. Because of carryover cooking, the final temperature will then be 150° to 155°F. You can serve the loin as is or with a complementary sauce or condiment.

Boston butt, either whole or a half, is best cooked slowly over indirect heat with a pan of water under the grill to provide a moist environment. A dry rub of your choice (see Seasoning Chart, page 577) adds flavor and juiciness. Use plenty of soaked hardwood chips or chunks for a pleasant smoky flavor. Ideally the pork butt should be cooked at 200° to 250°F for 4 to 6 hours, although this is not always possible. You can use the technique for slow-cooked barbecued ribs described on page 376 to regulate the heat using an instant-read thermometer inserted in the upper vent, if you wish. Or you can keep the coals low and feed them from time to time, checking the internal temperature of the pork butt with an instant-read thermometer. When it reads 155° to 160°F, the pork should be removed from the barbecue and allowed to rest, covered loosely with foil, for 15 to 30 minutes before carving. Carryover cooking should result in a final temperature of 160° to 165°F. Since pork butt has sufficient fat for long, slow cooking without drying out, you can cook it longer than loin, until it's almost falling off the bone, if you wish—that is, higher than 170°F. The pork is delicious chopped or sliced in your favorite barbecue sauce or as a leftover for a barbecued pork sandwich. Or you can serve it sliced with a sauce or condiment of your choice. Coleslaw (page 311) is the classic accompaniment.

Leg of Pork

The Finest Roast of All

FOR YOUR NEXT HOLIDAY FEAST, think about serving a roasted whole leg of pork instead of ham, turkey, or prime rib. It's equally spectacular and a whole lot cheaper, and it can provide wonderful leftovers for the family for Thai Red or Green Pork Curry (page 307) or roast pork sandwiches, to name just a couple.

This cut should be reserved for special occasions, since it weighs up to 20 pounds. To make for easy carving, have the butcher remove the aitch bone. If you really want to go all out with this roast and stuff it, ask him or her to remove the large leg bone as well, leaving the shank bone intact. This creates a large pocket that can be filled with a savory stuffing. Or you can double the recipe for the herb rub on page 263 and rub it inside the pork as well as out, and then tie up the leg for roasting.

If you get the enthusiastic response from guests that we always do, you may want to roast fresh leg of pork more frequently than just on holidays. Get your butcher to sell you a half or a third of a leg. If we asked for pieces of leg often enough, savvy marketers would soon discover how versatile it really is. If you purchase a half leg, keep in mind that the butt end is meatier than the shank end. If you buy it in pieces or want to cut it up yourself (see Making the Cut, page 351), the leg divides easily into butt and shank pieces. Rump and butt portions are the meatiest and should each weigh 4 to 6 pounds, a good-size roast for a family or dinner party. You can cook one of the roasts and freeze the other two for later use. You won't regret having this versatile meat in your freezer.

Some think that the crisp skin, or cracklings, is one of the best parts of the roast leg; others avoid eating the skin because of its fat content. If you are not interested in the skin, remove and discard it before roasting. Simply season the leg all over with the herb rub and roast it. If, like us, you love to eat the crunchy skin with pieces of the succulent meat, read on.

Roast Leg of Pork (Fresh Ham) with Cracklings

1 15-to-20-pound whole leg of pork, aitch bone removed, bone in or out and skin off or on

Whole leg serves 12 to 14, with leftovers; half leg, 6 to 7; third leg, 4 to 5
■ FIT FOR COMPANY ■ GOOD FOR A CROWD
■ GREAT LEFTOVERS ■ MOM'S COMFORT FOOD

STUFFING
Dried Cranberry and Apple Stuffing (page 330; triple the recipe) OR Sausage, Leek, and Onion Stuffing (page 518)

■ **Flavor Step** ■
FRESH HERB AND GARLIC RUB FOR ROAST PORK (double the quantities if you are not stuffing the boned roast)

20 fresh sage leaves or 2 tablespoons dried
20 sprigs fresh thyme or 1 tablespoon dried
8 large garlic cloves, finely chopped
2 tablespoons salt
1 tablespoon freshly ground black pepper

WE TOOK A WHOLE roast pork leg to a party once, removed it from the oven when it was 140°F, and didn't carve it until 1½ hours later. Even after all that time the meat was still warm—and the internal temperature had risen to a perfect 163°F. Figure that the internal temperature will rise 10° to 15°F after the whole leg is removed from the oven over a 30-to-45-minute resting period, the ideal time. If you plan to hold it longer than that, remove it from the oven when it's 140°F instead of 145°F.

Preheat the oven to 450°F. If you're stuffing the leg of pork, pack the stuffing into the cavity where the large leg bone was. Tie the roast together.

■ **Flavor Step** ■ Combine all the ingredients for the rub in a small bowl. Rub the herb mix on any exposed meat. If you are not stuffing it but have boned it, rub the cavity and any meat surfaces well with the herb mix and tie the roast together. If you have removed the skin, cut off the excess fat and rub the herb mix all over the surface of the meat. If you are a skin lover, brush the skin all over with a clean wire brush and/or pierce it all over with a skewer or tip of a knife so that there are literally hundreds of tiny punctures in the skin. Make 2-inch gashes through the skin at intervals all over the leg. Rub the herb mixture into the gashes but not onto the skin itself. Basically you want to season any exposed meat, not skin, with the herb mix.

Place the roast, skin side up if it is still on, fat side up if it is not, in a shallow roasting pan and put it in the lower third of the oven. After 15 to 20 minutes, lower the heat to 325°F. Check the roast—it should have started to brown. Turn the roasting pan around to ensure even browning. *Do not baste the roast,* as this will prevent the skin from crisping. Continue to roast for 3 more hours, then begin checking the internal temperature. After about 4¾ hours total cooking time, the internal temperature in the center of the meat should be about 145°F. At this point, transfer the meat to a large platter and cover it loosely with foil. Let it rest for 30 to 45 minutes for the juices to equilibrate and the temperature to rise. (This step is essential for any large roast.) After 15 minutes, the internal temperature of the roast should be above 150°F; after 30 minutes, it should reach 155°F. While the roast is resting, you can prepare your side dishes and make the gravy.

To make the optional Pan Sauce: Pour all the drippings (there will be quite a lot of fat) into a glass measuring cup or a fat separator. Remove and discard the fat, leaving behind plenty of brown meat juices. Add the herbs, garlic, and stock to the roasting pan and place it over low heat. Scrape up any browned bits from the bottom of the pan. Pour this liquid into a small saucepan. Put in the optional port wine and bring the sauce to a boil. Reduce it over high heat for a few minutes. Stir in the cornstarch mixture and boil the sauce until it begins to thicken. It should have the consistency of cream but not be too thick. Taste for salt and pepper.

To carve the roast, remove the cracklings if you've left the skin on, cut into small pieces, and serve separately. Carve the roast into thick slices and let the guests add their own gravy.

PAN SAUCE
(optional, but particularly good with stuffing)

2 teaspoons chopped fresh sage or 1 teaspoon dried
1 teaspoon chopped fresh thyme or ½ teaspoon dried
2 garlic cloves, finely chopped
1 cup pork or chicken stock
1 cup port wine (optional)
2 tablespoons cornstarch, dissolved in ¼ cup cold water
Salt and freshly ground black pepper

CRACKLINGS
(optional; page 350)

HOW TO MAKE CRACKLINGS

THE TRICK IS TO MAKE the skin crisp and crunchy without turning it hard and leathery. When we discussed the problem with Chinese chefs, who have mastered the technique, the first thing they told us to do was to dry out the skin of the leg as much as possible. Following their advice, we bought our leg of pork two days before we planned to cook it and stored it, skin side up and unwrapped, in the refrigerator.

The chefs also suggested that we prick the skin all over before roasting. (To do this, Chinese cooks whack it with a wire brush.) We also made a number of gashes in the skin to get the seasonings nearer the meat, although this is not necessarily traditional. The chefs' technique of roasting the pork in a hot (450°F) oven for a short period followed by long, slow roasting at 325°F turns the skin a lovely mahogany color and makes it delightfully crisp and crunchy. If the skin is not sufficiently crisp after roasting, you can turn the oven up to 450°F for the last 10 or 20 minutes.

MAKING THE CUT
Pork Leg (Fresh Ham)

CUTTING UP A PORK LEG can give you a number of tasty roasts and for meat braises and stir-fries. The technique is simple and requires only a sharp, stiff-bladed boning knife. You can buy a whole leg or fresh ham (20 pounds or more) or half legs (either the shank end or butt end). If you do buy a whole leg, have the butcher saw it in half into the butt end and the shank end for ease in cutting up (1). Cut away and discard the skin (or use it for cracklings; see opposite page) and most external fat.

Butt end   Shank end

Shank half: Lay the piece on a cutting board and cut away a large piece of boneless meat, running your knife along the shank bone and the leg bone. This will give you a large boneless pork roast and a meaty piece of bone-in shank (2). You can either braise the shank whole (see Caramelized Pork Shank and Braised Cabbage, page 389) or separate it into two hocks by cutting through the knuckle or stifle joint. These can be cooked (see Ham Hock and Split Pea Soup, page 406).

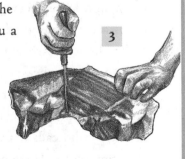

Butt half: This is even easier. Simply cut along the top of the leg bone, removing the largest piece of boneless meat you can. This will give you a boneless roast and a bone-in rump roast (3). You can roast any of these large pieces (4) whole, following any of our recipes for roast or braised pork. Or cut up the tender meat for kebabs, stir-fries, or pork cutlets. Fresh pork can be frozen successfully, tightly wrapped, for up to four to six months.

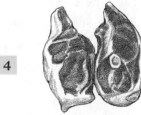

RISKING IT ALL FOR TONY LUKE'S

TONY LUKE'S is situated on Oregon Avenue, a wide and busy boulevard in a well-worn, truck-filled industrial section of South Philly. You pull your car up onto a strip of bare ground right smack in the middle of the street and park it as best you can. Your first challenge is to get in and out of the car without one of the massive semis roaring by, taking off a door with you flattened against it. Once you've slipped out, you watch for a break in the traffic and scamper across the road.

Is it worth the risk? Lots of folks seem to think so: the sidewalk outside the sandwich shop is crowded with guys in work clothes, joggers in shorts and $200 running shoes, businessmen in suits and ties, and women adorned at all levels of fashion from Gucci to Minnie Pearl on a bad day. People are seated at those ridiculously small plastic tables with built-in chairs you see in playgrounds, trying to eat thick, meaty sandwiches that fall apart as you bite them and cover you and your clothes with savory and very colorful juices.

Tony Luke's offers Texas hot dogs and chicken cutlet, veal cutlet, roast beef, and other sandwiches, but most folks shout out "Roast pork" when they finally get to the window. We watched the counterman as he prepared a roast pork sandwich with greens and cheese. First, a 12-inch-long crusty roll is split in half, leaving the two sides still attached. He sprinkles on a generous handful of coarsely grated provolone cheese—the aged kind that's so pungent it makes your mouth sweat. He wanders over to the steam table and spoons on a thick layer of steamed broccoli rabe or spinach over the cheese. The pork slices have been cut from the leg and are kept warm in a large rectangular pan filled with light brown meat juices. These tasty juices are replenished day after day from the roasting pans, and periodically whole garlic cloves and cherry peppers are added to enliven the flavors. The counterman tongs out some slices and weighs them on a perforated scale that lets the juices drip back into the pan. The pork is spread over the greens and several spoonfuls of juice are ladled on. He quickly folds foil around the sandwich and hands it to the register clerk, who calls out your name.

Sitting on the ledge of the counter are big jars of red and yellow sliced pickled peppers and assorted bottles of hot sauce. You add these to the sandwich and eat it fast since the juices have soaked into the bread and it disintegrates quickly. Everything is washed down with a South Philly specialty, birch beer. It's so good, you're thinking of ordering another when you're halfway through, but by the time you finish, you're just plain too full. All you can do is lick your fingers and cherish the memory.

B.A.

Tony Luke's Roast Pork, Greens, and Provolone Sandwich

■ In a Hurry ■ Mom's Comfort Food

FRESH LEG OF PORK is a great choice for these juicy sandwiches, but roast pork butt or loin will also be delicious.

To make the *Au Jus*: For the best results, add the stock to the pan the roast pork was cooked in and scrape up any browned bits from the bottom. Pour the stock into a small saucepan. Add the onion, garlic, and herbs and boil for 5 minutes. Add the cherry peppers and pickling liquid. (The *Au Jus* can be made up when the roast is first cooked—you can serve it as a pan gravy, if you wish—and kept refrigerated for 3 or 4 days. Before rewarming, remove any surface fat.)

Heat the pork in a shallow pan at a simmer in the *Au Jus* for 4 to 5 minutes. Split the roll open using your thumbs. Sprinkle the bottom of the roll with the cheese. Using a slotted spoon, spread the greens on top of the cheese. Remove the pork from the liquid with tongs and spread the slices over the greens. Ladle some of the juices over the pork. Season with salt and pepper. Seal the sandwich in foil and serve with the optional pickled peppers and hot sauce so guests can add their own.

Au Jus

2 cups pork, beef, or chicken stock

½ cup diced onion

4 garlic cloves

¼ teaspoon each dried sage, rosemary, and thyme

2-4 pickled cherry peppers, red or green or both, plus 2 tablespoons pickling liquid from the peppers

For Each Sandwich

¼ pound thinly sliced cooked pork, preferably from leftover roast pork leg, Boston butt, or boneless pork loin

1 10-inch Italian or French roll or piece of French baguette

¼ cup shredded aged provolone cheese

½ cup hot cooked broccoli rabe, flavored with olive oil, vinegar, and sautéed garlic, OR ½ cup other hot cooked greens such as collards or spinach, flavored as above

Salt and freshly ground black pepper

Pickled sweet yellow and red peppers, sliced (optional)

Hot sauce (optional)

WILD PIGS ON CREIGHTON RIDGE

OST FOLKS DON'T HAVE TO WORRY about wild pigs these days. After all, huge, hairy, tusked, and dangerous boars are just a part of myths and folklore, aren't they?

Well, not here on Creighton Ridge, five miles in and 1,500 feet up from the Pacific on California's Sonoma Coast. All along the ridges of the Coast Range, wild hogs feast on acorns from coastal oaks, tear up garden fences, rip hillsides apart, and consume huge quantities of expensive wine grapes just as soon as they get ripe. Up here feral pigs can be a damn nuisance, and if you run into a big boar when he's having a bad day or get between a sow and her piglets, they can be real trouble. There's one compensation, though: they do taste good and are often the featured meat at ridge country barbecues and get-togethers.

These wild pigs are the real thing, or close to it. If you look at Paleolithic cave paintings of *Sus scrofa*, the European wild boar, or depictions of boar hunts in Egyptian tombs or on Greek vases, you'll see it's all the same animal—a muscular and compact body with lots of hair and big, curving tusks that go with a long snout and a very aggressive attitude. There's a certain amount of discussion about the origin of these wild pigs along California's North and South Coasts: some say the Russians brought European wild boars to Fort Ross; others point to a rich sportsman who released some near Big Sur years ago. Most people think that what we have are simply feral pigs that escaped from farms over the years and bred back to the ancestral type. Wherever they came from, feral pigs are thriving all along the coast and have even moved down into Marin County, just north of the Golden Gate, where they're playing hell with suburban rhododendrons and the nerves of the BMW set.

Mark and Angie, friends of mine up on the ridge, adopted a cute little piglet that their dog dragged in one day, squealing and squirming in his jaws. It seemed like the right thing to do at the time and was just a minor addition to the flocks of ducks, geese, and chickens and the kittens, puppies, dogs, cats, goats, and a gregarious burro named Yo-Plait that inhabited their hillside farm. They named the baby pig Slammer, from his habit of butting ahead of everybody at the food trough, and he was quickly adopted by the donkey, who protected him from the dogs and from a pair of obnoxious ravens that were the bullies of the farmyard.

The pig and donkey became the talk of the neighborhood and were often seen trotting down the dirt road along the ridge, little Slammer scampering underneath the burro. A cute couple, we all said, but old hands predicted disaster. Slammer wasn't Babe. He was a male pig, after all, and the advice was: get him clipped in the necessary area quickly or put him on the barbecue without delay.

But of course they didn't, and Slammer the cute little piglet soon became Slammer the 300-pound boar, tusks and all, still hanging out with Yo-Plait, although no longer underneath and definitely no longer in need of protection. I remember opening my eyes one afternoon, after a long session of meditation—i.e., snoozing on the grass—to prepare myself for the arduous task of writing, to the sight of a wild boar's snout, curved tusks, and little red eyes about three inches from my face. Slammer, dripping and muddy from a wallow in my stream, was inspecting me carefully, sniffing and snorting assiduously. After a moment of calm reflection on both our parts, he waddled up the driveway toward home, the ever-faithful Yo-Plait at his side.

Well, as predicted, disaster ensued. Our friend Ron went to visit one day and noticed an eerie silence as he went up the steps. Nobody home, he thought. And then he heard a sound that he later described as "much like the sound of a charging 300-pound wild boar." He was right; it was Slammer on the prod, and Ron went flying over the side of the deck with a deep gash down the back of his leg. As the boar came around the house to finish him off, Ron grabbed a cement block and brought it down with maximum force on Slammer's head. That didn't faze the boar much, but it slowed him down just enough for Ron to get back to his truck and off to the emergency room for many stitches.

So the old hands were called in to do what had to be done, and Slammer ended up as delicious barbecue at the aptly named Wild Hog Vineyard a few ridges over. We all regretted not seeing the little piglet with the donkey anymore, but I think most of us were happy to bid farewell to the wild boar. Yo-Plait pined for a while, but then took up with a cute little goat named Kudra, who had a trick of perching on his back and peeking out coyly between his ears.   *D.K.*

Pork Marinated to Taste like Wild Boar

2 cups full-bodied red
   wine

¼ cup red wine vinegar

¼ cup port wine

1 medium onion, thinly
   sliced

1 cup chopped carrots

4 garlic cloves, chopped

1 tablespoon chopped
   fresh thyme or 1½
   teaspoons dried

1 tablespoon chopped
   fresh marjoram or
   1½ teaspoons dried

3 bay leaves

8 crushed juniper berries
   OR 2 tablespoons gin

6 crushed peppercorns

1 teaspoon salt

1 4-to-6-pound rump end
   or center cut of fresh
   pork leg or whole
   Boston butt, skin
   removed and trimmed
   of excess fat

1 cup beef, chicken, or
   pork stock
   Salt and freshly ground
   black pepper

Serves 6 to 8, with leftovers
■ Fit for Company ■ Great Leftovers

WILD PIG IS VERY TASTY if cooked properly. This recipe can also be applied to any good-size piece of domestic pork, however, and is especially good with Boston butt and fresh pork leg. The marinade will give most cuts of pork a little of the gamy flavors of the wild meat. This is a version of the French recipe called *à la façon de sanglier*, in which pork is marinated to taste like *sanglier*, or wild boar. Serve with mashed potatoes and turnips with maple-glazed carrots.

■ **Flavor Step** ■ Combine the marinade ingredients. Put the pork in a large bowl and pour the marinade over it. Pierce the meat with a carving fork or skewer all over to help the marinade penetrate. Cover and refrigerate for at least a day and up to 2 days, turning every so often.

Let the meat rest at room temperature for an hour or so before cooking. Preheat the oven to 325°F.

Remove the pork from the marinade and place in a roasting pan. Pour the marinade into the bottom of the pan. Roast the pork for about 2 hours, basting often with the marinade. Add a little water, stock, or wine to the pan if necessary. Test the roast at its thickest part with an instant-read meat thermometer—it should register 150° to 155°F. When it's done, remove the roast from the oven and cover it loosely with foil. The temperature should rise about 10°F while it rests.

To make a sauce, strain and degrease the pan drippings. In a small saucepan, mix with the stock. Bring to a boil and reduce until just syrupy. Taste for salt and pepper. Slice the meat and pour the sauce over and serve.

Chinese Red-Cooked Pork

Serves 6 to 8 as part of a Chinese meal
■ MOM'S COMFORT FOOD ■ REWARMS WELL
■ COOKING ON A BUDGET

EDY YOUNG learned to cook for her large Chinese-American family at an early age. Her father, a professional chef, taught her well, and she not only became an excellent home cook but also went on to become a professional baker and candymaker. Edy's recipe for this family favorite can stretch a little bit of meat a long way. Red-cooked pork is usually served Chinese style, with plenty of rice and two or three vegetable dishes such as braised baby bok choy or steamed broccoli. This recipe also works well with lamb shoulder: do use the chiles and garnish with chopped cilantro rather than green onions. Red-cooked lamb goes well with braised cabbage or cauliflower and is delicious with grilled green onions or baby leeks.

The red wine represents Edy's creative adaptation of the recipe.

1 tablespoon peanut oil

2 tablespoons sugar

2 pounds pork shoulder butt, cut into 2-to-3-inch chunks and trimmed of most external fat

4-6 large garlic cloves

1 2-inch piece of fresh ginger, peeled and sliced

½ cup soy sauce

½ cup red wine

6 star anise

2-3 small dried chile peppers (optional)

6 green onions or scallions

1 cup water

3 green onions or scallions, finely chopped, for garnish

Heat a heavy-bottomed pot or Dutch oven over medium-high heat. Add the oil and sugar and stir for about 5 minutes, until the sugar begins to turn a light brown. Add the pork, garlic, and ginger and stir until the meat is browned. Adjust the heat if necessary so the sugar does not burn. Add the soy sauce, wine, star anise, the optional chile peppers, and the whole green onions or scallions. Stir well to scrape up any browned bits from the bottom of the pan. Cook the mixture at a slow boil, stirring from time to time, for 10 minutes.

Add the water and reduce the heat to a simmer. Cover and cook for 1 hour, or until the meat is quite tender. Spoon the meat and juices into a shallow serving bowl and garnish with the chopped green onions or scallions.

Cuban Roast Pork

■ Flavor Step ■
CUBAN RUM AND CITRUS
MARINADE FOR PORK

(If cooking a whole leg, triple
the quantities)

2 tablespoons minced
garlic

1 tablespoon chopped
fresh oregano or 1
teaspoon dried

1 teaspoon ground cumin

¼ cup dark rum

¾ cup fresh orange juice

¼ cup fresh lime juice

3 tablespoons olive oil

2 teaspoons salt

1 teaspoon freshly ground
black pepper

1 4-to-6-pound bone-in
or boneless piece of
pork, such as rump
end of leg, blade end
of loin, sirloin end
of loin, or part of a
Boston butt, OR a
14-to-16-pound whole
leg of pork (fresh ham),
skin removed to be
crisped separately

About 1 cup chicken
stock or water
(optional)

Salt and freshly ground
black pepper (optional)

Small roast serves 6 to 8
Whole leg serves 12 to 16, with leftovers

■ GOOD FOR A CROWD ■ FIT FOR COMPANY
■ GREAT LEFTOVERS

CUBAN CHEFS do wonders with slowly cooked meats. They cook beef brisket until it is almost in shreds (they call it *ropa vieja*, "old clothes falling apart"), then flavor it with peppers, tomatoes, and chiles. They cook a whole leg of pork so that the meat is falling off the bone and yet the skin is crunchy. First they marinate the leg in orange juice and rum, then cook it to succulent perfection; they remove the skin and roast it in the oven until crisp.

You can make this dish with a whole leg if you want to serve a crowd or you can cut (or have the butcher cut) a section of the rump for a smaller group. Or better still, use a whole or half Boston butt, the shoulder of the pig. It's fattier than the leg but very juicy, and it holds up well to long cooking in the Cuban style. It doesn't come with the skin, however, so there won't be any cracklings. You can also use the blade end or the sirloin end of the pork loin for a small roast suitable for four to six. The only thing you need to vary is the cooking time for the different cuts.

To be traditional, serve the roast pork with black beans and steamed rice and, if you can find them, plantains, panfried in a little vegetable oil. And be sure to roast enough meat so that you'll have leftovers for roast pork sandwiches. If you use a whole leg of pork for a large crowd, remove the skin before cooking so you can crisp it separately, and triple the amount of marinade.

■ **Flavor Step** ■ Combine all the ingredients for the marinade in a small bowl. Put the meat in a large zipper-lock bag or bowl and pour the marinade over. (If you use a whole leg, you'll need a very large bowl.) Shake the bag or turn the meat until the pork is well coated. Refrigerate overnight, covered if in a bowl, turning occasionally.

The next day, remove the meat from the refrigerator 1 to 2 hours before roasting. Preheat the oven to 325°F.

If you're cooking a smaller roast, place it in a shallow roasting pan and pour the marinade over it. Roast for 1½ to 2½ hours, basting the meat occasionally. If the liquid evaporates from the pan during cooking, add a cup or so of water or stock. Test for doneness with an instant-read thermometer; the internal temperature should read 145° to 150°F for all cuts except Boston butt, which should read 150° to 155°F. When the roast reaches the desired doneness, remove it and let it rest, covered loosely with foil, for 15 to 20 minutes so the juices can be redistributed and the carryover heat will finish the cooking, resulting in a final temperature of 5° to 10°F higher.

Carve the meat into ½-inch-thick slices and arrange it on a platter. Skim any fat from the pan and pour the meat juices and any browned bits over the meat.

If you're cooking a whole leg, roast it for 2½ to 3 hours, basting from time to time. Add a cup or so of stock or water to the pan if the liquid evaporates. Check the internal temperature: it should read 145° to 150°F when the meat is ready. Remove the pork from the oven and let the leg rest, loosely covered with foil, for 30 to 45 minutes before carving. This allows the juices to redistribute and the carryover heat to finish cooking the roast to an internal temperature of 150° to 160°F.

While the leg is roasting, you can make the cracklings. Cut the skin into strips about 2 inches wide. Lightly salt and pepper them. Place them, fat side down, in a shallow roasting pan or on a baking sheet and bake alongside the roast for 1½ to 2 hours, until the strips are crisp and curled up.

Once the leg is cooked, turn off the oven and keep the

cracklings warm in the oven while the meat rests. Slice the meat and arrange it on a platter. Skim the fat from the juices in the roasting pan and pour the juices and any browned bits over the meat. Garnish the platter with the cracklings.

BUTCHERED ADVICE

A FRIEND OF OURS recently had an enlightening experience with a butcher shop—and a tony and expensive one at that. She was looking for a piece of Boston butt, a pork cut from the shoulder that has enough fat for making a braised pork dish, like Cuban Roast Pork with Mojo Sauce (see opposite page) or Braised Pork Butt with Port and Prunes (page 366). The butcher told her he couldn't sell pork butt in this neighborhood—all anyone wanted these days was loin of pork. The butcher then went on to tell our friend that pork loin would work just as well, since "all pork is the same."

A bit of balderdash if we've ever heard any, and we've heard plenty! Pork loin *would* be delicious roasted or grilled, but not braised; it becomes dry and hard because it's so lean. This butcher, obviously, wanted to sell some pork loin and didn't give a damn about the result. Or perhaps he genuinely didn't know any better.

Luckily our friend passed on the proffered loin and finally found a nice piece of pork butt in a store in a less fancy neighborhood. The lesson here? Avoid bad advice! Don't go back to balderdash-dispensing butchers, expensive or not. When in doubt or when you can't find a particular cut of meat, try to find a butcher who offers even the humblest, and often the most delicious, cuts.

Cuban Roast Pork Sandwich with Mojo Sauce

■ GREAT LEFTOVERS ■ IN A HURRY
■ COOKING ON A BUDGET

ANYONE WHO HAS SPENT some time in Miami or any Cuban community knows the joy of hearty Cuban sandwiches. They are made from a variety of meats and usually include cheese and ham. The sandwiches are heated on a griddle with a weight on top that compresses the bread to create a chewy, crunchy exterior and a luscious melted-cheese interior. One secret to these sandwiches is a tangy citrus concoction called Mojo Sauce. You can make it from scratch or use some of the leftover sauce from the Cuban Roast Pork.

To make the Mojo Sauce: Heat the oil in a small pan over medium heat and put in the garlic. Cook for a minute or two, stirring, until the garlic begins to color. Take the pan off the heat and stir in the remaining ingredients; there may be some sputtering, so be careful. Return the pan to the heat and cook for 1 minute more, stirring often. Cool the sauce before using. (Mojo will keep, covered, in the refrigerator for about a week.)

Split the roll in half and brush both cut sides with the mixture of mayonnaise and Mojo Sauce. Layer the meats, cheese, vegetables, and pickles, if desired, on the bottom half.

MOJO SAUCE

⅓ cup olive oil

6-8 garlic cloves, finely chopped

⅔ cup sour orange juice OR ½ fresh orange and ½ cup fresh lime juice

½ teaspoon ground cumin

1 teaspoon salt

½ teaspoon freshly ground black pepper

FOR EACH SANDWICH

1 soft sweet French roll, 6-8 inches long

1 tablespoon mayonnaise, mixed with 2 tablespoons leftover sauce from Cuban Roast Pork (page 358) or 2 tablespoons Mojo Sauce

3-4 thin slices leftover Cuban Roast Pork

1-2 large, thin slices prosciutto, Serrano, Westphalian, or other high-quality ham (optional)

2 slices Swiss or Fontina cheese

3 thin slices tomato (optional)

3 thin slices red onion (optional)

3-4 thin slices dill pickle

Melted butter
Coarsely chopped
  pickled peppers or
  jalapeños *en escabeche*
  (optional)

Cover the sandwich with the other half of the roll and brush the outside with melted butter.

Place the sandwich on a griddle or in a heavy nonstick pan over medium heat and place a weight on top. The weight can be a brick wrapped in foil, a small cast-iron skillet, or the bacon press used by professional grillmeisters. Grill the sandwich for 6 to 8 minutes per side, or until the roll is nicely browned. Lower the heat if it's cooking too fast or burning. The cheese should be soft and beginning to melt. Slice the sandwich in two and serve with the optional peppers or jalapeños.

MIAMI AIRPORT
Great Pork Sandwiches

MY WIFE, NANCY, and I were headed back home from the Bahamas with a two-hour layover in the Miami airport, a delay that would normally have made me angry as a bear. Like most travelers, I hate airports, and the thing I hate most about them is the abominable food served anywhere near them, either in the air or on the ground.

Except for Miami. I love the Miami airport so much that I grab every opportunity to choose routes that stop there. It's really Cuban, you see; Spanish is the first language of just about everybody, and the food is great (and cheap), from the strong, sweet cups of espresso for 30 cents each to the fantastic meals in the Cuban cafeteria. And if you're smart, you'll buy a bag of Cuban pork sandwiches to take on the next leg of the flight.

When everyone else stares down at the mystery meat in a gloppy sauce with frozen mashed potatoes, Nancy and I pull out fragrant Cuban pork sandwiches that make people turn in their seats and look longingly at our greasy bags. On one almost-empty flight, the captain got a whiff of what we were eating and asked over the P.A. system if he could invite himself to dinner. We took pity on him and sacrificed a sandwich or two to keep him happy, alert, and on course.   *B.A.*

Barbecued Pork Sandwich

■ COOKING ON A BUDGET ■ REWARMS WELL

BARBECUED PORK SANDWICHES are one of the best ways to use leftover pork. Although they can be made from just about any type of roasted or braised pork, the fattier cuts such as Boston butt and leg generally make the best barbecue. You can heat the pork up in the Coca-Cola and Chile Barbecue Sauce or use ½ recipe (about 1 cup) of Oakland-Style Barbecue Sauce (page 380), Mustardy Barbecue Sauce (page 379), Bourbon Barbecue Sauce (page 381), or your favorite barbecue sauce. Serve with Coleslaw (page 311), bread-and-butter pickles, and a cold pale ale.

For a quicker but less authentic sandwich, simply slice leftover pork and warm the slices in barbecue sauce. Layer the pork on a roll and serve slathered with sauce.

───────

To make the Coca-Cola and Chile Barbecue Sauce: Heat the oil over medium heat in a lidded 2-to-3-quart pot. Add the onion and garlic and cook until soft, about 5 minutes, stirring often. Add the remaining ingredients and bring to a boil. Simmer for 5 minutes. You can add the pork chunks now or, if you want to use the sauce later, simmer it for 45 minutes until it is thick and syrupy. It will keep for up to 2 weeks, covered, in the refrigerator.

Add the pork chunks to the sauce or to a mixture of 1 cup of any barbecue sauce plus ½ cup water. Simmer, covered, for 45 minutes, or until the meat is quite tender and easily shredded with a fork. Remove the pork with a slotted spoon and shred or chop it coarsely. Degrease the sauce and reduce it over high heat until syrupy. Spread a generous layer of meat on the bottom half of each roll. Spoon some sauce over the meat, close the sandwich, and serve.

COCA-COLA AND CHILE BARBECUE SAUCE

1 tablespoon salad oil
½ cup finely chopped onion
1 tablespoon finely chopped garlic
½ cup cider vinegar
1 tablespoon chile powder
½ cup Coca-Cola
1 cup ketchup
3 tablespoons yellow mustard
2 tablespoons Worcestershire sauce
2 teaspoons Tabasco sauce or to taste (optional)
1 teaspoon Liquid Smoke (optional) OR ½ recipe (about 1 cup) other barbecue sauce (see discussion) plus ½ cup water

1½ pounds leftover roast or braised pork, cut into 3-to-4-inch chunks
4 high-quality hamburger buns, Kaiser rolls, French rolls, or egg-sesame rolls

Casserole-Roasted Pork with 40 Cloves of Garlic

■ Flavor Step ■
Herb and Paprika Rub
for Beef (page 194)

1 2½-to-3-pound netted or
  tied boneless pork roast
  from the shoulder or
  leg OR a 2½-to-3-
  pound netted or tied
  veal shoulder roast
2 tablespoons olive oil
½ cup dry white wine
½ cup chicken stock
40 garlic cloves
1 teaspoon chopped fresh
  rosemary or ½ teaspoon
  dried
½ teaspoon dried sage
  Salt and freshly ground
  black pepper

Serves 6, with leftovers
■ REWARMS WELL ■ FIT FOR COMPANY

THIS METHOD OF CASSEROLE ROASTING is actually a form of braising, since it uses moist heat. The idea of using 40 cloves of garlic derives from the famous Provençal dish: a chicken is slowly roasted in a sealed pot with the whole garlic cloves, which mellow as they cook to give off a mouthwatering perfume and a savory flavor. The best cut to use here is a netted boneless pork roast from the shoulder or leg area. Do not use a loin roast, which will dry out with longer cooking. This dish is equally delicious made with a shoulder of veal.

For great results and an authentic Provençal feel, use a clay casserole or Römertopf. Soak it first in cold water for about a half hour or follow the manufacturer's directions. Serve with Oven-Roasted Potatoes (page 126) and steamed spinach or with mustard greens dressed with fresh lemon juice and olive oil.

■ Flavor Step ■ Rub the seasonings all over the meat. Let it rest, loosely covered, for 1 hour at room temperature before cooking.

Preheat the oven to 350°F. In a heavy skillet, heat the olive oil over high heat and brown the meat on all sides, about 5 minutes. Transfer it to a casserole just large enough to hold it. Pour off the oil from the pan and add the wine and stock. Bring to a boil, scraping up any browned bits from the bottom of the pan. Pour the liquid over the roast and scatter the garlic cloves and herbs in the casserole. Cover with foil and then cover tightly with a lid (if you are using a clay pot or

Römertopf, don't use foil; seal with flour and water paste or follow the manufacturer's directions).

Place the pot in the middle of the oven and cook for about 1 hour. Check the meat, which should be tender and register 160° to 165°F on an instant-read thermometer. Remove the roast and keep it warm, loosely covered with foil. After resting for 10 minutes, the final temperature will be 170° to 175°F.

Pour the pan juices and garlic into a small saucepan. Remove any grease from the surface and taste for salt and pepper. Keep warm over low heat. Remove the netting or string from the roast and carve the meat into ½-inch-thick slices. Spoon the sauce and garlic cloves over the meat and serve.

Braised Pork Butt with Port and Prunes

■ Flavor Step ■

HERB AND MUSTARD
RUB FOR PORK

½ teaspoon dried sage

½ teaspoon dried thyme

1 teaspoon dry mustard,
preferably Colman's

1½ teaspoons salt

1 teaspoon freshly ground
black pepper

1 4-to-6-pound boneless or
bone-in Boston butt or
pork shoulder butt,
trimmed of most
external fat

2 tablespoons olive oil

2 cups fresh or frozen
pearl onions, partially
defrosted if frozen

1 cup finely chopped leeks
(white part only)

½ cup finely chopped
carrots

1 cup port wine

½ cup beef or chicken
stock

1 cup pitted prunes

¼ cup Armagnac, slivovitz
(plum brandy), or other
brandy (optional)

2 bay leaves

Salt and freshly ground
black pepper

Serves 6 to 8, with leftovers
■ FIT FOR COMPANY ■ REWARMS WELL
■ COOKING ON A BUDGET

UNLIKE THE PORK LOIN, the Boston butt, or pork shoulder butt, is ideal for long, slow, moist cooking. Prunes, like many fruits, complement the sweet and succulent flavors of the pork, and port wine provides a nice undertone of sweetness and fruit. We recommend a rolled and tied boneless butt, since it's easier to carve and serve, but a bone-in roast will do as well. We like to serve this dish to company with brussels sprouts braised with chestnuts and an earthy red Burgundy from the Côtes de Nuits or a full-bodied Oregon Pinot Noir. *(See photograph, page 48.)*

■ **Flavor Step** ■ Combine all the herbs and spices in a small bowl and rub generously all over the meat.

Preheat the oven to 325°F. Heat the oil over high heat in a heavy casserole or Dutch oven just large enough to hold the pork. Brown the meat on all sides, 7 to 8 minutes. Remove it and set aside. Pour off all but about 1 tablespoon of the fat from the pot and add the pearl onions, leeks, and carrots. Lower the heat to medium, cover the pot, and cook until the vegetables have softened, about 5 minutes.

Pour in the port and stock and scrape up any browned bits from the bottom of the pot. Add the prunes, the optional brandy, and the bay leaves and bring to a boil. Put the pork back in and spoon some of the prunes and vegetables over the top. Cover the pot with foil and fit the lid on tightly.

Place the pot in the middle of the oven and cook for about 1½ hours, or until the pork is quite tender and registers 160° to 165°F on an instant-read meat thermometer. Remove the pork from the pot and cover loosely to keep warm. The final temperature of the meat after resting for 10 minutes or so may read 170° to 175°F.

Skim off any fat from the cooking juices. Remove 6 of the prunes and puree them in a food processor or blender. Stir the puree back into the sauce to thicken it. Remove the bay leaves and taste the sauce for salt and pepper. Remove the strings from the pork if necessary and carve into ½-inch-thick slices. Serve with the sauce and prunes and vegetables.

Caribbean Pork Braised with Limes and Oranges

½ cup rum, Grand
   Marnier, Triple Sec,
   or Curaçao (optional)
Juice from 2 oranges,
   preferably Valencias
   or other tart varieties,
   about 1 cup
Juice from 2 limes,
   about ¼ cup
1 tablespoon minced garlic
1 tablespoon minced fresh
   ginger
1 teaspoon crushed black
   peppercorns
½ teaspoon ground
   cinnamon
½ teaspoon ground allspice
½ teaspoon dried oregano
1 teaspoon salt

2 pounds boneless pork
   cut into 3-inch cubes,
   from the leg, butt,
   or shoulder
1 tablespoon peanut oil

Serves 4 to 6
■ REWARMS WELL ■ COOKING ON A BUDGET

THIS DELIGHTFULLY AROMATIC DISH is best made with large chunks of pork cut from the fresh ham, but you can also use boneless pieces of shoulder. Caribbean-flavored pork is best served with lots of rice and side dishes of black beans and fried plantains. The citrus marinade is equally good with other cuts of pork, beef, or split Rock Cornish hens. The preferred beverage: Red Stripe beer or rum sours.

■ **Flavor Step** ■ The day before cooking, mix all the marinade ingredients in a bowl. Place the pork in a zipper-lock bag, glass dish, or shallow bowl. Pour in the marinade and refrigerate overnight, covered if using a bowl. Shake the bag or turn the pork occasionally. The next day, remove the meat from the marinade, and save the marinade to use in cooking. Pat the pork dry with paper towels.

Heat the oil in a heavy, nonstick lidded skillet over high heat. Put in the pork and brown on all sides, for a total of 5 to 7 minutes. Remove the meat and set aside. Add the reserved marinade to the pan and bring it to a boil, scraping up any browned bits. Boil until the liquid is reduced by half.

Add the orange juice, tomatoes, bay leaves, stock, and reserved pork. Bring to a boil, reduce to a simmer, cover, and cook until the pork is tender, about 30 minutes. Remove the pork and keep it warm. Remove any fat from the surface of the sauce and boil it over high heat to reduce almost to a syrup. Taste for salt, pepper, and hot sauce. Serve the sauce over the pork with rice, black beans, and fried plantains on the side. Garnish with cilantro.

½ cup fresh orange juice
2 ripe tomatoes, peeled, seeded, and chopped, OR 2 canned Italian-style tomatoes, seeded, chopped, and drained
2 bay leaves
1 cup chicken stock
  Salt and freshly ground black pepper
  Bottled hot sauce to taste
½ cup chopped fresh cilantro, for garnish

CARNITAS TO REMEMBER

IN TIMES PAST, my old friends Alice and Steve Petersen were always looking for an excuse to hold a party, which they called a fiesta, since they considered themselves born-again Hispanics, although they're really WASPs. On one of their numerous trips from Santa Cruz to south of the border, they lugged back a huge cast-iron kettle. It was like the ones you see in the cartoons with the missionaries about to come to a boil—big and round and black, with little feet on it so you could build a fire under it.

In Mexico, this kettle had been used to make *carnitas*, chunks of highly seasoned deep-fried pork. First, the cauldron was used to render the lard. Then the meat was fried in the same cauldron. The whole pig, from ears to tail, ended up in the pot, and then everybody would take chunks of the succulent meat, along with bits of crackling, ears, or what you will, and put them into soft tacos, burritos, or tostadas. Or they might be added to enchiladas, chimichangas, gorditas, or tamales or eaten alone with beans, rice, and guacamole.

Once the rust was removed from the ancient kettle and it was properly cleaned and oiled, my friends decided to throw a party to break it in. You need a lot of folks to eat the food from a cauldron like that, so they invited the whole neighborhood. That memorable night, the Petersens served their own authentic *carnitas*, with platters of warm tortillas, various salsas, guacamole, radishes, chopped onions, black beans, salads, shredded cheese, and pickled chiles. We all made tacos and fell to, ate until we dropped, and listened to Alice and Steve's slightly off-key but enthusiastic renderings of Mexican folk songs for the rest of the evening.   *B.A.*

Carnitas

Serves 10 to 12 as part of a Southwestern meal
■ COOKING ON A BUDGET ■
■ MOM'S COMFORT FOOD ■ GOOD FOR A CROWD

THE TRADITIONAL WAY to make *carnitas* is to cook chunks of pork in lard, a bit too rich for most of us these days. Our friends Alice and Steve Petersen cook the pork in broth and then in milk for savory and delicious *carnitas* that are not as high in fat. The best cut of pork to use is the shoulder or Boston butt, which has sufficient fat to stay moist throughout the long cooking time. Serve *carnitas* wrapped in hot corn tortillas, with salsa and hot sauce.

■ **Flavor Step** ■ Mix all the seasonings together in a small bowl. Rub the mixture on all sides of the meat, using up the entire amount.

Heat the oil in a deep, heavy pot or Dutch oven over high heat. Put in the meat, in batches if necessary, and brown it on all sides, 7 to 10 minutes total. (If you cooked the meat in batches, return it all to the pot.) Add the onions and garlic, stir well, and reduce the heat to medium. Cook, stirring often, until the onions begin to soften, about 5 minutes. Add the bay leaves and water, cover, and simmer for 1½ hours.

Pour off the broth and save it to cook beans or to make a soup (degrease it before using). Pour the milk over the meat and simmer until the milk has curdled and caramelized and all the liquid has evaporated, 1 to 1½ hours. The milk will form a golden brown coating on the meat. Stir the sauce and meat from time to time and lower the temperature if it starts to burn.

When the pork is tender and browned, drain off the fat and discard the bay leaves. Serve at once, as described above. (To rewarm *carnitas*, bake in a 350°F oven for 15 to 20 minutes, or until just warmed through. The meat can also be warmed in a microwave.)

■ **Flavor Step** ■
SPICE RUB FOR *CARNITAS*

1 teaspoon ground cumin
½ teaspoon ground coriander
1 teaspoon dried oregano or 2 teaspoons chopped fresh
1 tablespoon salt
1 teaspoon freshly ground black pepper

4-6 pounds pork shoulder or Boston butt, cut into 3-inch chunks, not trimmed too closely (a little fat adds juiciness)
1 tablespoon vegetable oil
2 cups chopped onions
6 whole garlic cloves
2 bay leaves
2 cups water
1 quart milk
Corn tortillas

How to Choose Ribs

SPARERIBS

For meatiness and succulent pork flavor, you can't beat spareribs, the 13 ribs from the belly of the pig. The rest of the belly—that is, the bacon—has already been removed, leaving the ribs behind with a thin layer of meat. A slab of spareribs weighs 2 to 3 pounds or so and should have substantial meat on it, especially at the larger end. The best slabs weigh more than 3 pounds, and they often have a 2-inch-plus layer of meat at the larger end of the slab. There will be some fat, but the ribs should not be too fatty. Ask your butcher for a heavier slab, one with only a little fat. You will see a real difference among slabs, so it's worth taking the trouble. Don't buy previously frozen ribs or ones with discolored or dried-out edges. Figure on two to three servings per slab.

BABY BACK RIBS

These are pork chop bones from the upper portion of the rib section of the loin, with the boneless meat removed. Contrary to their name, they're not from baby pigs, and they have far less meat on them than the spareribs from the belly. In fact, some are trimmed so close to the bone that scarcely any meat remains. Baby back ribs are also leaner than spareribs, and the meat is quite tender because it comes from the loin. Restaurant owners love to serve these ribs because, with a couple of racks on a plate, it looks as if you are getting a lot of food. Once all of the bone and fat is accounted for, though, these small ribs are probably the most expensive part of the animal. Figure on a slab to feed one or two persons, more if there are plenty of other things to eat. Baby back ribs are ideal for cocktail party hors d'oeuvres (see Thai-Style Barbecued Baby Back Ribs, page 382). Because they're smaller, they take less time to cook than the other rib cuts. Look for lean ribs with plenty of meat on them. Avoid previously frozen ribs and any that are dried out or discolored.

COUNTRY-STYLE RIBS

Country-style ribs are actually pork chops from the blade end of the loin that have been butterflied or split. Since they contain enough fat, they can withstand long, slow grilling as well as braising. These meaty ribs have the additional advantage of being inexpensive.

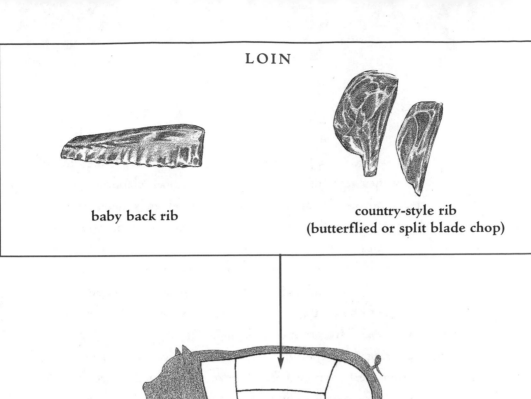

LOIN

baby back rib

country-style rib
(butterflied or split blade chop)

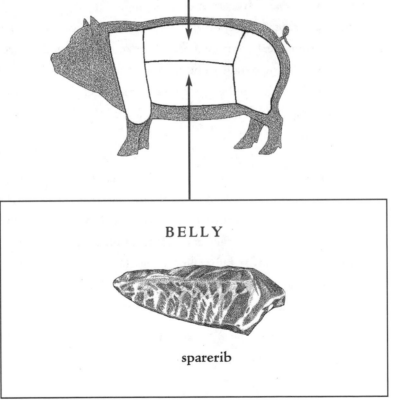

BELLY

sparerib

PORK RIBS
Slow-Cooked and Smoky

WHEN A GROUP OF FAMOUS CHEFS was recently asked to talk about their favorite foods, very few mentioned elaborate preparations with exotic ingredients. Most preferred simple, satisfying dishes. As I began thinking about how I might answer such a question, slow-cooked, juicy pork ribs flavored with wood smoke and smothered in a sweet and spicy sauce irresistibly came to mind. These are the ribs we find at our local barbecue joints in Oakland and San Francisco—they're so good that you can't get them home without digging in, and the red stains on the car seat and the greasy steering wheel are proof of your impatience.

The key to cooking these spareribs is a flavorful spice rub and long, slow cooking, the slower the better. See Slow-Cooked Barbecued Spareribs—The Real Way, page 376, for details. The barbecue sauce can vary—you can make your own (we provide a number of choices, on pages 379-81)—or there are plenty of good ones at the supermarket. You can also alter the flavor of the ribs by varying the spice rub.

If you don't have time to slow-cook the ribs on the barbecue (it can take four hours or more), there are two other acceptable alternatives. One way is to bake the ribs for one to two hours in a relatively low oven (this works well for Chinese marinades), sauce up the ribs toward the end of cooking, and eat them right from the oven. Or you can leave off the sauce and crisp the baked ribs to give them a smoky flavor by grilling over charcoal and brushing on some barbecue sauce during the last couple of minutes. Alternatively, you can crisp the ribs under a broiler after brushing with sauce.

B.A.

Good !!

SPICE RUB FOR PORK OR BEEF

Makes about 1 cup

THIS LIVELY MIX OF HERBS AND SPICES is the secret to great spareribs. It makes enough for two to four slabs, and any extra can be stored in a sealed jar for a couple of months. Sprinkle a little on the meat the next time you grill steaks or pork chops. For the best results, let the meat marinate in the rub for two hours at room temperature or overnight in the refrigerator.

> 2   tablespoons paprika, preferably Hungarian
> 2   tablespoons chile powder, preferably Gebhardt
> ~~1-2   teaspoons cayenne pepper (optional)~~
> 2   tablespoons granulated garlic or garlic powder
> 3   tablespoons light or dark brown sugar
> 1   tablespoon ground cumin
> 1   tablespoon dry mustard, preferably Colman's
> 1   teaspoon ground sage
> 1   teaspoon dried oregano
> ¼   cup salt
> ½   tablespoon freshly ground black pepper

Mix all the ingredients together in a small bowl or jar. Make a double or triple recipe if you like, and store it for up to a couple of months in a tightly sealed jar.

Slow-Cooked Barbecued Spareribs— The Real Way

■ Flavor Step ■

Spice Rub for Pork or
Beef (page 375)

2 2½-to-3-pound slabs of
spareribs OR three
1-to-1½-pound slabs
of baby back ribs
Mustardy Barbecue
Sauce (page 379),
OR Oakland-Style
Barbecue Sauce
(page 380), OR
Bourbon Barbecue
Sauce (page 381),
OR Coca-Cola and
Chile Barbecue Sauce
(page 363), OR
your favorite store-
bought sauce

Serves 4 to 6

■ MOM'S COMFORT FOOD ■ FIT FOR COMPANY

IF YOU'VE EVER WONDERED how they make those great spareribs in the world-renowned barbecue joints of Kansas City, the South Side of Chicago, Memphis, or Oakland, the secret is a flavorful spice rub and long, slow cooking with a spicy sauce slathered on just before serving. With a covered kettle barbecue, you can create equally wonderful results in your own backyard. The key elements: a flavor-packed spice rub, slow cooking at low temperatures (between 200° and 250°F) with a fairly long resting period to let the juices stabilize in the meat, and your favorite barbecue sauce or one of our recipes. You'll need to soak about 4 cups of wood chips such as hickory or oak, or 8 to 10 chunks.

We thank Cort Sinnes, who developed the details of this cooking technique for *Cook's Illustrated* magazine. We've adapted his method.

■ **Flavor Step** ■ Rub the spice rub all over both sides of the slabs or baby back ribs, using 3 to 4 tablespoons of the mixture for each slab. For the best results, place the ribs on a baking dish or platter and refrigerate them overnight, loosely wrapped with plastic wrap or foil; this will allow the flavors of the spices and herbs to permeate the meat. If you're in a hurry, cook the ribs after 1 hour in the spice rub at room temperature; this will at least give the outside of the ribs a good flavor. If you do refrigerate the ribs, remove them at least 30 minutes to 1 hour before you're ready to cook.

Prepare a covered barbecue for cooking: light a mound of 20 to 30 briquettes on one side of the grate and open the bottom vent fully. Place a roasting pan on the other side of the grate and add about 2 inches of water—the pan helps to catch any drippings, and the water provides moist heat to tenderize the meat. Meanwhile, if using wood chips, wrap about 2 cups of soaked hardwood chips in a foil packet and punch holes in the top to let the smoke escape (wrapping the chips in foil helps to keep the wood from burning up quickly when placed directly on the coals). Or you can place 4 or 5 hardwood chunks directly on the coals.

Once the coals are ready, lay the foil packet on the coals. Put on the rack and lay the ribs on it over the pan so that no meat is directly over the coals (see Grilling: Indirect Cooking, page 65). Cover the barbecue, with the lid vent about half open and opposite the coals, so that the smoke is drawn over the ribs. Stick an instant-read thermometer into a top vent hole, making sure that any plastic parts are not in direct contact with the metal lid, and leave it there. Ideally, you want the temperature to read 200° to 250°F; initially it can be higher, but it should not exceed 300°F; it should drop down to the lower range within a half hour or so. If not, partially close the lower vent to decrease the heat. Do not close this vent all the way, however, as this would cause the coals to die out. Regulate the temperature by adjusting the bottom vent, keeping the temperature registered in the upper vent in the desired range. Every 45 minutes, turn the ribs over and switch their places on the grill so that you alternate their exposure to the hotter edge near the coals. Add another 2-cup packet of chips or 4 or 5 hardwood chunks to the coals if the hardwood has burned up. If the temperature drops below 200°F, open all the vents fully, top and bottom, and check to see if the coals have burned out or need replenishing. If so, add 5 to 10 more briquettes. Once these coals get going, you may have to close the vents partially to regulate the heat.

After 1¾ to 2 hours (1½ hours for baby back ribs), check the ribs for doneness. When they are ready, the ends of the bones will be exposed and the meat will begin to pull away from the bone. If a rib bone is twisted, it should begin to turn and come loose from the meat. The surface of the ribs should be reddish brown. When tested with the instant-read meat thermometer, the meatiest section should have an internal temperature of 165° to 175°F. (Because ribs are so fatty, they can be cooked to a higher temperature than other pork cuts.)

When they are done, place the ribs on a baking sheet, large platter, or baking dish and cover them tightly with foil. Wrap the pan or platter with 10 to 20 sheets of unfolded newspaper and let the ribs rest for 20 to 40 minutes or up to an hour before serving.

Meanwhile, heat the barbecue sauce of your choice in a small saucepan. When you're ready to serve, slice the slabs into individual ribs and brush generously with the sauce. Serve with more sauce on the side and plenty of napkins and cold beer.

Mustardy Barbecue Sauce

Makes 2 to 3 cups

C ALLING THE SAUCE "mustardy" is somewhat misleading, since the mellow mustard provides a rich and savory undertone in one of the best barbecue sauces we've ever tasted. This type of sauce is popular in South Carolina and other areas where folks like a sauce with yellow mustard rather than tomatoes or vinegar as the dominant flavor. We prefer Dijon mustard, but if you like the yellow better, by all means use it. This is a tasty sauce for pork ribs of every type (see page 374) and equally good on beef brisket or barbecued lamb.

Heat the oil in a heavy saucepan over medium heat. Put in the onions, bell peppers, garlic, salt, and pepper. Cover the pan and cook, stirring from time to time, until the vegetables have softened, about 10 minutes. Put in the chile powder and stir until the vegetables are well coated. Add the remaining ingredients and stir well until blended. Bring to a boil, reduce the heat to a simmer, and cook for 30 to 45 minutes, stirring occasionally and adding water if the sauce gets too thick. It should be thick but easy to pour.

Taste the sauce for salt and pepper, and if you like it hotter, stir in some more Tabasco or other hot sauce. The sauce will keep in a tightly sealed jar in the refrigerator for up to 1 month.

2 tablespoons vegetable oil
1 cup finely chopped onions
½ cup finely chopped green bell peppers
1 tablespoon minced garlic
¼ teaspoon salt
1 teaspoon freshly ground black pepper
2 tablespoons chile powder, preferably Gebhardt
1 cup Dijon or prepared yellow mustard
2 tablespoons dry mustard, preferably Colman's
1 cup ketchup
2 cups beef stock
½ cup molasses
¼ cup fresh lemon juice
¼ cup Worcestershire sauce
2 tablespoons cider vinegar
¼ cup packed light or dark brown sugar
2 teaspoons Tabasco or other hot sauce, or more to taste
1 teaspoon ground coriander
1 teaspoon ground cumin
1-2 teaspoons Liquid Smoke (optional)

Oakland-Style Barbecue Sauce

2 tablespoons vegetable oil

2 cups finely chopped
  onions

1 cup finely chopped
  celery

½ cup finely chopped
  carrots

3 tablespoons chopped
  garlic

¼ teaspoon salt

2 teaspoons freshly ground
  black pepper

1 cup red wine

6 cups beef stock,
  preferably homemade

2 cups ketchup

⅓ cup Worcestershire sauce

¼ cup soy sauce, preferably
  low-sodium

3 tablespoons cider
  vinegar

1-2 teaspoons Liquid Smoke

¼ cup packed dark brown
  sugar

3 tablespoons dry mustard,
  preferably Colman's

2 teaspoons dried thyme

1 teaspoon dried oregano

1-2 teaspoons cayenne
  pepper (optional)

4 bay leaves

¼ teaspoon Tabasco or
  other hot sauce, or
  more to taste (optional)

Makes 2 to 3 cups

YOU'LL NEVER BUY barbecue sauce again after tasting this simple sauce. The meaty, smoky sauce gets its flavor from reduced beef stock and is not as tomato-y as many traditional sauces. Not only is it great over pork ribs, it is also delicious on grilled steaks or burgers. You can make it as mild or as hot as you like by varying the amount of (or leaving out) the cayenne or Tabasco. If you use canned beef stock, be careful about salt—most canned stock can become too salty when reduced. It's best to leave the salt out altogether and adjust at the end. And use a low-sodium soy sauce if you can find it.

Heat the oil in a large, heavy saucepan over medium heat. Add the onions, celery, carrots, garlic, salt, and pepper. Cover and cook, stirring occasionally, until the vegetables are soft and beginning to color, 10 to 15 minutes. Add the wine, bring to a boil, and boil for 2 to 3 minutes. Put in the remaining ingredients except the Tabasco and stir until everything is well blended. Reduce to a simmer and cook, uncovered, for 45 minutes to 1 hour, or until the sauce has thickened but can still be poured. Add a bit of water if it seems too thick.

Taste the sauce for salt and pepper and, if you wish, add Tabasco or other hot sauce. Remove the bay leaves. The sauce keeps, covered in the refrigerator, for up to 1 month.

Bourbon Barbecue Sauce

Makes 3 to 4 cups

THIS SAUCE IS understandably popular in Tennessee and Kentucky, where the best American whiskeys are made. The whiskey provides a smoky tang derived from the charred oak barrels it's aged in. The sauce is excellent with all types of grilled pork and delicious swabbed on beef or lamb toward the end of cooking.

———

Heat the oil in a large, heavy saucepan over medium heat. Add the onions and garlic, along with a pinch each of salt and pepper. Cover and cook, stirring frequently, until the onions are quite soft, about 10 minutes. Stir in the bell pepper and cook 1 minute more. Stir in the mustard, chile powder, paprika, and optional cayenne. Cook for 1 more minute, stirring well to coat the onions and bell pepper. Add the remaining ingredients and stir until everything is well blended. Bring to a boil, reduce to a simmer, and cook for 25 minutes, or until the sauce has thickened but can still be poured. Add water, if necessary, during cooking. Taste for salt, pepper, and Tabasco or other hot sauce. The sauce can be stored, covered, in the refrigerator for up to 1 month.

2 tablespoons vegetable oil
2 cups finely chopped onions
2 tablespoons minced garlic
Salt and freshly ground black pepper
¼ cup finely chopped green bell pepper
2 tablespoons dry mustard, preferable Colman's
1 tablespoon chile powder, preferably Gebhardt
1 tablespoon paprika, preferably Hungarian
2 teaspoons cayenne pepper (optional)
2 cups ketchup
¼ cup Worcestershire sauce
¼ cup cider vinegar
1-2 teaspoons Liquid Smoke (optional)
1 cup beer
½ cup bourbon or Tennessee whiskey
2 teaspoons ground cumin
¼ cup firmly packed light or dark brown sugar
2 tablespoons molasses
Tabasco or other hot sauce to taste

Thai-Style Barbecued Baby Back Ribs

■ Flavor Step ■

THAI MARINADE FOR
PORK

¼ cup Asian fish sauce
(*nam pla* or *nuoc mam*)

2 tablespoons Asian
peanut oil

2 tablespoons soy sauce

2 tablespoons fresh lime
juice

2 tablespoons minced
garlic

2 stalks lemongrass, outer
leaves removed and
tender center thinly
sliced

¼ cup chopped fresh
cilantro

1 tablespoon minced fresh
ginger

2 tablespoons sugar

2 teaspoons Asian sesame
oil

3 1-to-1½-pound slabs
of baby back ribs

**Serves 4 to 6 as a main course
Makes 35 to 40 ribs for hors d'oeuvres
■ FIT FOR COMPANY
■ GOOD FOR A CROWD (AS HORS D'OEUVRES)**

YOU CAN SERVE these succulent, habit-forming ribs as a course in a Thai banquet or as hors d'oeuvres at a cocktail party. They may be eaten as is or with the Thai Dipping Sauce. To make a meal out of the dish, serve the ribs over rice with Thai red onion and cucumber salad. *(See photograph, page 19.)*

This marinade also works well with spareribs, country-style ribs, pork chops, and lamb riblets. The Asian ingredients can be found in Asian groceries or specialty stores or by mail-order (see Sources, page 584).

■ **Flavor Step** ■ Mix all the marinade ingredients together in a small bowl and blend well. Put the ribs into a zipper-lock bag or shallow dish and pour the marinade over the meat. Cover if necessary and refrigerate the meat overnight, turning occasionally.

About 30 minutes before cooking, remove the ribs from the refrigerator. Preheat the oven to 300°F. Place a roasting pan half full of water in the bottom third of the oven.

Remove the ribs from the marinade and reserve the marinade. Shake off the excess marinade and place the ribs on a rack in a shallow roasting pan. Put the pan in the top third of the oven and roast for 45 minutes to 1 hour, basting the ribs from time to time with the reserved marinade. The ribs are done when they begin to pull away from the bone and the bone tips are exposed. The internal temperature of the thickest part should be 155° to 165°F.

Meanwhile, make the optional Thai Dipping Sauce: Combine the ingredients in a small bowl and stir until the sugar is dissolved.

After a 5-to-10-minute rest, cut the ribs into individual pieces.

Or you can grill the ribs over medium-hot coals (see Grilling, page 63) for 6 to 8 minutes total, turning them frequently to keep the sugar in the marinade from burning. Remove the ribs from the grill and let them rest for 5 to 10 minutes before cutting into individual pieces. Serve with the sauce or as is.

THAI DIPPING SAUCE
(OPTIONAL)

2 tablespoons fresh lime juice

2 tablespoons rice wine vinegar

1 tablespoon soy sauce

1 tablespoon *Sriracha* (Thai hot chili sauce) OR 1 teaspoon red pepper flakes

1 tablespoon sugar

1 teaspoon minced garlic

½ teaspoon Asian sesame oil

2 tablespoons chopped fresh cilantro

Precooking Grilled Spareribs for a Crowd

4-5 2½-to-3-pound slabs
of spareribs

BARBECUE SAUCE
(PAGES 379-81)

■ FIT FOR A CROWD

I F YOU'RE PREPARING many slabs of ribs for a large crowd, poaching the ribs over very low heat before grilling makes sense, but do not boil them.

Bring a large pot of salted water (1 teaspoon of salt per quart) to a slow boil. The pot should be large enough to hold several slabs. Put in the spareribs and turn the heat down so that the water does not even simmer (check with an instant-read thermometer: the temperature of the water should stay around 170°F, although it can range from 160° to 190°F). Poach the ribs, uncovered, at this low temperature for 1 hour, skimming and discarding any fat and foam from the surface of the water. Adjust the heat to keep the water in the desired range. You may even have to turn the heat off from time to time.

When the ribs are fully cooked, drain them (you may want to keep the stock for soup) and allow them to cool slightly. Pat the ribs dry and rub generously on both sides with the Spice Rub for Pork or Beef (page 375). You can wrap the ribs and refrigerate them overnight at this point or proceed directly to grilling.

Prepare a bed of medium-hot coals in a kettle barbecue. Just before adding the ribs, sprinkle the coals with 1 cup of hickory or oak chips that have been soaked in water for about 30 minutes. Place the ribs on the grill directly over the coals, cover the barbecue, and cook the ribs for a total of 10 to 15 minutes, turning frequently so they don't burn. (Ribs taken directly from the refrigerator will take a little longer.)

Place the ribs on a baking sheet or large platter and cover tightly with foil. Wrap with layers (10 sheets or more) of unfolded newspaper and let the ribs rest for 20 to 40 minutes or up to an hour to allow the juices to stabilize. This step will provide juicier and more flavorful ribs. When you're ready to eat, unwrap the ribs and slice them into individual pieces. Brush on your favorite barbecue sauce and serve.

MYTHBUSTING

DON'T PARBOIL SPARERIBS

MANY RECIPES FOR GRILLED SPARERIBS suggest boiling them first to partially cook the meat and remove some of the fat. We do not recommend this practice. Parboiling, or cooking in water at a boil, not only tends to toughen the meat but also leaches out valuable flavors. When the ribs are finally finished on the grill, the result is stringy meat that lacks juiciness and flavor.

Instead of parboiling, if you wish to precook the ribs, poach them in water that is never allowed to go above a simmer—the temperature stays below 170°F (boiling water is 212°F). This gentle cooking won't dry the meat out and will make the ribs tender, although it can leach out some flavor. A better way, we think, is to bake the ribs first in a slow oven and then grill them (see Chinese-Style Barbecued Spareribs, page 386).

Chinese-Style Barbecued Spareribs
(Oven-Roasted Marinated Spareribs)

CHINESE OYSTER SAUCE

MARINADE FOR PORK

¼ cup oyster sauce

¼ cup hoisin sauce

¼ cup soy sauce

¼ cup honey

2 tablespoons minced
   fresh ginger

2 tablespoons sweet sherry

1 tablespoon minced garlic

1 tablespoon Chinese
   brown bean paste or
   Chinese chili paste
   with garlic (optional)

2 teaspoons Asian peanut
   oil

2 2½-to-3-pound slabs of
   spareribs OR 3½ to 4½
   pounds of baby back
   ribs (3-4 slabs)

Serves 6 to 8

■ FIT FOR A CROWD

THE TECHNIQUE AND FLAVORS of this way of cooking spareribs are similar to those for Chinese Marinated and Roasted Pork (page 332). You can use the marinade from that recipe or this one, which gains a slightly more exotic flavor from the oyster sauce. You can cook these ribs entirely in the oven, but if you like a lightly smoky taste, they can be briefly seared over hot coals as a final step before serving. Take care not to burn the ribs, since the marinade has a high sugar content. The marinade is also delicious with thinly sliced pork loin for a stir-fry, or as a marinade and glaze for roasted pork tenderloin, or with lamb riblets.

■ **Flavor Step** ■ Combine all the ingredients for the marinade in a bowl and blend well. Place the ribs in a zipper-lock bag or shallow bowl and pour the marinade over them. Cover if necessary and refrigerate overnight or for up to 2 days, turning the meat occasionally to coat well.

Thirty to 60 minutes before cooking, remove the ribs from the refrigerator. Preheat the oven to 300°F. Place a baking pan of water on a rack in the lower third of the oven to increase the humidity.

Remove the ribs from the marinade and reserve the marinade. Lay the ribs, meaty side up, on a rack in a shallow roasting pan. Put them in the top third of the oven and roast for 1½ hours, basting the ribs from time to time with the reserved marinade. The ribs are done when the meat nearest the end begins to shrink away from the bone. The internal temperature should read 165° to 175°F. Slice the slabs into individual ribs and serve.

Overlooked but Delicious Cuts

W E'VE ALREADY MENTIONED the **leg of pork** (page 347) as a treasure trove of overlooked but delicious roasts and cutlets. The cured and smoked **picnic ham** from the foreleg is another often overlooked cut. It is usually a real bargain, too. It has more fat and waste than a back leg ham but has a great, hearty flavor. We like to braise it and serve it with beans, lentils, or sauerkraut.

If you can find butchers who cater to West Indian or African-American communities, be sure to pay them a visit. Here you can find such overlooked cuts as pork neckbones, pork jowl, pig's tails, ears and feet, or maybe even a whole pig's head. **Neck bones** are usually smoked and have very little meat on them, but they contribute fantastic flavors when braised with beans, black-eyed peas, lentils, or greens. We love them in pea soup or with braised cabbage. The **jowl** from the cheek and neck area of the pig is usually smoked like bacon and is also used to flavor dried legumes and vegetables. It is much fattier than bacon but gives a fantastic smoky taste.

Tails, **ears**, and **feet** are mostly skin and collagen. These parts of the pig require long, slow cooking to be tender enough to eat and generally have more bone, fat, and waste than most of us are willing to deal with today. But they add flavor and lots of body to the rest of the food in the pot. They are often used in classic peasant dishes like black bean *feijoada* from Brazil or Caribbean hot pot.

Southern and German-American cooks like to simmer the **whole pig's head** for hours with spices and then remove all the bones to make head cheese. These days most of us who love these gelatinous and spicy meats buy them already prepared in a deli. The same is true of pickled pig's feet, still found on beer bars all over the Midwest and South.

Smoked ham hocks are widely available. They are delicious as is after a long simmer in aromatic broth or cooked together with classic accompaniments such as lima beans, red beans, and sauerkraut. Some German-American butchers will sell you the **whole unsmoked hock** or **pork shank**, which is meaty and delicious and well worth trying (see Caramelized Pork Shank and Braised Cabbage, page 389).

PORK SHANK
A Feast Fit for the Flintstones

I FELL IN LOVE WITH THIS DELICIOUS CUT some years back when I was wandering around Eastern Europe. In Hungary one fall day, I found myself in a tiny village that had only one restaurant—a peasant cottage with a huge fireplace and smoke-blackened walls. I sat down with a glass of the traditional plum brandy and tried to figure out what to eat from a largely incomprehensible (to me, anyway) Magyar menu.

Suddenly, the door to the kitchen burst open, and a statuesque waitress swept into the room bearing huge platters of cabbage topped with what looked like beautifully browned dinosaur bones, a feast fit for the Flintstones. A table of Barney-size folks devoured the savory meat and cabbage in what seemed like a few seconds. This solved my dilemma—I pointed and licked my chops, the waitress beamed encouragingly, and I soon got my first taste of braised pork shank. In this restaurant of serious eaters, one shank of 2 to 3 pounds was considered a normal portion. In the United States, our shanks are smaller—one shank for two is a more reasonable serving.

Several years ago I came across a recipe for whole roasted pork shank by Alain Senderens, a three-star French chef, in his book *The Three-Star Recipes of Alain Senderens*. I've adapted it to reflect my first experience with pork shank in that unforgettable restaurant in the Hungarian countryside.   *B.A.*

Caramelized Pork Shank and Braised Cabbage

Serves 4 with hearty appetites
■ REWARMS WELL ■ FIT FOR COMPANY

UNFORTUNATELY, FRESH PORK SHANK is hard to find; most shanks these days are turned into smoked ham hocks. But fresh shank is worth seeking out, since, like veal and lamb shanks, the meat becomes quite silky and luscious when cooked slowly and thoroughly. In this recipe, the shank is briefly cured in salt and then coated with sugar, then caramelized in a hot oven to create a rich, dark, and lightly sweet glaze. You should be able to order fresh pork shank from a butcher or specialty pork store; if you can't find it, try this recipe with boned, rolled pork shoulder. Drink a mug or two of dark lager while you eat it.

The day before you are going to cook the shanks, trim off most of the external fat, leaving a thin layer to keep the meat moist and flavorful. Cut several 1-inch-deep diagonal slashes on the top and bottom of each shank. Pour kosher salt generously over the shanks and rub it into the slits. Place the shanks in a shallow glass pan or on a large plate. Cover with plastic wrap and refrigerate overnight.

The next day, preheat the oven to 425°F. Wash all the salt off the shanks and pat the meat dry. Rub the sugar all over the shanks and sprinkle generously with the black pepper. Oil a heavy, shallow roasting pan or 12-inch cast-iron skillet with 1 tablespoon of the oil. Put the shanks in the pan and roast in the middle of the oven for 20 minutes, basting a couple of times with any pan juices. Turn the shanks 2 or 3 times so they brown on all sides. Make sure the sugar does not burn; lower the oven temperature if necessary. Remove the shanks from the oven. Pour off all the pan juices and reserve. Set the shanks aside while you finish the cabbage. If you plan to use

2 fresh pork shanks
  (3-4 pounds total),
  skin removed
Kosher salt
¼ cup sugar
5 teaspoons freshly ground
  black pepper
2 tablespoons olive oil
2 medium onions, thinly
  sliced
2 carrots, diced
3 garlic cloves, chopped
1 2-pound cabbage,
  quartered, cored, and
  cut into ¼-inch shreds
1 pound sauerkraut, rinsed
  and drained
½ teaspoon caraway seeds
1 tablespoon mild
  Hungarian paprika
½ teaspoon dried marjoram
4 ripe tomatoes or canned
  Italian-style tomatoes,
  seeded and chopped
2 cups beef or chicken
  stock or water

the same pan or skillet to roast the shanks further, clean out any burned bits.

While the pork is roasting, heat the remaining 1 tablespoon oil in a heavy Dutch oven or casserole over medium-high heat. Put in the onions, carrots, garlic, and a pinch of salt. Cover the pot and cook until the vegetables soften, about 5 minutes. Stir in the remaining ingredients. Cover the pot and cook, stirring occasionally, until the cabbage wilts. Reduce the oven heat to 350°F. Spoon the mixture onto the bottom of the cleaned roasting pan or skillet (or a clean roasting pan) and place the browned pork shanks on top. Roast, uncovered, for 2 to 2½ hours, or until the meat is quite tender. Baste the shanks 2 or 3 times during cooking with juices from the pan and turn them from time to time.

To serve, taste the cabbage for salt and pepper and season to taste. Spoon the cabbage onto a serving platter. Place the pork shanks on top and carve chunks of the shank meat onto the cabbage. (Save any leftover cabbage and pork to serve as a side dish.)

How to Choose Ham

All You Need to Know

THERE WAS A TIME IN AMERICA when buying a ham was a commitment: you had to lug home a 20-pound piece of cured and smoked meat. The old-fashioned ham was lovely to look at and lovely to smell, but you needed to count on a dozen or more people to show up for dinner unless you wanted to eat nothing but ham for the next two weeks. Even then, you usually had to figure out what to do with the leftovers. Hence the famous comment by Mrs. Rombauer in the original *Joy of Cooking*: "Eternity is defined as two people and a ham." But in today's supermarket, you have no such difficulties: you can buy something labeled "ham" in 1-pound pieces— once again, technology has shortened eternity.

The idea of turning a fresh leg of pork into a ham goes far back in history. Long ago, Chinese cooks found that coating a leg of pork with salt for a few weeks and then letting it dry preserved the meat and also led to some very tasty results. And that's basically all there is to making ham. This drying and aging process can create some culinary masterpieces. Two of the world's finest hams, Serrano ham from Spain and *prosciutto di Parma* from Italy, are made with salt and salt only; skillful control of the hams' long and unique aging conditions is the secret.

Years ago, in the days before refrigerators, this heavy salting was necessary to preserve the meat. Today we don't need the salt for preservation, but we still cure meat to create a certain taste and texture. In the United States, there are still some traditionally made hams, called country hams, that use enough salt to ensure complete preservation without refrigeration, but these are the exceptions. Most hams these days are intended to be stored in the refrigerator.

Meat can be cured in two basic ways:

■ By coating with dry salt: This method is called **dry-curing** and is the most ancient. Examples of dry-cured meats are Smithfield ham and prosciutto. Dry cures are often sweetened with white, brown, or maple sugar, and sometimes the surface of the meat is coated with black pepper.

■ By soaking in brine: A high proportion of salt is dissolved in water and the meat is immersed in the brine; sometimes sugar and sodium nitrate are added. This is called **wet-curing**. Corned beef, ham hocks, and most ordinary smoked hams are examples of brine-cured meat.

In the old days, two or three weeks were needed for the salt to penetrate and cure the meat. Today's ham producers don't want to wait that long. They inject the brine directly into the meat using long needles, reducing the curing time to a day or two. Occasionally some of the old-time ham makers will combine both techniques: dry-curing the ham for one or two days and then switching over to brine-curing. Everybody has his or her own little secrets for making ham, and the best producers keep them well guarded.

Once the ham is cured, smoking it is optional, although most American ham is smoked. Many great European hams are only salted, air-dried, and aged. These and some other European hams are usually eaten raw—the dry-curing and aging process kills any trichinae that might be present in the pork. Traditional slow-smoking—hanging cured hams over smoldering hardwoods such as hickory, oak, or maple—adds a special flavor to the meat and creates an appetizing brownish-red color.

As with wet-curing, however, many of today's ham producers feel the need to hurry the process along using smokehouses with special temperature and humidity controls and a mist of liquid smoke vapor instead of real wood smoke. These modern hams may spend only a few hours rather than days in the smokehouse—just enough to provide a little smoky flavor and fully cook the hams to 148°F to destroy trichinae. These quickly processed hams have a mild flavor and are usually quite juicy because of the addition of water and phosphates.

Makers of country hams and some specialty producers and small regional smokehouses still use the long, slow process called **cold-smoking**, or bathing the ham in smoke for a long period of time without raising the temperature high enough to cook it. Some of the world's greatest hams are made this way: for example, Smithfield ham from Virginia, Westphalian ham from Germany, Austrian *Speck,* and traditional Polish ham (not the canned version). Like prosciutto and Serrano ham, these smoked hams are allowed to age and can be sliced very thin and eaten raw. They are expensive because of the time involved in processing and the weight lost through aging, but a little goes a long way, and the hams are well worth seeking out from quality delis or by mail-order (see Sources, page 584). At its best, meat from these hams is succulent, mildly smoky, and wonderfully silky.

What the pig eats (you are what you eat!) can produce subtle variations in the flavor of the resulting ham. The Iberico pig of Spain fattens on acorns, while the pigs of Westphalia thrive on sugar beets. Parma pigs consume the whey left over from making mountains of Parmesan cheese, and the pigs around Smithfield, Virginia, live on the local peanuts. Other great country hams from Kentucky, Tennessee, and the Carolinas come from pigs that eat acorns and peaches—but the happiest pigs of all get leftover sour mash from the whiskey distillers that dot the Southern hills.

HAM CUTS, SERVING PORTIONS, AND STORING

A whole ham, a 10-to-20-pound cured hind leg of pork with bone intact, is the most flavorful and least wasteful cut. It will serve 20 people, probably with leftovers—here comes eternity! A short, plump shape with a stubby rather than an elongated shank is the best choice. For smaller groups, you can buy a cut section of the whole ham: either the rounded part called the **butt** (the upper thigh of the animal) or the **lower shank end**. The butt half is somewhat more meaty but more difficult to carve because of the aitch bone. A 6-to-8-pound shank will serve 10 to 12 people, a 6-to-8-pound butt 12 or more. From the flat cut end of either butt or shank, several slices of individual ham steaks can be cut off and cooked separately (see Inspirations from a Ham, page 400).

Ham is also available in many boneless forms—whole, in halves, and in chunks of various sizes. These are not as flavorful as bone-in hams when baked. Small chunks or re-formed hams are best not baked at all (see Deli Hams, below). Allow 8 to 12 ounces for a bone-in ham per serving, 6 to 8 ounces for a boneless ham.

Ham is best served warm or cool; it is never as good chilled from the refrigerator. If a rainbow iridescence appears on sliced ham, it's merely due to light refraction on the film caused by the injected phosphates; it doesn't mean the ham is spoiled.

The rule is that all ham must be kept refrigerated—with two exceptions: small, unopened canned hams not labeled perishable and country hams, or Smithfield hams, which can be kept in a cool, dry, dark place indefinitely. For the best results, uncanned whole hams should not be stored in the original package in the refrigerator for more than 10 days before cooking. Smaller portions should not be kept longer than 3 to 5 days. Sliced ham is best used within 2 days. Freezing any ham is not recommended because of the rapid deterioration of quality and flavor; canned ham is especially vulnerable because of its high water content. Once it's been baked, you can keep ham lightly covered for an additional 7 to 10 days in the refrigerator.

THE NEW AMERICAN HAM

Old-fashioned, uncooked hams have mostly been replaced today by fully cooked hams, often laden with phosphates and pumped with water to add weight to make them appear cheaper to consumers.

■ **Deli Hams:** Also called sandwich hams, tavern hams, or buffet hams, these are boneless pieces of meat reshaped to form oval or large cylindrical "hams." They are meant to be eaten as is or sliced for sandwiches and are sold whole or in pieces in the meat departments of most supermarkets; they are also sold sliced in delicatessens. Although they can be reheated by steaming in a foil-covered roasting pan with a little water on the bottom, the taste and texture tend to be on the rubbery side, qualities that are not improved by heating. Deli hams containing no added water are simply labeled "ham" and should contain at least 20.5 percent protein by weight. Hams labeled "ham with natural juices" must have only 18.5 percent protein by weight and will contain added water.

■ **Fully Cooked Supermarket Hams:** These may or may not have a bone, but will have the natural shape of the pork leg or ham and will include some external fat and sometimes the skin. These hams are available whole at 10 to 20 pounds and can also be found in halves, either the butt end or shank end. Most of these hams contain added water and all contain phosphates. The best and most expensive are simply labeled "ham" and contain no added water, with at least 20.5 percent protein. Hams labeled "ham with natural juices" contain at least 18.5 percent protein. Those labeled "ham—water added" contain more water and at least 17 percent protein. The cheapest (and worst) of all these modern hams is labeled "ham and water product" and can contain as much added water as the manufacturer can pump into it. The vast majority of these hams will be labeled "fully cooked" or "ready to eat."

■ **Traditional Partially Cooked Hams:** These old-fashioned hams can be ordered by mail-order from small smokehouses in the Southeast, New England, and other parts of the country (see Sources, page 584). Expect to pay more for these hams since they will contain less waste and a higher proportion of protein. These hams should be cooked to 145° to 150°F so that the final internal temperature of the meat after resting is 155° to 160°F.

■ **Country Hams:** Less frequently found in this instant-everything age is the old-time country ham, often called Virginia, Kentucky, or Tennessee ham. The most famous (and some say the best) of all the country types is the Smithfield ham from Virginia. All country hams are dry-cured and heavily salted. They require extended soaking and long simmering before baking; see Buying a Country Ham, page 402.

■ **Canned Hams:** Most of the larger canned hams, including the superior types imported from Denmark, Holland, and Poland, must be kept under refrigeration before opening but can be stored in the refrigerator for a few months. Some of the smaller canned hams can be stored without refrigeration, but these hams have been sterilized (and overcooked) in the canning process, and taste and texture are the losers. Canned hams are usually sold under a manufacturer's label, and by sampling various brands, you may eventually find those you like.

■ **Other Hams:** The smoked arm, or shoulder, of the pig is known as a picnic ham, or cally. This is a less expensive cut than regular ham since it contains more fat, bone, and skin in proportion to lean meat. These "hams" can be a real bargain and generally have good flavor. The smoked Boston shoulder is a boneless cut from the neck and shoulder of the hog and may have several aliases: smoked Boston butt, cottage ham, or daisy ham. The butt can be roasted or simmered in a stock; sliced, it can be broiled, fried, or sautéed.

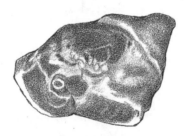

Whole Ham

Baked Ham—Fully Cooked or Ready to Eat

1 ready-to-eat ham of your choice, whole or half, bone-in or boneless

■ Flavor Step ■

GLAZES FOR BAKED HAM (optional; increase the quantity if you want to give the ham a final brushing of glaze)

1-2 cups packed light or dark brown sugar or granulated sugar,

OR

1 cup Dijon mustard plus 1 cup packed light or dark brown sugar,

OR

2 cups granulated or packed light or dark brown sugar, mixed with 3 tablespoons dry mustard, preferably Colman's

¼ teaspoon ground cloves

3 tablespoons cider vinegar or fruit juice,

OR

2 cups of your favorite jam or marmalade (apricot, peach, plum, orange, or lemon), diluted with a little water or white wine

1 cup dried bread crumbs (optional)

Serves 8 to 10 (half ham) or 16 to 20 (whole ham)

■ GOOD FOR A CROWD ■ GREAT LEFTOVERS ■ FIT FOR COMPANY

HAMS LABELED "FULLY COOKED" are safe to eat as is, but they benefit greatly both in flavor and texture from being roasted and glazed in the oven.

Hams suitable for baking can be bone-in or boneless. They usually have the natural shape of the leg as opposed to the re-formed oval shape of the deli hams, which shouldn't be baked. They're sold whole or in halves, from the shank end or butt end. Hams made from the foreleg or shoulder, called picnic hams, though fattier, can be used for baking as well.

How can you tell whether the ham you buy is suitable for baking? The answer is simple: buy one with the bone still in. If you require a boneless ham for some reason, look for one with the natural shape. Generally, if the ham seems to be the shape of a pig's leg and includes external fat and at least a little skin, it most likely can be successfully baked. Leave the rest of those unnaturally shaped lumps of salty pink rubber alone. You could also ask a specialty butcher to bone a ham for you; be sure to get the bone to make soup or cook with beans.

Besides baking the ham in the oven, you can cook it successfully in a covered kettle barbecue over indirect heat with smoke from hardwood chips. Most of these supermarket hams benefit enormously from the extra smoky flavor and slight drying effect of barbecuing (see Grilling, page 63, and Ham on the Grill, page 399).

Preheat the oven to 325°F. Cut away any skin and trim the fat to a thickness of ¼ to ½ inch. Place the ham, fat side up, in a shallow roasting pan. If you plan to glaze the ham, line the pan with foil, since the sugar in the glaze can burn. As a rough guide, roast a fully cooked ham for about 10 minutes per pound. A whole ham should cook in 2½ to 3 hours, a half ham in 1½ to 2 hours. Check the temperature after the minimum time with an instant-read meat thermometer. It should read 130° to 140°F (since the ham is fully cooked, you only have to heat it through). If the ham is not yet at the desired temperature, continue to bake and check it every 15 or 20 minutes. You can serve the ham as is after a 20-to-30-minute rest or proceed to glaze it.

To glaze the ham: When the ham is warmed through, raise the oven temperature to 425°F. Remove the ham from the oven and score the surface of the fat to make a crisscross grid. For a simple glaze, sprinkle the surface with the brown or granulated sugar. Or use any of the other glazes listed, spreading it generously over the surface of the ham. Bake for about 20 minutes, basting with the pan juices a few times. Brush on more glaze if you wish. Once the sugar melts in any of the glazes, you can also press dried bread crumbs onto the surface to make a more substantial crust. Remove the ham from the oven, cover loosely with foil, and let it rest for 20 to 30 minutes before carving. Serve with a sauce (see below) if desired.

SAUCES FOR BAKED HAM

Tangy Orange Sauce (page 272)
Blackberry and Black Currant Sauce (page 324)
Maple-Vanilla Sauce (page 339)
Apple and Cider Sauce (page 405)

Y OU CAN SERVE any of these sauces with a baked ham, whether or not you have glazed it. Expand the recipes as needed for larger groups. Ladle some sauce over the sliced ham and pass more in a gravy boat to your guests.

Partially Cooked Baked Ham

PLEASE READ HOW TO CHOOSE HAM: All You Need to Know (see page 391) to learn more about these tasty hams that are increasingly hard to find. In most cases, you will have to buy them from regional smokehouses by mail-order (see Sources, page 584), although they can still be found at quality butcher shops in some parts of the country.

The hams can vary considerably—some are well aged and can be as pungent and salty as a country ham, while others are tender and mild and are much like a fully cooked ham, although they must be cooked to 145° to 155°F before eating. For hams that are on the salty side, we recommend soaking and parboiling before baking as for country ham (see page 403). Slice off a small piece from the underside of the ham and fry it in a small pan. Give it a taste: if it's too salty, you should soak the ham overnight and parboil it for an hour or two before baking (although it should not need as much soaking and boiling as most country hams).

To bake a partially cooked ham, proceed exactly as directed for the fully cooked variety (see page 396), but allow about 12 minutes per pound before you check the temperature. Once the internal temperature of the meat reaches 145° to 155°F, you can glaze the ham if you wish or remove it from the oven. In any case, let the ham rest for 20 to 30 minutes, loosely covered with foil, before carving. The temperature will continue to rise by about 10°F.

If you soak and parboil the ham, bake it for about 1½ hours for a whole ham, or 1 hour for a half ham, before checking the internal temperature, which should be in the range of 145° to 155°F. You can glaze the ham at this point, if you wish, and serve it as described in the recipe for fully cooked ham.

Besides the glazes and sauces recommended on pages 396-97, try serving the ham with apple slices sautéed in butter.

Ham on the Grill

"FULLY COOKED" hams with various amounts of added water, either bone-in or boneless, can be improved by baking or barbecuing using indirect heat. The best way to prepare them is in a covered kettle barbecue, adding soaked hickory or oak chips to the coals from time to time. This additional smoking can improve the flavor and texture of these hams immensely, since the long, slow cooking dries them out a bit and reduces their sometimes excessive water content.

When the ham reaches an internal temperature of 130°F, it's ready for the final step. You can carve the meat and brush the slices with a glaze for the last few minutes of cooking. Or you can transfer the whole ham to a foil-lined baking dish, sprinkle it with a cup or two of light or dark brown sugar, and roast it in a conventional oven for 15 or 20 minutes at 425°F to provide a nice sweet glaze. Once it's cooked, make sure the ham rests for 20 to 30 minutes, loosely covered with foil, before slicing. By this time the internal temperature will be about 140°F. If you don't want to use a glaze, just cook the ham to 135° to 140°F, and it's ready to eat after a 20-to-30-minute rest.

INSPIRATIONS FROM A HAM

FOR US, the *raison d'être* of buying a ham is all that meat you have in the fridge the day after roasting it. There are many wonderful things that can be made with cooked ham. Fully cooked hams are about the only type of ham you can find in supermarkets these days. Thick slices of ham, or ham steaks, are also sold; they can also be cut from a baked ham.

While you can use cooked ham right out of the package—slicing it and using it in whatever "leftover" dish you have a hankering for—the flavor and texture of these hams are definitely improved by baking or grilling. This is especially true if you want to use the ham cold in sandwiches, salads, or hors d'oeuvres.

Sandwiches are a great way to use leftover baked ham. Besides the classic ham and Swiss on rye, try ham in a barbecued pork sandwich, using any of our barbecue sauces (pages 379-81) or a supermarket sauce. For a delicious ham sandwich dressing, combine some of the jellied cold pan drippings from the ham platter with mayonnaise and a little Dijon mustard.

A great variety of sauces (page 397) can be used to reheat baked ham, and slices or cubes of cooked ham can be incorporated into many family favorites. Turn your recipe for scalloped potatoes into a satisfying main dish by layering slices of leftover ham with the potatoes and onions. (This dish is particularly good with sharp white cheddar from upstate New York, Vermont, or Canada.) Or you can add some chunks of leftover ham to your family's traditional macaroni and cheese casserole. Or serve sliced ham with lightly poached broccoli in a light cheese sauce. Try mixing chunks of ham with blanched sliced green beans, thinly sliced onions, and grated cheddar; dot with butter and bake briefly. You can also add ham to baked beans or any of your favorite bean or lentil dishes.

Ham goes well with eggs, of course—in the time-honored combination of thickly sliced fried ham and fried eggs, in quiches of all sorts, and in eggs Benedict, with poached eggs and hollandaise sauce. Cooked ham can also be ground and mixed with pork or beef to make a ham loaf, or ground ham can be mixed with mushrooms and bread crumbs to make a forcemeat stuffing for vegetables such as mushrooms, bell peppers, or zucchini.

Classic cookbooks are great resources for other casseroles that use cooked ham. One favorite is a French *charcuterie* specialty, ham coronets: thin slices of smoked ham wrapped around a savory chopped vegetable salad. And ham improves soups and stews (especially the ham bone in pea or lentil soup) and flavors sauces and stocks.

Cooked ham, in slices, chopped, or in larger pieces, can be used in the following recipes as well: Smoked Ham Steak or Pork Chops in Apple and Cider Sauce (page 405), Baked Pork Steaks with Madeira, Ham, and Tomatoes (page 296), Braised Pork Chops, Steaks, and Other Slabs o' Pork (page 281), Ham Hock and Split Pea Soup (page 406), Caramelized Pork Shank and Braised Cabbage (page 389), Black Bean, Pork, and Sausage Stew (page 424), and Hammy Yammy Hash (page 408).

Buying a Country Ham

UNLESS YOU LIVE IN THE SOUTH, country ham is rarely found in the supermarket and must be ordered by mail from regional smokehouses or fancy food catalogues. Besides Virginia—which is famous for its Smithfield hams—Kentucky, Tennessee, Georgia, Missouri, Mississippi, Arkansas, and a few areas in New England and the Midwest produce superb country hams. Each style has its own nuances influenced by age, wood, and the cure, and these small producers offer a wonderful variety of flavors and types of ham and other smoked meats. We list a number of our favorites in Sources (page 584).

All country hams are quite salty, and they may be aged for as little as a few months to more than a year. Both the salt level and how long the ham has aged will affect how long you will need to soak and cook it. Unfortunately, it's difficult for us to generalize and for you to monitor the salt levels closely during the soaking and cooking. We recommend taking a conservative approach by trying to extract as much salt as possible from the ham. Don't worry—even then, the ham will be quite salty. Some country ham producers will sell you fully cooked hams that have been soaked and boiled at the smokehouse. This is a good way to begin if you're a novice or wish to send the ham as a gift.

Country hams are an acquired taste; they are not for the namby-pamby. They are always salty, even after being soaked and parboiled. And since they're aged, they take on some of the characteristics of other aged foods, such as cheese. Some will have a whitish mold on the outside. It's perfectly normal and completely harmless—just scrub it off before soaking and cooking the ham. Real ham lovers think nothing beats the aged flavors of a country ham, which intensify in your mouth, like a well-aged Parmesan.

Baked Country Ham

Serves 16 to 20
■ MOM'S HOME COOKING ■ GOOD FOR A CROWD
■ FIT FOR COMPANY

T HE BEST WAY TO SERVE COUNTRY HAM, hot
or cold, is sliced very thin.

1 12-to-16-pound country
ham
2 cups packed light or
dark brown sugar or
granulated sugar
1 teaspoon peanut
or vegetable oil

Wash the ham under cold water, scrubbing the skin with a
stiff brush to remove any black pepper coating and mold.
Many country hams are coated with black pepper, and the
formation of mold is a natural result of the aging process.

Put the ham in a very large pot or tub or into a clean sink
big enough so that it can be completely submerged in cold
water. Soak the ham for 48 hours, changing the water 6 to 8
times to extract as much of the salt as possible. Drain and
scrub the ham again to remove any remaining mold or pepper. Rinse the ham thoroughly.

Put the ham into a very large pot and cover it completely
with cold water. Bring to a boil and discard the water. Refill
the pot with water to cover the ham, bring the liquid to a boil,
and again discard the water. Do this one more time. Finally,
cover the ham again with cold water, bring it to a boil, and
reduce the heat to barely a simmer. Take care not to let the
water actually boil; it should read about 180°F on your
instant-read thermometer. Poach the ham, uncovered, for 4
hours at a slow simmer.

Slice off a bit of ham and taste it. It should be firm but tender and palatable, and it will probably still be quite salty. You
may need to cook it for 1 to 2 more hours, depending on its
salt level and how long it was aged. Taste it from time to time
to judge its progress.

At this point, you can let the ham cool in its poaching liquid, remove it, and wrap it loosely in foil and refrigerate it to
bake and glaze the next day. Or you can bake and glaze it as
follows. Discard the liquid.

Preheat the oven to 350°F. Put the ham on a platter or

clean work surface and carefully remove all the skin and any dark or discolored areas of the meat. Trim the fat, leaving a ⅛-to-¼-inch layer, and score a crisscross grid across the top of the fat if you want. Place the ham in a foil-lined roasting pan, fat side up, and bake for 30 minutes. Or, if you have refrigerated the boiled ham, bake it for 1 hour.

Increase the heat to 425°F. Spread a generous layer of sugar over the ham and roast it for 20 to 30 minutes more, or until the surface is glazed and browned.

Place the ham on a cutting board or platter and let it rest, covered loosely with foil, for 20 to 45 minutes. Cut into thin slices. Serve warm or at room temperature. Leftover ham can be served cold or rewarmed in one of the sauces listed on page 397. Thick slices of cooked country ham can be fried and served with steamed greens. The ham can also be used in any recipes calling for bacon or pancetta. For more ideas on using cooked ham, see Inspirations from a Ham (page 400).

Smoked Ham Steak or Pork Chops in Apple and Cider Sauce

Serves 4

■ IN A HURRY ■ LOW-FAT ■ REWARMS WELL

THIS EASY SAUCE GOES equally well with smoked pork chops and ham steaks. The sauce can also be used to liven up slices of leftover baked ham. We like to serve this dish alongside oven-baked sweet potatoes that have been thickly sliced, brushed with oil, and sprinkled with a pinch of cinnamon. Sweet potatoes can also be combined with thick slices of winter squash treated the same way. If you're using the sauce to reheat baked ham, cook the sauce separately, pour it over the thick slices of the ham, and bake in a covered pan in a 350°F oven for 20 to 25 minutes. Try this tangy dish with hard cider from England, France, or California or with a Riesling from Washington State, upstate New York, or Ontario's Niagara Peninsula.

1 1½-pound ham steak, trimmed of fat, OR four ¾-inch-thick smoked pork chops (6-8 ounces each), trimmed of fat

APPLE AND CIDER SAUCE

2 cups apple cider
½ cup packed light or dark brown sugar
1 cup chopped dried apples
½ teaspoon ground sage
¼ teaspoon ground cinnamon
¼ cup cider vinegar
1½ tablespoons Dijon mustard

Heat the oil in a large, heavy, nonstick or other nonreactive skillet over high heat. Put in the chops or steak and brown for 1 to 2 minutes on each side. Remove the meat.

To make the Apple and Cider Sauce: Add all the sauce ingredients to the skillet except the mustard. Boil rapidly until the liquid is reduced to about 1¾ cups. Whisk in the mustard and reduce to a simmer.

Return the chops or ham steak to the pan, cover, and cook over low heat for 10 to 15 minutes more. Transfer the meat to a platter. If the sauce is too thin, reduce it over high heat until it becomes syrupy. Pour the sauce over the meat and serve.

Ham Hock and Split Pea Soup
(*Ertesoupe*)

2 ham hocks
6-8 cups reserved ham hock
    stock (see discussion)

FRIED FRESH PORK
1 tablespoon vegetable oil
1 pound pork shoulder,
    cut into 1-inch dice
    Salt and freshly ground
    black pepper

1 pound dried split green
    peas
2 carrots, finely chopped
1½ cups finely chopped
    onions
1½ cups finely chopped leeks
    (white part only)
2 celery ribs, finely
    chopped
½ teaspoon dried sage
½ teaspoon dried thyme
1 bay leaf
½ teaspoon dried marjoram
    or oregano
1 pound smoked kielbasa,
    smoked bratwurst,
    or andouille, cut into
    ½-inch rounds
1 cup finely chopped
    green onions or
    scallions (white and
    green parts)
    Salt and freshly ground
    black pepper
1 cup chopped fresh chives
    (optional)
    Tabasco sauce (optional)

Serves 6 to 8
■ TWO FOR ONE ■ COOKING ON A BUDGET
■ GOOD FOR A CROWD ■ MOM'S COMFORT FOOD

CALLED *ERTESOUPE* IN HOLLAND, this substantial soup is hearty enough to serve as a main course for lunch or as a light supper with some crusty bread. Split pea soup always benefits from being made up to a day ahead so that the peas can turn creamy and the various flavor components marry.

Prepare the stock by cooking the ham hocks in water to cover for 2½ to 3 hours, until tender, following the directions on the next page.

To fry the pork shoulder: Heat the oil in a large soup pot or Dutch oven over high heat. Season the diced pork shoulder lightly with salt and pepper and fry it for 5 minutes, or until browned on all sides, stirring often. Pour off the fat, leaving the meat in the pot.

Put the ham hock stock in the pot and scrape up any browned bits. Bring to a boil, then reduce to a simmer. Add the split peas, carrots, onions, leeks, celery, and herbs. Cover the pot. Remove the meat and skin from the cooked ham hocks. If you want to serve the skin, finely chop it. (It adds flavor and body to the soup, but it also increases the fat level.) Coarsely chop the ham hock meat and add it and the optional skin to the soup pot. Cook over low heat for about 45 minutes, or until the peas are falling apart.

Put in the sausage and add the green onions or scallions. Cook for 10 minutes more. Remove the bay leaf and taste for salt and pepper. Garnish with the chives if you are using them. Offer your guests Tabasco to spice up the soup a bit.

COOKING HAM HOCKS

Makes 2 to 4 ham hocks

SERVE THE HAM HOCKS as is or remove the skin and bones and chop the meat coarsely before adding to soup or beans. Use the stock to prepare soup, beans, or lentils.

2-4	smoked ham hocks
1	medium onion, spiked with 3 cloves
3	garlic cloves
1	carrot, coarsely chopped
1	celery rib, coarsely chopped
3	bay leaves
1	teaspoon whole peppercorns

Cover the ham hocks with water in a large pot and add the vegetables, bay leaves, and peppercorns. Simmer over low heat for 2½ to 3 hours or more, until tender. Chill the stock and degrease it before using.

Hammy Yammy Hash

1½ cups peeled, diced
(½ inch) rutabagas

2-3 tablespoons olive oil
or melted butter

2 cups peeled, diced
(½ inch) butternut
squash

2½ cups peeled, diced
(½ inch) red yams
or peeled, diced
(½ inch) leftover
baked sweet potatoes
Salt and freshly ground
black pepper

½ teaspoon dried thyme
Pinch each of ground
ginger and cinnamon

2 cups chopped onions

2 cups diced (½ inch)
leftover smoked pork
chops or ham

½ cup Apple and Cider
Sauce (left over from
Smoked Ham Steak or
Pork Chops, page 405)
or maple syrup OR
2 tablespoons light or
dark brown sugar
dissolved in ½ cup
apple cider

¾ cup shredded sharp
cheddar cheese
(optional)

Serves 4 to 6
■ TWO FOR ONE ■ GREAT LEFTOVERS
■ MOM'S COMFORT FOOD

YOU CAN USE EITHER the leftovers from Smoked Ham Steak or Pork Chops in Apple and Cider Sauce (page 405) or diced leftover ham for this flavorful hash. In a pinch, you could buy slices of cooked ham from the deli.

Serve this dish as a light winter dinner or as a brunch along with scrambled or poached eggs. Red "yams" are actually a red-skinned variety of sweet potato but are usually called yams at the grocery store.

Preheat the oven to 350°F. In a large bowl, toss the rutabaga cubes with 1 to 1½ tablespoons of the oil or melted butter. Spread them in a large baking dish and bake for 10 minutes. In the same bowl, toss the squash and raw yams (if using leftover sweet potatoes, read on) in the remaining 1 to 1½ tablespoons of the oil or butter until well coated (add more oil or butter if necessary to coat thoroughly). Season with salt and pepper, thyme, ginger, and cinnamon and add to the rutabagas along with the onions and diced smoked pork chops or ham. Mix well and bake until all the vegetables are tender. This should take about 45 minutes—test the vegetables as they cook with a skewer or fork. If using leftover sweet potatoes, add them for the last 10 minutes of cooking. Turn over the vegetable-ham mixture occasionally with a spatula.

When it is done, combine with the Apple and Cider Sauce, maple syrup, or cider and brown sugar and mix until everything is well coated. Sprinkle with the optional shredded cheese. Bake for 5 to 10 minutes more, or until the sauce is heated through and the cheese is bubbly. Serve from the baking dish or transfer to a platter.

How to Choose Bacon

MOST BACON IN AMERICA is made from the belly of the pig after the rib bones (spareribs) have been removed. **Canadian bacon** is made from the boned pork loin, while **shoulder,** or **cottage, bacon** is made from the Boston butt. Almost all bacon is cured and smoked. While leanness is an important criterion in purchasing bacon, flavor is paramount. You can get some clues about the quality and flavor of bacon by reading the label. Is it made with "smoke flavorings" or is it naturally smoked? Are there many unknown chemicals on the ingredient list? Does the bacon contain phosphates? How cheap is it? Usually the better cured products cost more because they are more expensive to make, use quality ingredients, and are not pumped up with water and phosphates. Try many different brands and see which tastes best to you.

Good bacon should not shrivel up to nothing when cooked. Saltiness is a matter of taste and culture. To those used to its high salt level, dry-cured country bacon tastes great; others might find it too salty, even though it is usually well made. Some of the best bacon is sold by small mail-order smokehouses that often advertise in the back of cooking magazines. Try them out; they can offer excellent, hand-crafted products. We like to purchase our bacon in slab form so we can cut slices as thick or thin as we want or dice it and use it to flavor meat dishes, vegetables, beans, or soups.

Pancetta is cured but unsmoked pork belly flavored with aromatic herbs and spices. It is rolled into a cylinder and wrapped in casing. You can purchase pancetta sliced from Italian delis and specialty butcher shops. It is now frequently available in supermarket delis as well. Pancetta is used as a flavoring in many of our Italian-influenced recipes.

Pork Sausage

Simple Links to a Glorious Past

IT'S WITH MAKING SAUSAGE that the butcher's craft becomes an art form. The various combinations of spices and herbs, aromatic vegetables, and mushrooms, wines, and fruits that are mixed with the ground meat are the raw materials. Fine sausages come from a wealth of ethnic traditions and encompass a wide range of flavors.

The range and breadth of sausage are vast: virtually every country or region, and even in some cases an individual neighborhood, has its own variation. There are, literally, hundreds of different types throughout the world. The subject requires a shelf of books to describe it, and we wrote one of them, *Hot Links and Country Flavors*.

Making the sausage, however, is just the beginning, for although most of it can be enjoyed by itself, sausage is also an important element in dishes from soups and pastas to beans and stews, stuffings, and vegetable dishes. You can create the flavor of a cuisine by using a little bit of its traditional sausage in a dish. Add some spicy Italian sausage to steamed green beans and toss them with pasta and you're cooking Italian. Some fiery Louisiana sausage stirred into rice makes a Creole specialty, and so on.

We offer you a very brief look at making sausage: these recipes are not complicated and don't require any more equipment than a food processor or meat grinder. The sausage meat doesn't have to be stuffed into casings, since most recipes call for breaking up the sausage as it cooks. You can also form the meat into patties to pan-broil or grill. For those who want to make links, however, we will show you how with a minimum of fuss and bother.

In the spirit of keeping unnecessary fat out of our cooking, these recipes include a trick or two to allow you to make leaner sausage without sacrificing juiciness and texture. An added advantage of making your own sausage is that you control the ingredients and can eliminate the excess fat, salt, and additives often found in commercial sausages.

HYGIENE AND SAFETY
WHEN MAKING SAUSAGE

- Keep the meat cold at all times. Refrigerate it before beginning and between each step.
- Wash your hands frequently with very hot water and soap.
- Never taste raw sausage meat. Always fry up a small patty to adjust seasonings.
- Never leave the meat in the grinder or pastry bag for more than 10 minutes without refrigerating it.
- Wash all your utensils and equipment at once (not after you've taken just a short break).
- If you don't intend to use the sausage in the next two or three days, freeze it now. Don't wait for two or three days to pass and then freeze it.
- Clean everything. Chill everything. When in doubt, throw it out!

Sage and Pepper Pork Sausage

Makes 3 to 4 pounds

■ MOM'S COMFORT FOOD ■ MAKE AHEAD

MASTER RECIPE

MAKING SAUSAGE AT HOME gives you complete control over the type and freshness of the meat, the fat content, salt, and spices. With a food processor or meat grinder or even just a sharp knife, it's easy to make sausage at home.

By definition, sausage is simply a mixture of ground or chopped meat and spices. The meat can be red meat (pork, veal, beef, lamb, venison), poultry (chicken, turkey), innards (liver, chitlins, sweetbreads), and even seafood. The spices, herbs, and aromatics are myriad—just about any spice or herb you can think of has ended up in a sausage somewhere in the world.

This basic recipe provides a delicious breakfast-style sage and pepper sausage that accompanies country breakfasts through the South and Midwest. Like most sausage, it can be left in bulk and frozen for later use. It's best shaped into patties and panfried, but it can also be stuffed into casings (see page 416) and, if you like, smoked in a covered kettle barbecue for a fully cooked country-style smoked sausage. As with any sausage recipe, feel free to adjust or modify the spices to suit your own taste. The amount of fat in this sausage will be about 20 percent, under the level of most commercial sausage and about that of ground chuck. The low-fat versions made by adding fat-free ingredients such as onions or wild rice will have about 15 percent fat, the level of ground round and chicken thighs.

Before you make the sausage, read Hygiene and Safety When Making Sausage, page 411.

————————

To make sausage using a food processor: Cut the pork butt and fat into ¾-to-1-inch pieces. Spread the cubed meat and fat on a plate and place it in the freezer for 10 minutes to firm up the meat and make it easier to chop. Put the food processor bowl and blade in the freezer as well for the same amount of time.

Set up the food processor and add just enough meat to cover the blade (about 1 pound). Pulse to form chunks about ⅜ inch in size. Put the chopped meat into a large bowl and refrigerate.

Repeat the process for each batch of meat, adding the chopped meat to the bowl and keeping it cold. Finally, process the fat into smaller pieces, about ¼ inch, and mix it with the meat.

Add all the other ingredients, including any or all of the optional ones, to the meat and fat. Mix everything together with your hands, squeezing and kneading to blend the mixture well. Do not overmix, however, to the point where the fat begins to melt. The point of this kneading is just to get all the ingredients well distributed. Make a small patty of the sausage meat and fry it in a small pan over medium heat. Taste and adjust the salt, pepper, and sugar as necessary; if you added onions and/or rice, you'll probably need to add more of all three.

To make sausage in a meat grinder: You can use a hand-cranked or electric meat grinder to make sausage. (The grinder attachment to the KitchenAid mixer works very well.) You need to have the type of grinder with interchangeable plates with varying hole sizes. Chill the meat in the freezer as above before cutting up the meat and fat separately. You can cut the meat into strips rather than cubes to save a little time, but either will do. Chill the strips or cubes on a plate in the freezer for 10 minutes.

Using a ⅜-inch plate, grind the lean strips of meat and place the ground meat in a large bowl in the refrigerator.

2½ pounds lean pork butt
½ pound fat trimmed from pork butt and/or pork back fat

1 tablespoon salt, or more to taste
1½ teaspoons coarsely ground black pepper, or more to taste
2 teaspoons dried sage
½ teaspoon dried thyme
½ teaspoon ground ginger
⅛ teaspoon ground nutmeg
1 teaspoon light or dark brown sugar, or more to taste
½ teaspoon cayenne pepper, or to taste (optional)
½ cup finely chopped onions, blanched for 5 minutes, drained, and cooled (optional)
1 cup drained and cooled cooked wild rice (optional)
¼ cup cold water

Change to a ¼-inch grinder plate and grind the fat. Combine the meat, fat, and remaining ingredients and mix and knead as described above. Fry a small patty and adjust the salt, pepper, and sugar as necessary.

At this point, the sausage is ready to use, although its flavors will mellow and improve if allowed to rest for a day in the refrigerator in a bowl covered with plastic wrap. The sausage will keep for 2 to 3 days. Or you can wrap it in plastic wrap or foil in ½-pound packages and freeze it for up to 3 months. You can also stuff the mixture into sausage casings (see How to Make Sausage Links, page 416).

Pork and Apple Sausage

Makes 3 to 4 pounds

THIS SLIGHTLY SWEET SAUSAGE makes a mild, delicious breakfast patty or a savory addition to fruit stuffings.

Process the meat and mix the ingredients as directed in the Master Recipe. Include the optional onion and the wild rice if you wish to lower the percentage of fat in the sausage even more. Cook a patty, taste it, and adjust the salt and other seasonings if necessary.

To the Master Recipe
(page 412), add:

¼ teaspoon ground cinnamon

1 cup diced dried apples, soaked in warm water for 5 minutes and drained

¼ cup apple juice or cider

How to Make Sausage Links

TO STUFF SAUSAGE MEAT into casings, you will need either the sausage horn attachment for a meat grinder or a pastry bag fitted with a plain tip. You will need about 8 feet of medium hog casings, available from specialty butchers or by mail-order (see Note on the next page). Soak the casings, which come packed in salt, in warm water in a large bowl for 30 minutes to 1 hour. Then put one end of a casing over the end of a faucet and wash the inside with warm water. Change the water in the bowl and soak the casing again.

If you're using a grinder, remove the plate and knife and fit it with the sausage horn. Pull the entire length of soaked casing over the tip of the horn, gathering it up and leaving a little bit dangling. Tie a knot in the dangling end **(1)**. Fill the bowl of the grinder with chilled sausage meat and crank the meat through the grinder to fill the casing **(2)**. Continue to feed the meat through the grinder into the casing until all the meat is used up. Use a skewer, pin, or needle to prick any air bubbles that form as the casing fills. The casing should be full, but not too tightly packed, or it will burst when you form the links. Remove the casing from the horn.

If you're using a pastry bag, pull the entire length of casing over the end of the tip, gathering it up and leaving a little bit dangling. Tie a knot in the dangling end of the casing and fill the pastry bag with chilled sausage meat. Squeeze the bag with one hand to push the meat into the casing while you use your other hand to hold the casing on the metal tip. Fill the casing with all the meat, as described above. When it is filled, remove it from the pastry bag.

To form the links, begin at the knotted end and pinch the casing between your fingers about 5 inches from the end; you may vary the length if you wish **(3)**. Move down the casing another 5 inches and pinch again, about 10 inches from the knot. Twist the second 5-inch section with your fingers to make the first two links (twisting the link will twist both ends and seal both links). Proceed down the casing, twisting every other pinch to make links. When you reach the end, tie another knot.

To separate the chain into links, use a sharp knife to cut through the twisted casing to make individual sausages **(4)**. Refrigerate them right away and use within 2 to 3 days. Or wrap them in plastic wrap or foil and freeze for up to 3 months.

Note: *Casing won't be as hard to find as you may think. Look in the Yellow Pages under "Sausages, Supplies" or "Butcher's Supplies," or even "Sausage Casings," and you're likely to find them, especially if you live in a city with ethnic neighborhoods. Or ask your butcher if he makes his own sausage and will sell you some casing along with the pork and fat for making sausage. Or consult Sources (page 584). You may have to buy more casings than you need for a single recipe, but because they're packed in salt, they will last forever in the back of your refrigerator.*

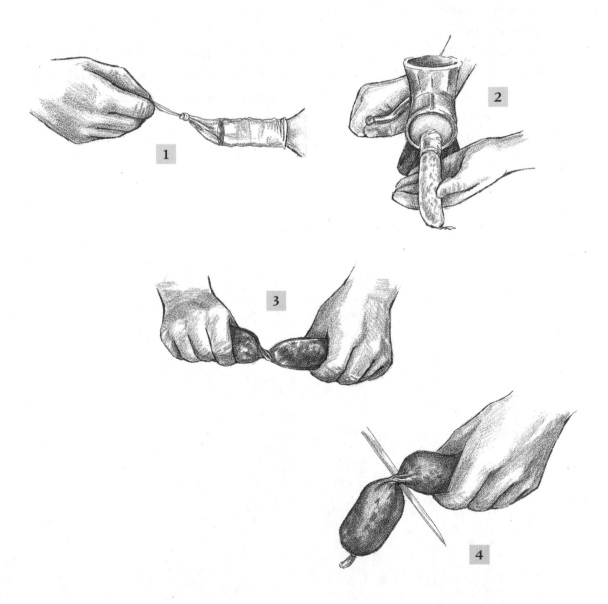

Fresh Bratwurst Wisconsin Style

2½ pounds lean pork butt

½ pound fat trimmed
from pork butt and/or
back fat

1 tablespoon salt, or
more to taste

1½ teaspoons coarsely
ground black pepper

1 teaspoon sugar

1 teaspoon dry mustard,
preferably Colman's

2 teaspoons mustard seeds

½ teaspoon dried sage

½ teaspoon ground
nutmeg or mace

¼ cup milk

2 cups ground raw
potatoes soaked in
lemon water (optional)

Makes about 4 pounds
■ MOM'S COMFORT FOOD ■ MAKE AHEAD

FRESH BRATWURST is a simple but delicious farmer's sausage that is very popular all through the Midwest, especially in Sheboygan, Wisconsin, the country's bratwurst capital. Try first poaching the tasty sausages in beer and then panfrying or grilling them. Use brats in any recipe calling for sauerkraut or in any stuffing.

Process the meat and fat and mix with the other ingredients as described in the Master Recipe (page 412). You can lower the fat content by adding the optional raw potato, but be sure to fry a patty to taste for salt and other seasonings.

Kielbasa Chicago Style

Makes about 3 pounds

■ MOM'S COMFORT FOOD ■ MAKE AHEAD

THIS FLAVORFUL FRESH SAUSAGE is much loved by Chicago's large Polish-American population. Use it in recipes with sauerkraut or anywhere you want a tangy, garlicky sausage.

————————

Process the meat and fat and combine with the other ingredients as described in the Master Recipe (page 412). For a lower fat content, drain and add the optional potatoes when you grind the meat. Fry and taste a patty, then adjust the seasonings if necessary.

1 pound lean beef, preferably chuck

1½ pounds lean pork butt

½ pound fat trimmed from butt and/or pork back fat

1 tablespoon salt

2 teaspoons coarsely ground black pepper

2 tablespoons minced garlic

1 teaspoon sugar

½ teaspoon ground cumin

1 teaspoon dried marjoram

½ teaspoon dried thyme

2 teaspoons dry mustard, preferably Colman's

¼ cup water

2 cups chopped raw potato soaked in lemon water (optional)

Southwest Chorizo

1 pound lean beef,
  preferably chuck

1½ pounds lean pork butt

½ pound fat trimmed from
  pork butt and/or
  pork back fat

2 dried New Mexico
  chiles, soaked in water,
  stemmed, and pureed,
  OR 2 tablespoons
  ground chiles

1 tablespoon salt

1 teaspoon coarsely
  ground black pepper

1 jalapeño pepper, seeded
  and finely chopped

1 green bell pepper OR
  2 Anaheim or poblano,
  fresh or canned, fire-
  roasted (see page 103),
  peeled and finely chopped

1 teaspoon cayenne pepper

2 teaspoons cumin seeds

2 teaspoons ground cumin

2 teaspoons dried oregano

2 tablespoons minced
  garlic

½ cup finely chopped
  onion, parboiled 5
  minutes, drained,
  and cooled

1 cup cooked and cooled
  long-grain rice (optional)

2 teaspoons sugar

2 tablespoons fresh lime
  juice

¼ cup dark Mexican beer

1 cup chopped fresh
  cilantro

Makes about 3 pounds
■ MAKE AHEAD ■ GREAT LEFTOVERS

USE THIS SPICY SAUSAGE in Black Bean, Pork, and Sausage Stew (page 424), as a filling for tacos, enchiladas, tamales, or with eggs in *huevos rancheros*. Chiles and other Southwest ingredients are available in Latino groceries or through mail-order (see Sources, page 584).

Process the meat and fat and mix together all the ingredients as in the Master Recipe (page 412). If you add the optional rice, fry a small patty of the sausage meat and adjust the salt, pepper, and other seasonings as needed.

Chaurice
(Spicy Creole Sausage)

Makes 3 pounds

■ MAKE AHEAD ■ GREAT LEFTOVERS

THIS SAUSAGE will give you a New Orleans accent in jambalaya, gumbo, or stews. It makes a great stuffing for vegetables or seafood when mixed with rice. It's also good with lentils or red beans. Chaurice can also be smoked and used in place of andouille.

———————————

Process the meat and fat and mix all the other ingredients as described in the Master Recipe (page 412). For a lower percentage of fat, add the optional rice. Fry a patty and taste to adjust the seasonings.

2½ pounds lean pork butt
½ pound fat trimmed from pork butt and/or pork back fat
1 tablespoon salt
2 teaspoons coarsely ground black pepper
1 teaspoon sugar
1 tablespoon garlic
½ teaspoon dried sage
1 teaspoon dried thyme
½ teaspoon ground bay leaves (pulverize in a spice grinder or with mortar and pestle)
½ teaspoon ground cumin
1 cup finely chopped onions, parboiled for 5 minutes, drained, and cooled
5 tablespoons paprika
1 teaspoon cayenne pepper
½ cup chopped fresh parsley
2 cups drained and cooled cooked long-grain rice (optional)

Louisiana Sausage and Seafood Ragout

1 tablespoon olive oil,
plus more as needed

1 medium onion,
cut into ¼-inch dice

½ red bell pepper,
cut into ¼-inch dice

¼ green bell pepper,
cut into ¼-inch dice

1 celery rib, cut into
¼-inch dice

3 garlic cloves, minced

1½ tablespoons paprika

3 fresh thyme sprigs or
1 teaspoon dried thyme

4 ripe tomatoes, peeled,
seeded, and diced

¾ cup white wine

1 cup fish stock or bottled
clam juice

½ cup whipping cream

¾ pound andouille sausage
or other spicy smoked
sausage, sliced in ¼-
inch rounds, OR ¾
pound Chaurice (page
421), fried and
crumbled

1 medium eggplant, cut
crosswise into ¼-inch-
thick rounds

**Serves 8 or more as an appetizer,
4 to 6 as a main course**

■ FIT FOR COMPANY ■ MEAT AS A CONDIMENT

LOUISIANA COOKS learned long ago that the tangy, smoky flavors of pork sausage such as andouille are a perfect complement to seafood. Many classic New Orleans dishes reflect this perfect marriage of sea and land. Cajun and Creole classics such as jambalaya, seafood gumbo, stuffed eggplant, and stuffed crab all link spicy sausage and seafood together. This elegant ragout bathes the seafood in a rich sauce flavored with andouille. The cream makes this an intense and delicious dish for a main course, or you can serve smaller portions as an elegant appetizer or first course at a Creole banquet. The sauce can be prepared up to a day ahead, which makes this a fast dish to put together.

Heat the olive oil in a large, heavy skillet over medium heat. Add the onion and sauté until it is golden, about 8 minutes. Add the bell peppers, celery, and garlic and sauté for 1 minute more. Mix in the paprika and thyme and cook for another minute. Add the tomatoes, wine, stock or clam juice, cream, and sausage and boil until the sauce thickens slightly, stirring occasionally, about 10 minutes. This sauce can be prepared up to 1 day ahead. Cover and refrigerate until needed. Bring it to a boil before continuing.

Preheat the oven to 400°F. Dip the eggplant rounds in olive oil and place on a cookie sheet. Bake until quite soft, turning the rounds from time to time, about 20 minutes. Set aside.

Add the red snapper and shrimp to the sauce. Reduce the heat to a simmer and cook for 3 minutes. Add the oysters and crabmeat and simmer for 1 or 2 minutes, until the oysters are plump. Season with salt and pepper to taste. Arrange the eggplant slices in the center of shallow bowls. Spoon the ragout over the eggplant, and serve the rice on the side.

1 pound red snapper fillets, cut into 1-inch pieces

18 raw medium shrimp, peeled and deveined

12 shucked medium oysters

¼ pound crabmeat

Salt and freshly ground black pepper

Freshly cooked rice

Black Bean, Pork, and Sausage Stew

2 pounds dried black
    beans

1½ pounds smoked sausage,
    such as andouille,
    linguiça, Portuguese
    chorizo, or kielbasa

½ pound smoked ham,
    diced (preferably
    country ham, Serrano,
    or Westphalian), or
    prosciutto, diced

2 ham hocks

3 cups chopped onions

1 cup chopped celery

2 tablespoons chopped
    garlic

3 bay leaves

1 teaspoon dried oregano

1 teaspoon ground cumin

2 dried red chiles OR 2
    canned chipotle chiles
    in *adobo*

1 cup tomato puree, OR
    2 cups peeled, seeded,
    and chopped fresh
    tomatoes, OR seeded
    and chopped canned
    tomatoes

Chopped stems and roots
    from two 10-ounce
    bunches of cilantro,
    leaves reserved

Serves 8 to 10, with leftovers
■ GOOD FOR A CROWD ■ COOKING ON A BUDGET

THE IDEA OF FLAVORING a big pot of beans with a small amount of highly seasoned sausage and meat is found in peasant cookery throughout the world. From our own Louisiana red beans and rice to Spanish *cocido*, French *cassoulet*, Tuscan white beans with sausage, and Brazilian *feijoada*, the concept is the same. Beans are a cheap source of protein and stick to the ribs; bits of meat and sausage provide intense flavors and added nutrition for just a little added cost.

These hearty peasant bean stews can be rewarmed easily. They take a while to cook, but they can provide at least two meals and can be served as side dishes at one or two others during the week. Remember to start the beans a day ahead.

In some cases, such as the Brazilian *feijoada completa*, the components are served individually, often as different courses—with the broth as a soup and the meats, beans, and vegetables as separate dishes. We prefer to serve this black bean stew as a one-pot meal, however; it makes a more relaxed presentation and saves on dishwashing. While our black bean stew is inspired by *feijoada*, we make no claims to authenticity, although the sliced oranges served on the side are definitely a Brazilian touch.

Soak the beans overnight in water to cover by 2 to 3 inches. The next day, drain the beans and rinse them well. Put them in a large pot and add enough water to cover by 2 to 3 inches. Bring to a boil and reduce to a simmer. Add ½ pound of the smoked sausage (in one piece), the chopped ham or prosciutto, ham hocks, onions, celery, garlic, bay leaves, oregano, cumin, chiles, tomato puree or tomatoes, and cilantro stems and roots. Cover and cook at a slow simmer for 1½ hours.

While the beans are cooking, season the pork ribs with salt and pepper. Heat the oil in a heavy skillet over medium-high heat and brown the spareribs on all sides. Remove them with a slotted spoon.

Add the spareribs to the beans. Cover and cook for 1 hour more, or until the beans are quite tender and the ham hocks and pork ribs are fully cooked. Add more water if needed during cooking. Stir the greens into the stew.

Meanwhile, pour off the fat from the skillet and add the chorizos or Italian sausages to the pan. Panfry for about 10 minutes, turning often, until they are firm. Remove and cool, then slice into 1-inch chunks and add to the pot. Cut the remaining smoked sausages into ½-inch rounds and add to the pot.

Remove the ham hocks and the large piece of smoked sausage from the stew. Cool, remove the meat from the ham hocks, and chop the meat and the sausage. Return them to the pot. Remove the bay leaves. If you wish, finely chop the ham hock skin and add it to the pot. Taste the beans for salt and pepper and add lime juice to taste, if you wish. Serve over steamed rice in large bowls with the suggested accompaniments on the side.

2-3 pounds country-style
   pork spareribs,
   cut into chunks
   Salt and freshly ground
   black pepper
1 tablespoon vegetable oil
3 cups chopped collard
   greens, kale, or green
   cabbage
8 Mexican chorizos or
   hot Italian sausages
   Fresh lime juice to taste
   (optional)

SIDE DISHES AND
ACCOMPANIMENTS
   Steamed rice
2-3 oranges, peeled
   and sliced
   Tabasco or other
   hot sauce
   Lime wedges
   Fresh cilantro leaves

▪ Lamb ▪

Ethnic Favorite and Epicure's Delight

I T'S NO ACCIDENT THAT LAMB HAS BEEN A POPULAR MEAT ever since the beginnings of domestication. Sheep herd easily and are not difficult to handle. They can also tolerate more severe conditions—extremes of heat and cold, hilly country with sparse pasturage—than cattle or pigs. And they provide a valuable, renewable crop, wool. But it's the flavor of the meat that makes this animal a favorite in cuisines all over the world.

Lamb's mild, earthy, and faintly gamy flavors stand up well to robust and exotic seasonings. No meat marries better with the pungent flavors of garlic, mustard, rosemary, thyme, oregano, savory, and fennel, to name just a few. Lamb goes wonderfully well with the exotic spices in Indian curries and North African tagines and couscous. And yet its delicate flavor can complement tender spring vegetables such as fresh peas, fava beans, baby carrots, or asparagus tips, as in the classic *navarin*. Like pork, lamb has an underlying sweetness that pairs beautifully with dried fruits and nuts—the prunes, figs, dates, apricots, roast almonds, and walnuts so popular in the fine lamb dishes of Morocco and North Africa.

These delicate yet robust flavors may explain the enthusiasm for expensive cuts like rack of lamb, which has become almost a cliché in fancy restaurants. But it's no wonder the elegant rack is so popular—the tender, juicy, and subtle meat is just plain delicious and easy to cook. The rack's flavors are nicely accented by the rich, reduced wine and fruit sauces created by modern chefs. The rack is often served with a host of mushrooms, including wild species like morels, porcini, and chanterelles. And best of all is the endless variety of potato dishes that go so well with rack of lamb: scalloped potatoes, peppery hash browns, mashed potatoes with garlic and truffle oil, oven-roasted new potatoes, and fried potatoes sprinkled with fresh herbs.

We don't actually eat a lot of lamb in the United States today—only a little more than a pound per person per year. But lamb is by far the most popular meat with many of America's ethnic populations; Greeks, the Middle Eastern and North African communities, Indians and Pakistanis, Basques, Spaniards, and the French all esteem lamb over other meats. It is also enjoyed by Americans whose ancestors came from southern and eastern Europe, South America, and parts of the British Isles. Lamb is not very popular, however, in the Midwest and the South or with groups whose origins lie in northern Europe. This lack of enthusiasm seems to be based on the misconception that lamb has a strong smell and taste—a confusion based on the very gamy flavors of mutton, or meat from mature sheep. This prejudice is unfortunate, since very little (if any) mutton is sold today, and lamb is in fact one of the most delicate, tasty, and healthful meats available.

Mutton and lamb have long been staples in Mediterranean cooking, and savory preparations are found throughout the Near East and North Africa and in Greece, Italy, Spain, and France. Young lamb is often associated with spring, and many cultures roast whole lambs to celebrate Easter and other spring festivals. Spain and Italy also feature lamb in many traditional dishes, such as Baked Leg of Lamb *Asadar* (page 494) and Lamb Shanks Osso Buco (page 516). English cooks favor lamb and mutton, and the Sunday "joint" for many households is often lamb leg or shoulder. Mutton chops are still a favorite at London clubs and restaurants, and Lancashire hot pot and Irish stew are regional specialties.

Rugged History

Range Wars and Woolybacks

Sheep, *Ovis aries,* were domesticated early in the Near East, most likely before the beginnings of settled agriculture. Early nomadic peoples followed and eventually controlled groups of the animals, feeding on their meat and exploiting their milk, wool, and hides. Most wild sheep are hairy rather than woolly—thistles, burrs, and other seeds are easily tangled in fleece, which is only an undercoat in the wild species. With domestication, sheep were bred selectively for economically beneficial characteristics such as their wool or meat and body configuration.

In the American West, sheep were herded in the millions and their meat and wool made huge profits for many ranchers. Sheep had some advantages over cattle: they thrived on sparse ranges, getting by on much less feed and water. They were also more amenable to herding and driving. While seven or eight cowboys were needed to drive a thousand cattle, one sheepherder with a good dog could handle that and many more animals at a time. And you had the double bonus: wool from breeds improved with the Merino bloodline brought in money year after year, and their meat, especially from sheep with English "Downs" ancestors, was a lucrative source of income if you could get the flock to market.

As with cattle, getting the meat on the hoof to the marketplace was the key. Enterprising ranchers and frontier speculators could buy sheep in New Mexico, where the descendants of Mexican herds thrived, for under a dollar a head. If they could survive the arduous, dangerous trek across deserts and mountains, braving thirst and Indians hungry for meat, drovers could sell the sheep to meat-deprived forty-niners in California for five or even ten dollars each. This wasn't a task for the meek sodbusters seen in Westerns, defended by the likes of Shane from black-hatted gunslingers. Mountain men such as Kit Carson fought Indians and the desert to make their fortunes in California with New Mexican sheep, but many others lost their lives and flocks on the trail.

As sheep spread out over the West, competition sparked range wars between sheepherders and cowboys, who believed that the "woolybacks" or "woolly monsters" destroyed and defiled the open range. Sheep will eat grass down to the roots, and they developed a reputation for destroying grassland by overgrazing.

One rancher warned a drover, "If you take sheep to Powder River, bring your coffin along. You will need it." Sheep were poisoned and shot, and sheep-

"Spring" Lamb

THE TERM "SPRING LAMB" refers to animals born in the spring, and it used to indicate freshness and quality. These days the word is rarely used, except as a slightly bogus marketing label. Improved animal husbandry practices allow lambs to be born year-round.

herders and settlers were killed in the battles fought for years across the West. Eventually the coming of barbed wire tamed the open range, and ranchers found that both cattle and sheep could bring a profit—although cattle ranching and sheep raising tend to be separate endeavors even today.

Western sheep raising owes much of its success to Basque immigrants, many of whom began as sheepherders in the nineteenth century and ended up owning large flocks over the years. The Basque tradition continues throughout the West, and their restaurants are some of the best places to eat savory lamb dishes today (see The Hotel Basque Great Lamb Stew, page 522, and Basque Sheepherders' Lamb Stew, page 524).

MODERN MEAT BREEDS

It was the English who developed most of the modern meat breeds, named Downs breeds for their place of origin. Yielding rather coarse wool, English sheep such as Southdown, Dorset, and Romney all have the compact, blocky, and early fattening characteristics desired for tender meat (similar in character to Angus cattle). These breeds formed the basis of the American lamb industry, spreading from early herds in the East, especially Vermont, to the main centers of lamb production in the Midwest today. Most of the sheep in western America developed from *churro* sheep from the original Mexican herds interbred with the Merino, a Spanish sheep bred for its fine wool, and the Rambouillet, a French version of the Merino with good wool and meat-production characteristics. Western sheep are often shipped to the Midwest for fattening and finishing before slaughter.

What Matters Most in Buying Lamb

ONCE YOU DECIDE to serve lamb, you are faced with a pleasant dilemma: there are so many good cuts and delicious ways to cook it that it's hard to make up your mind. The best way is to figure out what part of the lamb will work best for the dish you want to cook and for your budget.

Because British and American farmers have long bred sheep specifically for the quality of their meat, almost all of the lamb we buy today is tender and flavorful. Just about any part of the modern lamb except the shank and neck is tender enough to be cooked by dry-heat methods, although the shoulder area is often better when braised or cooked by other moist-heat methods.

Lamb comes from young animals between 5 and 12 months of age. This is the only lamb commonly available in American markets today. Older animals (12 to 24 months) called yearlings and mutton (older than 24 months) are rarely sold in the United States except by Islamic halal butchers and by a few specialty butchers in certain areas of the country. Particularly delicious and high-quality lamb comes from states such as Colorado, California, Vermont, and Washington; it is often labeled as such in supermarket meat cases or on restaurant menus.

Lamb meat should be light red and fine textured; mutton will be purplish.

LAMB AT A GLANCE

■ **Look for:** Light red, finely textured meat, bones that are reddish and moist. Fat should be smooth and white.

■ **Avoid:** Dark purple meat (indicates mutton), dry white bones, coarse yellow fat, strong-smelling meat or fat.

■ **Overlooked Cuts:** Lamb breast, lamb riblets, lamb flank steak, lamb shoulder roast, lamb neck (makes great stew).

■ **Best Buys:** Lamb sirloin chops and roasts, shoulder, butterflied leg.

■ **Luxury Cuts:** Rack of lamb (Frenched and trimmed), lamb tenderloin, crown roast, lamb T-bone chops, whole lamb loin (sliced, makes medallions, or *noisettes*).

■ **Storage:** Two to four days refrigerated; well wrapped and frozen, up to six months.

The ends of the bones should be red, moist, and porous; mutton bones are white and dry. Fat should be white and well trimmed and the meat should have no off odor. Lamb, like all meat, is highly perishable and should be stored in the refrigerator at 32° to 38°F. Ground lamb is the most perishable since, like any ground meat, it is exposed to more bacteria during grinding. Any ground meat should be used within 24 hours of purchase. Store ground lamb in its original package in the coldest part of the refrigerator. Other cuts of lamb, when refrigerated in the original package, should keep for one or two days. If you store uncooked lamb loosely wrapped in foil or plastic wrap in the coldest part of the refrigerator, it should last for two to four days. Once cooked, lamb will last, wrapped and refrigerated, for three to six days. Lamb freezes well, and frozen lamb will keep for six months. Frozen ground lamb is good for up to four months. Always defrost frozen lamb in the refrigerator for safety and the best taste and texture.

Besides American lamb, both Australian and New Zealand lamb are widely available in the United States. They are sold both fresh and frozen; try to find fresh lamb, if you can. Although New Zealand lamb tends to be the smallest, it is not necessarily the tenderest or mildest in flavor. Australian lamb has a pleasant flavor and tends to be leaner than the larger American lamb. But when it comes to flavor, tenderness, and overall quality, you can't beat lamb from the United States, especially California, Colorado, and Vermont. Since New Zealand and Australian lamb comes to market so much smaller than American lamb, individual cuts like the leg or rack of lamb may weigh only half to two-thirds of the American equivalent.

WHAT THE GRADES MEAN

Like beef, lamb is graded by yield and overall marbling of the fat. There are four grades: **Prime**, **Choice**, **Good**, and **Utility**. Unlike beef, however, lamb does not need a high level of marbling to be tender. Even meat showing minimal fat streaking will be quite palatable compared to similar cuts of beef. If you do find lamb with a greater than usual degree of marbling, it will have improved flavor and juiciness. There is very little Prime lamb, and most markets carry only the Choice grade; the others end up in canned products and pet food.

A Quick Anatomy Lesson
for the Busy Cook

SINCE A LAMB CARCASS is so much smaller than a beef carcass, its cuts are much simpler to understand. Most lamb is still delivered whole to the butcher; its five primal cuts are the **shoulder, forelegs and breast,** the **ribs** and **loin** along the back, and the hind **leg,** consisting of the leg section and the sirloin.

As with other meats, the most tender cuts come from the rib and loin area and should be cooked by dry-heat methods. The loin is usually cut up into T-bone-shaped chops.

The leg and sirloin are tender enough for dry-heat cooking. Leg of lamb is the most popular cut for dry-heat roasting, but it can also stay moist and delicious after long, slow braising. Often the sirloin area is cut into chops.

The shoulder produces cuts such as shoulder chops and square-cut shoulder roast. The meat has veins of fat, and because the muscles do more work than the back or leg, the shoulder has a good amount of connective tissue and is tougher than meat from the leg or loin. We prefer to use this meat for braises and for stew. The tough foreleg, or lamb shank, must be cooked by moist heat.

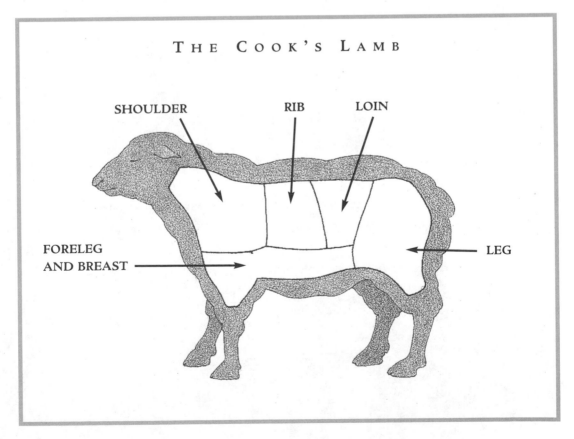

THE COOK'S LAMB

SHOULDER   RIB   LOIN

FORELEG AND BREAST   LEG

THE CUTS LISTED BELOW are not often found in supermarkets, but since lamb is still mostly sold as a whole carcass at the wholesale level, you may be able to persuade your butcher to cut them for you.

BONELESS TOP SIRLOIN

Where it comes from: This small, tender piece of meat is cut from the hip end of a leg and is usually sold attached to the leg. Ask your butcher to remove the hip bone. This will leave a solid chunk of meat composed of several muscles, the largest of which is the top sirloin. This can be cut out and grilled or roasted. It weighs 6 to 10 ounces and is delicious when marinated before cooking.

Why we like it: The meat from the top sirloin is firm, juicy, and tender. When sliced and served medium-rare, it makes an elegant and delicious presentation. Boning and removing the sirloin from the leg also makes the leg easier to roast and carve.

Price: Moderate, especially when sold as part of the leg. The trick is finding a butcher with enough skill to remove the hip bone.

AKA: Lamb block, sirloin roast (this is usually sold bone-in, but can be boned by the butcher and cut into individual muscles).

LAMB LOIN

Where it comes from: This is the large exterior strip of muscle on the T-bone rack, equivalent to the strip loin from beef.

Why we like it: This very tender and flavorful meat can be roasted whole for a small elegant dinner or cut into *noisettes*, or medallions, for quick sautéing and saucing.

Price: Very expensive, but suitable for a really special meal for two to four diners.

AKA: Lamb *noisettes*, lamb medallions.

SQUARE-CUT SHOULDER ROAST/ BONELESS LAMB SHOULDER ROAST

Where it comes from: The square-cut shoulder roast is the entire shoulder and upper arm of the lamb. A whole square-cut shoulder can weigh 6 to 8 pounds but can be trimmed to a smaller size by having the butcher cut off a few shoulder or arm chops. It can also be boned, rolled, and tied or netted to make a flavorful 3-to-5-pound roast.

Why we like it: Lamb shoulder is ideal for stews. The somewhat fatty meat has more flavor than the leaner leg meat. Because the shoulder consists of several muscles with veins of fat and gristle, cutting it up for stew may be time-consuming, but it's worth the extra effort. Both bone-in and boneless shoulder roasts may also be braised successfully. Use them in any of our braised lamb recipes.

Price: If you can find lamb shoulder before the butcher cuts it into chops, the price should be moderate. But remember, there will be a fair amount of waste from bones and fat. A rolled, boneless shoulder may be the best deal, since the bones and much of the fat will have been removed, even though the price may be a bit higher than the bone-in roast.

AKA: None, to our knowledge.

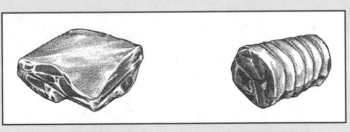

square-cut shoulder roast,
boneless

lamb shoulder roast,
rolled

Preparation and Cooking

THE PAPERY MEMBRANE that coats the lamb meat is called the fell and should be left intact (despite the many authorities who advise removing it) when cooking large cuts such as the leg or shoulder, since it helps to hold the meat in place. If you find much fell, however, on smaller cuts such as rack of lamb or chops, it should be removed, since it might make the meat curl when cooking.

Because most lamb is young and tender, almost any cut can be cooked by dry-heat methods. Most cuts cooked by dry heat—grilling, roasting, and broiling—benefit from being seasoned first with a dry rub, herb paste, or wet marinade (see Seasoning Chart, page 577). Lamb's popularity on the grill is increasing rapidly. This is not surprising, since grilling is the preferred mode of cooking in many of the cultures where lamb is the main red meat: Greece, the Near East, North Africa, Georgia, and the Caucasus.

Grilling is a particularly delicious way to cook lamb chops, especially when they have been marinated. Butterflied leg of lamb and lamb kebabs are also favorites. Except for braised dishes, lamb is best served medium-rare to medium. Consult the Doneness Chart (page 56) for exact details.

MYTHBUSTING

A BETTER WAY TO BROIL

WHEN IT COMES TO COOKING LAMB CHOPS, most home cooks sprinkle on a little salt and pepper and stick them under the broiler. This will do the job, but it's not the best way to cook them. Home broilers just don't put out enough heat to broil any meat adequately— the surface of the meat tends to sweat and dehydrate, losing the precious juices that make meat so appealing.

A better way is to pan-broil the chops in a heavy skillet without any oil, turning them once or twice until they reach the desired medium-rare stage (see Pan-Broiled Lamb Chops, page 449). The best type of pan is an old-fashioned, black cast-iron frying pan that's been seasoned over the years or a ridged skillet. The meat itself may get a brushing of oil, but no oil is added to the pan before cooking. Pan-broiled lamb chops develop a savory brown crust, especially if you've used a dry spice or herb rub, and all the delicious juices will stay in the meat.

KEEP LAMB HOT
AND HOLD THE ICE WATER

LAMB FAT is not particularly flavorful and can be downright nasty when cold. Cut as much off as possible before cooking and be sure to serve lamb while it is still hot. Many chefs use warm platters and plates when serving to keep the meat (and fat) warm. And don't serve ice water at the table with lamb, as the cold water can congeal the fat on the palate, with unpleasant results.

Moist-heat cooking makes lamb cuts such as the shoulder, leg, and shank soft and succulent. These cuts can be cooked to higher temperatures—150° to 160°F—than lamb cooked by dry-heat methods. In addition, there are wonderful flavors in the many sauces created by cooking lamb in water, wine, or other liquids. Many traditional lamb recipes, such as curry, tagines, Spanish *asadar,* and Chinese red-cooked lamb, benefit enormously from long, slow cooking. Often such dishes use exotic and flavorful spices, along with pungent, powerfully flavored ingredients such as garlic, tomatoes, olives, anchovies, and capers and aromatic vegetables like parsnips, carrots, onions, leeks, and turnips. The perfect cut for braising—and one increasingly popular in restaurants—is the shank, which, because of its convenient size, makes a single serving.

Like all braises and stews, these moist-cooked dishes are better when made ahead and rewarmed. An added advantage is that you can remove the congealed fat that forms on the surface when the dish is refrigerated.

Many restaurants these days are recognizing the rich flavors and fine textures of braised lamb dishes.

How to Choose Lamb Chops
and Lamb "Steaks"

ALMOST ALL LAMB CHOPS are sold on the bone, regardless of their size or what part of the lamb they come from. As with most other types of meat, the best and tenderest chops come from the loin and ribs. We prefer **rib chops** because they have more fat, and the meat therefore has more flavor. Some people find them a bit too fatty, though, and prefer the leaner **loin chops**. Loin chops contain the characteristic T-bone of the loin and are the most expensive. Lamb chops cut from both sides of the backbone are often called **double lamb chops**, or **English-cut lamb chops**. Look for these thicker chops, especially if you like your lamb rare or medium-rare. The thin chops that supermarkets try to pawn off on unsuspecting customers cook too quickly, and it's hard to keep them rare. Try to find chops that are at least ¾ inch thick; 1-to-1¼-inch-thick chops are even better.

Sirloin chops, cut from the sirloin end of the leg and hip, are considerably cheaper than loin or rib chops; they usually have less bone and are an excellent value. These delicious chops are tender enough to grill or broil medium-rare.

Sometimes butchers will slice the sirloin end of the leg into **leg steaks**. These circular chops have the characteristic round leg bone. They are particularly good marinated and grilled, but be sure they are at least ¾ inch thick.

Chops from the shoulder, or chuck, area are sold as **shoulder chops**, **shoulder blade chops**, or **shoulder arm chops**, with the round foreleg bone present. These chops are inexpensive but can vary a lot in quality and tenderness. Since the chuck is made up of several muscles, some of these chops can be quite chewy, especially those from the bottom side of the blade. If you wish to cook shoulder chops by dry heat (broiling, grilling, panfrying), look for chops cut near the rib—they will have a bit of the rib bone attached and the characteristic rib-eye near the bone. You can separate this rib meat from the other tougher meat with a knife. Grill or broil the rib meat and use the blade meat for kebabs or stews. The best way to handle shoulder chops is to braise them: brown them first and then finish cooking them in a savory liquid as in Lamb Shoulder Chops with Roasted Red Bell Peppers (page 464).

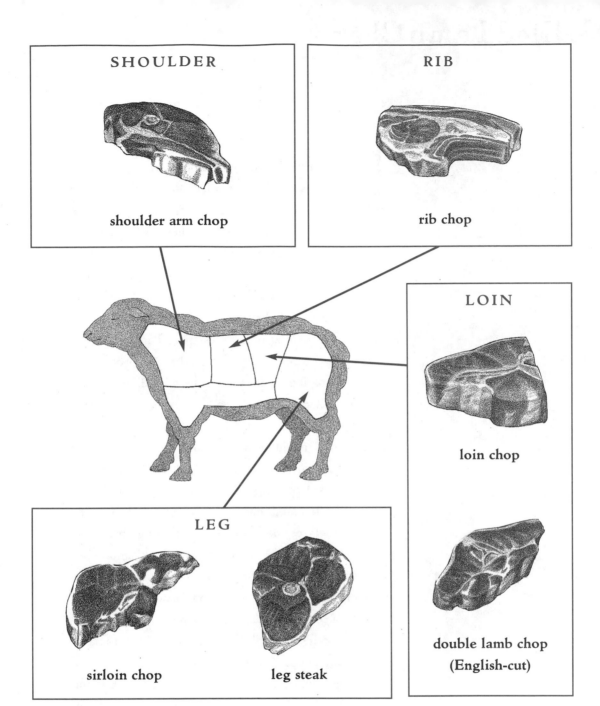

SHOULDER

shoulder arm chop

RIB

rib chop

LOIN

loin chop

double lamb chop
(English-cut)

LEG

sirloin chop

leg steak

Grilled Lamb Chops

Serves 4

■ **In a Hurry** ■ **Fit for Company**

IDEAL CHOPS FOR GRILLING are the T-bone (loin), rib, and sirloin. Shoulder and leg chops can be grilled when adequately marinated or cured. The chops should be at least 1 inch thick or, even better, 1 to 1¼ inches. All marinades for lamb kebabs are also suitable for lamb chops. Marinades with high acidity (those containing wine, vinegar, or citrus juice) can over-tenderize the fillet side of T-bone chops, so limit the marinating time to less than 16 hours in the refrigerator, and there should be no problems.

Cook lamb chops in a covered grill over medium-hot coals or in a gas barbecue with a cover. For best flavor and texture, don't cook them beyond medium-rare to medium. For internal temperatures to determine the degree of doneness, see the Doneness Chart (page 56).

Grilled lamb chops can be brushed with various glazes and sauces, including barbecue sauce. If the sauce contains a high amount of sugar, brush it on after the chops are cooked to prevent charring, or, if you prefer to apply the sauce before or during cooking, use the indirect method (see Grilling, page 63). Like rack of lamb, chops can be coated with an herb and bread crumb crust or a mustard or herb coating (see page 482) and then cooked over indirect heat. Chops do particularly well with flavorful herb rubs; to get the chops to form a tasty herb crust, brush them periodically with olive oil or melted butter as they grill.

■ **Flavor Step** ■ Brush the chops lightly with oil and season them with salt and pepper or the dry rub or marinade of your choice.

For medium-rare to medium chops, grill 1-to-1¼-inch-thick loin or rib chops over medium-hot coals for 3 to 5 minutes per side with the barbecue covered. For best results, use an instant-read meat thermometer to determine doneness. Grilled lamb chops really need no sauce, but they can be accompanied by various salsas, chutneys, and relishes, if you like.

6-8 lamb loin or rib chops, ¾ to 1¼ inch thick, trimmed of most external fat

■ **Flavor Step** ■
Olive oil
Salt and freshly ground black pepper OR dry rub or marinade of your choice (see Seasoning Chart, page 577)

BARBA YIANNI
Climbing the Acropolis the Back Way

I FIRST MET BARBA YIANNI—"Uncle John" in Greek—when I climbed up to the Acropolis by the back way. I was in Greece for the first time, down from a year in Paris at the Sorbonne, studying, among other things, modern Greek. I was eager to practice the language as much as possible and avoided all the tourist areas assiduously. But after about a week of hanging out in the sailors' bars of Piraeus and bargaining for ancient coins and bric-a-brac in the Monastiriaki flea market, I decided I had better take a look at the Acropolis. It's hard to miss it in Athens—a bit like the Eiffel Tower, the Pyramids, and the Empire State Building rolled into one; everywhere you go, there is the Acropolis looming over the city. If you visit Athens without seeing the Acropolis, you know people will look at you strangely, and your mother will never get the postcard she's expecting.

So I headed up through the Plaka, the old Turkish district on the slope of the hill. The Plaka is an ancient neighborhood with narrow, twisting streets, balconies shading the sidewalks, tiny cafes and restaurants, and lots of bouzouki joints and belly-dancing nightclubs for sailors on leave and tourists with a yen for adventure. I figured all I had to do was to head uphill, keeping my eyes on all those white temples up there, and I would eventually reach the Acropolis and see the sights so I could send that postcard home.

I kept climbing up and up through the maze of tiny streets, and suddenly I found myself at the base of a cliff. There was a little square with a fig tree and a cafe and a bunch of kids lounging around a fountain. "How do you get up to the Acropolis?" I yelled to the group. They all pointed to a tiny path, most likely made by goats, which curved up the steep and dusty hillside. "That's the way up," they said, pointing out the trail. "That's how we get there." "Well," I thought, "what the hell, it's the Acropolis after all," and set off up the path. After what seemed like hours of climbing, dusty and sweaty, I pulled myself up to the edge of the Acropolis and stared into the startled faces of bands of tourists, cameras and guidebooks in hand. They regarded me with wonder and a little fear as I scrabbled to my feet and looked down the wide staircase filled with hordes of leisurely ascending tourists. Of course, I had come up the back way, the way the neighborhood kids got there. Everyone else was using the main entrance, a broad and easy way up the hill. So I wandered casually around, looking at monuments and columns under their wary eyes, and then sauntered back to the path. With a nod to the assembled group, I stepped over the edge and slid rapidly down to the little square. The kids were rolling on the ground with laughter. I tried to look cool and thanked them for the wonderful directions.

And that's when I heard Barba Yianni for the first time—"*Ela, paide mou!*" (Come over here, my boy!) He was sitting under the fig tree, a huge man with a black fisherman's cap and a little pointed beard; he looked a little like Ali Baba or one of those fake genies in the movies. Barba Yianni was rolling up dolmades, grape leaves stuffed with spicy rice and mint. He had a large glass of wine in front of him and a copper pitcher with moisture beading the sides. He poured a glass of ice-cold retsina and held it out. "You must be a little thirsty," he said, "after your mountain-climbing expedition."

"Damn right," I said (literally, "Truly indeed, by the gods"), and I sat down gratefully, reaching for the glass.

That was the first of many long afternoons I spent with Barba Yianni, making dolmades, skewering souvlaki, chopping onions, drinking wine—usually his homemade retsina, but sometimes *krasi Kritis,* a rough red wine from the mountains of Crete, where he came from. He was a great cook, and his specialty was grilling: he would split and barbecue whole small lambs, kids, and suckling pigs that his cousins with a farm on Mount Hymettus would bring him almost every day. He liked to keep me around to help with the prep work and also to have an audience for his stories. It did a lot for my Greek, and the wine and food (and stories) were my pay.

Every time I got back to Greece, I'd go and see Barba Yianni. He got older and a little bigger around the middle, but he'd always greet me with, "*Ela, paide mou!*" and a glass of wine. I got married in Athens—my wife, Kathy, was working as an archeologist just outside Corinth—and naturally we had our wedding party at Barba Yianni's. He took some of his cousin's young lambs, cut the loin and shoulders into chops, and butterflied the legs. He marinated them all in olive oil and lemon juice with handfuls of chopped garlic and oregano and cooked them on his huge charcoal grill. We ate the lamb with *skordalia* (page 445), the garlicky yogurt and mint sauce, along with pan-roasted potatoes and *salada choriatiki,* country salad with spinach, fresh tomatoes, olives, and feta. We washed it all down with plenty of Cretan wine, danced the *hasapico* to wild bouzoukis, and ended the evening with the full moon high over the white temples above us, listening to mournful *rembetika* songs of dead captains, fierce bandits, heroes, and lovers lost long ago in the mountains. *D.K.*

Barba Yianni's Grilled Lamb

⅓ cup olive oil

Juice of 2 lemons

¼ cup dried oregano, preferably Greek, or ½ cup chopped fresh

6 garlic cloves, chopped

1 teaspoon salt

½ teaspoon freshly ground black pepper

3½ -4½ pounds lamb loin or rib chops, ¾-1¼ inch thick, trimmed, OR 4 pounds lamb for kebabs (see page 466), cut into 1½-inch chunks, OR a 3½-to-4½-pound leg of lamb, fat trimmed and butterflied

IF MAKING KEBABS

1 large onion, cut into 1-inch pieces

1 red or green bell pepper, cut into 1-inch pieces

Serves 6 to 8
■ Fit for Company

HERE'S OUR VERSION of Barba Yianni's grilled lamb. The marinade works equally well with lamb chops, kebabs, or butterflied leg of lamb. You can also use it on pork or chicken. *Skordalia* is often made with mashed potatoes or bread soaked in water, but we feel the yogurt gives it more flavor. *Skordalia* is also good with grilled fish or chicken breasts.

■ **Flavor Step** ■ Mix all the ingredients together into a paste in a small bowl and rub it all over the lamb. Place the lamb in a shallow bowl and cover with any remaining marinade. Marinate for about 2 hours at room temperature, or, preferably, cover the lamb and marinate overnight in the refrigerator, turning the meat from time to time.

To grill lamb chops: Depending on their thickness, grill the chops over medium-hot coals (see Grilling, page 63) for 3 to 5 minutes per side, turning once or twice. The chops should register 120° to 135°F at the thickest part for rare to medium-rare. You can also broil them 3 inches from the flame for 3 to 5 minutes per side, or until cooked as above.

To grill kebabs: Skewer the marinated lamb chunks on wooden or metal skewers, alternating with chunks of onions or peppers, if desired. Grill as directed in Kebabs in Cranberry-Onion Marinade (page 468) until the meat reaches 130° to 135°F for medium-rare to medium.

To grill a lamb leg: You may want to insert long metal skewers crosswise in the butterflied leg to hold it flat. Grill the leg over medium-hot coals (see Grilling, page 63), turning often, for 20 to 30 minutes. At its thickest point, the meat should register 120° to 130°F for rare to medium-rare; thinner parts will then be medium-rare to medium. Let the lamb rest, covered loosely with foil, for 5 to 10 minutes before slicing on the diagonal and serving. The internal temperature will rise 5° to 10°F more.

Meanwhile, make the *Skordalia:* Mix the ingredients together in a small bowl. Serve with the lamb.

SKORDALIA

1   cup plain yogurt
4   garlic cloves, pressed
1   tablespoon fresh lemon
    juice
2   tablespoons chopped
    fresh mint or 1
    tablespoon dried
    **Salt and freshly ground
    black pepper to taste**

GREEK GRAPE LEAF AND MINT SAUCE

Makes 2 to 3 cups

This sauce is excellent for grilled or roasted lamb and also with grilled pork or veal.

⅓   cup chopped, bottled Greek grape leaves, stems removed
3   tablespoons chopped fresh mint or 2 tablespoons dried
1   tablespoon chopped fresh oregano or 2 teaspoons dried
    Greek oregano
2   teaspoons minced garlic
1   teaspoon salt
1   cup chopped fresh parsley
¼   cup fresh lemon juice
2   tablespoons chopped capers
1   tablespoon freshly ground black pepper
¼   cup chopped green onions (white and green parts)
1½ cups olive oil

Blend or process all the ingredients in a blender or food processor. The sauce will keep refrigerated in a closed jar for 1 to 2 weeks.

Lamb and Bean Salad with Olive and Lemon Dressing

BEAN SALAD

1   pound green beans

2   cups cooked white
    beans, such as great
    northern or cannellini,
    cooked dried or
    canned, OR 2 cups
    cooked chickpeas
    (garbanzos), cooked
    dried or canned

1   medium red onion,
    thinly sliced

1   cup chopped fresh
    parsley

½   basket (½ pound) cherry
    tomatoes, cut in half

1   fire-roasted and peeled
    red bell pepper
    (see page 103) or
    bottled red pepper,
    cut into strips

20 kalamata or other
    Mediterranean olives,
    pitted

Serves 4 to 6, 6 to 8 with pasta
■ **Cooking on a Budget** ■ **In a Hurry**

YOU CAN SERVE THIS SUBSTANTIAL Greek salad warm or at room temperature or spooned over freshly cooked pasta. Use any leftover roast lamb, but Barba Yianni's Grilled Lamb (page 444) is particularly good.

To make the Bean Salad: Stem the green beans and break them into 2-inch pieces. Boil for 4 to 5 minutes in salted water to cover until fairly tender. Drain and cool under cold running water. In a large bowl, mix together the beans with the other salad ingredients.

To make the Olive and Lemon Dressing: In a food processor, blend together the mustard, lemon zest, oregano, garlic, pepper, vinegar, lemon juice, and water until smooth. With the processor running, add the oil, blending to make a homogeneous dressing. Pour the dressing into a small bowl and stir in the chopped olives. You will have about 1 cup. The dressing will keep for 1 week, covered, in the refrigerator.

To assemble the salad: Toss the Bean Salad with the dressing. Arrange it on a shallow serving platter or bowl. Sprinkle with the feta cheese and place the lamb strips on top.

To serve the salad over pasta: Cook the pasta until al dente. Drain and toss with a little oil and then mix into the dressed Bean Salad. Place the salad on a serving dish and top with the cheese and lamb strips.

OLIVE AND LEMON DRESSING

1 tablespoon Dijon mustard

2 teaspoons finely chopped lemon zest

2 teaspoons dried oregano, preferably Greek

2 teaspoons minced garlic

½ teaspoon freshly ground black pepper

1 tablespoon red wine vinegar

3 tablespoons fresh lemon juice

2 tablespoons water

½ cup olive oil

2 tablespoons pitted, chopped kalamata or other Mediterranean olives

½ cup diced or crumbled feta cheese

1 pound cooked leg of lamb, sliced and cut into 1-inch strips

1 pound rotelle or small shells (optional)

Dan's Grilled Rosemary-Cured Lamb Shoulder Chops

■ Flavor Step ■
HERB-FLAVORED DRY
CURE FOR LAMB

- 2 tablespoons chopped
  fresh rosemary
- 1 tablespoon freshly
  ground black pepper
- 10 juniper berries, chopped
  (optional)
- 2 tablespoons sugar
- ¼ cup kosher salt

- 4 ¾-1-inch-thick lamb
  shoulder, leg, or sirloin
  chops
  Olive oil

Serves 4
■ COOKING ON A BUDGET

D AN STRONGIN, a hotel chef who is currently in charge of catering and deli operations for a popular, upscale Berkeley grocery chain, is a consummate grill chef—and he's especially enthusiastic about Greek grilling recipes and techniques. In this recipe, he adapts Greek flavorings to the newly rediscovered art of curing; he dry-cures inexpensive and chewy lamb shoulder chops in a rosemary-accented salt and sugar mixture to add flavor and promote tenderness.

For the best results, use shoulder blade chops, especially those from next to the rib. Arm, leg, and sirloin chops will also work well. It's critical that you choose chops that are at least ¾ inch thick, as thinner chops may become too salty during curing.

■ **Flavor Step** ■ Combine the cure ingredients in a small bowl. Sprinkle 1 to 1½ tablespoons over both sides of each chop. (You can keep any extra rub in a sealed jar in the refrigerator for up to 2 weeks.) Place the chops on a plate and wrap loosely. Cure the chops for 12 to 16 hours in the refrigerator. Bring to room temperature before cooking.

Wash off the salt and pat the chops dry. Brush them with the olive oil. You can grill (see page 63), broil (see page 58), or sauté (page 61) the chops, but they're best grilled and cooked medium-rare, or until the internal temperature reaches 130° to 135°F.

Pan-Broiled Lamb Chops

Serves 4
■ IN A HURRY

MASTER RECIPE

THE IDEAL LAMB CHOPS for pan-broiling are T-bone (loin) or rib chops. Sirloin chops are tender enough for this method, but blade shoulder chops may be too chewy. The times for doneness are only approximate, since variations in the thickness of the chops, the pan, and the heat of your stove burners are critical. In general, we provide a minimum time.

6-8 ¾-1¼-inch-thick T-bone (loin), rib, or sirloin lamb chops, trimmed of most external fat

■ **Flavor Step** ■
Olive oil
Salt and freshly ground black pepper OR dry rub of your choice (see Seasoning Chart, page 577)

■ **Flavor Step** ■ Brush the chops lightly with oil and season them with salt and pepper or the dry rub of your choice. If you're using a dry rub, let the chops marinate for 1 to 2 hours at room temperature or for 1 to 2 days, wrapped, in the refrigerator. If they've been refrigerated, let the chops come back to room temperature before cooking.

Heat a heavy frying pan or ridged skillet over high heat. The pan should be large enough to hold all the chops; if not, cook them in two batches to avoid overcrowding. Test the pan by pressing a corner of a chop onto the surface. The chop should begin to sizzle immediately. Put the chops into the pan and sear them for 1½ to 2 minutes, until browned on the bottom. Turn the chops and sear the other side for 1½ to 2 minutes. Reduce the heat to medium (the chops should continue to sizzle, but not as vigorously as before). Cook the chops an additional 1 to 2 minutes for rare, 2 to 3 minutes for medium-rare, or 3 to 4 minutes for medium, turning them one to three times as they cook. The internal temperatures should read 120° to 130°F for rare, 130° to 135°F for medium-rare, or 135° to 150°F for medium. Let the chops rest for 5 minutes and serve as is or with a pan sauce (see next page).

PAN SAUCES FOR PAN-BROILED, BROILED, OR GRILLED LAMB CHOPS

Wilted Greens, Pine Nuts, and Raisins (page 268)
Vermouth and Mustard Sauce (page 269)
Green Olive, Artichokes, and Lemon Sauce (page 270)
Sweet Apple and Mustard Sauce (page 275)
Pearl Onion and Red Wine Sauce (page 460)

CONDIMENTS

Tomato-Olive Salsa (page 109)
Orange-Pineapple Salsa (page 295)
Cilantro Chutney (page 320)
Greek Grape Leaf and Mint Sauce (page 445)

Pan-Broiled Lamb Chops with Eggplant, Tomatoes, and Feta

Serves 4
■ IN A HURRY

ANY LEFTOVERS can be cut up and incorporated into a Greek rice pilaf. The eggplant sauce is also delicious cold as an appetizer or in a pita sandwich with the garlic and yogurt sauce called *Skordalia* (page 445). Serve the lamb chops with couscous or steamed rice.

■ **Flavor Step** ■ Season the lamb chops with olive oil and salt and pepper. Cook as directed in the Master Recipe (page 449), adding the oregano.

To make the Pan Sauce: While the lamb is cooking, in another skillet heat the oil over medium-high heat. Add the eggplant and season with salt and pepper. Fry the eggplant for 2 to 3 minutes per side, until quite soft; fry in batches if necessary and add more olive oil if needed. Arrange the eggplant in a decorative fashion on a serving platter. Cover loosely with foil to keep warm.

When the chops are done, remove them from the pan and cover loosely to keep warm. Pour off all but 1 tablespoon of the fat from the pan and reduce the heat to medium. Add the onion, along with the water. Scrape up any browned bits from the bottom of the pan, cover, and cook until all the water has evaporated, stirring occasionally, about 5 minutes. Add the tomatoes, spices, and lemon juice and taste for salt and pepper. Cook, stirring often, for 2 to 3 minutes, or until the tomatoes have just begun to release some of their juices.

Spoon the tomatoes and onion over the eggplant, sprinkle with the feta cheese and oregano, top with the chops, and serve.

6-8 ¾-1¼-inch-thick loin, rib, or sirloin lamb chops, trimmed of most external fat

■ **Flavor Step** ■
Olive oil
Salt and freshly ground black pepper
½ teaspoon dried oregano

PAN SAUCE
About ¼ cup olive oil
2 Japanese eggplants or 1 small eggplant, cut lengthwise into ¼-inch-thick slices
Salt and freshly ground black pepper
½ cup thinly sliced onion
¼ cup water
4 very ripe tomatoes, diced
½ teaspoon turmeric
½ teaspoon ground coriander
Pinch of ground cinnamon
1 tablespoon fresh lemon juice
3 tablespoons crumbled feta cheese
2 teaspoons dried oregano

Pan-Broiled Lamb Chops with Creamy Spinach Sauce

6-8 ¾-1¼-inch-thick
     T-bone (loin), rib,
     or sirloin lamb chops,
     trimmed of most
     external fat

PAN SAUCE

2 teaspoons chopped garlic
½ cup chicken stock
2 10-ounce bunches fresh
     spinach, cooked,
     chopped, and squeezed
     dry, OR two (10-ounce)
     packages frozen
     chopped spinach,
     defrosted and squeezed
     dry
1 cup plain nonfat yogurt
½ teaspoon ground
     coriander
½ teaspoon dried dill
2 tablespoons chopped
     fresh mint or 1
     teaspoon dried
     Salt and freshly ground
     black pepper

Serves 4
■ IN A HURRY

SERVE THESE TASTY CHOPS with steamed new potatoes and dill or your favorite mashed potatoes.

■ **Flavor Step** ■ Season the lamb chops as in the Master Recipe (page 449) and cook as directed. Remove them from the pan and keep warm while you make the sauce.

To make the Pan Sauce: Pour off all but 1 tablespoon of fat from the pan and reduce the heat to medium. Add the garlic and cook for 1 minute, stirring well. Pour in the stock and scrape up any browned bits from the bottom of the pan. Bring to a boil and reduce the stock to a few tablespoons. Add the spinach and stir in the yogurt, coriander, dill, and half of the mint. Cook, uncovered, over medium heat until the mixture is no longer watery, about 5 minutes, stirring often. The yogurt will curdle, but that's all right. Taste for salt and pepper.

Return the lamb chops to the pan, spoon the mixture over them, and heat through. Arrange the chops on a platter and spoon any remaining sauce over them. Garnish with the remaining mint. You can serve with additional yogurt or *Skordalia* (page 445).

Broiled Lamb Chops

Serves 2 to 4

■ IN A HURRY ■ FIT FOR COMPANY

MASTER RECIPE

Broiling is an adequate method for cooking lamb chops, especially if they're not too thin. It also has the advantage of allowing you to coat the chops with a savory crust. All the recipes for grilled lamb chops are also suitable for broiling, although cooking times may vary. For the best results, broil chops as close as possible to the flame in a preheated broiler, about 3 inches. Chops for broiling can be marinated in the same rubs or marinades suggested for grilling. They can also be given any of the coatings used for Roast Rack of Lamb (page 482).

The best chops for broiling are T-bone (loin), rib chops, or sirloin chops. Shoulder chops are a bit too chewy and are better braised.

───────────

■ **Flavor Step** ■ Salt and pepper the chops generously and rub with the cut edge of the garlic clove or use one of the marinades or rubs. If using a marinade, marinate the chops for 2 hours at room temperature or overnight in the refrigerator. If you're going to apply one of the coatings for Roast Rack of Lamb, simply salt and pepper the chops on both sides and proceed as directed for a coating on the next page.

Preheat the broiler for at least 15 minutes. If you're using a marinade, remove the chops and pat dry with paper towels. Place the chops on the broiling pan as close to the flame as possible and broil for 3 to 4 minutes per side, depending on the thickness and the degree of doneness you prefer: 2½ to 3 minutes will yield rare chops, while 4 minutes should give you medium-rare to medium. Better still, cook the chops for

■ **Flavor Step** ■
Salt and freshly ground black pepper plus a cut garlic clove OR a marinade or dry rub of your choice (see Seasoning Chart, page 577)

4   1-1¼-inch-thick T-bone (loin), rib, or sirloin lamb chops

COATINGS
(OPTIONAL)
See page 454

3 to 4 minutes per side and check the interior with an instant-read meat thermometer. When the temperature reaches about 5°F below your desired range (about 120° for rare, 135°F for medium), remove the chops from the pan and let them rest for 5 minutes or so before serving, loosely covered with foil, to allow the temperatures to equilibrate and the juices to stabilize.

COATINGS FOR BROILED CHOPS

THESE COATINGS form a nice crust and help keep the interior of the chops juicy. Fresh Herb Crust and Black Bean-Mustard Coating (page 482) are especially good with broiled lamb chops. Make the coatings as directed and then proceed as follows:

Broil the seasoned chops for 3 to 4 minutes on one side, then turn and broil them for 1½ minutes more. Remove the broiling rack with the chops and spoon or brush the coating on top of the chops. Put the rack with the chops, coating side up, back in the broiler and broil for 2 to 3 minutes more, or until the chops reach the desired degree of doneness. If the coating begins to burn, move the broiling rack farther away from the flame or lower the heat slightly and cook until done. Once the coating has been applied, don't turn the chops over again. Remove the chops and let them rest for 5 minutes before serving.

LONI'S FLAVORED BUTTER
(Burro Rosso)

Makes about ¾ cup, enough for 30 to 40 lamb or veal chops or 10 to 12 good-size T-bone beefsteaks

GRILLED OR PAN-BROILED STEAKS, lamb chops, or veal chops need little accompaniment when properly seasoned. A dollop of this butter, however, will always enhance the flavor. If you trim the excess fat from the meat, a bit of butter will not make much difference in the overall fat profile.

This recipe comes from our good friend and San Francisco cooking teacher Loni Kuhn, who told us, "Not only is this great on steaks, but it makes a nice hors d'oeuvre with bread sticks, and it's good as an impromptu sauce for pasta."

You can simply put a piece of the flavored butter on top of a steak or chop when you serve it. Or you can cut gashes in the surface of an almost-done steak—a 2-inch-thick T-bone, for example: Spread the butter into the gashes and then crisp the steak under a broiler for a minute or two.

1-2	anchovy fillets, to your taste
1	garlic clove
1	teaspoon dry mustard, preferably Colman's
1	teaspoon Dijon mustard
2	tablespoons freshly grated Parmesan cheese
1	tablespoon paprika, preferably sweet Hungarian
1	teaspoon freshly ground black pepper
1	tablespoon Worcestershire or A-1 steak sauce
8	tablespoons (1 stick) butter, softened
	Salt

In a food processor, process the anchovies, garlic, mustards, and cheese to make a paste. Add the paprika, pepper, Worcestershire or steak sauce, and butter and process until smooth. Taste for salt.

If you are going to use it within an hour or so, keep the butter at room temperature. Otherwise, shape it into a roll in plastic wrap and refrigerate or freeze to use later. Wrapped well, the butter will keep for a week to 10 days in the refrigerator or several months in the freezer. Cut off slices as needed. Use 2 to 3 teaspoons per steak.

STUFFED LAMB CHOPS

ONE WAY OF ADDING FLAVOR to grilled, broiled, or pan-broiled lamb chops is by cutting a pocket in the chop and filling it with an intensely flavored stuffing. Since the lamb chops are cooked only to the rare to medium stage, you can expect that whatever you stuff inside will not cook. Therefore anything you put into the chop should either be already cooked or able to be eaten raw. This leaves out raw sausage but still provides many tasty possibilities.

Ideal chops for stuffing are thick (1¼-to-1½-inch) rib chops or T-bone (loin) chops. Place the chop on a flat surface and make a small slit in the larger piece of meat parallel to the surface. Then use your knife and fingers to expand the pocket. You can also stuff a rack of lamb by cutting a hole down the center of the loin meat and poking a stuffing in with the handle of a wooden spoon. Whatever you use to stuff the chop should be small enough not to cause the sides and surface to bulge out—this makes it difficult to brown the chop evenly.

Here's a list of possible stuffings. You may want to pair a stuffing with a complementary herb or spice rub or marinade, such as dates with Moroccan spices or basil and garlic with Italian flavors. Use your own imagination and experiment as you wish:

- Any fresh herb paste or rub
- A basil leaf wrapped around a large slice of blanched garlic (raw is too strong)
- A coarse tapenade of chopped olives, garlic, and anchovies (see page 483)
- Chopped capers
- A couple of sage or mint leaves
- A mixture of chopped parsley and chopped lemon zest
- A drained sun-dried tomato packed in oil
- Tomato-Olive Salsa (page 109)
- Mushroom duxelles: finely chopped mushrooms sautéed with butter and chopped garlic
- A few thin slices of highly flavored cooked smoked sausage such as andouille
- A thin slice or chopped prosciutto, tasso, Westphalian, or cooked country ham
- Chopped, cooked, and seasoned chard, spinach, or other greens with pine nuts
- Oven-Roasted Tomatoes (see page 299).

- Chopped raisins, currants, and/or pine nuts (especially with Greek/Mideast seasonings)
- Mild goat cheese with or without herbs
- Provolone or other mild cheese
- Anchovy fillet, rinsed and chopped
- Anchovy fillet chopped with sun-dried tomatoes and pine nuts
- Fire-roasted peppers or chiles (see page 103)
- Chopped braised onions with some toasted bread crumbs
- Chopped or whole dried figs, dates, or apricots
- Strips of marinated artichoke hearts
- Pesto

Once the chop has been stuffed and seasoned, you can broil (see page 58), grill (see page 63) or pan-broil (see page 60) it as you would an unstuffed chop in any recipe of your choice.

Sautéed Lamb Chops with Balsamic Vinegar and Fresh Mint Vinaigrette

6-8   1-1¼-inch-thick
rib or T-bone (loin)
lamb chops (2-3 pounds
total), trimmed of most
external fat

      Salt and freshly ground
black pepper

¼   cup olive oil, or more
if necessary

⅓   cup beef or chicken
stock

2   tablespoons balsamic
vinegar

¼   cup packed fresh mint
leaves

8   cups washed and dried
frisée, arugula, or other
greens (optional)

Serves 4

■ IN A HURRY ■ FIT FOR COMPANY

HERB- AND FRUIT-FLAVORED OILS and vinegars, which have become popular in restaurants, provide quick and simple ways to add flavor to fish, meat, and poultry. Sometimes the oil and vinegar are combined to make a light vinaigrette. The main dish may then be served on a bed of greens, and the vinaigrette becomes a sauce for the meat and a dressing for the greens. This type of meal is easy to prepare at home, yet elegant. You can also served it with Nancy's Mushroom Vinaigrette (page 108) and a side dish of roasted new potatoes or French fries dusted with chopped fresh herbs. *(See photograph, page 18.)*

In this recipe, we've taken advantage of the pan juices and added stock to give the minty vinaigrette a pleasant meaty flavor. Instead of steeping the mint leaves in the vinaigrette, you could add freshly chopped mint at the end to give the sauce a burst of flavor.

Season the chops well with salt and pepper. Heat a large, heavy skillet over high heat and add 1 tablespoon of the oil. Put in the chops (in batches if necessary, adding more oil as needed) and cook for 3 minutes. Turn and cook them for 2 to 3 minutes longer for rare (120° to 130°F). For medium chops, add 2 more minutes per side, turning the chops two or three times. Remove the chops from the pan and cover loosely with foil to keep warm while you make the vinaigrette. The meat's internal temperature will rise about 5°F or so as the chops rest.

Pour off all the fat from the pan, leaving any meat juices behind. Put in the stock and scrape up any browned bits from the bottom of the pan. Boil until the stock and juices are reduced to about 1 tablespoon. Add the vinegar and take the pan off the heat. Whisk in the remaining 3 tablespoons oil to make a vinaigrette. Taste for salt and pepper.

Place the mint leaves in a small bowl and pour the vinaigrette over them. Steep for 3 minutes.

Spread the optional greens on a platter, arrange the lamb chops on top, and pour the vinaigrette and mint leaves over it all. If you're not using the greens, arrange the chops on a platter and pour the sauce and mint leaves over them. Serve at once.

Lamb Chops with Pearl Onions and Red Wine

■ **Flavor Step** ■
Herb Rub for Pork,
Lamb, or Beef
(page 263)

2 pounds shoulder, sirloin,
   loin, or rib lamb chops,
   ¾-1¼ inches thick
1 tablespoon olive oil

**PEARL ONION AND RED
   WINE SAUCE**
½ cup dry red wine
½ cup chicken stock
2 tablespoons balsamic
   vinegar
1 teaspoon chopped fresh
   mint or 1 teaspoon
   dried
40 fresh pearl onions,
   peeled and trimmed;
   or frozen
   Salt and freshly ground
   black pepper

Serves 4 to 6
■ IN A HURRY (RIB OR LOIN CHOPS)
■ REWARMS WELL (SHOULDER AND SIRLOIN CHOPS)

THERE ARE TWO WAYS you can prepare this dish, depending on the cut of lamb chops you buy. If you use chewier shoulder or sirloin chops, finish the cooking by braising them for 35 to 45 minutes in the sauce. If you use tender rib or loin chops, you can pan-broil them until done, then remove them and make a pan sauce. Either way, this is a delicious and easy way to serve lamb. Accompany the dish with some of the wine you use in the sauce—a medium-bodied Pinot Noir or Chianti would be just right.

■ **Flavor Step** ■ Rub the herb rub all over the lamb chops. Let them rest for 20 minutes or so.

Heat the oil in a large, heavy skillet over medium-high heat. Put in the chops. If you're using shoulder or sirloin chops, brown them for 3 minutes per side, remove, and set aside. If you're using loin or rib chops, cook them for 4 to 5 minutes on one side, turn, and cook for 3 to 4 minutes more on the other. When tested with an instant-read meat thermometer, the center of the meatiest part should read 130° to 135°F for medium-rare, 135° to 150°F for medium. Remove the chops and set aside.

To make the Pearl Onion and Red Wine Sauce: Pour off any grease from the pan and add the wine, stock, vinegar, and mint. Bring to a boil and scrape up any browned bits from the bottom of the pan. Put in the onions.

If you're using shoulder or sirloin chops, return them to the pan. (Do not put in loin or rib chops.) Reduce the heat and cover the pan. Cook over low heat until the lamb is tender and the onions are soft, shaking the pan from time to time to ensure even cooking, 35 to 45 minutes more. Remove the chops when they are tender and keep them warm. Skim any fat from the sauce and reduce it over high heat until it is just syrupy. Taste for salt and pepper, pour over the chops, and serve.

If you're using loin or rib chops, cook the pan sauce for 35 to 45 minutes, shaking the pan occasionally, until the onions are soft and the sauce is syrupy. Put in the loin or rib chops and cook for 1 minute to heat them through before serving.

Braised Lamb Chops in a Piquant Sausage and Anchovy Sauce

■ **Flavor Step** ■
Fennel-Sage Rub for
Pork or Veal
(page 340)

4-6 blade, arm, sirloin,
  or leg lamb chops,
  at least ¾ inch thick
  (2-3 pounds total),
  trimmed of excess fat
1 tablespoon olive oil
1 tablespoon minced garlic
¼ cup finely chopped
  onion
3 tablespoons water

Serves 4 to 6
■ COOKING ON A BUDGET ■ REWARMS WELL
■ GREAT LEFTOVERS

THIS PIQUANT ITALIAN SAUCE is more typically served with duck, but the robust shoulder, leg, and sirloin lamb chops are complemented nicely by the intense flavors and underlying spice. Serve the braised chops with bow-tie or pinwheel pasta. Any leftover meat can be chopped, mixed with the sauce and cooked pasta, sprinkled with pecorino cheese, and baked in a buttered casserole for a delicious and easy family dinner.

■ **Flavor Step** ■ Mix the seasonings in a small bowl and rub generously all over the chops. Set them aside to marinate at room temperature for an hour or so or overnight, wrapped, in the refrigerator. Let the chops come to room temperature before cooking.

Heat the oil over high heat in a heavy, lidded pan large enough to hold the chops. Or you can cook them in two batches in a smaller pan. Add the chops and brown them for 2 minutes per side. Set them aside.

Pour off all but 1 tablespoon of the fat from the pan and reduce the heat to medium. Put in the garlic and onion and cook over medium-high heat until the onion just begins to color, stirring often, about 5 minutes. Add the water and scrape up any browned bits from the bottom of the pan. Cook, stirring often, until the liquid is absorbed, about 2 minutes.

Add the sausage and fry for 5 minutes, breaking the meat up with a fork as it cooks. Add the anchovies, sage, and vinegar. Bring to a boil and add the stock. Put the chops back in, reduce the heat to a simmer, cover, and cook for 30 to 45 minutes, or until the lamb is quite tender.

Remove the chops and keep them warm. Degrease the sauce and season with salt and pepper. Arrange the chops on a platter, pour the sauce over them, and serve.

1 raw hot or mild Italian sausage, removed from casing

2 anchovy fillets, well rinsed with water, chopped

1 teaspoon chopped fresh sage

½ cup sherry vinegar, white wine vinegar, or red wine vinegar

1 cup beef or chicken stock

Salt and freshly ground black pepper

Lamb Shoulder Chops with Roasted Red Bell Peppers

2 large red bell peppers, fire-roasted (see page 103), OR 1 cup packed bottled roasted red peppers or pimentos (bottled Greek peppers, such as the Peloponnese brand, are quite good)

4 lamb blade shoulder chops (6-8 ounces each) OR 1½-2 pounds rib or loin lamb chops, trimmed of excess fat
Salt and freshly ground black pepper

1 tablespoon olive oil

½ cup finely chopped onion

1 tablespoon minced garlic

1 cup dry white wine

1 tablespoon tomato paste

½ teaspoon dried marjoram or oregano

1 cup sour cream or crème fraîche (optional)

¼ cup chopped fresh parsley

1 pound pasta, cooked

Serves 4
■ COOKING ON A BUDGET
■ IN A HURRY ■ REWARMS WELL

THE EARTHY FLAVORS of roasted bell peppers provide an ideal accompaniment to lamb chops, but this sauce would be equally good with veal or pork chops. You can use shoulder, rib, or loin chops. Take care to adjust the cooking times so that they're appropriate to the type of meat you use.

If you're in a hurry or feeling particularly lazy, you can use bottled roasted red peppers or pimentos. Otherwise, roast the peppers yourself. Use fire-roasted green or yellow bell peppers instead, if you like, or any combination. And try this recipe with fire-roasted mild green chiles, such as Anaheim or poblano. Serve the lamb chops with large pasta such as bow-ties or pinwheels tossed in the pepper sauce.

Cut half a roasted or bottled bell pepper or pimento lengthwise into strips about ⅛ inch wide. Set aside. Put the rest of the peppers into a food processor or blender and puree them. Set the puree aside.

Season the chops well with salt and pepper. In a heavy skillet large enough to hold all the chops without crowding, heat the olive oil over high heat. Put in the chops and brown on each side for 3 minutes. Remove the chops and set aside. Pour off all but 1 tablespoon of the fat from the pan and add the onion and garlic. Reduce the heat to medium and cook, stirring often, for 3 minutes. Add the wine, tomato paste, and marjoram and bring to a boil, scraping up any browned bits from the bottom of the pan.

Reduce the heat and return the browned chops to the pan. If you're using chewier shoulder chops, braise them over low heat for 45 minutes, or to an internal temperature of 145° to 150°F. For the more tender rib or loin chops, braise for 7 to 10 minutes, until medium—135° to 150°F internal temperature. Remove the chops and cover them loosely to keep warm.

Skim any fat from the pan and add the pureed peppers. If necessary, boil the sauce to reduce and thicken it. Stir in the sour cream or crème fraîche, if you wish, and add the reserved pepper strips and chopped parsley. Spoon two-thirds of the sauce over the cooked pasta of your choice and arrange the chops on top. Spoon on the remaining sauce and serve.

How to Choose and Prepare
Lamb Kebabs

WHEN WE THINK OF KEBABS, lamb always comes first to mind. It must have been a clever and frugal fellow who figured out how to cook and enjoy small morsels of marinated meat impaled on skewers. The first kebab chefs were probably nomadic Mongols marauding over the steppes, with little time to prepare food except for the odd chunk of lamb or mutton grilled over the fire on their sword points. Most likely they enlivened the probably gamy meat a bit with some exotic spices looted from far Cathay and carefully guarded in their saddlebags. The technique probably goes further back than that—our hunter-gatherer ancestors must have cooked bits of meat on sticks over the fire, but we doubt they used many spices. And it's the marinating and spicing of the meat that makes kebabs so special.

Marinating allows the budget-minded cook to use less expensive cuts of meat in kebabs, since many marinades not only flavor the chunks of meat but also tenderize them. The best cuts of lamb to use are the inexpensive sirloin, shoulder, or leg. The more expensive rib and loin are not very suitable for marinating as they can become too tender and mushy, especially in acidic marinades.

Skewering lamb is a favorite way of cooking this savory meat in the Mideast: Georgian *shaslik,* Greek *souvlaki,* and Turkish *sis kebabi* are all virtually the same dish, with variations in the marinade. There are many more different marinade ingredients from all over the world, however, and these give kebabs variety and interest. Some are based on wine, lemons, or vinegar; others use minced onions as a dominant flavor. Some marinades are based on fruit juices such as pomegranate; others use yogurt with exotic spices. You can even find marinades incorporating beer, soy sauce, chiles, and other pungent and powerful ingredients. In addition to these wet marinades, lamb kebabs can be marinated with a dry rub or in brine (see Seasoning Chart, page 577, for suggestions for lamb).

Once marinated, the chunks of meat are threaded onto skewers with pieces of onion, mild peppers, or other vegetables or fruits. The list is endless and may include mushrooms, tomatoes, squash of various types, eggplant, dried figs, prunes, and apricots. Sometimes whole fresh herb leaves such as bay, sage, or basil are tucked between the pieces of lamb; the meat can also be wrapped in grape or spinach leaves.

Once the skewers are filled, grill them over medium-hot coals or on a gas grill. Kebabs should be turned frequently and can be brushed with the marinade during cooking. Although you can cook them in a broiler, they're never quite as good as grilled. Pan-broiling doesn't work either; the kebabs tend to ooze juices in the pan and fail to brown properly.

Kebabs in Cranberry-Onion Marinade

1 medium onion, coarsely
    chopped
3 garlic cloves, peeled
1 teaspoon dried marjoram
    or oregano
2 teaspoons salt
1 teaspoon freshly ground
    black pepper
½ cup cranberry or
    pomegranate juice
2 tablespoons olive oil

2 pounds boneless lamb
    from sirloin, shoulder,
    or leg, gristle and
    external fat removed,
    cut into 1½-inch cubes
2 red onions, cut into
    1-inch chunks
1 green bell pepper, cut
    into 1½-inch squares
1 red bell pepper, cut into
    1½-inch squares

Serves 4 to 6

■ FIT FOR COMPANY ■ GOOD FOR A CROWD

MASTER RECIPE

IN MANY MIDDLE EASTERN COUNTRIES, lamb is marinated in a mixture based on minced or grated onion. In Iraq and Iran, pomegranate juice is also added to flavor and tenderize the meat. Pomegranate juice is hard to find, although it is carried by Middle Eastern specialty stores and some health food stores. Cranberry juice makes a more than adequate substitute. This tasty recipe was inspired by one that San Francisco food celebrity Narsai David used for rack of lamb at his fine Kensington restaurant, Narsai's.

You can also use this as a master recipe; substitute whatever other dry rub or marinade you wish (see Seasoning Chart, page 577).

■ **Flavor Step** ■ Blend the onion, garlic, marjoram or oregano, salt, and pepper to a coarse paste in a food processor. Pour in the cranberry or pomegranate juice and oil and pulse once or twice to mix. Place the meat in a zipper-lock bag or bowl and cover with the marinade. Seal the bag or cover the bowl and marinate for 2 to 3 hours at room temperature or overnight in the refrigerator. Shake the bag or turn the meat from time to time (or prepare your favorite marinade or dry rub and marinate the meat as described in the recipe).

When you're ready to grill, light the charcoal (see Grilling, page 63). If the meat has been refrigerated, allow it to come to room temperature.

Remove the meat, reserving the marinade, and pat it dry. Thread the meat onto skewers, alternating it with the pieces of onion and pepper in any order you wish. When the coals are medium-hot, put the skewers directly over the heat. Grill them for 4 to 5 minutes per side for medium, 3 to 4 minutes for medium-rare. Make sure not to burn the meat—if there are any flare-ups, cover the grill or move the skewers to a cooler part of the fire. Brush with the reserved marinade from time to time, rotating the skewers to hotter or cooler areas of the grill as needed. Serve the skewers with pilaf or steamed rice, accompanied by warm pita bread and yogurt.

KEBABS IN GARLIC, LEMON, AND HERB MARINADE

Serves 4 to 6
■ FIT FOR COMPANY ■ GOOD FOR A CROWD

YOU CAN USE this classic Middle Eastern marinade for kebabs, lamb chops, or butterflied leg of lamb. Sumac is a tangy red spice popular in Iran; it can be found in Middle Eastern specialty stores or by mail-order (see Sources, page 584).

■ Flavor Step ■ Puree the onions with the salt in a food processor or blender or grate them by hand and mix with the salt. Pour the mixture into a strainer and place it over a bowl. Let sit until ⅓ to ½ cup of onion juice has dripped into the bowl. Press the onions through a sieve to extract all of the juice and discard them. Stir the rest of the ingredients into the onion juice. Place the meat in a zipper-lock bag or bowl and marinate the meat as described in the Master Recipe (opposite page).

Prepare the kebabs and grill as directed.

■ Flavor Step ■
GARLIC, LEMON, AND
HERB MARINADE FOR
LAMB

3 cups coarsely chopped
onions
1 tablespoon salt
¼ cup fresh lemon juice
2 teaspoons minced garlic
1 teaspoon freshly ground
black pepper
2 teaspoons dried oregano,
marjoram, or basil
3 tablespoons olive oil
1-2 teaspoons sumac
(optional)

2 pounds boneless lamb
from sirloin, shoulder,
or leg, gristle and
external fat removed

How to Choose Ground Lamb

GROUND LAMB IS WIDELY AVAILABLE and can be used in many dishes calling for ground beef (see Greek Burger, page 159). The problem is that much of the ground lamb sold in supermarkets is very fatty because it usually comes from the breast, belly, or flank. We suggest that you purchase a piece of shoulder or leg and have the butcher grind it for you or that you grind it yourself at home in a grinder or food processor (see Sage and Pepper Pork Sausage, page 412, for grinding tips).

YOGURT CUCUMBER SAUCE
Makes 2 cups

1   cup plain yogurt
1   cup diced (¼-inch dice) cucumber
2   teaspoons chopped fresh dill or 1 teaspoon dried
2   teaspoons fresh mint or 1 teaspoon dried
    Salt and freshly ground black pepper

In a medium-size bowl, mix all the ingredients. Taste for salt and pepper. Serve at once.

Turkish Lamb Burgers in Pita Bread

Serves 6

■ COOKING ON A BUDGET ■ GOOD FOR A CROWD

THESE GROUND LAMB BURGERS are a delicious alternative to the American variety— but if you and your family prefer lean ground beef, use it instead. Rather than trying to stuff the mixture into a split pita, just shape an oval patty and wrap the whole warm pita around it. This recipe also makes delicious meatballs—serve them in a tomato sauce flavored with fresh mint and cinnamon.

This recipe comes from our friend and San Francisco cooking teacher Loni Kuhn. Grilled food became so popular with her five children that she installed a grill inside her house so they could use it year-round.

To make the Burgers: In a large bowl, combine all the ingredients, kneading the mixture well. Cover and refrigerate for several hours or overnight.

Form the ground meat into 6 oval patties, not packing the meat too tightly. Grill over a medium charcoal fire (see Grilling, page 63) or sauté (see Sautéing, page 61) until the meat is still slightly pink in the center.

Fold a warm pita bread in half around each cooked burger. Add the sliced tomatoes, onions, and a bit of feta to each. Let guests spoon on the Yogurt Cucumber Sauce. Serve with lots of napkins.

BURGERS

- 2 pounds lean ground lamb
- ½ cup fresh bread crumbs
- 1 large egg, lightly beaten
- 1 cup minced onions
- 2 teaspoons minced garlic
- ⅓ pound feta cheese, crumbled
- 2 teaspoons chopped fresh oregano or 1 teaspoon dried
- ½ cup chopped fresh mint or 2 tablespoons dried
- 1 tablespoon ground cumin
- 2 tablespoons fresh lemon juice
- ¼ cup chopped fresh parsley or cilantro
- 2 teaspoons salt
- 1 teaspoon freshly ground black pepper

- 6 pita breads, warmed
  Sliced tomatoes
  Thinly sliced red onions
  OR Lime-Pickled Red
  Onions (page 104)
- ½ cup crumbled feta cheese
  Yogurt Cucumber Sauce
  (see opposite page)

Grilled Indian Ground Lamb Kebabs

KEBABS

¼ cup chopped fresh
cilantro

1 pound lean ground lamb
or beef

¼ cup finely minced onion

2 teaspoons minced garlic

2 teaspoons minced fresh
ginger

½ teaspoon ground cumin

½ teaspoon ground
coriander

½ teaspoon ground
cardamom

¼ teaspoon ground allspice

½ teaspoon turmeric

¼ teaspoon cayenne pepper

1½ teaspoons salt

½ teaspoon freshly ground
black pepper

¼ cup plain yogurt

1 tablespoon cornstarch

8 pita breads, warmed
Lime-Pickled Red
Onions (page 104)
Cilantro Chutney (page
320)

Serves 4
■ COOKING ON A BUDGET
■ FIT FOR COMPANY ■ GREAT LEFTOVERS

THESE INDIAN-INSPIRED kebabs can be shaped into oval patties or long cylinders around flat or square metal skewers and grilled.

Make sure to use very lean ground lamb. You can also use lean ground beef or a combination of the two.

To make the Kebabs: Place all the ingredients in a large bowl and knead and squeeze the mixture until everything is well blended. Either shape the meat into 8 oval patties or mold it around 4 flat or square metal skewers into long cigar shapes about ¾ inch in diameter.

Cook the patties or kebabs over hot coals or on a gas barbecue (see Grilling, page 63) or in a broiler (see Broiling, page 58), turning frequently until the inside is just faintly pink, a total of 8 to 10 minutes.

Serve in warm pita bread with the onions and chutney.

Indian Ground Lamb with Chinese Long Beans and Potatoes
(*Kheema*)

Serves 8

■ GOOD FOR A CROWD ■ REWARMS WELL
■ FIT FOR COMPANY

THIS RECIPE COMES FROM a talented friend, Seattle chef Jeff Bergman. He says, "*Kheema* is a simple way to serve last-minute guests or provide for a special Sunday supper. It's also a great buffet dish that feeds a lot of hungry folks. Serve it with plenty of condiments: a *raita* made from grated cucumber, yogurt, ground cumin, and salt; tomato chutney; and/or Cilantro Chutney" (see page 320). This recipe calls for curry paste, a superior product to curry powder. Patak's brand is widely available in Indian groceries or by mail-order (see Sources, page 584). Garam masala is an aromatic mix of Indian spices (for mail-order sources, see page 584; for homemade, see page 321). Serve *kheema* with basmati rice cooked with saffron and raisins.

---

1 cup peeled and diced (½-inch dice) white potatoes
1 cup plain regular or low-fat yogurt
1 tablespoon plus ½ teaspoon ground cumin
Salt
1 cup 1-inch lengths Chinese long beans or other green beans
Freshly ground black pepper
2 tablespoons peanut or vegetable oil
1 cinnamon stick (about 2 inches long)
6 whole cloves
2 medium onions, chopped
1 2-inch piece of fresh ginger (2 ounces), peeled and minced
4 garlic cloves, minced
½ cup minced green onions or scallions (white and green parts)

Blanch the potatoes in boiling water for 10 minutes, or until almost tender. Drain, toss with ½ cup of the yogurt, ½ teaspoon of the ground cumin, and ¼ teaspoon salt and set aside. Blanch the green beans in boiling water for 2 minutes or just until al dente. Drain, toss with salt and pepper to taste, and set aside.

Heat the oil in a heavy 12-inch skillet or a Dutch oven over medium-high heat. Put the cinnamon stick and cloves into the hot oil. When the cinnamon starts to uncurl, add the onions, ginger, garlic, and green onions or scallions. Sauté for 10 minutes, stirring frequently. The onions should be a light nut-brown color.

1 tablespoon ground
    coriander
1 teaspoon turmeric
1 teaspoon Garam Masala
    (page 321)
1 teaspoon curry paste,
    preferably Patak's
3 tablespoons canned or
    homemade tomato
    sauce
2 pounds lean ground
    lamb or beef
¼ teaspoon cayenne pepper
1½ cups water
¼ cup chopped fresh
    cilantro

Lower the heat to medium and add the coriander, the remaining 1 tablespoon cumin, the turmeric, garam masala, and curry paste. Sauté for 3 minutes, stirring all the time. Add the remaining ½ cup yogurt and cook for 1 more minute. Put in the tomato sauce and cook, stirring for 3 minutes.

Put in the ground lamb or beef. Raise the heat to medium-high and sauté the meat, breaking it up with a fork as it cooks until it is browned, about 8 minutes. Add 2 teaspoons salt, the cayenne, and ½ cup of the water and stir well. Bring to a boil, cover the pan, reduce the heat to low, and simmer for 30 minutes.

Put in the potatoes with the remaining 1 cup water and continue cooking, uncovered, for 15 minutes. Add the green beans and cook, uncovered, for 5 minutes, or until the beans are tender and heated through. There should be just a little sauce in the pan, with most of the juices absorbed by the meat. Stir in the chopped cilantro and remove the cinnamon stick. Taste for salt and pepper.

Note: *Leftover* kheema *makes a great filling for chapatis, pita bread, or flour tortillas. Heat the* kheema *and garnish the sandwiches with yogurt, diced tomatoes, and thinly sliced red onions.*

COOKING RED MEAT ON A VEGETARIAN BUDGET

ALONG ABOUT MY JUNIOR YEAR at the University of California at Berkeley, I declared financial independence from my parents. I got a part-time job packing greeting cards (it paid a whopping $80 per month) and another job washing pots for meals at a boardinghouse. One day I showed up for work to find another hungry student at my pot-washing station. When I queried the cook, she informed me that my all-too-frequently greasy pots had forced her to relieve me of my duties. As an act of pure generosity, however, she did let me partake of dinner one last time before I was sent on my way.

I was now faced with a dilemma—here I was with a red meat appetite and a vegetarian budget. And the kitchen facilities in my shared room in an old Victorian on College Avenue consisted of an electric skillet, a hot plate with frayed wires, and two battered pots from a secondhand store. Needless to say, I ate a whole hell of a lot of pasta. Occasionally friends would chip in, and I'd cook up a big batch of chicken cacciatore (even with my limited facilities, I was a better cook than most of my friends).

One day a friend invited me to celebrate his birthday at an Afghan restaurant called the Khyber Pass. It was a revelation—much like the Indian food I already liked, but heartier and earthier. In particular, I fell in love with a dish of ground lamb and eggplant that was served on ribbons of handmade pasta and garnished with yogurt. After several tries, I learned to master this dish, called *kofta,* which lent itself very well to my two-pot cookery and limited budget.   *B.A.*

Afghani Ground Lamb and Eggplant Pasta
(Kofta)

¼ cup vegetable or olive oil, or more if needed

1 medium eggplant, peeled and cut into ½-inch cubes

Salt and freshly ground black pepper

2 cups finely chopped leeks or onions

1 cup finely chopped carrots

¾ pound lean ground lamb or beef

1 tablespoon chopped garlic

1 tablespoon chopped fresh ginger

2 tablespoons water

2 tablespoons chile powder, preferably Gebhardt

1 tablespoon ground coriander

1 tablespoon paprika

1 tablespoon turmeric

½ teaspoon ground cumin

¼ teaspoon ground cinnamon

⅛ teaspoon ground cloves

½ teaspoon chopped lemon zest

2 tablespoons fresh lemon juice, or more to taste

2 canned Italian-style tomatoes, chopped

½ cup tomato puree

Serves 4 to 6

■ COOKING ON A BUDGET ■ GOOD FOR A CROWD ■ MEAT AS A CONDIMENT

THIS RECIPE is a slightly more elegant version of a dish I used to make as a starving student, but it's still economical enough to squeeze into a limited budget, since it only uses ¾ pound of meat.

Heat the oil in a large, heavy skillet over medium heat and add the eggplant. Sprinkle with salt and pepper. Cook, turning the eggplant often, until it is quite soft, about 7 minutes. Using a slotted spoon, remove the eggplant and set it aside. Add a little more oil to the pan if necessary and add the chopped leeks or onions and carrots. Cover and cook over medium heat until soft, stirring often, about 5 minutes. Put in the lamb or beef, 1 teaspoon salt, ½ teaspoon pepper, the garlic and ginger and sauté for 5 minutes, breaking up the lamb with a fork as it browns. Add the water and scrape up any browned bits from the bottom of the pan.

Put the eggplant back in the pan and stir in the chile powder, spices, lemon zest, lemon juice, tomatoes, tomato puree, and ¼ cup of the yogurt. Bring to a simmer and stir to mix everything well. Cover and cook over low heat for 30 minutes.

Remove the cover and check to see if most of the liquid has been absorbed. If the mixture seems too dry, add a little more water. If it seems too liquid, boil to concentrate slightly. Stir in the cilantro. Skim any fat from the surface and taste for salt and pepper.

Meanwhile, cook the pasta until al dente in lots of salted boiling water. Drain and divide among individual plates. Spoon the eggplant and lamb mixture over the pasta and garnish with a dollop of the remaining yogurt and chopped fresh mint. Serve at once.

¾ cup plain yogurt
½ cup chopped fresh
    cilantro
1½ pounds fresh pasta, wide
    noodles, or
    dried fettuccine
    Chopped fresh mint,
    for garnish

How to Choose Rack of Lamb, Lamb Loin, and Lamb Shoulder Roasts

WHILE LEG IS THE MOST COMMON CUT for roasting, there are smaller roasts that are tender and delicious—suitable for two to four diners. The most popular small roast is the **rack of lamb**. The rack is an elegant and flavorful treat and is the favorite way to eat lamb in a restaurant. It is quite expensive but worth it for a special dinner for two. This is the equivalent of a beef standing rib roast, but the 7-bone racks are much smaller than the beef roast, usually only enough for two.

If you wish to roast a rack of lamb, have your butcher remove the chine bone and trim the fat and thin flap of meat from the outside of the rack, leaving the rib-eye of meat intact. He should also remove all the intercostal meat and any fat between the ribs. This trimmed rack of lamb, ready for the oven, is called **frenched.** New Zealand and Australian racks of lamb are now sold frenched and individually wrapped in Cryovac. A trimmed American rack usually weighs 1 to 1½ pounds; New Zealand and Australian racks weigh in at less than a pound. A rack will feed two people and should be roasted quickly in a hot oven (see page 480).

Occasionally you may find a butcher who is willing to bone out a **whole loin of lamb** from a rack of T-bone lamb chops. This is another elegant, tender, and expensive lamb roast. Weighing about 2 pounds, it is perfect for a small dinner party of four or five. The other muscle that makes up the loin, the small and very tender **tenderloin**, is sometimes sold by expensive butchers. It weighs only about ½ pound and is too small to roast successfully, but it is ideal grilled or quickly sautéed.

Some butchers sell the **whole lamb sirloin** separated from the leg. It weighs about 2 pounds and can be roasted bone-in or boned, rolled, and tied. Like leg of lamb, the sirloin makes a juicy roast for four to six and can be eaten rare.

If you wish to dry-roast **lamb shoulder**, purchase a boneless rolled and tied shoulder. Sear it first in a hot oven (450°F) to brown for 15 minutes or so and then roast very slowly in a 250° to 300°F oven to medium-rare to medium. This slow roasting will make this tougher cut tender and juicy.

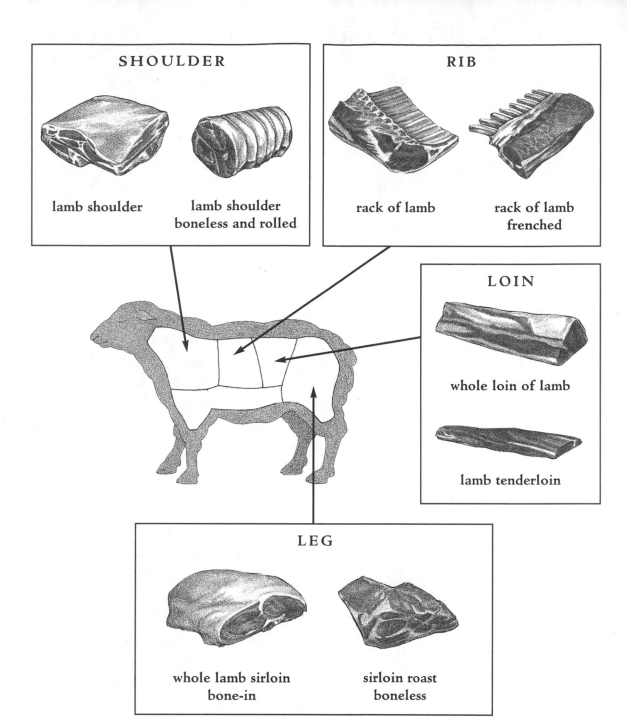

SHOULDER

lamb shoulder

lamb shoulder
boneless and rolled

RIB

rack of lamb

rack of lamb
frenched

LOIN

whole loin of lamb

lamb tenderloin

LEG

whole lamb sirloin
bone-in

sirloin roast
boneless

Roast Rack of Lamb

1 7- or 8-bone rack of
    lamb, trimmed and
    frenched (1-1¼ pounds)
    Salt and freshly ground
    black pepper
1-2 tablespoons olive oil

■ Flavor Step ■
(optional)
Use one of the coatings
or crusts listed on pages
482-83

Serves 2 to 4
■ FIT FOR COMPANY

MASTER RECIPE

WE SEEM TO EAT RACK OF LAMB most often in restaurants, but a rack cooked at home is perfect for a romantic dinner for two. Properly prepared by the butcher, it's very easy to cook and serve (see page 478).

The techniques for searing and roasting are always the same, but the seasonings and final coatings can vary. Because rack of lamb is so tender and delicate, we don't recommend a wet marinade, which can make tender meat mushy and obliterate the subtle flavors of the lamb. You can season it with a rub such as Herb Rub for Pork, Lamb, or Beef (page 263) to enhance the flavors if you don't use one of the coatings on pages 482-83.

Since the rack is first seared at a high temperature, the Flavor Step is added afterward so that the coating or crust won't burn. Rack of lamb is best eaten rare to medium. Remember that it should rest a bit before carving; this means there will be some carryover cooking after the rack is removed from the oven: the internal temperature will rise 5° to 10°F. Be sure to remove the roast from the oven at 5°F or so lower than the required doneness to compensate. For best results, always use an instant-read thermometer. The final temperatures after resting should be as follows:

Blood-rare	115° to 125°F
Rare	125° to 130°F
Medium-rare	130° to 140°F
Medium	140° to 150°F

PAN SAUCE FOR RACK OF LAMB (OPTIONAL)

- 1 teaspoon minced garlic
- ½ cup red wine
- ½ cup lamb, beef, or chicken stock
- 1 teaspoon chopped fresh thyme or 1 teaspoon dried
- 1 teaspoon Dijon mustard
- 2 tablespoons butter (optional)
- Salt and freshly ground black pepper

Preheat the oven to 475°F. Season the rack all over with salt and pepper. Place a heavy 10-inch ovenproof skillet over high heat and film the bottom with the oil. Put the rack in the skillet fat side down and sear for 1 to 2 minutes. Then, using tongs, hold the rack with the bones vertical and sear the top meat for 1 to 2 minutes. Finally, sear the bone side for 1 to 2 minutes. Remove the pan from the heat and let the lamb rest for a few minutes, uncovered. (If you don't have an ovenproof skillet, sear the rack in a pan and then transfer it to a small roasting pan or pie plate.) Roast the rack as is or apply a coating now. Cover the ends of the bones with foil to prevent charring.

Arrange the rack bone side down in the skillet (or roasting pan). Roast the lamb in the middle of the oven for 15 to 20 minutes, depending on the degree of doneness you want. Take a reading in the center of the meat after 12 to 15 minutes and remove the meat, or let it cook longer to your taste. Let it rest for 5 to 7 minutes, loosely covered, before carving between the ribs and serving 3 to 4 chops per person.

To make the Pan Sauce, if desired: Pour off any fat from the skillet or roasting pan, leaving any juices behind. Place the pan over medium heat and add the garlic. Cook for 15 seconds, pour in the wine, raise the heat to high, and stir to scrape up any browned bits from the bottom of the pan. Boil the wine to reduce it by half. Add the stock and thyme and boil the sauce until it just begins to turn syrupy. Whisk in the mustard until the sauce is smooth. If you'd like a richer sauce with a velvety texture, whisk in the optional butter. Season to taste with salt and pepper. Serve over the lamb.

BLACK BEAN-MUSTARD COATING FOR LAMB

1 tablespoon Chinese fermented black beans, finely chopped, OR 1 tablespoon soy sauce

2 teaspoons finely chopped fresh rosemary

2 tablespoons Dijon mustard

1 teaspoon minced garlic

½ teaspoon freshly ground black pepper

Mix all the ingredients in a small bowl or process in a food processor to form a paste. Once the rack is seared as described in the Master Recipe (page 480), brush the mixture thickly all over the meat. If you use this coating, the lamb is best served without a sauce.

FRESH HERB CRUST FOR LAMB

2 tablespoons fresh rosemary leaves

2 tablespoons fresh thyme leaves

2 garlic cloves

½ teaspoon salt

¼ teaspoon freshly ground black pepper

2 tablespoons olive oil

Combine all the ingredients in a food processor and blend to form a coarse paste. Sear the lamb as described in the Master Recipe (page 480) and coat as directed above.

HERB AND BREAD CRUMB CRUST FOR LAMB

½ cup fresh bread crumbs

2 teaspoons minced garlic

2 tablespoons chopped fresh rosemary, savory, thyme, or oregano

1 teaspoon salt

¼ teaspoon freshly ground black pepper

2 tablespoons olive oil

2 tablespoons Dijon mustard

SEE PHOTOGRAPH, PAGE 23.

Combine all the ingredients except the oil and mustard in a small bowl or blend in a food processor. Moisten the mixture by tossing in the olive oil. Spread the herbed crumbs in a shallow pan or on a deep platter. Once the rack is seared as directed on page 481, brush it all over with the mustard. Roll it in the bread crumb mixture so that it is well coated. Roast and serve as described in the Master Recipe. To make the crumb coating crispier, place the rack under a broiler for 1 to 2 minutes.

PARMESAN AND MINT COATING FOR LAMB

Combine everything except the butter in a shallow bowl. Stir in the melted butter. Coat the seared rack with the mixture and roast as directed in the Master Recipe (page 480).

¼ cup freshly grated Parmesan cheese

1 tablespoon chopped fresh mint or 2 teaspoons dried

1 teaspoon chopped fresh thyme or ½ teaspoon dried

1 teaspoon minced garlic
Pinch of freshly ground black pepper

2 tablespoons butter, melted

TAPENADE

This tangy olive spread from Provence is delicious as an appetizer with crostini—toasted Italian bread rounds—or as a dip with fresh vegetables. As a coating, it's wonderful for broiled or roast lamb. It also adds a lot of flavor to grilled fish or chicken breasts.

Soak the pitted olives and anchovy fillets separately in cold water for 10 minutes or so. Drain and add them to the bowl of a food processor along with the garlic, oregano or marjoram, and pepper. With the motor running, add the oil to make a creamy paste. Once the lamb has been seared, smear the rack with the tapenade and roast and serve as in the Master Recipe (page 480).

30 kalamata or other ripe Greek, Italian, or French olives, rinsed and pitted

6 anchovy fillets, rinsed

2 garlic cloves

1 teaspoon chopped fresh or dried oregano or marjoram

¼ teaspoon freshly ground black pepper

½ cup olive oil

How to Choose a Leg of Lamb

THE LEG IS THE MOST VERSATILE cut of lamb. It is a tender cut, though not as tender as meat from the rib or sirloin. A **whole leg** may weigh 5 to 9 pounds, depending on how much of the sirloin is included and whether it has been cut in America, Australia, or New Zealand.

The leg can be completely boned; it is often sold **butterflied** for grilling or **boneless, rolled, and tied** (or netted) for roasting. This type of roast is perfect for stuffing: just remove the net, fill the cavity left by the bone with a savory dressing, and tie it up again.

Half legs of lamb are also sold: the **shank** end is less meaty and a bit chewy; the **sirloin** end has more meat and is more tender, making it perfect for kebabs or chops. Either makes an ideal roast for a family of four since they usually weigh 3 to 4 pounds. The whole sirloin, in particular, can be cut off the leg, boned, and rolled to make a 2-pound roast, just right for a small family or dinner party. To cook these roasts, follow the directions for whole legs and adjust the cooking times, using internal temperatures as your guide (see the Doneness Chart, page 56). The **short leg**, which has the sirloin and hip bone removed, is also a good choice.

The most economical choice is a full leg of lamb; ask the butcher to cut three or four ¾-to-1¼-inch-thick sirloin chops off the sirloin end. This gives you some nice chops for one meal and the remaining leg to roast for another.

Most leg of lamb dishes are cooked by dry heat; roasting and grilling are the usual methods. Braised leg can also be delicious, though, as in Baked Leg of Lamb *Asadar* (page 494). You can also cut leg of lamb into chunks to use in stews such as Lamb Braised with Fresh Coriander and Fenugreek (page 527) and *Rogan Josh* (Indian Spiced Lamb with Yogurt, page 510).

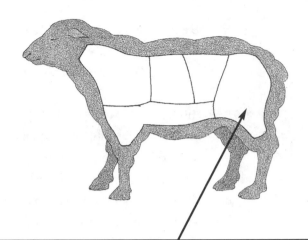

LEG

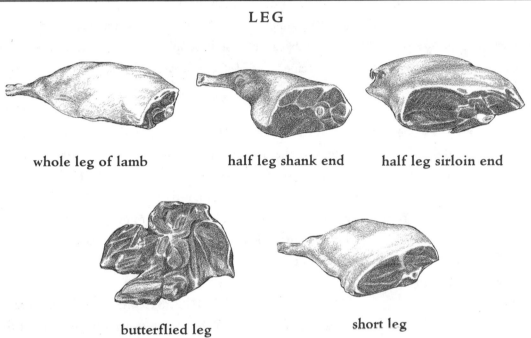

whole leg of lamb   half leg shank end   half leg sirloin end

butterflied leg   short leg

Roast Leg of Lamb

■ Flavor Step ■
MUSTARD-ROSEMARY PASTE FOR LAMB

1 tablespoon olive oil

¼ cup Dijon mustard

1 tablespoon chopped
   fresh rosemary

1 teaspoon kosher salt

½ teaspoon freshly ground
   black pepper

1 tablespoon minced garlic
   OR
   Any of the coatings or
   crusts for lamb on
   pages 482-83

1 6-to-8-pound whole leg
   of lamb, shank intact,
   hip bone removed, OR
   a 5-pound boned and
   rolled leg, OR a short
   leg (about 4 pounds),
   OR a semiboneless
   shank half (about 3½
   pounds)

Serves 6 to 8, with leftovers
■ FIT FOR COMPANY ■ GOOD FOR A CROWD
■ GREAT LEFTOVERS

THERE IS NO MORE FESTIVE DISH than a roast leg of lamb, accompanied by oven-roasted herbed potatoes and barely cooked fresh green beans with garlic and walnut oil. We think Pinot Noir was made to go with lamb—try one from California's Russian River region or a Volnay from the Côte de Beaune in Burgundy. Any of the coatings and crusts for lamb can be used; simply double or triple the recipe. *(See photograph, page 43.)*

■ **Flavor Step** ■ If you're using the mustard-rosemary paste, mix the ingredients in a small bowl and set aside.

Trim most of the visible fat from the lamb. If using a whole leg with the hip bone removed, skewer or sew together the flaps of meat where the bones were removed. Brush the meat with the mustard-rosemary paste or other coating and let it sit for up to 2 hours at room temperature.

Preheat the oven to 350°F. Roast the lamb in the middle of the oven for 1 hour. When the internal temperature of the thickest part reads 115° to 120°F, remove it from the oven if you want beautiful, rosy, rare lamb. A temperature of 130° to 140°F will yield a medium roast. A shank half will take about 1 hour, a whole leg 1¼ to 1½ hours, a boned and rolled leg 1½ to 2 hours, and a short leg 1 to 1¼ hours. All these times are approximate; the most important determinant of doneness is the internal temperature (see the Doneness Chart, page 56).

Let the roast rest for at least 20 minutes, loosely covered with foil, before carving and serving.

Fattoush
(Lebanese Bread and Lamb Salad)

Serves 4 as a main course, 6 as a side dish
■ Cooking on a Budget ■ In a Hurry

THIS HEARTY SALAD is delicious when made with leftover or freshly grilled flank steak with Middle Eastern Rub for Lamb (page 527), but you can use any spicy, leftover beef or lamb.

Fattoush tastes best when made with stale pita bread and very ripe, late summer tomatoes. Traditionally it would use *za'atar*, a Mediterranean herb similar to oregano and marjoram. Middle Eastern grocers sell the herb as well as a spice blend, *zahtar*, which is a mixture of sumac, sesame seeds, and thyme. You can substitute oregano or marjoram for *za'atar* in the salad or leave it out altogether—the salad will still be very tasty.

Preheat the oven to 400°F. Place the pieces of pita on a cookie sheet and toast them in the oven for about 10 minutes, or until they are crisp and light brown. Set aside.

Put the meat, cucumber, tomatoes, onion, bell pepper, parsley, and mint in a large salad bowl. Whisk together the lemon juice, olive oil, garlic, and salt. Whisk in the pepper and optional herbs. Add the toasted pita to the salad and toss with the dressing just before serving. Season with additional black pepper, if desired.

4 stale pita breads, separated and torn into 1-inch pieces

1-1½ pounds leftover cooked lamb or beef, cut into ¼-inch strips

1 English cucumber, seeded and cut into ½-inch pieces

3 large ripe tomatoes, peeled, seeded, and diced

½ cup diced red onion

1 green or red bell pepper, cut into ¼-inch dice

1 cup finely chopped fresh parsley

¼ cup finely chopped fresh mint

¼ cup fresh lemon juice

½ cup olive oil

1 teaspoon minced garlic

1 teaspoon kosher salt

¼ teaspoon freshly ground black pepper

2 teaspoons *za'atar* OR 2 teaspoons chopped fresh oregano or marjoram or 1 teaspoon dried (optional)

Lamb and Caponata Sandwich

CAPONATA

1 medium eggplant (about 1 pound), cut into ¾-inch cubes
   Salt
½ cup extra-virgin olive oil
3 cups thinly sliced onions
2 cups finely chopped celery
½ cup finely chopped carrots
2 tablespoons chopped garlic
⅓ cup red wine vinegar
1 teaspoon sugar
2 large ripe tomatoes, peeled, seeded, and chopped (about 2 cups)
2 tablespoons coarsely chopped drained capers
2 tablespoons chopped fresh basil or 2 teaspoons dried
⅓ cup sliced pimento-stuffed green olives
¼ cup pitted, chopped black olives, such as kalamata or an Italian variety
2 anchovy fillets, finely chopped (optional)
¼ cup chopped fresh parsley
1 teaspoon crushed fennel seeds
   Freshly ground black pepper

Serves 4
■ GREAT LEFTOVERS ■ IN A HURRY

CAPONATA, a sweet-and-sour Sicilian eggplant and tomato dish, makes a great sandwich when combined with lamb on a crusty French or Italian roll or focaccia. Caponata is also delicious when served with hot roast lamb or as part of an Italian buffet. The key to this spicy salad is to make sure the eggplant is sufficiently cooked: it should be quite soft and creamy. Caponata is best after a day or two in the refrigerator.

To make the Caponata: Toss the eggplant cubes with salt so that they are well coated. Let them drain in a colander in the sink for at least 30 minutes. Rinse the salt from the eggplant and pat the cubes dry. Set aside. Heat 3 tablespoons of the oil in a large skillet over medium heat. Add the onions, celery, and carrots. Cover and cook for 10 minutes, stirring occasionally, until the vegetables are soft. Stir in the garlic and cook for 1 minute more. Remove the vegetables from the pan and set aside.

Add ¼ cup of the oil to the skillet. Add the eggplant cubes and fry until they are quite soft, stirring often, for 10 to 15 minutes, adding more olive oil as needed.

While the eggplant is cooking, combine the vinegar, sugar, and tomatoes in a small saucepan. Bring to a boil, then reduce to a simmer, stirring the tomatoes to make a smooth sauce. If it seems too thick, add a little water.

Add the onion mixture to the eggplant and pour in the tomato sauce. Add the capers, basil, both kinds of olives, optional anchovies, parsley, and fennel seeds. Simmer for about 20 minutes, diluting the sauce with a little water if necessary. Taste for salt, pepper, vinegar, and sugar. The sauce should be sweet-and-sour. You can make the caponata up to a week ahead. Cool and refrigerate.

To assemble the sandwiches: Let the caponata come to

room temperature. Split the rolls or focaccia pieces. Cover both sides with the caponata and several thin slices of roast lamb. Garnish with thinly sliced onions and pepperoncini, if you wish. Close the sandwiches and serve.

4   French or Italian rolls
    OR pieces of focaccia
1   pound roast lamb, sliced
    Sliced red onions
    (optional)
    Pepperoncini (optional)

Butterflied Leg of Lamb Tejano Style
(Borrego Tejano)

■ Flavor Step ■

TEJANO MARINADE FOR
LAMB, PORK, OR BEEF

2 tablespoons minced
   garlic

2 teaspoons ground cumin

1 teaspoon cumin seeds

2 teaspoons dried oregano,
   preferably Mexican

2 tablespoons sesame seeds

1 tablespoon pure vanilla
   extract

½ cup fresh lemon juice

2 tablespoons salt

1 teaspoon freshly ground
   black pepper

¼ cup olive oil

1 3-to-4½-pound leg
   of lamb, boned,
   butterflied, and
   trimmed of most
   external fat

Serves 8 or more
■ FIT FOR COMPANY ■ GREAT LEFTOVERS

ANA CANALES grew up on the Texas-Mexico border. Part of her family were fourth-generation sheep ranchers from Bugle Pass, Texas, and the other part came from Piedra Negra, Mexico. The large extended families and many friends often dropped by for impromptu celebrations and outdoor barbecues. With this solid background, Ana became a successful caterer when she moved to the Napa Valley.

One of her favorite dishes from childhood, and now one of the favorites of her clientele, is this marinated leg of lamb, which shows the strong influence of Tejano, or northern Mexican, spicing. For best results, marinate the lamb overnight or, better still, for up to two days in the refrigerator. The marinade is also excellent for lamb, pork, or beef kebabs. Serve it with black or pinto beans, warm tortillas, and an assortment of salads and salsas (see the suggestions for Nogales Steak Tacos, page 102). Have a butcher butterfly the leg of lamb.

■ **Flavor Step** ■ Mix all the marinade ingredients except the oil in a bowl. Briskly stir in the olive oil. Put the lamb, fat side down, in a shallow bowl or baking dish and pour the marinade over it. Cover with plastic wrap, refrigerate, and marinate for up to 2 days. Turn the lamb occasionally.

Build a medium-hot charcoal fire in a covered kettle barbecue or light a covered gas grill (see Grilling, page 63). Remove the lamb from the marinade and shake off any excess. Grill it directly over the coals, with the barbecue covered, turning it frequently. It should take a total of 30 to 35 minutes to get the lamb medium-rare. To be sure, test the lamb in a thick area with an instant-read meat thermometer: it should read 125° to 130°F. This will give you medium-rare meat at the thickest parts and medium at the thinner areas. Let the meat rest for 10 to 15 minutes, loosely covered with foil, before slicing.

BARBECUED MUTTON
AT THE MOONLIGHT CAFE

M Y FRIEND TOM JAMISON and I were spending some time wandering around Murfreesboro, Tennessee, near Nashville, which, as you might know, is great 'cue country. Tom had just moved into an old farmhouse outside town, and I was helping him break in the kitchen by splattering grease around and dripping barbecue sauce on the newly sanded counters. We'd been sampling pulled pork—long-cooked shredded pig meat with hot sauce slathered on—for about a week when we heard about a place in Owensboro, Kentucky, called the Moonlight Cafe that served great barbecued mutton. We had had enough of pork, for that week anyway, so we decided to "get an early start" so that we could have either a late lunch or, if we showed up too late, an early dinner. We figured we could kill an hour or two watching the Ohio River float by if we had to wait for dinner. We had neglected to find out, though, that it's almost 300 miles from Murfreesboro to Owensboro.

Our plan was to get on the road about eight o'clock on a Sunday morning, but what with sampling the local home-smoked bacon and backyard eggs, we didn't get rolling till about ten or so. Tom may be a bit slow starting, but he's no slouch on the road. We soon reached our cruising speed of 75 miles an hour on the winding country roads. After whizzing through tiny hamlets and past many a country store and farmhouse, we arrived at the Moonlight Cafe at exactly 3:01 P.M. The time was significant, since it turned out they don't serve Sunday dinner—only lunch—and they close at 3 P.M. sharp. The doors were locked and the shades were drawn.

We pounded on the door until a kindly looking lady opened it up. She explained that they were closed, but I begged shamelessly, telling her that I had come all the way from California to taste her food. She relented, apologized that the fried chicken was sold out, but opined that they probably had a bit of barbecued mutton left. We said that that would be all right with us, so she ushered us into the biggest buffet I had ever seen. The 30-foot table was still set up with salads (more Jell-O salads than you could ever imagine), hot side dishes like the eternal macaroni and cheese, collard greens, braised cabbage, green beans, black-eyed peas, and creamed corn. And then there were barbecued pork ribs, platters of pulled pork, and a whole mound of barbecued mutton with bowls of smoky sauce on the side. As we headed for the table, I noticed a table of equal size next door filled with desserts.

The mutton was falling off the bone, very smoky and tangy, especially delicious when doused with the spicy sauce. We sampled around, of course, passing up the macaroni and the Jell-O salads. The pork ribs were fantastic, succulent, and sweet in a tomato-y sauce, and we tasted a bit of the pulled pork, just for comparison's sake. We averted our eyes from the dessert table, although Tom whispered longingly, "I think there's pecan pie over there, and peach cobbler and ambrosia cake." I silenced him with an imperious (and somewhat greasy) hand: "Let's not get carried away; we might spoil our dinner."

After a tour of the kitchen, which had a huge smoke oven that could easily handle a whole herd of sheep, and a peek in the walk-in fridge loaded with 150-pound sheep carcasses, we paid the bill. I think it came to less than $15 for us both. We then headed for the Ohio River. We wanted to say we'd been to Ohio, and besides, there was this place I'd heard about that served great barbecued goat. After all, we still had dinner to think about. *B.A.*

Baked Leg of Lamb *Asadar*

■ Flavor Step ■
ASADAR HERB-GARLIC PASTE FOR LAMB OR PORK

- 2 teaspoons chopped fresh rosemary or 1 teaspoon dried
- 1 teaspoon chopped fresh marjoram or ½ teaspoon dried
- 2 tablespoons minced garlic
- 2 tablespoons olive oil
- 2 teaspoons salt
- 1 teaspoon freshly ground black pepper

- 1 large leg of lamb (6 pounds plus) OR a large boned and tied lamb shoulder
- 2 tablespoons olive oil
- 2 cups sliced onions
- 3 bay leaves
  Salt and freshly ground black pepper
- 1 cup water
- ½ cup Spanish or California brandy (optional)

Serves 6 to 8
■ REWARMS WELL ■ FIT FOR COMPANY

WE HAVE FOUND that by roasting a leg of supermarket lamb in a covered roasting pan for five to six hours we can approximate Spanish *asadar* cooking. While the lamb takes a long time to cook, it requires very little preparation. This is just the dish to make on a cold winter Sunday with company coming for dinner. When they arrive, the lamb will be done and the house filled with wonderful aromas. You can make the dish up to a day or so ahead, since it rewarms very well. In Spain, the lamb is served with large white boiled beans and chunks of crisp oven-roasted potatoes and pimentos. Drink an aged Rioja with it, a Châteauneuf du Pape, or one of California's Rhône-style blends.

■ **Flavor Step** ■ Mash all the ingredients together in a bowl to make a dry paste. Trim most of the external fat from the meat. Tie the leg tightly with cotton string every 2 or 3 inches to keep it from falling apart during the long cooking. Rub the paste all over the meat.

Preheat the oven to 250°F. Heat the olive oil in a roasting pan or Dutch oven over medium heat. Strew the onions and bay leaves over the bottom and sprinkle with salt and pepper. Cook, covered, for 5 minutes, stirring occasionally. Add the water and the optional brandy.

Place the lamb on top of the onions. Cover the pot and place it in the middle of the oven. The liquid should remain below a simmer while the lamb bakes; from time to time, check to see if it is simmering—if it is, turn the oven down to 225°F. Every 1½ hours or so, check to see if there is enough liquid in the pot; if not, add some more. Turn the lamb over each time you check.

After 5 hours, carefully remove the lamb from the pot and cover to keep it warm. Skim off any fat from the surface of the sauce and taste it—if it is not intense and rich, transfer it to a saucepan and boil it down a bit. It does not need to thicken. Remove the strings from the lamb and cut it into thick slices or chunks. Serve with the pan sauce on the side.

AFICIONADOS DEL ASADAR

A COUPLE OF MILES NORTH of Madrid, around the city of Segovia, is *asadar* country. *Asadar* is a special way of roasting baby lamb, pig, and, occasionally, goat that has made the region famous among gourmands the world over. The whole animal is seasoned with herbs and garlic and then roasted slowly in a wood-fired brick oven. The secret to the cooking is slow heat and frequent basting with water. When you sit down to the table, you get a pitcher of the local red wine and a quarter of the roasted animal. Since Spanish animals tend to be lean, the shoulder is preferred because it has a higher fat content and juicier meat than the leg. The local *aficionados del asadar* try for the left shoulder, claiming that it is more succulent and tender because the animal always sleeps on the left side.

The lamb is served with a delicious, slightly watery, but intensely flavorful sauce. When we asked the proprietor of the tavern the secret of his sauce, he told us it was made just from the basting water and natural juices from the roasting meat.

Braised Boneless Leg of Lamb with 20 Garlic Cloves

SPINACH STUFFING FOR LAMB (OPTIONAL)

- 1 cup chopped cooked spinach (1 bunch fresh or a 10-ounce package frozen), water squeezed out
- ½ pound ground lamb, beef, or veal
- 1 cup fresh bread crumbs
- ¼ cup minced onion
- ½ teaspoon chopped fresh thyme or ¼ teaspoon dried
- ½ teaspoon chopped fresh rosemary or ¼ teaspoon dried
- 1 teaspoon salt
- ½ teaspoon freshly ground black pepper
- ½ cup freshly grated Parmesan cheese
- 1 large egg, lightly beaten

- 1 3½-to-5-pound boneless leg of lamb, rolled and tied or netted

ALTHOUGH LAMB is quite delicious when cooked so that the meat is lusciously pink and juicy (medium-rare to medium), it can also be braised or roasted with wonderfully succulent results. Because the leg has sufficient fat and sturdy enough muscle, it can still be juicy when cooked long and slowly in moist heat.

You can purchase a boned and rolled whole leg of lamb from your butcher. You can then cook it as is or untie it and spread it with a savory stuffing, our favorite way. If you choose to stuff the lamb, it should be rolled back up and tied, not a difficult task. This dish works equally well with a boned and rolled lamb shoulder, which may require additional cooking time to reach tenderness.

To make the Spinach Stuffing: Combine all the stuffing ingredients in a mixing bowl. Untie and unroll the lamb roast and spread the cut side with the stuffing. Roll the roast back up and tie it in 4 or more places on the short diameter with a couple of loops around the long diameter.

Preheat the oven to 350°F.

■ **Flavor Step** ■ Combine all the ingredients in a bowl and rub the entire mixture over the lamb.

Heat a heavy, lidded casserole or Dutch oven just large enough to hold the lamb over high heat. Add the oil and brown the roast evenly on all sides for a total of 7 to 10 minutes. Remove the lamb and pour off all but 1 tablespoon of fat. Add the onions, carrots, and garlic cloves. Cover the pan, reduce the heat to medium-low, and cook for 10 minutes, stirring occasionally, until the vegetables begin to soften. Put in the rosemary and wine and scrape up any browned bits from the bottom of the pan. Put the lamb back in, seal the pot with foil, and cover it tightly with the lid. Place the pot in the oven and cook for 1½ hours. It should be medium to well-done and quite tender.

Remove the lamb and keep it warm. There should be about 1 cup of highly flavored juices in the pan. Skim off any fat from the surface. Slice the lamb and spoon over the pan juices and garlic.

■ **Flavor Step** ■
Fresh Herb Rub for
Lamb (page 518)

2 tablespoons olive oil
1 cup finely chopped
   onions
½ cup finely chopped
   carrots
20 garlic cloves, peeled
½ teaspoon fresh chopped
   rosemary or ¼ teaspoon
   dried
½ cup white wine

Bulgur and Lamb Salad

2-3 cups cooked bulgur
    wheat

1 cup finely chopped
    fresh parsley

¼ cup finely chopped
    red onion

4 medium tomatoes,
    seeded and diced

3 scallions, thinly sliced

¼ cup chopped fresh mint

1 cup cooked chickpeas
    (garbanzos), cooked,
    dried, or canned

½ cup dried cranberries
    or currants

¼ cup toasted almonds
    (page 121; optional)

⅓ cup extra-virgin olive oil
    About ¼ cup fresh
    lemon juice
    Salt and freshly ground
    black pepper
    Thin slices of leftover
    roast lamb, cut into
    strips

Serves 4
■ MEAT AS A CONDIMENT ■ IN A HURRY

SERVE LEFTOVER BULGUR WHEAT with thin slices of roast lamb on top for an excellent light lunch or first course. You can also use leftover roast beef, veal, or chicken—or leave the meat out altogether.

In a large mixing bowl, combine the bulgur, parsley, onion, tomatoes, scallions, mint, chickpeas, cranberries or currants, and almonds. Toss with the olive oil and lemon juice. Taste for salt, pepper, and lemon juice. Arrange in a serving bowl and top with the lamb.

How to Choose the
Best Cuts for Braised Lamb
and Lamb Stew

WHENEVER YOU SEE A PACKAGE of cut-up meat in the butcher's case labeled "stew meat," pass it by. Usually, it's leftover trimmings that the butcher wants to get rid of. Cut up your own stew meat so you'll know exactly what you're getting.

Our favorite cut for lamb stew is **lamb neck**, usually sold sliced through the bone with meat attached. The meat has plenty of collagen, which softens and dissolves to provide a rich, silky sauce and tender, flavorful meat much like oxtails. But, like oxtails, lamb neck contains a lot of bone, which may put some people off. Lamb neck is quite cheap, but you'll need to buy at least a pound per person because of all the bone.

If you are looking for boneless lamb stew, buy a chunk of **lamb shoulder** sold on the bone as **square-cut lamb shoulder roast** or sometimes as **boneless lamb shoulder roast**. Cut out the areas of fat, gristle, and bone, then cut the meat into 1½-to-3-inch cubes. If you're using bone-in shoulder, it may take a bit of time and effort, but it is well worth it, since the shoulder provides really flavorful stew meat. Cutting up a boneless roast is easier, of course, and you may find a butcher who will cut up a shoulder for you. As with other stews, try not to cut the meat into cubes smaller than 1½ inches, as smaller chunks can fall apart during the long cooking. Remember, meat shrinks while cooking, so the cubes won't seem as big when they're done. Boned shoulder can also be stuffed with a savory dressing and braised.

Some people use meat from the **lamb leg** for stew. This is not only expensive but the meat will not be as moist and full of flavor as the shoulder or neck. The leg is easier to cut up than either shoulder or neck, however, since there's a lot less fat, gristle, and bone to contend with. If you must use leg meat, buy the less tender end, the **shank half roast**.

Lamb shanks are superb for long braises and provide great flavor and meat that becomes soft and succulent after long, moist cooking. They can be braised whole or cut across the bone into 2-inch rounds for any lamb stew.

Middle Eastern Lamb Baked with Eggplant and Tomatoes

■ Flavor Step ■
MIDDLE EASTERN
MARINADE FOR LAMB
OR BEEF

1 teaspoon turmeric

1 teaspoon paprika, preferably Hungarian (hot or mild)

½ teaspoon ground coriander

½ teaspoon ground cumin

¼ teaspoon ground ginger

1 teaspoon minced garlic

2 tablespoons fresh lemon juice

1½ teaspoons salt, preferably kosher

1 teaspoon freshly ground black pepper

2 pounds boneless lamb shoulder, cut into 2-to-3-inch pieces, OR 3 pounds shoulder lamb chops, OR 4 pounds lamb neck, cut into 1-inch slices

6 tablespoons olive oil

Serves 4
■ REWARMS WELL ■ COOKING ON A BUDGET ■ FIT FOR COMPANY

USE SHOULDER LAMB CHOPS or 2-to-3-inch chunks of meat cut from the lamb shoulder for this spicy Middle Eastern dish. If you want to go the budget route, use lamb neck. All three cuts benefit from long, slow cooking, which allows the meat to develop a silky, luscious quality and lets it absorb the exotic spices. Serve over steamed couscous, rice, or bulgur wheat. The dish can be started a day ahead and then refrigerated for finishing off the next day. Serve with *harissa*, the fiery Middle Eastern sauce of hot peppers and vinegar.

■ **Flavor Step** ■ Combine all the marinade ingredients in a bowl to make a thick paste. If it seems too dry, add a few drops of water. Put the meat into another bowl and rub the marinade all over it. Cover and marinate for 2 hours at room temperature or, better still, for 1 or 2 days in the refrigerator.

Preheat the oven to 350°F. Heat a large skillet over high heat and put in 2 tablespoons of the oil. Brown the meat, in batches if necessary so that it is not crowded, for 6 to 7 minutes total. Remove with tongs to a shallow roasting pan or a casserole.

Pour off any fat from the pan. Add the water to the pan and bring to a boil, scraping up any browned bits from the bottom. Pour the liquid into a large bowl and stir in the onions, garlic, ginger, and cinnamon.

Heat the remaining ¼ cup oil in a clean, heavy skillet over high heat and brown the eggplant cubes on all sides. Sprinkle the eggplant with salt and pepper and continue to cook until it begins to soften, stirring often, about 7 minutes. Add the eggplant to the onions along with the tomatoes and lemon juice. Spoon the mixture over the lamb and seal the pan with foil. (You can refrigerate the pan at this point for cooking later or the next day.)

Put the covered pan in the oven and cook for 1 to 2 hours, or until the lamb is quite tender. Neck will take the longest time to cook; lamb chops should take the least time. Transfer the meat to a platter and cover loosely with foil to keep it warm. Remove any grease from the surface of the sauce. If necessary, pour the sauce into a pan and reduce it by boiling it down. It should be fairly liquid and not too concentrated. Taste for salt and pepper.

Put the lamb on a bed of cooked couscous, rice, or bulgur and pour the sauce over. Garnish with lemon wedges and coarsely chopped cilantro or mint and pass *harissa* or another hot sauce, if you like.

½ cup water

2 large onions, thinly sliced

1 tablespoon chopped garlic

Pinch of ground ginger

Pinch of ground cinnamon

1 medium eggplant, cut into 1-inch cubes

Salt and freshly ground black pepper

3 cups peeled, seeded, and chopped vine-ripened tomatoes OR a 28-ounce can Italian-style tomatoes, drained and chopped

2 tablespoons fresh lemon juice

GARNISH

Lemon wedges and chopped fresh cilantro or mint

Harissa (page 505) or other hot sauce (optional)

The Versatile Tagine

I T'S NOT SURPRISING to find that tagines and couscous come from the same region: Morocco and the neighboring North African countries. Savory tagines with meat and fruit and spicy stews ladled over steamed pasta grains or couscous are common at North African banquets, often with a side of fiery *harissa* to heat things up a bit. The word *tagine* refers to the pot that the stew is traditionally cooked and served in—a shallow bowl with straight sides and a tall, conical lid.

Tagines are stews of lamb, beef, or fowl in which the usually unbrowned meat is simmered with exotic spices and water. These stews can then be enhanced with a whole range of vegetables such as carrots, artichoke hearts, squash of various types, pumpkin, cauliflower, root vegetables, or beans. And that's not all: many tagines combine meat with fruits such as lemons, figs, dates, prunes, or apricots. The fruits are usually added in dried form and contribute a savory sweetness to the overall flavor. Often tagines contain preserved or salted lemons, which give the dish a special tang not provided by fresh lemons. Preserved lemons and *harissa* can be purchased from Middle Eastern shops or by mail-order (see Sources, page 584, or see the recipes on pages 505 and 507).

Couscous is the name for both the grainy semolina-based pasta and the stew served over the steamed pasta. The recipes here are for the stews. Couscous (the stew) is very similar to a tagine, but it often contains chickpeas and usually has a wider variety of vegetables. Couscous stews are always served over the steamed grains of pasta, while tagines can be eaten as is or over couscous, bulgur wheat, or steamed rice.

We don't claim that our recipe that follows is particularly authentic. It does, however, represent our variations and adaptations of a range of traditional recipes that we've come across over the years, many of them in the extraordinary writings on Middle Eastern cooking by Claudia Roden and Paula Wolfert.

Moroccan Lemon Tagine

Serves 4 to 6, with leftovers
■ FIT FOR COMPANY ■ GOOD FOR A CROWD
■ REWARMS WELL

MASTER RECIPE

THIS TANGY VERSION uses preserved lemons, but you can use fresh ones if you wish. Serve the tagine over steamed rice, couscous, or bulgur. *(See photograph, page 47.)*

Combine the lamb, onions, garlic, spices, saffron, mint, and cilantro stems in a large, heavy pot or Dutch oven. Add the water and bring to a boil, adding more water if necessary to cover lamb. Reduce the heat to a simmer. Cover the pot and cook for 1 to 1½ hours, or until the lamb is tender.

Add the carrots and fresh lemons, if using them, to the pot, making sure they are covered with liquid (add more water if needed), and cook for 10 minutes more.

Add the preserved lemons, if using them, the lemon juice, olives, and squash and cook, covered, for 10 to 15 minutes more, or until the carrots and squash are tender.

Remove the solids from the pot with a slotted spoon. Arrange the meat and vegetables in a shallow serving dish or a deep platter. Degrease the sauce and boil to reduce it and concentrate the flavors. It should not get too thick, however—it should have a souplike consistency. Taste for salt, pepper, and lemon and adjust if necessary. Pour the sauce over the meat and vegetables. Garnish with cilantro leaves and let your guests heat it up as much as they want with *harissa* or another hot sauce.

3 pounds boneless lean lamb shoulder, cut into 2-inch chunks
1½ cups finely diced onions
1 tablespoon minced garlic
1 tablespoon paprika
1½ teaspoons ground ginger
½ teaspoon ground cumin
½ teaspoon turmeric
1 teaspoon salt, or more to taste
½ teaspoon freshly ground black pepper, or more to taste
Pinch of saffron (optional)
1 teaspoon dried mint
¼ cup chopped fresh cilantro stems (save the leaves for garnish)
1½ cups water
3 carrots, cut into 1½-inch chunks
2 preserved lemons, rinsed and cut into eighths, OR 1 fresh lemon, cut into eighths and seeded
2 tablespoons fresh lemon juice, or more to taste
20 kalamata or mild green olives, well rinsed and pitted
2 cups 1½-inch chunks crookneck squash or yellow zucchini
Harissa (page 505) or other hot sauce

A BERBER'S TENTFUL OF VARIATIONS

YOU CAN VARY THE RECIPES for tagine and couscous in the following ways:

- Add tomatoes, chopped fresh or canned, at the beginning of the cooking or when you add the summer squash.
- Enrich the sauces with a few tablespoons of olive or vegetable oil or butter, added at the beginning of the cooking.
- Add cooked dried beans such as favas, chickpeas (garbanzo beans), or red beans at the beginning of cooking.
- When you add the carrots, put in any or all of the following vegetables, cut into chunks: celery, fennel, potato, sweet potato or yam, cauliflower, artichoke heart, cardoon, turnip, rutabaga, parsnip, celery root, Jerusalem artichokes, bok choy, winter squash of all sorts, quartered onions or whole baby onions, and quartered cabbage.
- Omit the olives from the tagine.
- When you add the summer squash, add to it (or replace the squash with) any combination of: okra, sautéed eggplant, zucchini, pattypan squash, green beans, spinach, chard, bitter greens, fire-roasted peppers and chiles, peas, snow peas, sugar snap peas, fresh fava beans, and runner (pole) beans.
- Add chopped fresh herbs such as oregano, marjoram, thyme, mint, and cilantro toward the end of cooking.
- Garnish the tagine or couscous stew with roasted almonds, walnuts, or sesame seeds, fresh mint leaves or cilantro sprigs, yogurt, crispy fried onions, chopped raw onions, or chopped fresh green chiles.

HARISSA
(NORTH AFRICAN HOT SAUCE)

Makes ⅓ cup

ACTUALLY MORE A PASTE than a sauce, *harissa* is used as a condiment with couscous and other North African and Middle Eastern dishes. You can use the commercial product, sold canned or in jars in specialty groceries, or make your own. Make it as hot as you want (it's usually very hot) by varying the amount of hot paprika and cayenne.

1	tablespoon hot Hungarian paprika
1-2	teaspoons or more cayenne pepper OR
	1 teaspoon or more crushed red pepper flakes
½	teaspoon ground cumin
½	teaspoon ground coriander
½	teaspoon ground fennel seeds
1	teaspoon salt
½	teaspoon freshly ground black pepper
1	tablespoon red wine vinegar or more
2	tablespoons olive oil

In a small bowl, combine the spices and salt and pepper. Dribble in the vinegar to make a paste. Add the olive oil, stirring well, to smooth it out. *Harissa* can be stored, covered, in the refrigerator for up to 2 weeks.

Couscous
(Moroccan Stewed Lamb and Vegetables)

3 pounds boneless lean
    lamb shoulder, cut
    into 2-inch chunks

1½ cups finely diced onions

1 tablespoon minced garlic

1 tablespoon paprika

1½ teaspoons ground ginger

½ teaspoon ground cumin

½ teaspoon turmeric
    About 1 teaspoon salt
    About ½ teaspoon freshly
    ground black pepper
    Pinch of saffron (optional)

1 teaspoon dried mint

¼ cup chopped fresh
    cilantro stems (save the
    leaves for garnish)

3 cups coarsely chopped
    onions

4 cups water

3 carrots, cut into
    1½-inch chunks

2 cups cooked chickpeas
    (garbanzos), homemade
    or canned

3 cups 2-inch chunks
    peeled winter squash,
    such as butternut,
    banana, or acorn

2 cups 1-inch chunks
    peeled turnip

1 cup raisins (optional)
    Pinch of ground
    cinnamon (optional)

2 teaspoons *Harissa*
    (page 505), or other
    hot sauce, or to taste
    (optional)

Serves 8, with leftovers
■ FIT FOR COMPANY ■ GOOD FOR A CROWD
■ REWARMS WELL

THIS SAVORY STEW is a variation on the recipe for Moroccan Lemon Tagine: the ingredients are slightly different. In general, the stew served over couscous uses more vegetables than a tagine and meat is not the main ingredient. Vary this recipe as you will, using beef or chicken instead of lamb and adding or subtracting vegetables. The heat level is also optional: *harissa* or another hot sauce can be used more copiously if you like spicy food or left out altogether if you want a milder stew. The easiest thing is to stir in just a touch of fiery hot sauce and let your guests add more if they wish.

Prepare the stew as in the Master Recipe (page 503). When adding the carrots, add the chickpeas, winter squash, turnips, and the optional raisins, cinnamon, and *harissa* or other hot sauce. The water should just cover the vegetables; add more if necessary. Put the zucchini in the pot when you add the crookneck squash. Simmer the stew for 5 to 10 minutes, until the squash is tender. Taste for more *harissa* or hot sauce and salt and pepper.

Almost all the couscous available in the United States is already cooked or instant. Once you've added the squash to the stew, cook the couscous following the directions on the box.

Spoon the couscous into a large, shallow serving bowl and ladle the stew over it. Pass *harissa* or another hot sauce at the table.

2 cups 2-inch zucchini pieces

2 cups 1½-inch chunks crookneck squash or yellow zucchini

2-3 cups instant couscous

PRESERVED LEMONS
Makes 1 quart

THIS MOROCCAN DELICACY is easy to make and adds an intense lemony flavor to tagines (see page 503). Allow about a week at room temperature for the salt and lemon juice to pickle and preserve the lemons.

8 lemons
1 cup salt
1½-2 cups fresh lemon juice
Olive oil

Wash the lemons well, using plenty of hot water to get rid of any dirt and wax. Dry them well. Cut each lemon into 8 wedges lengthwise. Remove any visible seeds. Put the wedges into a bowl and toss with the salt. Pack them into a 1-quart jar with a glass or plastic lid (metal will rust). Scrape any salt or juice from the bowl into the jar. Cover the lemons with lemon juice, leaving about ½ inch space at the top. Put the lid on loosely and let the jar sit at cool room temperature for a week to pickle. Shake the jar from time to time to redistribute the salt and juices.

After a week at room temperature, add enough olive oil to fill the air space at the top. Cover tightly and refrigerate. The preserved lemons keep well in the refrigerator for up to six months.

Indian Lamb and Lentils

½ teaspoon ground cumin

½ teaspoon ground coriander

2 teaspoons salt

1 teaspoon freshly ground black pepper

2 pounds lean lamb from the leg or shoulder, cut into 1½-inch cubes

Serves 6 to 8
■ REWARMS WELL ■ COOKING ON A BUDGET
■ MEAT AS A CONDIMENT

CERTAIN FOODS SEEM TO HAVE a natural affinity for one another: corned beef and cabbage, hot dogs and sauerkraut, strawberries and cream—and lentils and lamb. The earthy lentils absorb the savory flavors of the lamb perfectly and combine with spices and herbs to create memorable dishes in many different cuisines. Lamb and lentils take to Indian spices wonderfully. This dish is particularly flavorful when made with coconut milk. You can find it in some supermarkets and in Asian grocery stores or by mail-order (see Sources, page 584), but if you can't get coconut milk, you can use chicken stock. The dish will have a slightly different flavor profile but will be equally enjoyable. Another advantage of the lentil and lamb combination is that it's thrifty with meat; with only a little and plenty of flavorful lentils you can feed a crowd easily and cheaply.

This utterly simple and delicious recipe was given to us by our friend Loni Kuhn, a San Francisco cooking teacher. She served it with saffron rice. Small green French lentils are preferable because they hold their shape well during cooking.

■ **Flavor Step** ■ Combine the spices, salt, and pepper in a small bowl. Toss with the lamb on a deep platter or in a shallow bowl until the meat is well coated. You can let it marinate in the spices for up to 2 hours at room temperature or proceed with the recipe directly.

Preheat the oven to 325°F. Put the onions, ginger, garlic, and mint into a blender or food processor and blend to a coarse paste. In a heavy pan or Dutch oven large enough to hold the lamb, heat the oil over high heat. Put in the lamb and brown on all sides, about 3 to 5 minutes. Reduce the heat to medium and add the onion and garlic paste. Stir and continue to cook for about 5 minutes. Stir in the coriander, cumin, and cardamom and cook for 1 minute more. Add the coconut milk or stock, tomato paste, tomato puree, and water, along with the lentils. Stir well and bring to a simmer.

Cover the pan and put it in the middle of the oven to bake for 1 to 1½ hours. Stir two or three times while cooking. Add more water if the lentils seem too dry. The dish is ready when the lentils and meat are quite tender. Taste for salt and pepper. Garnish with the chopped fresh mint and serve.

2 medium onions, coarsely chopped

1 2-inch piece of fresh ginger, peeled

8 garlic cloves

¾ cup fresh mint leaves

2 tablespoons peanut or vegetable oil

1 teaspoon ground coriander

1 teaspoon ground cumin

1 teaspoon ground cardamom

1 14-ounce can unsweetened coconut milk OR chicken stock

2 tablespoons tomato paste mixed with ½ cup water

½ cup tomato puree

1 cup water

1 cup brown, green (French), or red lentils
Salt and freshly ground black pepper

GARNISH
Chopped fresh mint

Rogan Josh
(Indian Spiced Lamb with Yogurt)

■ Flavor Step ■
INDIAN DRY RUB FOR LAMB

1 teaspoon Garam Masala (page 321)
2 teaspoons turmeric
2 teaspoons salt
1 teaspoon freshly ground black pepper

2 pounds boneless lamb from the shoulder or leg, trimmed of fat and cut into 2-inch cubes

SPICES FOR ROASTING

1½ tablespoons coriander seeds
1 tablespoon cumin seeds
2 teaspoons fenugreek or fennel seeds
6 whole cloves
  Seeds from 6 cardamom pods

2 tablespoons vegetable oil or *ghee* (clarified butter)
3 medium onions, thinly sliced
3 tablespoons minced garlic
2 tablespoons minced fresh ginger
1 tablespoon ground dried chiles, OR Hungarian hot paprika, OR paprika with a pinch of cayenne pepper

Serves 4 to 6
■ REWARMS WELL ■ COOKING ON A BUDGET

ROGAN JOSH (or *Ghost*) is often found in Indian restaurants and consists of lamb stewed in spices and yogurt. In our recipe, the yogurt eventually curdles to give the sauce a pleasantly thick consistency. Tomatoes are not classic in the cuisine, but we think they help to sweeten and round out the spiciness of the dish. We suggest using ground dried chiles (ancho or pasilla), available in Latino groceries, or Hungarian hot paprika (see Sources, page 584). If you can't find these, use regular paprika with a pinch or two of cayenne pepper.

■ **Flavor Step** ■ Combine all the rub ingredients in a small bowl. Smear the mixture all over the lamb cubes to coat them thoroughly. You can let the lamb marinate in the spices for up to 2 hours at room temperature or proceed with the recipe immediately.

To prepare the roasting spices: Heat a small, heavy skillet over medium-high heat. Put in the spices and shake the pan and stir until they are fragrant but have not begun to brown, about 3 minutes. Put them into a mortar and pulverize them to a coarse powder or grind them in a spice grinder or an electric coffee grinder reserved for that purpose.

Heat the oil or *ghee* in a deep, heavy pot or Dutch oven over high heat. Put in the lamb and brown it on all sides, about 5 minutes. Remove the lamb and set it aside. Pour off all but about 2 tablespoons of the fat from the pot. Add the onions, garlic, and ginger. Stir well, cover, and reduce the heat to medium. Cook, stirring occasionally, for about 5 minutes.

Add the roasted spices along with the ground chiles or paprika mixture, garam masala, turmeric, and bay leaves. Stir well to coat the onions and cook for 1 minute. Stir in the lamb, yogurt, lemon juice, tomato puree, cilantro stems, and the optional chiles or cayenne. Add the water and bring to a boil.

Reduce the heat to a simmer, cover, and cook for 45 minutes to 1 hour, or until the lamb is completely tender and the sauce is nicely thickened. If the sauce gets too thick, add more water.

Degrease the sauce and remove the bay leaves. If it's not thick enough, remove the solids and boil to reduce. Season with salt and pepper. Serve the meat, vegetables, and sauce with basmati rice and garnish with the chopped cilantro leaves.

2 teaspoons Garam Masala (page 321)
1 teaspoon turmeric
2 bay leaves
1 cup plain low-fat yogurt
2 tablespoons fresh lemon juice
⅓ cup tomato puree
1 10-ounce bunch of cilantro, stems finely chopped, leaves coarsely chopped and kept separate
2 small dried red chiles OR 1 teaspoon cayenne pepper (optional)
1 cup water
Salt and freshly ground black pepper

A LAST-MINUTE LIFT

IN OUR OPINION, no culture has taken lamb cookery to a higher level than those of India and Pakistan. Using a wide range of spices and side dishes, vegetables, and condiments, Indian and Pakistani chefs have created myriad ways to accent the meat's rich flavor. Many of these world-class dishes are lumped together under the title of "lamb curry," one of the world's great lamb stews, which comes in all shapes and forms.

The word *curry* refers to the process of long, slow cooking in a blend of aromatic spices rather than any one particular spice or curry powder. Most Indian cooks blend spices together for each specific dish and wouldn't be caught dead using a prepared curry powder. This blend of aromatic spices is referred to as *masala*, and the most popular type, used to give Indian dishes a last-minute aromatic lift, is garam masala. You can buy the spice blend in paste or powdered form from an Indian or Pakistani grocery or by mail-order (see Sources, page 584) or you can make your own (see page 321).

Curries are best made one or two days ahead and refrigerated to allow the flavors to mellow and any excess fat to congeal for easy removal. They can then be quickly rewarmed and served.

Foil-Baked Lamb Shanks

Flavor Step
PANCETTA AND ROSEMARY PASTE

¼ pound pancetta, chopped

1 tablespoon fresh rosemary leaves

2 teaspoons minced garlic

4 large lamb shanks (4-6 pounds total), trimmed of external fat
Salt and freshly ground black pepper

2 tablespoons olive oil

½ cup dry white wine

1 medium onion, thinly sliced

4 fire-roasted, medium red or green bell peppers (see page 103), unpeeled and left whole

Serves 4
■ FIT FOR COMPANY ■ REWARMS WELL

IN HER SAN FRANCISCO RESTAURANT, Boulevard, Nancy Oakes presents these succulent shanks in a spectacular fashion: still wrapped in foil, draped with a bell pepper, and rising from the center of large, shallow bowls with couscous or soft polenta spread over the bottom. She then gently removes the wrappings and lets the rich juices flow out and swirl through the surrounding pasta or polenta base.

Don't remove the papery skin, or fell, when cooking lamb shanks. It keeps them from falling apart.

Cooking meat in foil seems like one of Mom's cliché recipes from the '50s, but for foods suited to moist cooking, it gives juicy and tasty results, since all the flavors stay locked in the meat during the cooking.

■ **Flavor Step** ■ In a food processor, process all the ingredients to make a paste. Cut gashes across the grain in the meaty part of the lamb shanks and rub the paste into the gashes. Lightly salt and pepper the remaining areas of the shanks.

Preheat the oven to 325°F. Heat the oil in a large, heavy skillet over medium-high heat and brown the shanks on all sides, about 10 minutes total. Remove the shanks. Add the wine and scrape up any browned bits from the bottom of the pan. Cook for about 2 minutes, stirring well. Set the pan sauce aside.

Lay out four 12-inch squares of foil, shiny side up. Sprinkle a quarter of the onion onto the center of each and spoon the pan sauce over it. Cut around the stem of each bell pepper and gently remove it and any attached seeds without tearing the pepper apart (1). Cut a 1-inch slit in the bottom of each bell pepper opposite the stem. Slide a pepper over and down the bone of each shank so that it drapes over the meaty part (2). Place the shank straight up in the center of each piece of foil and pull the foil up around the meat and pepper, twisting it around the bone to seal. Leave some of the bone exposed (3).

Place the shanks in a deep casserole, tall enough to hold them upright. Roast for 2 hours, or until the meat is almost falling from the bone. Serve in shallow bowls with couscous or polenta.

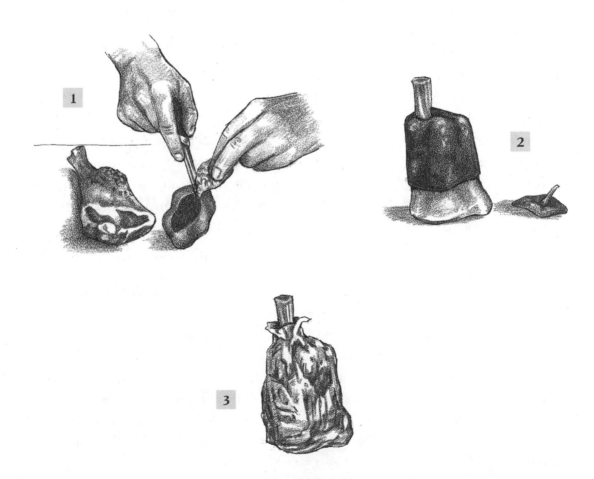

Braised Lamb Shanks with Fennel and Small White Beans

1½ cups small white beans, such as rice beans

4 lamb shanks, trimmed of most external fat (total weight 4-5 pounds)
 Salt and freshly ground black pepper

4 tablespoons olive oil

1 medium fennel bulb (about ¾ pound), cut into small dice

2 carrots, peeled and cut into small dice

2 medium leeks, quartered lengthwise, washed, and sliced

6 large garlic cloves, sliced

4 ounces pancetta, cut into ⅛-by-½-inch strips

1 teaspoon fennel seeds, lightly crushed with a mortar and pestle

4 cups lamb, beef, or chicken stock, preferably homemade

6 large sprigs of fresh thyme or 2 teaspoons dried

2 tablespoons chopped fennel tops

4 large fresh or canned Italian-style tomatoes, peeled, seeded, and diced

Serves 4
■ REWARMS WELL ■ FIT FOR COMPANY ■ COOKING ON A BUDGET

JEFF BERGMAN, who gave us this recipe, oversees the prepared food at Larry's Markets in Seattle. He says, "After long, slow braising in stock, these shanks melt away from the bone. The beans absorb the lamb juices and the delicate flavor of the vegetables." If you want to make eating this dish easier for your guests, remove the meat from the shank bone in large pieces and place them on the beans. Serve with Fennel Gremolata (see opposite page) and a glass of Washington State Merlot from the Yakima Valley.

Rice beans are available from specialty groceries or by mail-order (see Sources, page 584). Rice beans have a nice texture, but if you can't find them, use the smallest white bean you can get and adjust the cooking time accordingly. Remember to start the beans the night before you plan to serve this dish. *(See the photograph on the cover.)*

The night before you cook the lamb shanks, wash and pick over the beans, cover them with cold water, and soak them overnight. Season the shanks with salt and pepper. In an 8-to-10-quart Dutch oven or casserole with a tight lid, heat 2 tablespoons of the olive oil over medium-high heat. Put in the shanks and cook for 10 minutes, turning them frequently. The shanks should be well browned on all sides. Remove them to a platter. Discard all the fat from the pan.

Add the remaining 2 tablespoons olive oil to the pan, heat until lightly smoking, and stir in the fennel, carrots, leeks, garlic, pancetta, and fennel seeds. Cover and cook over medium heat, stirring well to scrape up any browned bits from the bottom of the pan. Continue to cook until the vegetables are lightly brown and translucent, 10 to 12 minutes. Drain and rinse the beans and stir them into the pot with the vegetables. Add the stock, thyme, fennel tops, and diced tomatoes. Bring to a boil, stirring well. Set the browned shanks on top of the beans and reduce the heat to a gentle simmer. Cover and simmer undisturbed for 1 hour 15 minutes. At this stage the meat should have shrunk away from the bones and be very tender.

Remove the lamb shanks to a large, ovenproof platter. Cover the shanks with foil and keep warm in a 200°F oven. Taste the beans—they should be tender but still firm. Cook longer, if needed. Adjust the salt, pepper, and seasonings. Check the liquid in the pan—if it's too brothy, raise the heat and cook it down slightly. Spoon the beans and the cooking liquid onto 4 large, warm plates, remove the shanks from the oven, and place 1 shank on top of the beans on each plate. Garnish liberally with the Fennel Gremolata, and place a small dish of gremolata on the table for guests to add to taste.

Fennel Gremolata (recipe follows)

FENNEL GREMOLATA

Makes ¼ cup

THIS SAVORY GARNISH can also be used on grilled chicken and fish or sprinkled over pasta in place of grated Parmesan cheese.

1 tablespoon minced fennel tops
2 tablespoons chopped flat-leaf parsley
Zest of 1 lemon, chopped
1 large garlic clove, minced

Combine all the ingredients in a small bowl. The gremolata will keep for 2 to 4 hours refrigerated.

Lamb Shanks Osso Buco

■ **Flavor Step** ■
Herb Rub for Pork,
Lamb, or Beef
(page 263)

4-6 large lamb shanks,
    trimmed of fat and
    sawed into 2-inch-
    thick slices
2 tablespoons olive oil

BRAISING SAUCE
1 ounce prosciutto,
    chopped (about ¼ cup)
2 medium onions,
    thinly sliced
1 carrot, finely chopped
2 tablespoons minced
    garlic
1 cup dry white wine
1½ cups peeled, seeded, and
    diced fresh tomatoes or
    seeded and diced
    canned tomatoes
2 cups lamb, beef, or
    chicken stock
2-3 small strips of lemon
    peel
1 bay leaf
1 teaspoon chopped fresh
    rosemary or ½
    teaspoon dried
1 teaspoon chopped fresh
    thyme or oregano
    or ½ teaspoon dried
    Salt and freshly ground
    black pepper
    Basil Gremolata
    (recipe follows)

Serves 4 to 6
■ **REWARMS WELL** ■ **MOM'S COMFORT FOOD**
■ **TWO FOR ONE**

IN ITALY, VEAL SHANK, or osso buco, is traditionally served with risotto. For a special treat, serve these savory lamb shanks with bulgur wheat cooked with lots of onions. You'll want to cook the shanks until the meat is falling from the bone and takes on a soft, silky texture. Instead of the traditional gremolata garnish—grated lemon zest, parsley, and garlic—try the variation on the next page, which mixes lemon zest, garlic, fresh basil, and black pepper. Serve the shanks on a bed of risotto, steamed rice, or bulgur wheat with a Pinot Noir from Oregon or a Chianti Classico from Tuscany.

■ **Flavor Step** ■ Rub the herb mixture generously over the shanks.

Preheat the oven to 325°F. In a large skillet or a Dutch oven, heat the oil over high heat. Add the shanks and brown them on all sides, turning often, 5 to 7 minutes. Remove the meat and set it aside.

To make the Braising Sauce: Pour off all but 2 tablespoons of fat from the pan. Turn the heat down to medium, add the prosciutto, onions, and carrot, cover, and cook for 10 minutes, stirring often, until the vegetables are quite soft. Put in the garlic and cook for 1 minute more. Add the wine, tomatoes, and stock and bring to a boil. Put in the lemon peel, bay leaf, rosemary, thyme or oregano, and the shanks.

Cover the pot and put it in the center of the oven. Bake for 1½ to 2 hours, or until the meat is quite tender, turning it from time to time during cooking. Remove the shanks and cover them loosely to keep warm. Degrease the sauce and discard the bay leaves and lemon peel. Reduce the sauce by half over high heat. Taste for salt and pepper.

Sprinkle the gremolata generously over the top and serve.

BASIL GREMOLATA

Makes 3 tablespoons

THIS SAVORY GARNISH can also be used on grilled chicken and fish or sprinkled over pasta in place of grated Parmesan cheese.

    2   teaspoons chopped lemon zest
    ½   teaspoon chopped garlic
    2   tablespoons chopped fresh basil
    ½   teaspoon freshly ground black pepper
        Pinch of salt

Finely chop all the ingredients together by hand or in a food processor. The gremolata will keep for 2 to 4 hours refrigerated.

Ale-Basted Stuffed Lamb Shoulder

■ **Flavor Step** ■

FRESH HERB RUB FOR LAMB

1   tablespoon chopped
    fresh oregano,
    rosemary, sage, savory,
    basil, or tarragon
2   teaspoons salt
½   teaspoon freshly ground
    black pepper

SAUSAGE, LEEK, AND ONION STUFFING

1   tablespoon olive oil
2   mild Italian sausages,
     removed from casings
1½   cups chopped leeks
     (white parts only)
¾   cup chopped onions
1   tablespoon chopped
     garlic
1   cup diced dry bread
½   teaspoon dried sage
1   large egg, lightly beaten
     Salt and freshly ground
     black pepper

■ REWARMS WELL ■ MOM'S COMFORT FOOD ■ COOKING ON A BUDGET

THIS SLIGHTLY CHEWY CUT is roasted uncovered on a bed of aromatic vegetables infused with ale, which serves as a basting sauce. The ale provides a moist environment: the oven will fill with steam from the evaporating liquid, tenderizing the meat nicely during the long cooking. Frequent basting with the savory pan juices gives the roast a delicious flavor and creates a browned crust that it wouldn't get if the pot were covered. You can also use this technique with beef rump, chuck, and bottom round. Instead of ale, you can use wine or stock. Accompany this dish with some of the ale you used in the pan sauce.

The sausage, leek, and onion stuffing is hearty and substantial and will also work as a stuffing for fresh pork, veal, or poultry.

─────────────

■ **Flavor Step** ■ Mix the herbs, salt, and pepper in a small bowl. Set aside while you make the stuffing.

To make the Sausage, Leek, and Onion Stuffing: In a large skillet, heat the oil over medium heat. Put in the sausage and fry for about 5 minutes, breaking it apart with a fork as it browns. Add the leeks, onions, and garlic, cover the pan, and cook for 10 more minutes, stirring from time to time, until the vegetables are tender. Spoon the meat and vegetable mixture and any liquid into a large bowl, stir in the bread cubes, sage, and egg, and mix well. The dressing should be slightly moist, not sopping wet. Add a little water if it seems too dry. Taste for salt and pepper and refrigerate to cool the mixture. (The stuffing can be made a day ahead and refrigerated, but *do not stuff the meat a day ahead*, as spoilage could easily occur.)

Preheat the oven to 425°F. Spread the lamb shoulder out flat on a clean surface, cut side up.

Place the stuffing in the pocket and any crevices left by the bones, roll the roast around the stuffing to form a cylinder, and tie in four or five places and around the ends. Rub the outside of the roast with the herb rub.

Scatter the leeks, carrots, onions, and garlic cloves over the bottom of a shallow roasting pan. Put the meat on top and roast in the hot oven for 15 minutes to brown.

Turn the oven down to 325°F. Add the bay leaf, ale, stock, and Worcestershire sauce and spoon over the meat. Stir in the mustard. There should be about ¼ inch of liquid in the bottom of the pan at all times. If not, add more ale and/or stock as needed. Roast, uncovered, basting with the pan juices every 20 or 30 minutes or so.

After 2 hours, check the internal temperature of the roast: when it reaches 150° to 155°F, remove the meat and keep it covered loosely with foil while you finish the sauce. Let the roast rest for at least 10 minutes before carving.

You may strain the sauce and discard the vegetables or leave them in the sauce. Remove and discard the bay leaf. Degrease the sauce and taste it. It should have an intense, delicious flavor. If not, boil it over high heat to reduce it slightly and concentrate the flavors. Taste for salt and pepper and adjust the seasonings as needed.

Cut away the string and slice the meat into ½-to-¾-inch-thick slices. Arrange the slices, with stuffing enclosed, on a platter and pour the pan sauce, and the vegetables if you saved them, over the meat.

1 boneless lamb shoulder (4-6 pounds), removed from netting or string, trimmed of most external fat

1 cup split and thinly sliced well-washed leeks (white parts only)

½ cup diced carrots

½ cup thinly sliced onions

3 garlic cloves

1 bay leaf

½ 12-ounce bottle of ale, or more if needed

½ cup beef or chicken stock, or more if needed

2 teaspoons Worcestershire sauce

1 tablespoon coarse-grained mustard

Salt and freshly ground black pepper

Baked Pasta with Lamb

¾ pound pasta of choice

½ pound low-fat ricotta

2 cups chopped cooked
  Swiss chard or spinach
  (optional)

2 leftover lamb shanks,
  meat removed from
  bones and chopped
  (1½-2 cups)

1-2 cups sauce left over from
  Lamb Shanks Osso
  Buco (page 516) or
  other lamb recipe
  Olive oil

¾ cup freshly grated
  Romano, pecorino,
  or Parmesan cheese

Serves 4
■ COOKING ON A BUDGET ■ REWARMS WELL

I
F YOU HAVE A COUPLE OF LAMB SHANKS
left over from Lamb Shanks Osso Buco (page
516) or Braised Lamb Shanks with Fennel and
Small White Beans (page 514) and 1 to 2 cups
of sauce, they can easily be turned into a delicious baked pasta. You can also use leftover
roasted leg or shoulder of lamb with gravy in
this versatile dish. A large pasta such as penne,
ziti, bow-ties, rigatoni, fusilli, or elbow macaroni
works best. You can put the pasta, meat, and
sauce together ahead of time, refrigerate it,
then bake it just before serving. Leftover pasta
can be reheated in the oven.

Cook the pasta in a large pot of boiling salted water until
al dente, following the instructions on the package. Drain
and put the pasta into a large mixing bowl while still hot. Stir
in the ricotta, optional greens, meat, and sauce. The ricotta
can be in clumps.

Preheat the oven to 350°F.

Oil a 2-to-3-quart baking dish or ovenproof casserole and
spoon in the pasta mixture. Sprinkle the grated cheese on top.
Bake for 20 to 30 minutes, uncovered, until the cheese is bubbly. Pasta cooked directly from the refrigerator will take 5 to
10 minutes more to heat through. For a crisp top, brown
under the broiler for 2 to 3 minutes. Serve hot.

Overlooked but Delicious Cuts

CULTURES THAT REALLY LOVE LAMB, such as Middle Eastern, North African, Greek, and Indian, cut up the breast and lamb ribs for stew. They don't mind the fatty character of the meat because it is so full of flavor.

Lamb breast includes the spareribs and some meat above the ribs. One of the cheapest cuts on the animal, it can be boned, stuffed, and braised in a spice-laden broth. The breast is particularly delicious when stuffed with rice and dried fruits. When braising lamb breast, it's best to make the dish ahead of time and refrigerate it so that you can remove the congealed fat before serving. The **spareribs**, or **riblets**, from the breast can be grilled or broiled and go well with a tomato-based barbecue sauce. The lamb ribs can be substituted for baby back ribs and spareribs in any of our recipes, although the cooking times should be reduced.

Lamb neck is cheap and bony, but like oxtails, it makes great stew and exquisite curry. It's best to cook these dishes a day ahead and refrigerate them to remove any congealed fat.

Lamb tongues are quite tasty. They don't take as long to cook as beef tongues and end up extremely tender. They are delicious warm or sliced and served cold.

THE HOTEL BASQUE GREAT LAMB STEW
But Watch Out for *Maman!*

THE WESTERN SHEEP INDUSTRY was created by the labor and hardiness of Basque sheepherders, who endured lonely and sometimes dangerous conditions to protect and nurture huge herds of sheep in a rough landscape. From the late nineteenth century to the present day, Basque immigrants have lived with their sheep for months on end, protecting them against predators and the elements with only the companionship of a faithful sheepdog and lots and lots of woolybacks.

So naturally, when Basque sheepherders arrived in the big city (or anyplace at all, for that matter), they needed somewhere to celebrate with good food and wine and to enjoy some human company. Old-fashioned Basque hotels and restaurants can still be found throughout the West—in San Francisco and Elko, Reno and Winnemucca, Fresno and Los Baños—where you can sit down to huge, multicourse meals with lots of hearty red wine for very little money. You'll most likely be served at communal tables filled with friendly folk who like to eat and drink and sometimes sing and tell stories in a lively mixture of English, Spanish, French, and even Uskera, or Basque, an ancient language with no connection to any other tongue.

One of these gathering places was the Hotel Basque in San Francisco, where they served huge amounts of delicious food for many years to a sometimes raucous mix of sheepherders, college students, hungry bohemians, and occasional bewildered tourists. I was a frequent visitor in my college days, since the food was great and plentiful and cheap and I got to practice my newly learned French (I was just back from Quebec) with the lads at the bar and the pretty waitresses who served the long tables.

One night, however, I made a big mistake that got me barred from this gastronomic and romantic heaven forevermore: I tried to speak Basque. A friend who hailed from Elko, Nevada, where Basques make up a large part of the population, had taught me a few words of the ancient language—phrases that my good pal said were friendly greetings such as, "Howdy, how are things going?" or "How have you been lately, old friend?" I practiced them assiduously so I could impress the pretty waitresses.

On the fateful night, after lubricating my tongue with wine, I tried out my Basque. I started by asking the loveliest waitress, with pale skin, raven hair, and dark eyes, if she was *uzkaldi*, or Basque. She was charmed, to say the least, that I knew at least one Basque word and asked me if I knew any more.

Encouraged, I bellowed out my carefully practiced Basque phrases. The room grew suddenly silent: the waitress dropped her platter to the floor, threw her apron over her face, and ran toward the kitchen, crying out, *"Maman!"* This was not the reaction I was looking for.

Several big men in berets who looked like her brothers or cousins advanced toward me from the bar. I was looking for the exits when suddenly, with a loud cry of Gallic rage, a formidable woman in a flowered apron with a large cleaver in her hand burst from the kitchen. "Who has said those words of infamy?" she cried in French (it loses something in the translation). *"C'est moi,"* I croaked, searching for the French words to explain the infamous Basque words and not finding an answer in any language.

As Maman and the growing crowd of enraged Uzkaldis advanced, I retreated and soon found myself moving rapidly out the door onto the sidewalk, which soon filled up with angry Basques yelling, "And don't ever come back!" in as many languages as I could understand.

To this day, I have never learned what those words meant. I have met many Basques since then and dined often at Basque restaurants (but never again the Hotel Basque, alas). But I have never had the courage to ask, and besides, I just couldn't repeat the infamous words—I didn't want to be exiled from Basque food ever again.

Here is a recipe that gives the flavor of the spicy and delicious lamb stew that was a specialty at the Hotel Basque. I didn't get it from Maman, of course, but from other Basque cooks with whom I carefully spoke only English.   *D.K.*

Basque Sheepherders' Lamb Stew

■ **Flavor Step** ■
BASQUE CHILE AND
HERB RUB FOR LAMB

1   teaspoon chile powder,
       preferably Gebhardt
1   tablespoon paprika,
       preferably sweet
       Hungarian
1   teaspoon dried oregano
       or thyme
2   teaspoons salt
¼   teaspoon freshly ground
       black pepper

3-4   pounds lamb stew meat
        from the neck,
        shoulder, or leg, with
        or without bones, cut
        into 2-inch pieces
1   fire-roasted red bell
        pepper (see page 103)
        OR 2 canned or bottled
        red peppers or pimentos
2   tablespoons red wine
        vinegar
2   tablespoons olive oil
1   medium onion, chopped
6   garlic cloves, chopped
1   fire-roasted mild green
        chile, such as Anaheim
        (see page 103),
        chopped, OR ¼ cup
        chopped canned green
        chiles
2   bay leaves
        About 1 cup red wine
        About 1 cup beef stock
        Salt and freshly ground
        black pepper

■ REWARMS WELL ■ COOKING ON A BUDGET

SERVE THIS SPICY STEW with Oven-Roasted Potatoes (page 126) and a hearty red wine such as California Zinfandel.

———

■ **Flavor Step** ■ Mix the rub ingredients in a small bowl. Put the meat in a zipper-lock bag or a bowl, add the rub, and toss to coat thoroughly. Marinate the meat for up to 2 hours at room temperature or overnight, covered if necessary, in the refrigerator. If the meat has been refrigerated, bring it to room temperature before cooking.

In a blender or food processor, blend the red pepper and vinegar to a puree. Set aside.

In a large skillet or heavy pot, heat the olive oil over medium-high heat. Brown the lamb on all sides, stirring often, about 10 minutes. Remove the lamb and pour off all but about 2 tablespoons of the fat from the pan. Reduce the heat to medium and sauté the onion, garlic, and green chile, stirring often, for about 5 minutes. Add the lamb, the pureed red peppers, the bay leaves, wine, and stock, reduce the heat to a simmer, and cook, uncovered, for about 1½ hours, or until the meat is tender. Stir once in a while and add more wine or stock if necessary; the liquid should barely cover the meat.

Remove the meat with a slotted spoon and set aside. Degrease the sauce and reduce it over high heat to thicken slightly. It can still be a bit on the soupy side. Remove and discard the bay leaves. Taste for salt and pepper. Return the meat to the pan to warm through, and serve.

Joe Nouhan's Warm Lamb Salad

Serves 4 to 6
■ REWARMS WELL ■ FIT FOR COMPANY

DETROIT HAS THE LARGEST Arab-American community in the United States. Joe Nouhan, former executive chef of the Bay Wolf Restaurant in Oakland, California, grew up in Detroit and learned how to cook from his parents, who prepared meals for a large family. They made this delicious salad from lamb tongues when they were available. Boneless lamb shoulder, well trimmed of fat and cooked until very tender, can be used instead. Although hard to find, lamb tongues are well worth the effort. They have a soft, silky texture and mild flavor that blend well with the lemon in this dish. Serve this tangy salad as a first course or lunch main dish with pita bread.

1 pound lamb tongues
   OR a 1-pound piece
   of lean, boneless lamb
   shoulder, trimmed
   of all fat
1 medium onion,
   unpeeled, split in half
2 bay leaves
6 garlic cloves, unpeeled
1 carrot, unpeeled, cut in
   half lengthwise
½ teaspoon dried thyme
½ teaspoon coriander seeds
½ teaspoon cumin seeds
2 teaspoons salt
1 teaspoon freshly ground
   black pepper
3 cups water or chicken
   stock

To prepare the lamb: Wash the meat and place in a large kettle with the remaining ingredients. Bring to a boil, reduce to a simmer, and cover. Simmer lamb tongues for 2 to 3 hours, shoulder for 1½ to 2 hours, or until the meat is quite tender. Remove the meat, discard the vegetables, and let the meat cool, covered, in the stock. Save the stock for soup.

When the tongues are cool enough to handle, make a long slit starting from the base. With your fingers, peel away the skin. Or trim the shoulder of any fat or gristle.

Cut the meat into ¼-inch-thick slices and reserve.

SALAD DRESSING

3 tablespoons fresh lemon
  juice
3 tablespoons extra-virgin
  olive oil
1 garlic clove, crushed
½ teaspoon salt
¼ teaspoon freshly ground
  black pepper

3 cups cubed, cooked red
  potatoes
½ cup chopped flat-leaf
  parsley, packed
4 green onions or
  scallions, finely
  chopped
  Salt and freshly ground
  black pepper

To make the Salad Dressing: Whisk all the ingredients together in a bowl or pulse briefly in a food processor.

To assemble the salad: Gently toss the meat, potatoes, parsley, and green onions with the dressing, preferably while the lamb and potatoes are still slightly warm. Add salt and pepper to taste. Serve at once.

Note: *You can also make the dish ahead of time, refrigerate it, and place the meat and salad in the microwave to get warm, not hot, just before serving.*

Lamb Braised with Fresh Coriander and Fenugreek

Serves 4 to 6
■ COOKING ON A BUDGET ■ REWARMS WELL ■
■ GREAT LEFTOVERS ■

I WAS FIRST SERVED THIS DISH in London at the home of a gifted Middle Eastern cook and food writer, Sami Zabaida. He made it with lamb tongues, and although I still prefer the tongues with their silky texture for this dish, they are often hard to find. Chunks of boneless lamb shoulder make a more than adequate substitute. Serve the lamb over cooked basmati rice flavored with chopped fresh dill. Try a red wine from Greece such as Vin Noir de Naoussa or Château Musar from Lebanon for an authentic and delicious accompaniment. A medium-bodied California Merlot would also be very nice.

B.A.

■ **Flavor Step** ■ Combine the seasonings and sprinkle generously over all the surfaces of the meat.

If using lamb shoulder, heat the oil over medium-high heat in a Dutch oven or a heavy, high-sided skillet with a lid. Add the shoulder and brown on all sides for 5 to 7 minutes. Remove and reserve the meat, leaving about 2 tablespoons of oil in the pot. Add the carrots and onion along with a pinch of salt and pepper. Cover and cook over medium heat until the vegetables are soft, about 10 minutes, stirring occasionally and scraping up any bits from the bottom of the pot. Stir in the garlic and fenugreek and cook 1 minute more.

■ **Flavor Step** ■
MIDDLE EASTERN RUB
FOR LAMB
(for lamb shoulder only)

½ teaspoon ground coriander

1 teaspoon salt

½ teaspoon freshly ground black pepper

2 pounds lamb tongues, cooked and peeled (page 525), cut into 1-inch cubes, OR 2 pounds boneless lamb shoulder, fat removed, cut into 2-inch cubes

2 tablespoons olive oil

3 carrots, cut into ½-inch chunks

1 medium onion, thinly sliced
Salt and freshly ground black pepper

4 garlic cloves, finely chopped

1 teaspoon ground fenugreek or 6-8 dried fenugreek leaves, crumbled, OR a mixture of ½ teaspoon each dried coriander, cumin, and cardamom

2 bunches cilantro (about
   8 ounces each), stems
   finely chopped, leaves
   coarsely chopped and
   kept separate
1 cup water

Put the shoulder or lamb tongues in the pot with all the cilantro stems and about two-thirds of the leaves along with the water. Bring to a boil, reduce to a simmer, cover, and cook slowly for ½ hour, if using cooked lamb tongues, or 1½ hours if using shoulder, until the lamb is quite tender. Add more water if needed. Taste for salt and pepper.

Garnish with the remaining chopped cilantro leaves.

Note: *Use any leftovers as a filling for flour tortillas or pita bread; garnish with yogurt and Lime-Pickled Red Onions (page 104). You can also make a simple biriani, or Indian rice dish, by combining leftover meat and rice in a buttered casserole and heating. Garnish with toasted almonds and raisins.*

· Veal ·

A Tender Delicacy

IT'S A SHAME THAT VEAL, meat from calves slaughtered at about four months or less, has never been as popular in America as in Europe. Veal's mild character combines well with intense flavors in sauces, and its delicate taste provides a nice contrast with herbs and spices. Because of their high collagen content, tough cuts such as shank, shoulder, and breast provide a fine base for stews and other braised dishes; no other meat develops such a silky texture. And from a nutritional point of view, veal is one of the leanest meats you can buy. The many delicious ways it can be prepared should motivate cooks to give it another try. You can do almost anything with veal: grill it, roast it, sauté it, braise it.

Italian cooks are the masters of veal cookery today, and Italians eat by far the most veal, consuming over 15 pounds per capita a year compared to about 1 pound per capita in America and only a little over 2 pounds per capita in England. Italians love veal for its mild character, which goes so well with the sauces that the country's cooks are known for. As Waverly Root says in *The Food of Italy:*

> Most persons think of the French as the great sauce makers; but it was Italians who first developed this art. . . . In France, a sauce is an adornment, even a disguise, added to a dish more or less as an afterthought. In Italy, it is *the dish,* its soul, its raison d'être, the element which gives it character and flavor. The most widespread Italian foods are bland, neutral; they would produce little impact on the tastebuds unassisted. . . . Even the favorite meat of Italy is the most neutral of all—veal.

HUMANE VEAL

MANY AMERICANS OBJECT TO VEAL on moral grounds, since milk- or formula-fed calves are confined to stalls throughout their brief life. If the thought of stall-raised veal bothers you, choose grass-fed or range-fed veal from animals that are allowed to roam. You can usually recognize this meat by its reddish, rather than pale pink, color. Grass-fed veal has a more pronounced flavor than the blander milk- or formula-fed veal, and many prefer it for its "meaty," slightly chewier character.

Veal scallopini is a good example. Thin slices of tender veal are quickly sautéed, then a pan sauce provides the signature of the dish: lemons and capers for *piccata,* mushrooms and Marsala for *alla Marsala,* meat and tomatoes for *bolognese.* One of the most popular veal dishes in the world is osso buco. The meat is tasty, yes, but what we really love about it is spooning up the velvety, luscious sauce, mixing risotto into it, and rubbing the plate clean with the last bit of crusty bread.

Other countries, especially Austria and Germany, have taken veal cookery to great heights. Their famous Wiener schnitzel is a thin slice of veal, pounded even thinner (you're supposed to be able to read a newspaper through the meat), encased in a savory coating and fried quickly to crisp succulence. But this is just the start: Viennese and German chefs surround the schnitzel with garnishes and sauces that create a whole menu: *Kaiserschnitzel,* with a sauce of sour cream, lemon, and capers; *Paradies schnitzel,* with tomato sauce; and *Holsteinerschnitzel,* with fried eggs and anchovies. Try Veal Chops Milanese (page 544) for an Italian-accented version of this classic preparation.

French chefs have created their own classics: *blanquette de veau,* pale veal simmered with mushrooms and onions; *noisettes de veau,* tender morsels of veal fillet with savory sauces; *paupiettes de veau,* thin scallops with savory stuffings; and *tête de veau*—calf's head simmered in stock, boned, and served cold in its own jelly as an appetizer. Veal's gelatinous quality is one of the reasons it makes such fine sauces.

Veal is showing up more and more in American restaurants and increasingly on the home table. Grilled veal chop, usually seasoned with fresh sage and cooked medium-rare, is a popular restaurant dish, and osso buco, with its rich sauce and robust flavors, is a sell-out on many menus.

The History of an Elite Meat

VEAL HAS BEEN A LUXURY ITEM ever since the Sumerians first penned up and subdued the wild cattle that roamed the plains of Mesopotamia. In early times, cattle were valued mainly for milk and as draft animals. When their milking or working days were over, older cattle were slaughtered for their tough, stringy meat, often consumed at religious or other village festivals. But the tender meat of the calves was reserved for those who could afford to sacrifice a valuable worker to satisfy their taste buds. Nobles and priests ate veal and drank wine (another luxury product—the peasants drank beer) at the elaborate banquets portrayed in great detail on mosaics and bas-relief sculptures.

The taste for the tender meat of young animals was passed on to the Romans, whose gourmandizing reached the point where the Emperor Alexander Severus had to issue a decree forbidding the slaughter of young animals—suckling pigs, lambs, calves—since the herds were being deprived of breeding stock. Roman chefs prized veal for its ability to take well to complex sauces. One recipe in Apicius' *De Re Coquinaria* includes "pepper, lovage, caraway, celery seed, cumin, oregano, onions, honey, vinegar, wine, broth, oil, and reduced must." This dish, *Vitellina Fricata,* or fried veal steak, while a bit on the fussy side, could fit into a modern Italian chef's scallopini repertoire with few changes.

Nutritional Profile

OF ALL THE RED MEATS, veal is the leanest. A three-ounce cooked portion of veal has slightly less fat than a boneless, skinless chicken breast. A serving of veal also has 10 percent fewer calories (128 vs. 140) than chicken breast and about the same amount of saturated fat (1.04 g vs. 0.86 g).

MYTHBUSTING

THE YOUNGEST IS NOT THE BEST

MANY MISTAKENLY BELIEVE that the youngest veal is the best; they assume that very young animals will have extremely tender and juicy meat. But the opposite is true: very young calves, sold as "bob veal" by some butchers, should be avoided. The veal is so bland as to be almost tasteless, and the meat has a soft but chewy texture that we find unpleasant. Even the cuts from the loin and rib become chewy and dry when grilled or broiled. You can braise the tougher cuts of "bob veal" such as shank, breast, or shoulder, but we prefer to use meat from older animals in any recipe.

"Bob veal," which is usually sold bone-in, is often labeled as such in the butcher case and can be significantly cheaper than other veal. You can usually recognize it by the small size of the cuts (tiny chops, for example) and by its very pale, anemic-looking meat.

What Matters Most in Buying Veal

AGE AND DIET both affect the appearance and quality of veal. The meat industry's distinction between "veal" and "calf" is based on feed: pale veal is fed a special formula, reddish calf is grass-fed. Typically, veal comes from calves less than four months old, while calf meat is from older animals, whose meat is darker. Formula-fed veal is easy to find; range-fed may take a little searching out.

Formula-fed veal has pale pink flesh and creamy white fat and should come from animals less than four months old. Formula-fed, or Provimi (see page 535), veal carcasses, although still from animals less than four months old, are quite large, coming to market at about 350 pounds. Grass- or range-fed calves are somewhat smaller, with reddish-gray to red meat and yellowish fat. The animal has been allowed to graze and has had more muscular activity.

Frequently you will find meat labeled "bob veal." This is meat from very young (less than a few weeks old) or newly born calves. Cuts will be quite small, and the meat has little or no taste. We don't recommend it.

A Quick Anatomy Lesson
for the Busy Cook

WHOLE VEAL CARCASSES can vary considerably in size—from less than 80 pounds for very young "bob veal" to the large 350-pound-plus animal produced by the Dutch-formula feeding process (Provimi). Most range-fed animals will fall somewhere in between. Thus the size of individual cuts can vary considerably and cause confusion.

The veal carcass is divided into six large primal cuts. The **shoulder** is good for roasts, stews, and blade chops. The **front leg** yields veal shank, or osso buco. From the **rib** and **loin** areas come the best chops, roasts, and scallopini. The **breast** is often stuffed and braised. The **leg** area gives us roasts, scallopini, and shanks.

Most veal is tender enough for dry-heat cooking, but the shoulder is improved by braising. The **breast,** shank, and neck are chewy and should always be braised. Home cooks can usually find only a limited selection of expensive cuts such as scallopini or loin chops in the veal section of the butcher's case. Be persistent, shop around, and don't shy away from cheaper cuts such as veal shank or, especially, veal breast.

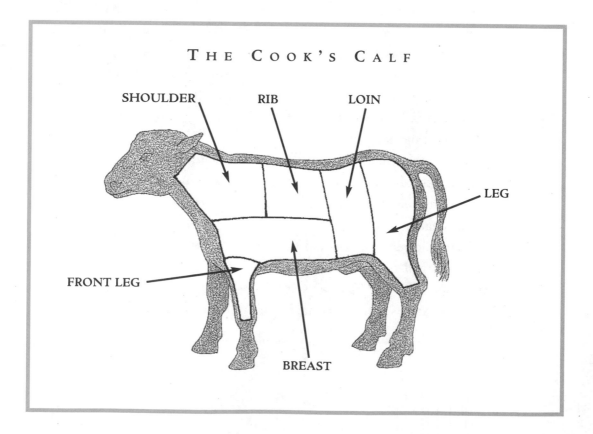

THE COOK'S CALF

SHOULDER · RIB · LOIN · LEG · FRONT LEG · BREAST

FORMULA-FED, OR DUTCH-PROCESS, VEAL

I T WAS DUTCH DAIRY FARMERS who originally discovered that feeding calves skim milk and other dairy by-products resulted in meat that was pale, juicy, and succulent. The veal they produced became popular throughout Europe and is preferred by Italian and French gourmets. In the 1960s, this process was introduced to the United States with a trademarked formula called Provimi (from *protein/vitamin/mineral*) and was an instant success. A bonus is that calves raised by the Dutch process attain weights of 350 pounds, providing large and tender cuts.

Dutch-process veal will be labeled as Provimi or Dutch Valley, or with some other indicator, and the meat will be very pale. Grass-fed or range-fed veal is reddish in color and has a flavor and character that some prefer to the blander meat of formula-fed veal.

Grades and Brands

V EAL CAN BE GRADED like beef, but very little actually is. Quality is determined by the conformation, or physique, of the carcass (the more loin, the better) and by what is called feathering—fat intermingled with lean meat between the ribs and fat streaking in the flank muscles. Veal is USDA-graded **Prime, Choice, Good, Standard, Utility**, and **Cull**. Usually only Choice and Good make it into the retail marketplace; most Prime goes to the restaurants. Since so little veal ends up being graded, though, it's probably more reliable to look for branded veal to ensure getting the best meat.

Much good veal is sold under brand names such as Provimi (Blue Delft brand), Dutch Valley, Plume de Veau, and several other brands. Pale and tender formula-fed veal is sold at premium prices in fine butcher shops and is used by many restaurants. The flavor and texture are excellent. Try to find a butcher that sells either formula-fed white veal such as Provimi or, if you prefer, the redder range-fed variety.

MANY BUTCHERS don't buy much veal because they think it is too expensive and won't sell well. Veal *is* expensive but worth seeking out because no other meat is so well suited to quick sautés or long braising, depending on the cut.

VEAL SHOULDER BLADE ROAST

Where it comes from: This bone-in roast is cut from the shoulder or chuck area and looks just like a miniature version of the larger beef chuck blade roast. A 2-inch-thick veal blade roast will weigh 1½ to 2 pounds, about half the size of a comparable beef blade roast.

Why we like it: Like its beef counterpart, the veal blade roast makes the best pot roast. Veal's delicate meat absorbs the rich flavors of the braising liquid, and the collagen, softened through long cooking, provides a soft and silky texture in the meat and sauce. Use the veal blade as a substitute for beef in any pot roast recipe, or use it in recipes calling for braised shoulder roasts.

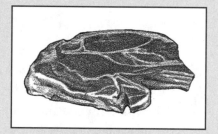

Price: Very reasonable and worth seeking out. A 1½-to-2 pound roast is enough for two to four people.

AKA: Veal pot roast.

VEAL CHEEKS

Where they come from: From the head, cheeks are the small muscles used for chewing. Each cheek is a boneless piece 2 to 3 inches in diameter. Four to six cheeks will make a serving.

Why we like them: Like beef cheeks, veal cheeks are heavily used muscles and are loaded with collagen. When slow-cooked by moist heat, the collagen softens and turns to gelatin, providing soft and succulent meat. Use veal cheeks in any veal stew recipe. You can also substitute them for pork in any pork stew recipe. Increase the cooking time accordingly. Veal cheeks will need more time than veal or pork shoulder to reach tenderness.

Price: Inexpensive, but many packers do not bother to remove the cheek meat. Veal cheeks must be special-ordered but are worth it.

AKA: None.

CALVES' LIVER

Where it comes from: Usually sold in slices, true calves' liver will be quite pale—light brown to brown and never red like beef liver. Avoid "baby beef liver," which is just beef liver by another name from a mature steer.

Why we like it: True calves' liver is unsurpassed for its delicate, mild flavor and smooth texture. It is very important to avoid overcooking it, as it will become dry and chalky. Lightly floured and sautéed with white wine, mushrooms, and Dijon mustard, calves' liver is exquisitely delicious. It is expensive but worth looking for. The real thing is also hard to find: most authentic calves' liver ends up on the restaurant table or goes home with the butcher.

AKA: Veal liver. *Never* baby beef liver.

Preparation and Cooking Methods

MEAT FROM YOUNG ANIMALS is usually more tender than meat from older ones because their muscles have not had time to perform much work. Meat from young calves has almost no marbling and a high percentage of collagen that is easily softened to gelatin by moist-heat cooking.

DRY-HEAT COOKING

Just as with other animals, the most tender cuts come from the back (ribs and loin). Chops and roasts from this area are ideal for dry-heat cooking. In addition, thin slices cut from the leg and sirloin, called veal scallopini, escalopes, or scallops, are also delicious when panfried or sautéed.

Care must be taken when cooking veal by dry heat because it's so lean. Err on the side of undercooking rather than risk drying it out. With all tender cuts of veal such as chops or scallops, aim toward the medium-rare stage (130° to 140°F) to ensure flavor and juiciness. Don't be worried if the veal is still a bit pink inside; that's fine.

We don't recommend broiling for veal chops but prefer pan-broiling or grilling them medium-rare. Thick (1½-inch) veal chops are delicious when marinated in olive oil and fresh herbs and then grilled (see Grilled Veal Chops, page 542). We think the reddish meat of range-fed veal is especially good when grilled.

Thin slices of veal, or scallopini, are ideal for sautéing because the meat easily absorbs the flavors of a sauce. Often these slices (*schnitzels* in German) are coated with flour or bread crumbs to protect the meat from overcooking. They are then panfried to create a lightly browned crust. Thinly sliced lean pork can stand in for veal in many of the classic recipes, especially scallopini and schnitzels in all their guises. Turkey cutlets are another popular alternative.

Usually only a select few "fancy butchers" or Italian butchers offer veal roast. Most of the time, all you find in the meat case are chops and scallops, although more and more markets now offer veal shanks and breast. If you'd like a delicious roast rack of veal, ask your butcher not to cut the rib section into chops. A whole rib section consisting of 8 ribs (equivalent to a standing rib roast, although much smaller) is by far the best cut of veal for dry-heat roasting. You can purchase the entire rack or a 3-to-7-rib piece. This is expensive but absolutely delicious when rubbed with a savory paste of herbs and pancetta (see Tuscan Roast Rack of Veal, page 552). To keep the meat from drying out, veal should not be roasted beyond medium doneness (140° to

150°F). We prefer to take the roast out of the oven at medium-rare (125° to 130°F) and let it sit for 5 to 15 minutes, depending on the size. Other roasts are cut from the loin or leg. These are expensive but very tasty when served medium-rare to medium. Some butchers sell shoulder roasts that they recommend for dry-heat roasting, but we think this chewier cut is better when braised.

MOIST-HEAT COOKING

Tougher cuts such as breast or shank—whether milk-fed, formula-fed, or range-fed—should be braised to the "falling-off-the-bone" stage, which is 165° to 170°F. Many veal classics such as osso buco, stuffed veal breast, and *blanquette de veau* fall into this category. The key to a delicious braise is the liquid the meat is cooked in: besides aromatic herbs and vegetables, it can include rich stocks, white wine, vermouth, lemon juice, and mushroom soaking liquids, if dried mushrooms are used. Braised veal roasts from the shoulder, rump, or leg are best cooked to a temperature of 155° to 160°F.

How to Choose the Best Veal Chops

CHOPS ARE VEAL'S EQUIVALENT of steaks from beef. Fortunately, because of veal's smaller size, there is less confusion about names than among steaks. For dry-heat cooking, the best chops come from the loin and back. Shoulder chops cut from the arm or blade sections are best braised.

Our favorite veal chops are **rib chops** cut 1¼ to 1½ inches thick. Rib chops have adequate fat, and the meat has a firm texture. We prefer bone-in chops with a piece of the rib attached, but veal chops are also sold as boneless rib chops.

Veal loin chops are very expensive, but we don't think they're as flavorful and juicy as those from the rib. They have a characteristic T-bone shape and include a piece of the tenderloin and a larger piece of top loin. Occasionally these are sold with a slice of veal kidney attached and are called **veal kidney chops**. Chops containing just the large top loin side of the T-bone are called **top loin chops** and may or may not include the bone. If seasoned well and not overcooked, they can be very tasty, however. They should be cut 1¼ to 1½ inches thick. Italian chefs often season thick veal T-bones with sage, brush them with olive oil, and grill them over charcoal with excellent results. Take care not to overcook veal chops because they can dry out easily. They are best cooked medium-rare to medium, 130° to 150°F.

Sirloin veal steaks, cut from the sirloin area of the leg, are sold bone-in or boneless. Like loin chops, sirloin chops are quite lean and can dry out when overcooked. Look for chops that have the pin bone, which means that they are located next to the loin chops and will be more tender. Sirloin chops can be grilled or pan-broiled; they are also excellent when braised.

Veal blade steaks and **veal arm steaks** are cut from the forearm and blade sections of the shoulder and are much cheaper than those cut from the rib and loin. These chops are still tender enough to be cooked by dry heat, but they are best when browned and braised in a tasty liquid like wine or stock.

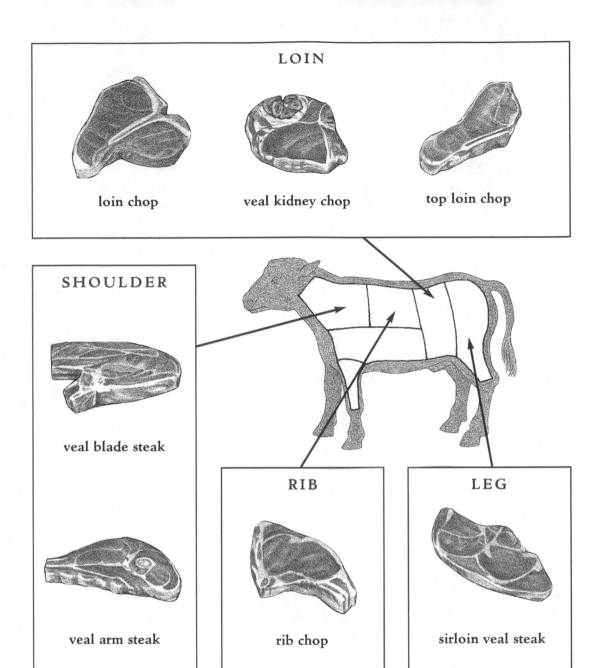

LOIN

loin chop

veal kidney chop

top loin chop

SHOULDER

veal blade steak

veal arm steak

RIB

rib chop

LEG

sirloin veal steak

Grilled Veal Chops

■ Flavor Step ■

HERB MARINADE FOR
GRILLED VEAL

½ cup olive oil

1 tablespoon minced garlic

2 tablespoons chopped
fresh herbs: sage,
thyme, tarragon,
rosemary, savory, or
marjoram, alone or
in combination, or
1 tablespoon dried

2 teaspoons salt

1 teaspoon freshly ground
black pepper OR any
of the marinades or
rubs on the opposite
page

4 1¼-to-1½-inch-thick
veal T-bone or rib
chops, excess fat
trimmed to ¼ inch
Olive oil (if using a
dry rub)

Serves 4
■ FIT FOR COMPANY

TO OUR TASTE, the best type of veal for grilling is range-fed veal, which is darker in color (usually a pale red) than formula-fed veal such as Provimi. It's tastier and juicier than paler veal when grilled to medium-rare, our recommended degree of doneness, where it still shows some pink inside.

Since veal is blander than beef, it benefits mightily from a flavor enhancer such as a marinade or spice rub. You can prepare veal chops as you would Beefsteak Florentine (page 106), or marinate the chops in any of the suggested marinades or rubs, or follow the recipe here. If you do choose a dry rub, be sure to brush the chops on both sides with olive oil to help seal in the flavors and juices. Serve the chops on a bed of arugula dressed with Nancy's Mushroom Vinaigrette (page 108) along with oven-roasted potatoes and sautéed spinach.

_____

■ **Flavor Step** ■ If using the herb marinade, combine the ingredients. If using a wet marinade, place the meat in a zipper-lock bag or bowl and cover with the marinade. Marinate, covered if necessary, for up to 2 hours at room temperature or overnight in the refrigerator. If using a dry rub, smear generously all over the chops. Cover and marinate at room temperature for up to 2 hours or overnight in the refrigerator. If the meat has been refrigerated, bring it to room temperature before grilling.

Prepare a charcoal fire for direct grilling (see Grilling, page 63). When the coals are medium-hot, remove the meat from a wet marinade, shake off any excess, and place over the coals. If using a dry rub, brush the chops with olive oil on both sides and place over the coals.

Cover the grill and sear the chops for 3 minutes per side, turning every minute or so. Grill the chops for another 2 minutes per side for medium-rare or 5 minutes per side for medium. The internal temperature will be 130° to 135°F for medium-rare, 135° to 150°F for medium. Remove the chops from the heat and let them rest for 5 minutes, covered loosely with foil.

MARINADES AND DRY RUBS FOR GRILLED VEAL

MARINADES
Olive Oil and Garlic Marinade for Steak (page 106)
Spicy Beer Marinade (page 138)
Chipotle-Orange Marinade (page 138)
Yucatán Marinade (page 294)
Tandoori Marinade (page 319)
Greek Marinade for Lamb (page 444)

DRY RUBS
Southwestern Spice Rub (page 128)
Dry Herb Rub for Tenderloin (page 300)
Spice Rub for Pork or Beef (page 375)
Garlic and Herb Rub for Veal or Pork (page 554)

Veal Chops Milanese

2 cups fresh bread crumbs
or Japanese *panko*
(see discussion)

¾ cup freshly grated
Parmesan cheese

1 teaspoon chopped fresh
thyme or ½ teaspoon
dried (you can
substitute rosemary,
basil, oregano,
marjoram, savory,
or tarragon or any
combination of herbs)

½ teaspoon salt

½ teaspoon freshly ground
black pepper

4 ¾-inch-thick veal rib
chops, pounded
Salt and freshly ground
black pepper
Flour for dredging

3 large eggs, lightly
beaten with ⅓ cup
water
Olive or vegetable oil
for panfrying
Lemon wedges
Arugula tossed with
lemon and olive oil
(optional)

Serves 4

■ IN A HURRY ■ FIT FOR COMPANY

THIS WONDERFULLY LIGHT AND CRUNCHY veal dish is Italy's answer to Wiener schnitzel. It can be made with thin veal rib chops, as here, or with boneless veal scallops. You can also use thin slices of pounded pork loin or beef sirloin, if you prefer. In the classic version, the meat is simply coated with an egg batter and bread crumbs, but we prefer to add some freshly grated Parmesan cheese and some aromatic herbs to our coating. If you're a purist and would rather make the traditional dish, you can leave these out.

We like to present this dish as they would in Milan, with a large, thin piece of meat attached to the rib bone. To prepare the chop this way, have your butcher remove the chine bone so that the meat is attached to the rib bone on only one side. This way the meat can be easily pounded into a thin piece much larger than its original size. Have the butcher flatten the meat to a thickness of ¼ inch, or do it yourself with the flat side of a cleaver, a rolling pin, or a meat mallet. Take care not to tear the meat.

Panko, finely crumbled Japanese bread crumbs that brown easily, makes an excellent breading material. It is available in Asian markets or by mail-order (see Sources, page 584).

■ **Flavor Step** ■ Mix the coating ingredients and spread the bread crumbs in a pie plate.

Season both sides of the meat generously with salt and pepper. Put the flour in one pie pan and the eggs in another one or in a shallow bowl. Dredge a chop on both sides in the flour, shake off any excess, and then dip into the eggs, making sure that both sides are coated well. Finally, dredge the chop in the bread crumbs, making sure both sides of the meat are covered. Place the chop on a wire rack to allow the coating to dry for 15 to 20 minutes. Repeat the process for all the chops.

Pour enough oil into a 12-inch skillet to reach a depth of ¼ inch. Heat over medium-high heat until it sizzles when a bit of flour is tossed in or to a temperature of 375°F. Fry one chop at a time and regulate the heat so that the coating browns evenly and does not burn. This should take 3 to 4 minutes for the first side. Turn the chop over and cook for 2 to 3 more minutes, or until the other side is nicely browned. Drain the chops on paper towels as you cook them and keep warm.

Serve garnished with lemon wedges and, if you wish, a small salad of arugula leaves dressed with olive oil and lemon mounded in the center of each chop.

How to Choose the
Best Veal Scallopini

VEAL SCALLOPINI is the Italian name for thin slices of tender veal that are quickly sautéed, either breaded or sauced. Other names are veal scallops, veal cutlets, *escallopes de veau*, or Wiener schnitzel. Even though scallopini can be quite expensive, there is no waste, and 3 ounces is an adequate portion for most people. Avoid slices cut too thin because they will dry out in the few seconds it takes to cook them. Ideally, scallopini should be cut ¼ inch to ⅜ inch thick.

Usually the part the scallopini is cut from is not recognizable. Try asking for the larger-diameter scallopini cut from the top round for schnitzel; slices from the bottom round, eye of the round, and sirloin tip all seem to have comparable tenderness, flavor, and texture. They vary in size: slices from the eye of the round are the smallest in diameter.

Some of the best scallopini come from the boneless top loin (very expensive). The top loin is tender enough that thicker ¾-inch slices can be cut as steaks and medallions. The whole sirloin or hip area is boned and separated into three individual muscles: the tenderloin, top sirloin, and the bottom sirloin. These pieces are then thinly sliced to ¼-to-⅜-inch thickness. The hind leg also provides expensive and desirable scallopini. They will be larger in diameter than those cut from the top loin or small sirloin muscles. The leg is separated into four individual muscles, and each is sliced thinly into scallopini.

We don't think that pounding, called for in many classic scallopini recipes, is necessary; scallopini today are very tender, but if you want to, pound away!

Sautéed Veal Scallopini

Serves 4

■ IN A HURRY ■ FIT FOR COMPANY ■ LOW-FAT

1 pound ¼-inch-thick
   veal scallops
   Salt and freshly ground
   black pepper
   Flour for dredging

3 tablespoons olive oil

MASTER RECIPE

THE KEY TO SUCCESSFULLY SAUTÉING scallopini is to make sure that the oil is quite hot so the veal will sear quickly and not lose precious juices. If the pan isn't hot enough, the meat steams and sweats and can become dry. Veal scallops should be well seasoned and can be dredged lightly in flour on one side before cooking. Thin slices of pork can be substituted for veal in these recipes; conversely, veal scallops can be used in any recipe calling for thin pork chops.

If you like, pound the veal scallops lightly with the flat side of a cleaver or a meat mallet to a thickness of ⅛ inch—or leave them as is. Season both sides with salt and pepper and dredge one side with flour.

In a large skillet, heat 1½ tablespoons of the oil over high heat and add half the scallopini, floured side down, making sure the pan is not crowded. Fry until small beads of moisture appear on the surface of the meat, 1 to 2 minutes. The bottom side should just be turning a light brown. Flip the scallops over and sauté for another 1 to 2 minutes more. Remove the scallopini as they brown and cover loosely to keep them warm. Add the remaining 1½ tablespoons oil to the pan and repeat the process with the rest of the scallopini.

PICCATA SAUCE

1 teaspoon minced garlic

½ cup dry white wine

1 teaspoon grated
   lemon zest

   Juice of 1 lemon

2 teaspoons chopped
   drained capers

1 tablespoon chopped
   fresh parsley (optional)

   Salt and freshly ground
   black pepper

To make the Piccata Sauce: Pour off all but a drop of oil from the pan and put in the garlic. Reduce the heat to medium and stir the garlic for 15 seconds. Pour in the white wine and scrape up any browned bits from the bottom of the pan. Reduce the wine over high heat until it begins to turn syrupy. Stir in the lemon zest, lemon juice, and capers and cook for 1 to 2 minutes more. Add the optional parsley and taste for salt and pepper. Pour any juices that have accumulated around the veal into the pan.

Arrange the scallopini on a serving platter, spoon the sauce over the veal, and serve at once.

Veal Scallopini with Tomatoes and Mushrooms

Serves 4
▪ IN A HURRY ▪ FIT FOR COMPANY

YOU CAN USE VEAL SCALLOPINI, sliced pork loin, or thin veal chops in this recipe. The only adjustments needed are for the cooking times: veal chops will take 9 to 12 minutes in the braising liquid, depending on their thickness, to get to the medium stage. Serve with cooked egg noodles or spaetzle.

Season the meat on both sides with salt and pepper. In a large skillet, heat the oil over high heat (if using veal scallops or slices of veal or pork loin, heat half the oil and cook half the meat, then repeat with the remaining oil and meat) and sear the meat until lightly browned on both sides. Sear veal scallops for 1 to 2 minutes per side, chops for about 3 minutes per side. Remove the meat from the pan and set aside.

Reduce the heat to medium. Add the garlic, ham, mushrooms, and a pinch each of salt and pepper. Sauté for 2 minutes, then stir in the wine. Bring to a boil and reduce to about ¼ cup. Add the stock and tomatoes. Continue to boil until the sauce becomes syrupy. Return the meat to the pan, reduce the heat to low, and cover. Cook the veal scallops or pork loin slices for about 2 minutes, chops for 9 to 12 minutes. Add a little more stock or water if the sauce gets too thick. Remove the meat and stir in the optional sour cream. Taste the sauce for salt and pepper.

Arrange the meat on a platter, pour the sauce over, and serve.

1 pound ¼-inch-thick veal scallops, OR slices of veal or pork loin, OR four ¾-to-1-inch-thick veal rib or T-bone chops
Salt and freshly ground black pepper
3 tablespoons olive oil
2 teaspoons minced garlic
¼ cup diced mild smoked ham
⅓ pound mushrooms, sliced
1 cup dry white wine
½ cup veal or chicken stock
¼ cup Oven-Roasted Tomatoes (page 299), OR canned tomato puree, OR tomato sauce, homemade or canned
½ cup low-fat or regular sour cream (optional)

How to Choose the Best Veal Roast

ALMOST ALL VEAL from the shoulder, rib, loin, sirloin and leg is tender enough to dry-roast. But to our taste, only the **rib**, or **rack**, and **loin** offer sufficient meaty flavor and lack of connective tissue to be flavorful when dry-roasted. All other large cuts should be braised so that the flavor of the meat is enhanced by some of the flavorful liquid the meat is braised in.

For braising, the best cuts are the same as our favorites for beef pot roast. They all come from the shoulder, or chuck, section and are comparable in flavor and texture. Boneless formula-fed shoulder roasts go by names such as **veal square, chuck neck off boneless,** and **veal chuck shoulder clod roast.** Bone-in roasts that braise well are **veal blade roast** and **veal arm roast.** Very good but somewhat expensive roasts for braising come from the sirloin and hind leg and go by names like **veal sirloin roast, veal rump roast, veal round roast,** and **leg of veal top roast.**

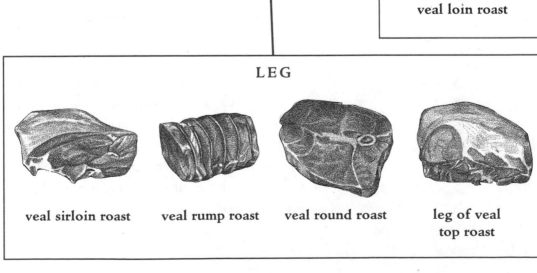

SHOULDER

veal chuck neck off
boneless roast

veal chuck
shoulder clod roast

veal blade roast

RIB

veal rib roast (rack)

LOIN

veal loin roast

LEG

veal sirloin roast

veal rump roast

veal round roast

leg of veal
top roast

Tuscan Roast Rack of Veal

■ Flavor Step ■
SAGE AND SHALLOT PASTE FOR VEAL

1 tablespoon olive oil

4 shallots, finely chopped

3 garlic cloves, finely
  chopped

  Salt and freshly ground
  black pepper

16 fresh sage leaves or
  2 teaspoons dried

4-5 ounces pancetta, cut
  into small cubes

1 4-to-6-pound rack of
  veal (6 bones), chine
  bone and most external
  fat removed

Serves 6 to 8
■ FIT FOR COMPANY

DAVID SHALLET, an accomplished chef, formerly of the now-defunct bistro Lulu-bis in San Francisco, prepared his special-ty, *arrosto misto*, for a celebration of my fiftieth birthday. The *arrosto misto* is one of the great Tuscan *secondi*, or main, courses. As many as five or six roasts usually make up the authen-tic preparation. If you want to reproduce the entire experience, use our recipes for *Arista*, Tuscan Herb-Infused Roast Pork (page 335) and Baked Leg of Lamb *Asadar* (page 494). Typical accompaniments are garlic roast pota-toes, stewed cannellini beans with extra-virgin olive oil, sautéed spinach with garlic and lemon, and slow-baked garden tomatoes with herbs and bread crumbs. *B.A.*

(See photograph, page 21.)

■ **Flavor Step** ■ In a small skillet, heat the oil over medi-um heat. Add the shallots and garlic and a pinch each of salt and pepper. Cover and cook for 3 to 4 minutes, stirring from time to time. Set the pan aside to cool. Place the sage, pancetta, and some pepper in a food processor and chop to a paste. Blend in the shallots and garlic.

Preheat the oven to 450°F. Cut ½-inch-deep gashes 1 to 2 inches long at an angle all over the surface of the meat. Partially separate the bones from the meat. Fill each gash with some of the sage and shallot paste. Rub the remaining paste all over the meat and in between the bones and meat wherever possible. Tie the roast with string in several places to hold the bones in place.

Place the roast bone side down in a shallow roasting pan. Put it in the middle of the oven and roast for 15 minutes to sear the outside. Reduce the heat to 350°F and continue to roast for 30 minutes more. Check the internal temperature; the roast is done at 125° to 140°F for medium-rare to medium. If necessary, continue to roast, checking the temperature every 15 minutes. (You can baste if you wish, but it isn't necessary.)

When the roast reaches the desired temperature, remove it from the oven and let it rest for 10 to 20 minutes, covered loosely with foil. Remove the string and carve between each bone into thick chops and two end pieces. Serve one chop or more per person.

Braised Shoulder of Veal

■ **Flavor Step** ■
GARLIC AND HERB RUB FOR VEAL OR PORK

4 garlic cloves, finely chopped

2 teaspoons chopped fresh thyme or other herb or 1 teaspoon dried

2 teaspoons chopped fresh tarragon or other herb or 1 teaspoon dried

2 teaspoons salt

½ teaspoon freshly ground black pepper

1 teaspoon finely chopped lemon zest (optional)

1 2½-to-3½-pound boneless veal shoulder roast, tied or netted, OR a 3-4 pound bone-in blade shoulder roast

BRAISING LIQUID

2 tablespoons olive oil

2 large onions, finely chopped

½ cup finely chopped carrots

½ cup chopped leeks

¼ cup diced prosciutto, smoked ham, dry coppa, pancetta, lean bacon, or salt pork

MASTER RECIPE

VEAL, ESPECIALLY A CUT that comes from the shoulder or breast, makes excellent pot roast. Its high collagen content makes a richer gravy than beef, and its mild flavor is complemented by a whole host of flavors. Our recipe provides a savory roast that can be easily enhanced or changed by adding other ingredients such as mushrooms or by varying the herbs and spices. We've provided some variations, but let your own imagination, culinary interests, and the contents of your larder guide your choices.

■ **Flavor Step** ■ Combine the garlic, herbs, salt, pepper, and optional lemon zest in a small bowl. Using the tip of a paring knife, make 1-inch-deep slits all over the roast, taking care not to cut the string or netting. Fill each slit with the garlic and herb mixture and rub the remainder over the meat. (If you wish, you can remove the string or netting, rub the roast, and retie it.)

To make the Braising Liquid: Heat the olive oil in a heavy pot over medium-high heat. Put the roast in and brown it all over for about 10 minutes. Remove and set aside. Pour off all but about 2 tablespoons of the fat and add the vegetables and ham, along with any extra herb mixture. Cover the pot and cook over medium heat until the vegetables soften, about 5 minutes, stirring often and scraping up any browned bits from the bottom of the pan.

Add the wine or vermouth, stock, veal, and herbs and bring to a boil. Cover tightly; if the fit is not snug, cover the pan with foil and replace the lid to fit tightly. (At this point you can continue to cook the dish or refrigerate the pot to complete cooking later or the next day.)

Preheat the oven to 350°F.

Put the pot in the oven and bake the veal for 1½ to 2 hours, or until the meat is tender. The veal should register 155° to 160°F when measured with an instant-read thermometer. Remove the meat and keep it warm, loosely wrapped with foil. Spoon off any accumulated fat from the surface of the sauce. If using the whipping cream, add it at this time. Reduce the sauce by boiling until it just turns syrupy. If you're using low-fat sour cream, whisk it in off the heat. Season to taste with salt and pepper.

Cut the string or netting from the veal and slice into ⅜-inch-thick slices. Pour the sauce over and serve.

½ cup dry white wine or vermouth

½ cup veal or chicken stock (low-sodium if canned)

2 tablespoons chopped fresh herbs such as thyme, tarragon, rosemary, sage, or marjoram OR 1 teaspoon dried

½ cup whipping cream or low-fat sour cream (optional)
Salt and freshly ground black pepper

Braised Shoulder of Veal with Mushroom Gravy

■ Flavor Step ■
Garlic and Herb Rub
for Veal or Pork
(page 554)

1   2½-to-3½-pound
     boneless veal shoulder
     roast, tied or netted,
     OR a 3-4 pound bone-
     in blade shoulder roast

2   tablespoons olive oil

½   pound fresh domestic or
     wild mushrooms, sliced,
     OR ½ ounce dried
     mushrooms, soaked in
     boiling water for at
     least 30 minutes

2   tablespoons chopped
     shallots

     Braising Liquid
     (page 554): omit
     the prosciutto

½   cup whipping cream or
     low-fat sour cream
     (optional)
     Salt and freshly ground
     black pepper

Serves 4 to 6, with leftovers
■ REWARMS WELL ■ MOM'S COMFORT FOOD
■ FIT FOR COMPANY

MORELS, FRESH OR DRIED, are really fantastic here. Use them if you can find them.

Season and brown the veal roast as in the Master Recipe (page 554). Strain the mushroom liquid if using, leaving any grit behind. Add the mushrooms, shallots, and reserved mushroom water (if using), along with the other ingredients for the braising liquid.

When the veal is done, remove from the pot and keep warm. Finish the sauce as in the Master Recipe, adding cream if desired. Season to taste with salt and pepper and serve.

Braised Shoulder of Veal with Apples

Serves 4 to 6, with leftovers

■ Mom's Comfort Food ■ Fit for Company

T HE CREAM DESCRIBED in the Master Recipe is still optional, but it really does make a difference here if you want an authentic Norman flavor. Serve this dish with braised savoy cabbage and a glass of hard cider from Devon, Normandy, or California.

———

Season and brown the veal shoulder as described in the Master Recipe (page 554).

Strain the mushroom liquid, leaving any grit behind. Add the mushrooms, the reserved mushroom liquid (if using), and the apples and shallots. Add the cider and Calvados instead of the wine.

When the veal is done, remove from the pot and keep warm. Finish the sauce as in the Master Recipe, using the cream. Season to taste with salt and pepper and serve.

■ **Flavor Step** ■

Garlic and Herb Rub
for Veal or Pork
(page 554)

1 2½-to-3½-pound
   boneless veal shoulder
   roast, tied or netted,
   OR a 3-4 pound bone-
   in blade shoulder roast

2 tablespoons olive oil

½ pound fresh domestic or
   wild mushrooms, sliced,
   OR ½ ounce dried
   mushrooms, soaked
   in boiling water for
   at least 30 minutes

BRAISING LIQUID

½ cup dried apples or 2
   cups sliced fresh tart
   apples

2 tablespoons chopped
   shallots

½ cup apple cider

2 tablespoons Calvados
   or apple brandy

½ cup whipping cream
   or low-fat sour cream
   Salt and freshly ground
   black pepper

Braised Shoulder of Veal Stuffed with Porcini Mushrooms

■ **Flavor Step** ■
Garlic and Herb Rub
for Veal or Pork
(page 554)

**PORCINI STUFFING FOR
VEAL OR PORK**

1   ounce dried porcini or
    other mushrooms,
    soaked in boiling water
    to cover for at least
    30 minutes
1   cup fresh bread crumbs
¼   cup finely chopped
    onion
    Pinch of dried thyme
    Pinch each of salt and
    freshly ground black
    pepper

1   2½-to-3½-pound
    boneless veal roast, tied
    and netted, OR a 3-4
    pound bone-in blade
    shoulder roast
2   tablespoons olive oil
    Braising Liquid
    (page 554)

½   cup whipping cream
    or low-fat sour cream
    (optional)
    Salt and freshly ground
    black pepper

Serves 4 to 6, with leftovers
■ REWARMS WELL ■ MOM'S COMFORT FOOD
■ FIT FOR COMPANY

VEAL SHOULDER is very easy to stuff, adds flavor, and stretches the dish to serve more diners. If you can't find dried porcini, use dried shiitakes or any other dried mushrooms.

To make the Porcini Stuffing: Season and brown the veal shoulder as directed in the Master Recipe, page 554. Drain the mushrooms, leaving any grit behind. Strain and save the soaking liquid to use in the braising liquid. Chop the mushrooms and mix two-thirds of them with the bread crumbs, onions, thyme, and salt and pepper.

Remove the string or netting from the roast. Spread the bread crumb mixture on the inside of the meat. Roll the roast back up and tie it securely. Prepare and cook it as in the Master Recipe, adding the reserved mushroom water and mushrooms along with the wine and stock.

When the veal is done, remove from the pot and keep warm. Finish the sauce as in the Master Recipe, adding cream or sour cream if using. Season to taste with salt and pepper and serve.

How to Choose Meat for Veal Stew

VEAL CAN BE MADE INTO EXCELLENT STEWS, for its mild flavor marries well with many different spices. With its higher collagen, veal also holds up during long, moist cooking without falling apart, and the texture of the meat is soft and silky. We think **veal breast**, boned and cut up into stewing pieces, makes the best stew because it is more fatty than most veal cuts, with a high level of connective tissue. When the collagen melts and softens during the cooking, it not only provides excellent flavor and texture but also helps to make the sauce more luscious and rich. We add the breast bones to the stew to give the sauce even more body and flavor. They can be removed and discarded after cooking. When you ask your butcher to bone and cut up a veal breast for you, don't forget to ask for the bones. Or do it yourself; it's not as hard as you may think.

As with beef, other excellent meat for stew comes from the shoulder, or chuck, area. Buy a roast such as boneless **veal chuck shoulder clod roast, veal square,** or **chuck neck off boneless roast,** or bone-in roasts such as **veal arm roast, veal blade roast,** or **veal shoulder roast** and cut it up yourself into 1½-to-2½-inch cubes. If your butcher cuts up his own veal, ask him to give you some stew meat from the neck area. It has lots of collagen, and the meat becomes deliciously succulent. Sometimes veal from the **hind leg** and **sirloin** is cut up for stew, but it is less flavorful and unnecessarily more expensive than stew from the shoulder. But if this is all you can find, it still makes a good stew.

Veal shanks are usually sold sliced into rounds on the bone and make a delicious stew when cooked as whole pieces. This braised dish usually goes by the Italian name of *osso buco.* Shanks are great in all stew recipes, and there is the bonus of the rich marrow.

Don't buy cubes of meat labeled stewing veal. It always costs more than the original cuts. Cutting the meat up yourself lets you control the fat content, origin of the meat, size of the pieces—in a word, the quality.

Oven-Braised Veal with Portobello Mushrooms

2 pounds veal shoulder
or veal cheeks, trimmed
of fat and cut into
2-inch chunks
Salt and freshly ground
black pepper
1 tablespoon olive oil
¾ pound portobello
mushrooms, stems and
gills removed, cut into
½-inch slices, OR
¾ pound shiitake
mushrooms, stems
removed, cut into
½-inch slices, OR 1
pound white or brown
mushrooms, cut into
½-inch slices
2 tablespoons minced
garlic
1 teaspoon chopped fresh
or dried tarragon
½ teaspoon chopped fresh
or dried thyme
1½ cups dry vermouth, white
wine, or dry sherry
½ cup whipping cream or
low-fat sour cream
(optional)

Serves 4 to 6
■ REWARMS WELL ■ FIT FOR COMPANY
■ LOW-FAT (WITHOUT THE CREAM)

PORTOBELLO MUSHROOMS are the large, mature caps of brown crimini mushrooms. They have become popular lately because of their intense flavor and rich, meaty texture. Their only drawback is that their dark gills give off a blackish liquid as they cook that some find unappealing. To avoid this, trim off the gills with a small sharp knife. If you can't find portobellos, use fresh shiitake or brown or white button mushrooms. All will taste fine, although a little less intense.

You can prepare this dish ahead and finish the final cooking just before serving. Cream gives the sauce a nice silky texture and some extra flavor, but you can leave it out. Or you can whisk in some low-fat sour cream off the heat just before serving the sauce. Serve with fresh noodles, spaetzle, or a dried pasta of your choice.

Use any cut of veal shoulder such as bone-in blade roast or boneless roast. Veal cheeks would also make an excellent substitute.

Season the veal well with salt and pepper and brown on all sides in hot olive oil in a heavy skillet over high heat, about 5 to 7 minutes.

Transfer the veal to a baking dish and stir into the skillet the mushrooms, garlic, tarragon, thyme, and a pinch each of salt and pepper. Cook briefly over high heat, stirring often, for 2 to 3 minutes. Pour in the vermouth or wine and bring to a boil, scraping up any browned bits from the bottom of the skillet. Add to the veal in the baking pan and mix well. Cover tightly with foil. At this point, you can proceed with the recipe or refrigerate the dish overnight.

Preheat the oven to 350°F. Place the roasting dish in the middle of the oven and bake for 1 to 1½ hours, or until the veal is quite tender. Transfer the meat to a platter with a slotted spoon and keep warm. Pour the sauce into the pan and skim any grease from the surface. Bring it to a boil and add the optional cream. Reduce the sauce over high heat until it just begins to turn syrupy. If you're using low-fat sour cream, remove the pan from the fire and whisk it into the sauce. Taste for salt and pepper. Spoon the sauce and mushrooms over the veal and serve as suggested above.

Veal and Asparagus Stew in Lemon Sauce

1 tablespoon olive oil

¼ pound mild Italian
  sausage (turkey or
  pork), removed from
  casings

2 cups chopped leeks
  (white part only)

2 teaspoons chopped garlic

¾ cup finely chopped
  carrots

½ cup finely chopped
  celery

  Salt and freshly ground
  black pepper

2½ pounds boneless veal
  shoulder or bone-in
  breast, cut into 2-inch
  cubes

2 teaspoons chopped fresh
  tarragon or 1 teaspoon
  dried

1 teaspoon chopped fresh
  thyme or ½ teaspoon
  dried

2 teaspoons chopped
  lemon zest

1¼ cups chicken or veal
  stock

1 cup dry white wine

1 tablespoon butter

24 small boiling onions

½ pound whole button
  mushrooms or large
  mushrooms, quartered

1 pound asparagus, woody
  stems removed, cut into
  2-inch pieces

Serves 4 to 6
■ FIT FOR COMPANY

THE CLASSIC FRENCH VEAL STEW, *blanquette de veau*, combines tender veal chunks with baby onions and mushrooms in a white wine and cream sauce. It's delicious but far too rich for our modern palates. In this stew, we've substituted a tangy white wine and lemon sauce for the cream. It not only complements the veal but also makes a lovely accompaniment to blanched asparagus, which are stirred into the stew just before serving. The sauce is enhanced with a little crumbled, cooked Italian sausage for extra flavor. Serve this stew with dumplings or egg noodles. *(See photograph, page 20.)*

In a large, heavy pot or Dutch oven, heat the oil over medium heat. Put in the sausage and cook it for 3 to 4 minutes, breaking the meat apart with a fork. Add the leeks, garlic, carrots, and celery along with a pinch each of salt and pepper. Cook, stirring often, for 5 to 10 minutes, until the vegetables are soft.

Season the veal with salt and pepper and cook it for 1 to 2 minutes, not to brown the meat but to let it absorb some of the flavors. Stir in the tarragon, thyme, and lemon zest and cook for 1 minute more. Pour in 1 cup of the stock and the wine. Bring to a simmer and cook, uncovered, for 1½ hours, or until the veal is quite tender.

Meanwhile, heat the butter in a medium skillet over medium heat. Add the onions and a pinch each of salt and pepper. Cover the pan and cook for 5 minutes, shaking the pan from time to time to keep the onions from sticking. Add the remaining ¼ cup stock. Cover the pan and continue cooking for 15 minutes. Add the mushrooms and cook, uncovered, for 5 more minutes, stirring often, until the onions and mushrooms are fully cooked. Set the pan aside.

Blanch the asparagus in a pot of boiling salted water for 3 minutes. Drain and cool the asparagus under cold running water. Set aside.

If the stew liquid has not become slightly syrupy during cooking, remove the meat with a slotted spoon and boil the sauce to thicken it slightly. Take the pot off the heat. Beat together the lemon juice and egg yolks in a small bowl. Stir in 1 cup of the stew liquid. Add the reserved meat, onions, mushrooms, and asparagus to the pot. Without reheating the stew, stir in the egg and lemon mixture to thicken the sauce slightly and give it a creamy texture. Take care when you add the egg and lemon mixture: the eggs will curdle if the liquid is too hot or the stew is allowed to come to a boil afterward. Taste the sauce for salt and pepper and lemon juice. Serve at once. Reheat gently over low heat, if necessary.

2 tablespoons fresh
    lemon juice
2 large egg yolks

Northern Italian Veal Stew with Peas and Roast Portobello Mushrooms

■ Flavor Step ■
HERB RUB FOR VEAL

½ teaspoon dried sage
1 teaspoon dried tarragon
2 teaspoons salt
1 teaspoon freshly ground
    black pepper

2 pounds veal shoulder,
    cut into 1½-inch cubes
    Flour
¼ cup olive oil
½ cup finely chopped
    onion
¼ cup finely chopped
    carrot
¼ cup finely chopped
    celery
1 tablespoon minced garlic
    Salt and freshly ground
    black pepper
1 cup dry white wine
4 ripe fresh tomatoes,
    peeled, seeded, and
    chopped, OR canned
    Italian-style tomatoes,
    seeded and chopped
1 tablespoon tomato paste
1 cup chicken or veal stock

Serves 4 to 6
■ REWARMS WELL ■ GREAT LEFTOVERS
■ FIT FOR COMPANY

SERVE THIS HEARTY stew with Ricotta Dumplings (page 566) or soft polenta. Simple it may be, but it makes a great party dish when served with Chianti Classico and some crusty bread. Any leftovers can be rewarmed and served over your favorite pasta.

When using portobello mushrooms, it's a good idea to cut away the black gills so that the sauce doesn't turn a dirty gray.

■ Flavor Step ■ Combine the ingredients in a small bowl. Toss with the veal cubes to season thoroughly.

Dredge the veal in the flour, shaking off any excess. In a large skillet or Dutch oven, heat 2 tablespoons of the olive oil over medium-high heat. Brown the veal cubes on all sides, in batches if necessary, about 8 minutes. Remove with a slotted spoon. Put the onion, carrot, celery, garlic, and a pinch each of salt and pepper in the pan. Cover and cook for 5 minutes to soften the vegetables, stirring often. Pour in the wine and bring to a boil, scraping up any browned bits from the bottom of the pan. Stir in the tomatoes, tomato paste, and stock. Put the veal back in the pan and bring to a simmer. Cover and cook until the veal is fork-tender, about 1½ hours.

Meanwhile, roast the mushrooms. Preheat the oven to 425°F. Toss the mushrooms with the remaining 2 tablespoons olive oil and sprinkle with salt and pepper. Spread them out on a baking sheet and roast for 10 to 12 minutes, or until the mushrooms are soft. Set aside.

When the veal is tender, remove it with a slotted spoon. Degrease the sauce, if necessary, and boil it down until it just begins to turn syrupy. Add the peas and the mushrooms with any liquid. Return the meat to the pot, and cook for 1 minute over medium heat. Taste for salt and pepper and serve.

1 pound portobello mushrooms, gills removed and caps cut into ½-inch-thick slices

1 package frozen peas, thawed

OSSO BUCO

THIS IS ONE OF THE MOST POPULAR dishes in Italian restaurants today—its silky sauce and luscious meat makes osso buco a perfect match for a creamy risotto. Serve with Vino Nobile di Montepulciano—a soft and fragrant wine from southern Tuscany—or a California Sangiovese made from Tuscany's great red grape variety.

Use Lamb Shank Osso Buco (page 516) as a Master Recipe: substitute veal shanks for the lamb and use chicken or veal stock in the braising sauce.

RICOTTA DUMPLINGS

Makes about 18 dumplings

THESE FLAVORFUL DUMPLINGS can be eaten with a stew such as Northern Italian Veal Stew with Peas and Roast Portobello Mushrooms (page 564). They go well with virtually all braised meat dishes, including Veal and Asparagus Stew in Lemon Sauce (page 562). They can also be served as a separate course, with a little butter and sprinkled with grated Parmesan cheese and fresh sage, or in chicken broth like exotic matzoh balls.

⅔ cup fresh bread crumbs
¼ cup whole milk
⅔ cup whole-milk ricotta cheese
4 large egg yolks
2 large egg whites
1 teaspoon salt
½ teaspoon freshly ground black pepper
¾ cup flour
1 tablespoon baking powder
8 cups chicken stock or water

Stir the bread crumbs and milk together in a medium-size mixing bowl. Let stand for 3 minutes so the crumbs absorb the milk. Mix in the ricotta, egg yolks and whites, salt, and pepper, whisking to blend everything well. Stir in the flour and baking powder until well blended.

Bring the stock or water to a simmer in a large pot. Shape about 1 tablespoon of the dumpling dough on a tablespoon and drop into the simmering liquid. Repeat until all the dough is used. Cook for about 8 minutes, until the dumplings are cooked through. You may need to cut one in half to check. Serve immediately.

Pam's Veal Meatballs

Serves 4
■ COOKING ON A BUDGET ■ GREAT LEFTOVERS

PAM STUDENT is the lunch chef at Nancy Oakes's restaurant, Boulevard, in San Francisco. Like many people who cook for a living, she prefers to eat simply at home with her own family. These versatile and delicious veal meatballs are a favorite with Pam's family and friends. They can be combined with a homemade or a supermarket tomato sauce to serve over pasta. They can also be added to chicken soup or a platter of steamed vegetables. Or they can be served with a simple brown gravy over rice or mashed potatoes. The cooked meatballs freeze well and can be used for a quick party snack. You can also make them from a mixture of beef and ground turkey, although veal has a lighter texture than beef.

———

Heat 1 tablespoon of the olive oil in a small skillet over medium-high heat. Add the onion and cook, stirring often, for 5 minutes. Stir in the garlic and cook for 1 minute more. Set aside to cool.

In a large bowl, combine the veal, eggs, bread, parsley or spinach, cheese, herbs, salt, and pepper. Add the onion and garlic and any juices from the pan. Knead the mixture with your hands until everything is thoroughly blended. Shape the meat into balls the diameter of a quarter.

Preheat the oven to 350°F. In a large, nonstick skillet, heat the remaining oil and brown the meatballs in batches over medium-high heat. Transfer them to a baking dish as they brown. Bake uncovered for 10 minutes, or until they're cooked through, and serve.

¼ cup olive oil

1 medium onion, finely chopped

2 garlic cloves, minced

1 pound ground veal OR ¾ pound ground beef chuck plus ¼ pound ground turkey

2 large eggs, lightly beaten

3 slices stale French bread, crusts removed, soaked in water, squeezed dry, and shredded

1 bunch (6 ounces) parsley, chopped, OR 1 bunch (10 ounces) spinach, trimmed, cooked, and chopped and water squeezed out

½ cup freshly grated Asiago or Parmesan cheese

1 teaspoon chopped fresh thyme or ½ teaspoon dried

1 teaspoon chopped fresh tarragon or ½ teaspoon dried

1 teaspoon salt

½ teaspoon freshly ground black pepper

Braised Veal Shanks North African Style

4 meaty veal shanks, cut
into sections 2-3 inches
thick (2-2½ pounds
total)

■ Flavor Step ■
North African Marinade
(page 114)

BRAISING LIQUID

2 tablespoons olive oil
3 cups chopped onions
2 celery ribs, chopped
2 medium carrots, diced
2 tablespoons chopped
garlic
1 tablespoon Hungarian
paprika
1 teaspoon ground cumin
1 teaspoon ground
coriander
1 teaspoon turmeric
½ teaspoon ground ginger
1 teaspoon dried marjoram
Salt and freshly ground
black pepper
3 cups chicken or veal
stock
1 cup dry white wine

Serves 4
■ REWARMS WELL ■ FIT FOR COMPANY

ONE OF THE REASONS long-simmered veal shanks are so appealing is that the meat becomes very tender with an almost buttery texture and absorbs lots of flavor from the cooking liquid. Here we've used an exotic mixture of spices in the sauce, much different from that in the traditional northern Italian osso buco. Serve this North African version on a bed of bulgur wheat, couscous, or the small rice-shaped pasta called orzo.

You could also use this recipe to cook lamb shanks, adjusting the cooking time accordingly.

■ **Flavor Step** ■ Put the veal shanks in a zip-lock bag or shallow bowl, cover with the marinade, and refrigerate overnight, covered if necessary. Turn the meat occasionally as it marinates.

Preheat the oven to 350°F. Remove the shanks from the marinade and pat them dry. Heat the oil in a Dutch oven or large casserole over medium-high heat. Put in the shanks and brown them on both sides, 5 to 6 minutes. Remove the shanks as they brown and set them aside.

Add the onions, celery, carrots, and garlic to the pot. Cover, reduce the heat to medium, and cook until the vegetables are soft, stirring from time to time, 10 to 15 minutes. Add a little water if the vegetables begin to stick. Stir in the spices and the marjoram along with a hefty pinch each of salt and pepper. Stir until the vegetables are well coated. Cook for 1 minute, then pour in the stock and wine, stirring well to scrape up any browned bits from the bottom of the pot. Stir in the tomato paste and return the veal to the pot. Stir in the lemon juice. Bring to a boil, cover, and place in the center of the oven.

Check the meat after 1 hour and baste it with some of the liquid in the pot. Turn the shanks over, cook for 30 to 40 minutes more, and then turn them again in the sauce. The shanks are done when they're completely tender. If not, continue to cook them. At this point they can be cooled and refrigerated for a day or so. Or you can finish the sauce and serve the shanks.

To proceed, degrease the sauce. If the shanks have been refrigerated, remove any congealed fat from the surface. Bring the sauce to a boil and put in the squash, carrots, and chickpeas. Reduce the heat to a simmer and cook until the vegetables are tender, 15 to 20 minutes.

Taste the sauce. If it seems watery, remove the solids with a slotted spoon and reduce until it begins to become syrupy. Taste for salt, pepper, and lemon juice. Return the solids to the sauce and reheat for 1 minute. Serve over bulgur, couscous, or orzo, garnished with chopped fresh mint.

2 tablespoons tomato paste

2 tablespoons fresh lemon juice, or more

3 cups peeled and diced winter squash, such as butternut, hubbard, or banana

4 medium carrots, cut into 2-inch pieces

1 cup cooked chickpeas (garbanzos) or canned

Chopped fresh mint to garnish

Stuffed Veal for Passover

■ Flavor Step ■

1 tablespoon kosher salt

2 tablespoons minced garlic

1 teaspoon ground ginger

2 teaspoons freshly ground black pepper

1 8-to-10-pound breast of veal with bones attached, pocket cut for stuffing, OR a 5-pound boneless breast of veal, pocket cut for stuffing

STUFFING

4 tablespoons rendered chicken fat or vegetable oil

2 large onions, chopped

4 garlic cloves, minced

¾ pound mushrooms, sliced

1 pound ground veal or turkey

2 bunches of spinach, cooked, drained, and squeezed dry, OR a 10-ounce package of chopped spinach, defrosted and squeezed dry

½ cup matzoh meal OR 1 cup small pieces of matzoh

2 tablespoons minced fresh parsley

2 large eggs, lightly beaten

VEAL BREAST is an economical cut of meat that can withstand long cooking and holding or reheating. It can also be dressed up nicely for entertaining. Lisa Weiss, our recipe tester, serves this rich dish to her family at the Passover Seder, and everyone loves it. The stuffing can be varied at will: bread can be substituted for matzoh, sausage for ground veal. It is also delicious in roast chicken or turkey.

■ **Flavor Step** ■ Crush the salt and garlic together with a mortar and pestle or mix them well in a small bowl. Stir in the ginger and pepper. Rub the mixture all over the veal breast, making sure that the inside of the pocket is well coated. Allow the meat to sit at room temperature, loosely covered, for 2 hours or refrigerate overnight. Do not stuff the veal until you are ready to cook it.

To make the Stuffing: In a large skillet, heat 2 tablespoons of the chicken fat or oil over medium heat. Add the onions and cook until softened, stirring frequently, 5 to 7 minutes. Increase the heat to medium-high and cook until the onions begin to turn golden, about 4 minutes more. Stir in the garlic and cook for 2 minutes. Remove the onions and garlic to a large bowl and set aside.

Heat the remaining 2 tablespoons chicken fat or oil in the pan over high heat and add the mushrooms. Sauté until they have exuded their liquid and begin to color, stirring and tossing frequently, about 6 minutes. Add the mushrooms, along with any liquid, to the onions and garlic. Allow the mixture to cool slightly and add the rest of the stuffing ingredients. Stir everything gently until well combined.

Preheat the oven to 350°F. Stuff the pocket of the veal

breast with the stuffing. Do not pack too tightly; allow room for expansion during cooking. Any leftover dressing can be baked in a covered casserole for 30 to 40 minutes. Sew or skewer the pocket closed.

Scatter the remaining chopped onion, the celery, and the carrot over the bottom of a roasting pan just large enough to hold the veal breast. Place the veal on top of the vegetables, pour in the white wine and stock, and cover the pan with foil. Seal the edges as tightly as possible. Roast the veal for 2 hours, then remove the foil.

Roast for another hour, or until the veal is golden brown and fork-tender. Remove from the roasting pan and allow it to rest, loosely covered with foil.

To make a pan sauce, degrease the juices in the pan. Bring to a simmer over medium-high heat and reduce to a syrup. Strain and discard the vegetables. Taste for salt and pepper. Cut the veal into thick slices, between the bones if they've been left in. Moisten each serving with a little of the pan sauce.

2 teaspoons kosher salt
2 teaspoons coarsely ground black pepper

1 large onion, coarsely chopped
1 celery rib, coarsely chopped
1 large carrot, coarsely chopped
1 cup dry white wine
1 cup veal or chicken stock
  Salt and freshly ground black pepper

OVERLOOKED BUT DELICIOUS CUTS

Breast of veal is not only wonderful with a savory stuffing but also makes excellent meat for stews. Because it has so much connective tissue, veal breast is a great base for the velvety sauce that results from long, slow braising. See Veal and Asparagus Stew in Lemon Sauce (page 562) and Northern Italian Veal Stew with Peas and Roast Portobello Mushrooms (page 564).

Liver owes its undeserved, much-maligned reputation to the fact that most Americans overcook meat of all types, especially organ meats. Our mothers suffered from this habit, cooking liver so thoroughly that it ended up dry and tough.

When properly cooked, though, liver is slightly pink on the inside, tender, and wonderfully succulent. The flavor of calves' liver is delicate and mild; beef, lamb, and pork livers are slightly stronger in flavor but can be delicious when seasoned well.

The best liver comes from young animals, with calves' liver being the most sought after. True calves' liver is often hard to find: it should be pale red to yellow brown in color, and it will be smaller than beef liver. Beef livers are much larger and are usually a dark reddish brown. Both are tender, with calves' liver lighter in color and flavor.

Liver is encased in a membrane that should be peeled away. This is usually done by the butcher (most liver is sold sliced), but if the membrane is left on, do remove it, since it will toughen during cooking. Also remove any veins or sinews you see. If the liver is not sliced, slice it thinly before cooking. Good liver should have a fresh smell and no strong or off odors. It does not freeze well, so never buy frozen liver.

Sweetbreads have a delicious mild taste and a soft, slightly chewy texture. They take well to a host of flavors, from mushrooms to slightly sweet sauces. Sweetbreads can be either the thymus glands from the neck of a young calf or the pancreas. Unlikely as these organs sound, they are elegant, expensive, and very rich. That's why we think they are best served as an appetizer or first course for a special dinner.

Soak beef sweetbreads in cold salted water to remove any last residue of blood and "organy" flavor, then parboil them to firm them up. Since veal sweetbreads are milder than those of beef, you can omit the soaking, if you wish. Some recipes suggest weighting sweetbreads in the refrigerator to improve texture, but that's not necessary. Sweetbreads are especially good as part of a salad with arugula, curly endive, or frisée, as in the recipe on page 574.

Calves' or Beef Liver in Mustard Sauce

Serves 4
■ **IN A HURRY**
■ **COOKING ON A BUDGET (BEEF LIVER)**

CLASSIC LIVER AND ONIONS is hard to beat when it's properly cooked. Try it and see if you don't agree. Serve the liver and sauce with hash browns or mashed potatoes. *(See photograph, page 22.)*

■ **Flavor Step** ■ Mix the ingredients in a shallow bowl or pie pan. Dredge both sides of the liver in the seasoned flour and shake off the excess.

Heat 2 tablespoons of the oil in a skillet over medium-high heat and fry the slices, in batches if necessary, adding more oil as needed, for 2 to 3 minutes per side, until the inside is just slightly pink. Cut into a slice to make sure you are not overcooking it. Remove the slices from the pan as they are done and cover loosely to keep warm. Pour off all but 2 tablespoons of oil from the pan. Reduce the heat to medium and add the onions. Cover and cook until soft, about 5 minutes, stirring from time to time. Stir in the garlic and mushrooms and cook for 5 minutes, stirring occasionally. Add the parsley, sherry or wine, and mustard, bring to a boil, and cook until the sauce begins to turn syrupy. Taste for salt and pepper. Add the optional butter if you want a smoother, richer sauce.

Put the liver back in the pan and rewarm for 30 seconds over medium heat. Serve immediately.

■ **Flavor Step** ■
SEASONED FLOUR FOR LIVER, VEAL SCALLOPS, OR THIN PORK CHOPS

- ½ cup flour
- 2 teaspoons paprika, preferably Hungarian
- 2 teaspoons dry mustard, preferably Colman's
- ½ teaspoon dried thyme
- ½ teaspoon dried sage
- 2 teaspoons salt
- 1 teaspoon freshly ground black pepper

- 1½ pounds calves' or beef liver, thinly sliced, membranes and sinews removed
    About ¼ cup olive oil
- 3 cups thinly sliced onions
- 1 teaspoon chopped garlic
- ½ pound mushrooms, sliced
- 2 tablespoons chopped fresh parsley
- ¼ cup dry sherry or dry white wine
- 2 tablespoons Dijon mustard
    Salt and freshly ground black pepper
- 1 tablespoon butter (optional)

Port-Glazed Sweetbreads with Wine-Pickled Shallots

1 pair veal sweetbreads
  (¾-1 pound)
  Salt and freshly ground
  black pepper
  Flour for dredging
2 tablespoons butter
½ cup chicken or veal stock
2 tablespoons balsamic
  vinegar
½ cup port wine

WINE-PICKLED SHALLOTS

2 tablespoons olive oil
  or unsalted butter
20 shallots, peeled
  Salt and freshly ground
  black pepper
1 cup dry red wine
¼ cup balsamic vinegar

  Arugula, curly endive,
  or frisée for serving
  (optional)

**Serves 4 to 6 as an appetizer,
2 to 3 as a main course**
■ FIT FOR COMPANY

YOU CAN SERVE these slightly sweet, delicious morsels as an appetizer or as a main dish over rice or rice pilaf, garnished with the Wine-Pickled Shallots.

Put the sweetbreads in a bowl. Dissolve 1 teaspoon of salt in 3 cups of cold water and pour it over the sweetbreads. Soak for 1 to 2 hours in the refrigerator. Discard the water.

In a saucepan, bring enough lightly salted water to cover the sweetbreads to a boil. Put in the sweetbreads, reduce to a simmer, cover the pan, and cook for 5 to 7 minutes. Remove the sweetbreads and cool them under cold running water. If necessary, use sharp scissors or a paring knife to remove any tough outer membranes or blood vessels.

Cut the sweetbreads into ½-inch-thick slices. Sprinkle both sides with salt and pepper and dredge in flour, shaking off any excess. Melt the butter in a large nonstick skillet over medium heat. Brown the sweetbreads on both sides, about 4 minutes per side.

Put in the stock, vinegar, and port, shaking the pan to loosen any browned bits on the bottom of the pan. Bring to a low boil and cook until the sauce is thick enough to coat and glaze the sweetbreads, about 10 minutes. Taste for salt and pepper.

Meanwhile, make the Wine-Pickled Shallots: In a small saucepan or skillet, heat the oil or butter over medium heat. Add the shallots and a pinch each of salt and pepper. Cover the pan and cook for 2 to 3 minutes, shaking the pan to turn the shallots as they cook. Add the wine and vinegar and bring to a boil. Cook at a low boil until most of the liquid has evaporated and the shallots are glazed with the sauce, about 12 minutes. The shallots should be quite tender. (You can make them up to a day ahead and refrigerate them until serving. Reheat when ready to serve.)

Scatter the sweetbreads on a bed of lettuce or frisée, if you like, and garnish with the pickled shallots and all the sauce.

Seasoning Chart

Dry Rubs

Southwestern Spice Rub, page 128
—All beefsteaks, pork chops, pork steaks, lamb chops, lamb steaks

Herb Rub for Swiss Steak, page 148
—All cuts of beef, pork, lamb, and veal suitable for braising

Dry Rub for Roast Beef, page 178
—All beef, pork, lamb, and veal roasts

Thyme and Garlic Paste for Beef, page 181
—All beef, pork, lamb, and veal cuts

Herb and Garlic Paste for Roast Beef, page 189
—All roasting cuts of beef, lamb, pork, and veal

Herb and Paprika Rub for Beef, page 194
—All cuts of beef for braising and stewing, short ribs

Spicy Herb Rub for Beef, page 222
—Short ribs, country-style ribs, grilled lamb

Herb Rub for Braised Beef, page 227
—All braising cuts for beef and lamb

Herb Rub for Pork, Lamb, or Beef, page 263
—All lamb, beef, and pork cuts suitable for roasting, grilling, broiling, and pan-broiling

Fennel Rub for Pork Tenderloin, page 298
—Pork tenderloin, lamb chops

Dry Herb Rub for Tenderloin, page 300
—All cuts of pork and lamb suitable for grilling and sautéing

Asian Sesame Coating, page 302
   —Pork tenderloin for sautéing, pork chops, lamb chops, boneless lamb loin

Rosemary and Fennel Rub for Pork, page 318
   —Pork tenderloin, pork chops, lamb chops, culotte steak, top loin steak,
   fillet steak, veal chops, boneless veal for grilling

Creole Spice Rub for Pork, Beef, or Lamb, page 328
   —All cuts of pork loin suitable for pan-broiling, grilling, broiling, and
   roasting

***Arista* Herb Rub for Pork Loin,** page 335
   —All pork roasts, pork chops for grilling or pan-broiling, all lamb chops
   and veal chops

Garlic and Herb Paste for Pork Loin, page 336
   —All pork roasts, all lamb roasts, small beef roasts such as tri-tip and fillet,
   crown roast of pork, or lamb

Fennel-Sage Rub for Pork or Veal, page 340
   —Pork tenderloin, pork chops, pork loin, veal chop, pork shoulder,
   pork leg, veal roast, veal shoulder roast

Fresh Herb and Garlic Rub for Roast Pork, page 348
   —All pork and veal roasts

Herb and Mustard Rub for Pork, page 366
   —All cuts of beef and pork suitable for braising

Spice Rub for *Carnitas,* page 371
   —All pork ribs, all cuts of pork and lamb suitable for braising

Spice Rub for Pork or Beef, page 375
   —Pork ribs, beef ribs, brisket for barbecuing, whole pork loin, pork shoulder

Herb-Flavored Dry Cure for Lamb, page 448
   —Shoulder lamb chops, lamb shanks, lamb sirloin chops, pork country-style
   spareribs, beef short ribs

Mustard-Rosemary Paste for Lamb, page 486
—Pork loin roasts, rack of lamb

***Asadar* Herb-Garlic Paste for Lamb or Pork,** page 494
—Lamb leg, pork leg, pork shoulder, pork loin, rack of lamb, rack of veal, all lamb, pork, and veal roasts

Indian Dry Rub for Lamb, page 510
—Lamb, beef, and pork cuts suitable for braising

Pancetta and Rosemary Paste, page 512
—Eye of round for braising, roast fillet, or strip loin, roasts, pork loin, veal loin, leg of lamb, lamb shanks

Fresh Herb Rub for Lamb, page 518
—All cuts of lamb and veal suitable for braising

Basque Chile and Herb Rub for Lamb, page 524
—Beef stews and pot roasts, lamb stews and other lamb cuts suitable for braising

Middle Eastern Rub for Lamb, page 527
—All cuts of lamb and pork for grilling

Sage and Shallot Paste for Veal, page 552
—Rack of veal, veal chops, rack of lamb, pork loin, beefsteaks for grilling

Garlic and Herb Rub for Veal or Pork, page 554
—Veal shoulder, all cuts of braised veal and pork

Marinades

Nogales Steak Marinade, page 102
—Chuck steak, flank steak, rib steak, sirloin steak, pork steak, country-style spareribs, lamb shoulder chops, all types of kebabs, skirt steak, hanger steak

Olive Oil and Garlic Marinade for Steak, page 106
—Porterhouse steak, rib-eye steak, top loin steak, lamb chops, veal chops

North African Marinade, page 114

—Flank steak, beef ribs, chuck steak, rib steak, sirloin steak, lamb steak, lamb shoulder and rib chops, butterflied leg of lamb, lamb kebabs, veal shanks, lamb shanks

Teriyaki Marinade, page 115

—All beef steaks, pork fillets, pork steaks

Bourbon Marinade for Steak, page 124

—Top round steak, sirloin steak, chuck steak, flatiron steak, flank steak, hanger steak, beef kebabs, lamb sirloin chops, lamb shoulder chops, ham slices, fatty pork such as ribs

Chipotle-Orange Marinade, page 138

—Chuck steak, flatiron steak, flank steak, skirt steak, top round steak, pork steak, pork kebabs, beef kebabs, country-style spareribs, beef ribs

Spicy Beer Marinade, page 138

—Chuck steak, flank steak, skirt steak, beef ribs, beef tri-tip, butterflied leg of lamb, all kebabs

Satay Marinade for Beef, page 153

—Skirt steak, all types of kebabs, boneless thin-cut beef, pork, or lamb

Orange-Ginger Marinade for Beef, page 186

—Fillet roast, chuck steak, pork chops, pork tenderloin, tri-tip

Fresh Basil and Garlic Marinade for Beef, page 224

—All cuts of beef and veal suitable for dry-roasting

***Adobo* Marinade,** page 286

—Pork stew meat, pork chops, boneless pork, boneless beef, flank steak, beef stew meat, lamb stew, boneless lamb for grilling

Korean Marinade for Beef, page 217

—Flank steak, skirt steak, chuck steak, culotte steak, hanger steak, beef short ribs, beef ribs, pork tenderloin, beef and lamb kebabs

Tequila and Lime Marinade, page 292

—All types of kebabs, fajitas, butterflied leg of lamb, beef, pork, and lamb steaks, any meats suitable for grilling, pork butt for roasting

Yucatán Marinade, page 294

—Pork steaks, pork kebabs, fajitas, beef kebabs, chuck steak, flank steak, country-style spareribs, beef ribs, spareribs

Tamarind Marinade for Pork, page 306

—Boneless pork, thin pork chops, pork for stir-frying, boneless lamb, strips of beef from flank steak, skirt steak, top loin steak for stir-frying

Tandoori Marinade, page 319

—Pork tenderloin, pork, lamb, and veal kebabs, all cuts of pork, lamb, and veal for grilling

Chinese Ginger-Lemon Marinade, page 325

—Pork tenderloin, pork chops, veal chops, pork and veal kebabs, baby back ribs

Apple Brandy Marinade for Pork, page 326

—Pork chops for grilling, pork tenderloin, pork kebabs, veal chops

Chinese Barbecued Pork Marinade, page 332

—Pork tenderloin, all pork ribs, strips from pork butt, lamb riblets, boneless pork, pork chops, ham steaks, smoked pork chops

"Wild Boar" Marinade, page 356

—Leg of pork, pork shoulder, leg of lamb (whole or butterflied), chuck blade roast, cross-rib roast, beef sirloin tip, bottom round, top round

Cuban Rum and Citrus Marinade for Pork, page 358

—Fresh pork leg, pork loin, pork tenderloin pork chops, pork kebabs, pork butt, beef kebabs

Caribbean Marinade for Pork or Beef, page 368

—Flank steaks, skirt steaks, hanging tender, braised pork cuts, pork blade chops, pork kebabs

Thai Marinade for Pork, page 382

    —Baby back ribs, spareribs, country-style spareribs, pork kebabs, boneless beef, flank steak, skirt steak, lamb riblets, lamb shoulder chops

Chinese Oyster Sauce Marinade for Pork, page 386

    —Pork tenderloin, all pork ribs, pork butt strips, lamb riblets, lamb shoulder chops, flank steak, skirt steak

Greek Marinade for Lamb, page 444

    —Lamb kebabs, butterflied leg of lamb, lamb chops for grilling, lamb riblets, veal chops, veal kebabs

Cranberry-Onion Marinade, page 468

    —Lamb kebabs, rack of lamb, lamb chops, butterflied leg of lamb, veal kebabs, veal chops, boneless pork leg

Garlic, Lemon, and Herb Marinade for Lamb, page 469

    —All lamb and veal cuts for grilling, chuck steaks, flank steaks, top sirloin, top round steaks, culotte steaks

Tejano Marinade for Lamb, Pork, or Beef, page 490

    —Butterflied leg of lamb, lamb shoulder, lamb kebabs, flank steak, top round steak, chuck steak, rib steak, pork loin, country-style spareribs, spareribs

Middle Eastern Marinade for Lamb or Beef, page 500

    —All cuts of lamb and beef suitable for braising

Herb Marinade for Grilled Veal, page 542

    —All cuts of veal, lamb, and pork for grilling

Brines

Nancy's Vanilla Brine, page 255
   —Pork loin, thick-cut pork chops, pork shoulder strips, pork tenderloin, eye
   of the round, individual roasts from pork leg, pork sirloin

Boulevard's Maple Syrup and Apple Cider Brine for Pork, page 256
   —Same as Vanilla Brine, above

Honey and Chili Flavor Cure for Pork, page 257
   —Pork loin, thick-cut pork chops, pork shoulder strips, pork tenderloin, eye
   of the round, individual roasts from pork leg, pork sirloin

Fennel and Mustard Flavor Cure, page 258
   —Pork loin, thick-cut pork chops, pork shoulder strips, pork tenderloin, eye
   of the round, individual roasts from pork leg, pork sirloin, butterflied leg of
   lamb

Beer, Chili, and Sage Brine for Pork, page 259
   —Same as Vanilla Brine, above, plus brisket, short ribs, beef chuck blade
   roasts, butterflied leg of lamb

Sources

ASIAN INGREDIENTS

House of Rice
4112 University Way NE
Seattle, WA 98105
(206) 545-6956

Kim Man Food
200 Canal Street
New York, NY 10013
(212) 571-0330

Oriental Pantry
423 Great Road
Acton, MA 01720
(800) 828-0368

Tokyo Fish Market
122 San Pablo Avenue
Berkeley, CA 94706
(510) 524-7243

CREOLE AND CAJUN SEASONINGS

Catahoula
1457 Lincoln Avenue
Calistoga, CA 94515
(707) 942-2275
New Orleans red gravy

Catfish Wholesale
PO Box 759
Abbeville, LA 70510
(318) 643-6700

Louisiana Fish Fry Products
5267 Plank Road
Baton Rouge, LA 70805
(504) 356-2905

COUNTRY HAMS

Burger Smokehouse
32819 Highway 87
California, MO 65018
(800) 624-5426

Early's Honey Stand
PO Box 908
Spring Hill, TN 37174
(800) 523-2015

Finchville Farms
PO Box 56
Finchville, KY 40022
(800) 678-1521

Gratton Farms
Father's Country Ham
Bremen, KY 42325
(502) 525-3437

Gwaltney's
PO Box 1
Smithfield, VA 23431
(800) 292-2773

Johnston County Country Hams
204 North Bright Leaf Blvd.
Smithfield, NC 27577
(800) 543-4267

Scott Hams
1301 Scott Road
Greenville, KY 42345
(502) 338-3402

Smithfield Collection
PO Box 497
Smithfield, VA 23430
(800) 628-2242

Stadler's Country Ham
PO Box 397
Elon College, NC 27244
(800) 262-1795

Tripp Country Hams
PO Box 527
Brownville, TN 38012
(901) 772-2130

Wallace Edwards & Sons
PO Box 25
Surry, VA 23883
(800) 222-4267

MEXICAN/SOUTHWEST INGREDIENTS

Carmen's of New Mexico
PO Box 7310
Albuquerque, NM 87194
(800) 851-4852

The Chile Shop
109 East Water Street
Santa Fe, NM 87501
(505) 983-6080

El Nopalito #1
560 Santa Fe Drive
Encinitas, CA 92024
(760) 436–5775

The Kitchen Food Shop
218 Eighth Avenue
New York, NY 10011
(212) 243-4433

Texas Spice Company
PO Box 3769
Austin, TX 78764-3769
(800) 880-8007
(512) 444-2223

SAUSAGES AND SPECIALTY MEATS

Aidells Sausage Company
1625 Alvarado Street
San Leandro, CA 94577
(800) 546-5795

Balducci's
424 Avenue of the Americas
New York, NY 10011
(800) 822–1444

Summerfield Farm
10044 James Monroe Highway
Culpeper, VA 22701
(540) 547-9600

SAUSAGE-MAKING SUPPLIES AND EQUIPMENT

Carlson Butcher Supply
50 Mendell #12
San Francisco, CA 94124
(415) 648–2601

The Sausage Maker
1500 Clinton Street
Buffalo, NY 14206
(716) 824-6510

SPECIALTY PRODUCTS, HERBS, AND SPICES

Adriana's Caravan
409 Vanderbilt Street
Brooklyn, NY 11218
(800) 316-0820

Dean & DeLuca
560 Broadway
New York, NY 10012
(800) 221-7714
(212) 431-1691

Kalustyan's
123 Lexington Avenue
New York, NY 10016
(212) 685-3451

Penzey's, Ltd.
PO Box 933
Muskego, WI 53150
(414) 574-0277

Zingermans
422 Detroit Street
Ann Arbor, MI 48104
(313) 663-3354
(888) 636-8162

Acknowledgments

WE'D LIKE TO THANK OUR EDITOR, Rux Martin, for her unflagging enthusiasm, good sense, and ability to get things done; our agent, Martha Casselman, for her constant encouragement and sage counsel; our publisher, Barry Estabrook, for his support and advice; Lisa Weiss, for carefully testing recipes (and feeding us all that great food); and Nancy Oakes, for her fantastic recipes and constant help with all phases of the book. Thanks also to Fran McCullough, who provided prudent guidance and great editing for an earlier version, and to Maria Guarnaschelli and Jane Rosenman at Scribner, who aided in the conception and development of the book's early stages. We'd also like to thank the following friends, fellow cooks, and cookbook writers for contributing recipes, advice, and help: John Alamilla, Pam Barnett, Jan Birnbaum, Jeff Bergman, Bucci, Ana Canales, Gordon Heyden, Loni Kuhn, David Shalleck, Cort Sinnes, Dan Strongen, Pam Student, Faith Willinger, Priscilla Yee, Edy Young, and Sam Zabaida. We'd like to express our appreciation to Rosemary Mucklow at the National Meat Association, and to the National Pork Producer's Council, the National Cattleman's Beef Association, and the American Lamb Council for providing charts, facts, figures, and general information about meat in America. Thanks also to Susan McClellan for her design, to Beatriz Da Costa for terrific food photography, to Anne Disrude and Betty Alfenito for styling, and to Bill Reitzel for the back cover photo. And thanks to the Authors' Guild for support when we needed it.

Index

Numbers in boldface denote illustrations or photographs.

broiling, 59; best cuts for, 58-59

dry-heat cooking, preparing meat for, 59

flavor brining, 254

grilling (direct, over coals), 64; best cuts for, 63

grilling (indirect, with coals surrounding), 65-66; best cuts for, 65

pan-broiling, 60-61; best cuts for, 60

panfrying, 62; best cuts for, 62

sautéing, 61; best cuts for, 61

stir-frying, 62; best cuts for, 62

Matambre (Rolled Stuffed Flank Steak), 120

meat. *See also* Beef; Lamb; *name of meat cut;* Pork; Veal

brined, storing, 256

brining, 39

about buying, 31, 34

in agriculturally based civilization, 27-28

basting, 67

choosing, 34

cooking, 51

cuts, recommended marinades for, 579-82

Doneness Chart for, 56-57

dry heat or moist heat, 51-52

factors affecting flavor, 31

flavor (increasing) steps for, 36

and healthy diet, 13

history (short) of, 25-28

how to buy, 13

how to read retail label, 36

how to use recipes, 14

and the industrial revolution, 28

in modern diet, 28

new approach to, 12

nutrients in, 52

picking the right cut, 35

primal cuts of, 35

and pressure cookers, 52

safety of, 53-54

salt and pepper, for seasoning, 37

seasoning, 12-13, 36-37, 49. *See also* seasoning

tenderness and flavor of, 31, 51, 85-86

thermometer for meat cookery, 53, 55

Meat Loaf

Beef, Turkey, and Andouille, 165

Not-Like-Mom's, 166

Meatballs

Italian-American, Bucci's, 168

Veal, Pam's, 567

Mediterranean Brisket, 200

Mexican seasoning flavors, 30

microwaving meat, 73

Middle Eastern Lamb Baked with Eggplant and Tomatoes, 500

mock tender (chuck), 134

moist-heat, cooking, 51-52, 70-73

Moroccan

Lemon Tagine, **47** (master recipe), 503; variations, 504;

Stewed Lamb and Vegetables (Couscous), 506

Mozzarella and Pesto-Stuffed Burger, 162

Mushroom

Burger, Chinese, 158

and Onion-Stuffed Burgers, Teriyaki, 164

-Stuffed Burger, 162

Vinaigrette, Nancy's, 108

Mustardy Barbecue Sauce, 379

mutton, 428, 431-32

"natural" meat, 34

neck bones (pork), 387

Neolithic agricultural revolution, 27

New York steak, 95, 98

New York Strip

loin steak, 93, **94,** 98

Whole Roast Top Loin with Herb Crust, 189

no-roll beef, 87

North African

Braised Veal Shanks, 568

Marinade, Marinated Flank Steak with, 114

Not-Like-Mom's Meat Loaf, 166

nutrients in meat, affected by cooking, 52

Oakland-Style Barbecue Sauce, 380

oil, in recipes, 15

Onions, Red, Lime-Pickled, 104

Orange-Pineapple Salsa, 295

Osso Buco with Veal Shanks, 565

outdoor grills, 63

Oven-Roasted, Marinated Spareribs (Chinese-Style), 386

oven-roasting, best cuts for, 66. *See also* roasting

oxen, 77; wild ox (aurochs or urus), 76

Oxtails, 226; Braised, 227

pan-broiling meat, master technique, 60-61; best cuts for, 60

Pan Sauce. *See name of recipe*

panfrying meat, master technique, 62; best cuts for, 62

Pasta with Lamb, Baked, 520